praise for u n r i g

"*Unrig* is, simply, the unmissable book. Daniel Newman—a national treasure and a tireless defender of democracy—explains in graphic style and easy-to-follow language, how democracy's tools are made 'boring' and opaque on purpose—how the system undermines candidates who just want to serve the people—and, most inspiringly of all, what we can all do to fix this. **This should be required reading** (and luckily, it's engaging, powerful reading) for every student and every citizen."

—**Naomi Wolf,** bestselling author of *The Beauty Myth* and *The End of America*

"By clearly illustrating the toughest problems that threaten our system of government, *Unrig* has the potential to be this generation's **most influential book on American democracy**. It is a must read."

—**Spencer Overton,** Professor of Law, The George Washington University
and author of *Stealing Democracy: The New Politics of Voter Suppression*

"Everyone knows that our democracy is broken, but what's less clear is how we got into this mess and what we should do about it. Newman's *Unrig* explains both in an accessible and entertaining way, **leaving the reader equipped and inspired to get involved in unrigging our democracy** and putting it to work for people and the planet."

—**Annie Leonard,** Executive Director, Greenpeace USA

"Can a graphic novel save America from the billionaires and giant corporations that have hijacked our democracy? Thanks to Daniel G. Newman and George O'Connor the answer is an emphatic 'YES!' But only if enough of us **read this great new book and take action**."

—**John Sellers,** co-founder of The Other 98%

"**This brilliant book** explains the need and urgency for reform powerfully and with **great insight**."

—**Lawrence Lessig,** Harvard Law professor and bestselling author of *Republic, Lost*

"Daniel Newman and George O'Connor's gripping account of the battles to fix our democracy paints a graphic picture of this ongoing struggle. This **informative and inspiring must-read** spotlights the movement of modern-day American patriots on the front lines of the fight to save our democracy."

—**Greg Moore,** former Executive Director, NAACP National Voter Fund

"I love it—**stories of real citizens making historic change**. *Unrig* enables readers to move from the notion of 'dutiful' citizen to taste the excitement of becoming a democracy hero. Yes. I'm hooked!"

—**Frances Moore Lappé,** bestselling author of *Diet for a Small Planet*

"**An urgent gem of a graphic novel**. A smart, fun, artful guide to how government got so broken and—even more important—how we can fix our ailing democracy so that it finally works for all the people. Read *Unrig* ASAP!"

—Nancy MacLean, author of *Democracy in Chains: The Deep History of the Radical Right's Stealth Plan for America*

"Fixing our country's most pressing issues is going to require working together. *Unrig* is not only **fun and clarifying**, it highlights opportunities to improve our democracy that people from across the political spectrum can get behind. That is exciting!"

—Joan Blades, co-founder, MoveOn.org, LivingRoomConversations.org, and MomsRising.org

"*Unrig* is entertaining, alarming, and actionable as it diagnoses the pressing problems in our democracy. The unique combination of understandable explanations and powerful art make *Unrig* **a one-of-a-kind tool to improve our country**. Anyone who wants a more accountable and responsive government, while having fun along the way, should read this book."

—Ann Ravel, former Chair, Federal Election Commission

"The most fundamental issue in politics today is the institutional (and legal!) corruption that plagues the electoral system. With their engaging, entertaining, and enlightening graphic novel, *Unrig*, Daniel Newman and George O'Connor transform this abstract subject into compelling real-world stories—and give us dramatic and inspiring tales of champions of democracy fighting for and implementing practical solutions. It's a great read—with **important lessons for any citizen who gives a damn**."

—David Corn, Washington bureau chief, *Mother Jones*

"Daniel Newman gives us **a solidly researched look at our governing system**, its myriad broken parts and ways those parts might be fixed. His insights and George O'Connor's upbeat art make the situation seem surprisingly un-grim."

—Peter Overby, former Power, Money and Influence Correspondent for National Public Radio

"*Unrig* powerfully demonstrates the potential of a graphic novel format for teaching citizens about the flaws in our democracy and equipping them to be an active part of the solution. **Lucid, entertaining, and compelling**."

—Thomas E. Mann, senior fellow at Brookings and co-author of *It's Even Worse Than It Looks*

unrig

how to
fix our
BROKEN
DEMOCRACY

★

written by DANIEL G. NEWMAN
art by GEORGE O'CONNOR
color by FRANK REYNOSO

First Second

NEW YORK

First Second

Text copyright © 2020 by Daniel G. Newman
Illustration copyright © 2020 by George O'Connor
Portions of "Running for Congress" text copyright © 2018 by First Look Media. Used with permission
Published by First Second
First Second is an imprint of Roaring Brook Press,
a division of Holtzbrinck Publishing Holdings Limited Partnership
120 Broadway, New York, NY 10271

Visit UnrigBook.com to find out how you can get involved in fixing our democracy.

Don't miss your next favorite book from First Second!
For the latest updates go to firstsecondnewsletter.com and sign up for our enewsletter.

Library of Congress Control Number: 2019930675
ISBN: 978-1-250-29530-9

Our books may be purchased in bulk for promotional, educational, or business use.
Please contact your local bookseller or the Macmillan Corporate and Premium Sales Department at
(800) 221-7945 ext. 5442 or by email at MacmillanSpecialMarkets@macmillan.com.

First edition, 2020
Edited by Mark Siegel and Robyn Chapman
Cover design by Kirk Benshoff and Andrew Arnold
Interior book design by Molly Johanson
Lettering by Chris Dickey
Color by Frank Reynoso

Printed in Singapore

The art for *Unrig* was created digitally on a Cintiq with Adobe Photoshop and Clip Studio.

1 3 5 7 9 10 8 6 4 2

BY ART
WE LIVE

contents

introduction

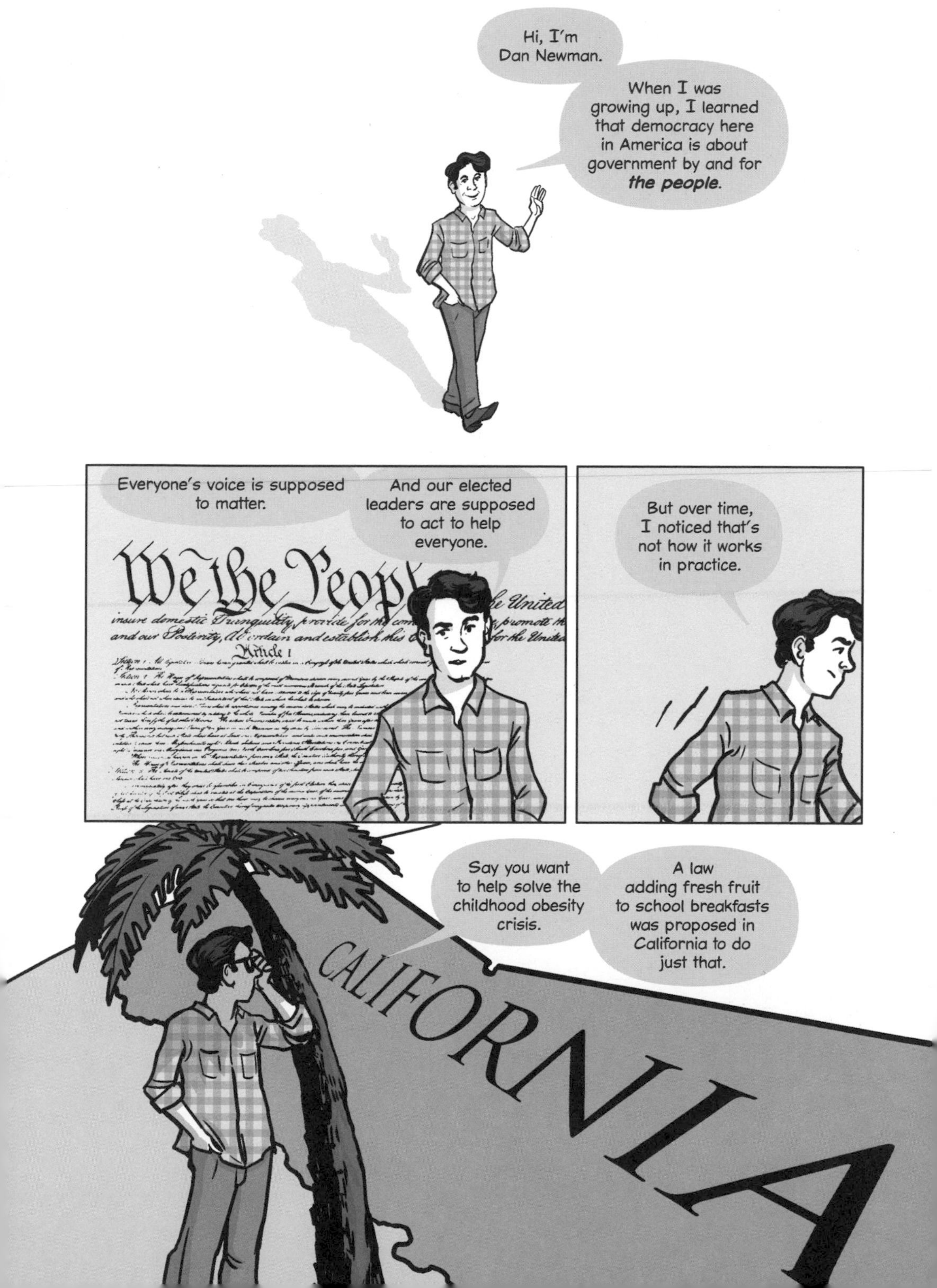
Hi, I'm Dan Newman.
When I was growing up, I learned that democracy here in America is about government by and for ***the people***.
Everyone's voice is supposed to matter.
And our elected leaders are supposed to act to help everyone.
But over time, I noticed that's not how it works in practice.
Say you want to help solve the childhood obesity crisis.
A law adding fresh fruit to school breakfasts was proposed in California to do just that.
CALIFORNIA

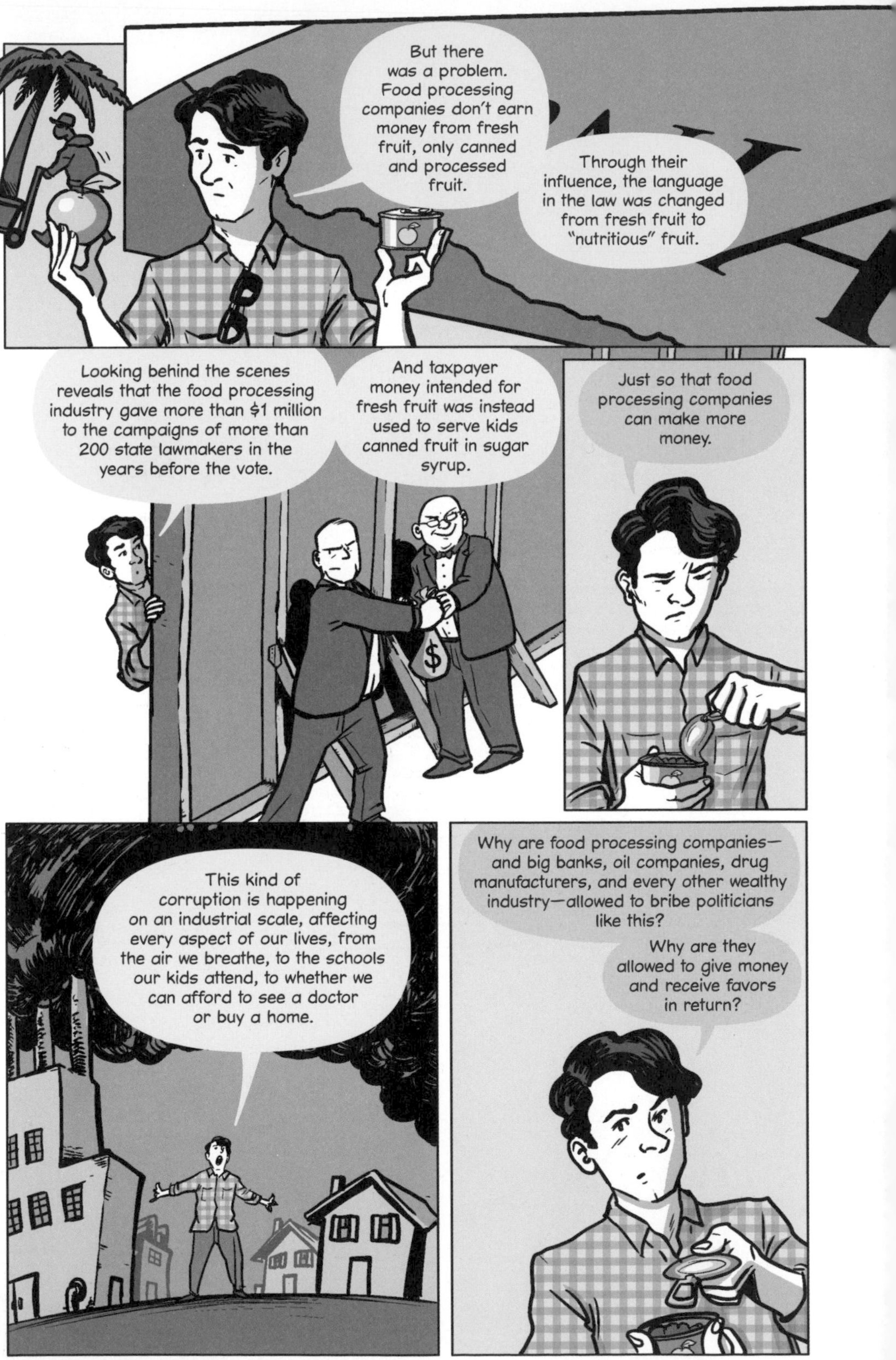
But there was a problem. Food processing companies don't earn money from fresh fruit, only canned and processed fruit.
Through their influence, the language in the law was changed from fresh fruit to "nutritious" fruit.
Looking behind the scenes reveals that the food processing industry gave more than $1 million to the campaigns of more than 200 state lawmakers in the years before the vote.
And taxpayer money intended for fresh fruit was instead used to serve kids canned fruit in sugar syrup.
Just so that food processing companies can make more money.
This kind of corruption is happening on an industrial scale, affecting every aspect of our lives, from the air we breathe, to the schools our kids attend, to whether we can afford to see a doctor or buy a home.
Why are food processing companies—and big banks, oil companies, drug manufacturers, and every other wealthy industry—allowed to bribe politicians like this?
Why are they allowed to give money and receive favors in return?

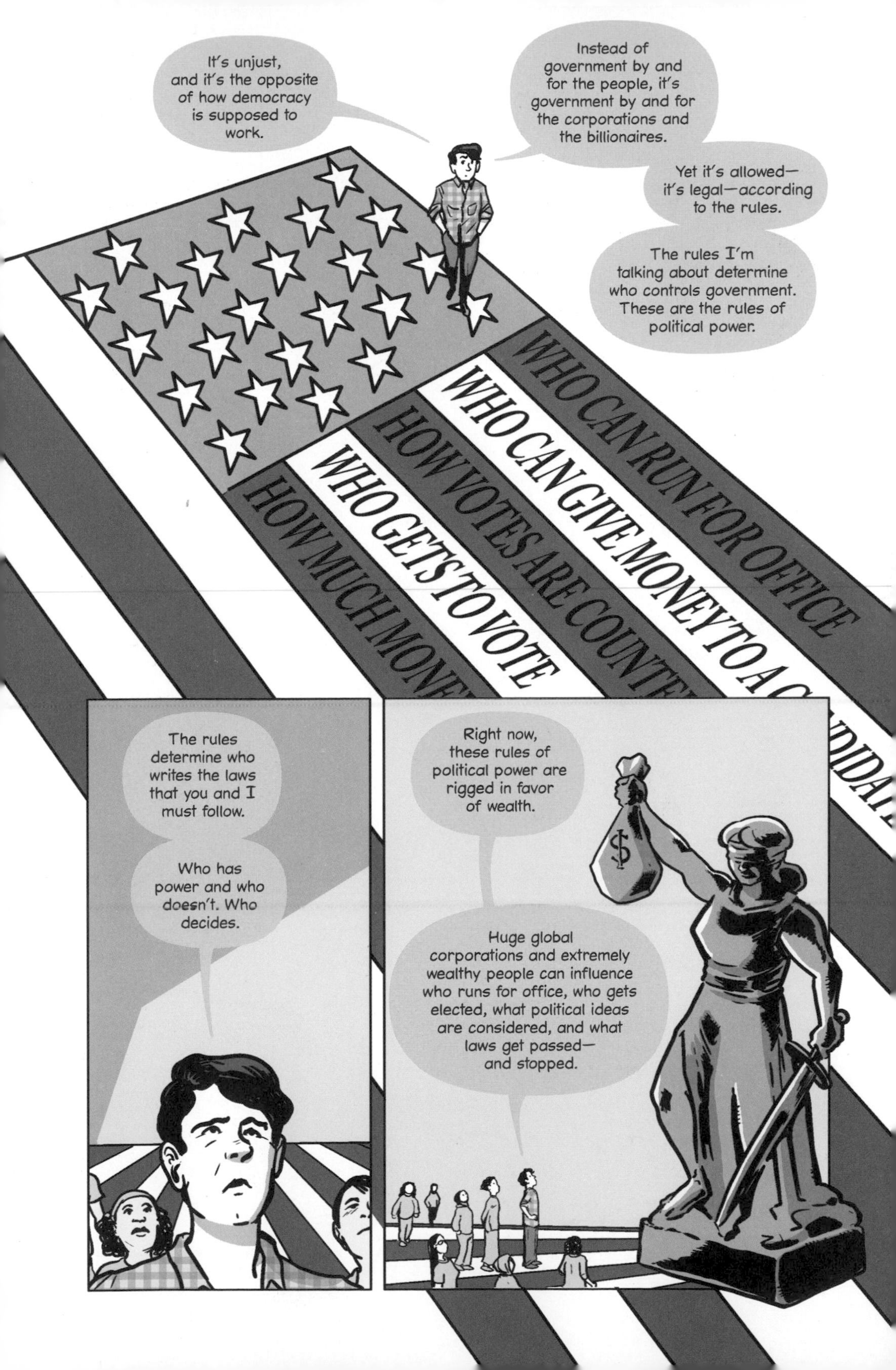

It's unjust, and it's the opposite of how democracy is supposed to work.
Instead of government by and for the people, it's government by and for the corporations and the billionaires.
Yet it's allowed— it's legal—according to the rules.
The rules I'm talking about determine who controls government. These are the rules of political power.
WHO CAN RUN FOR OFFICE
WHO CAN GIVE MONEY TO A
HOW VOTES ARE
WHO GETS TO VOTE
HOW MUCH
The rules determine who writes the laws that you and I must follow.
Who has power and who doesn't. Who decides.
Right now, these rules of political power are rigged in favor of wealth.
Huge global corporations and extremely wealthy people can influence who runs for office, who gets elected, what political ideas are considered, and what laws get passed— and stopped.

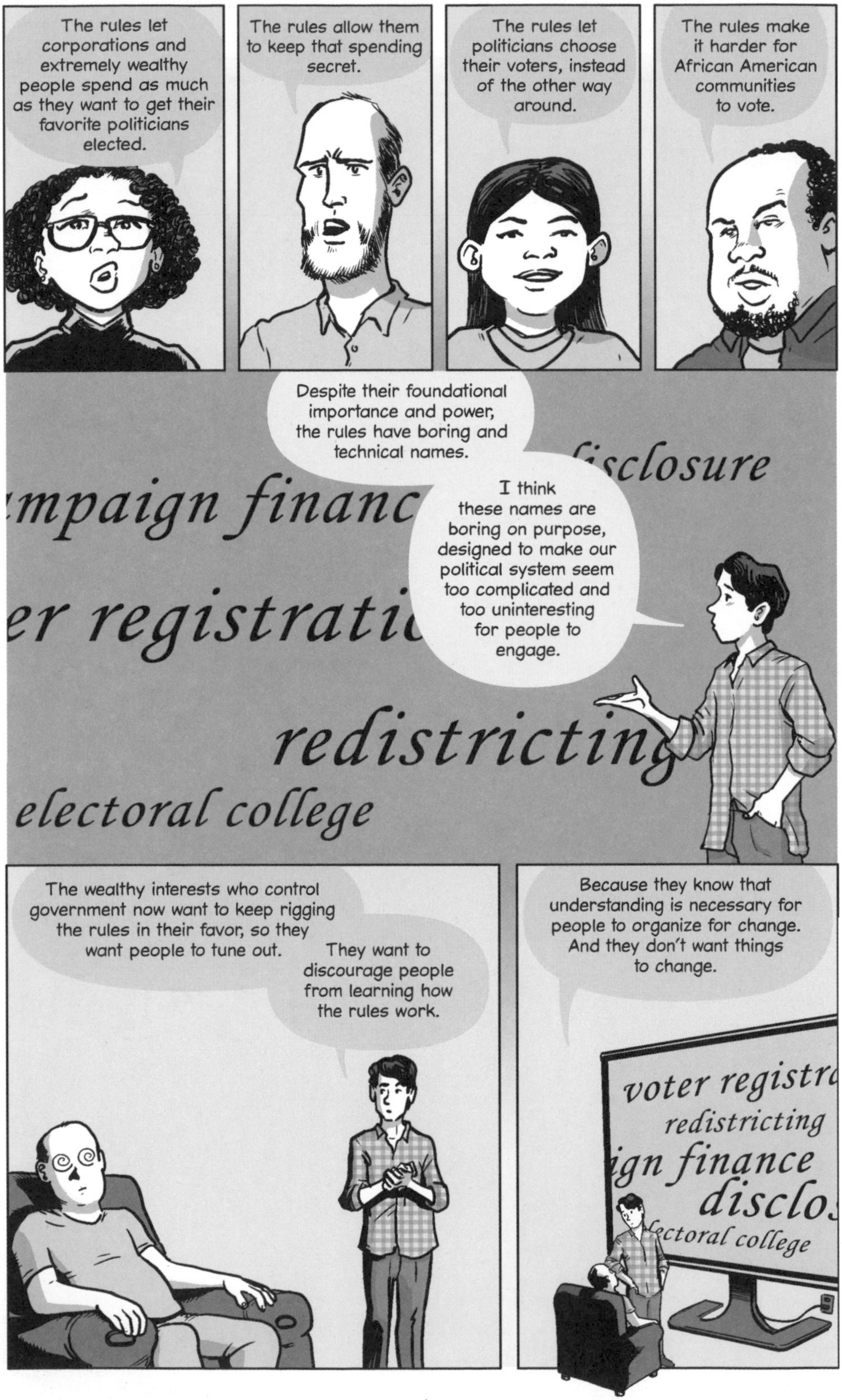
The rules let corporations and extremely wealthy people spend as much as they want to get their favorite politicians elected.
The rules allow them to keep that spending secret.
The rules let politicians choose their voters, instead of the other way around.
The rules make it harder for African American communities to vote.
Despite their foundational importance and power, the rules have boring and technical names.
I think these names are boring on purpose, designed to make our political system seem too complicated and too uninteresting for people to engage.
disclosure
redistricting
electoral college
The wealthy interests who control government now want to keep rigging the rules in their favor, so they want people to tune out.
They want to discourage people from learning how the rules work.
Because they know that understanding is necessary for people to organize for change. And they don't want things to change.
voter registr
redistricting
ign finance
disclo
ectoral college

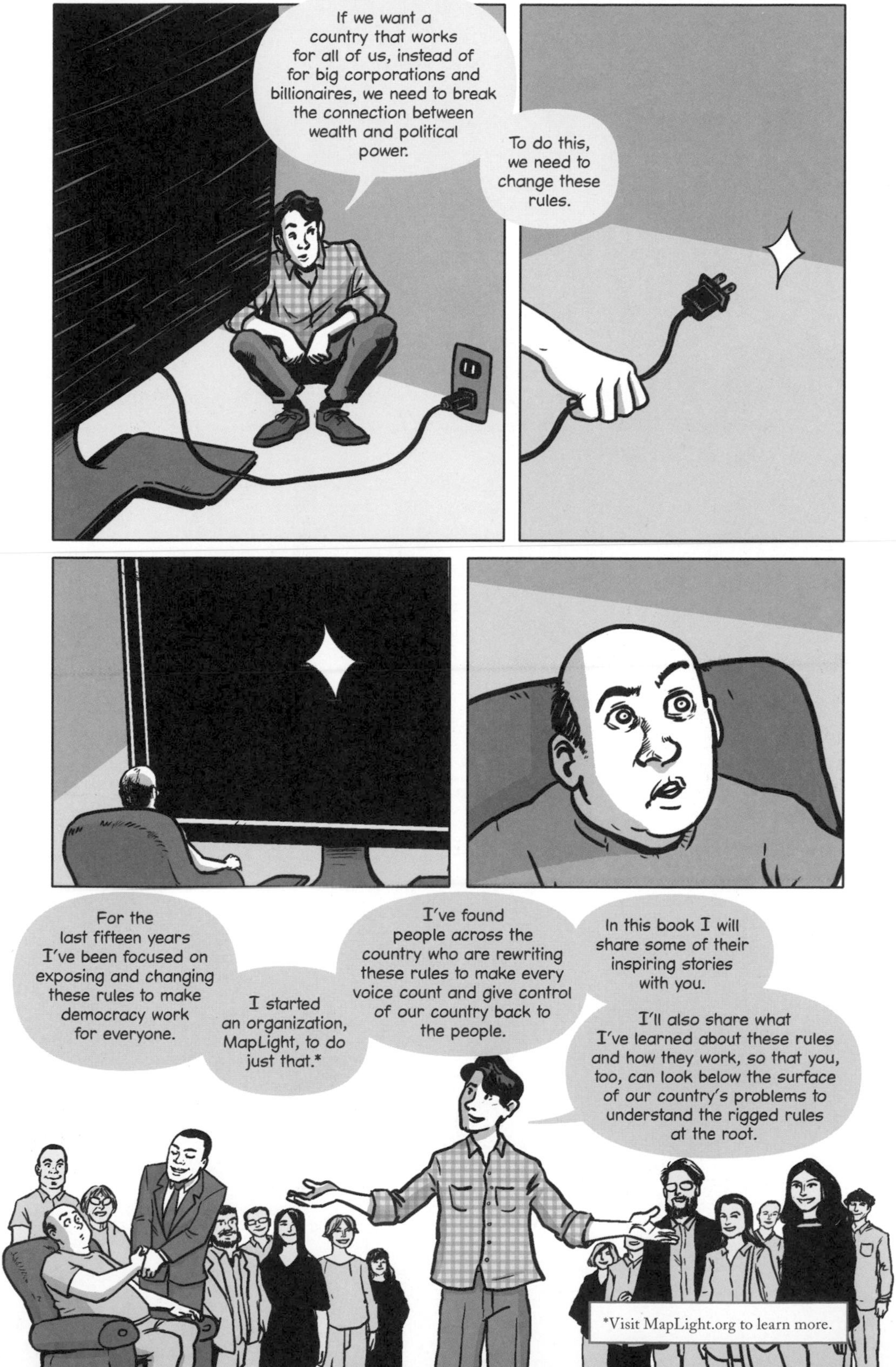
If we want a country that works for all of us, instead of for big corporations and billionaires, we need to break the connection between wealth and political power.
To do this, we need to change these rules.
For the last fifteen years I've been focused on exposing and changing these rules to make democracy work for everyone.
I started an organization, MapLight, to do just that.*
I've found people across the country who are rewriting these rules to make every voice count and give control of our country back to the people.
In this book I will share some of their inspiring stories with you.
I'll also share what I've learned about these rules and how they work, so that you, too, can look below the surface of our country's problems to understand the rigged rules at the root.

*Visit MapLight.org to learn more.

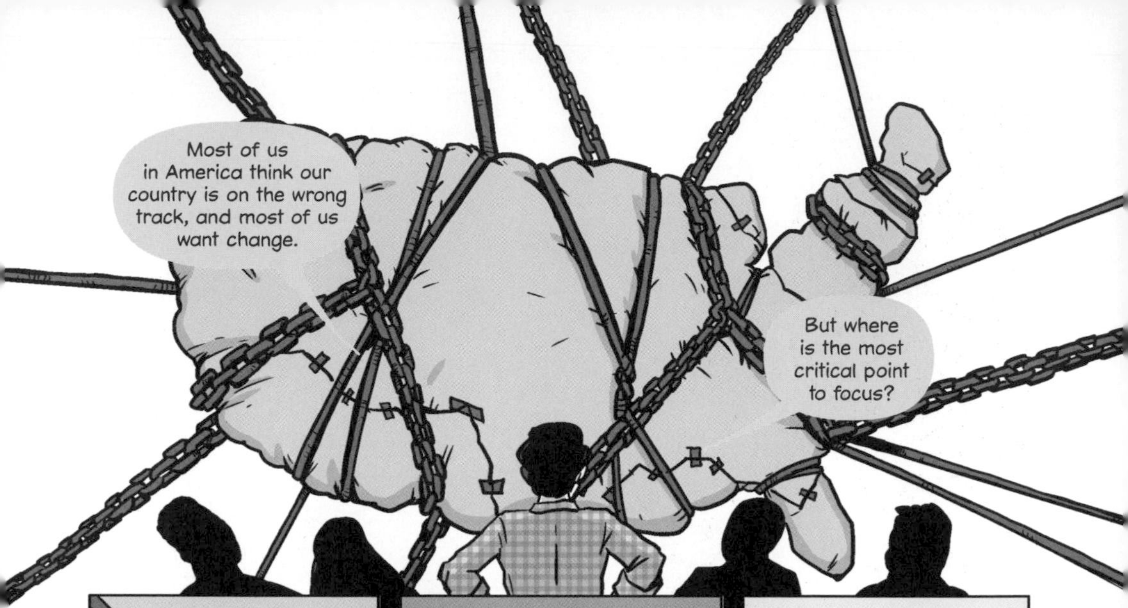
Most of us in America think our country is on the wrong track, and most of us want change.
But where is the most critical point to focus?

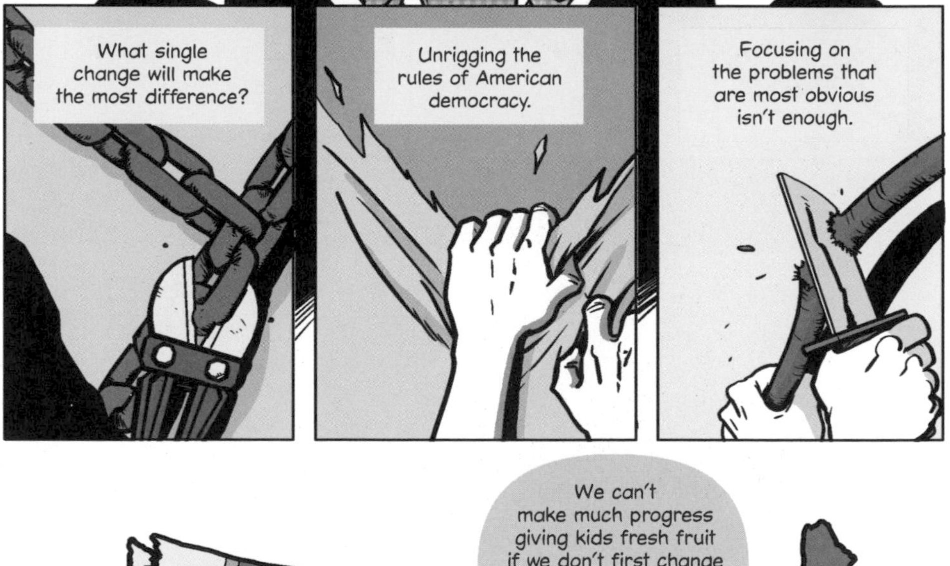
What single change will make the most difference?
Unrigging the rules of American democracy.
Focusing on the problems that are most obvious isn't enough.

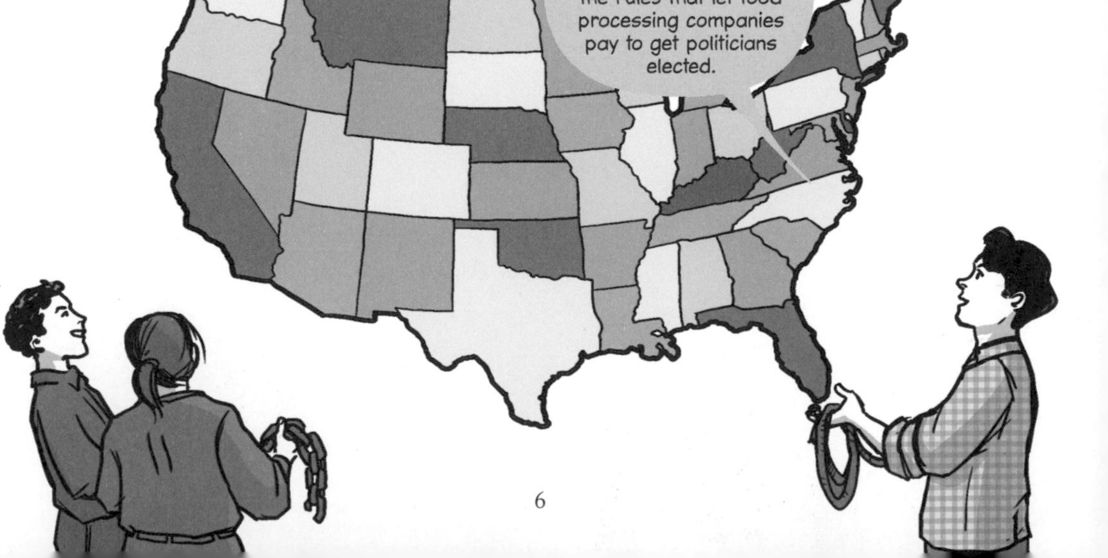
We can't make much progress giving kids fresh fruit if we don't first change the rules that let food processing companies pay to get politicians elected.

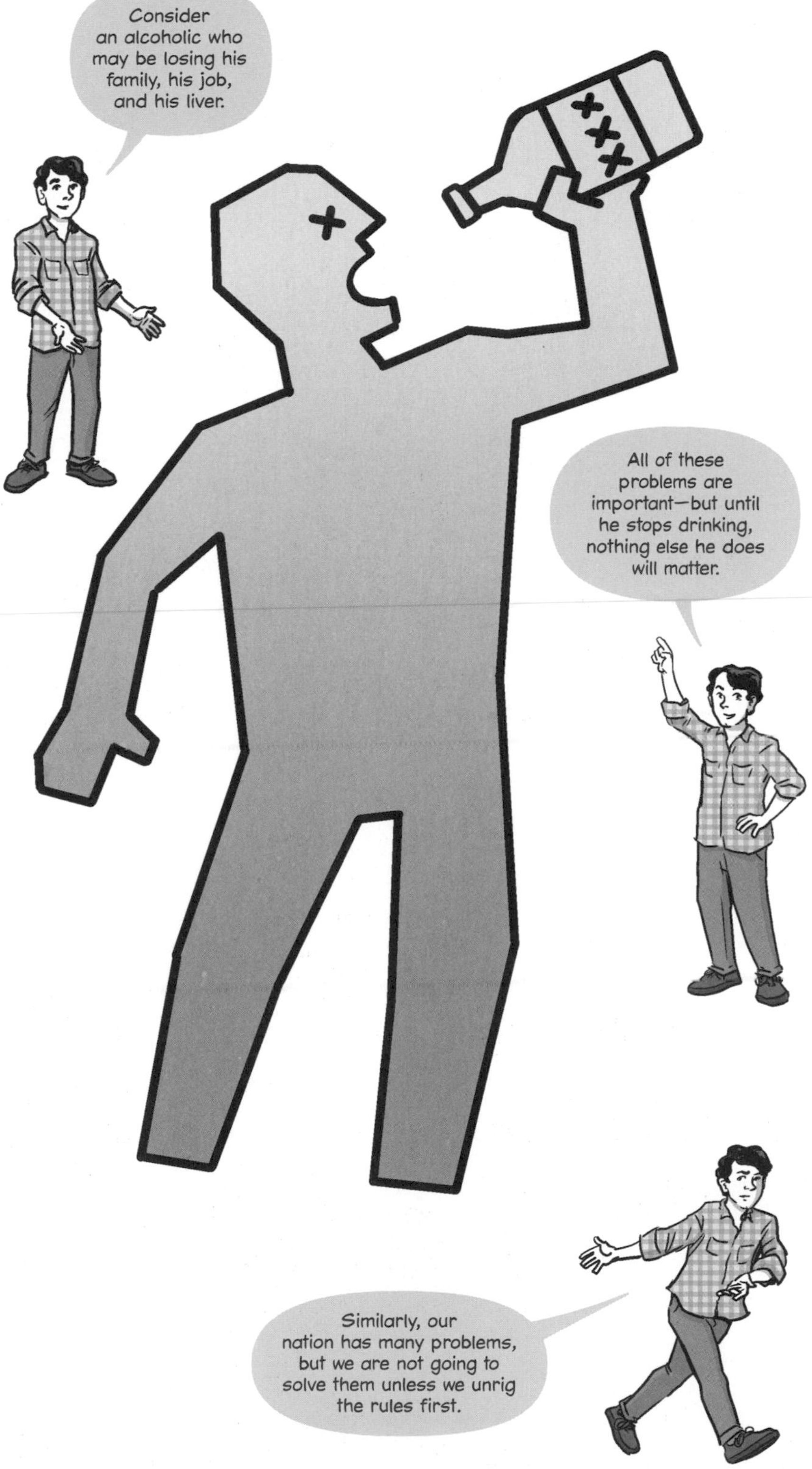
Consider an alcoholic who may be losing his family, his job, and his liver.
All of these problems are important—but until he stops drinking, nothing else he does will matter.
Similarly, our nation has many problems, but we are not going to solve them unless we unrig the rules first.

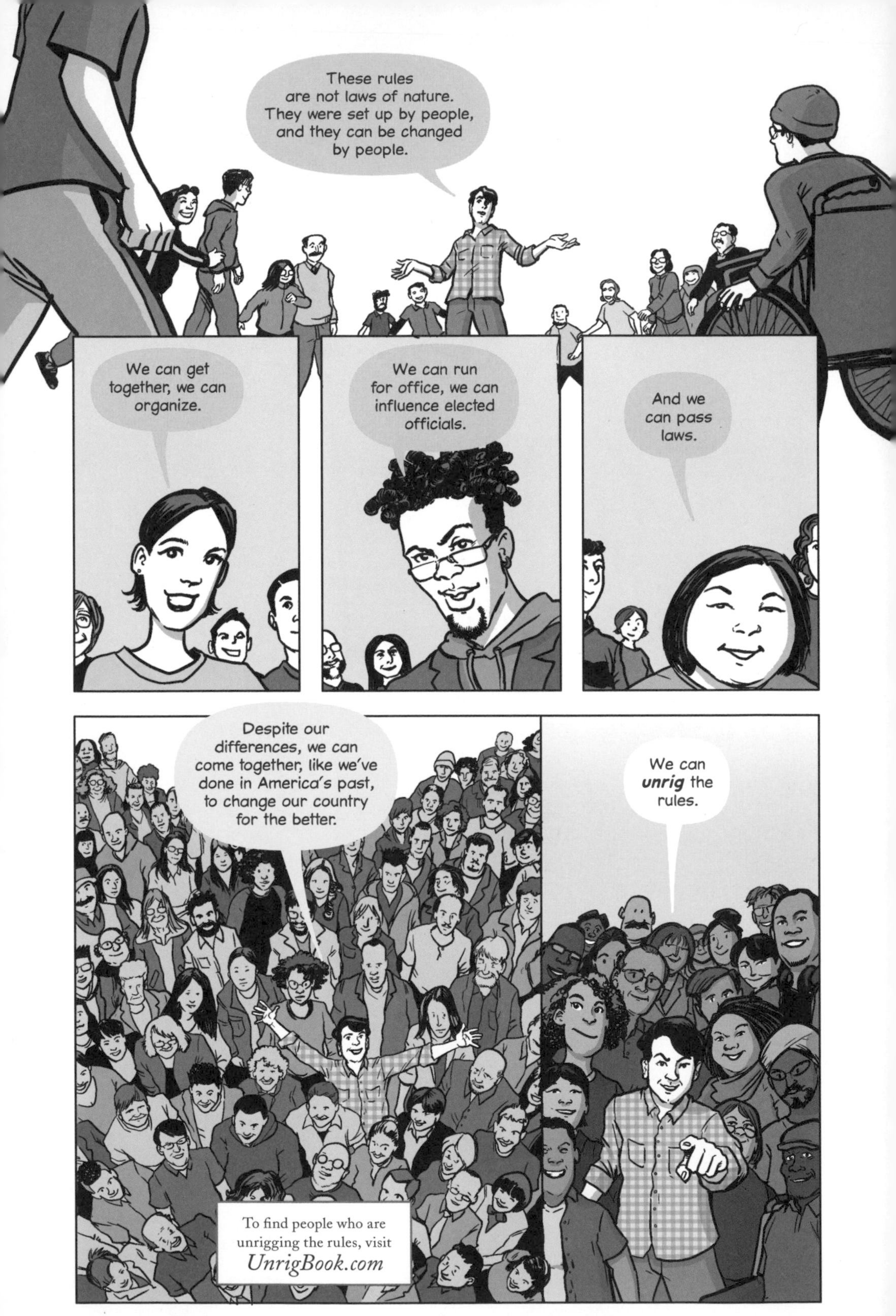
These rules are not laws of nature. They were set up by people, and they can be changed by people.
We can get together, we can organize.
We can run for office, we can influence elected officials.
And we can pass laws.
Despite our differences, we can come together, like we've done in America's past, to change our country for the better.
We can **unrig** the rules.
To find people who are unrigging the rules, visit *UnrigBook.com*

1
unrigging
the rules

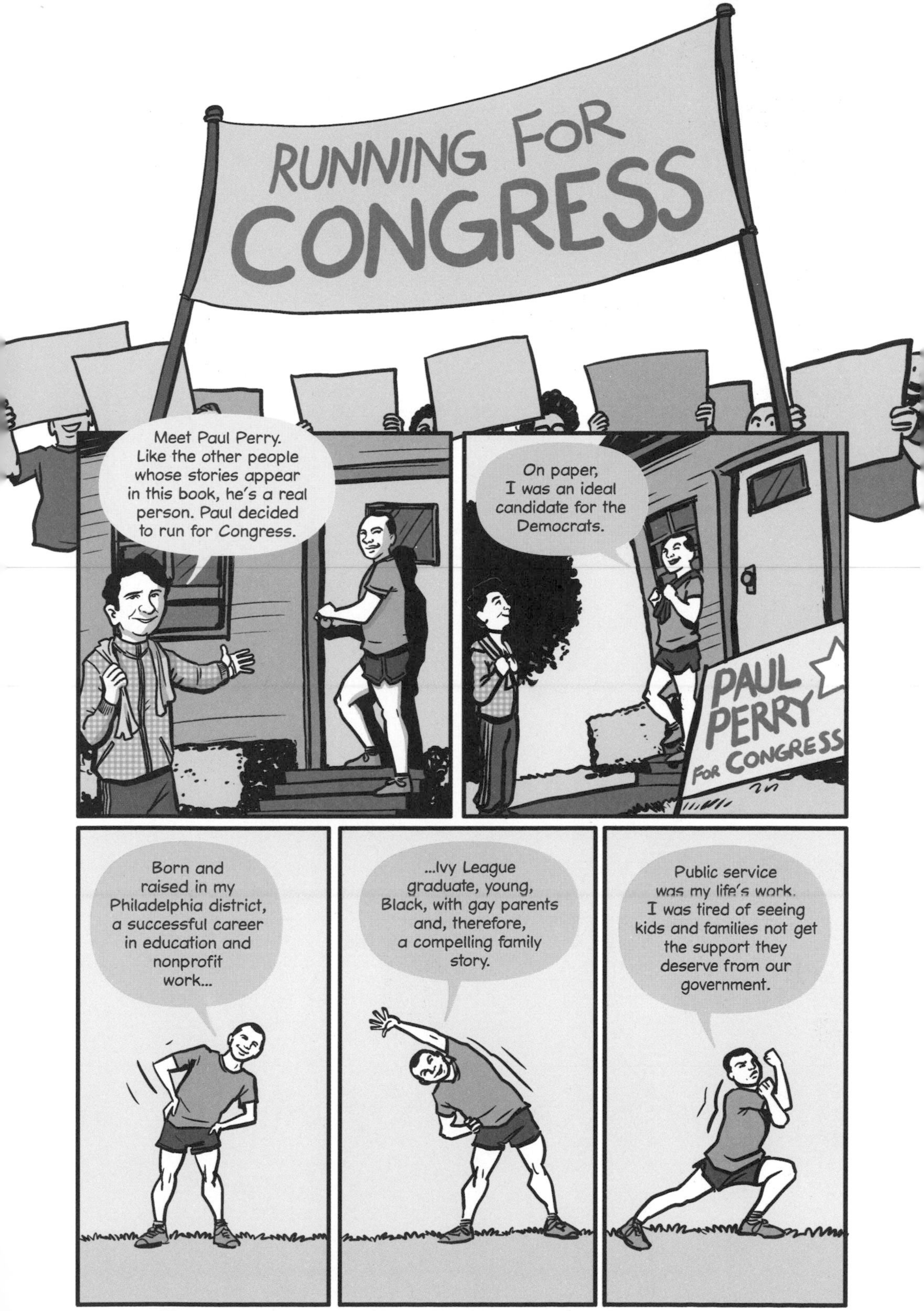
RUNNING FOR CONGRESS
Meet Paul Perry. Like the other people whose stories appear in this book, he's a real person. Paul decided to run for Congress.
On paper, I was an ideal candidate for the Democrats.
PAUL PERRY FOR CONGRESS
Born and raised in my Philadelphia district, a successful career in education and nonprofit work...
...Ivy League graduate, young, Black, with gay parents and, therefore, a compelling family story.
Public service was my life's work. I was tired of seeing kids and families not get the support they deserve from our government.

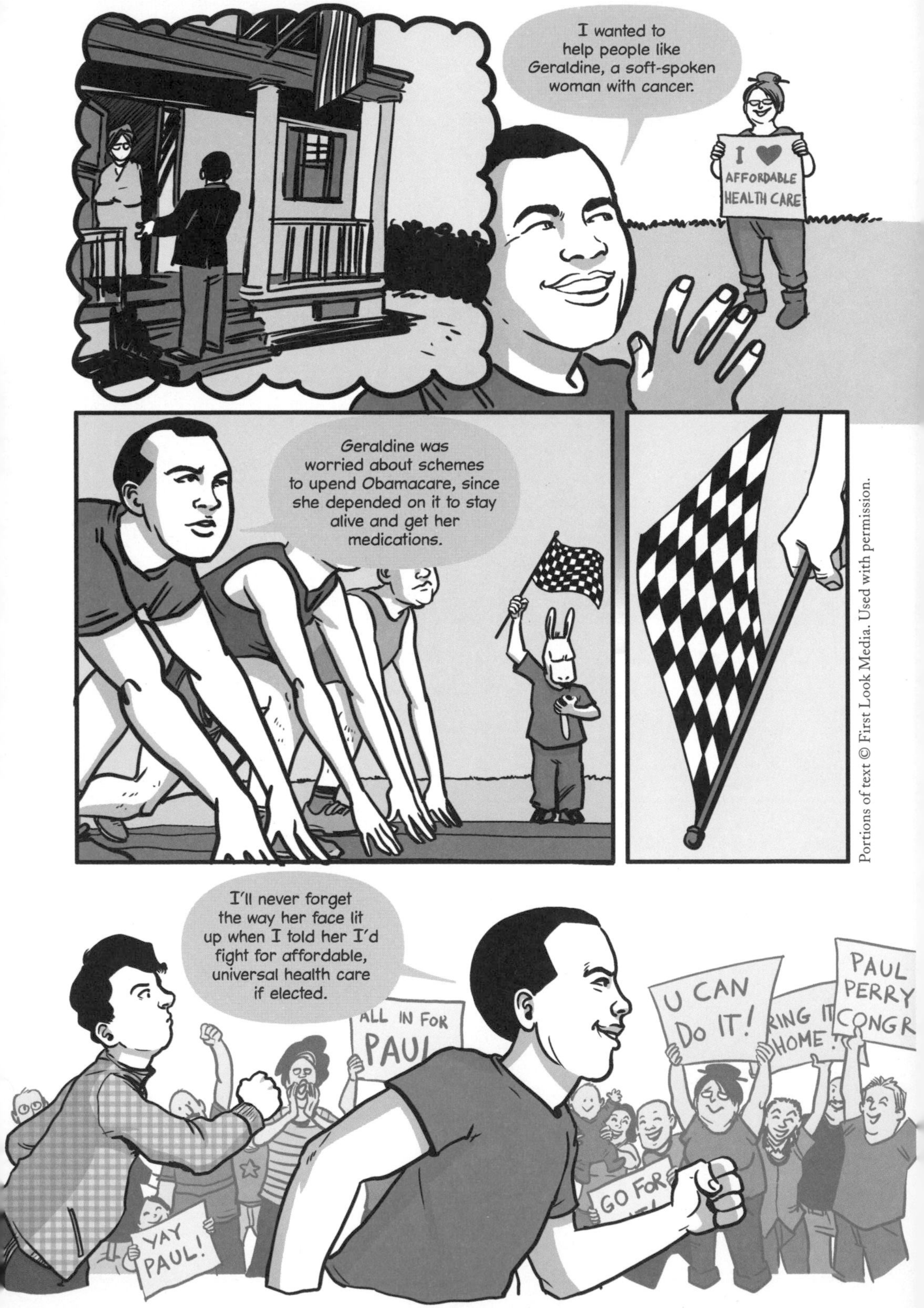
I wanted to help people like Geraldine, a soft-spoken woman with cancer.
I ♥ AFFORDABLE HEALTH CARE
Geraldine was worried about schemes to upend Obamacare, since she depended on it to stay alive and get her medications.
I'll never forget the way her face lit up when I told her I'd fight for affordable, universal health care if elected.
ALL IN FOR PAU
U CAN DO IT!
RING IT HOME!
PAUL PERRY CONGR
GO FOR
YAY PAUL!

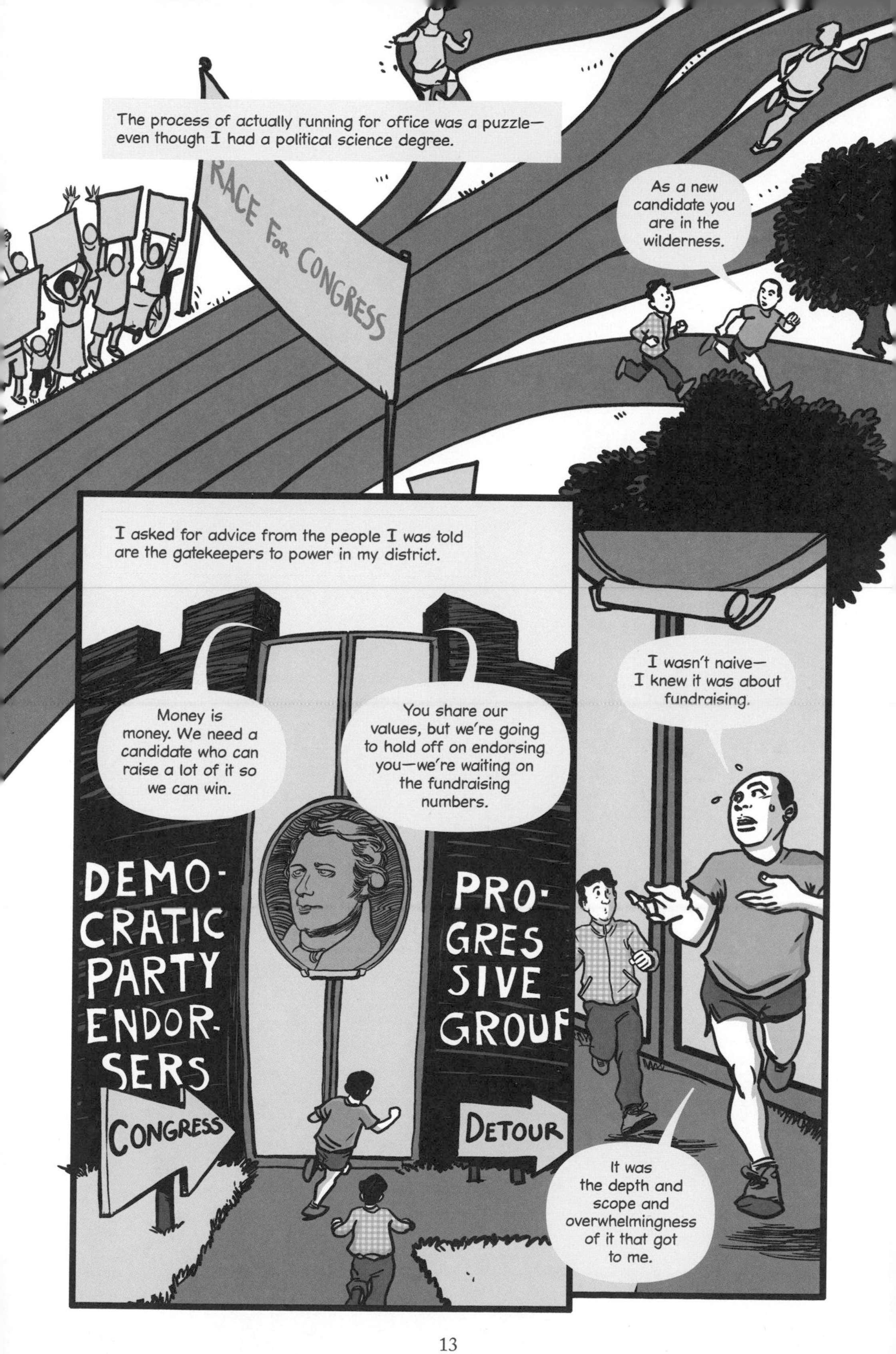
The process of actually running for office was a puzzle—even though I had a political science degree.
RACE FOR CONGRESS
As a new candidate you are in the wilderness.
I asked for advice from the people I was told are the gatekeepers to power in my district.
Money is money. We need a candidate who can raise a lot of it so we can win.
You share our values, but we're going to hold off on endorsing you—we're waiting on the fundraising numbers.
DEMO-CRATIC PARTY ENDOR-SERS
PRO-GRES SIVE GROUP
CONGRESS
DETOUR
I wasn't naive—I knew it was about fundraising.
It was the depth and scope and overwhelmingness of it that got to me.

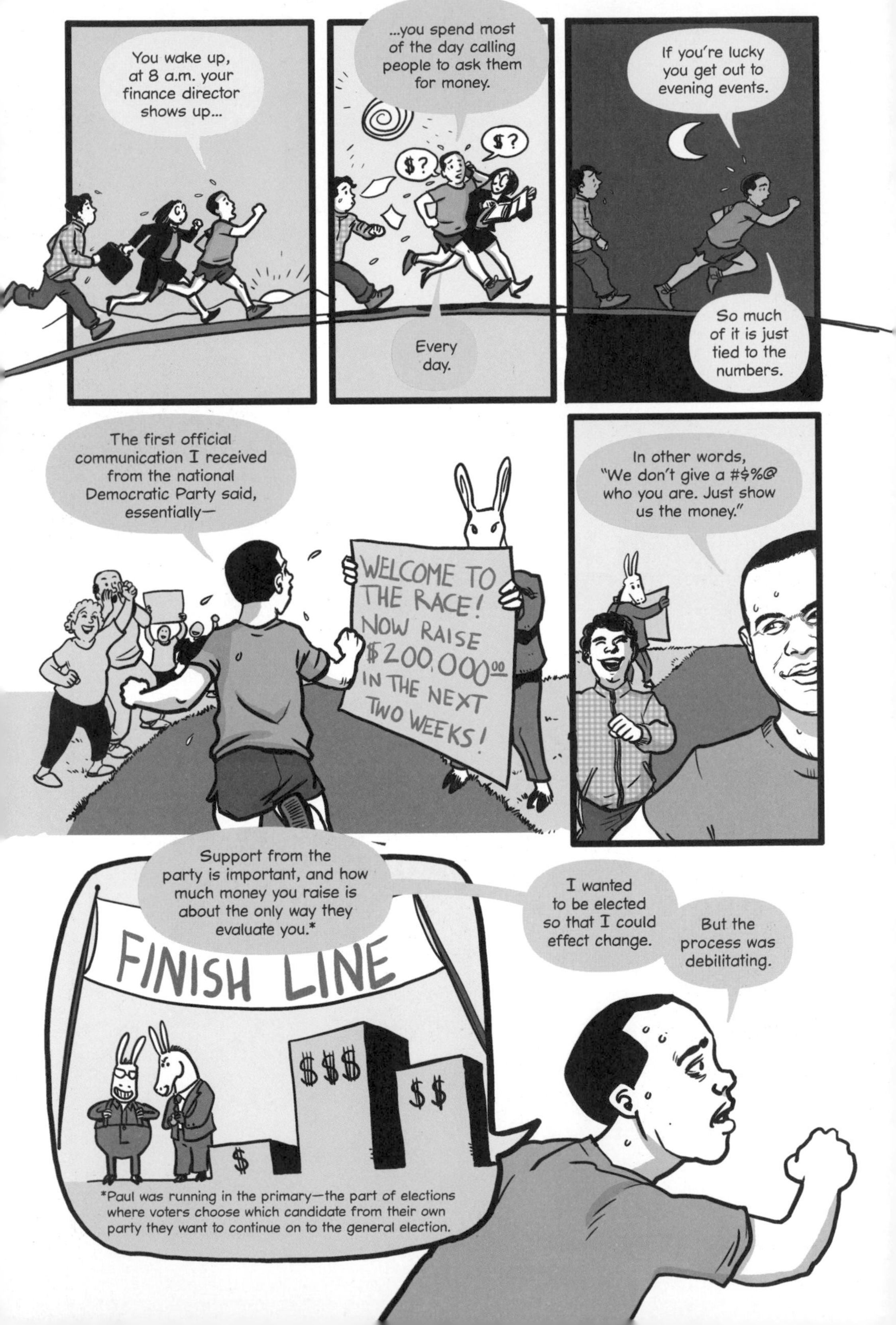
You wake up, at 8 a.m. your finance director shows up...
...you spend most of the day calling people to ask them for money.
$?
$?
Every day.
If you're lucky you get out to evening events.
So much of it is just tied to the numbers.
The first official communication I received from the national Democratic Party said, essentially—
WELCOME TO THE RACE! NOW RAISE $200,000.00 IN THE NEXT TWO WEEKS!
In other words, "We don't give a #$%@ who you are. Just show us the money."
Support from the party is important, and how much money you raise is about the only way they evaluate you.*
I wanted to be elected so that I could effect change.
But the process was debilitating.
FINISH LINE
$$$
$$
$
*Paul was running in the primary—the part of elections where voters choose which candidate from their own party they want to continue on to the general election.

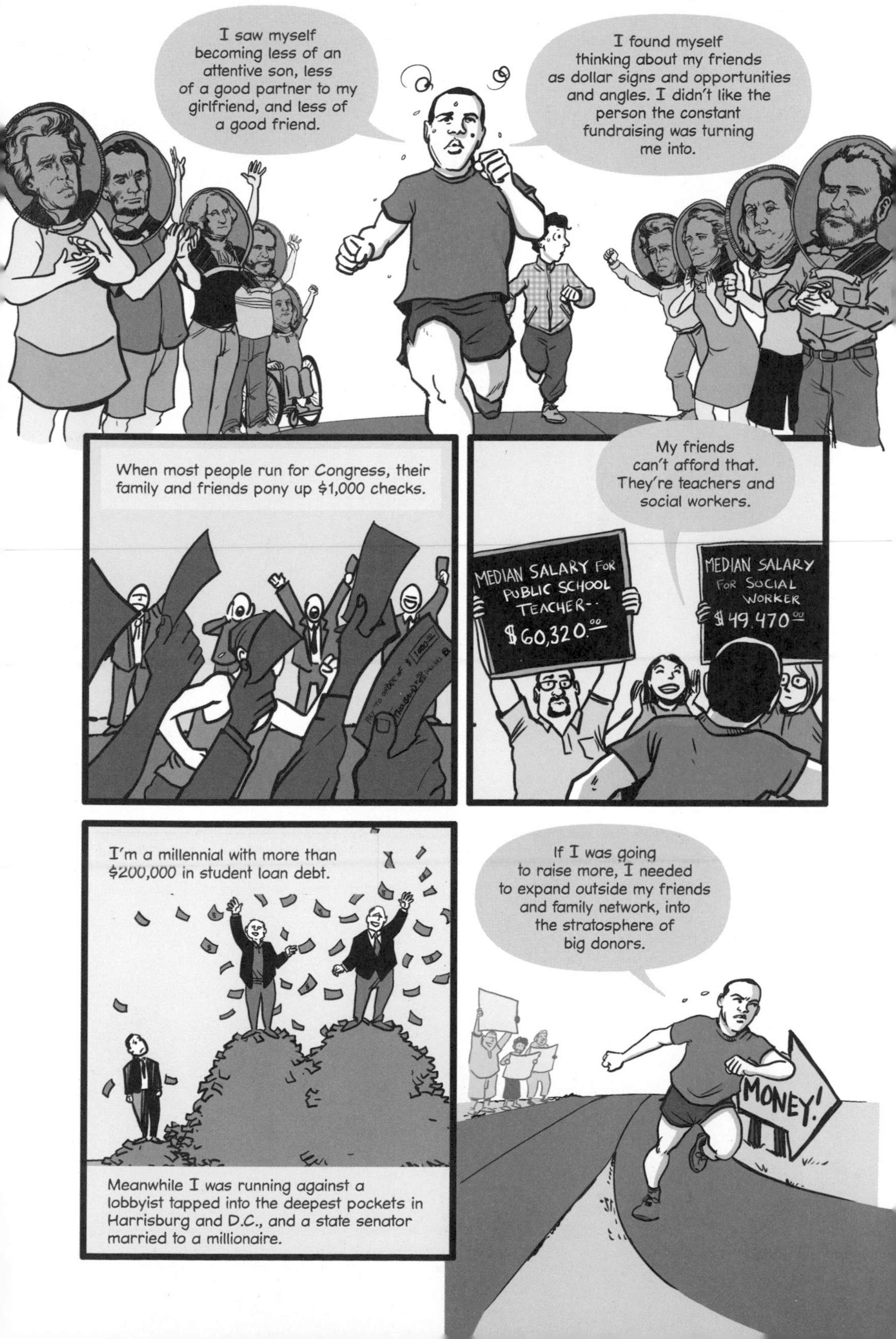
I saw myself becoming less of an attentive son, less of a good partner to my girlfriend, and less of a good friend.
I found myself thinking about my friends as dollar signs and opportunities and angles. I didn't like the person the constant fundraising was turning me into.
When most people run for Congress, their family and friends pony up $1,000 checks.
My friends can't afford that. They're teachers and social workers.
MEDIAN SALARY FOR PUBLIC SCHOOL TEACHER-- $60,320.00
MEDIAN SALARY FOR SOCIAL WORKER $49,470.00
I'm a millennial with more than $200,000 in student loan debt.
Meanwhile I was running against a lobbyist tapped into the deepest pockets in Harrisburg and D.C., and a state senator married to a millionaire.
If I was going to raise more, I needed to expand outside my friends and family network, into the stratosphere of big donors.
MONEY!

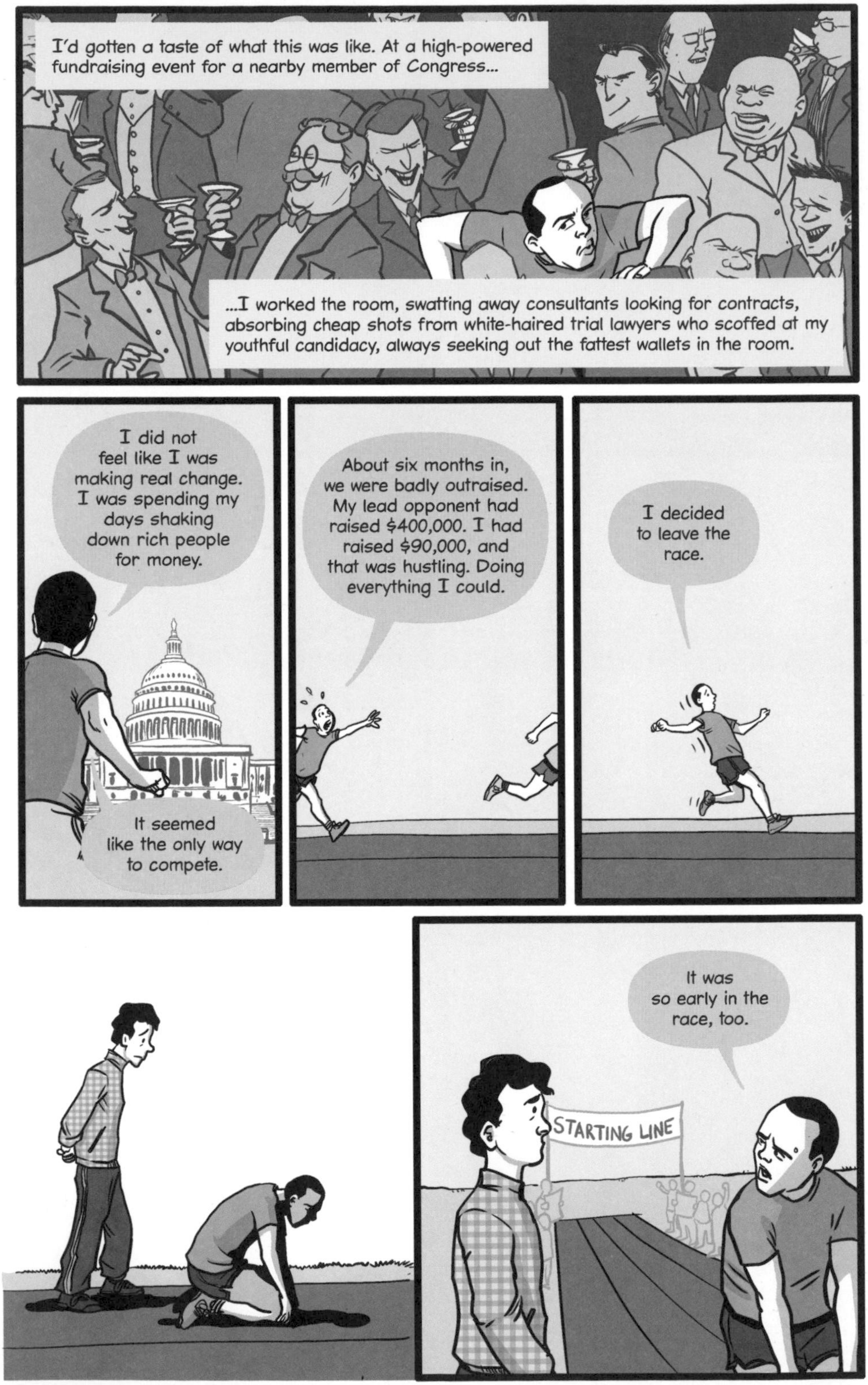
I'd gotten a taste of what this was like. At a high-powered fundraising event for a nearby member of Congress...
...I worked the room, swatting away consultants looking for contracts, absorbing cheap shots from white-haired trial lawyers who scoffed at my youthful candidacy, always seeking out the fattest wallets in the room.
I did not feel like I was making real change. I was spending my days shaking down rich people for money.
It seemed like the only way to compete.
About six months in, we were badly outraised. My lead opponent had raised $400,000. I had raised $90,000, and that was hustling. Doing everything I could.
I decided to leave the race.
It was so early in the race, too.
STARTING LINE

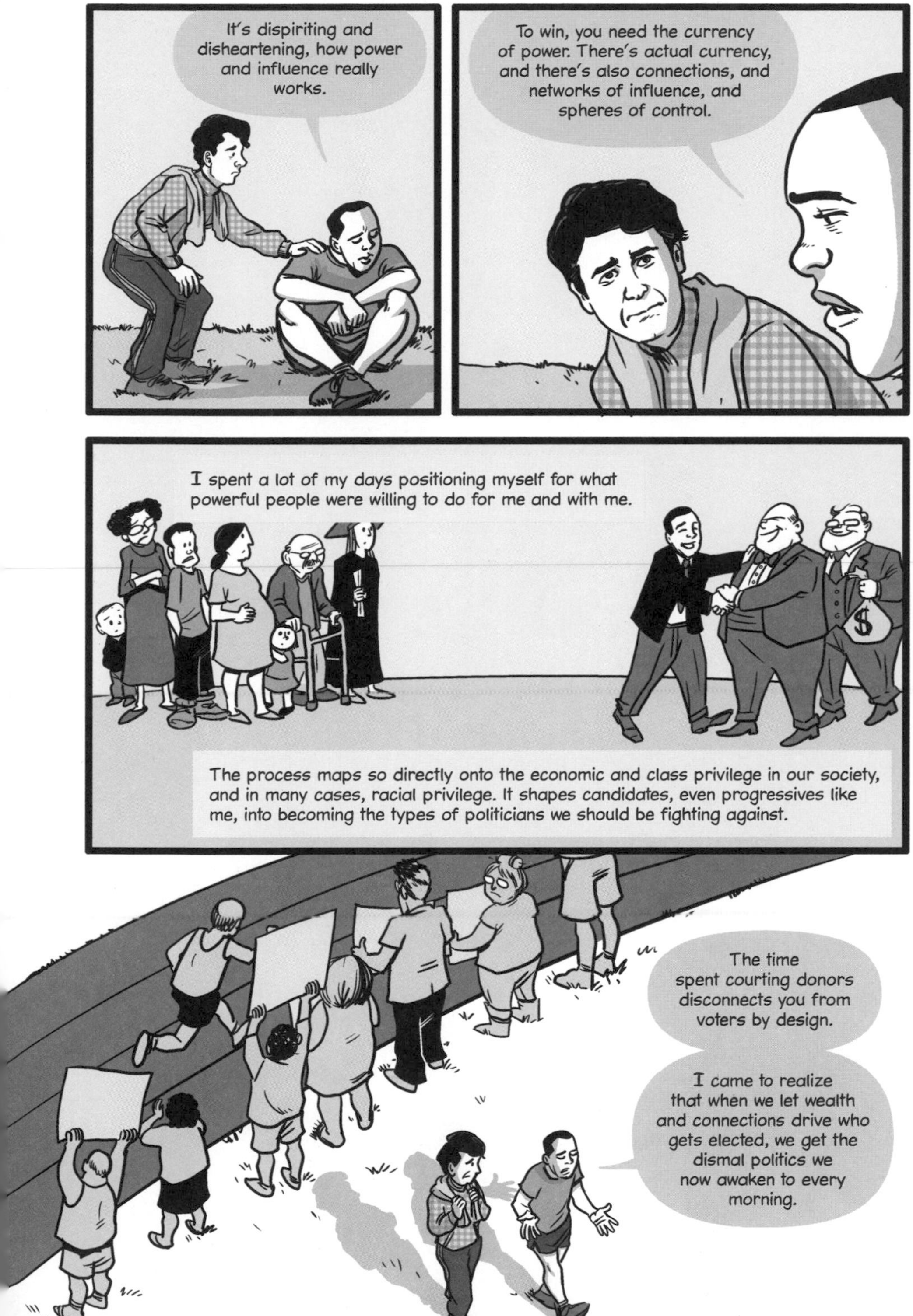
It's dispiriting and disheartening, how power and influence really works.
To win, you need the currency of power. There's actual currency, and there's also connections, and networks of influence, and spheres of control.
I spent a lot of my days positioning myself for what powerful people were willing to do for me and with me.
$
The process maps so directly onto the economic and class privilege in our society, and in many cases, racial privilege. It shapes candidates, even progressives like me, into becoming the types of politicians we should be fighting against.
The time spent courting donors disconnects you from voters by design.
I came to realize that when we let wealth and connections drive who gets elected, we get the dismal politics we now awaken to every morning.

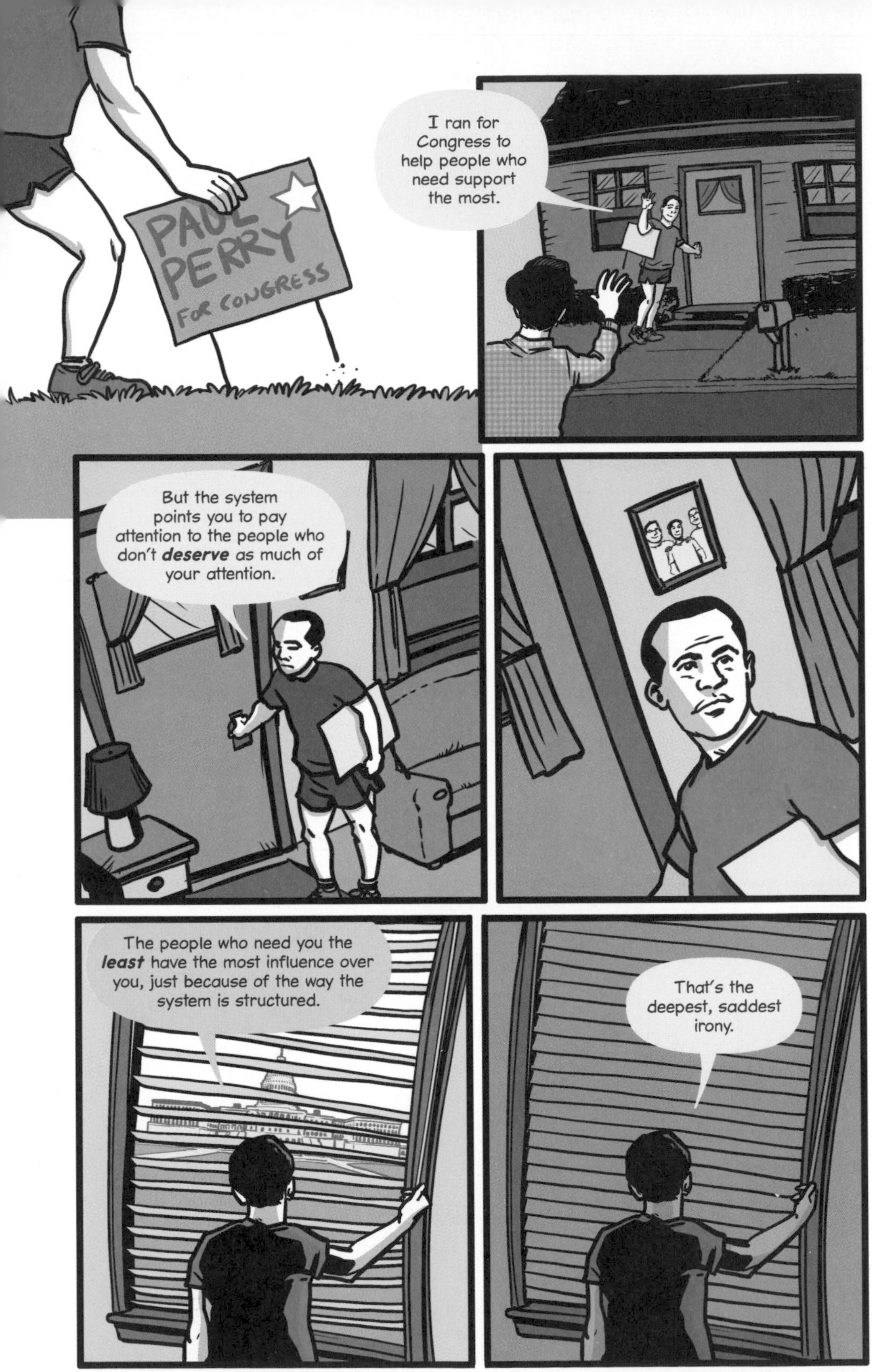
PAUL PERRY FOR CONGRESS
I ran for Congress to help people who need support the most.
But the system points you to pay attention to the people who don't ***deserve*** as much of your attention.
The people who need you the ***least*** have the most influence over you, just because of the way the system is structured.
That's the deepest, saddest irony.

democracy vouchers

Paul Perry found that running for Congress forces candidates to focus on the people funding their campaigns. In most elections, that means people with fat wallets.

But what if campaign money came from the community instead?

Welcome to Seattle

Meet Teresa Mosqueda.

Hi!!!

A third-generation Mexican American and daughter of educators and activists, Teresa grew up in the Pacific Northwest.

As a leader in the Washington State labor movement and a public health advocate, Teresa helped raise the state minimum wage and pass paid sick leave...

...and led a program to make sure every child in Washington could receive health care.

We've covered 96% of the kiddos in our state.

RAISE UP WASHINGTON YES

I AM HO A SIGN

VOTE Y 1433

R Wa YES1

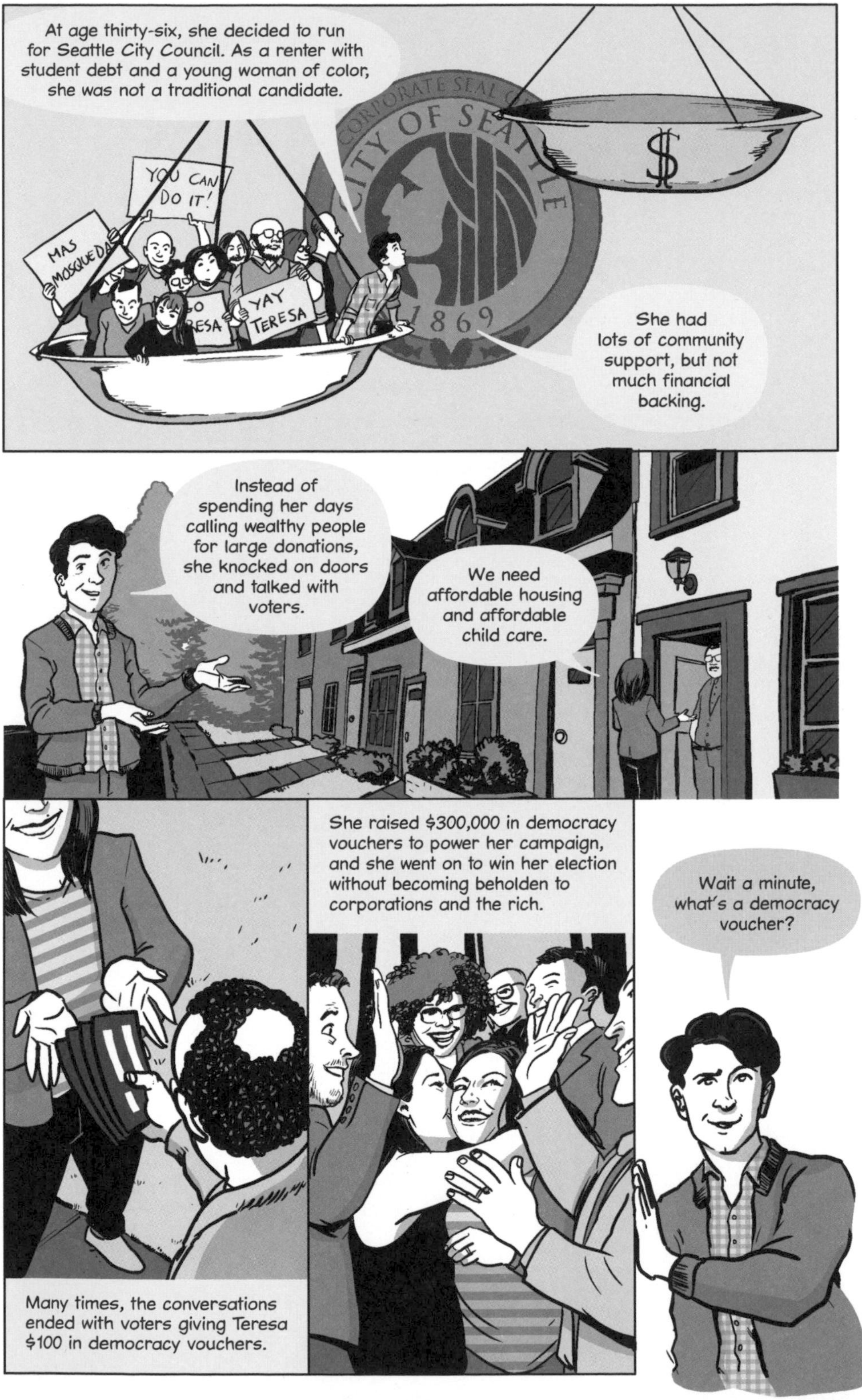
At age thirty-six, she decided to run for Seattle City Council. As a renter with student debt and a young woman of color, she was not a traditional candidate.
CORPORATE SEAL OF CITY OF SEATTLE 1869
YOU CAN DO IT!
YAY TERESA
$
She had lots of community support, but not much financial backing.
Instead of spending her days calling wealthy people for large donations, she knocked on doors and talked with voters.
We need affordable housing and affordable child care.
Many times, the conversations ended with voters giving Teresa $100 in democracy vouchers.
She raised $300,000 in democracy vouchers to power her campaign, and she went on to win her election without becoming beholden to corporations and the rich.
Wait a minute, what's a democracy voucher?

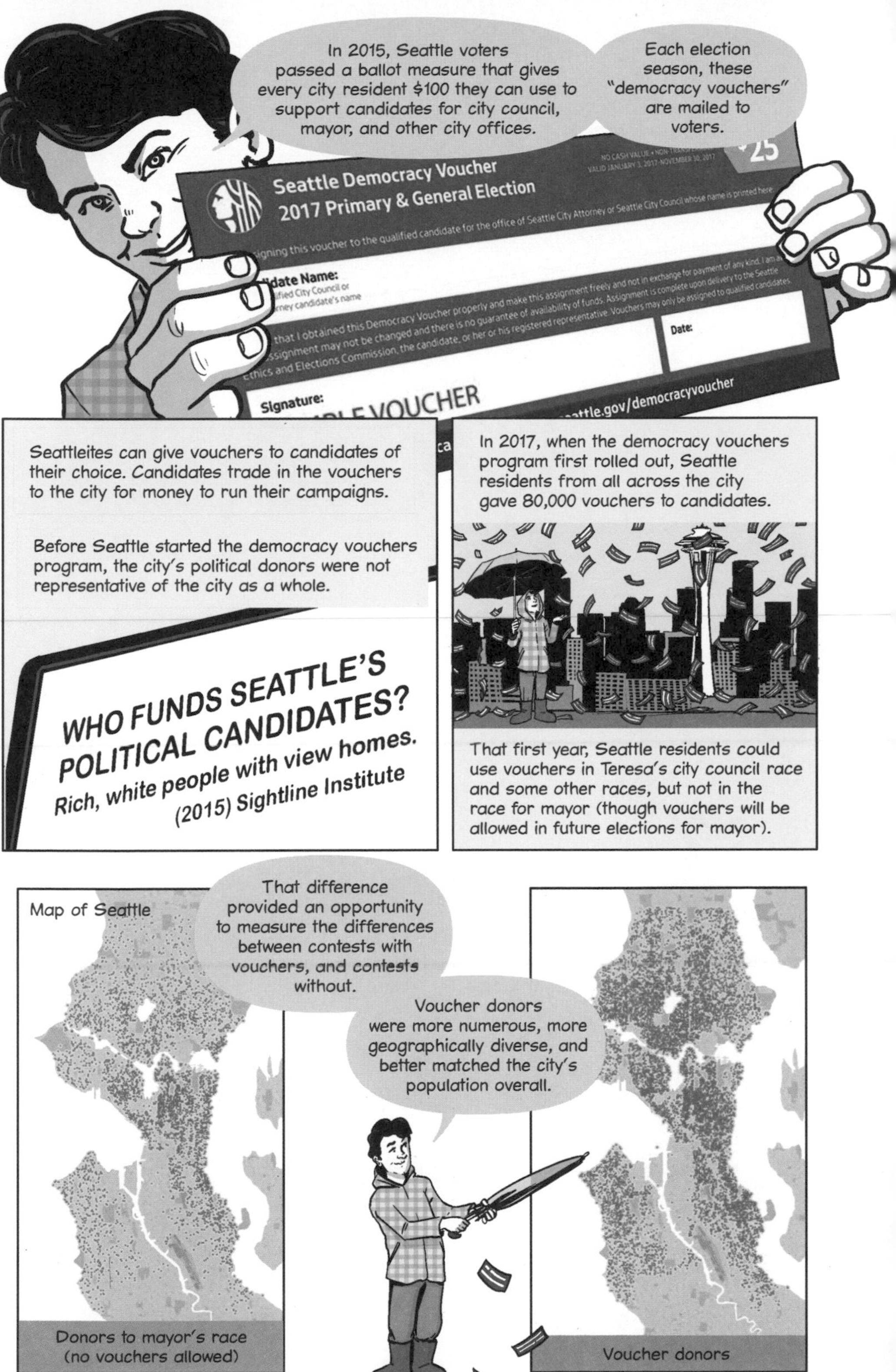
In 2015, Seattle voters passed a ballot measure that gives every city resident $100 they can use to support candidates for city council, mayor, and other city offices.
Each election season, these "democracy vouchers" are mailed to voters.
Seattle Democracy Voucher
2017 Primary & General Election
$25
Signature:
Date:
seattle.gov/democracyvoucher
Seattleites can give vouchers to candidates of their choice. Candidates trade in the vouchers to the city for money to run their campaigns.
Before Seattle started the democracy vouchers program, the city's political donors were not representative of the city as a whole.
WHO FUNDS SEATTLE'S POLITICAL CANDIDATES?
Rich, white people with view homes.
(2015) Sightline Institute
In 2017, when the democracy vouchers program first rolled out, Seattle residents from all across the city gave 80,000 vouchers to candidates.
That first year, Seattle residents could use vouchers in Teresa's city council race and some other races, but not in the race for mayor (though vouchers will be allowed in future elections for mayor).
Map of Seattle
That difference provided an opportunity to measure the differences between contests with vouchers, and contests without.
Voucher donors were more numerous, more geographically diverse, and better matched the city's population overall.
Donors to mayor's race (no vouchers allowed)
Voucher donors

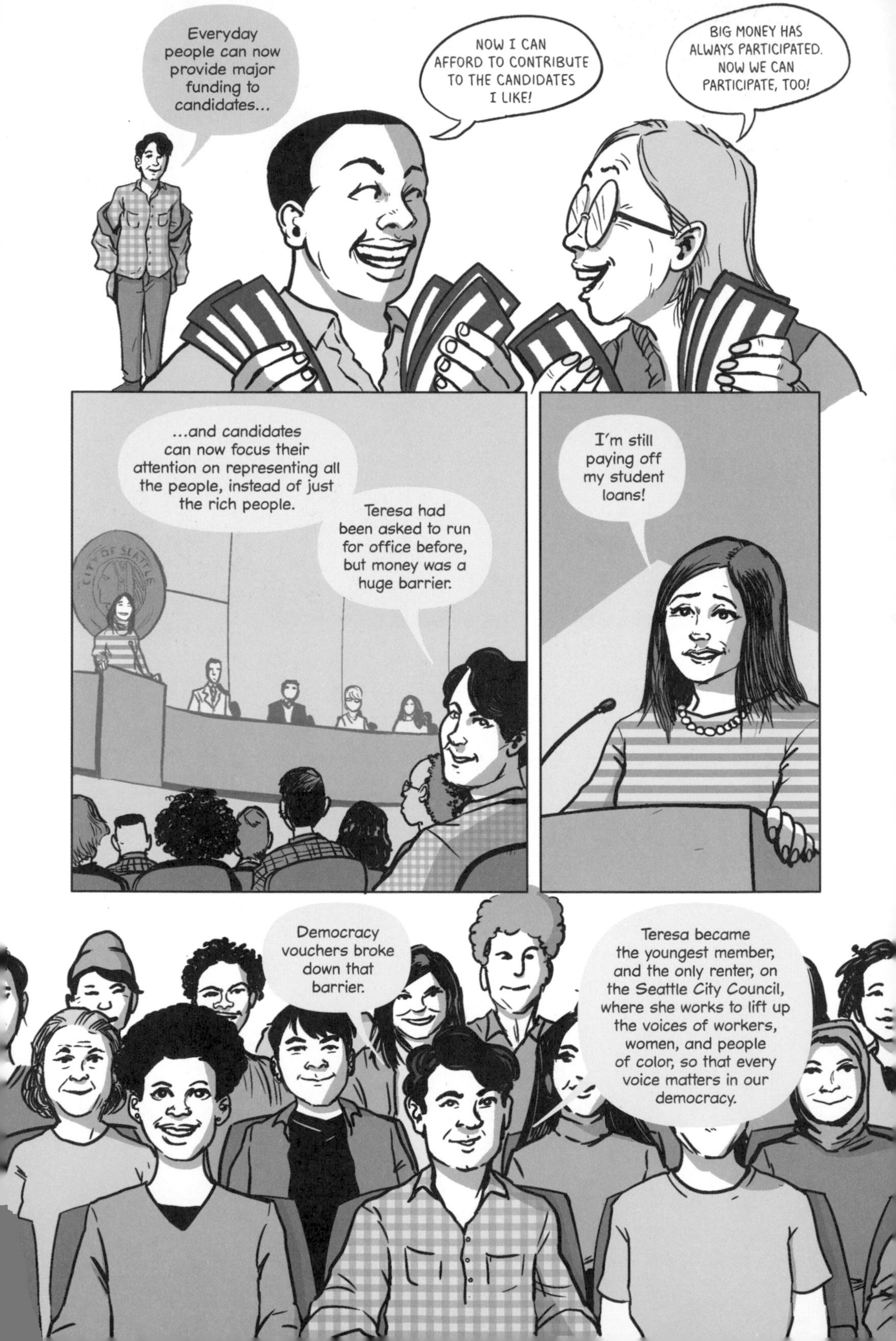
Everyday people can now provide major funding to candidates...
NOW I CAN AFFORD TO CONTRIBUTE TO THE CANDIDATES I LIKE!
BIG MONEY HAS ALWAYS PARTICIPATED. NOW WE CAN PARTICIPATE, TOO!
...and candidates can now focus their attention on representing all the people, instead of just the rich people.
Teresa had been asked to run for office before, but money was a huge barrier.
CITY OF SEATTLE
I'm still paying off my student loans!
Democracy vouchers broke down that barrier.
Teresa became the youngest member, and the only renter, on the Seattle City Council, where she works to lift up the voices of workers, women, and people of color, so that every voice matters in our democracy.

clean elections

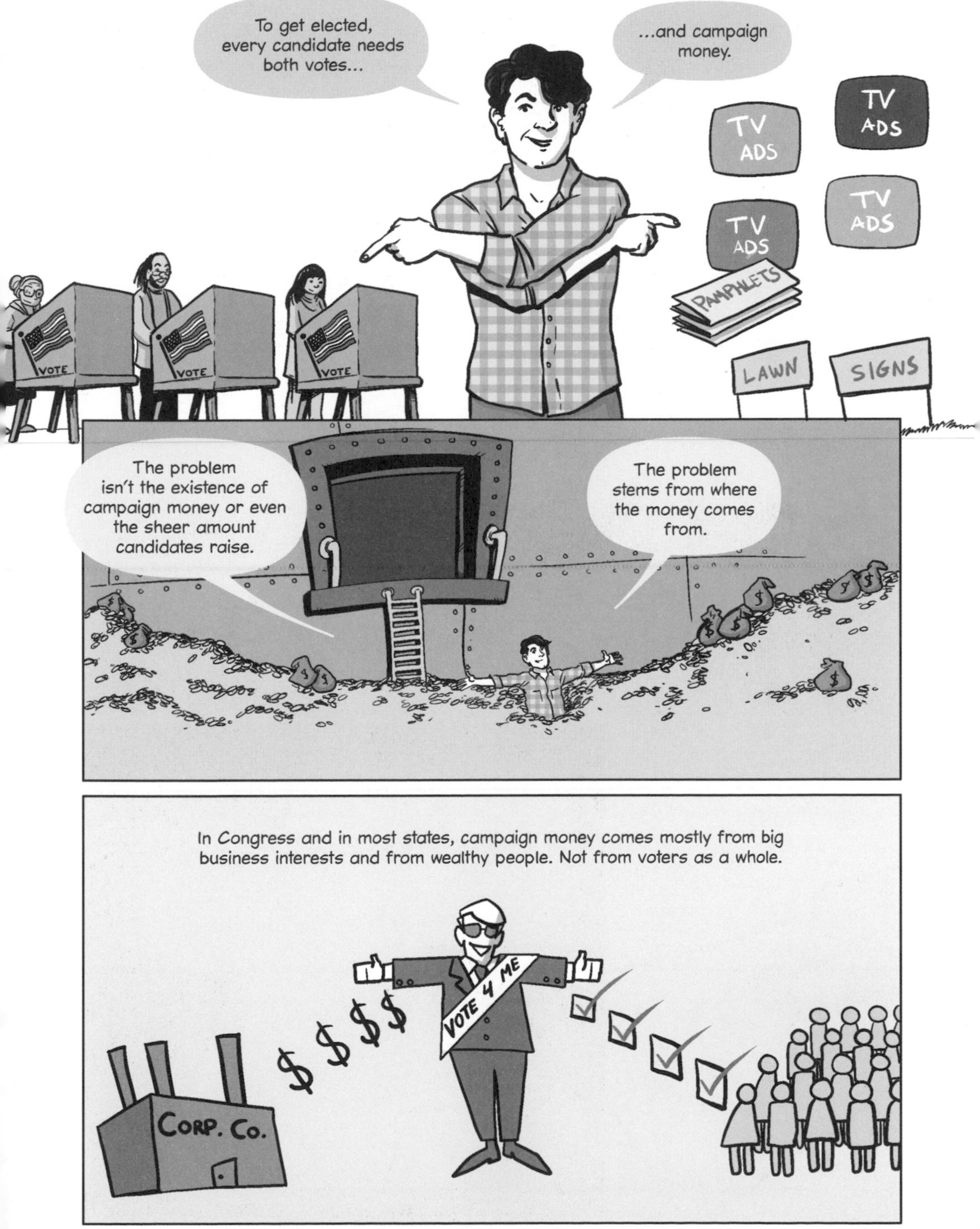

To get elected, every candidate needs both votes...
...and campaign money.
VOTE
VOTE
VOTE
TV ADS
TV ADS
TV ADS
TV ADS
PAMPHLETS
LAWN
SIGNS
The problem isn't the existence of campaign money or even the sheer amount candidates raise.
The problem stems from where the money comes from.
In Congress and in most states, campaign money comes mostly from big business interests and from wealthy people. Not from voters as a whole.
VOTE 4 ME
CORP. Co.

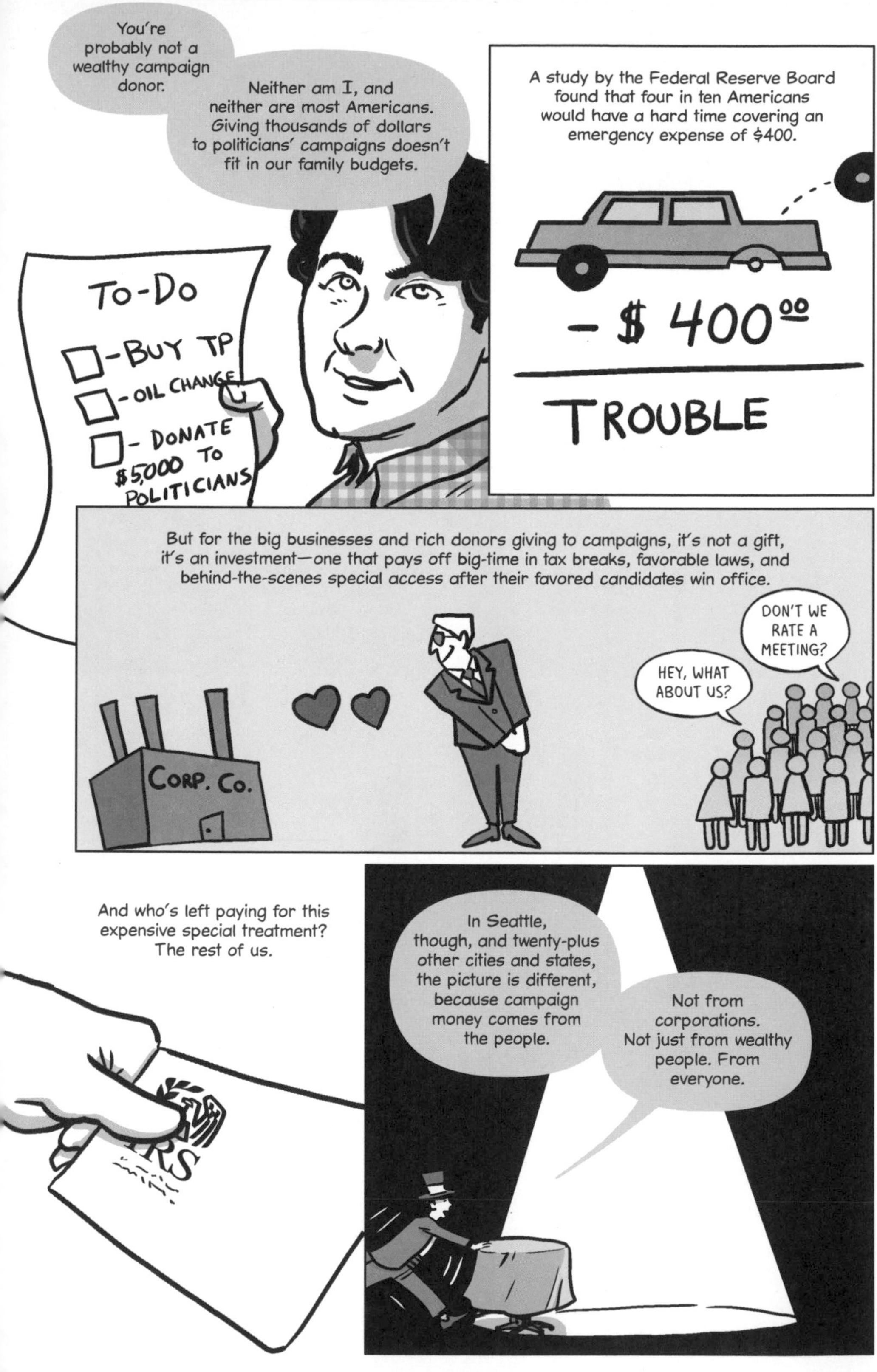
You're probably not a wealthy campaign donor.
Neither am I, and neither are most Americans. Giving thousands of dollars to politicians' campaigns doesn't fit in our family budgets.
TO-DO
-BUY TP
-OIL CHANGE
-DONATE $5,000 TO POLITICIANS
A study by the Federal Reserve Board found that four in ten Americans would have a hard time covering an emergency expense of $400.
- $ 400.00
TROUBLE
But for the big businesses and rich donors giving to campaigns, it's not a gift, it's an investment—one that pays off big-time in tax breaks, favorable laws, and behind-the-scenes special access after their favored candidates win office.
CORP. CO.
HEY, WHAT ABOUT US?
DON'T WE RATE A MEETING?
And who's left paying for this expensive special treatment? The rest of us.
IRS
In Seattle, though, and twenty-plus other cities and states, the picture is different, because campaign money comes from the people.
Not from corporations. Not just from wealthy people. From everyone.

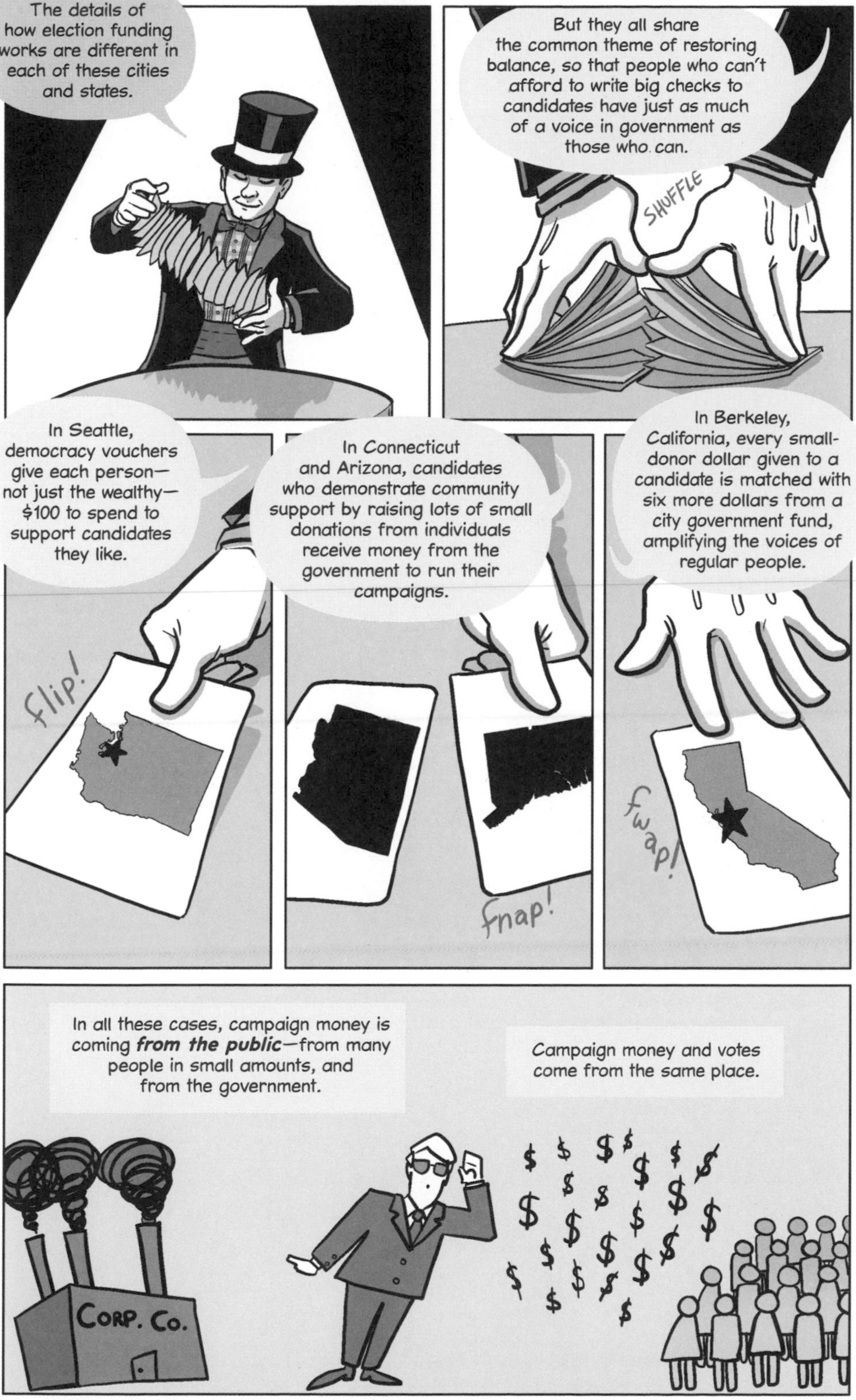
The details of how election funding works are different in each of these cities and states.
But they all share the common theme of restoring balance, so that people who can't afford to write big checks to candidates have just as much of a voice in government as those who can.
SHUFFLE
In Seattle, democracy vouchers give each person—not just the wealthy—$100 to spend to support candidates they like.
flip!
In Connecticut and Arizona, candidates who demonstrate community support by raising lots of small donations from individuals receive money from the government to run their campaigns.
fnap!
In Berkeley, California, every small-donor dollar given to a candidate is matched with six more dollars from a city government fund, amplifying the voices of regular people.
fwap!
In all these cases, campaign money is coming *from the public*—from many people in small amounts, and from the government.
Campaign money and votes come from the same place.
CORP. CO.

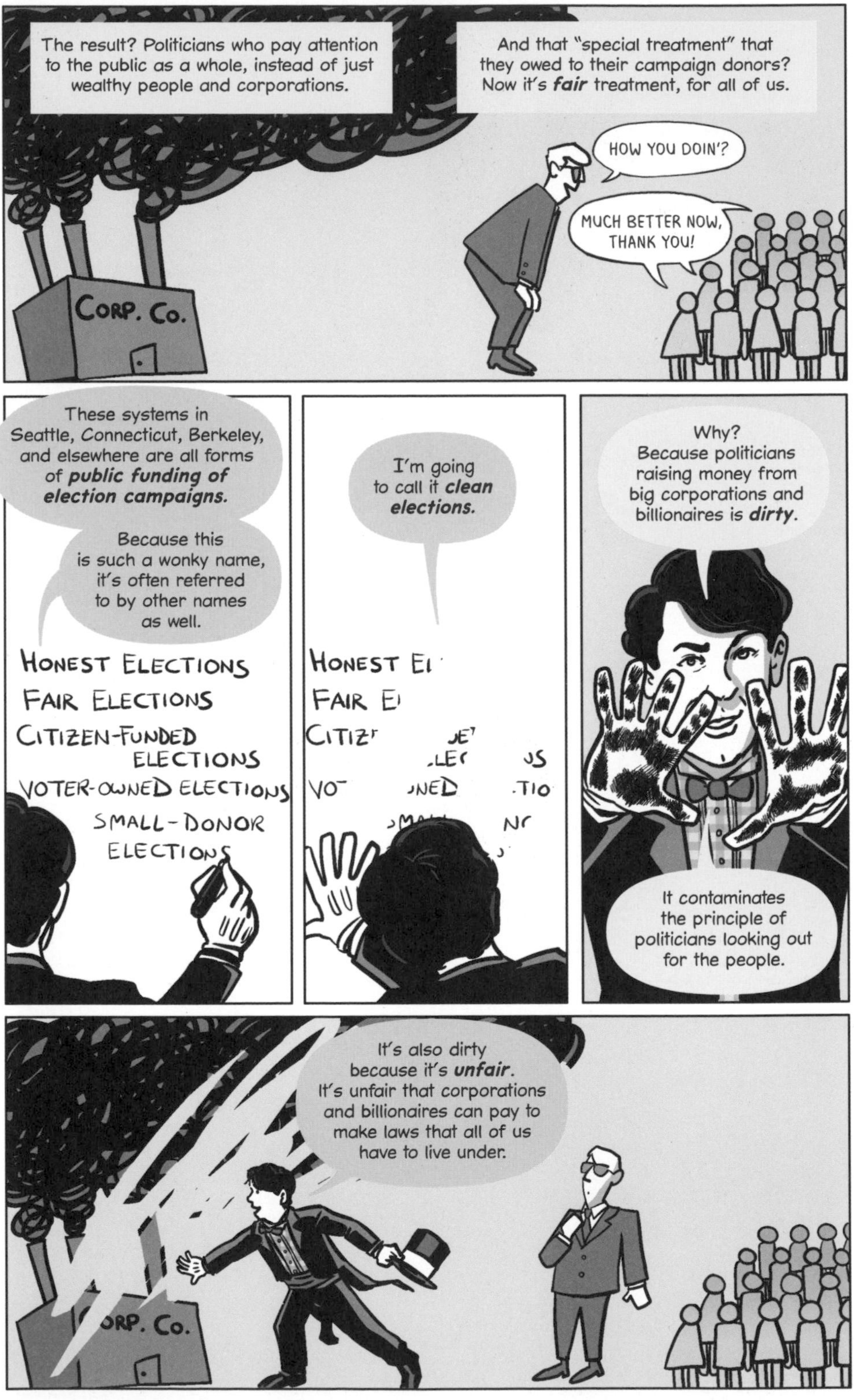

The result? Politicians who pay attention to the public as a whole, instead of just wealthy people and corporations.
And that "special treatment" that they owed to their campaign donors? Now it's ***fair*** treatment, for all of us.
HOW YOU DOIN'?
MUCH BETTER NOW, THANK YOU!
CORP. CO.
These systems in Seattle, Connecticut, Berkeley, and elsewhere are all forms of ***public funding of election campaigns.***
Because this is such a wonky name, it's often referred to by other names as well.
HONEST ELECTIONS
FAIR ELECTIONS
CITIZEN-FUNDED ELECTIONS
VOTER-OWNED ELECTIONS
SMALL-DONOR ELECTIONS
I'm going to call it ***clean elections.***
Why? Because politicians raising money from big corporations and billionaires is ***dirty.***
It contaminates the principle of politicians looking out for the people.
It's also dirty because it's ***unfair.*** It's unfair that corporations and billionaires can pay to make laws that all of us have to live under.
ORP. CO.

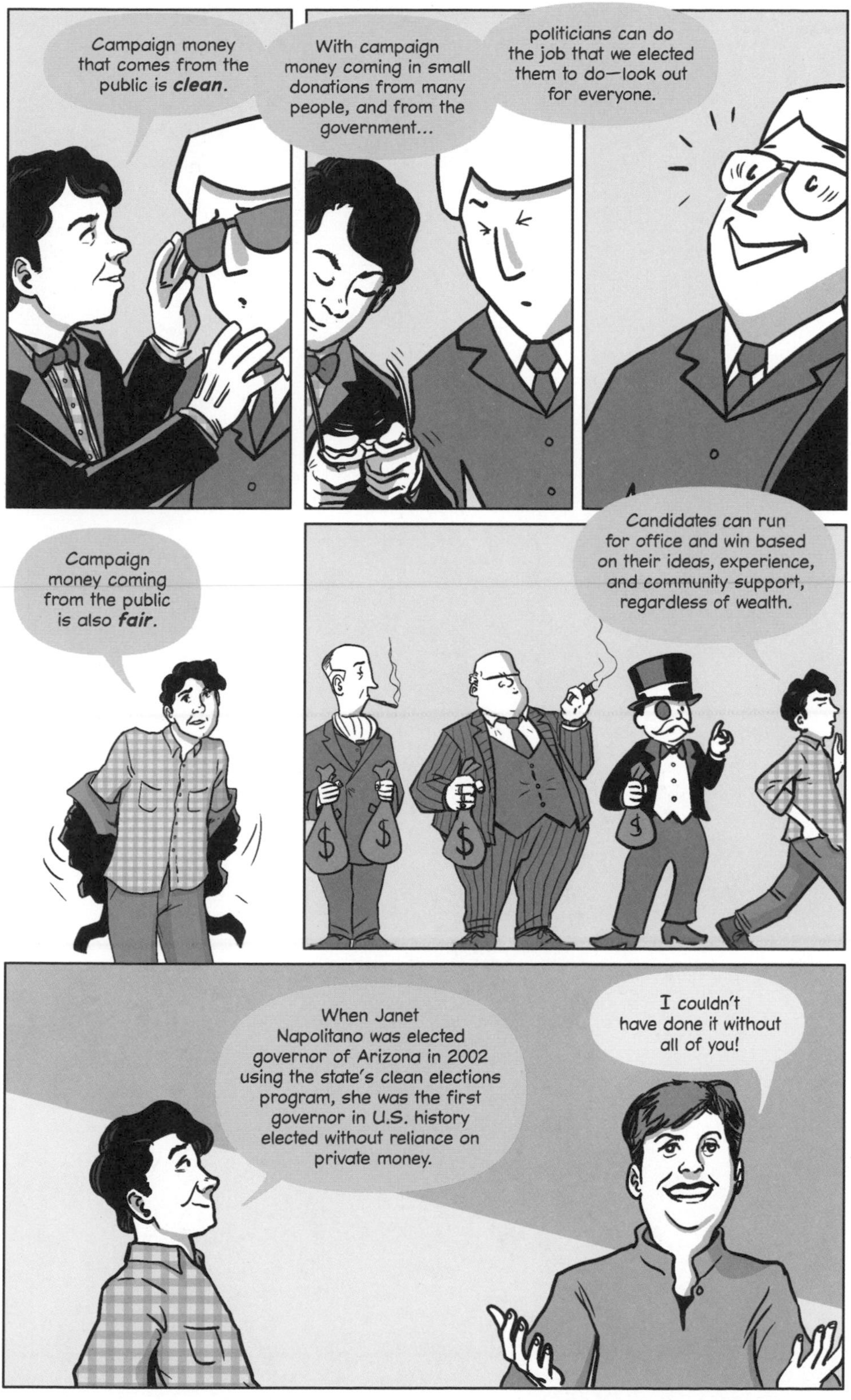
Campaign money that comes from the public is ***clean***.
With campaign money coming in small donations from many people, and from the government...
politicians can do the job that we elected them to do—look out for everyone.
Campaign money coming from the public is also ***fair***.
Candidates can run for office and win based on their ideas, experience, and community support, regardless of wealth.
When Janet Napolitano was elected governor of Arizona in 2002 using the state's clean elections program, she was the first governor in U.S. history elected without reliance on private money.
I couldn't have done it without all of you!

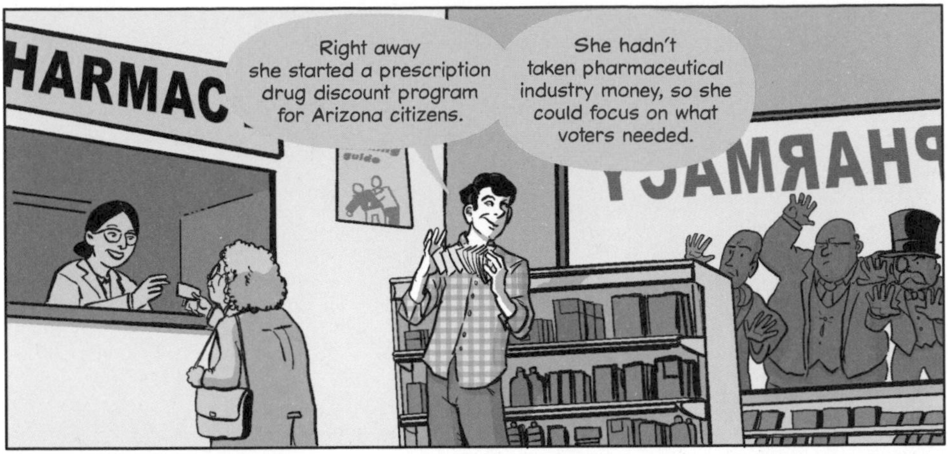
HARMAC
Right away she started a prescription drug discount program for Arizona citizens.
She hadn't taken pharmaceutical industry money, so she could focus on what voters needed.

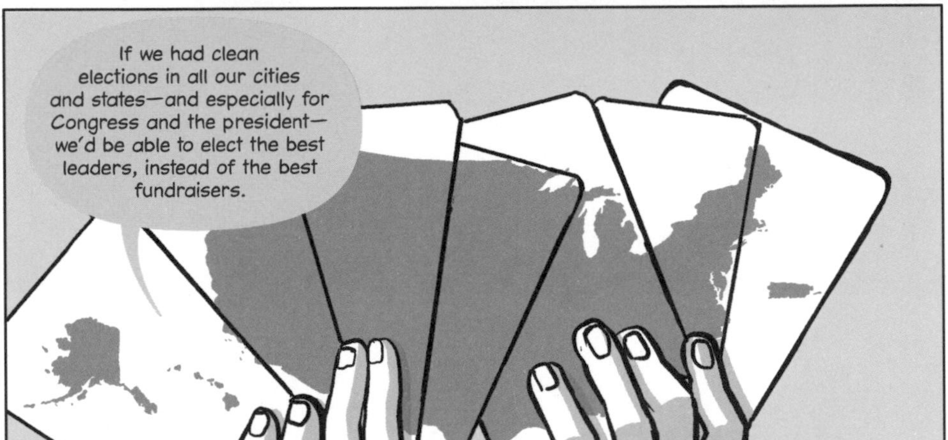
If we had clean elections in all our cities and states—and especially for Congress and the president—we'd be able to elect the best leaders, instead of the best fundraisers.

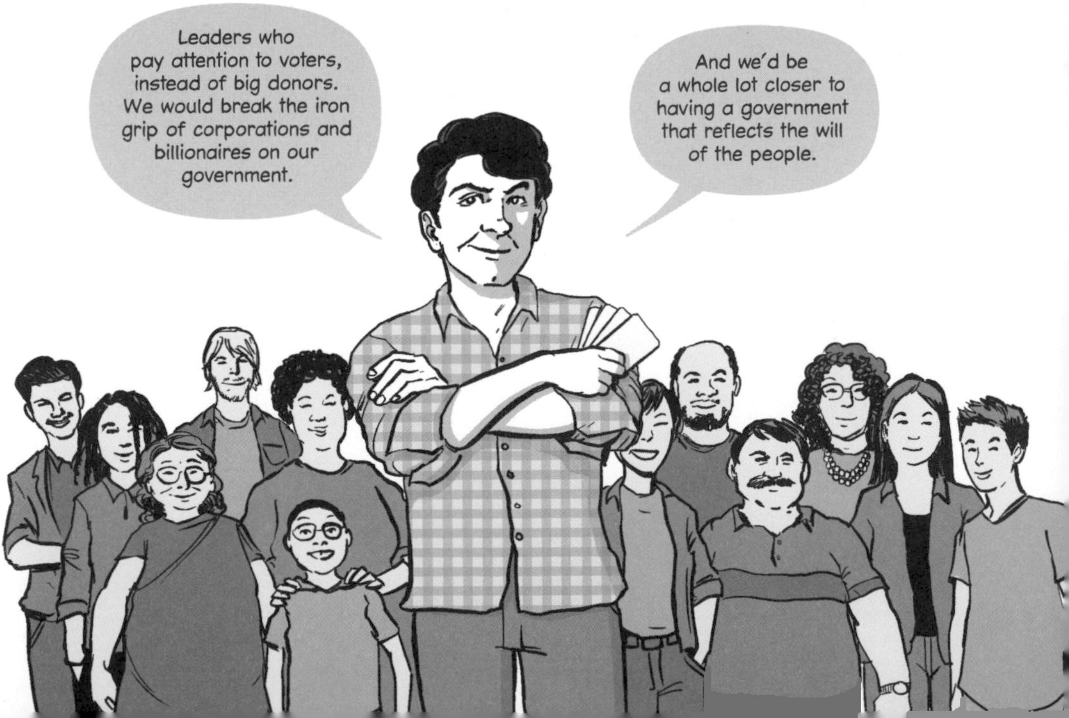
Leaders who pay attention to voters, instead of big donors. We would break the iron grip of corporations and billionaires on our government.
And we'd be a whole lot closer to having a government that reflects the will of the people.

power to the public

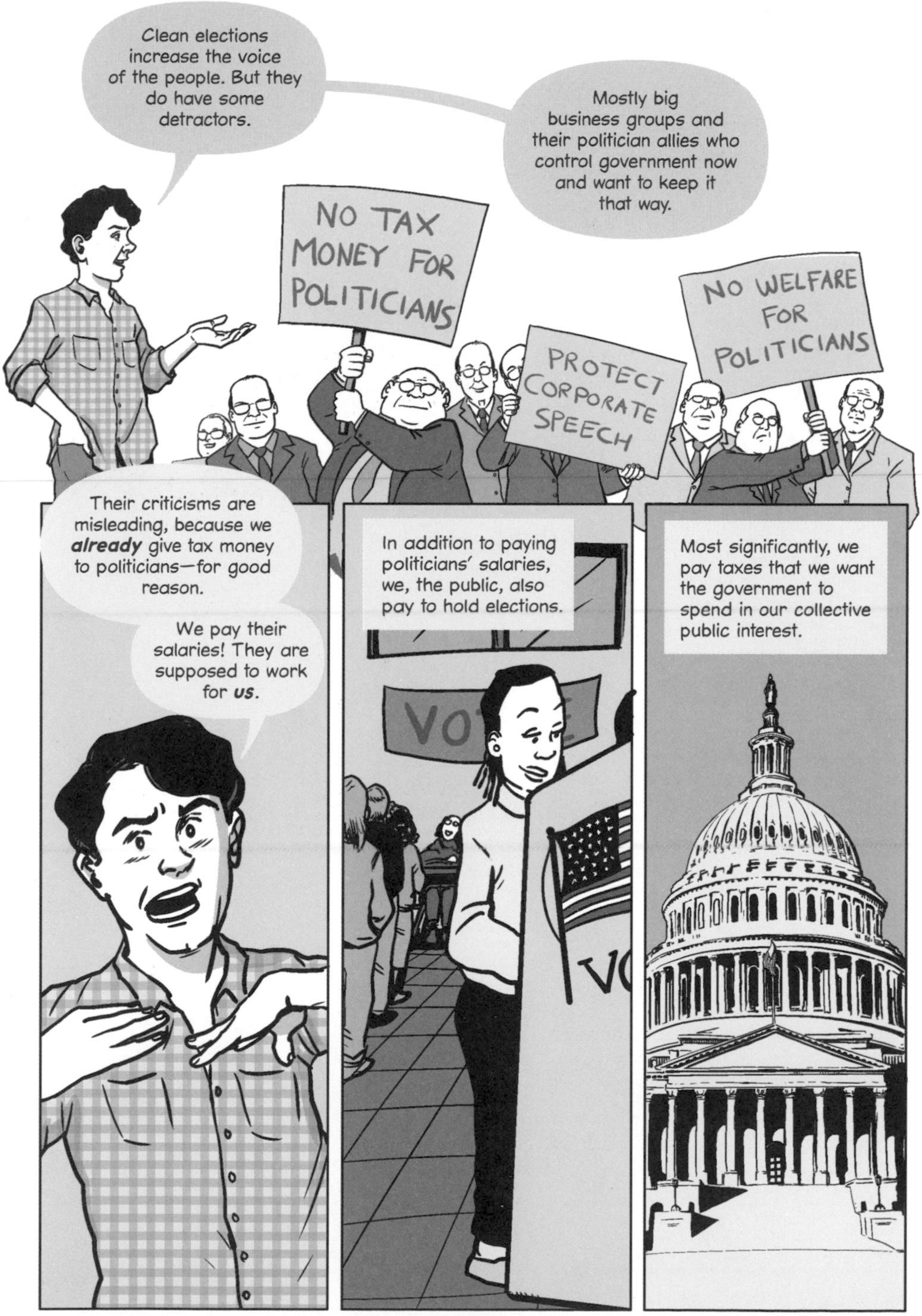

Clean elections increase the voice of the people. But they do have some detractors.
Mostly big business groups and their politician allies who control government now and want to keep it that way.
NO TAX MONEY FOR POLITICIANS
PROTECT CORPORATE SPEECH
NO WELFARE FOR POLITICIANS
Their criticisms are misleading, because we ***already*** give tax money to politicians—for good reason.
We pay their salaries! They are supposed to work for ***us***.
In addition to paying politicians' salaries, we, the public, also pay to hold elections.
VOTE
Most significantly, we pay taxes that we want the government to spend in our collective public interest.

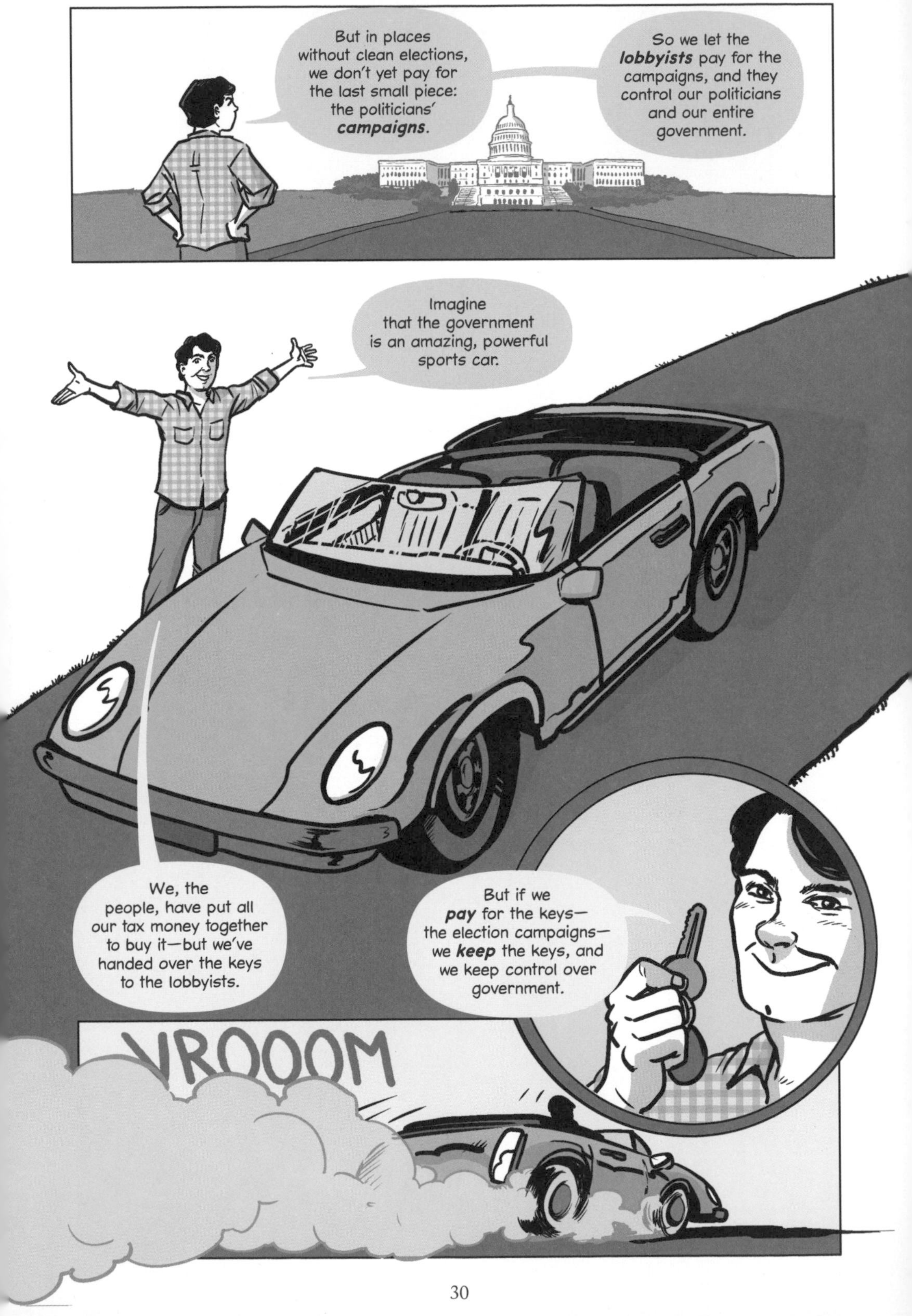
But in places without clean elections, we don't yet pay for the last small piece: the politicians' **campaigns**.
So we let the **lobbyists** pay for the campaigns, and they control our politicians and our entire government.
Imagine that the government is an amazing, powerful sports car.
We, the people, have put all our tax money together to buy it—but we've handed over the keys to the lobbyists.
But if we **pay** for the keys—the election campaigns—we **keep** the keys, and we keep control over government.
VROOOM

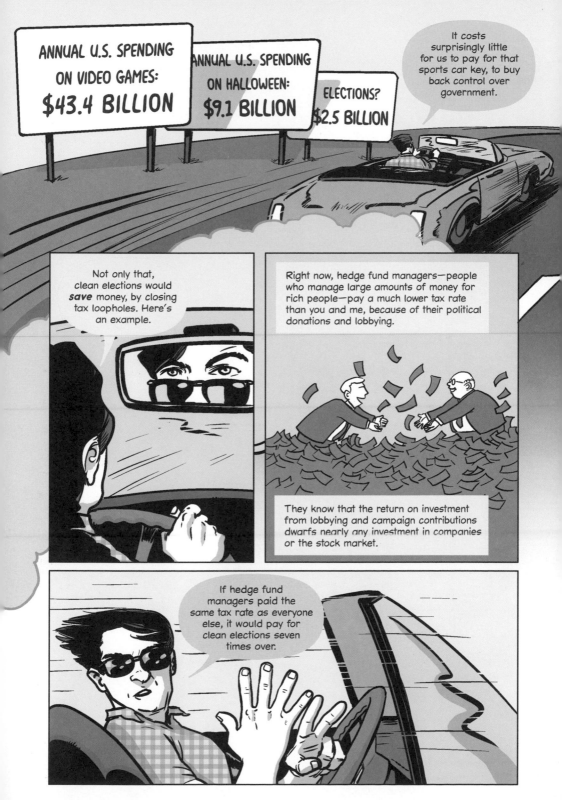

ANNUAL U.S. SPENDING ON VIDEO GAMES: **$43.4 BILLION**

ANNUAL U.S. SPENDING ON HALLOWEEN: **$9.1 BILLION**

ELECTIONS? $2.5 BILLION

It costs surprisingly little for us to pay for that sports car key, to buy back control over government.

Not only that, clean elections would *save* money, by closing tax loopholes. Here's an example.

Right now, hedge fund managers—people who manage large amounts of money for rich people—pay a much lower tax rate than you and me, because of their political donations and lobbying.

They know that the return on investment from lobbying and campaign contributions dwarfs nearly any investment in companies or the stock market.

If hedge fund managers paid the same tax rate as everyone else, it would pay for clean elections seven times over.

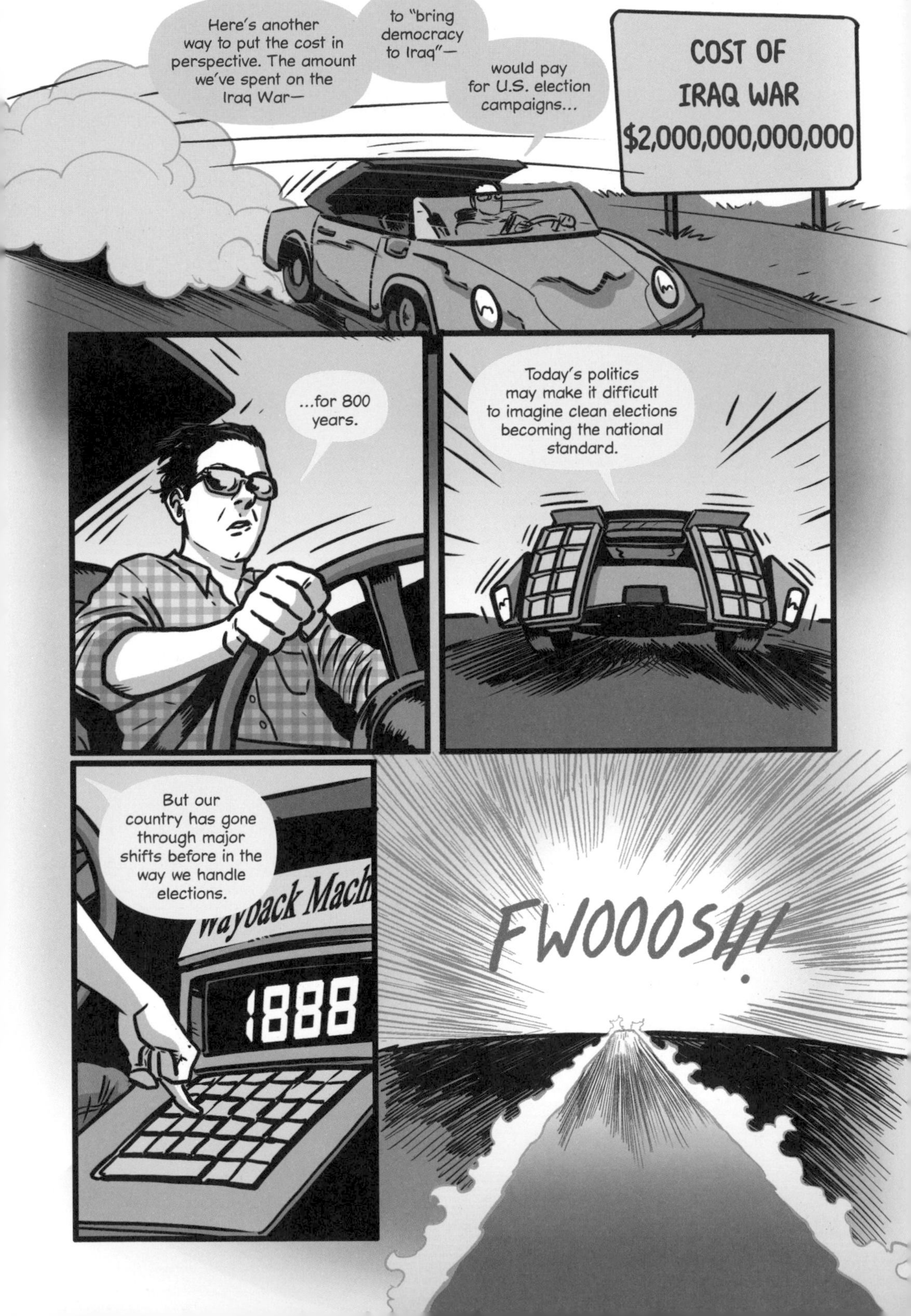
Here's another way to put the cost in perspective. The amount we've spent on the Iraq War—
to "bring democracy to Iraq"—
would pay for U.S. election campaigns...
COST OF IRAQ WAR $2,000,000,000,000
...for 800 years.
Today's politics may make it difficult to imagine clean elections becoming the national standard.
But our country has gone through major shifts before in the way we handle elections.
Wayback Mach
1888
FWOOOSH!

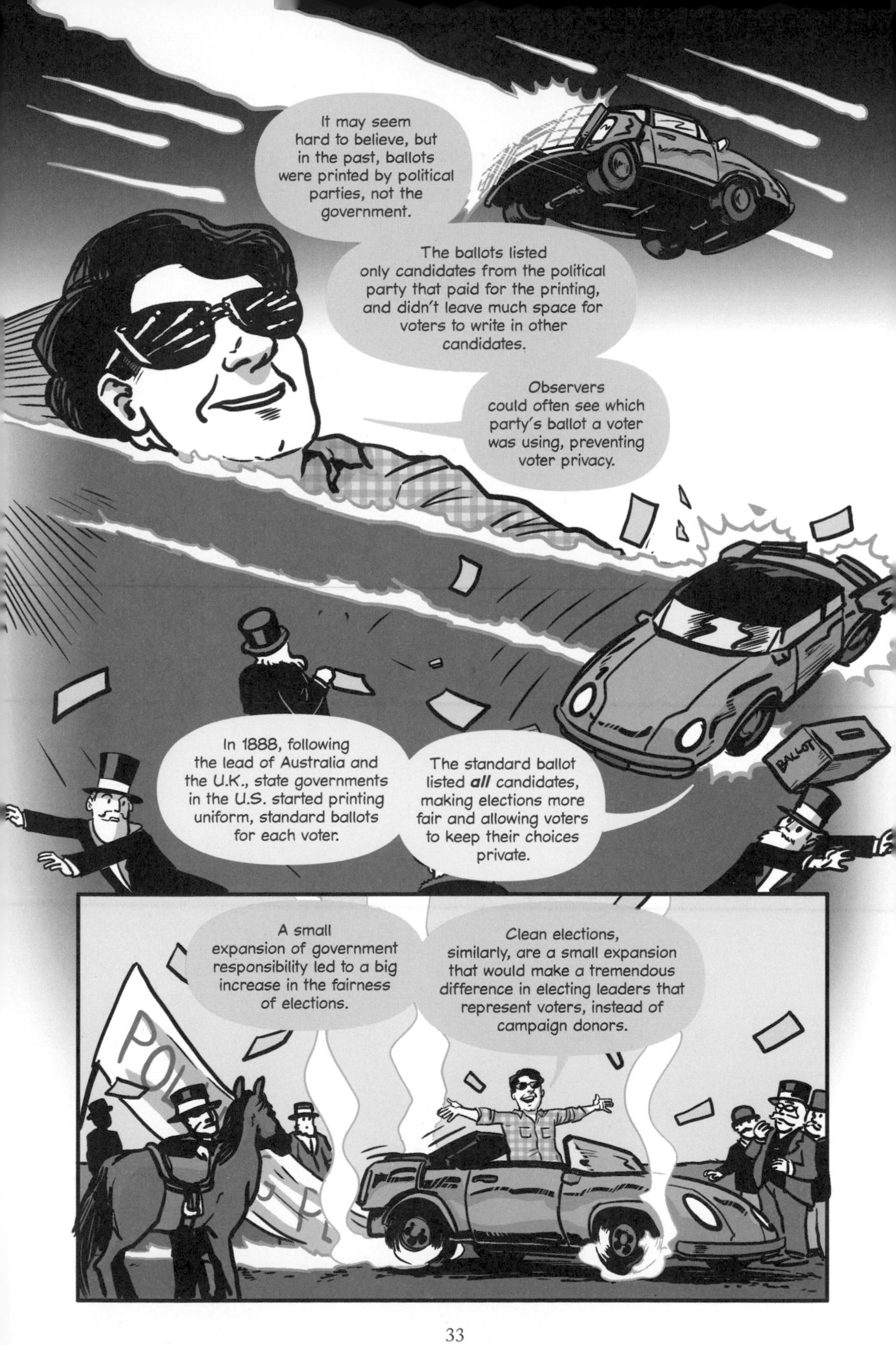
It may seem hard to believe, but in the past, ballots were printed by political parties, not the government.
The ballots listed only candidates from the political party that paid for the printing, and didn't leave much space for voters to write in other candidates.
Observers could often see which party's ballot a voter was using, preventing voter privacy.
In 1888, following the lead of Australia and the U.K., state governments in the U.S. started printing uniform, standard ballots for each voter.
The standard ballot listed ***all*** candidates, making elections more fair and allowing voters to keep their choices private.
BALLOT
A small expansion of government responsibility led to a big increase in the fairness of elections.
Clean elections, similarly, are a small expansion that would make a tremendous difference in electing leaders that represent voters, instead of campaign donors.

unrigging seattle elections

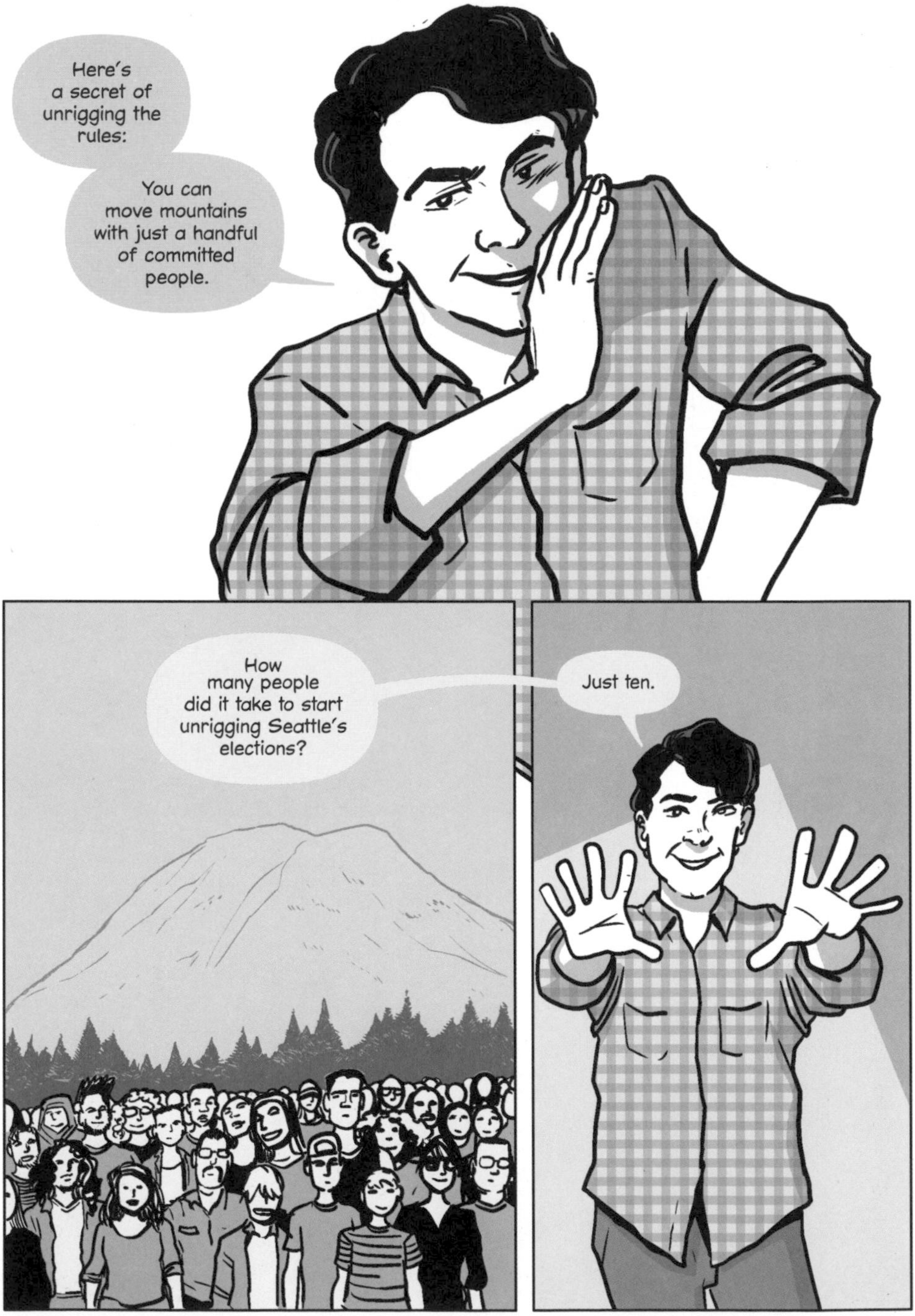
Here's a secret of unrigging the rules:
You can move mountains with just a handful of committed people.
How many people did it take to start unrigging Seattle's elections?
Just ten.

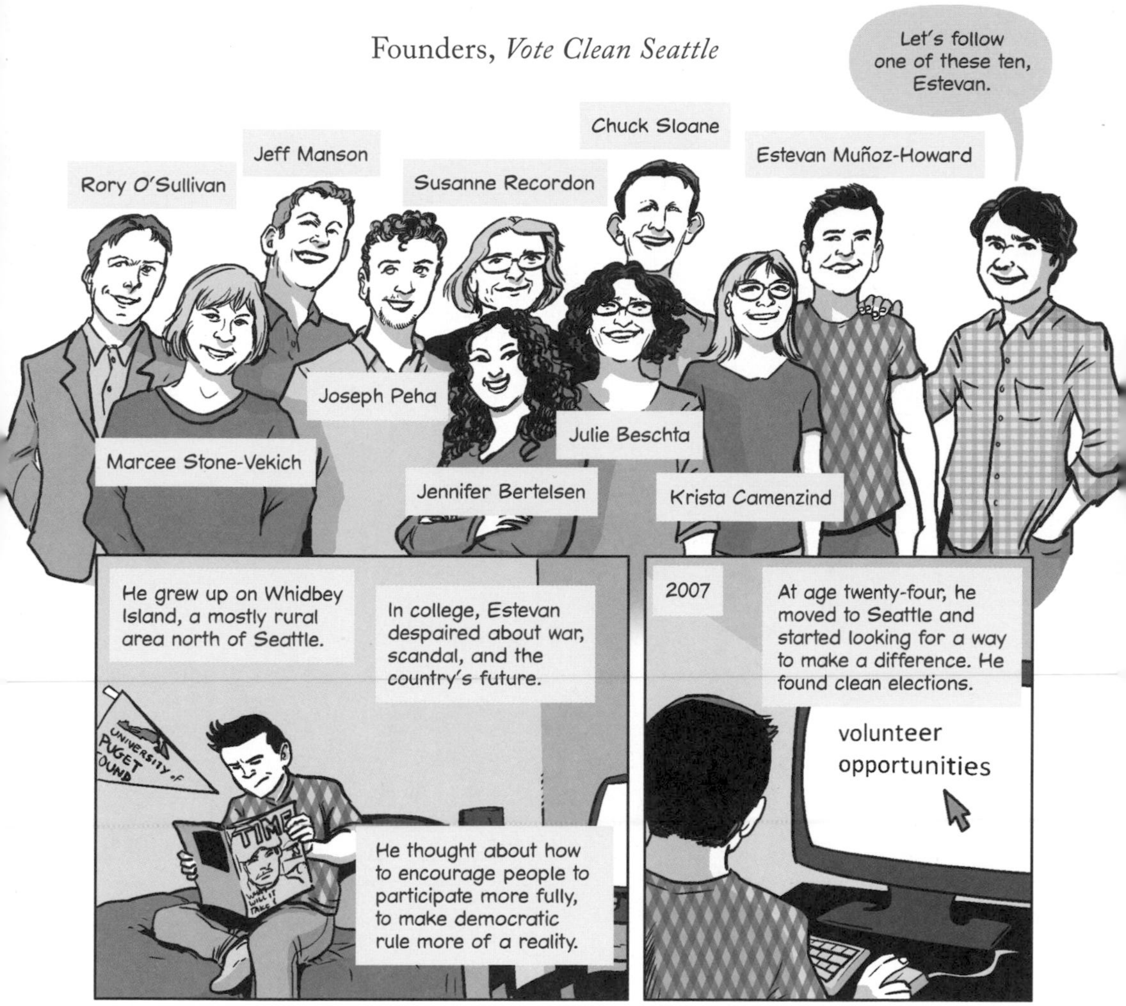
Founders, *Vote Clean Seattle*
Let's follow one of these ten, Estevan.
Rory O'Sullivan
Jeff Manson
Susanne Recordon
Chuck Sloane
Estevan Muñoz-Howard
Joseph Peha
Marcee Stone-Vekich
Julie Beschta
Jennifer Bertelsen
Krista Camenzind
He grew up on Whidbey Island, a mostly rural area north of Seattle.
In college, Estevan despaired about war, scandal, and the country's future.
UNIVERSITY of PUGET SOUND
TIME
He thought about how to encourage people to participate more fully, to make democratic rule more of a reality.
2007
At age twenty-four, he moved to Seattle and started looking for a way to make a difference. He found clean elections.
volunteer opportunities

THE RIGHT POLICY? THE RIGHT TIME?

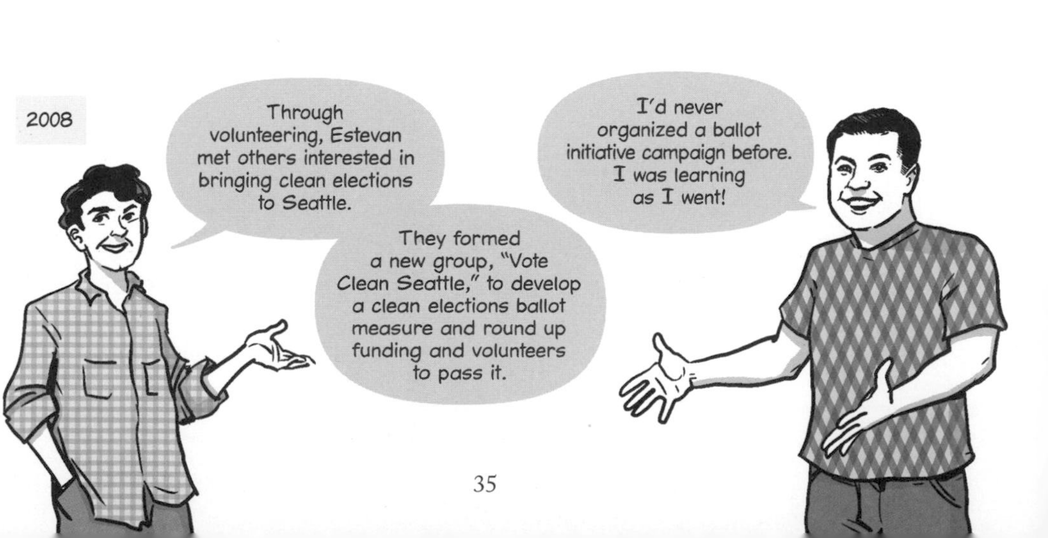
2008
Through volunteering, Estevan met others interested in bringing clean elections to Seattle.
They formed a new group, "Vote Clean Seattle," to develop a clean elections ballot measure and round up funding and volunteers to pass it.
I'd never organized a ballot initiative campaign before. I was learning as I went!

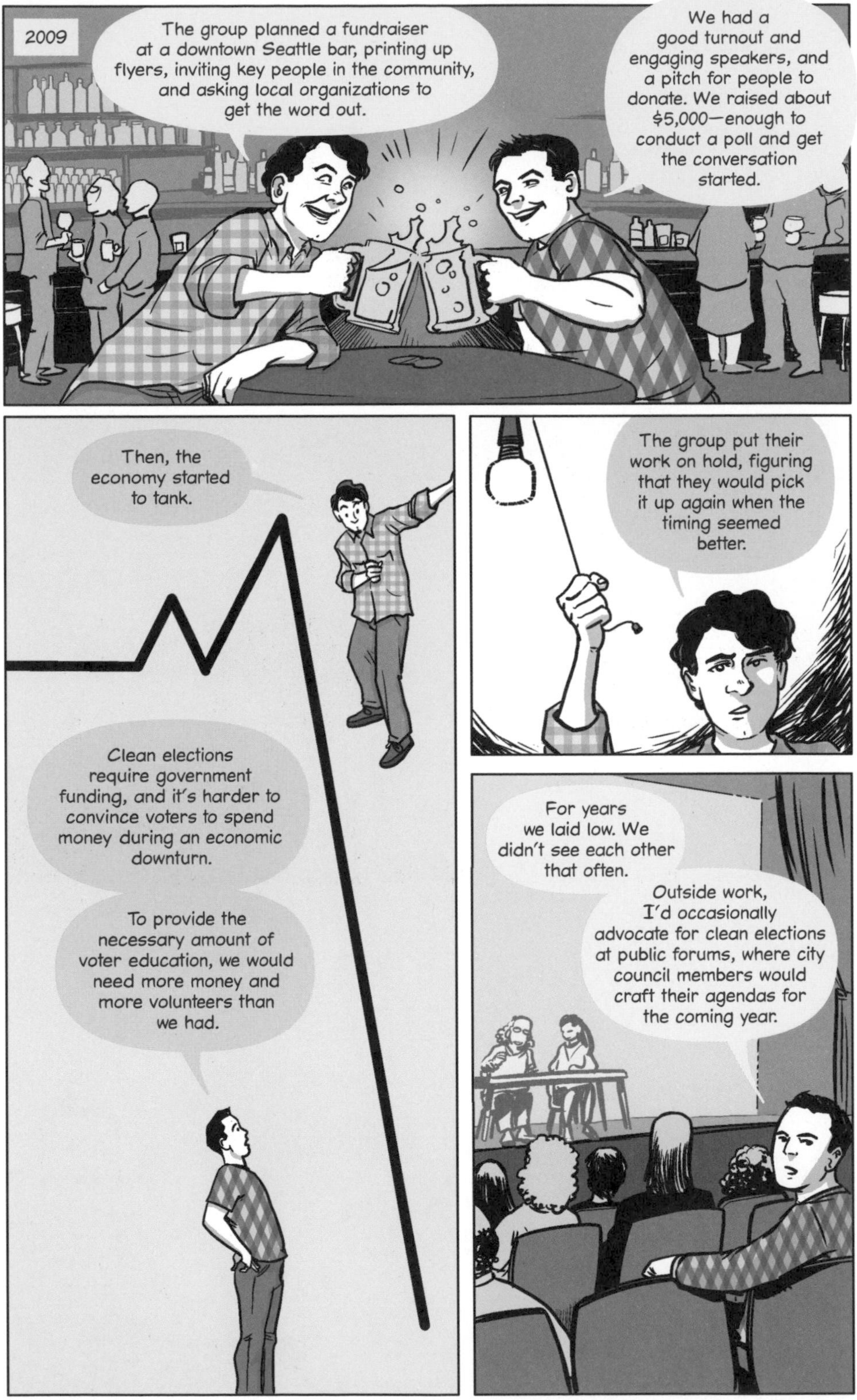
2009
The group planned a fundraiser at a downtown Seattle bar, printing up flyers, inviting key people in the community, and asking local organizations to get the word out.
We had a good turnout and engaging speakers, and a pitch for people to donate. We raised about $5,000—enough to conduct a poll and get the conversation started.
Then, the economy started to tank.
Clean elections require government funding, and it's harder to convince voters to spend money during an economic downturn.
To provide the necessary amount of voter education, we would need more money and more volunteers than we had.
The group put their work on hold, figuring that they would pick it up again when the timing seemed better.
For years we laid low. We didn't see each other that often.
Outside work, I'd occasionally advocate for clean elections at public forums, where city council members would craft their agendas for the coming year.

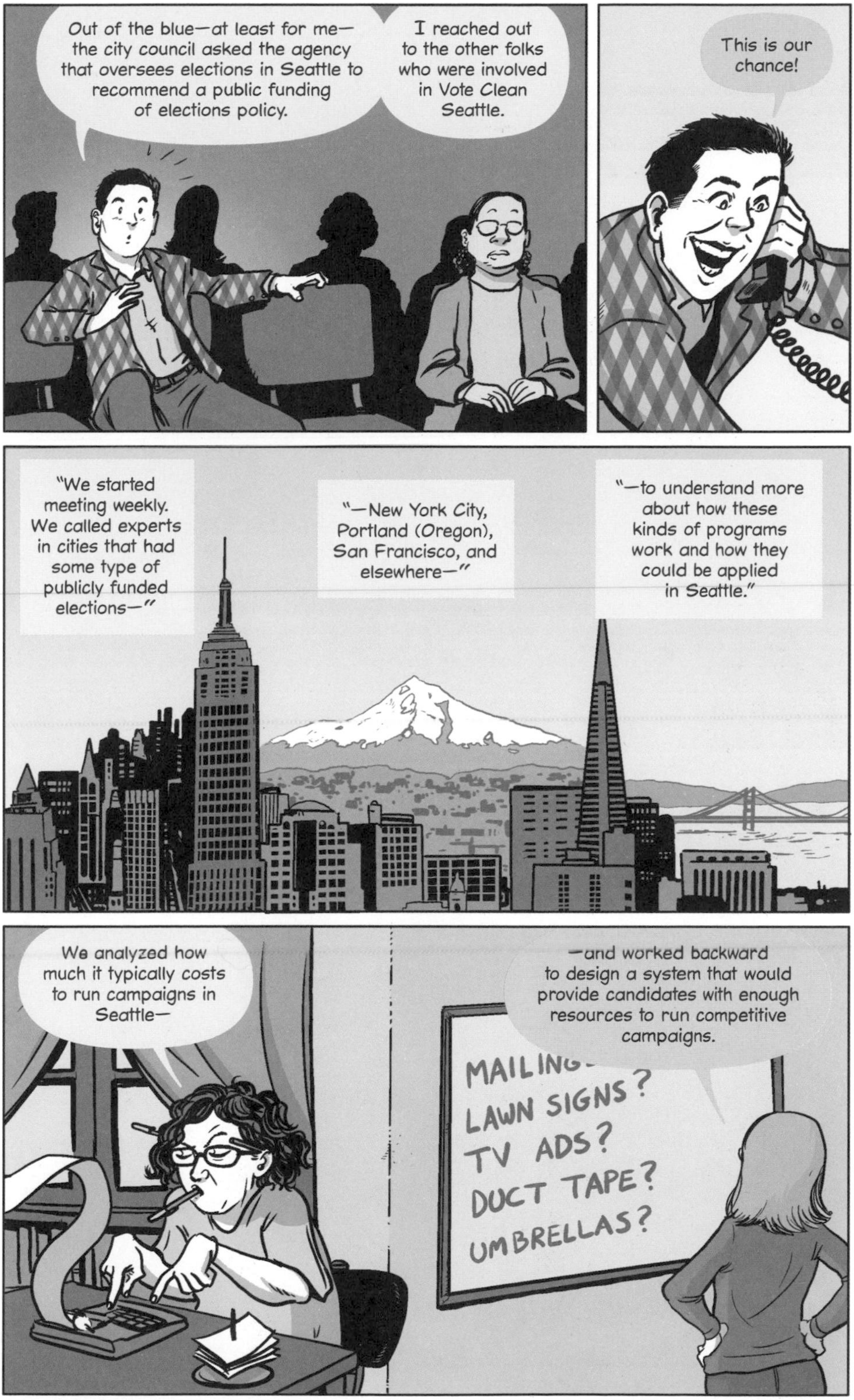
Out of the blue—at least for me—the city council asked the agency that oversees elections in Seattle to recommend a public funding of elections policy.
I reached out to the other folks who were involved in Vote Clean Seattle.
This is our chance!
"We started meeting weekly. We called experts in cities that had some type of publicly funded elections—"
"—New York City, Portland (Oregon), San Francisco, and elsewhere—"
"—to understand more about how these kinds of programs work and how they could be applied in Seattle."
We analyzed how much it typically costs to run campaigns in Seattle—
—and worked backward to design a system that would provide candidates with enough resources to run competitive campaigns.
LAWN SIGNS?
TV ADS?
DUCT TAPE?
UMBRELLAS?

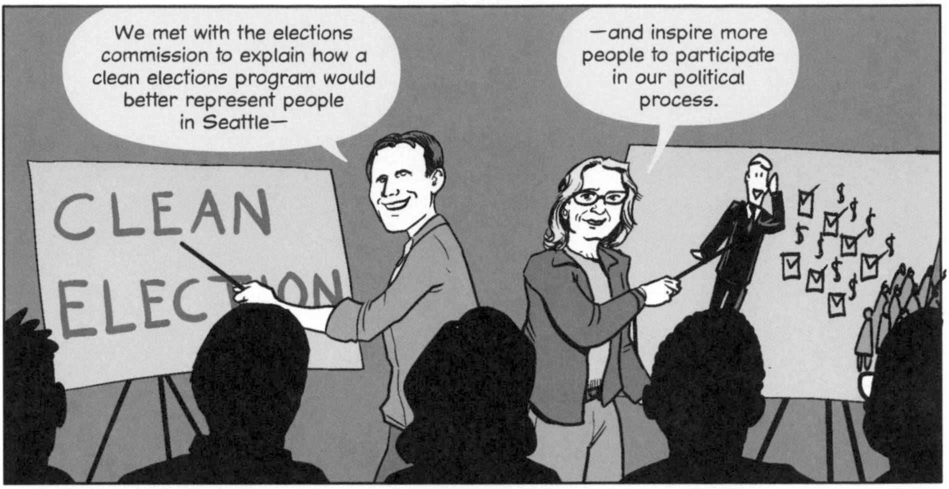
We met with the elections commission to explain how a clean elections program would better represent people in Seattle—
—and inspire more people to participate in our political process.
CLEAN ELECTION

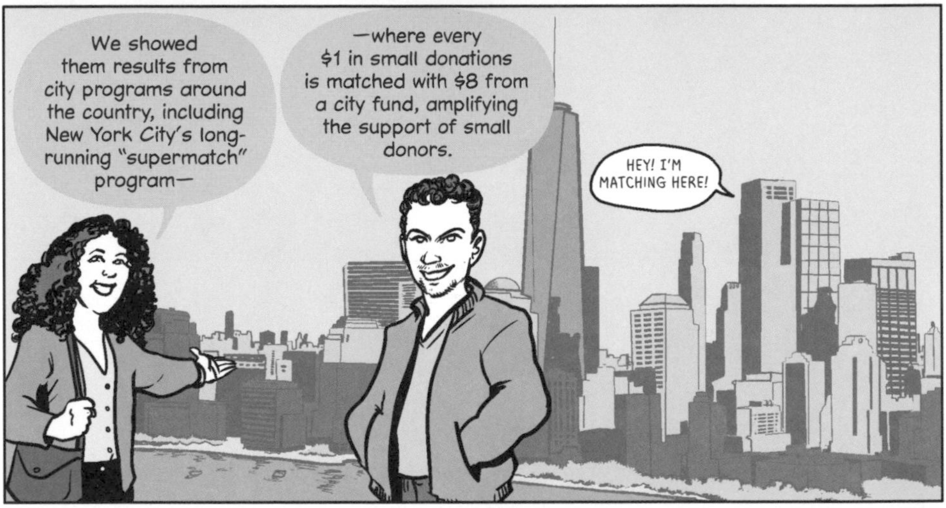
We showed them results from city programs around the country, including New York City's long-running "supermatch" program—
—where every $1 in small donations is matched with $8 from a city fund, amplifying the support of small donors.
HEY! I'M MATCHING HERE!

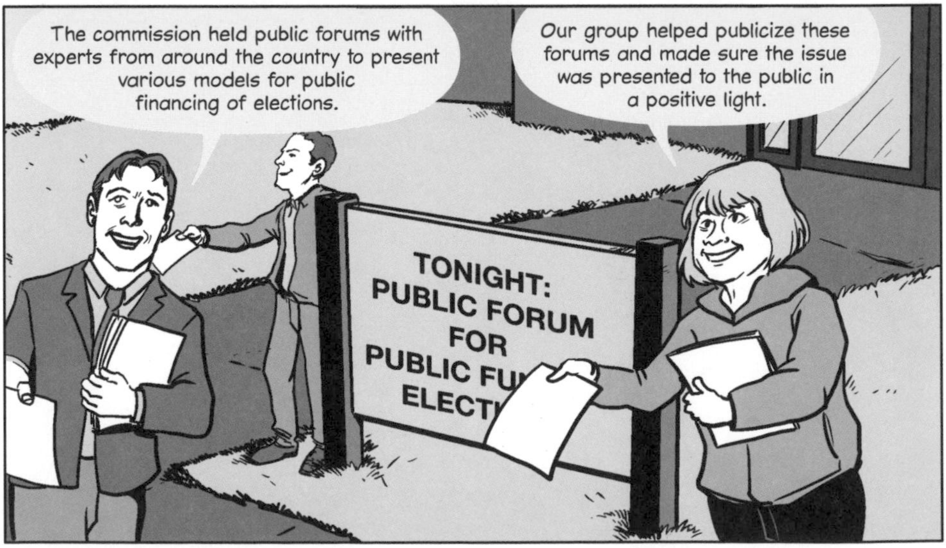
The commission held public forums with experts from around the country to present various models for public financing of elections.
Our group helped publicize these forums and made sure the issue was presented to the public in a positive light.
TONIGHT: PUBLIC FORUM FOR PUBLIC FU ELECTI

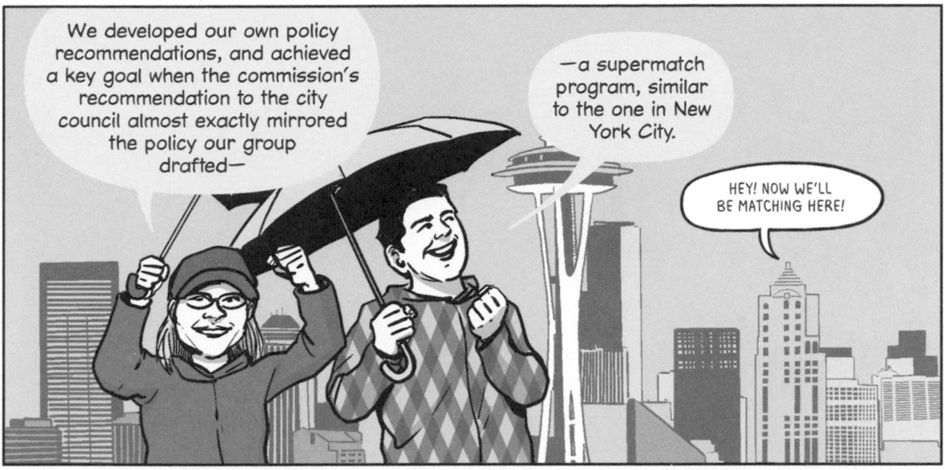
We developed our own policy recommendations, and achieved a key goal when the commission's recommendation to the city council almost exactly mirrored the policy our group drafted—
—a supermatch program, similar to the one in New York City.
HEY! NOW WE'LL BE MATCHING HERE!

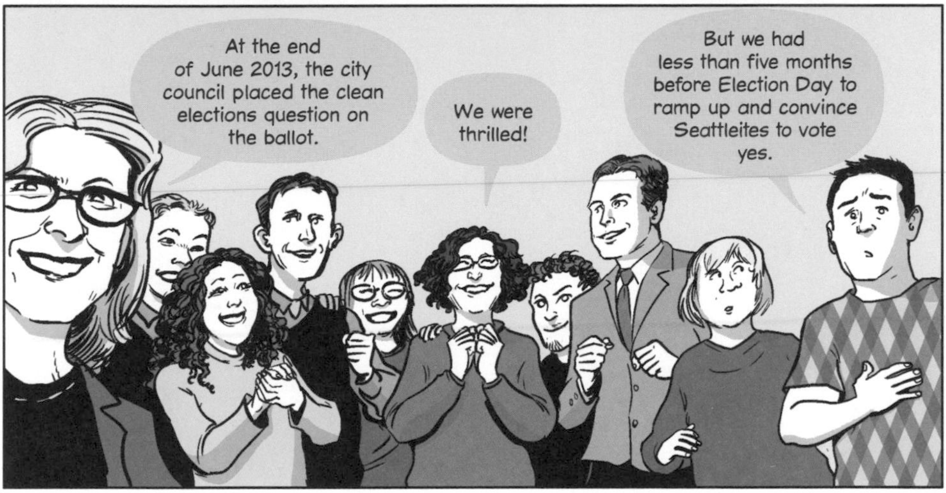
At the end of June 2013, the city council placed the clean elections question on the ballot.
We were thrilled!
But we had less than five months before Election Day to ramp up and convince Seattleites to vote yes.

LESSONS LEARNED FROM A SHORT CAMPAIGN

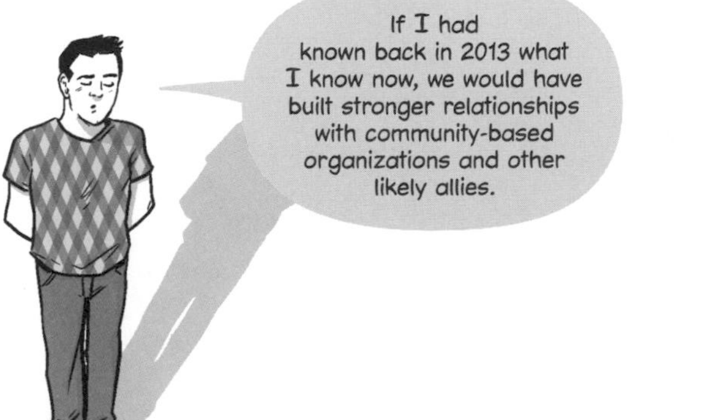
If I had known back in 2013 what I know now, we would have built stronger relationships with community-based organizations and other likely allies.

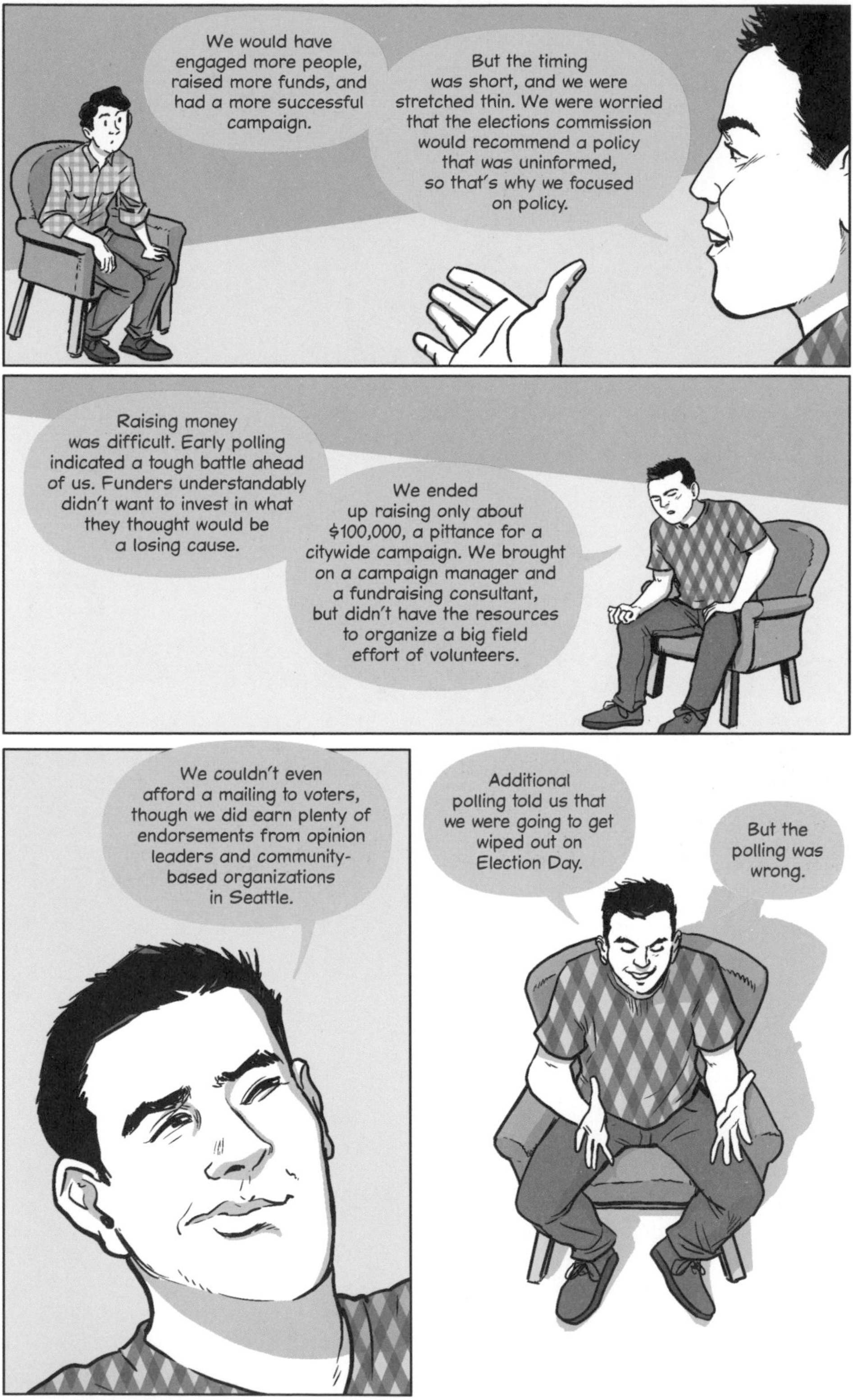

We would have engaged more people, raised more funds, and had a more successful campaign.
But the timing was short, and we were stretched thin. We were worried that the elections commission would recommend a policy that was uninformed, so that's why we focused on policy.
Raising money was difficult. Early polling indicated a tough battle ahead of us. Funders understandably didn't want to invest in what they thought would be a losing cause.
We ended up raising only about $100,000, a pittance for a citywide campaign. We brought on a campaign manager and a fundraising consultant, but didn't have the resources to organize a big field effort of volunteers.
We couldn't even afford a mailing to voters, though we did earn plenty of endorsements from opinion leaders and community-based organizations in Seattle.
Additional polling told us that we were going to get wiped out on Election Day.
But the polling was wrong.

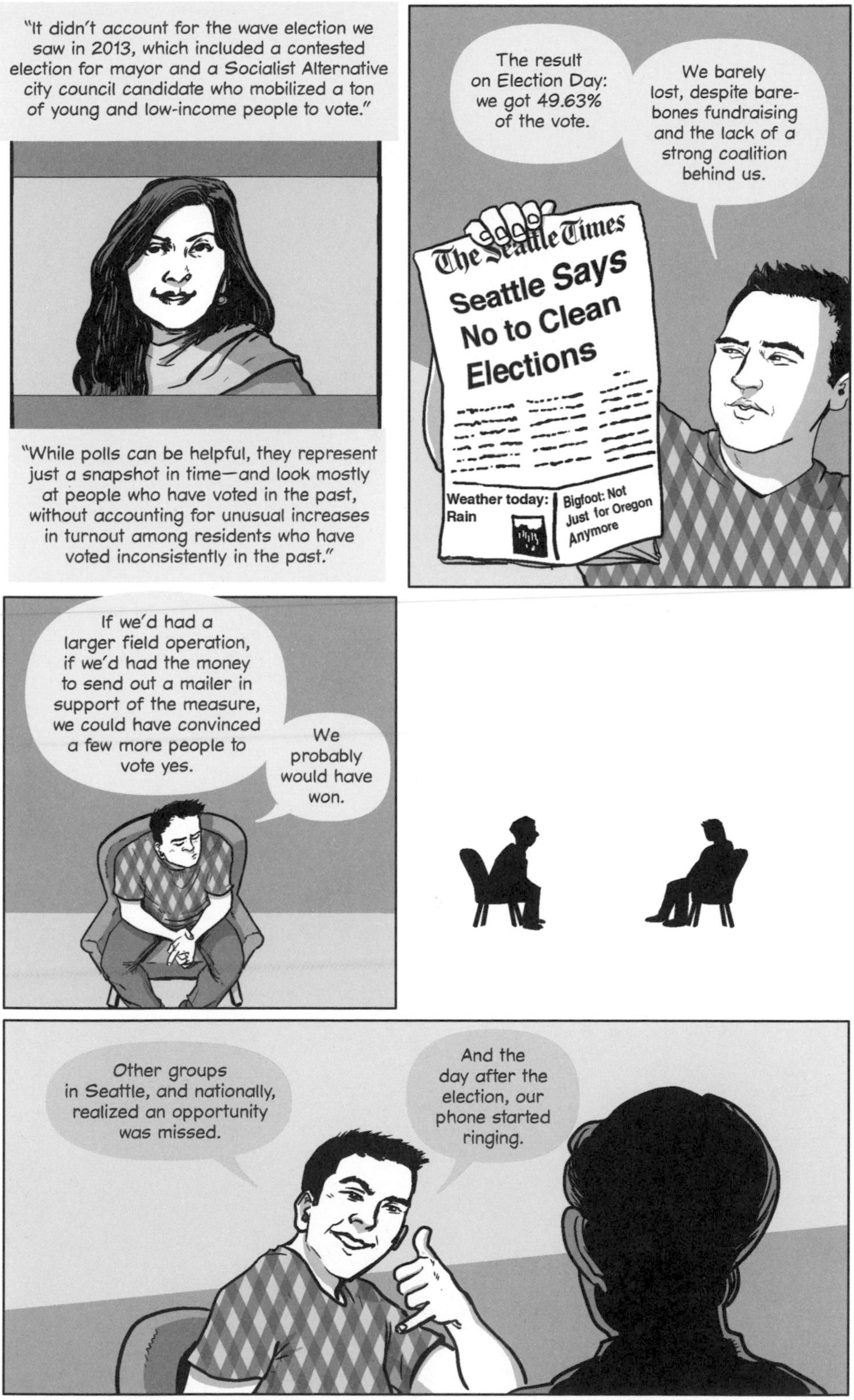
"It didn't account for the wave election we saw in 2013, which included a contested election for mayor and a Socialist Alternative city council candidate who mobilized a ton of young and low-income people to vote."
"While polls can be helpful, they represent just a snapshot in time—and look mostly at people who have voted in the past, without accounting for unusual increases in turnout among residents who have voted inconsistently in the past."
The result on Election Day: we got 49.63% of the vote.
We barely lost, despite bare-bones fundraising and the lack of a strong coalition behind us.
The Seattle Times
Seattle Says No to Clean Elections
Weather today: Rain
Bigfoot: Not Just for Oregon Anymore
If we'd had a larger field operation, if we'd had the money to send out a mailer in support of the measure, we could have convinced a few more people to vote yes.
We probably would have won.
Other groups in Seattle, and nationally, realized an opportunity was missed.
And the day after the election, our phone started ringing.

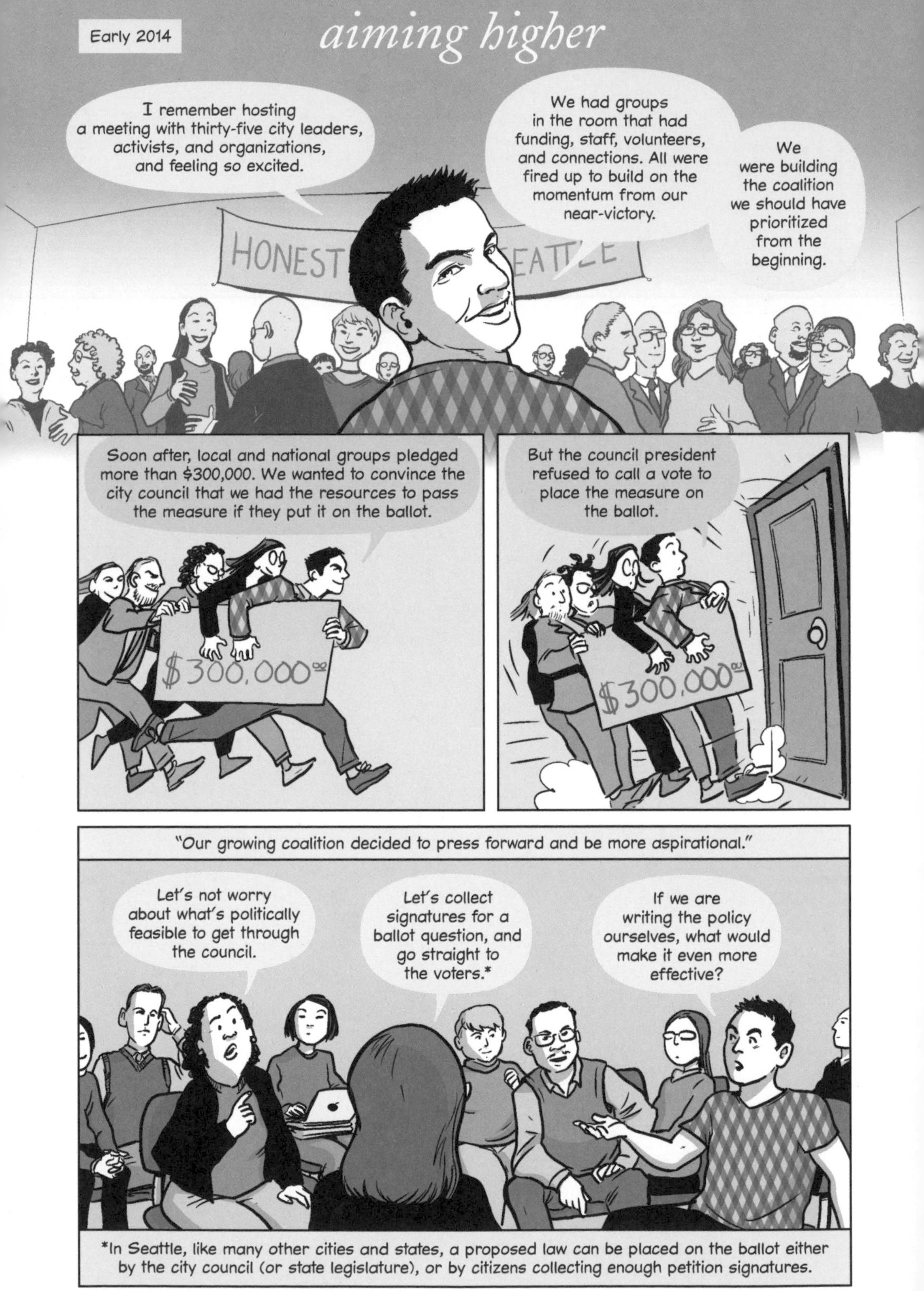
Early 2014
aiming higher
I remember hosting a meeting with thirty-five city leaders, activists, and organizations, and feeling so excited.
We had groups in the room that had funding, staff, volunteers, and connections. All were fired up to build on the momentum from our near-victory.
We were building the coalition we should have prioritized from the beginning.
HONEST
EATTLE
Soon after, local and national groups pledged more than $300,000. We wanted to convince the city council that we had the resources to pass the measure if they put it on the ballot.
$300,000
But the council president refused to call a vote to place the measure on the ballot.
$300,000
"Our growing coalition decided to press forward and be more aspirational."
Let's not worry about what's politically feasible to get through the council.
Let's collect signatures for a ballot question, and go straight to the voters.*
If we are writing the policy ourselves, what would make it even more effective?
*In Seattle, like many other cities and states, a proposed law can be placed on the ballot either by the city council (or state legislature), or by citizens collecting enough petition signatures.

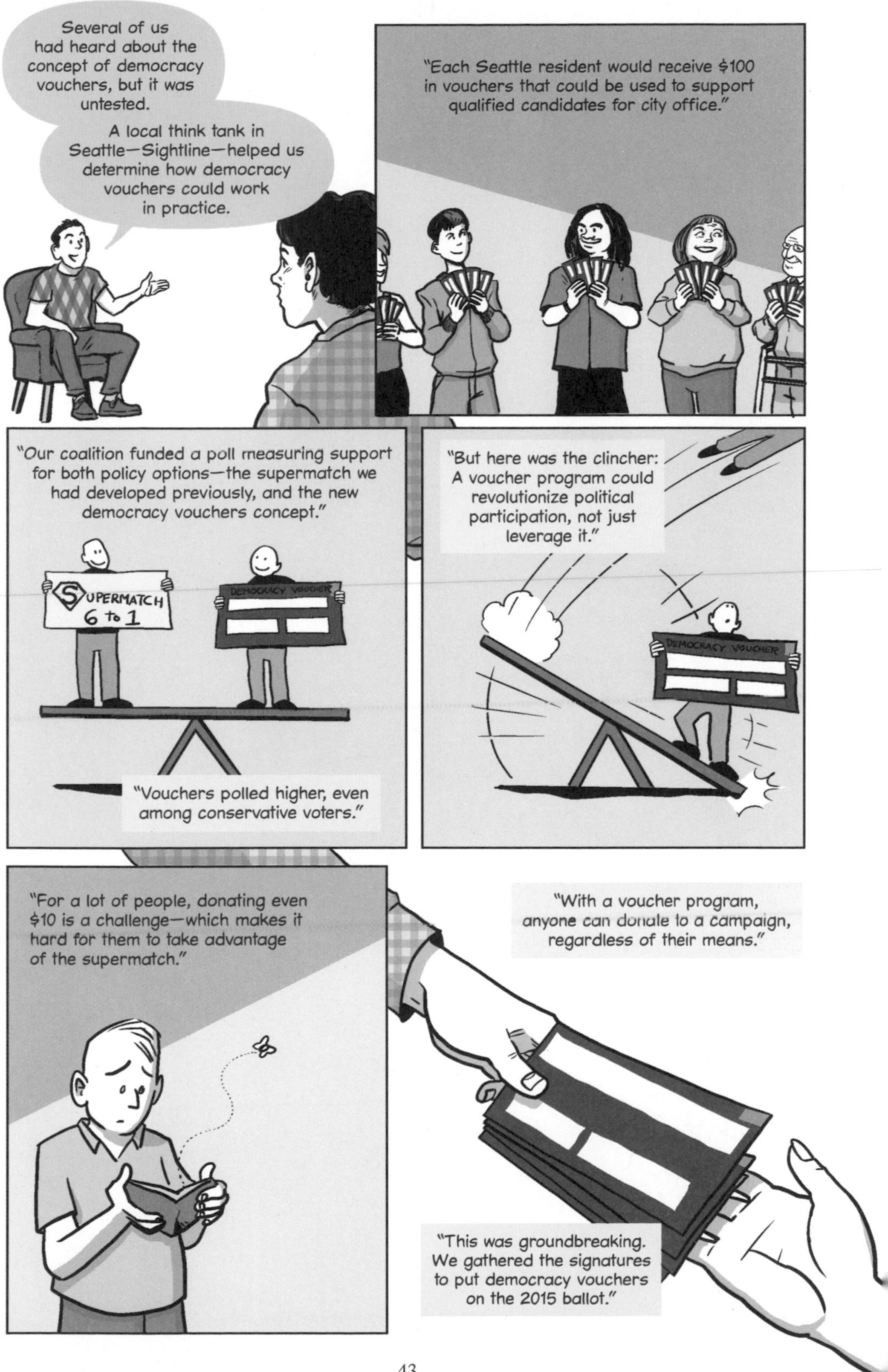
Several of us had heard about the concept of democracy vouchers, but it was untested.
A local think tank in Seattle—Sightline—helped us determine how democracy vouchers could work in practice.
"Each Seattle resident would receive $100 in vouchers that could be used to support qualified candidates for city office."
"Our coalition funded a poll measuring support for both policy options—the supermatch we had developed previously, and the new democracy vouchers concept."
SUPERMATCH
6 to 1
DEMOCRACY VOUCHER
"Vouchers polled higher, even among conservative voters."
"But here was the clincher: A voucher program could revolutionize political participation, not just leverage it."
DEMOCRACY VOUCHER
"For a lot of people, donating even $10 is a challenge—which makes it hard for them to take advantage of the supermatch."
"With a voucher program, anyone can donate to a campaign, regardless of their means."
"This was groundbreaking. We gathered the signatures to put democracy vouchers on the 2015 ballot."

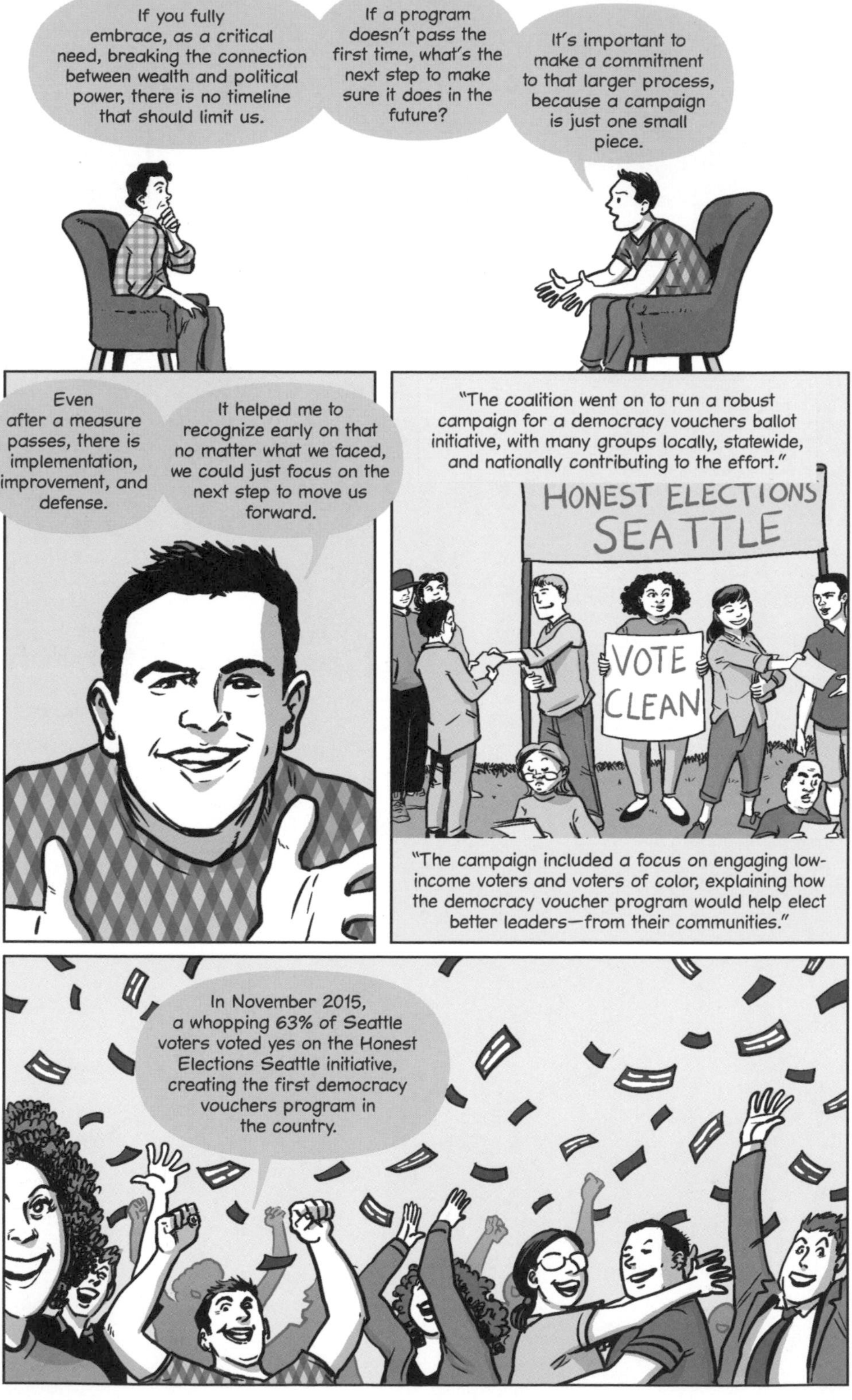
If you fully embrace, as a critical need, breaking the connection between wealth and political power, there is no timeline that should limit us.
If a program doesn't pass the first time, what's the next step to make sure it does in the future?
It's important to make a commitment to that larger process, because a campaign is just one small piece.
Even after a measure passes, there is implementation, improvement, and defense.
It helped me to recognize early on that no matter what we faced, we could just focus on the next step to move us forward.
"The coalition went on to run a robust campaign for a democracy vouchers ballot initiative, with many groups locally, statewide, and nationally contributing to the effort."
HONEST ELECTIONS SEATTLE
VOTE CLEAN
"The campaign included a focus on engaging low-income voters and voters of color, explaining how the democracy voucher program would help elect better leaders—from their communities."
In November 2015, a whopping 63% of Seattle voters voted yes on the Honest Elections Seattle initiative, creating the first democracy vouchers program in the country.

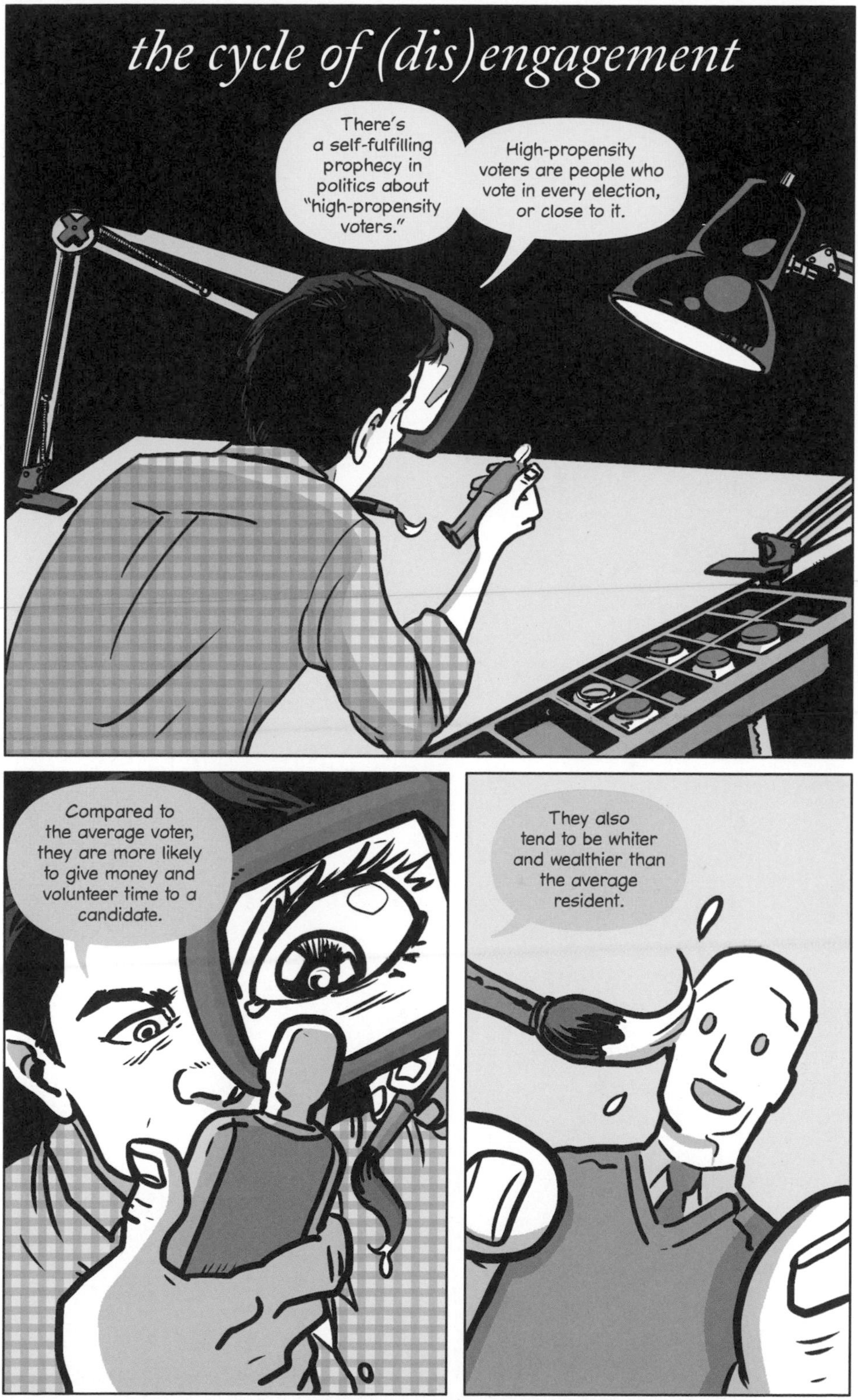
the cycle of (dis)engagement
There's a self-fulfilling prophecy in politics about "high-propensity voters."
High-propensity voters are people who vote in every election, or close to it.
Compared to the average voter, they are more likely to give money and volunteer time to a candidate.
They also tend to be whiter and wealthier than the average resident.

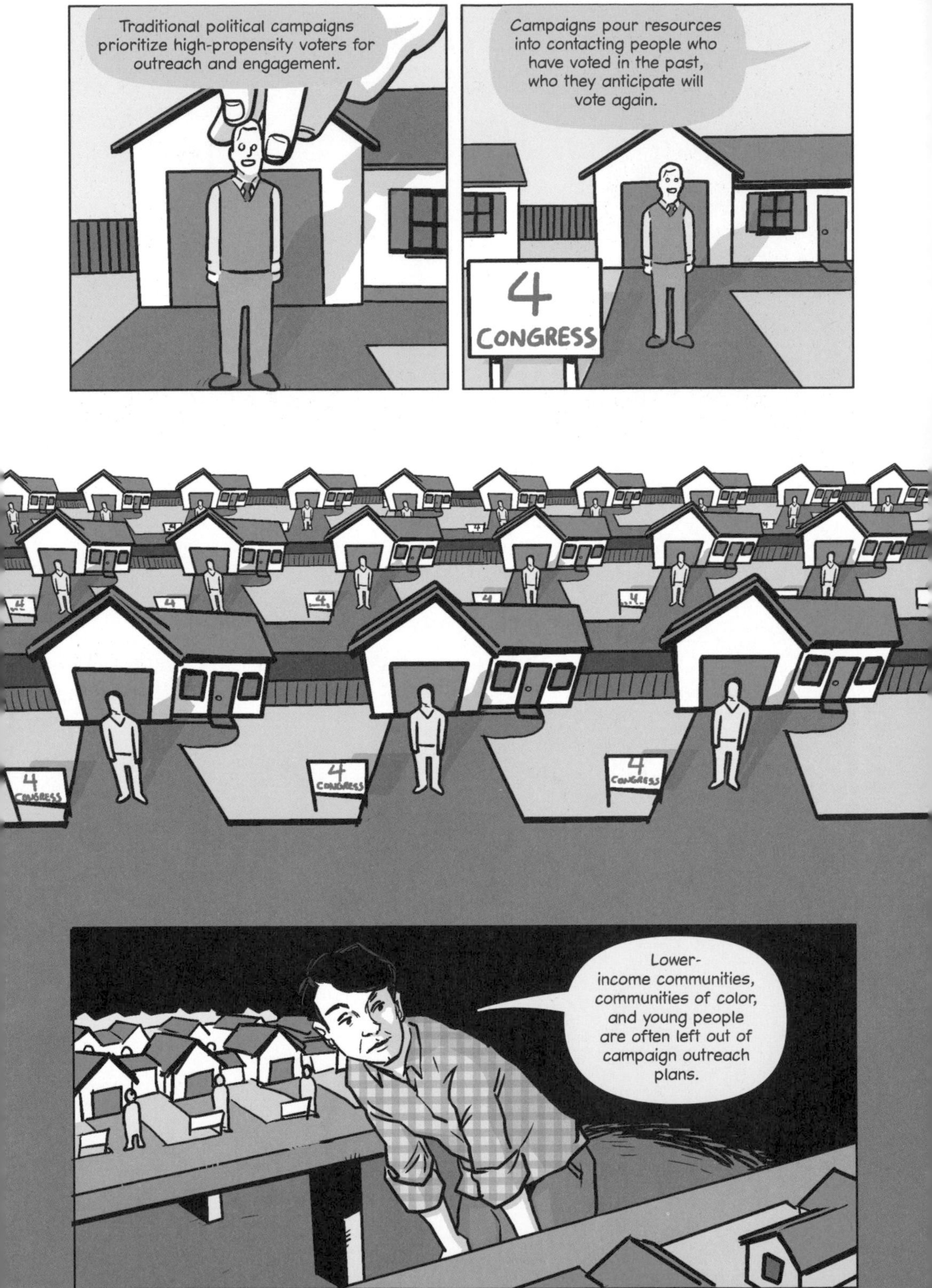
Traditional political campaigns prioritize high-propensity voters for outreach and engagement.
Campaigns pour resources into contacting people who have voted in the past, who they anticipate will vote again.
4 CONGRESS
Lower-income communities, communities of color, and young people are often left out of campaign outreach plans.

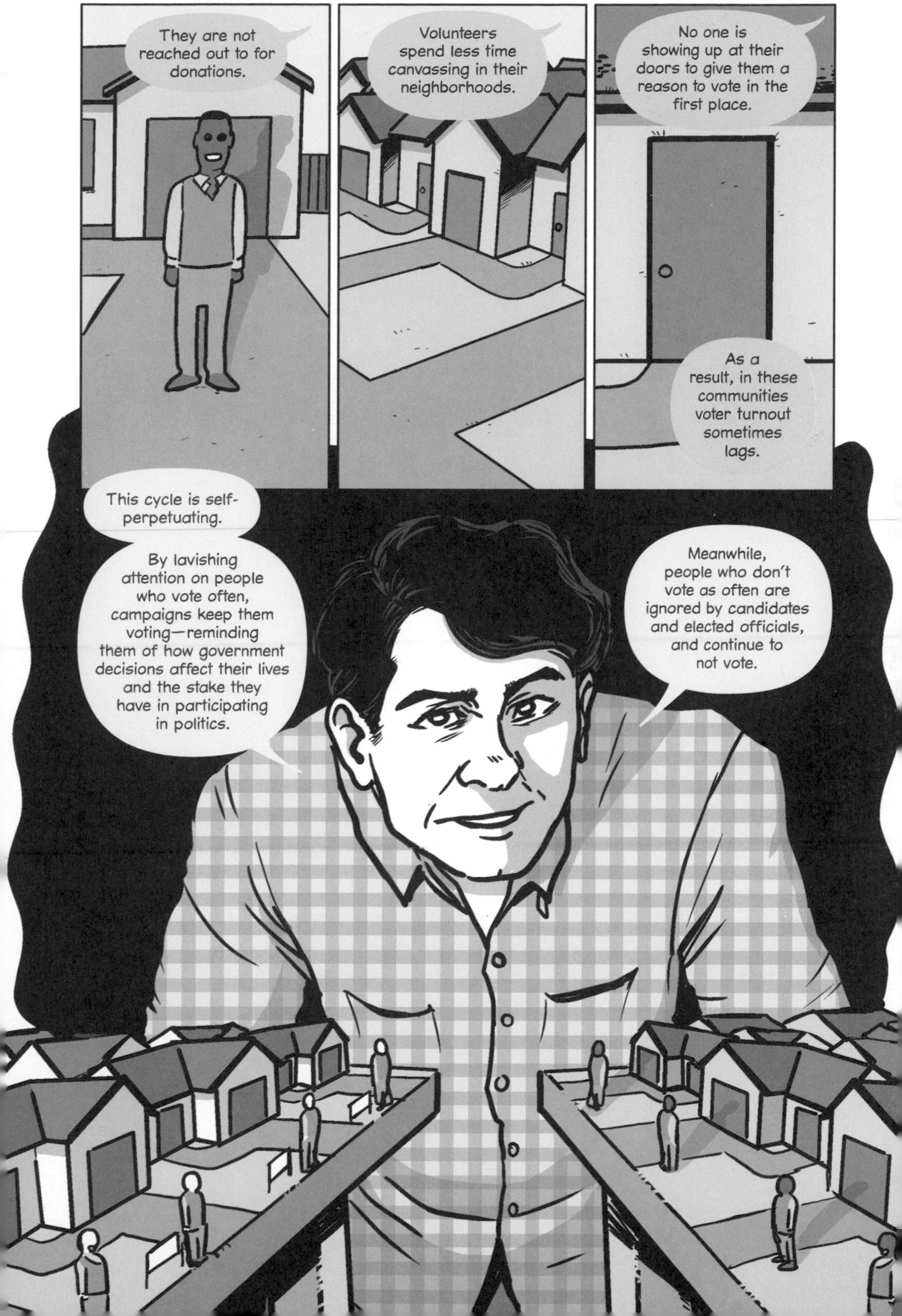
They are not reached out to for donations.
Volunteers spend less time canvassing in their neighborhoods.
No one is showing up at their doors to give them a reason to vote in the first place.
As a result, in these communities voter turnout sometimes lags.
This cycle is self-perpetuating.
By lavishing attention on people who vote often, campaigns keep them voting—reminding them of how government decisions affect their lives and the stake they have in participating in politics.
Meanwhile, people who don't vote as often are ignored by candidates and elected officials, and continue to not vote.

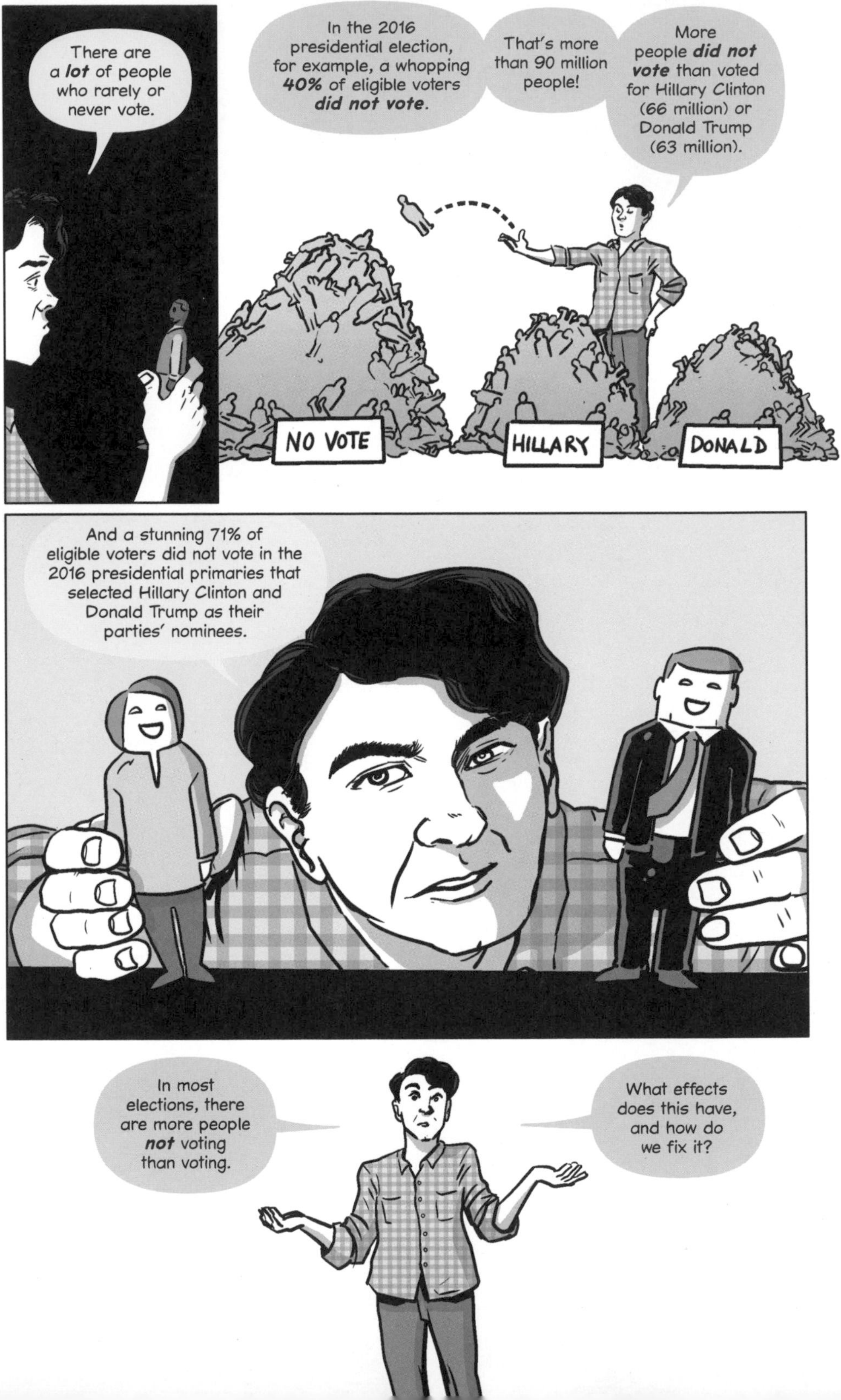
There are a ***lot*** of people who rarely or never vote.
In the 2016 presidential election, for example, a whopping ***40%*** of eligible voters ***did not vote***.
That's more than 90 million people!
More people ***did not vote*** than voted for Hillary Clinton (66 million) or Donald Trump (63 million).
NO VOTE
HILLARY
DONALD
And a stunning 71% of eligible voters did not vote in the 2016 presidential primaries that selected Hillary Clinton and Donald Trump as their parties' nominees.
In most elections, there are more people ***not*** voting than voting.
What effects does this have, and how do we fix it?

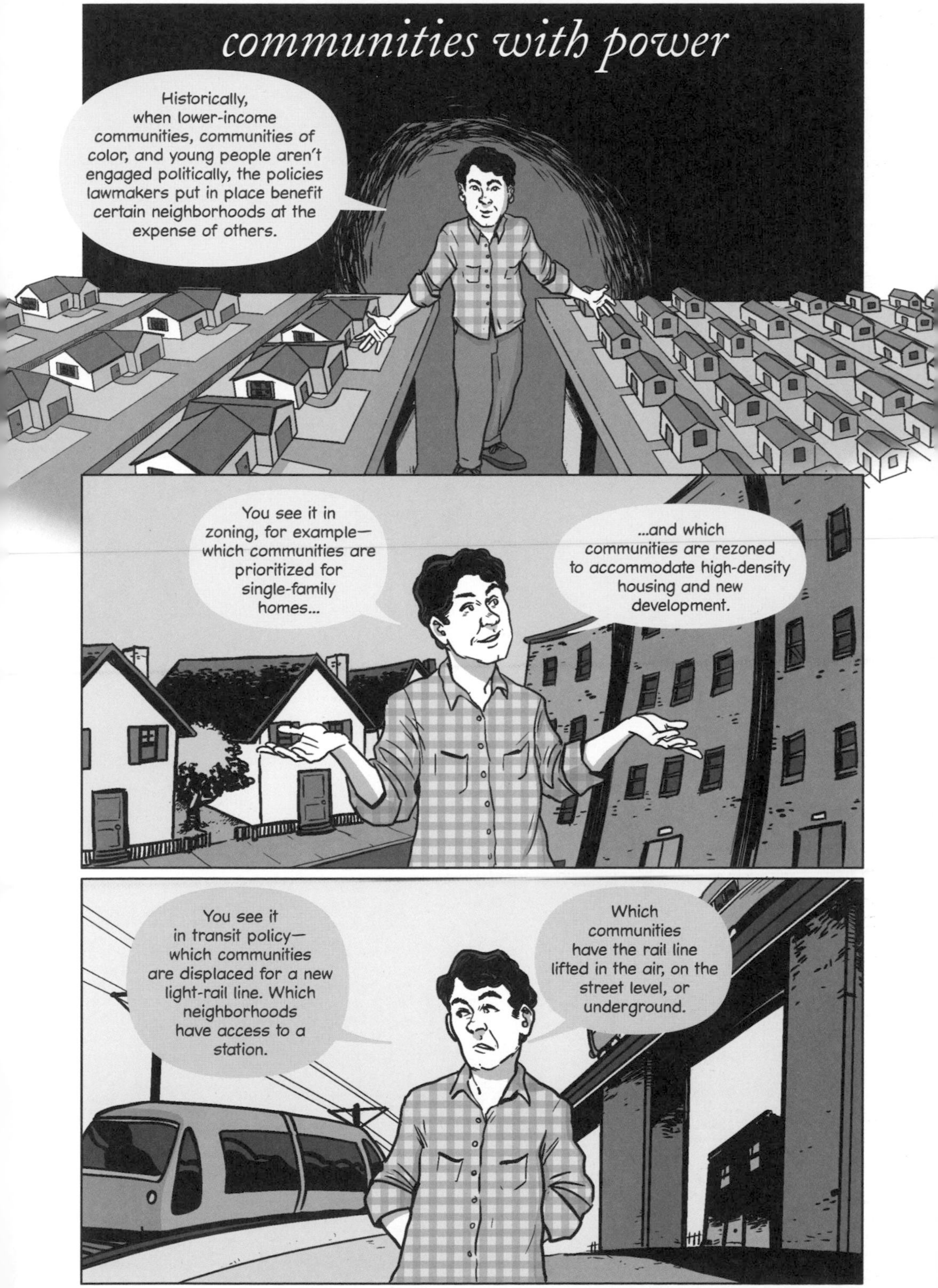
communities with power
Historically, when lower-income communities, communities of color, and young people aren't engaged politically, the policies lawmakers put in place benefit certain neighborhoods at the expense of others.
You see it in zoning, for example—which communities are prioritized for single-family homes...
...and which communities are rezoned to accommodate high-density housing and new development.
You see it in transit policy—which communities are displaced for a new light-rail line. Which neighborhoods have access to a station.
Which communities have the rail line lifted in the air, on the street level, or underground.

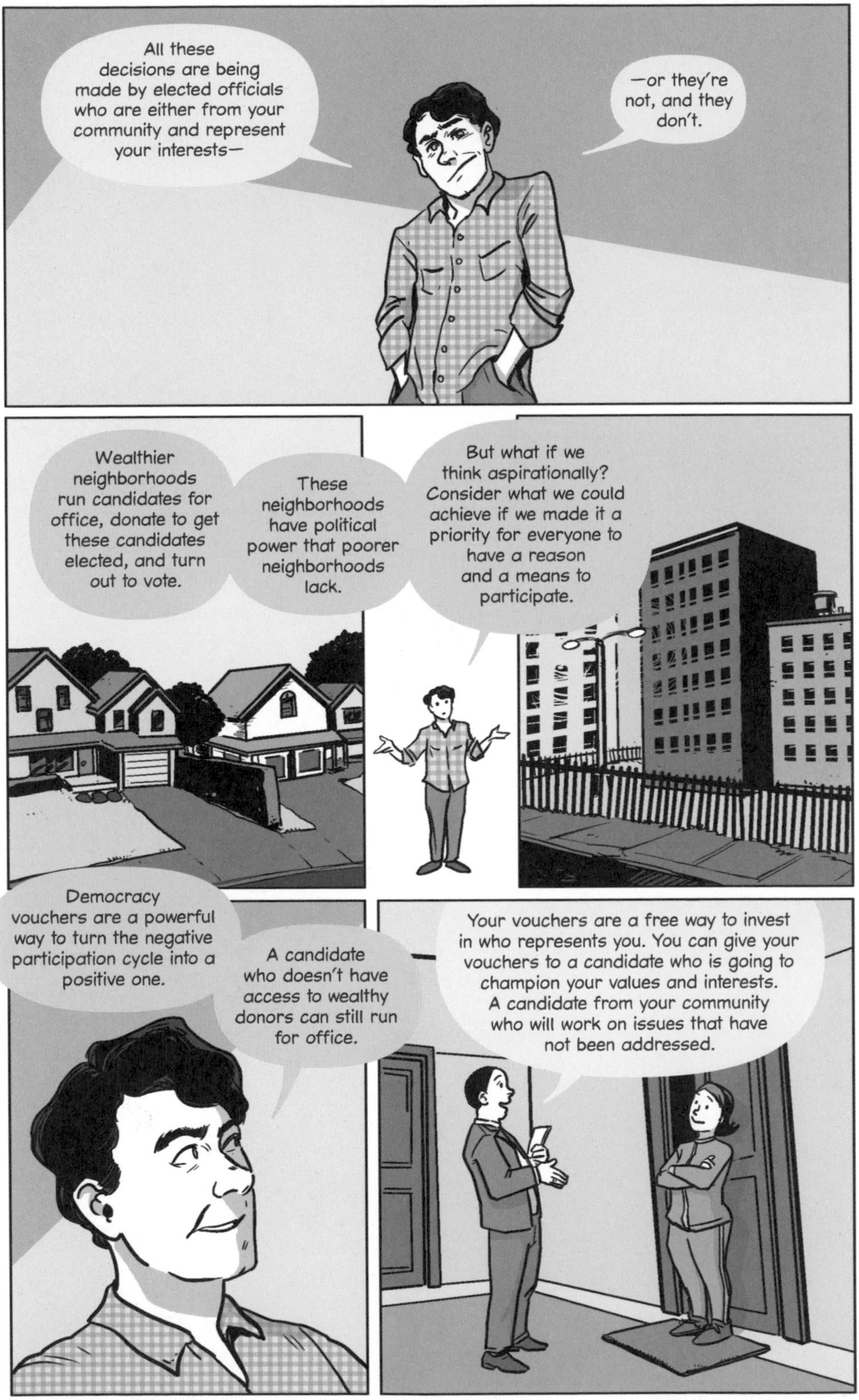
All these decisions are being made by elected officials who are either from your community and represent your interests—
—or they're not, and they don't.
Wealthier neighborhoods run candidates for office, donate to get these candidates elected, and turn out to vote.
These neighborhoods have political power that poorer neighborhoods lack.
But what if we think aspirationally? Consider what we could achieve if we made it a priority for everyone to have a reason and a means to participate.
Democracy vouchers are a powerful way to turn the negative participation cycle into a positive one.
A candidate who doesn't have access to wealthy donors can still run for office.
Your vouchers are a free way to invest in who represents you. You can give your vouchers to a candidate who is going to champion your values and interests. A candidate from your community who will work on issues that have not been addressed.

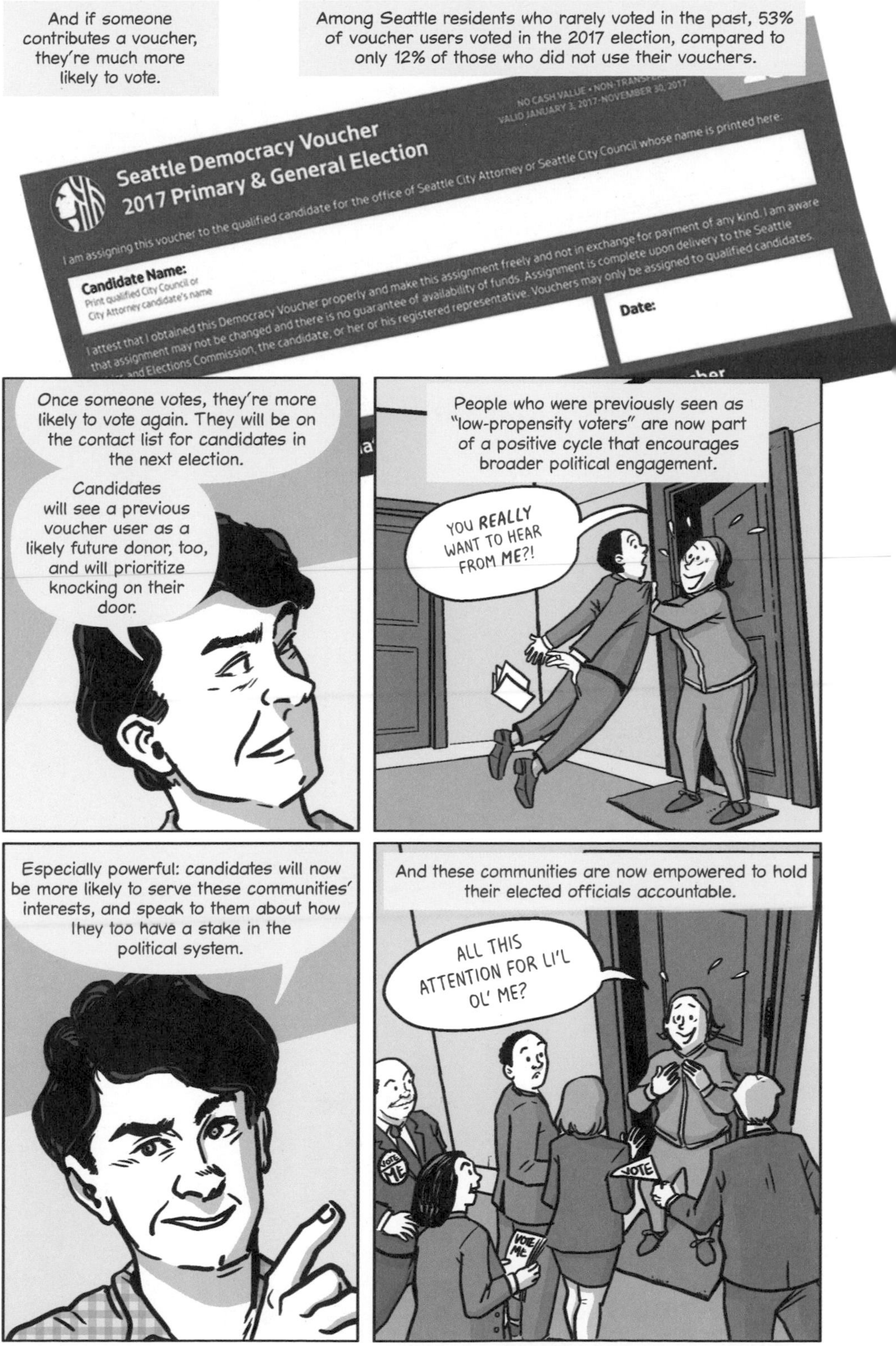

And if someone contributes a voucher, they're much more likely to vote.
Among Seattle residents who rarely voted in the past, 53% of voucher users voted in the 2017 election, compared to only 12% of those who did not use their vouchers.
VALID JANUARY 3, 2017-NOVEMBER 30, 2017
Seattle Democracy Voucher
2017 Primary & General Election
I am assigning this voucher to the qualified candidate for the office of Seattle City Attorney or Seattle City Council whose name is printed here:
Candidate Name:
Print qualified City Council or City Attorney candidate's name
I attest that I obtained this Democracy Voucher properly and make this assignment freely and not in exchange for payment of any kind. I am aware that assignment may not be changed and there is no guarantee of availability of funds. Assignment is complete upon delivery to the Seattle
and Elections Commission, the candidate, or her or his registered representative. Vouchers may only be assigned to qualified candidates.
Date:
Once someone votes, they're more likely to vote again. They will be on the contact list for candidates in the next election.
Candidates will see a previous voucher user as a likely future donor, too, and will prioritize knocking on their door.
People who were previously seen as "low-propensity voters" are now part of a positive cycle that encourages broader political engagement.
YOU REALLY WANT TO HEAR FROM ME?!
Especially powerful: candidates will now be more likely to serve these communities' interests, and speak to them about how they too have a stake in the political system.
And these communities are now empowered to hold their elected officials accountable.
ALL THIS ATTENTION FOR LI'L OL' ME?
VOTE ME
VOTE
VOTE ME

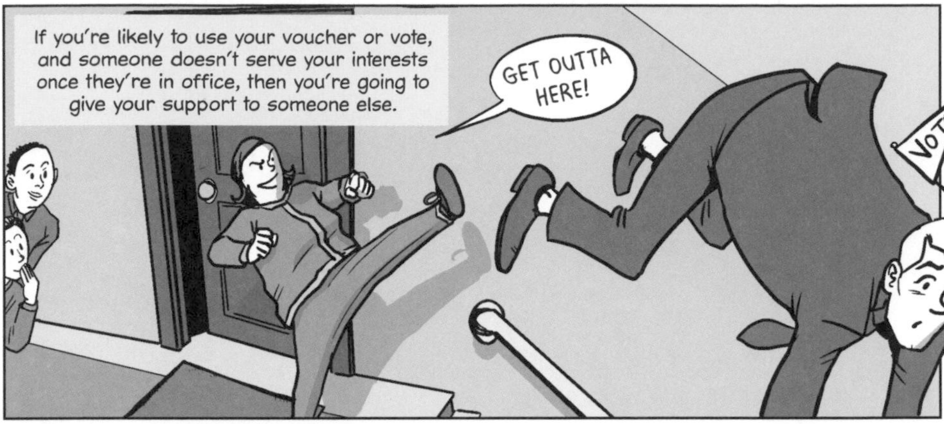
If you're likely to use your voucher or vote, and someone doesn't serve your interests once they're in office, then you're going to give your support to someone else.
GET OUTTA HERE!
VOTE

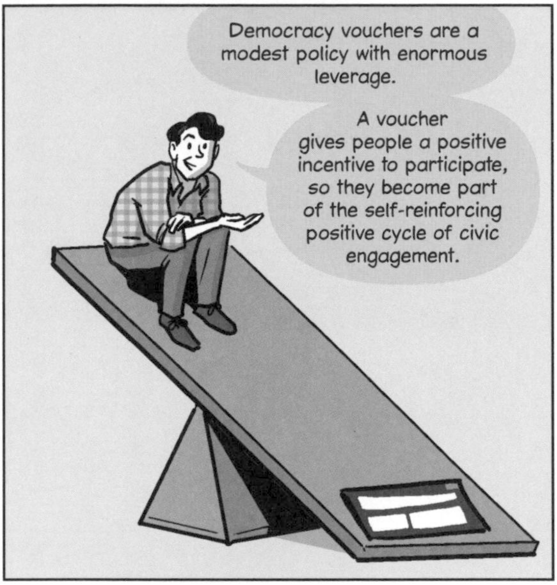
Democracy vouchers are a modest policy with enormous leverage.
A voucher gives people a positive incentive to participate, so they become part of the self-reinforcing positive cycle of civic engagement.

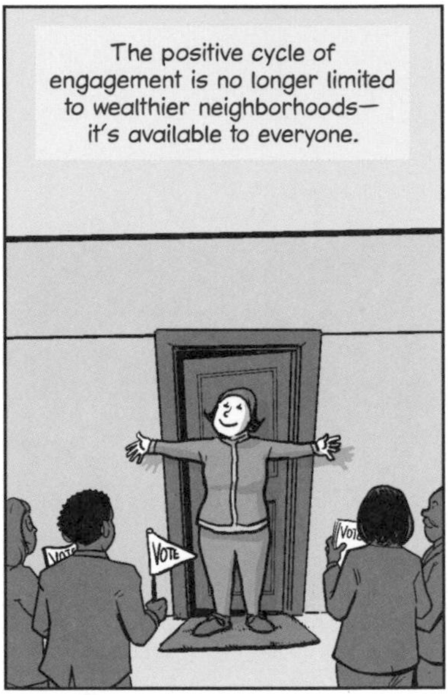
The positive cycle of engagement is no longer limited to wealthier neighborhoods—it's available to everyone.
VOTE
VOTE
VOTE

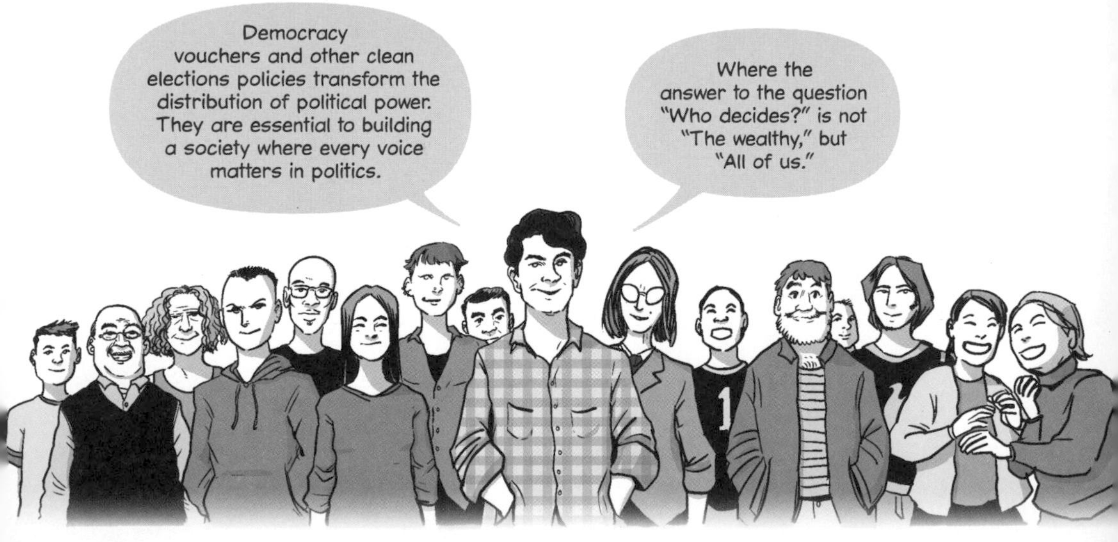
Democracy vouchers and other clean elections policies transform the distribution of political power. They are essential to building a society where every voice matters in politics.
Where the answer to the question "Who decides?" is not "The wealthy," but "All of us."

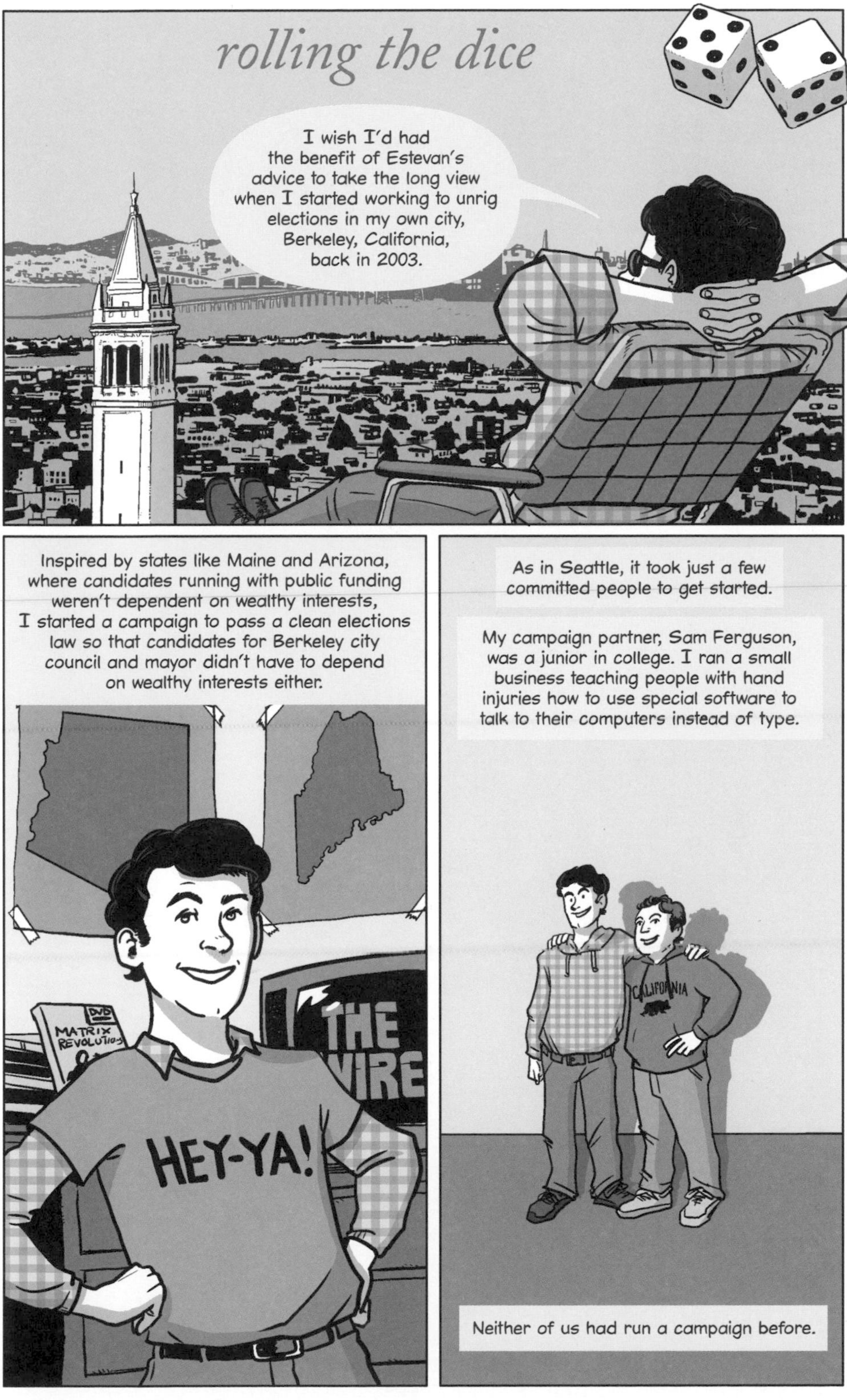
rolling the dice
I wish I'd had the benefit of Estevan's advice to take the long view when I started working to unrig elections in my own city, Berkeley, California, back in 2003.
Inspired by states like Maine and Arizona, where candidates running with public funding weren't dependent on wealthy interests, I started a campaign to pass a clean elections law so that candidates for Berkeley city council and mayor didn't have to depend on wealthy interests either.
DVD
MATRIX REVOLUTIONS
THE WIRE
HEY-YA!
As in Seattle, it took just a few committed people to get started.
My campaign partner, Sam Ferguson, was a junior in college. I ran a small business teaching people with hand injuries how to use special software to talk to their computers instead of type.
CALIFORNIA
Neither of us had run a campaign before.

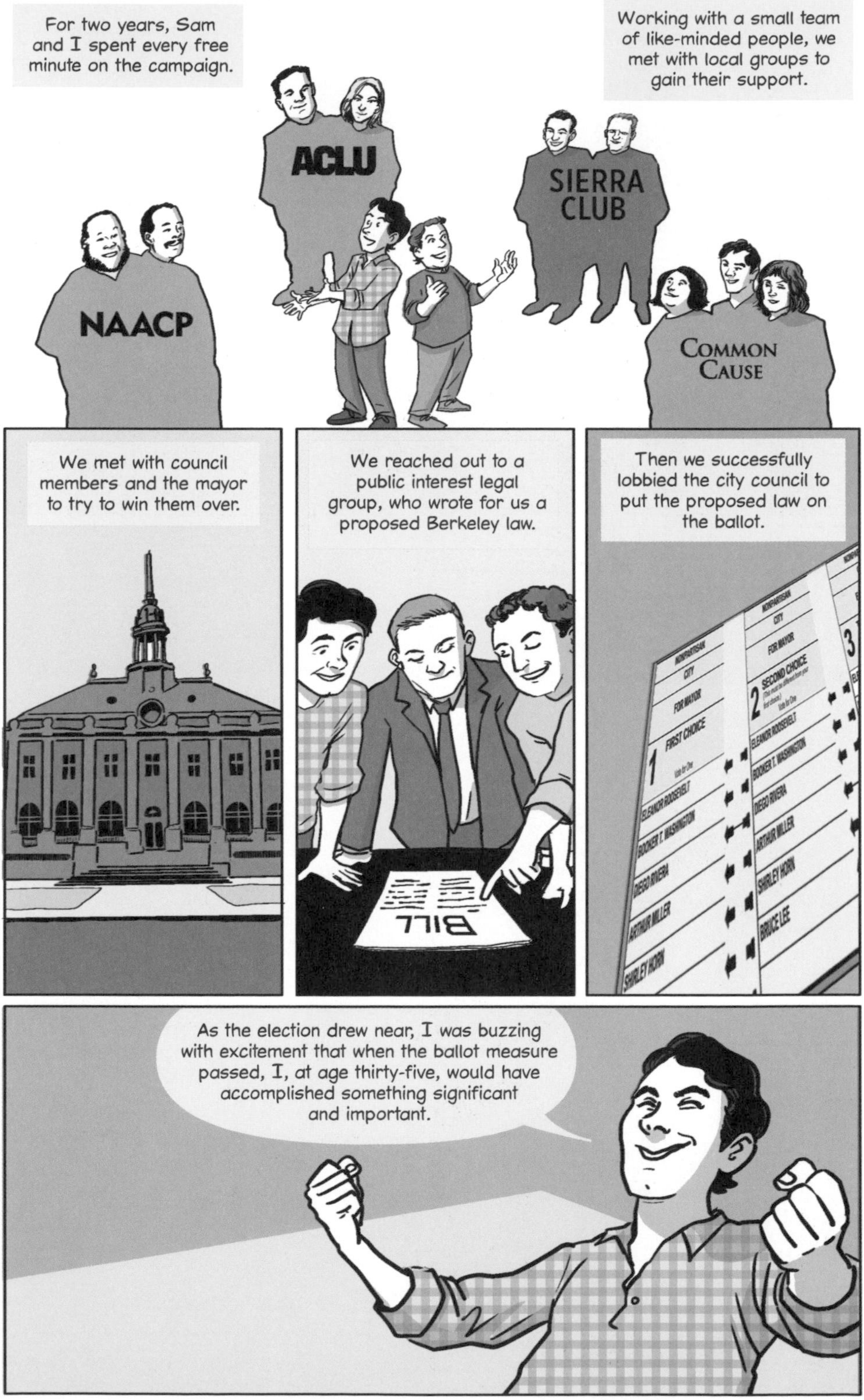
For two years, Sam and I spent every free minute on the campaign.
Working with a small team of like-minded people, we met with local groups to gain their support.
NAACP
ACLU
SIERRA CLUB
COMMON CAUSE
We met with council members and the mayor to try to win them over.
We reached out to a public interest legal group, who wrote for us a proposed Berkeley law.
Then we successfully lobbied the city council to put the proposed law on the ballot.
As the election drew near, I was buzzing with excitement that when the ballot measure passed, I, at age thirty-five, would have accomplished something significant and important.

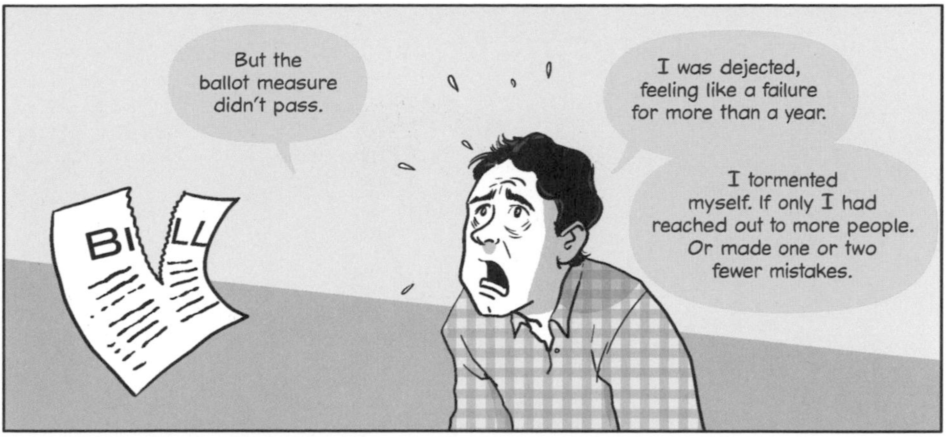
But the ballot measure didn't pass.
I was dejected, feeling like a failure for more than a year.
I tormented myself. If only I had reached out to more people. Or made one or two fewer mistakes.
BILL

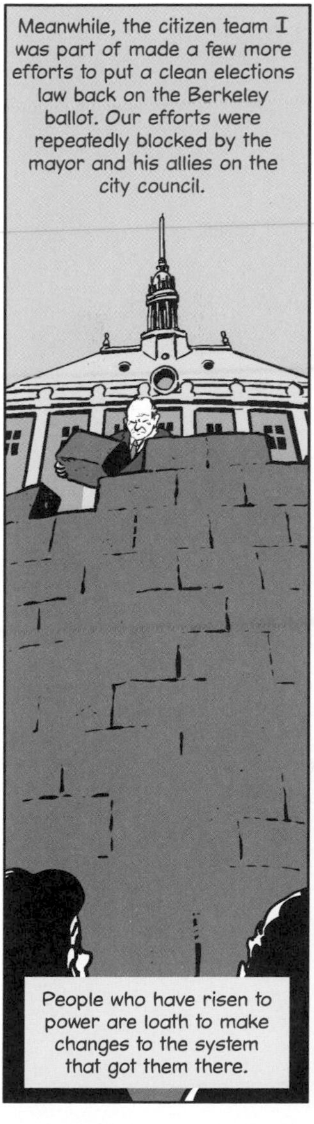
Meanwhile, the citizen team I was part of made a few more efforts to put a clean elections law back on the Berkeley ballot. Our efforts were repeatedly blocked by the mayor and his allies on the city council.
People who have risen to power are loath to make changes to the system that got them there.

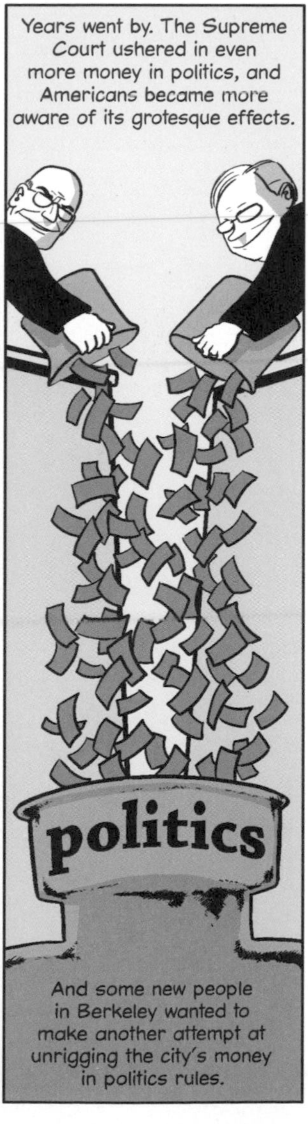
Years went by. The Supreme Court ushered in even more money in politics, and Americans became more aware of its grotesque effects.
politics
And some new people in Berkeley wanted to make another attempt at unrigging the city's money in politics rules.

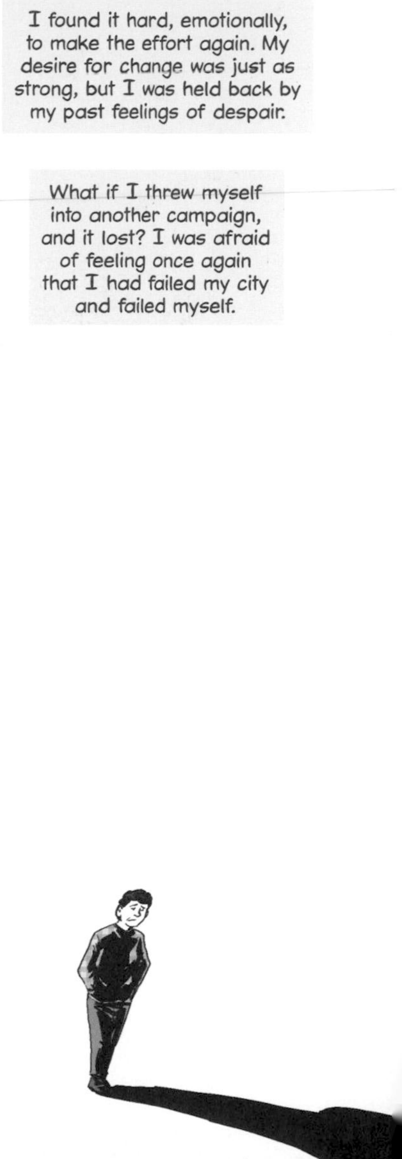
I found it hard, emotionally, to make the effort again. My desire for change was just as strong, but I was held back by my past feelings of despair.
What if I threw myself into another campaign, and it lost? I was afraid of feeling once again that I had failed my city and failed myself.

humility

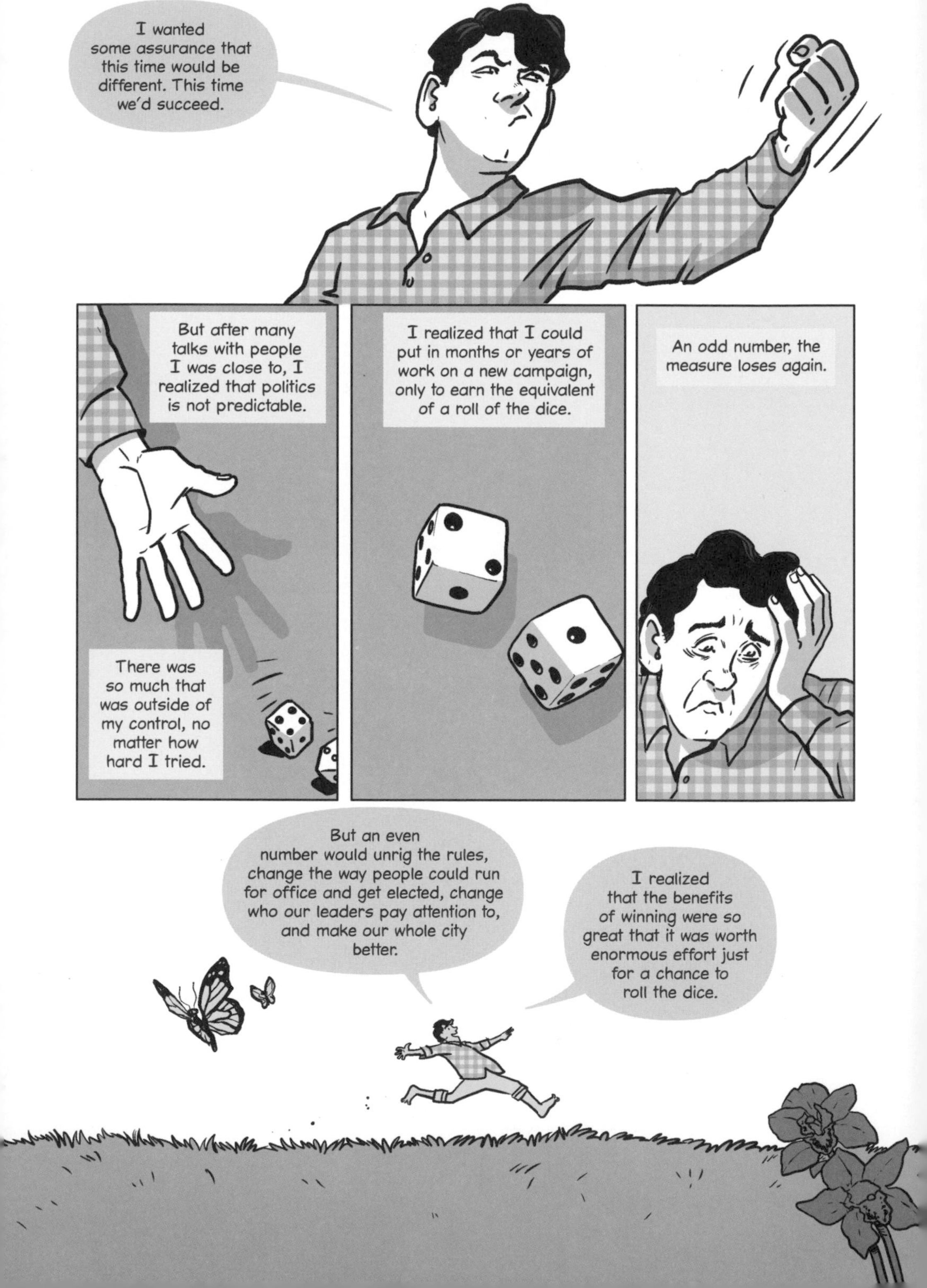
I wanted some assurance that this time would be different. This time we'd succeed.
But after many talks with people I was close to, I realized that politics is not predictable.
There was so much that was outside of my control, no matter how hard I tried.
I realized that I could put in months or years of work on a new campaign, only to earn the equivalent of a roll of the dice.
An odd number, the measure loses again.
But an even number would unrig the rules, change the way people could run for office and get elected, change who our leaders pay attention to, and make our whole city better.
I realized that the benefits of winning were so great that it was worth enormous effort just for a chance to roll the dice.

And I realized that I could separate my success as a person from the success of the campaign. My job was to make the best effort I could, regardless of the outcome.

It took this shift in perspective—you might call it humility, or maturity, in the face of the world's uncertainty—for me to throw myself into the new campaign.

We drafted a new proposed law, and for three years a dedicated group of four of us lobbied the city council to put it on the ballot.

Finally, in 2016, they did.

The proposed law was simple and powerful, a "supermatch" to amplify the support of small donors.

I threw myself into the campaign with a core steering group of fifteen, and more than 100 volunteers who knocked on doors, made phone calls, and talked with voters. On Election Day, we came through with a victory!

POSITION	YES	NO	PASS/FAIL
MEASURE TI	86.5%	13.5%	PASSES
MEASURE UI	74.1%	25.9%	PASSES
MEASURE VI	87.2%	12.8%	PASSES
MEASURE WI			PASSES
MEASURE XI	64.8%	35.2%	PASSES
MEASURE YI			PASSES
MEASURE ZI	82.6%	17.4%	PASS
MEASURE AA	72.3%	27.7%	FAILS
MEASURE BB	34.0%	66.0%	FAIL
MEASURE CC	34.1%	65.9%	FAIL
MEASURE DD	29.2%	70.8%	FAI
MEASURE EI	88.3%	11.7%	PA

A whopping 65% of voters supported clean elections, and the new, unrigged system became part of Berkeley's city constitution.

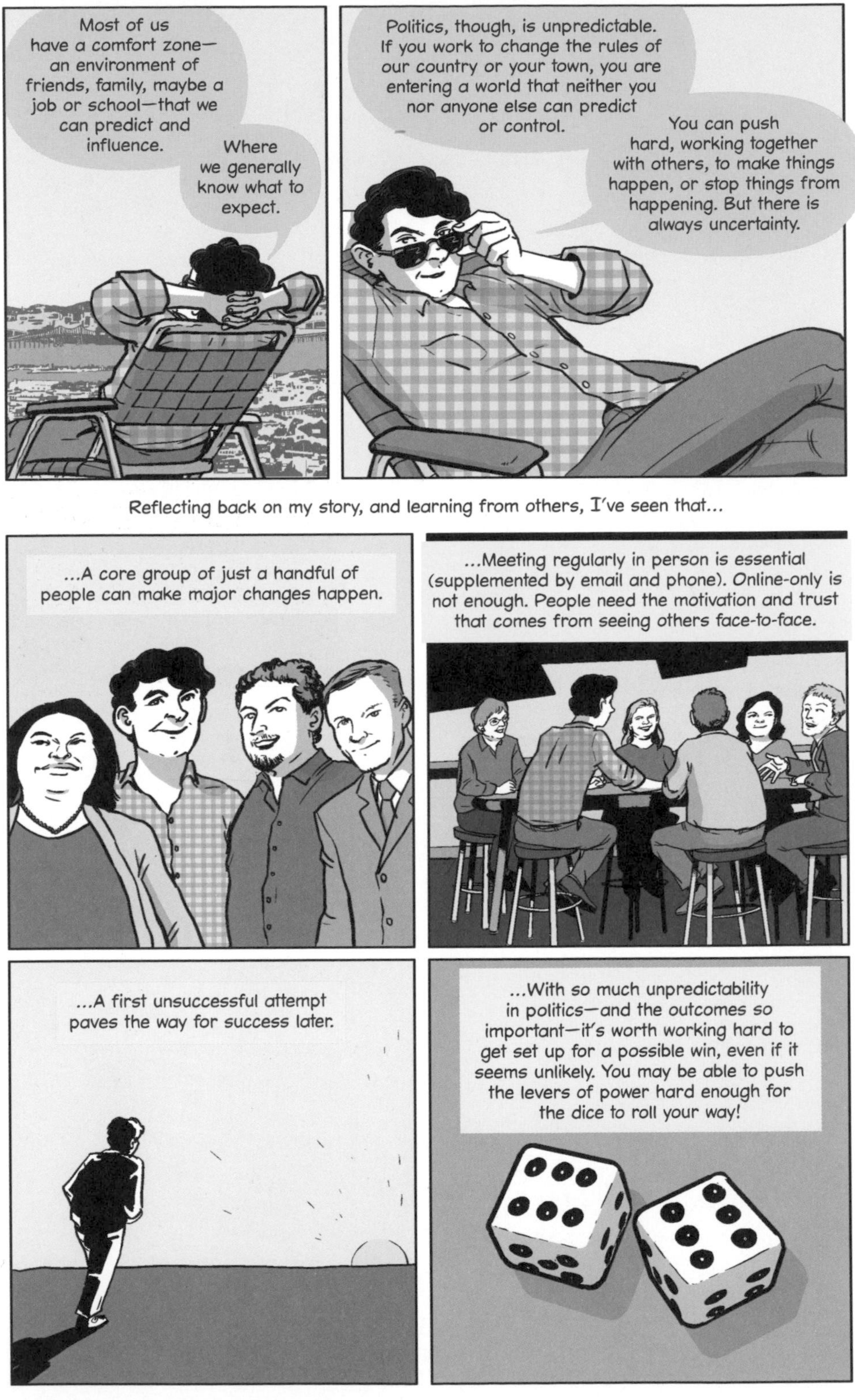
Most of us have a comfort zone—an environment of friends, family, maybe a job or school—that we can predict and influence.
Where we generally know what to expect.
Politics, though, is unpredictable. If you work to change the rules of our country or your town, you are entering a world that neither you nor anyone else can predict or control.
You can push hard, working together with others, to make things happen, or stop things from happening. But there is always uncertainty.
Reflecting back on my story, and learning from others, I've seen that...
...A core group of just a handful of people can make major changes happen.
...Meeting regularly in person is essential (supplemented by email and phone). Online-only is not enough. People need the motivation and trust that comes from seeing others face-to-face.
...A first unsuccessful attempt paves the way for success later.
...With so much unpredictability in politics—and the outcomes so important—it's worth working hard to get set up for a possible win, even if it seems unlikely. You may be able to push the levers of power hard enough for the dice to roll your way!

2

congress
and
lobbying

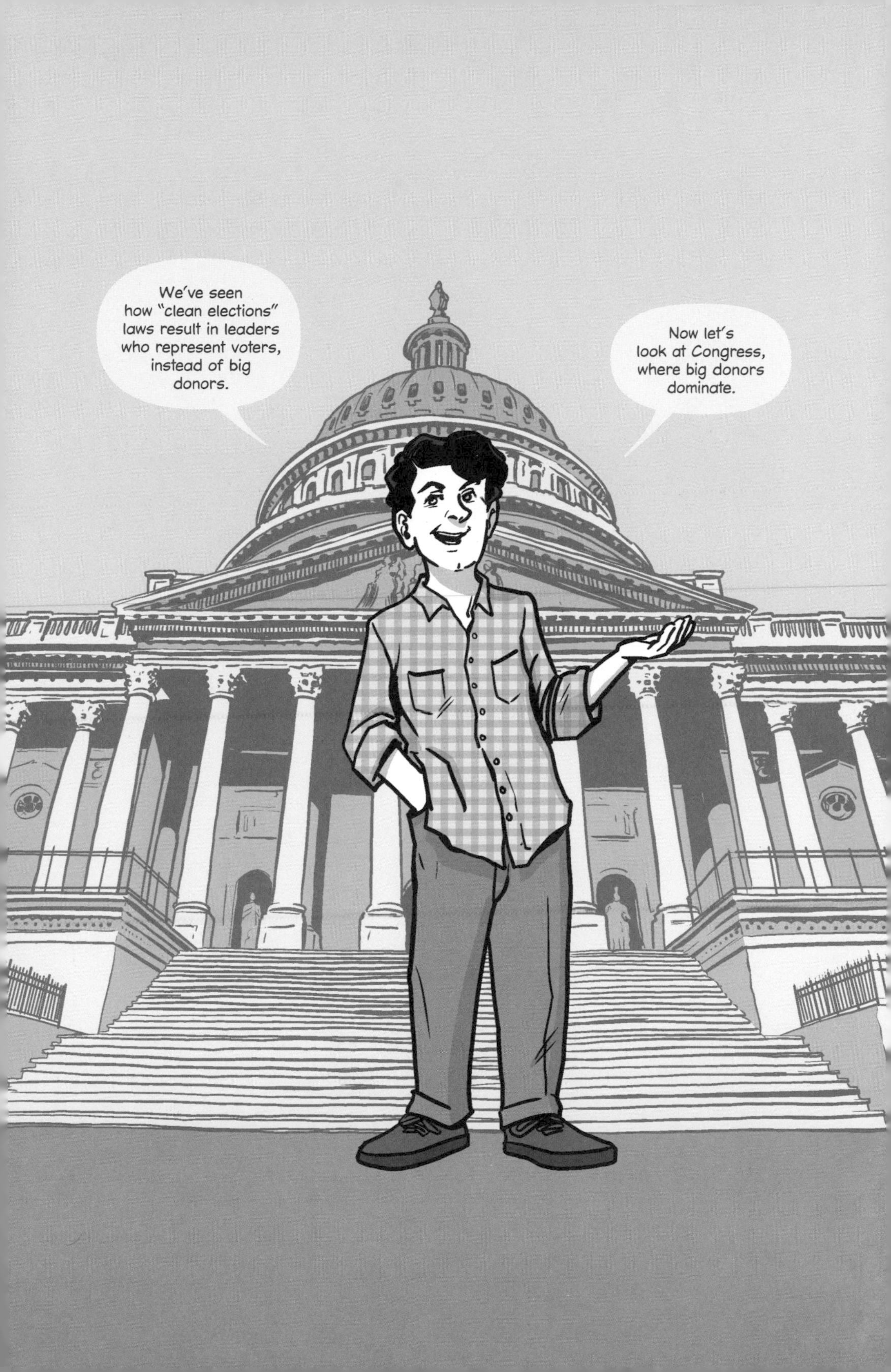
We've seen how "clean elections" laws result in leaders who represent voters, instead of big donors.
Now let's look at Congress, where big donors dominate.

life as a member of congress

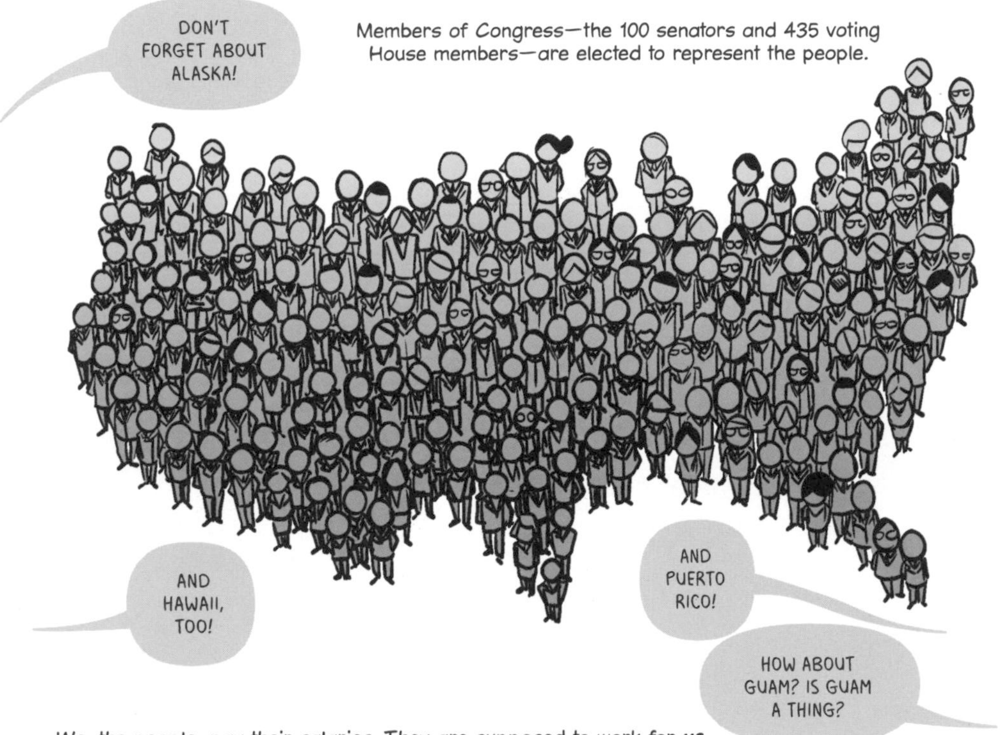
DON'T FORGET ABOUT ALASKA!
Members of Congress—the 100 senators and 435 voting House members—are elected to represent the people.
AND HAWAII, TOO!
AND PUERTO RICO!
HOW ABOUT GUAM? IS GUAM A THING?

We, the people, pay their salaries. They are supposed to work for ***us***.
So how do members of Congress spend their time?

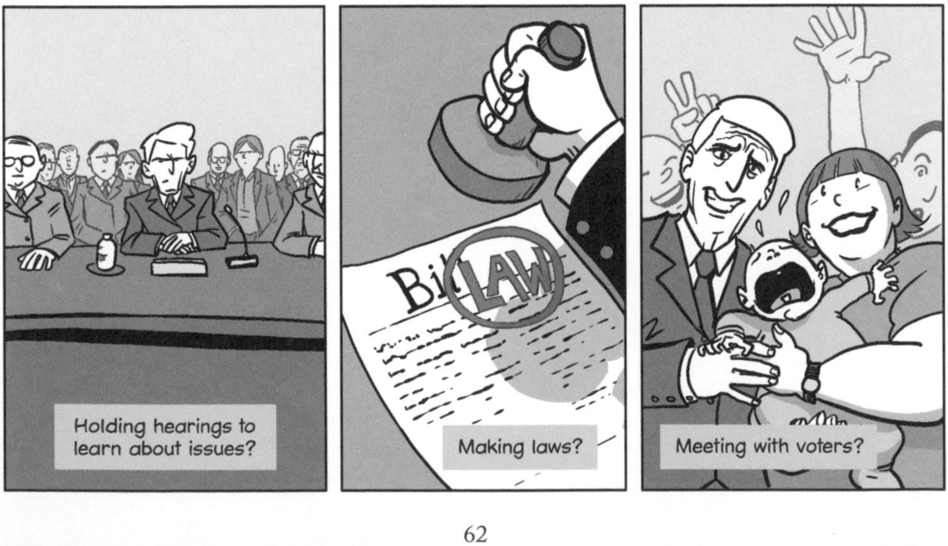
Holding hearings to learn about issues?
Bill
LAW
Making laws?
Meeting with voters?

Members of Congress spend some time on these things, but overwhelmingly, they spend their time raising money for their reelection campaigns.

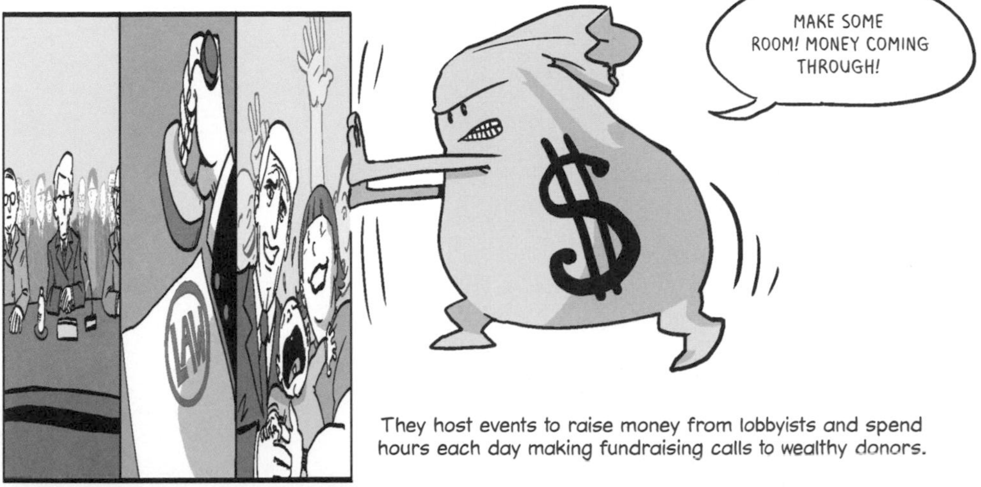

MAKE SOME ROOM! MONEY COMING THROUGH!
LAW
They host events to raise money from lobbyists and spend hours each day making fundraising calls to wealthy donors.

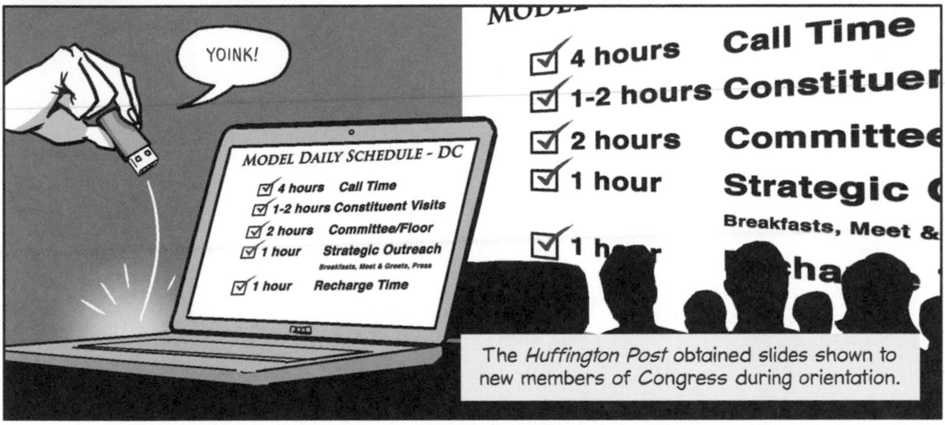

YOINK!
MODEL DAILY SCHEDULE - DC
4 hours Call Time
1-2 hours Constituent Visits
2 hours Committee/Floor
1 hour Strategic Outreach
1 hour Recharge Time
The *Huffington Post* obtained slides shown to new members of Congress during orientation.

MODEL DAILY SCHEDULE - DC

- ☑ **4 hours** **Call Time**
- ☑ **1-2 hours** **Constituent Visits**
- ☑ **2 hours** **Committee/Floor**
- ☑ **1 hour** **Strategic Outreach**
  Breakfasts, Meet & Greets, Press
- ☑ **1 hour** **Recharge Time**

This 2013 presentation was by the Democratic Party for their newly elected members of Congress. Similar fundraising work is expected by the Republican Party.

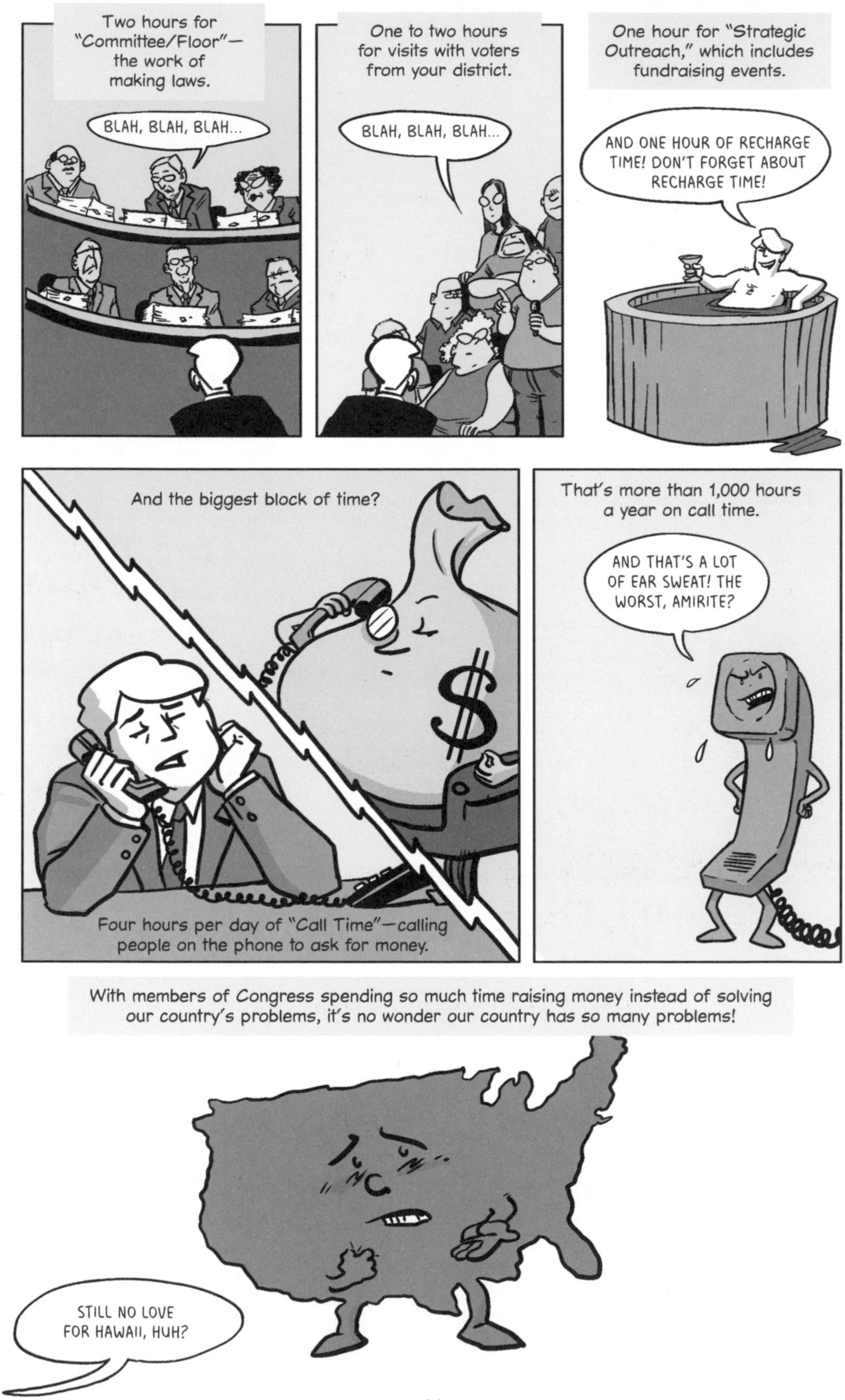
Two hours for "Committee/Floor"—the work of making laws.
BLAH, BLAH, BLAH...
One to two hours for visits with voters from your district.
BLAH, BLAH, BLAH...
One hour for "Strategic Outreach," which includes fundraising events.
AND ONE HOUR OF RECHARGE TIME! DON'T FORGET ABOUT RECHARGE TIME!
And the biggest block of time?
Four hours per day of "Call Time"—calling people on the phone to ask for money.
That's more than 1,000 hours a year on call time.
AND THAT'S A LOT OF EAR SWEAT! THE WORST, AMIRITE?
With members of Congress spending so much time raising money instead of solving our country's problems, it's no wonder our country has so many problems!
STILL NO LOVE FOR HAWAII, HUH?

call time

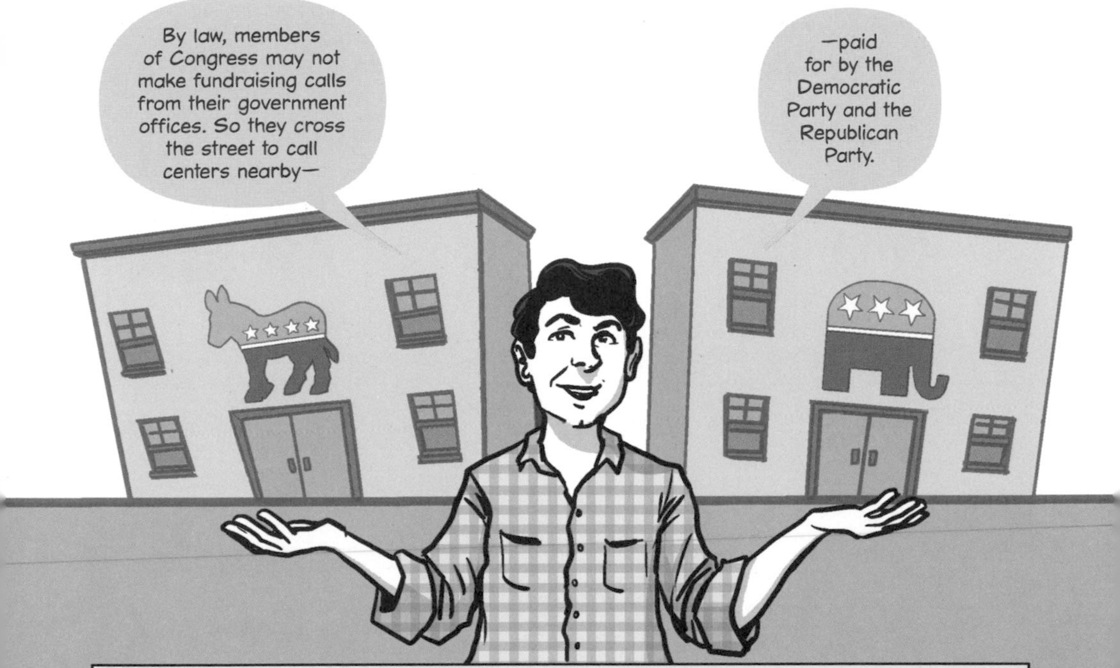
By law, members of Congress may not make fundraising calls from their government offices. So they cross the street to call centers nearby—
—paid for by the Democratic Party and the Republican Party.

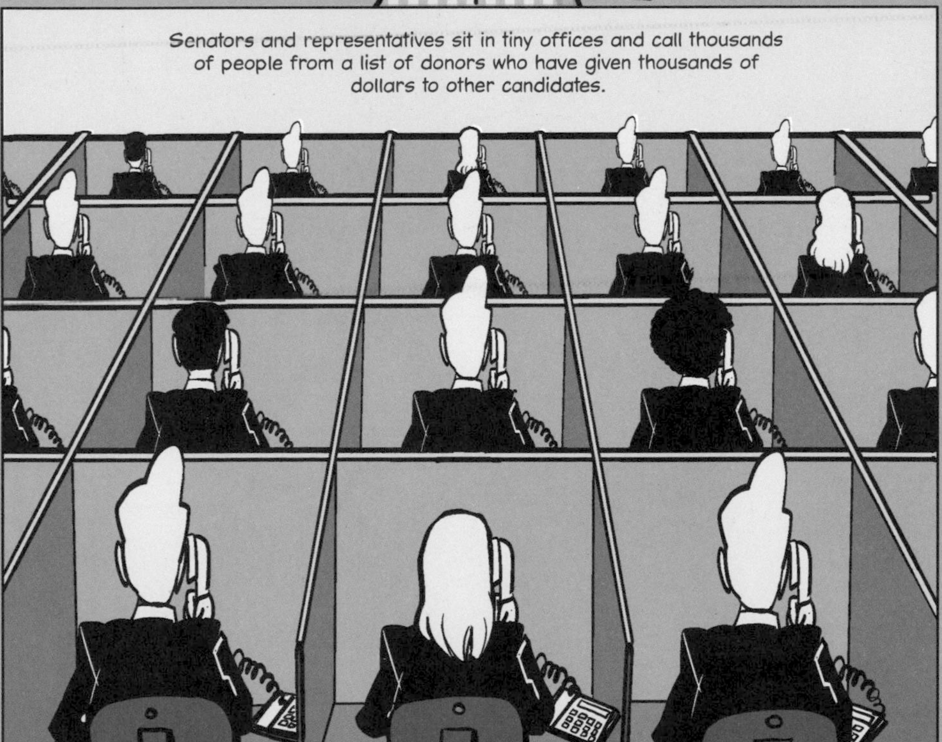
Senators and representatives sit in tiny offices and call thousands of people from a list of donors who have given thousands of dollars to other candidates.

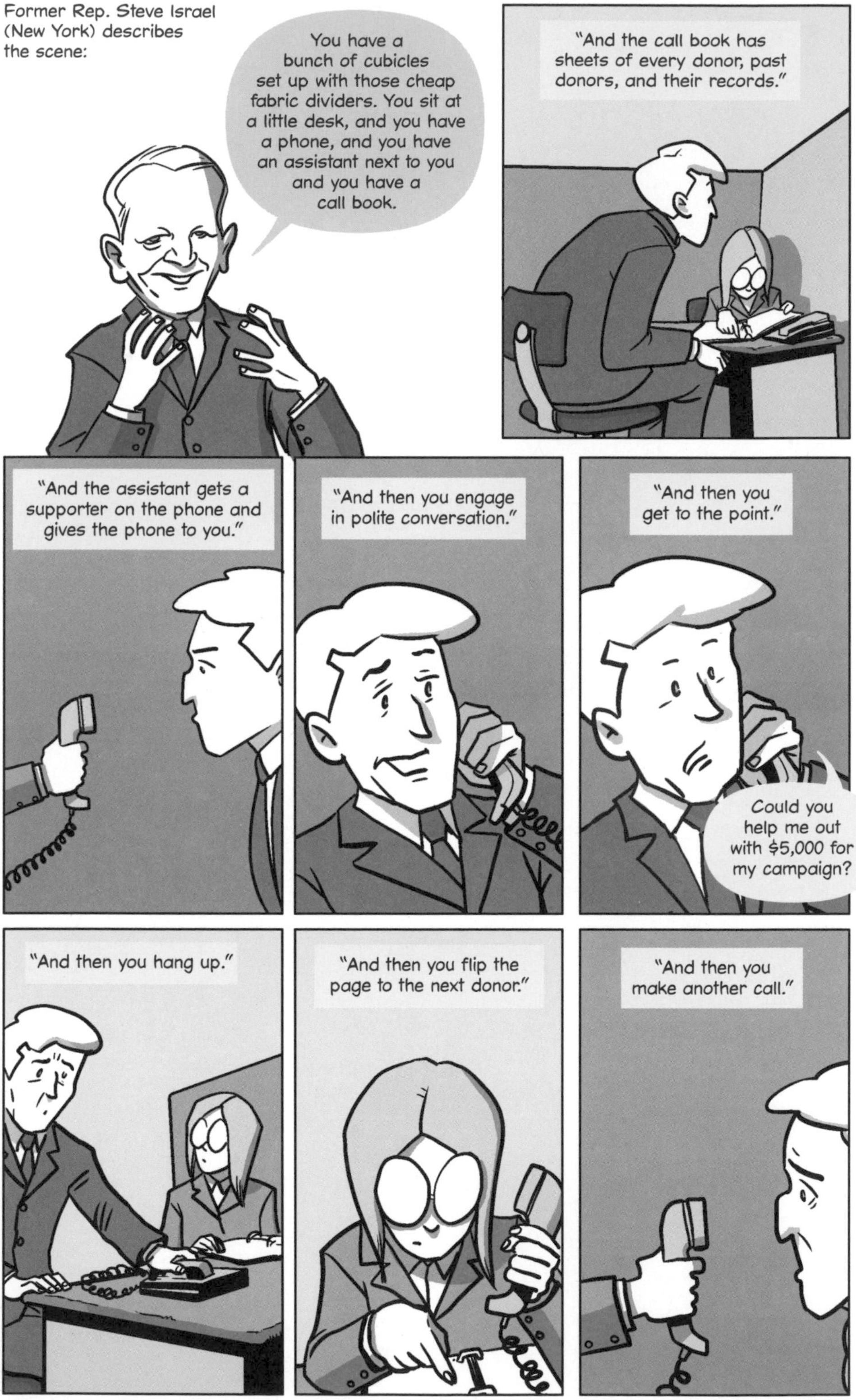
Former Rep. Steve Israel (New York) describes the scene:
You have a bunch of cubicles set up with those cheap fabric dividers. You sit at a little desk, and you have a phone, and you have an assistant next to you and you have a call book.
"And the call book has sheets of every donor, past donors, and their records."
"And the assistant gets a supporter on the phone and gives the phone to you."
"And then you engage in polite conversation."
"And then you get to the point."
Could you help me out with $5,000 for my campaign?
"And then you hang up."
"And then you flip the page to the next donor."
"And then you make another call."

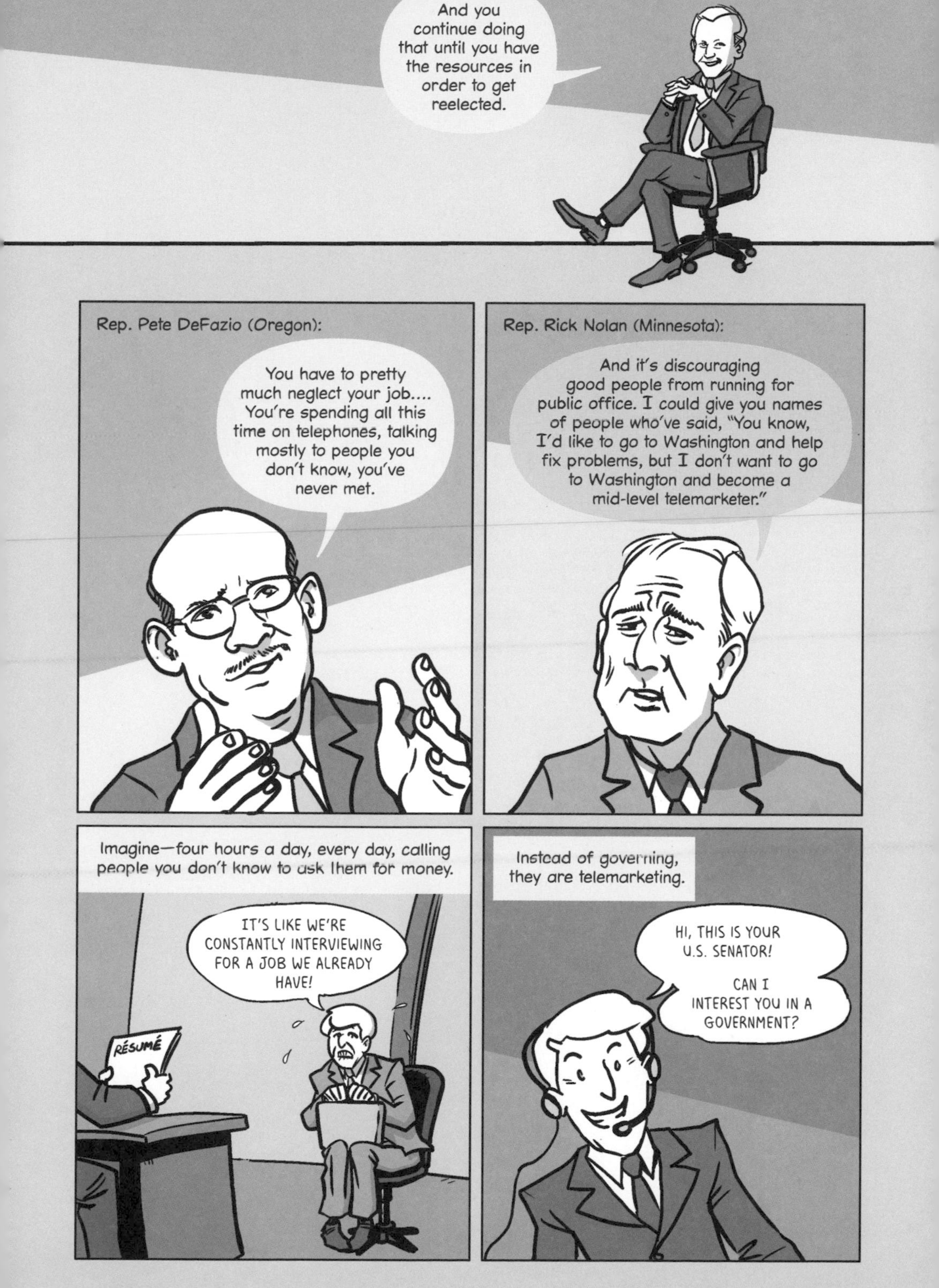
And you continue doing that until you have the resources in order to get reelected.
Rep. Pete DeFazio (Oregon):
You have to pretty much neglect your job.... You're spending all this time on telephones, talking mostly to people you don't know, you've never met.
Rep. Rick Nolan (Minnesota):
And it's discouraging good people from running for public office. I could give you names of people who've said, "You know, I'd like to go to Washington and help fix problems, but I don't want to go to Washington and become a mid-level telemarketer."
Imagine—four hours a day, every day, calling people you don't know to ask them for money.
IT'S LIKE WE'RE CONSTANTLY INTERVIEWING FOR A JOB WE ALREADY HAVE!
RÉSUMÉ
Instead of governing, they are telemarketing.
HI, THIS IS YOUR U.S. SENATOR!
CAN I INTEREST YOU IN A GOVERNMENT?

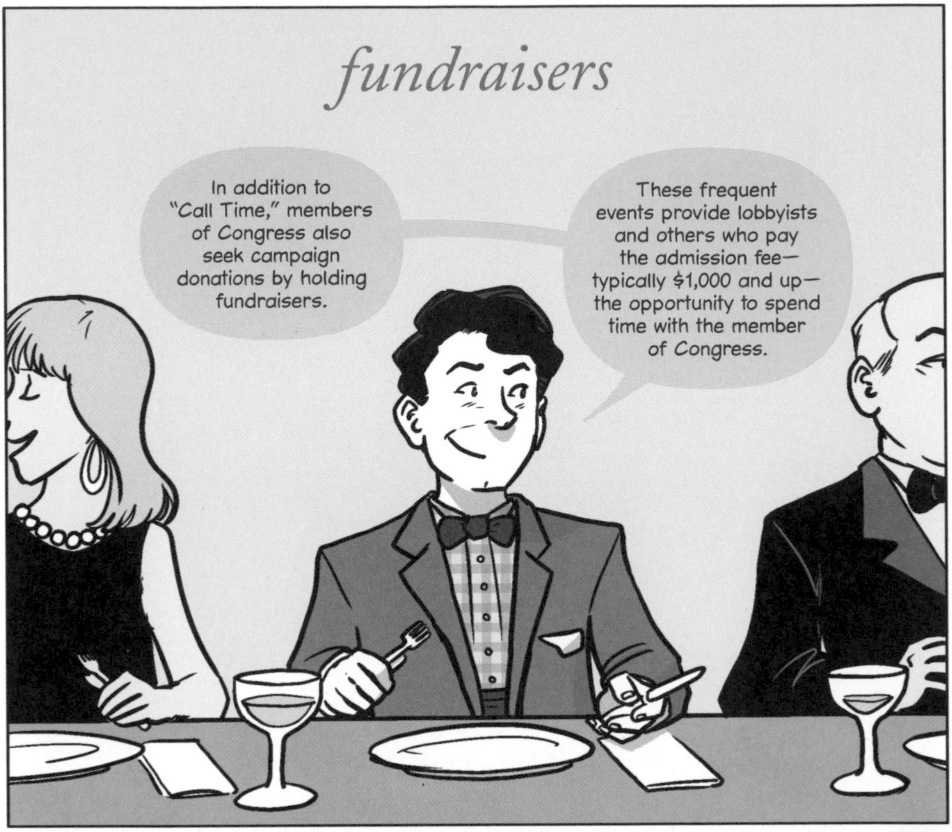
fundraisers
In addition to "Call Time," members of Congress also seek campaign donations by holding fundraisers.
These frequent events provide lobbyists and others who pay the admission fee—typically $1,000 and up—the opportunity to spend time with the member of Congress.

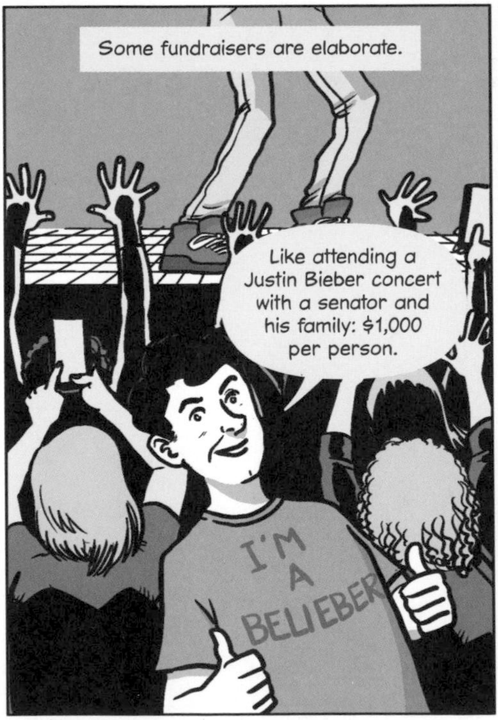
Some fundraisers are elaborate.
Like attending a Justin Bieber concert with a senator and his family: $1,000 per person.
I'M A BELIEBER

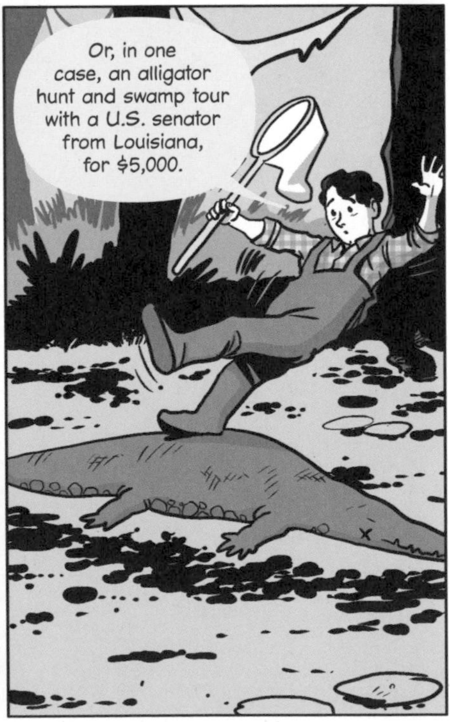
Or, in one case, an alligator hunt and swamp tour with a U.S. senator from Louisiana, for $5,000.

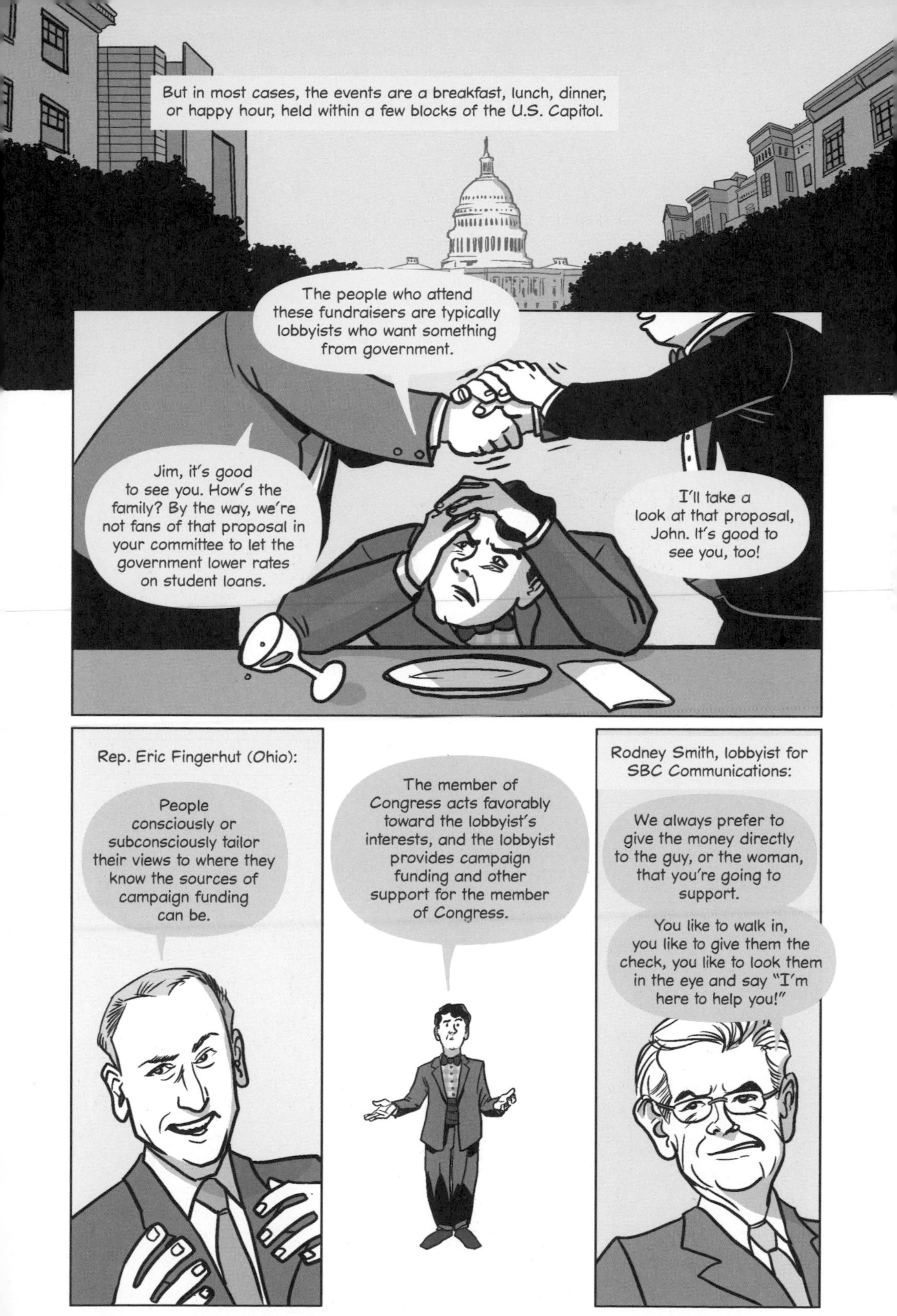
But in most cases, the events are a breakfast, lunch, dinner, or happy hour, held within a few blocks of the U.S. Capitol.
The people who attend these fundraisers are typically lobbyists who want something from government.
Jim, it's good to see you. How's the family? By the way, we're not fans of that proposal in your committee to let the government lower rates on student loans.
I'll take a look at that proposal, John. It's good to see you, too!
Rep. Eric Fingerhut (Ohio):
People consciously or subconsciously tailor their views to where they know the sources of campaign funding can be.
The member of Congress acts favorably toward the lobbyist's interests, and the lobbyist provides campaign funding and other support for the member of Congress.
Rodney Smith, lobbyist for SBC Communications:
We always prefer to give the money directly to the guy, or the woman, that you're going to support.
You like to walk in, you like to give them the check, you like to look them in the eye and say "I'm here to help you!"

little time for bipartisanship, or ordinary voters

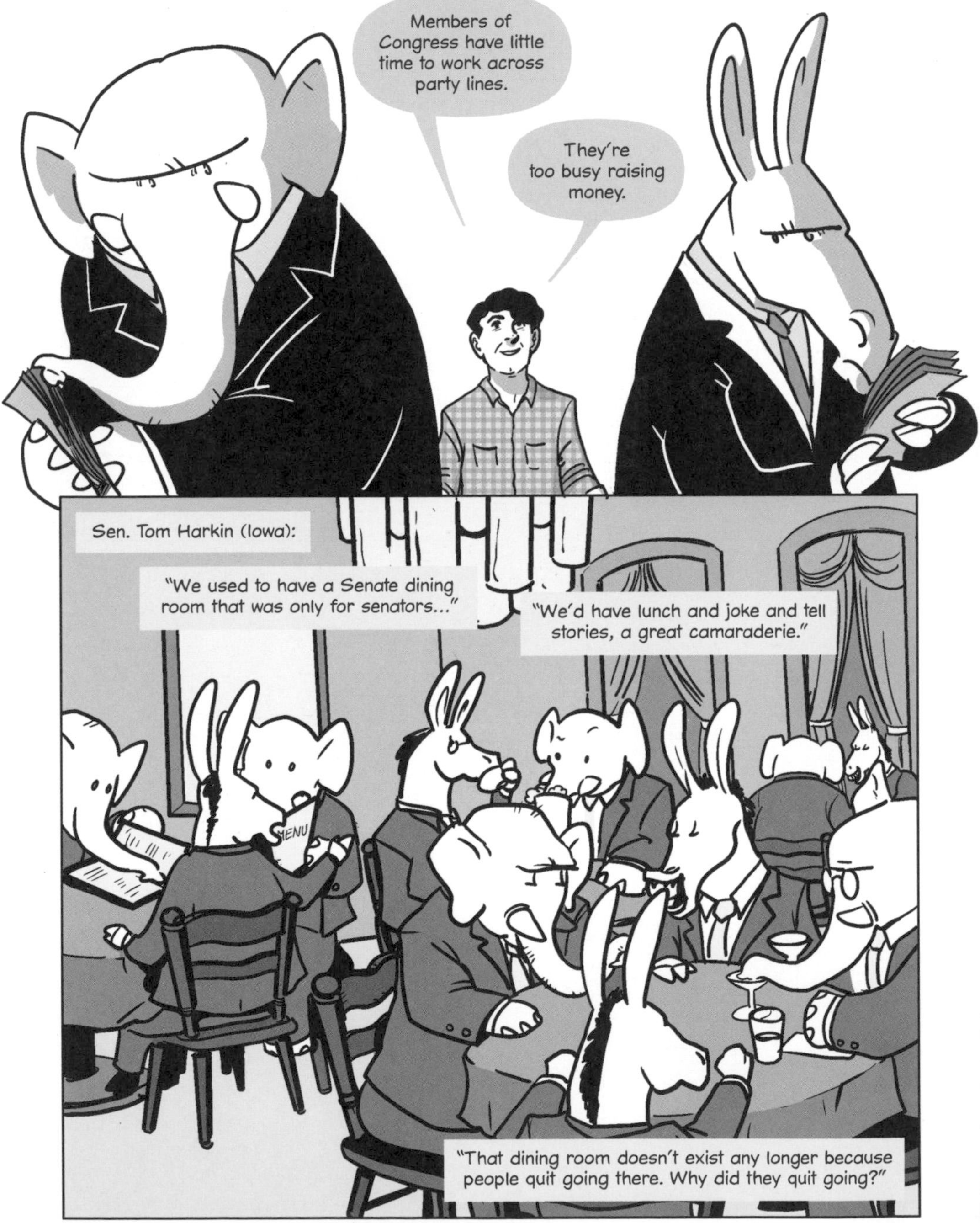
Members of Congress have little time to work across party lines.
They're too busy raising money.
Sen. Tom Harkin (Iowa):
"We used to have a Senate dining room that was only for senators..."
"We'd have lunch and joke and tell stories, a great camaraderie."
MENU
"That dining room doesn't exist any longer because people quit going there. Why did they quit going?"

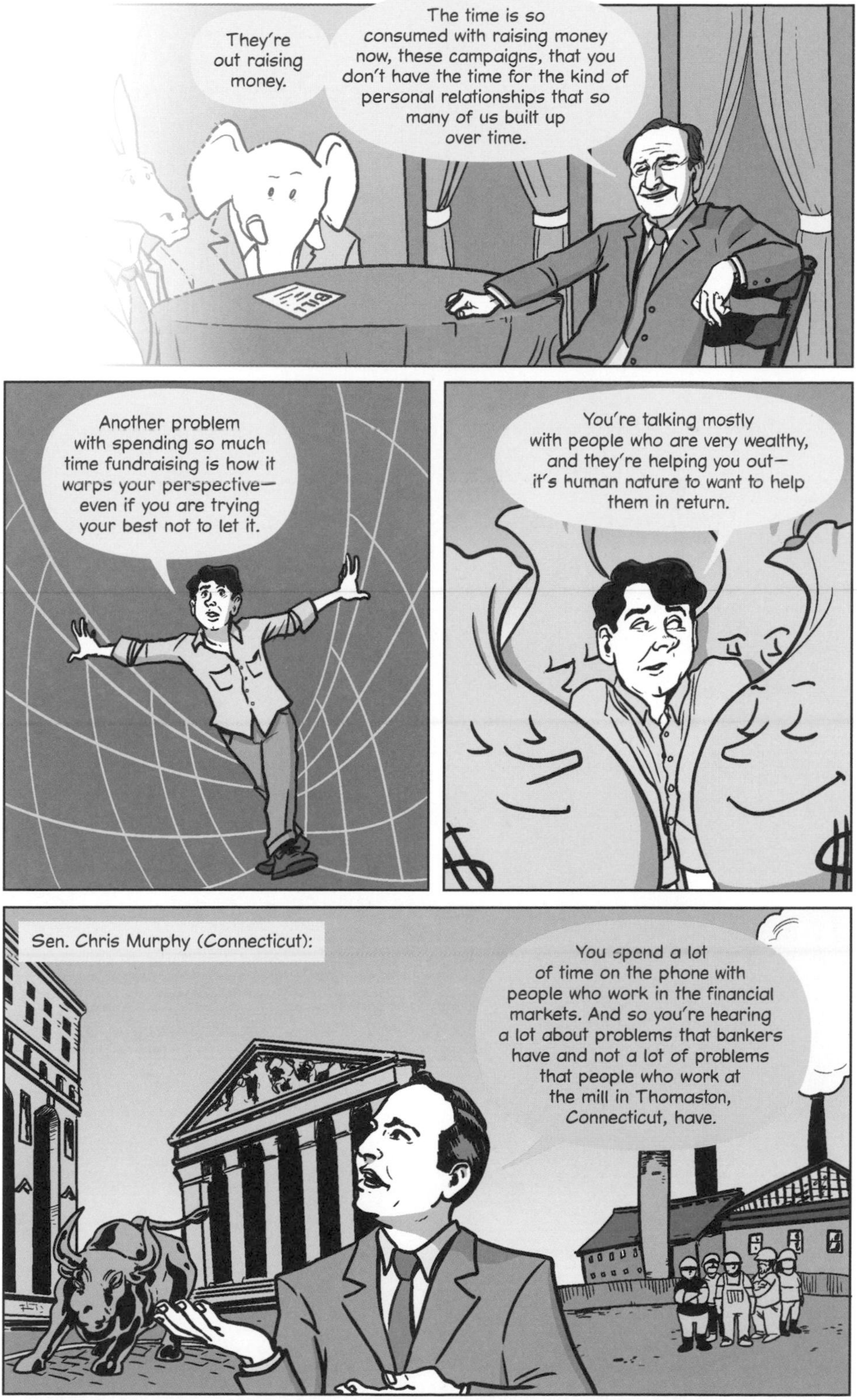
They're out raising money.
The time is so consumed with raising money now, these campaigns, that you don't have the time for the kind of personal relationships that so many of us built up over time.
BILL
Another problem with spending so much time fundraising is how it warps your perspective—even if you are trying your best not to let it.
You're talking mostly with people who are very wealthy, and they're helping you out—it's human nature to want to help them in return.
Sen. Chris Murphy (Connecticut):
You spend a lot of time on the phone with people who work in the financial markets. And so you're hearing a lot about problems that bankers have and not a lot of problems that people who work at the mill in Thomaston, Connecticut, have.

how much money?

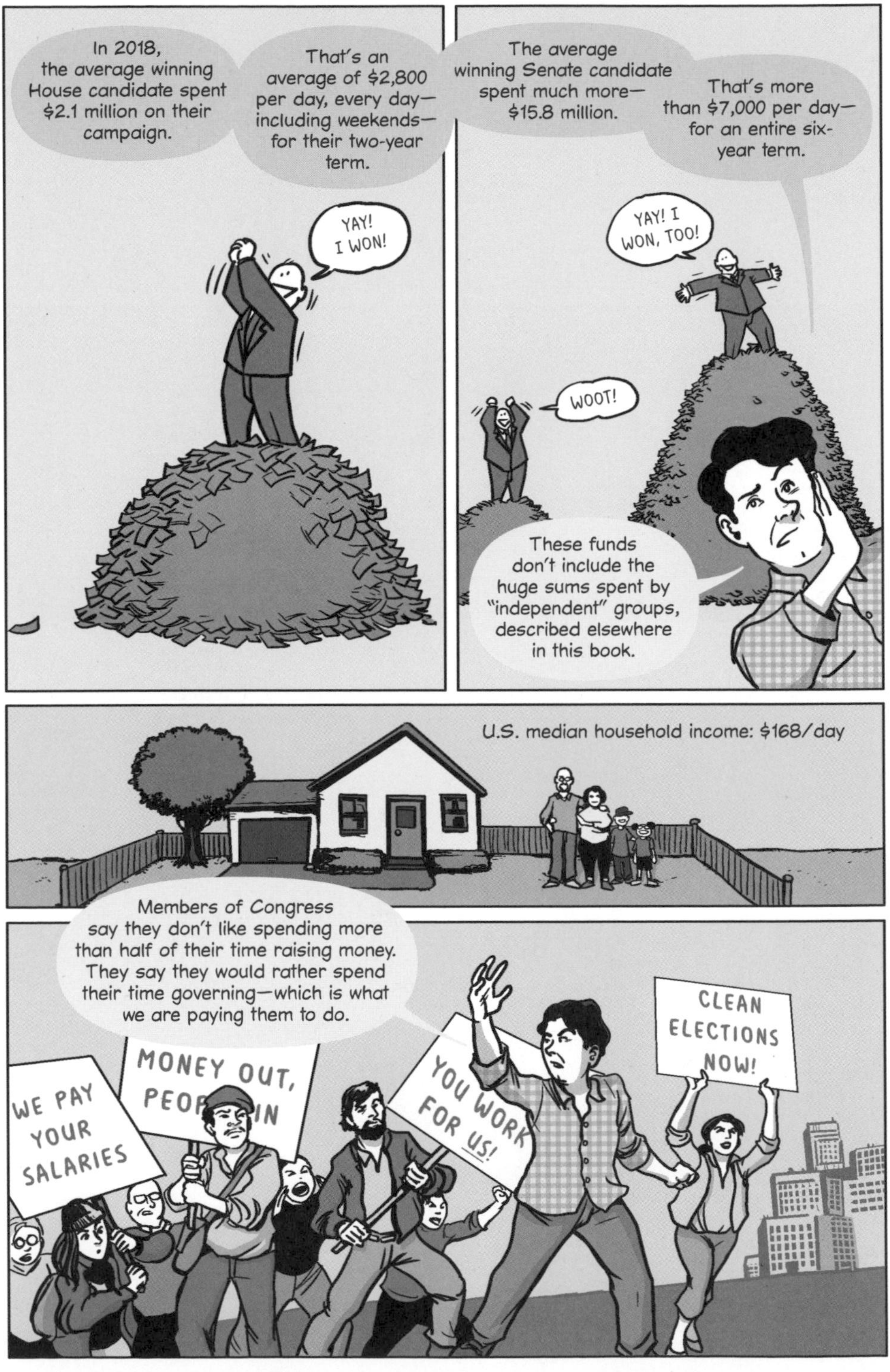

In 2018, the average winning House candidate spent $2.1 million on their campaign.
That's an average of $2,800 per day, every day—including weekends—for their two-year term.
YAY! I WON!
The average winning Senate candidate spent much more—$15.8 million.
That's more than $7,000 per day—for an entire six-year term.
YAY! I WON, TOO!
WOOT!
These funds don't include the huge sums spent by "independent" groups, described elsewhere in this book.
U.S. median household income: $168/day
Members of Congress say they don't like spending more than half of their time raising money. They say they would rather spend their time governing—which is what we are paying them to do.
WE PAY YOUR SALARIES
MONEY OUT,
YOU WORK FOR US!
CLEAN ELECTIONS NOW!

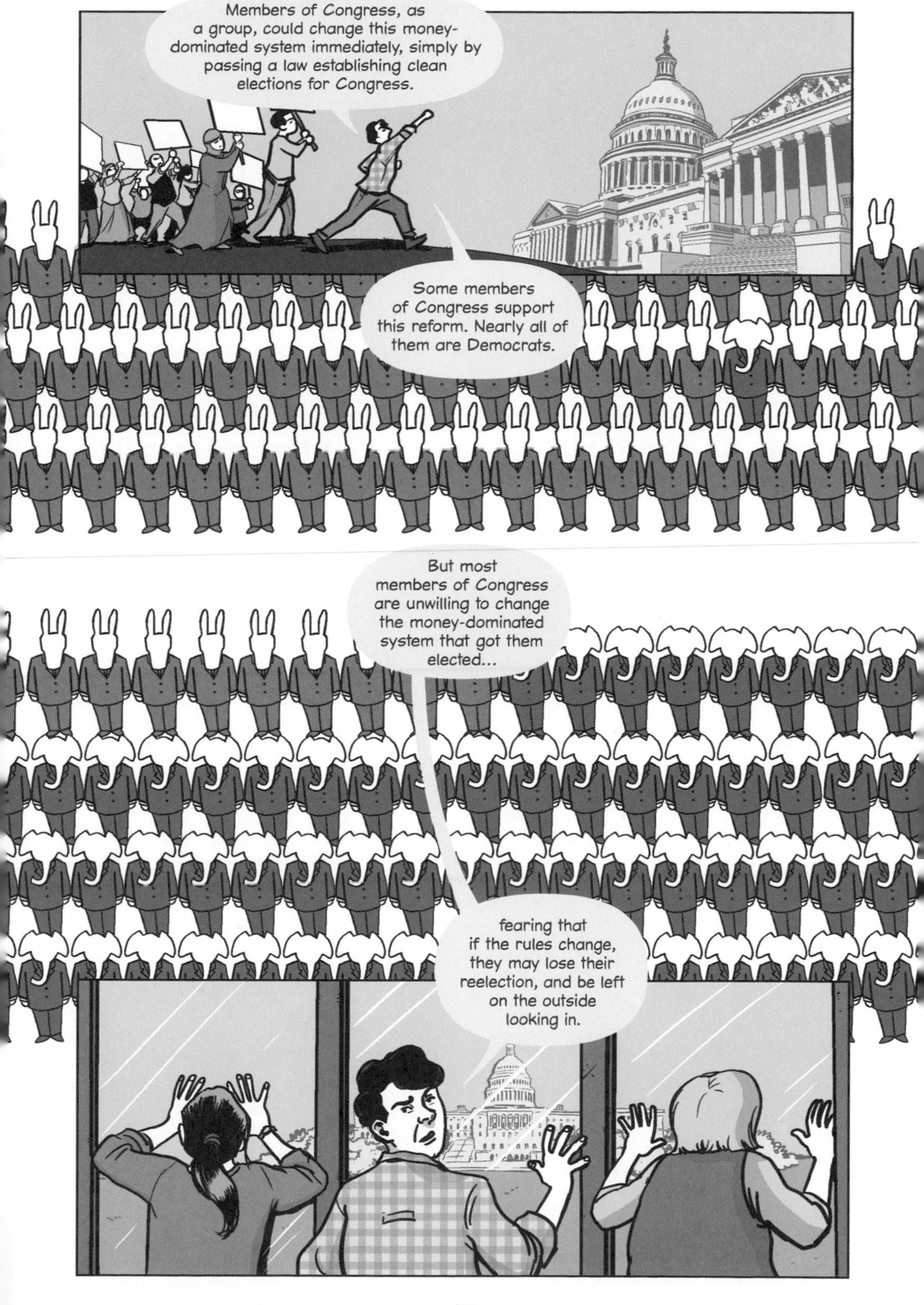
Members of Congress, as a group, could change this money-dominated system immediately, simply by passing a law establishing clean elections for Congress.
Some members of Congress support this reform. Nearly all of them are Democrats.
But most members of Congress are unwilling to change the money-dominated system that got them elected...
fearing that if the rules change, they may lose their reelection, and be left on the outside looking in.

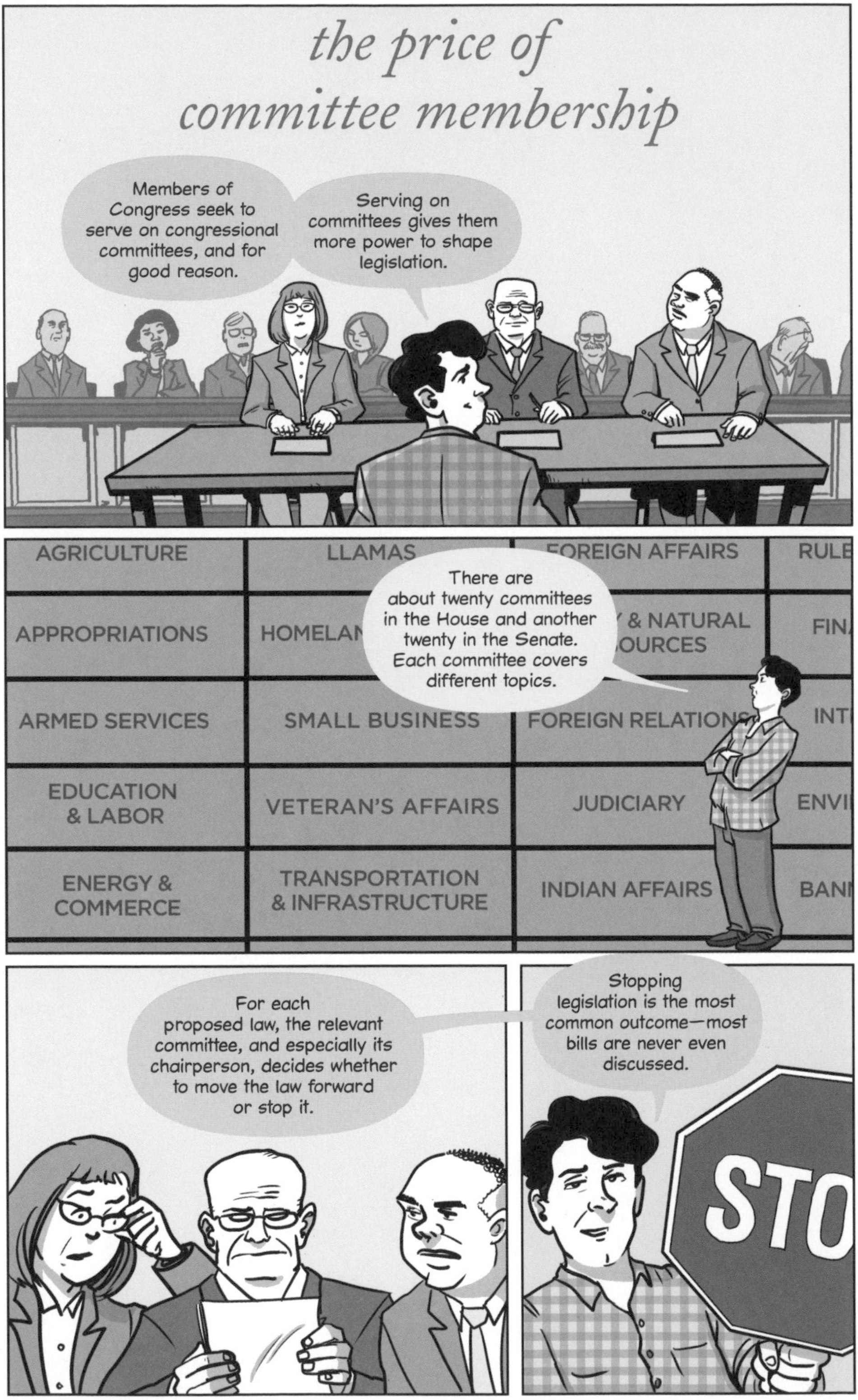
the price of committee membership
Members of Congress seek to serve on congressional committees, and for good reason.
Serving on committees gives them more power to shape legislation.
AGRICULTURE
LLAMAS
APPROPRIATIONS
ARMED SERVICES
SMALL BUSINESS
EDUCATION & LABOR
VETERAN'S AFFAIRS
JUDICIARY
ENERGY & COMMERCE
TRANSPORTATION & INFRASTRUCTURE
INDIAN AFFAIRS
There are about twenty committees in the House and another twenty in the Senate. Each committee covers different topics.
For each proposed law, the relevant committee, and especially its chairperson, decides whether to move the law forward or stop it.
Stopping legislation is the most common outcome—most bills are never even discussed.

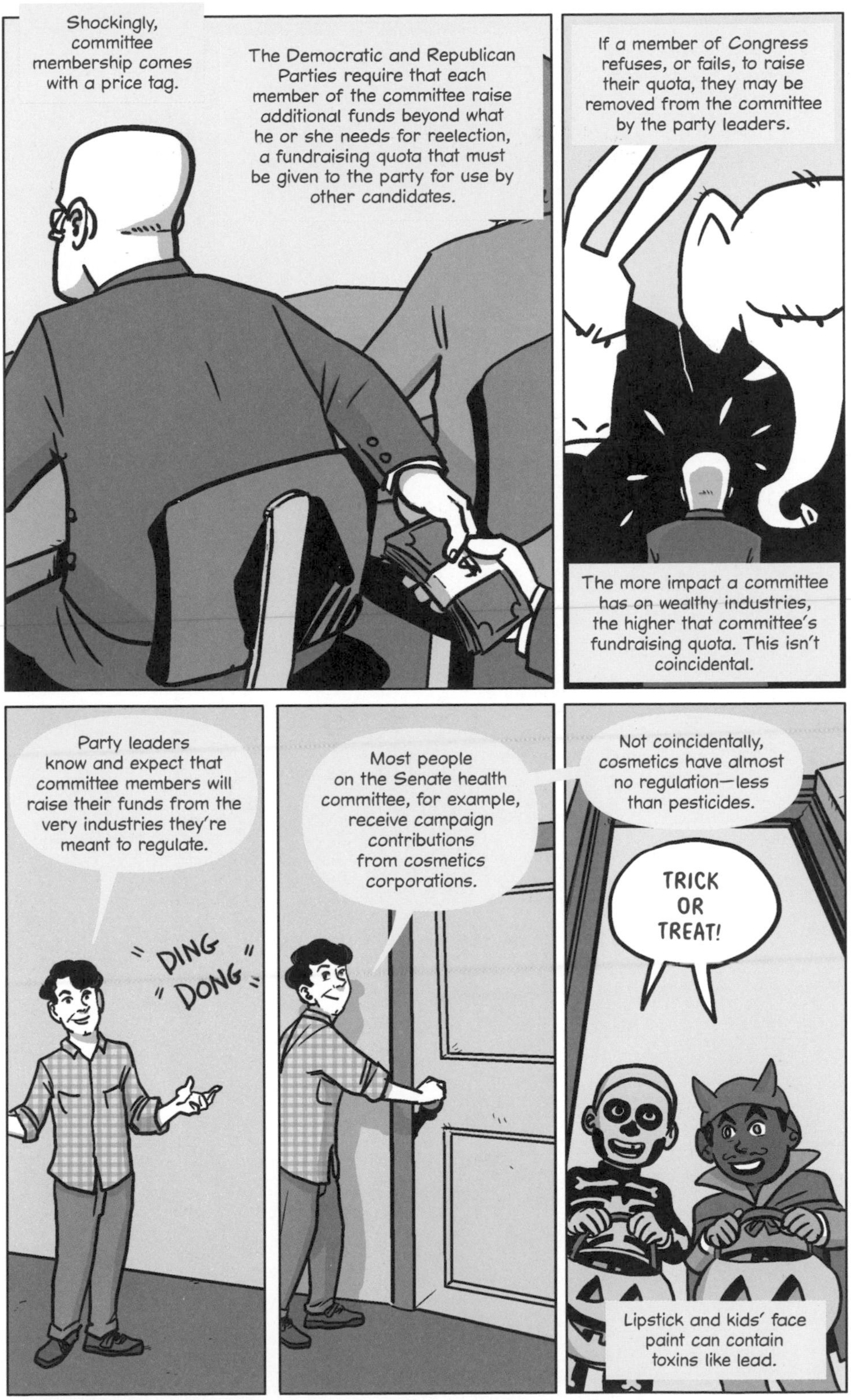
Shockingly, committee membership comes with a price tag.
The Democratic and Republican Parties require that each member of the committee raise additional funds beyond what he or she needs for reelection, a fundraising quota that must be given to the party for use by other candidates.
If a member of Congress refuses, or fails, to raise their quota, they may be removed from the committee by the party leaders.
The more impact a committee has on wealthy industries, the higher that committee's fundraising quota. This isn't coincidental.
Party leaders know and expect that committee members will raise their funds from the very industries they're meant to regulate.
DING DONG
Most people on the Senate health committee, for example, receive campaign contributions from cosmetics corporations.
Not coincidentally, cosmetics have almost no regulation—less than pesticides.
TRICK OR TREAT!
Lipstick and kids' face paint can contain toxins like lead.

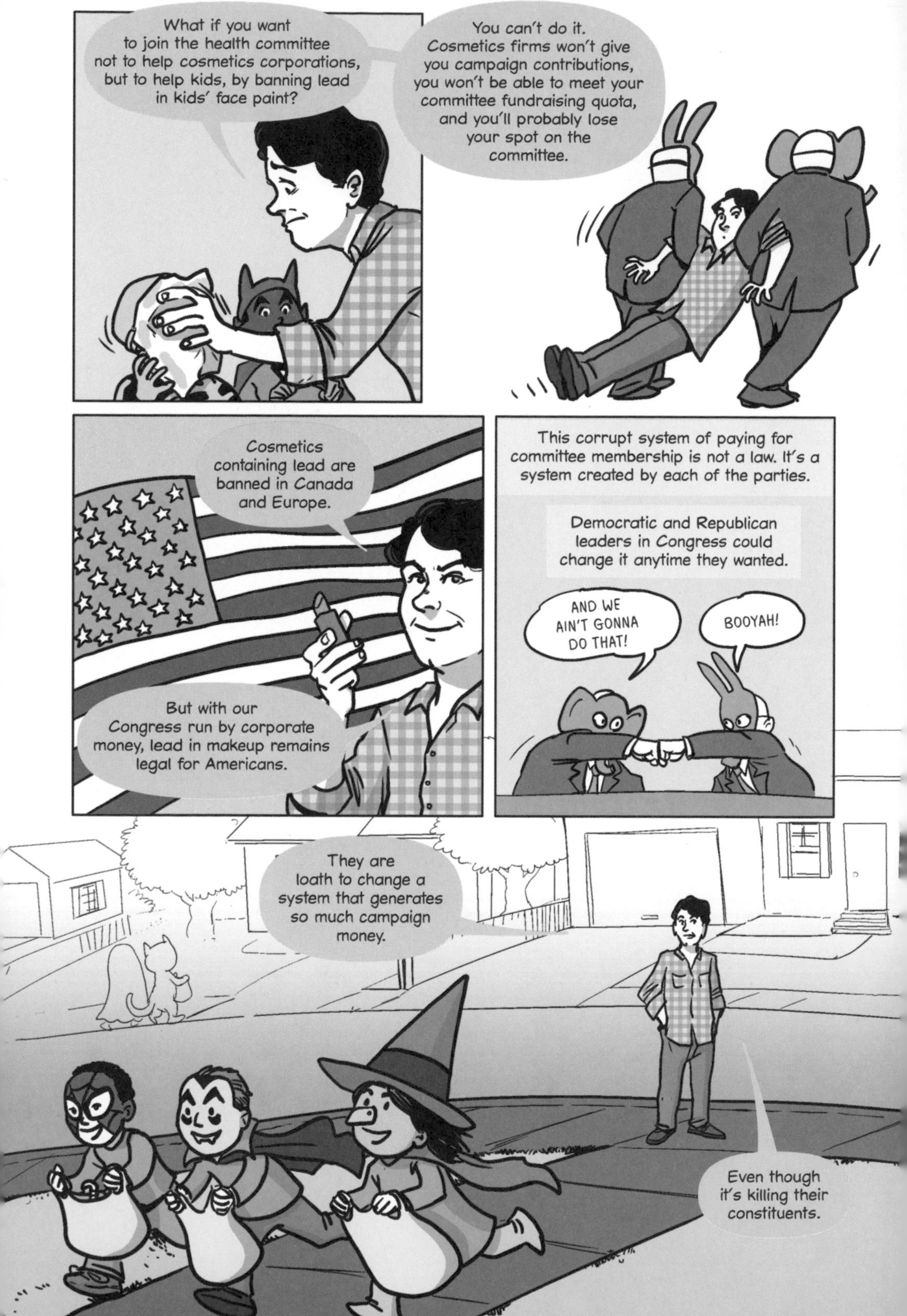

What if you want to join the health committee not to help cosmetics corporations, but to help kids, by banning lead in kids' face paint?
You can't do it. Cosmetics firms won't give you campaign contributions, you won't be able to meet your committee fundraising quota, and you'll probably lose your spot on the committee.
Cosmetics containing lead are banned in Canada and Europe.
But with our Congress run by corporate money, lead in makeup remains legal for Americans.
This corrupt system of paying for committee membership is not a law. It's a system created by each of the parties.
Democratic and Republican leaders in Congress could change it anytime they wanted.
AND WE AIN'T GONNA DO THAT!
BOOYAH!
They are loath to change a system that generates so much campaign money.
Even though it's killing their constituents.

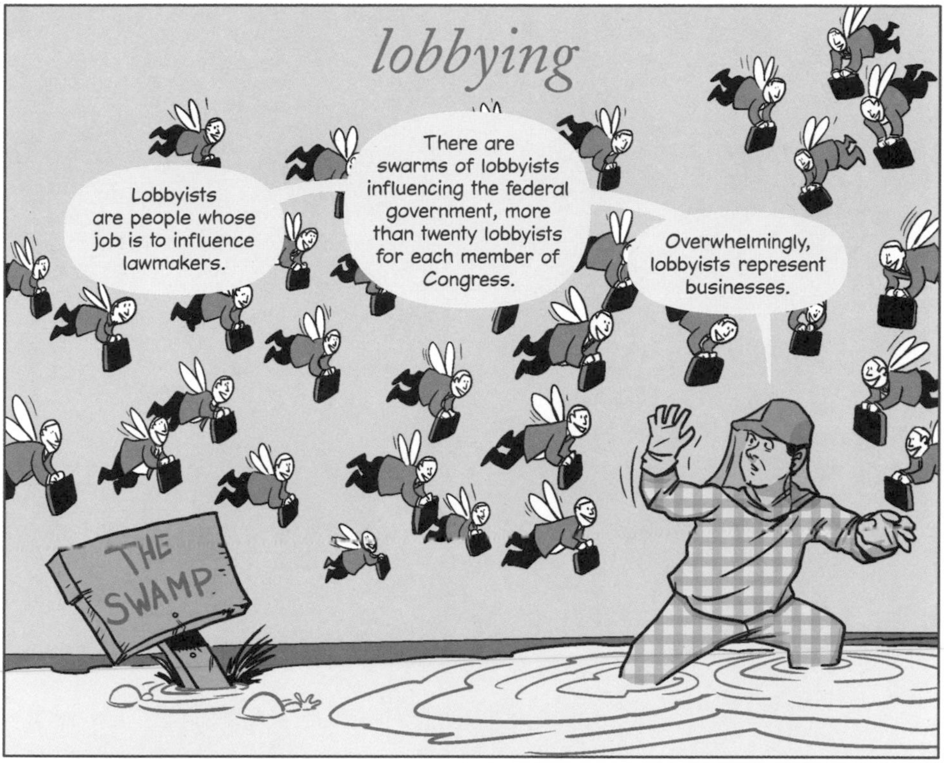
lobbying
Lobbyists are people whose job is to influence lawmakers.
There are swarms of lobbyists influencing the federal government, more than twenty lobbyists for each member of Congress.
Overwhelmingly, lobbyists represent businesses.
THE SWAMP

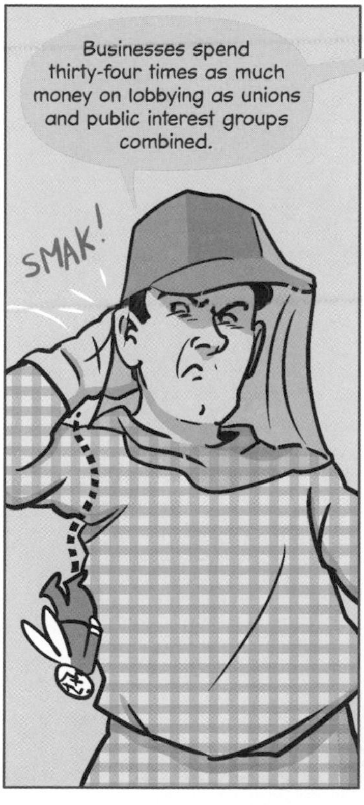
Businesses spend thirty-four times as much money on lobbying as unions and public interest groups combined.
SMAK!

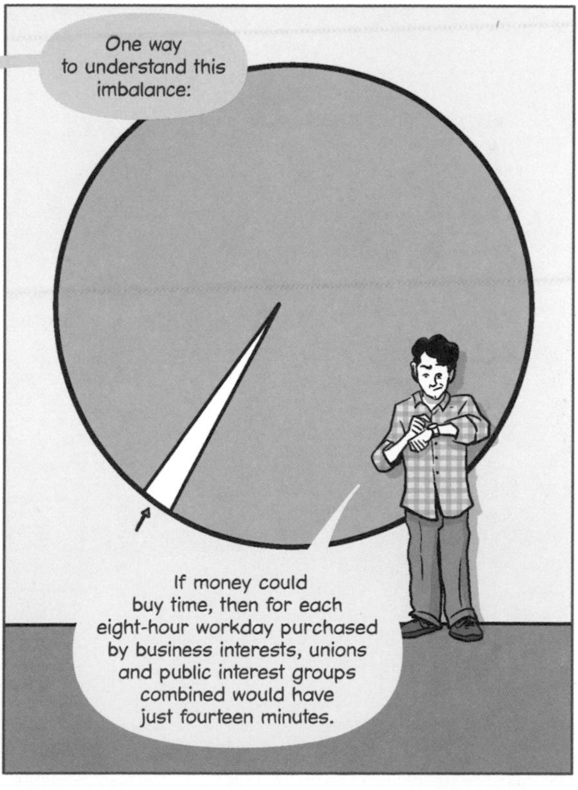
One way to understand this imbalance:
If money could buy time, then for each eight-hour workday purchased by business interests, unions and public interest groups combined would have just fourteen minutes.

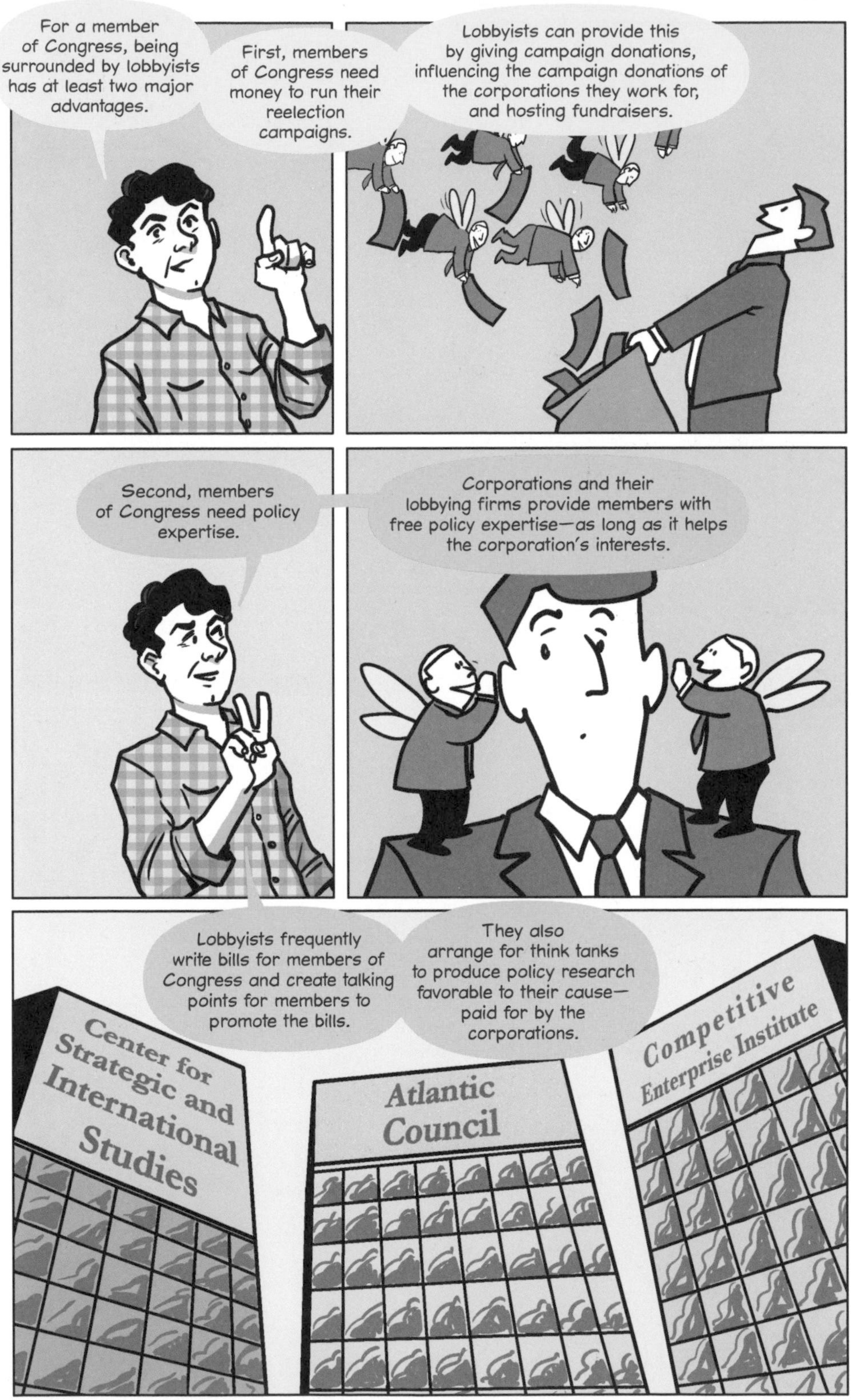
For a member of Congress, being surrounded by lobbyists has at least two major advantages.
First, members of Congress need money to run their reelection campaigns.
Lobbyists can provide this by giving campaign donations, influencing the campaign donations of the corporations they work for, and hosting fundraisers.
Second, members of Congress need policy expertise.
Corporations and their lobbying firms provide members with free policy expertise—as long as it helps the corporation's interests.
Lobbyists frequently write bills for members of Congress and create talking points for members to promote the bills.
They also arrange for think tanks to produce policy research favorable to their cause—paid for by the corporations.
Center for Strategic and International Studies
Atlantic Council
Competitive Enterprise Institute

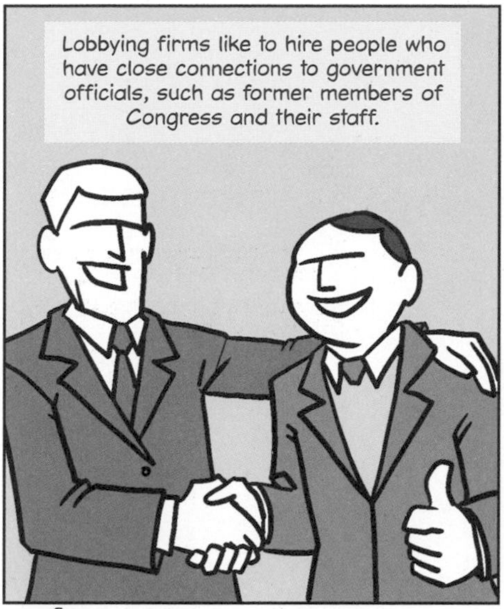
Lobbying firms like to hire people who have close connections to government officials, such as former members of Congress and their staff.

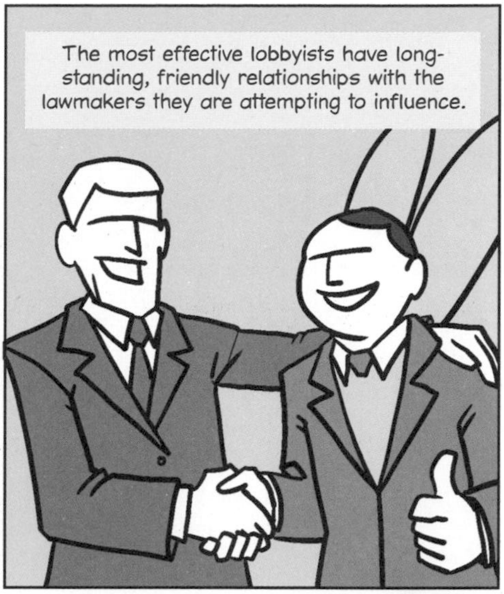
The most effective lobbyists have long-standing, friendly relationships with the lawmakers they are attempting to influence.

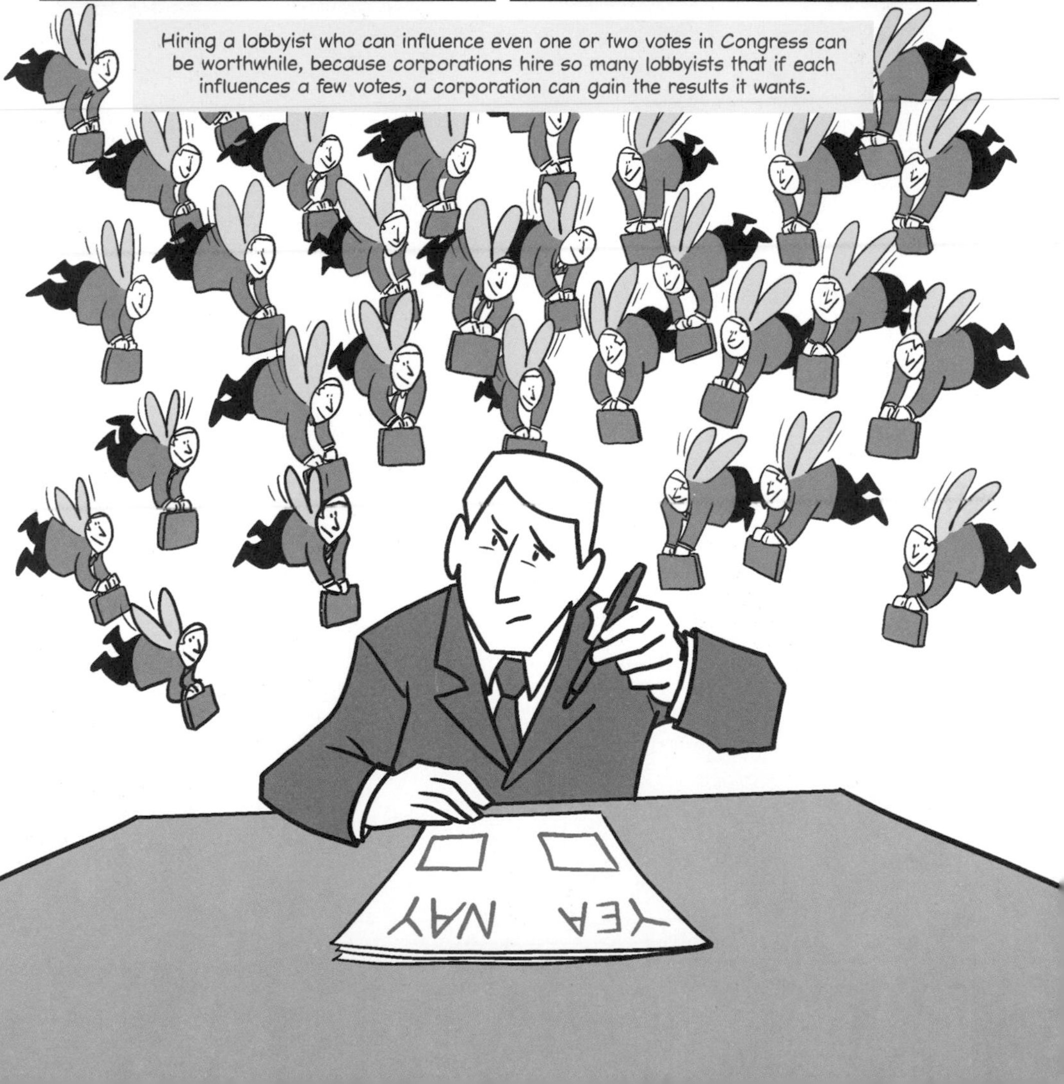
Hiring a lobbyist who can influence even one or two votes in Congress can be worthwhile, because corporations hire so many lobbyists that if each influences a few votes, a corporation can gain the results it wants.
YEA
NAY

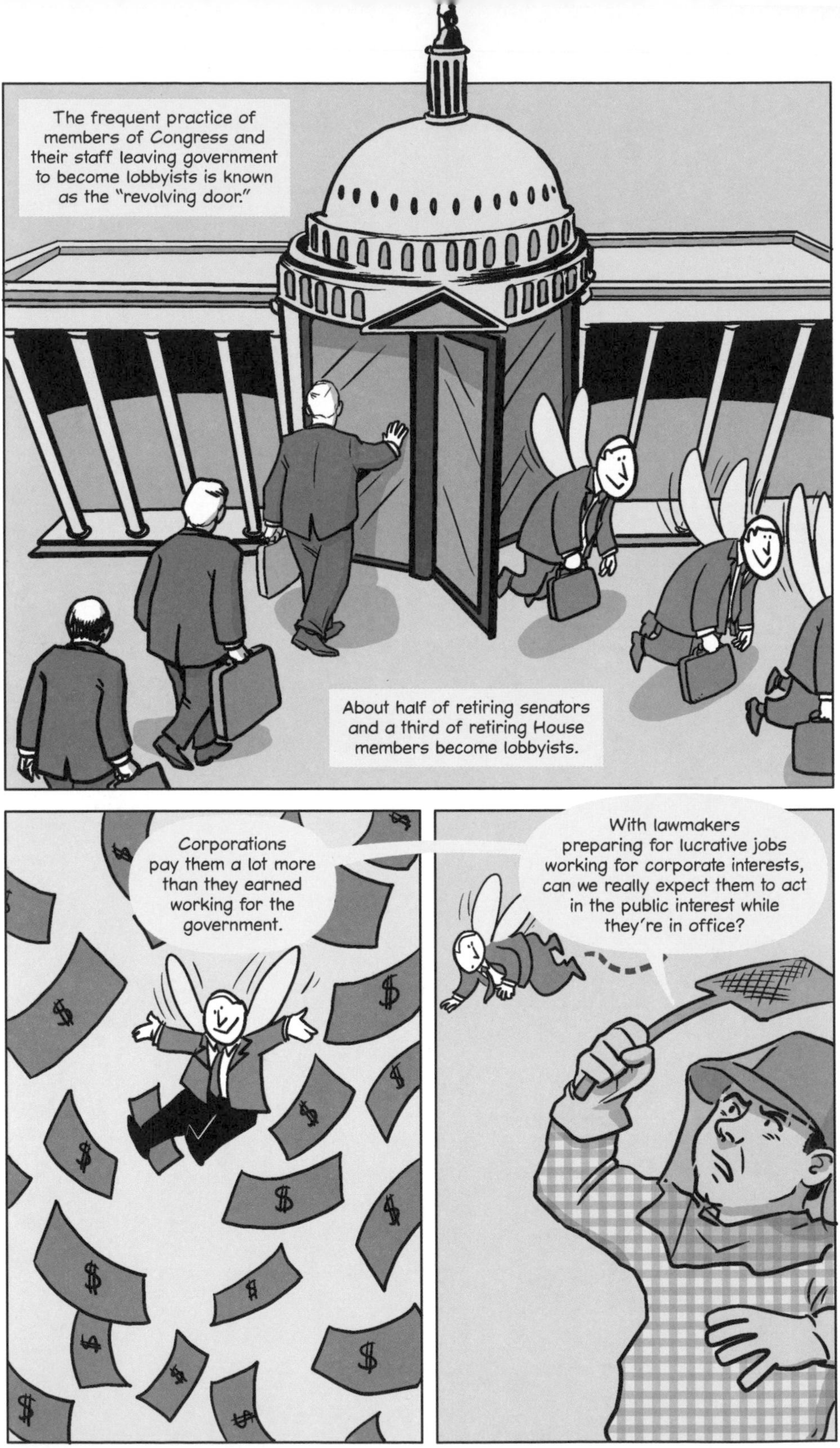
The frequent practice of members of Congress and their staff leaving government to become lobbyists is known as the "revolving door."
About half of retiring senators and a third of retiring House members become lobbyists.
Corporations pay them a lot more than they earned working for the government.
With lawmakers preparing for lucrative jobs working for corporate interests, can we really expect them to act in the public interest while they're in office?

lobbying's effects

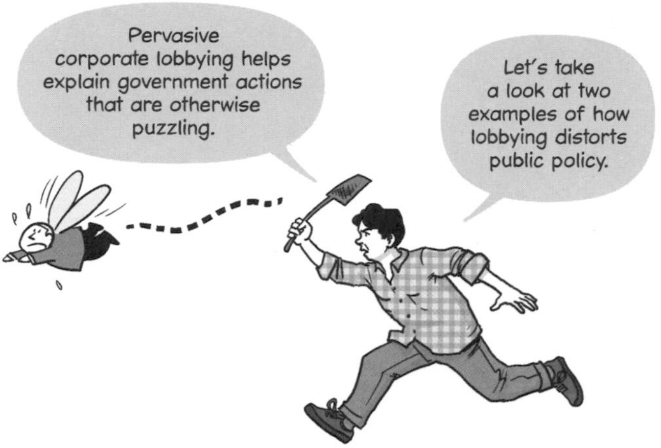
Pervasive corporate lobbying helps explain government actions that are otherwise puzzling.
Let's take a look at two examples of how lobbying distorts public policy.

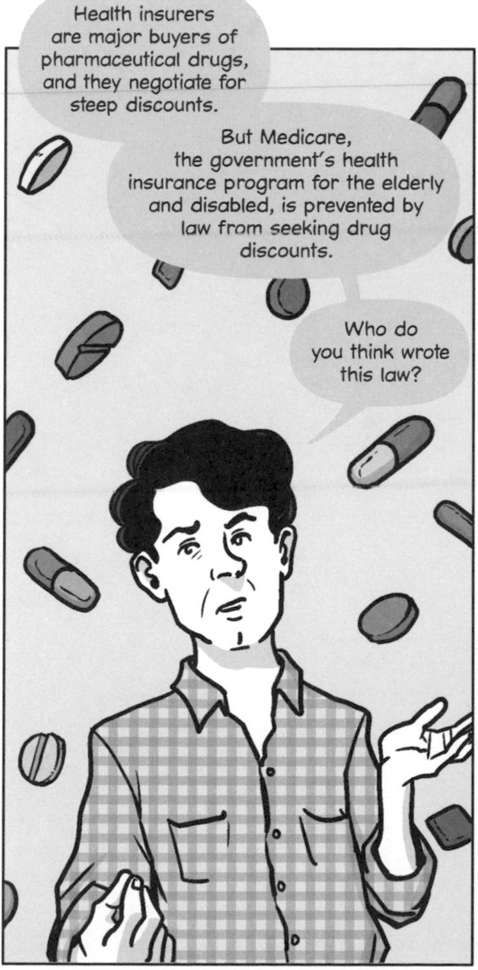
Health insurers are major buyers of pharmaceutical drugs, and they negotiate for steep discounts.
But Medicare, the government's health insurance program for the elderly and disabled, is prevented by law from seeking drug discounts.
Who do you think wrote this law?

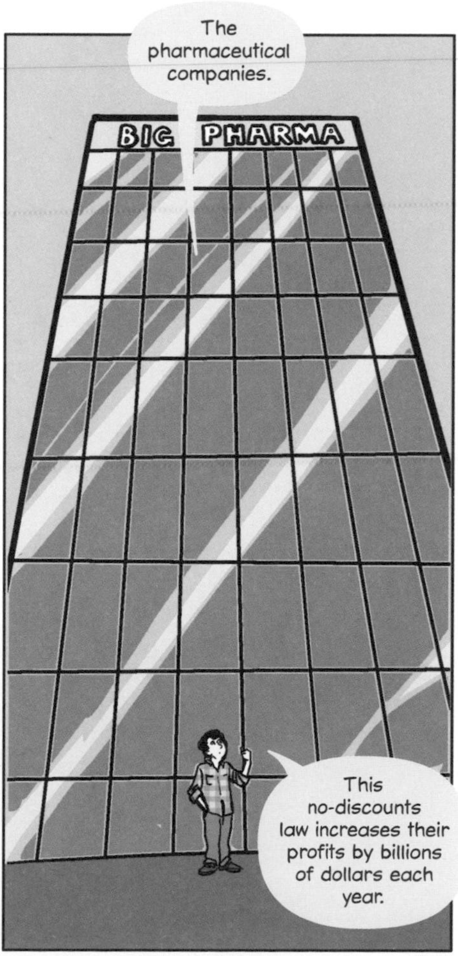
The pharmaceutical companies.
BIG PHARMA
This no-discounts law increases their profits by billions of dollars each year.

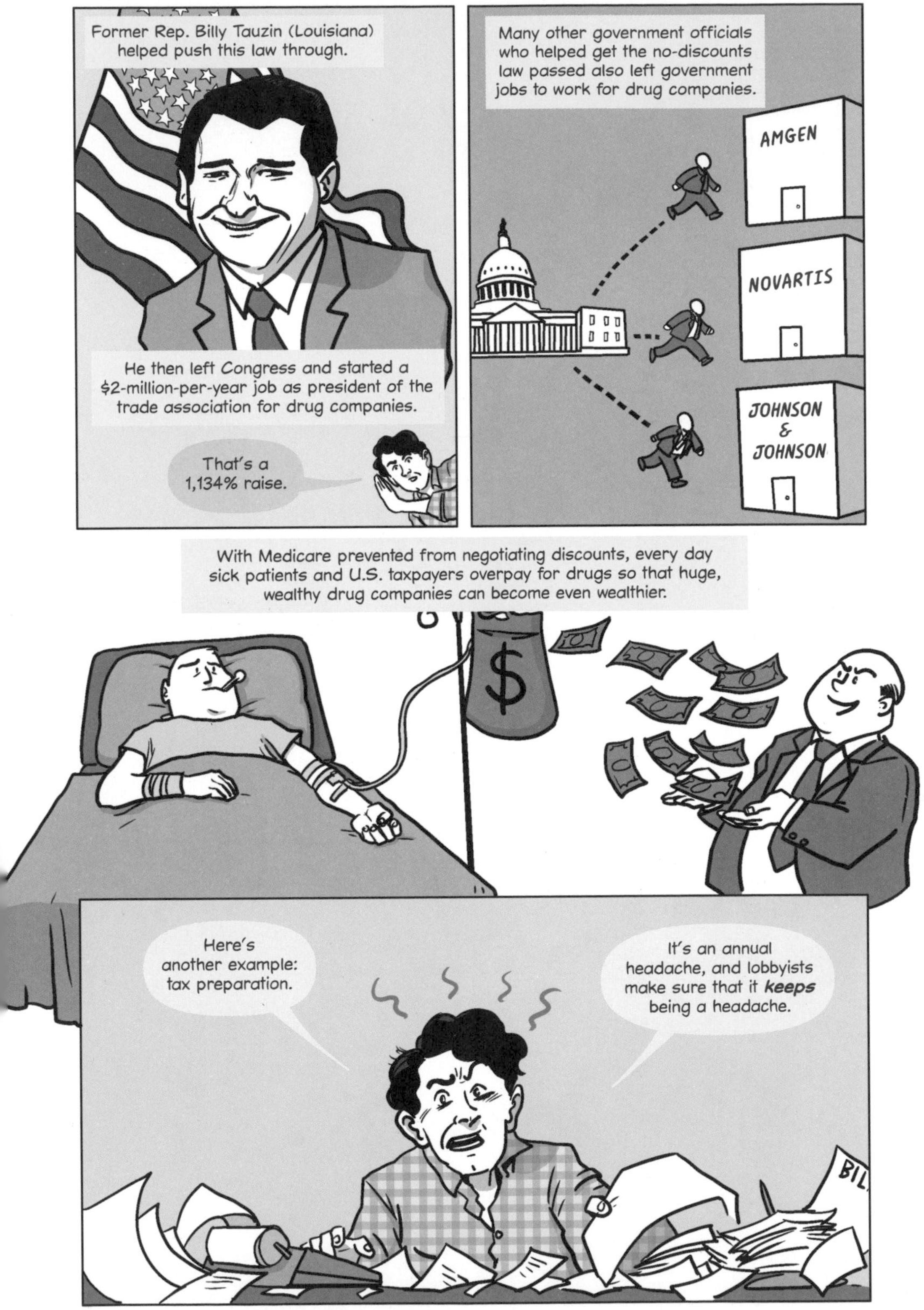
Former Rep. Billy Tauzin (Louisiana) helped push this law through.
He then left Congress and started a $2-million-per-year job as president of the trade association for drug companies.
That's a 1,134% raise.
Many other government officials who helped get the no-discounts law passed also left government jobs to work for drug companies.
AMGEN
NOVARTIS
JOHNSON & JOHNSON
With Medicare prevented from negotiating discounts, every day sick patients and U.S. taxpayers overpay for drugs so that huge, wealthy drug companies can become even wealthier.
$
Here's another example: tax preparation.
It's an annual headache, and lobbyists make sure that it ***keeps*** being a headache.

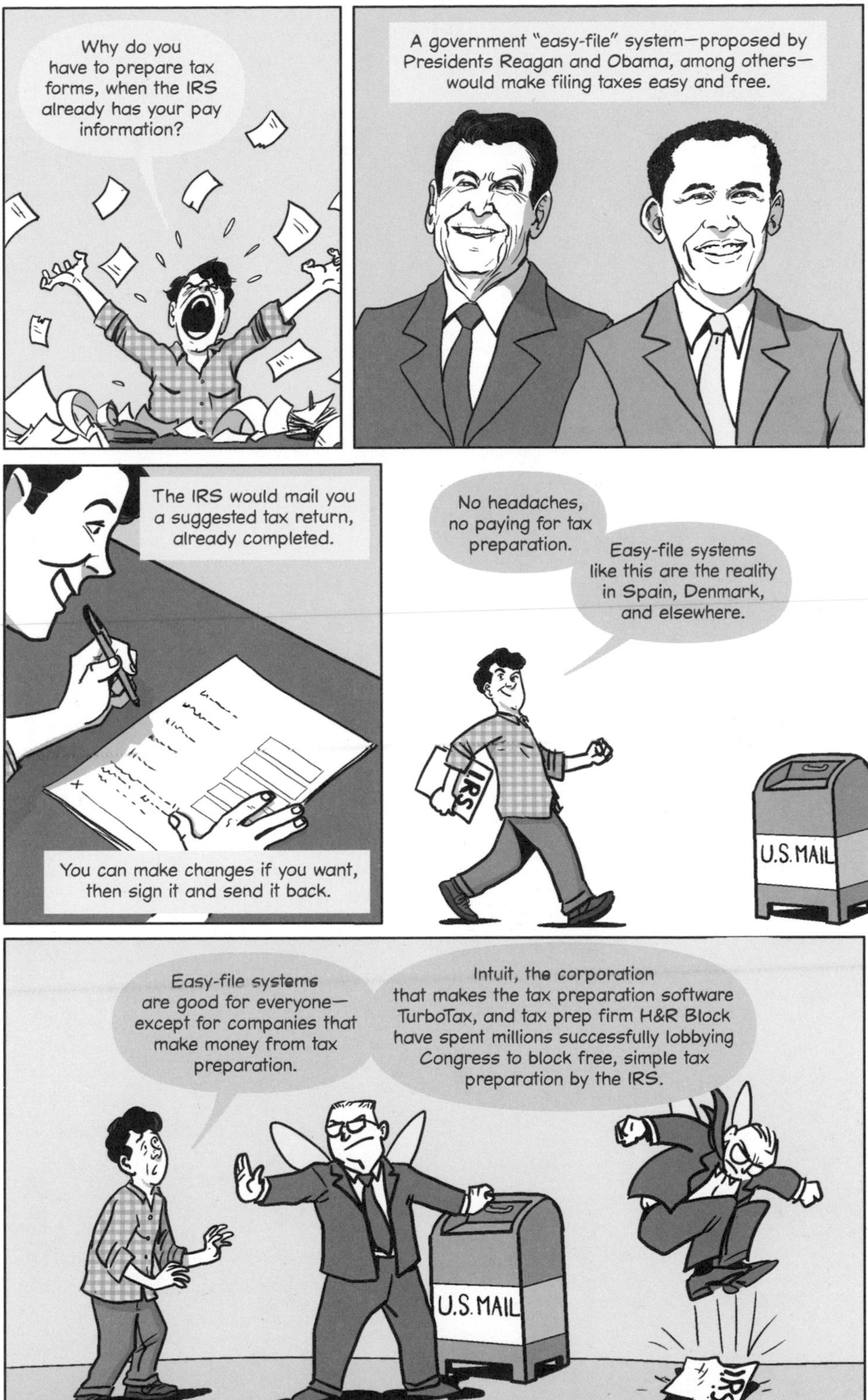
Why do you have to prepare tax forms, when the IRS already has your pay information?
A government "easy-file" system—proposed by Presidents Reagan and Obama, among others—would make filing taxes easy and free.
The IRS would mail you a suggested tax return, already completed.
You can make changes if you want, then sign it and send it back.
No headaches, no paying for tax preparation.
Easy-file systems like this are the reality in Spain, Denmark, and elsewhere.
IRS
U.S. MAIL
Easy-file systems are good for everyone—except for companies that make money from tax preparation.
Intuit, the corporation that makes the tax preparation software TurboTax, and tax prep firm H&R Block have spent millions successfully lobbying Congress to block free, simple tax preparation by the IRS.
U.S. MAIL
IRS

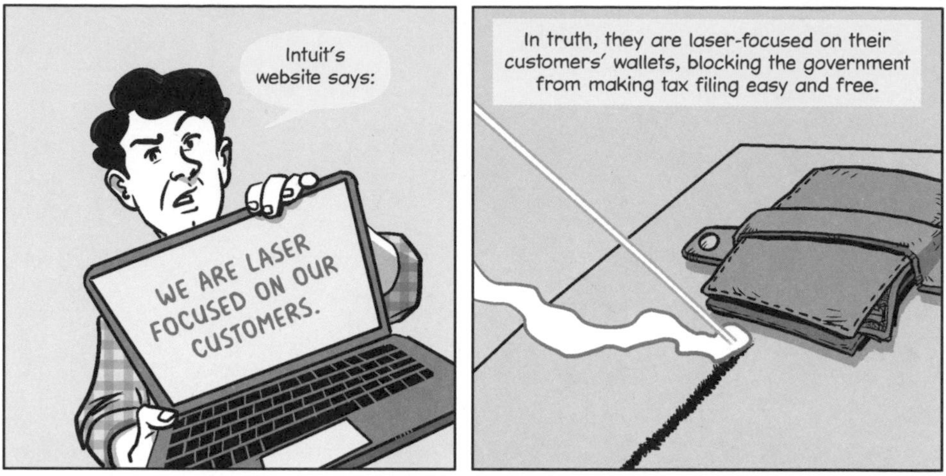
Intuit's website says:
WE ARE LASER FOCUSED ON OUR CUSTOMERS.
In truth, they are laser-focused on their customers' wallets, blocking the government from making tax filing easy and free.

Looking at the big picture of influence, here is how Washington works:

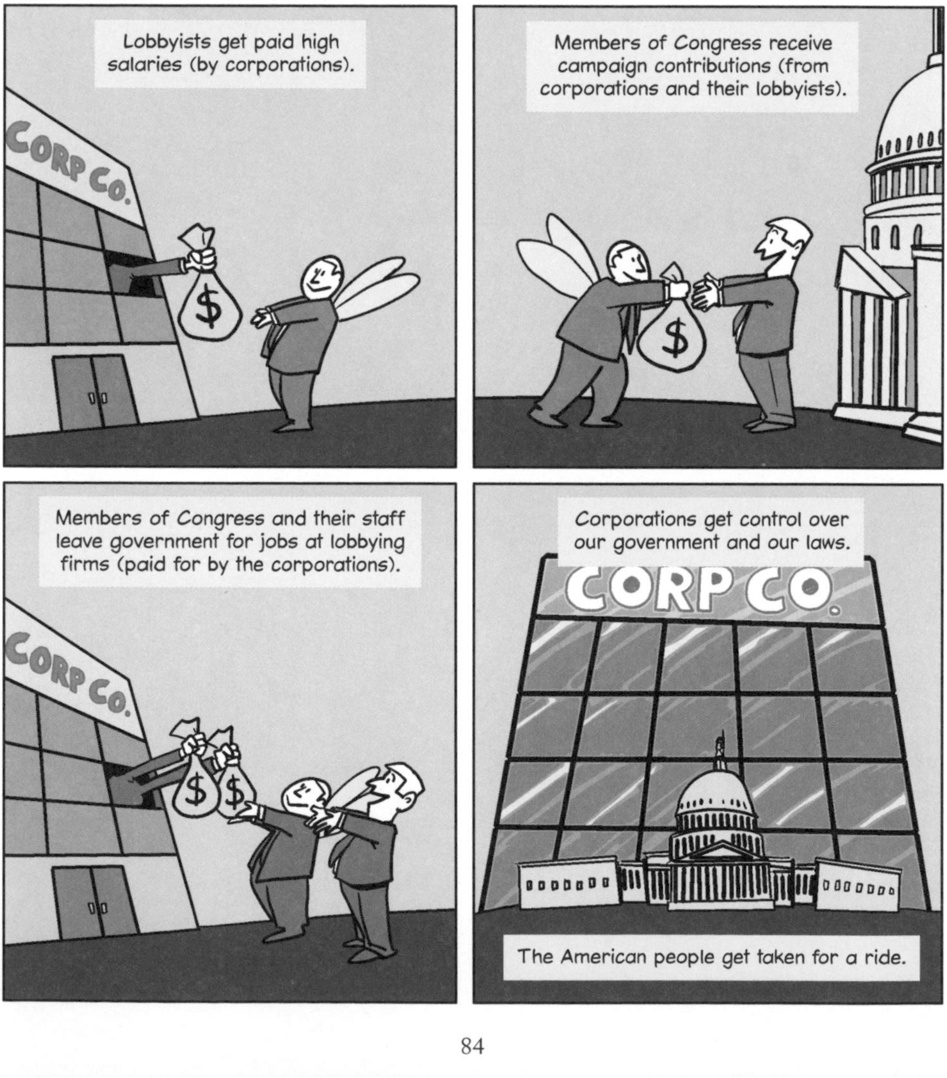
Lobbyists get paid high salaries (by corporations).
CORP CO.
$
Members of Congress receive campaign contributions (from corporations and their lobbyists).
$
Members of Congress and their staff leave government for jobs at lobbying firms (paid for by the corporations).
CORP CO.
$
$
Corporations get control over our government and our laws.
CORP CO.
The American people get taken for a ride.

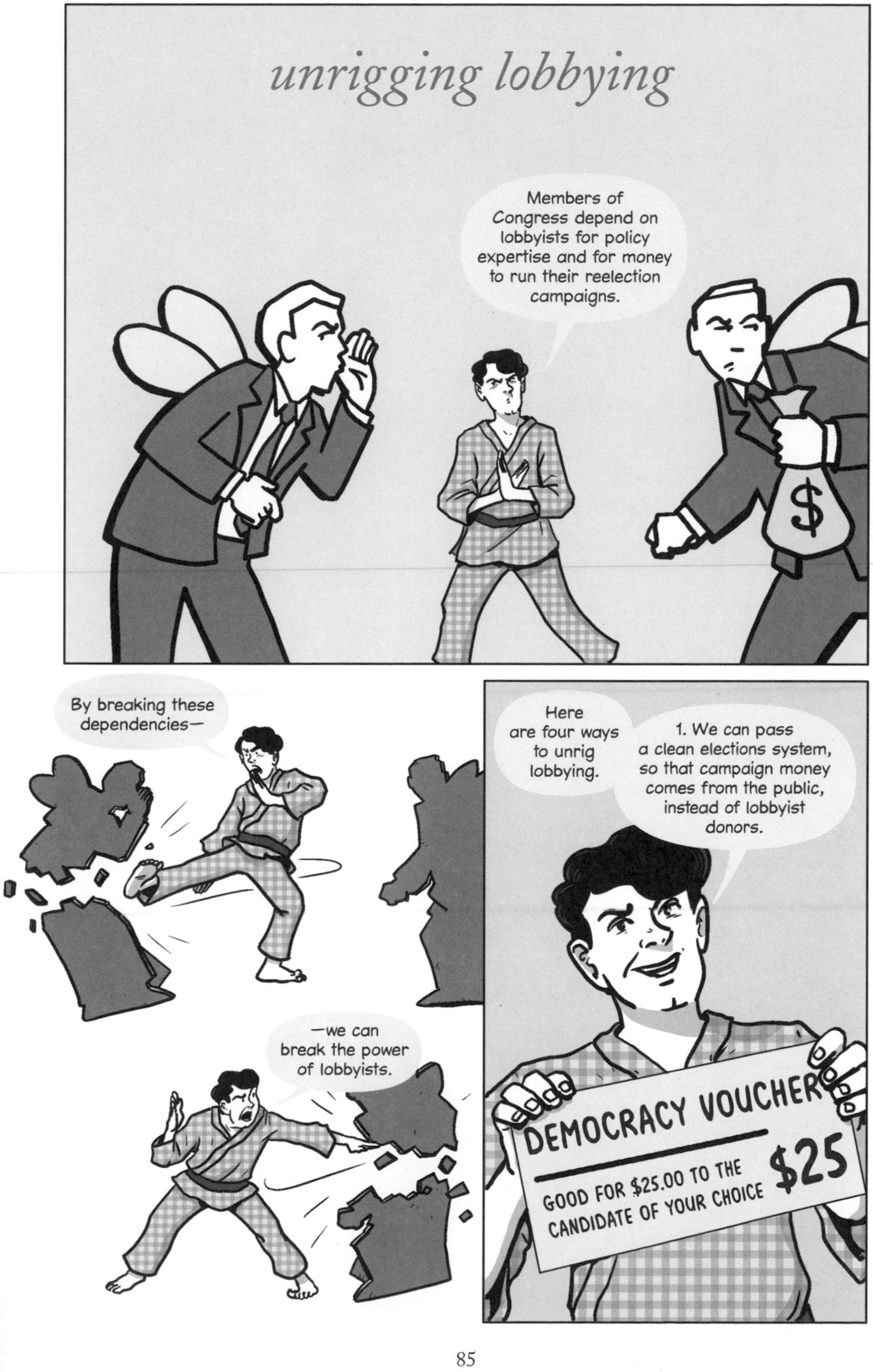
unrigging lobbying
Members of Congress depend on lobbyists for policy expertise and for money to run their reelection campaigns.
By breaking these dependencies—
—we can break the power of lobbyists.
Here are four ways to unrig lobbying.
1. We can pass a clean elections system, so that campaign money comes from the public, instead of lobbyist donors.
DEMOCRACY VOUCHER
GOOD FOR $25.00 TO THE CANDIDATE OF YOUR CHOICE
$25

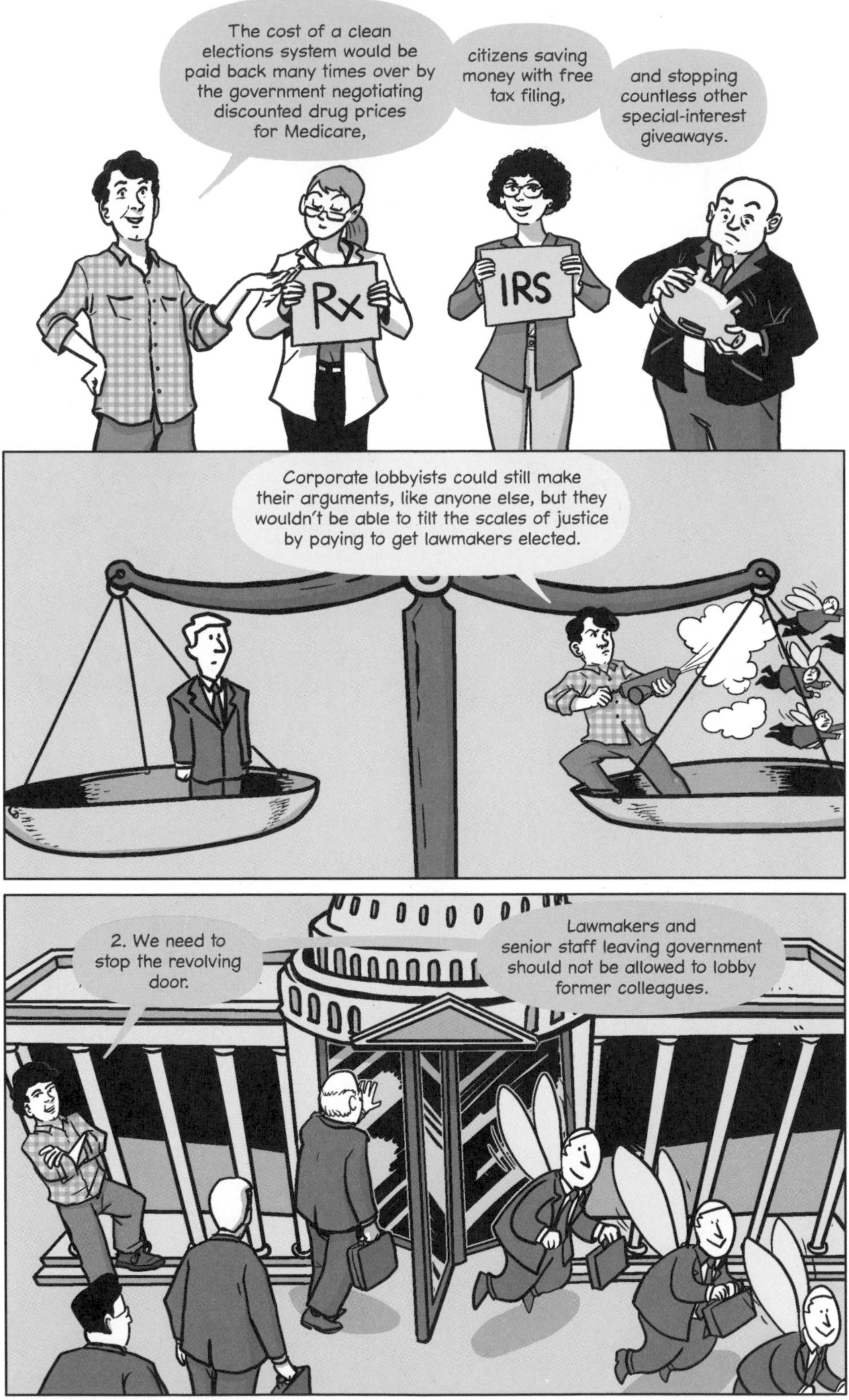
The cost of a clean elections system would be paid back many times over by the government negotiating discounted drug prices for Medicare,
citizens saving money with free tax filing,
and stopping countless other special-interest giveaways.
Rx
IRS
Corporate lobbyists could still make their arguments, like anyone else, but they wouldn't be able to tilt the scales of justice by paying to get lawmakers elected.
2. We need to stop the revolving door.
Lawmakers and senior staff leaving government should not be allowed to lobby former colleagues.

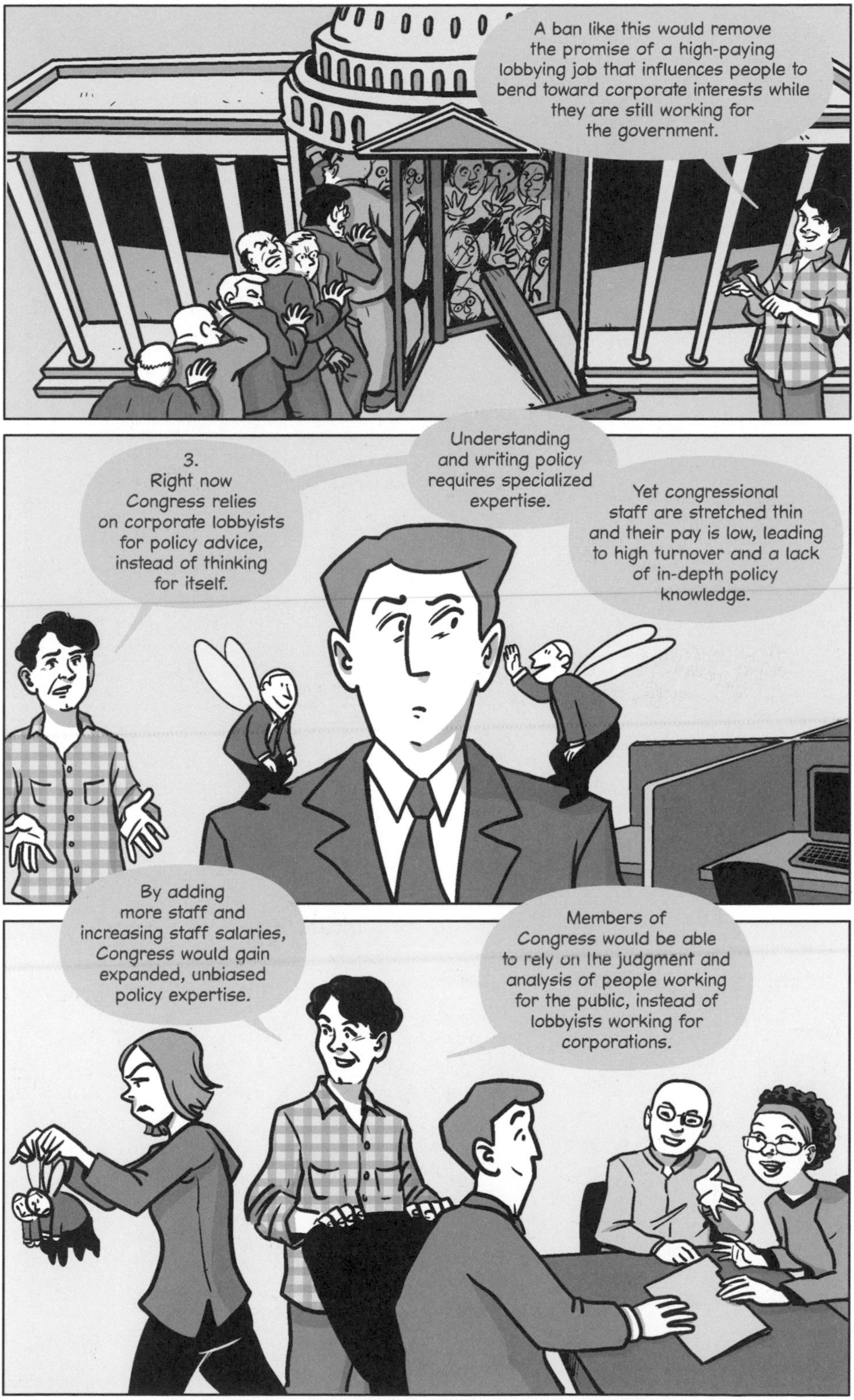
A ban like this would remove the promise of a high-paying lobbying job that influences people to bend toward corporate interests while they are still working for the government.
3. Right now Congress relies on corporate lobbyists for policy advice, instead of thinking for itself.
Understanding and writing policy requires specialized expertise.
Yet congressional staff are stretched thin and their pay is low, leading to high turnover and a lack of in-depth policy knowledge.
By adding more staff and increasing staff salaries, Congress would gain expanded, unbiased policy expertise.
Members of Congress would be able to rely on the judgment and analysis of people working for the public, instead of lobbyists working for corporations.

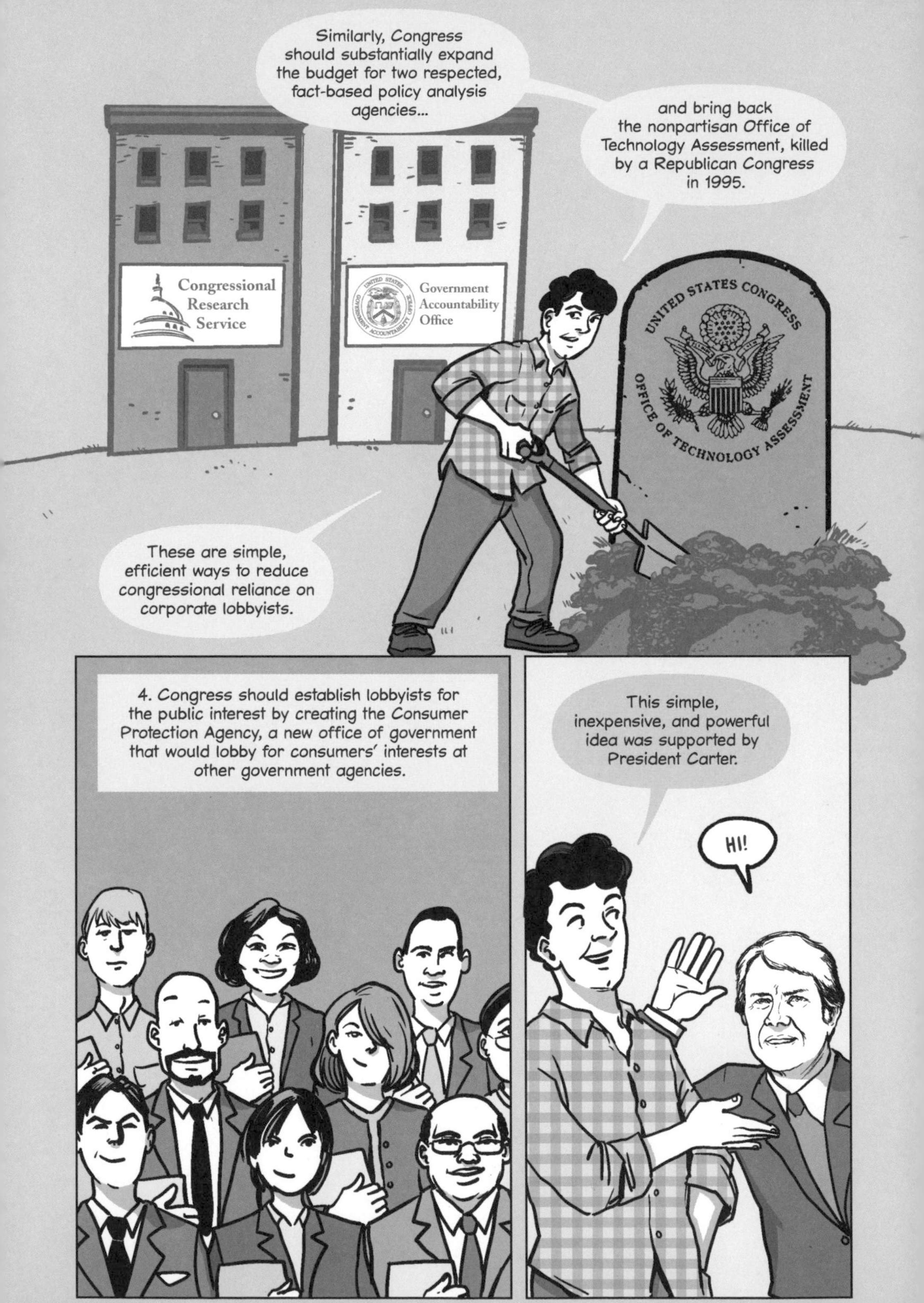
Similarly, Congress should substantially expand the budget for two respected, fact-based policy analysis agencies...
Congressional Research Service
Government Accountability Office
and bring back the nonpartisan Office of Technology Assessment, killed by a Republican Congress in 1995.
UNITED STATES CONGRESS
OFFICE OF TECHNOLOGY ASSESSMENT
These are simple, efficient ways to reduce congressional reliance on corporate lobbyists.
4. Congress should establish lobbyists for the public interest by creating the Consumer Protection Agency, a new office of government that would lobby for consumers' interests at other government agencies.
This simple, inexpensive, and powerful idea was supported by President Carter.
HI!

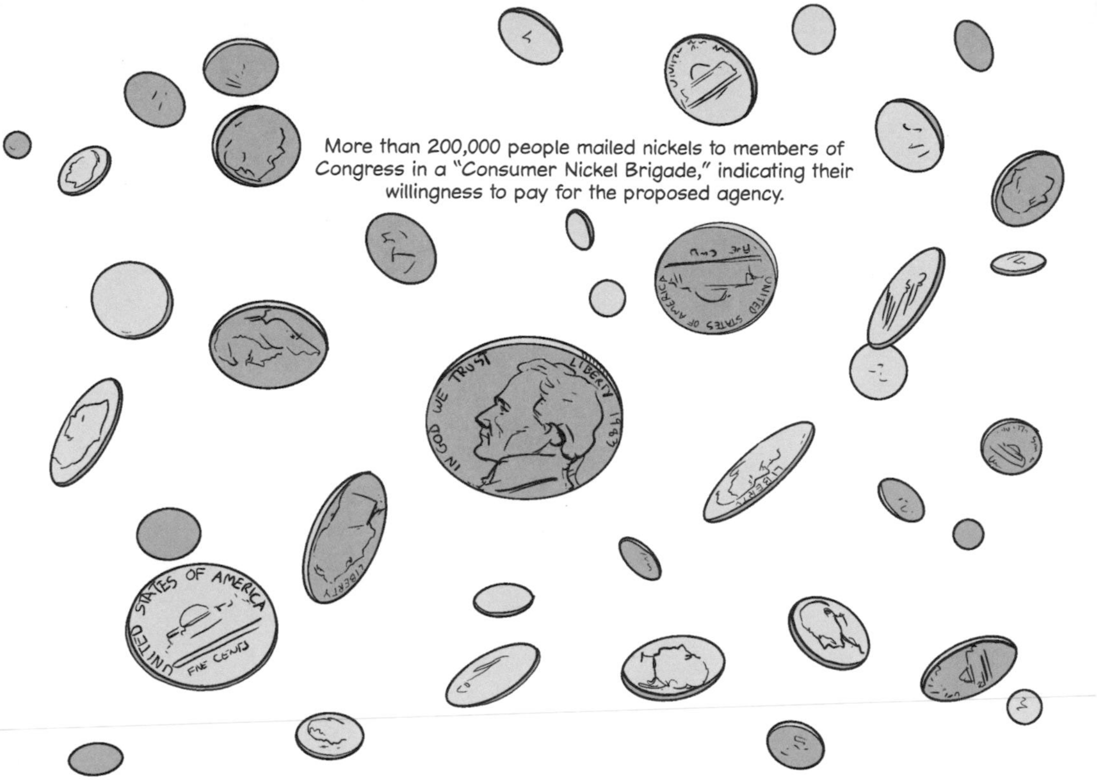
More than 200,000 people mailed nickels to members of Congress in a "Consumer Nickel Brigade," indicating their willingness to pay for the proposed agency.
IN GOD WE TRUST
LIBERTY
STATES OF AMERICA
UNITED
FIVE CENTS

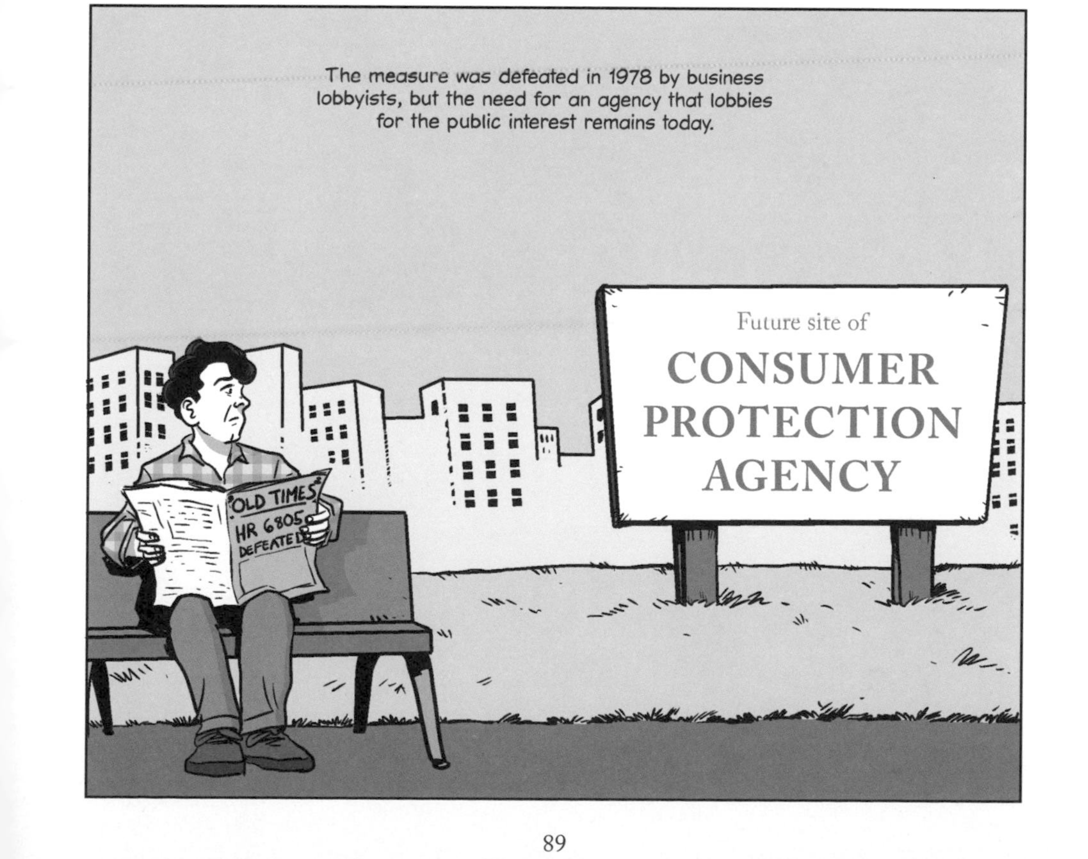
The measure was defeated in 1978 by business lobbyists, but the need for an agency that lobbies for the public interest remains today.
OLD TIMES
HR 6805
DEFEATED
Future site of
CONSUMER
PROTECTION
AGENCY

3
political money

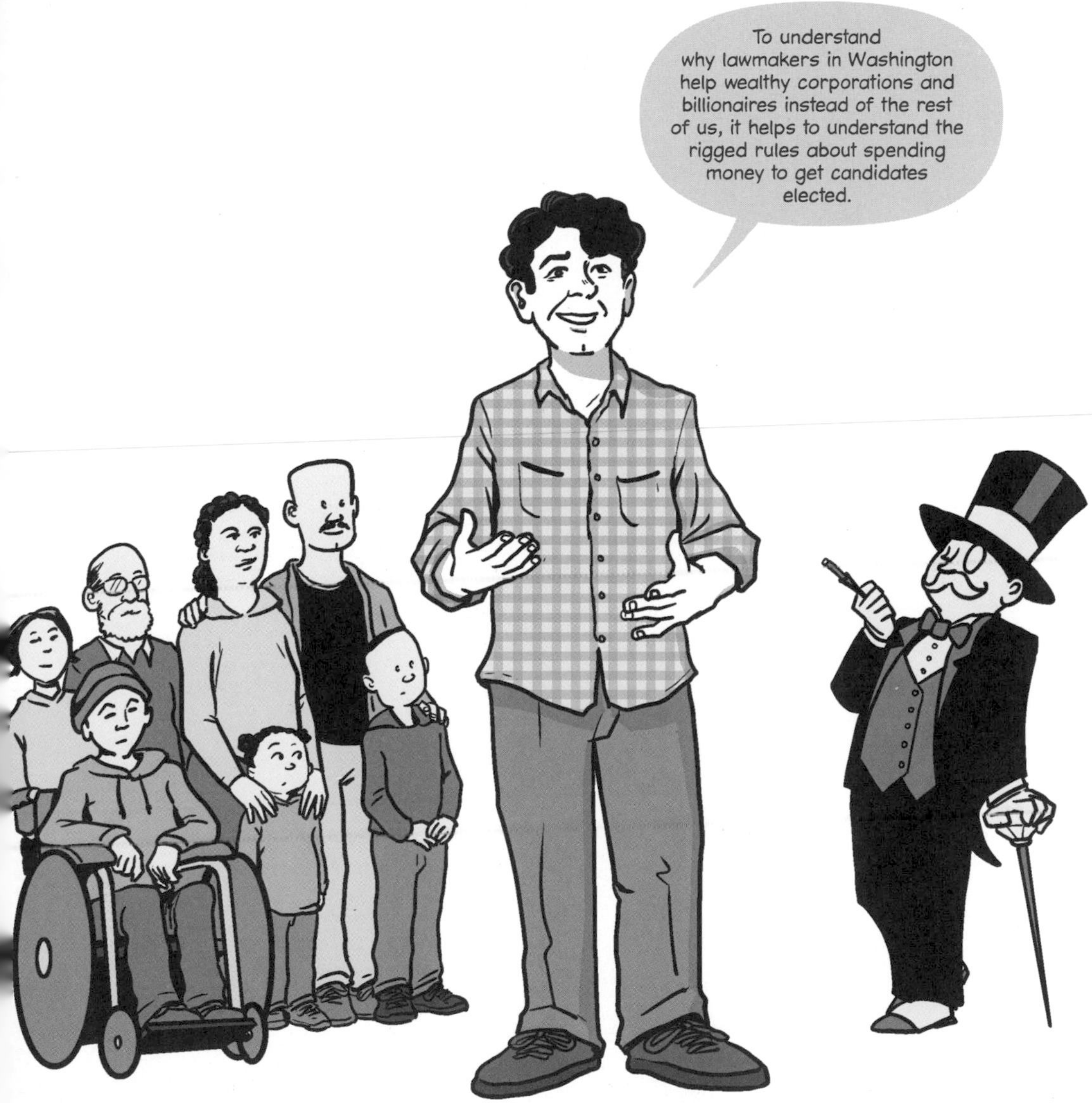
To understand why lawmakers in Washington help wealthy corporations and billionaires instead of the rest of us, it helps to understand the rigged rules about spending money to get candidates elected.

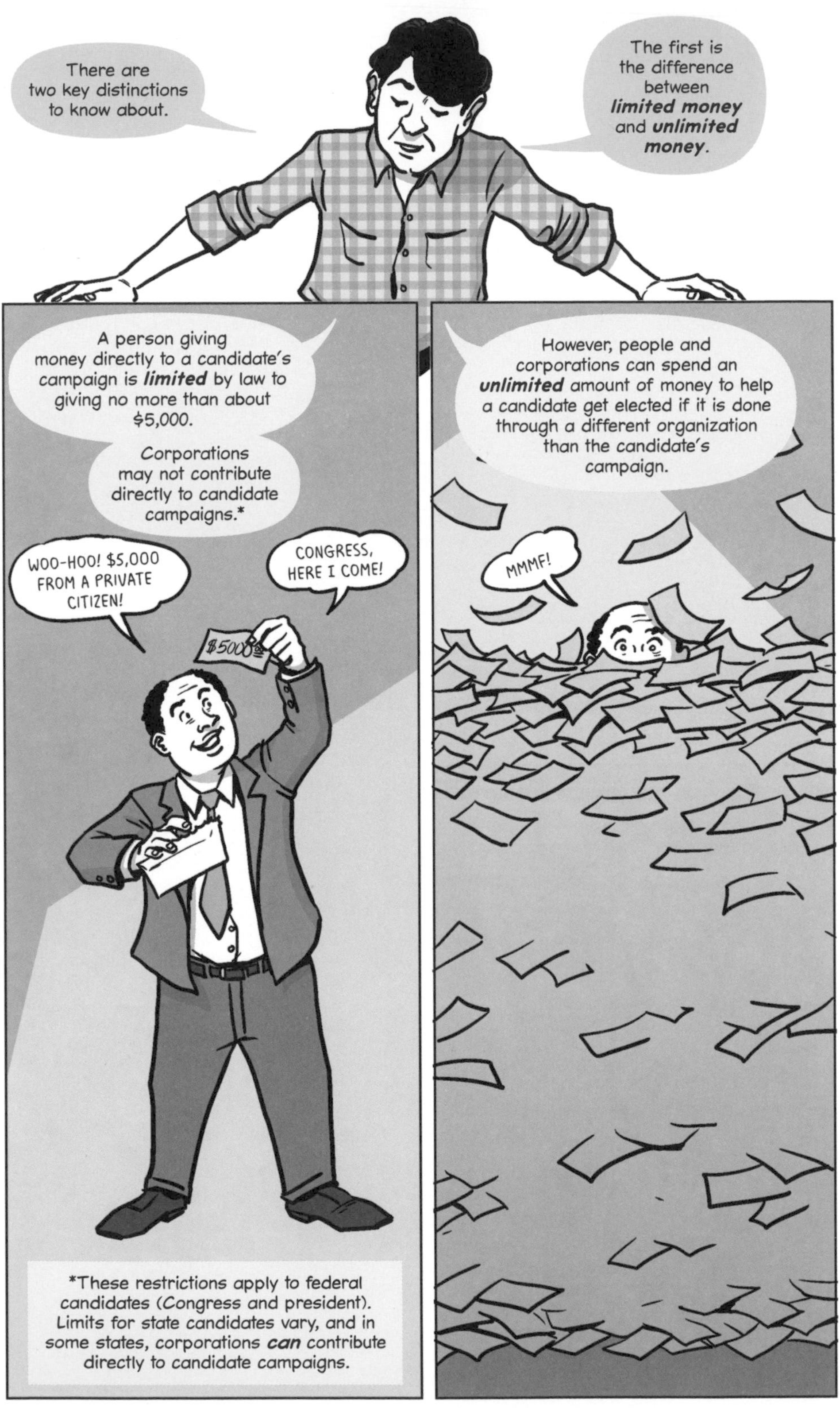
There are two key distinctions to know about.
The first is the difference between **limited money** and **unlimited money**.
A person giving money directly to a candidate's campaign is ***limited*** by law to giving no more than about $5,000.
Corporations may not contribute directly to candidate campaigns.*
WOO-HOO! $5,000 FROM A PRIVATE CITIZEN!
CONGRESS, HERE I COME!
$5000
*These restrictions apply to federal candidates (Congress and president). Limits for state candidates vary, and in some states, corporations ***can*** contribute directly to candidate campaigns.
However, people and corporations can spend an ***unlimited*** amount of money to help a candidate get elected if it is done through a different organization than the candidate's campaign.
MMMF!

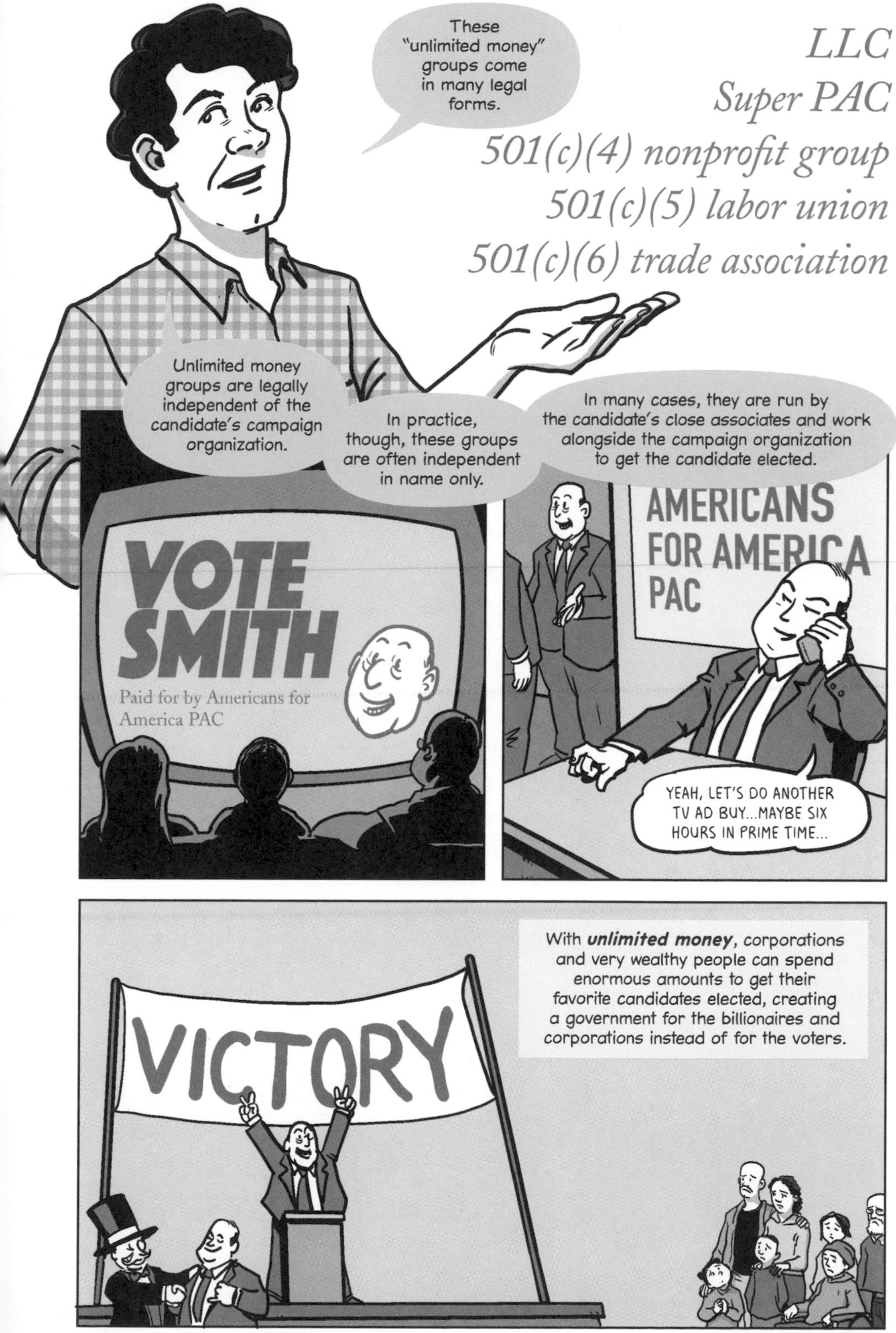

These "unlimited money" groups come in many legal forms.
LLC
Super PAC
501(c)(4) nonprofit group
501(c)(5) labor union
501(c)(6) trade association
Unlimited money groups are legally independent of the candidate's campaign organization.
In practice, though, these groups are often independent in name only.
In many cases, they are run by the candidate's close associates and work alongside the campaign organization to get the candidate elected.
VOTE SMITH
Paid for by Americans for America PAC
AMERICANS FOR AMERICA PAC
YEAH, LET'S DO ANOTHER TV AD BUY...MAYBE SIX HOURS IN PRIME TIME...
With ***unlimited money***, corporations and very wealthy people can spend enormous amounts to get their favorite candidates elected, creating a government for the billionaires and corporations instead of for the voters.
VICTORY

dark money

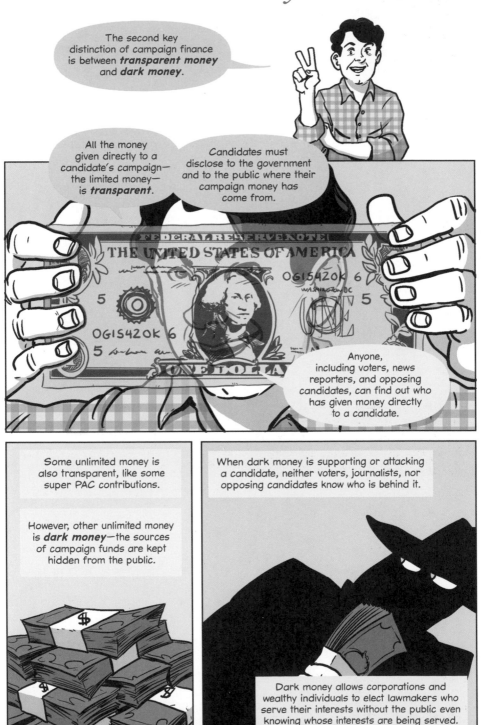

The second key distinction of campaign finance is between *transparent money* and *dark money*.

All the money given directly to a candidate's campaign—the limited money—is *transparent*.

Candidates must disclose to the government and to the public where their campaign money has come from.

Anyone, including voters, news reporters, and opposing candidates, can find out who has given money directly to a candidate.

Some unlimited money is also transparent, like some super PAC contributions.

However, other unlimited money is *dark money*—the sources of campaign funds are kept hidden from the public.

When dark money is supporting or attacking a candidate, neither voters, journalists, nor opposing candidates know who is behind it.

Dark money allows corporations and wealthy individuals to elect lawmakers who serve their interests without the public even knowing whose interests are being served.

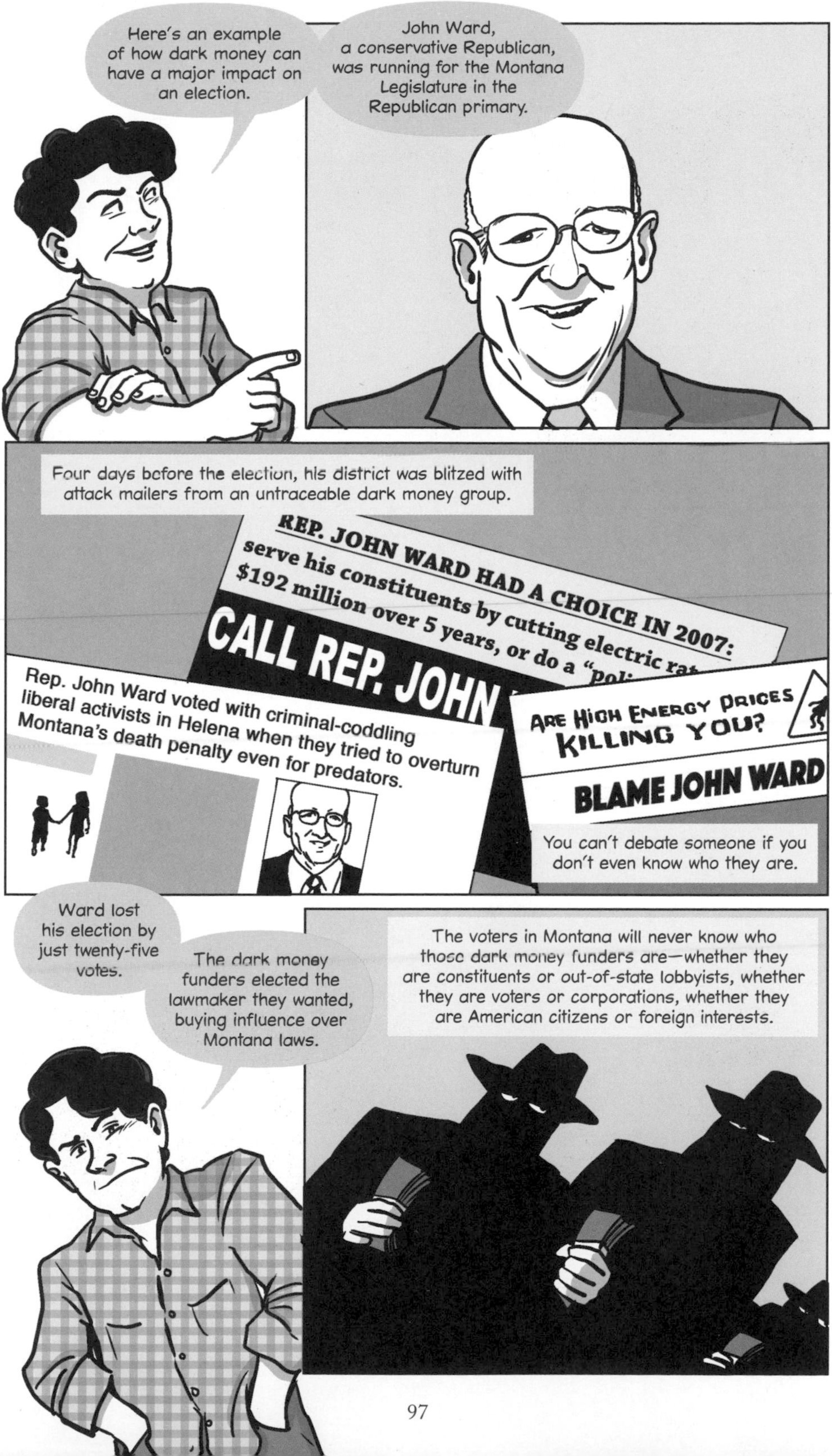
Here's an example of how dark money can have a major impact on an election.
John Ward, a conservative Republican, was running for the Montana Legislature in the Republican primary.
Four days before the election, his district was blitzed with attack mailers from an untraceable dark money group.
REP. JOHN WARD HAD A CHOICE IN 2007:
serve his constituents by cutting electric
$192 million over 5 years, or do a
CALL REP. JOHN
Rep. John Ward voted with criminal-coddling liberal activists in Helena when they tried to overturn Montana's death penalty even for predators.
ARE HIGH ENERGY PRICES KILLING YOU?
BLAME JOHN WARD
You can't debate someone if you don't even know who they are.
Ward lost his election by just twenty-five votes.
The dark money funders elected the lawmaker they wanted, buying influence over Montana laws.
The voters in Montana will never know who those dark money funders are—whether they are constituents or out-of-state lobbyists, whether they are voters or corporations, whether they are American citizens or foreign interests.

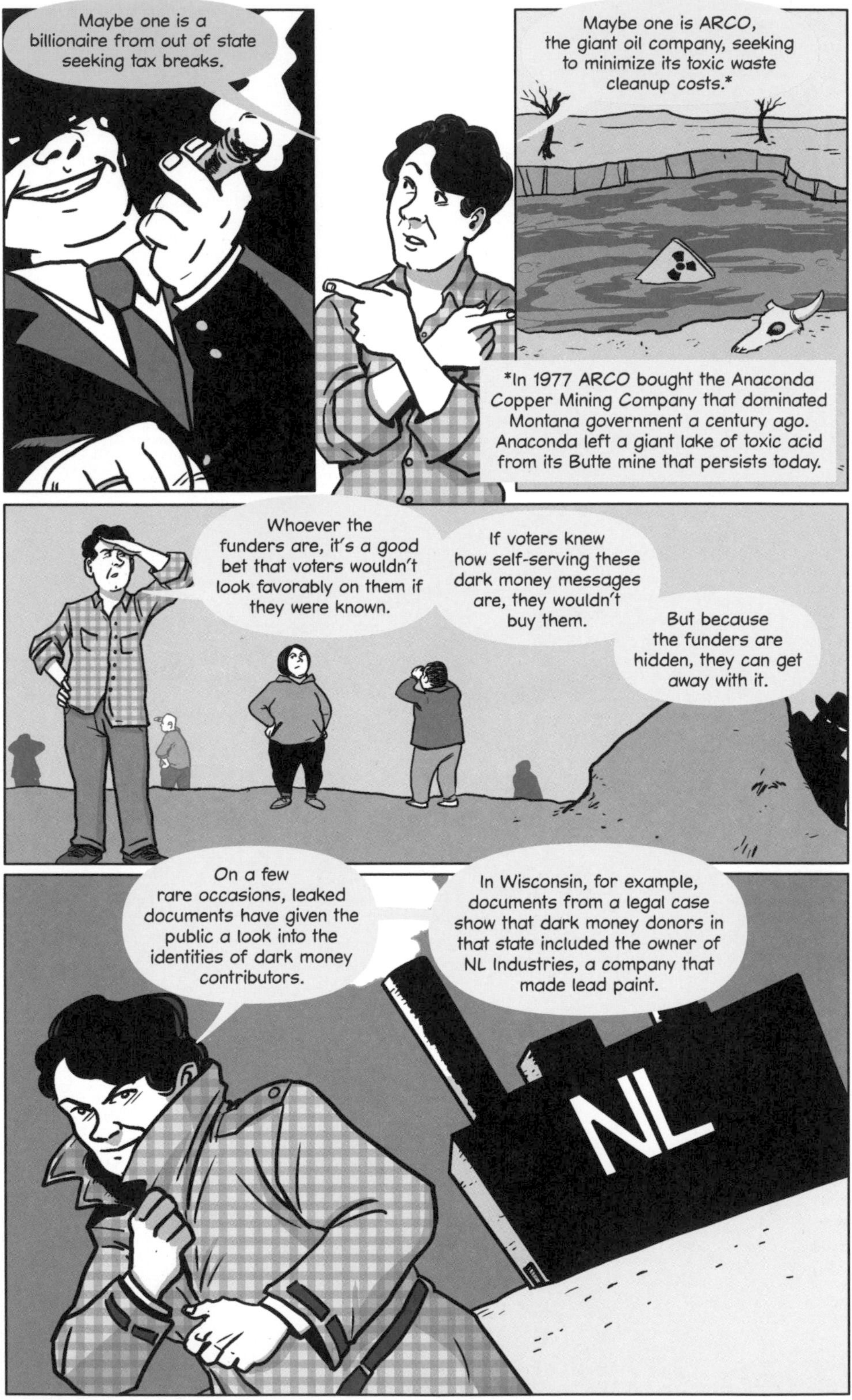
Maybe one is a billionaire from out of state seeking tax breaks.
Maybe one is ARCO, the giant oil company, seeking to minimize its toxic waste cleanup costs.*
*In 1977 ARCO bought the Anaconda Copper Mining Company that dominated Montana government a century ago. Anaconda left a giant lake of toxic acid from its Butte mine that persists today.
Whoever the funders are, it's a good bet that voters wouldn't look favorably on them if they were known.
If voters knew how self-serving these dark money messages are, they wouldn't buy them.
But because the funders are hidden, they can get away with it.
On a few rare occasions, leaked documents have given the public a look into the identities of dark money contributors.
In Wisconsin, for example, documents from a legal case show that dark money donors in that state included the owner of NL Industries, a company that made lead paint.
NL

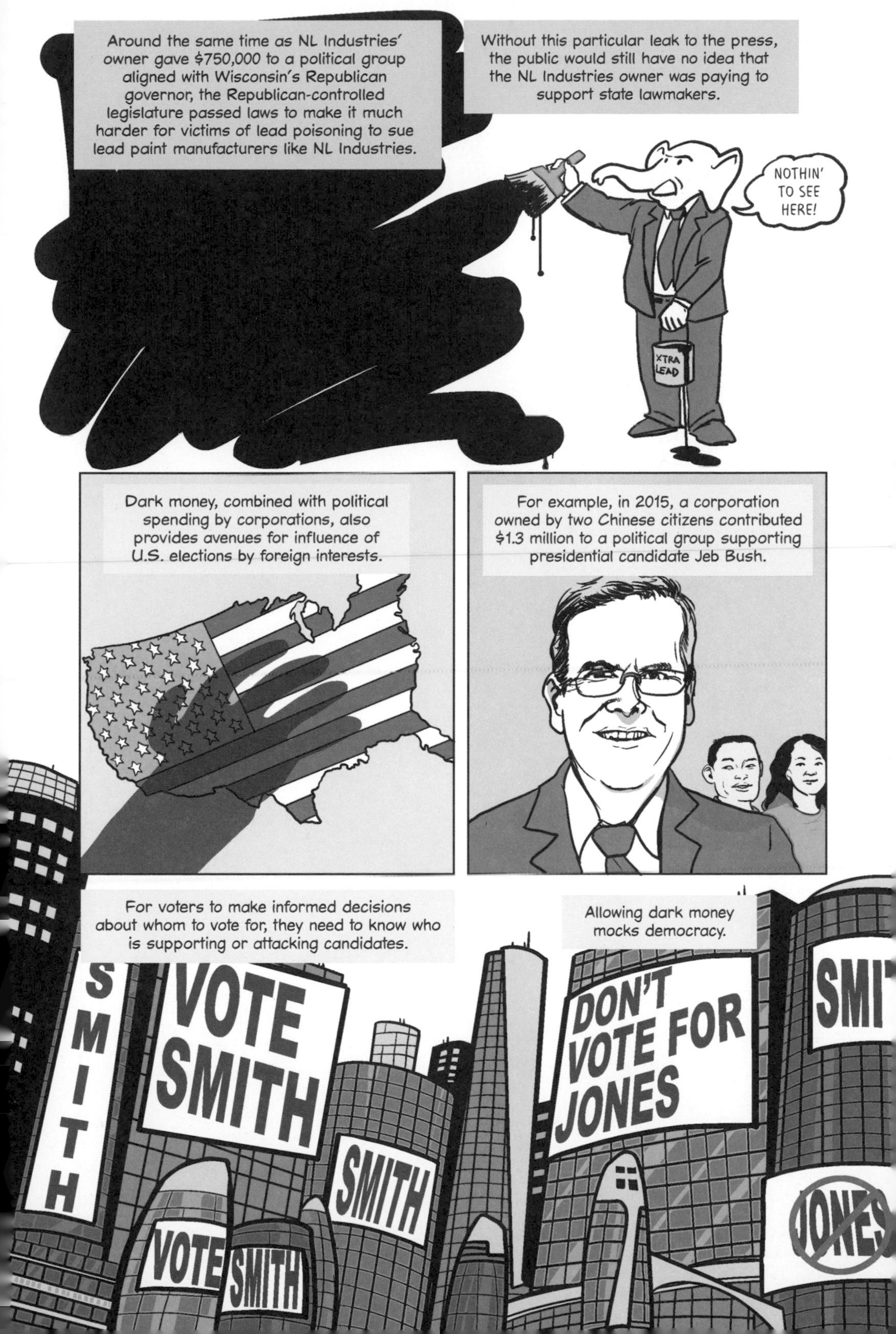
Around the same time as NL Industries' owner gave $750,000 to a political group aligned with Wisconsin's Republican governor, the Republican-controlled legislature passed laws to make it much harder for victims of lead poisoning to sue lead paint manufacturers like NL Industries.
Without this particular leak to the press, the public would still have no idea that the NL Industries owner was paying to support state lawmakers.
NOTHIN' TO SEE HERE!
XTRA LEAD
Dark money, combined with political spending by corporations, also provides avenues for influence of U.S. elections by foreign interests.
For example, in 2015, a corporation owned by two Chinese citizens contributed $1.3 million to a political group supporting presidential candidate Jeb Bush.
For voters to make informed decisions about whom to vote for, they need to know who is supporting or attacking candidates.
Allowing dark money mocks democracy.
SMITH
VOTE SMITH
SMITH
VOTE
SMITH
DON'T VOTE FOR JONES
JONES

ending dark money

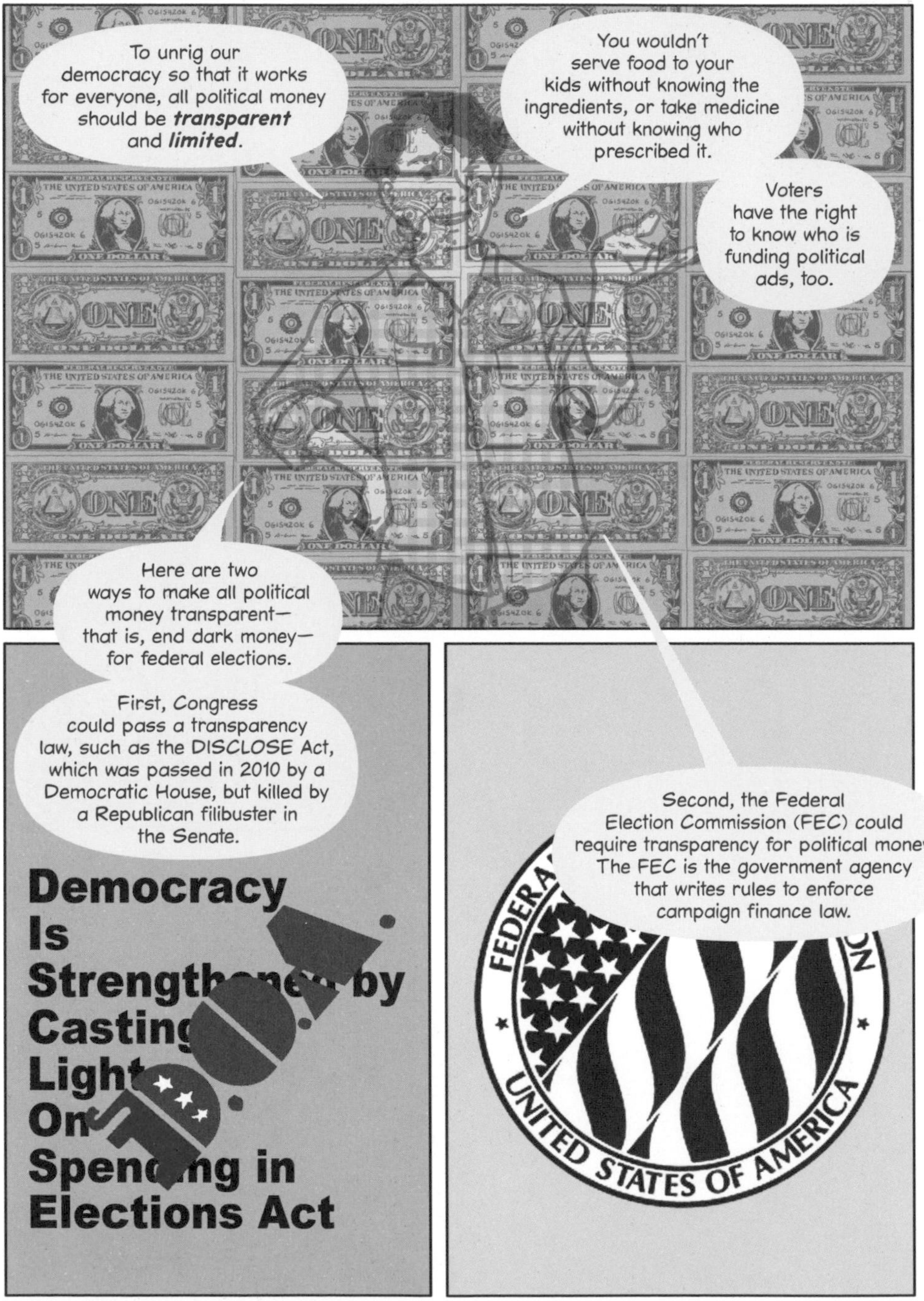
To unrig our democracy so that it works for everyone, all political money should be ***transparent*** and ***limited***.
You wouldn't serve food to your kids without knowing the ingredients, or take medicine without knowing who prescribed it.
Voters have the right to know who is funding political ads, too.
Here are two ways to make all political money transparent—that is, end dark money—for federal elections.
First, Congress could pass a transparency law, such as the DISCLOSE Act, which was passed in 2010 by a Democratic House, but killed by a Republican filibuster in the Senate.
Democracy
Is
Strength by
Casting
Ligh
On
Spen ng in
Elections Act
Second, the Federal Election Commission (FEC) could require transparency for political money. The FEC is the government agency that writes rules to enforce campaign finance law.
UNITED STATES OF AMERICA

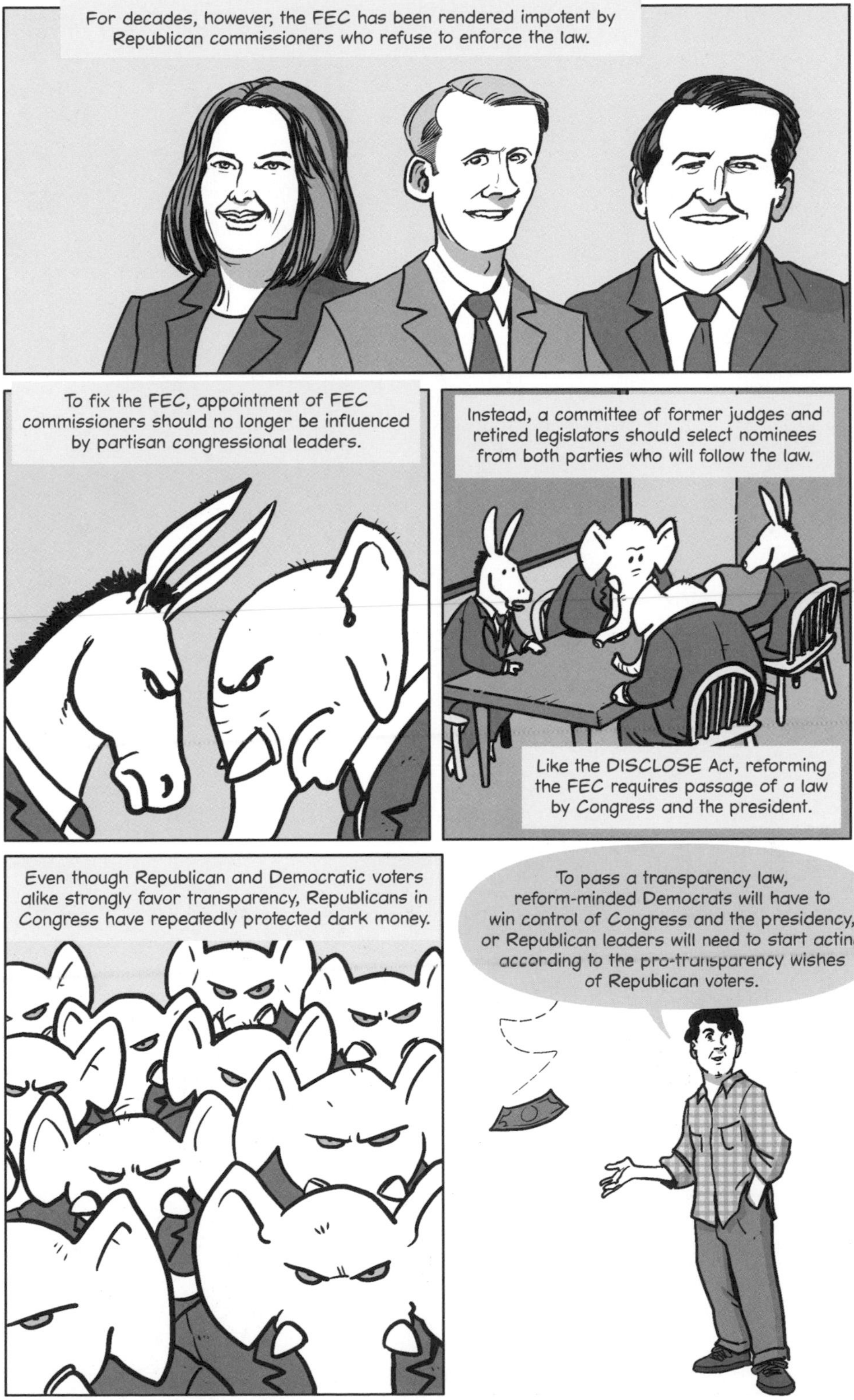
For decades, however, the FEC has been rendered impotent by Republican commissioners who refuse to enforce the law.
To fix the FEC, appointment of FEC commissioners should no longer be influenced by partisan congressional leaders.
Instead, a committee of former judges and retired legislators should select nominees from both parties who will follow the law.
Like the DISCLOSE Act, reforming the FEC requires passage of a law by Congress and the president.
Even though Republican and Democratic voters alike strongly favor transparency, Republicans in Congress have repeatedly protected dark money.
To pass a transparency law, reform-minded Democrats will have to win control of Congress and the presidency, or Republican leaders will need to start acting according to the pro-transparency wishes of Republican voters.

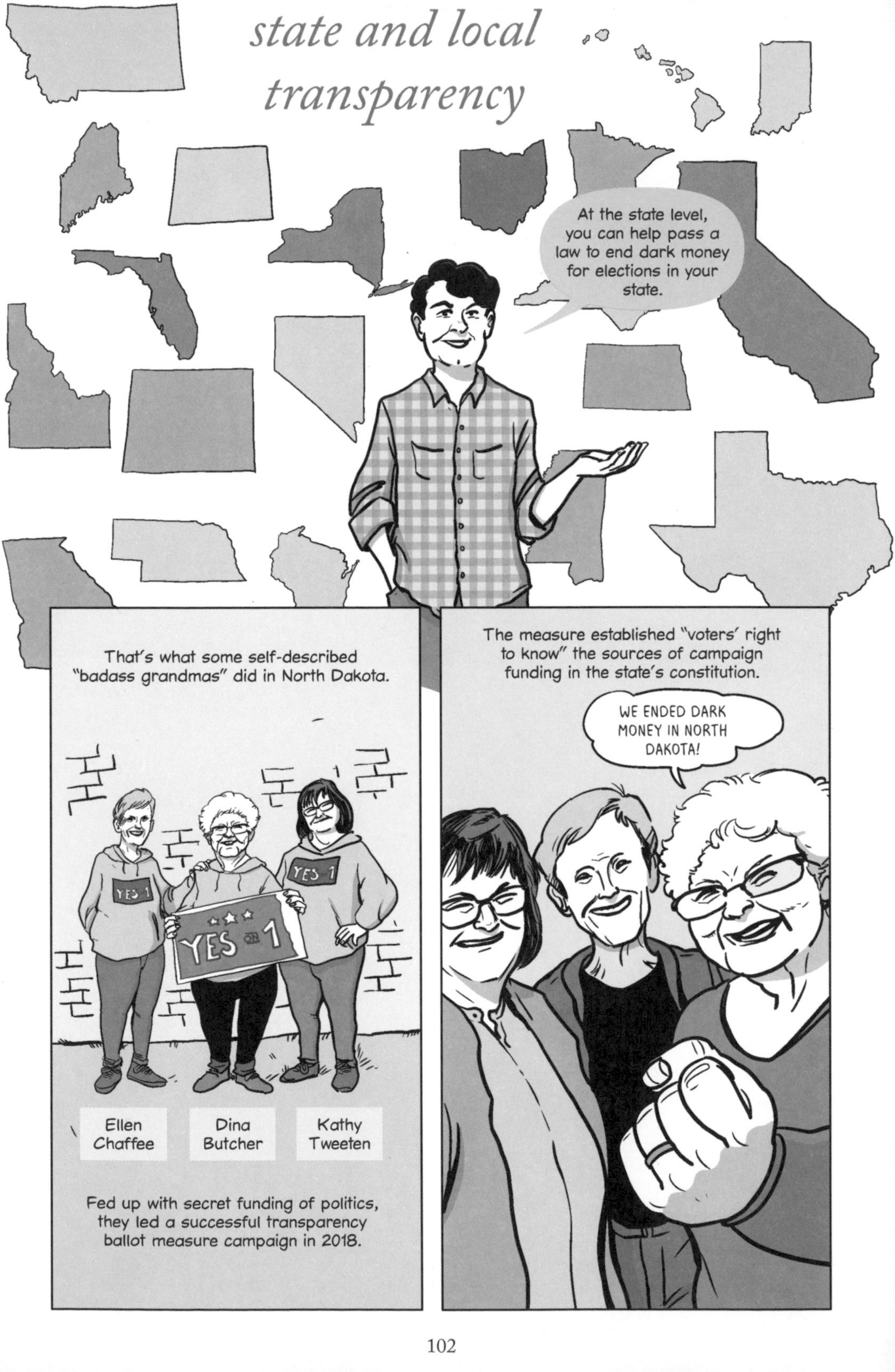
state and local transparency
At the state level, you can help pass a law to end dark money for elections in your state.
That's what some self-described "badass grandmas" did in North Dakota.
YES 1
YES 1
YES ON 1
Ellen Chaffee
Dina Butcher
Kathy Tweeten
Fed up with secret funding of politics, they led a successful transparency ballot measure campaign in 2018.
The measure established "voters' right to know" the sources of campaign funding in the state's constitution.
WE ENDED DARK MONEY IN NORTH DAKOTA!

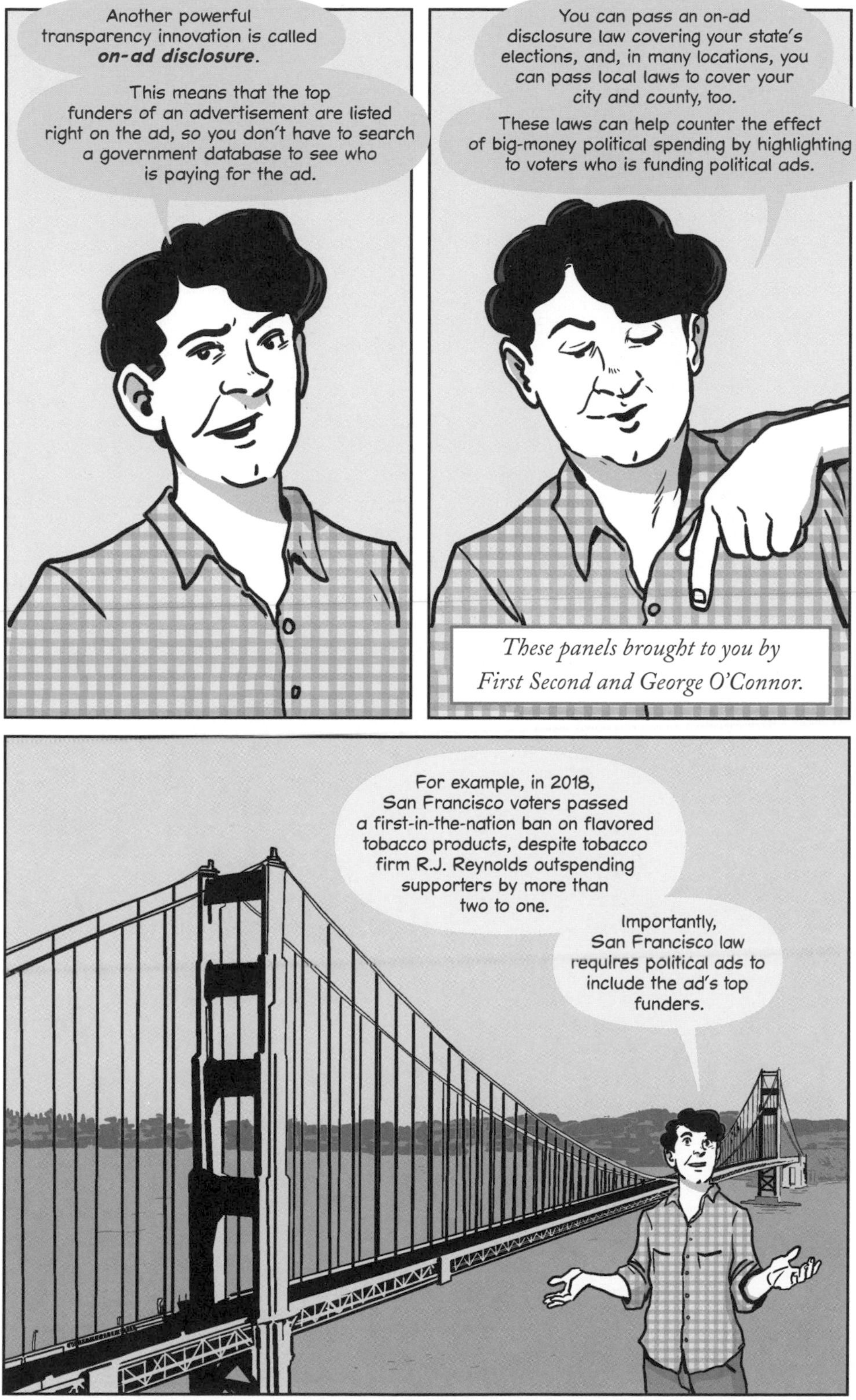
Another powerful transparency innovation is called ***on-ad disclosure***.
This means that the top funders of an advertisement are listed right on the ad, so you don't have to search a government database to see who is paying for the ad.
You can pass an on-ad disclosure law covering your state's elections, and, in many locations, you can pass local laws to cover your city and county, too.
These laws can help counter the effect of big-money political spending by highlighting to voters who is funding political ads.
These panels brought to you by First Second and George O'Connor.
For example, in 2018, San Francisco voters passed a first-in-the-nation ban on flavored tobacco products, despite tobacco firm R.J. Reynolds outspending supporters by more than two to one.
Importantly, San Francisco law requires political ads to include the ad's top funders.

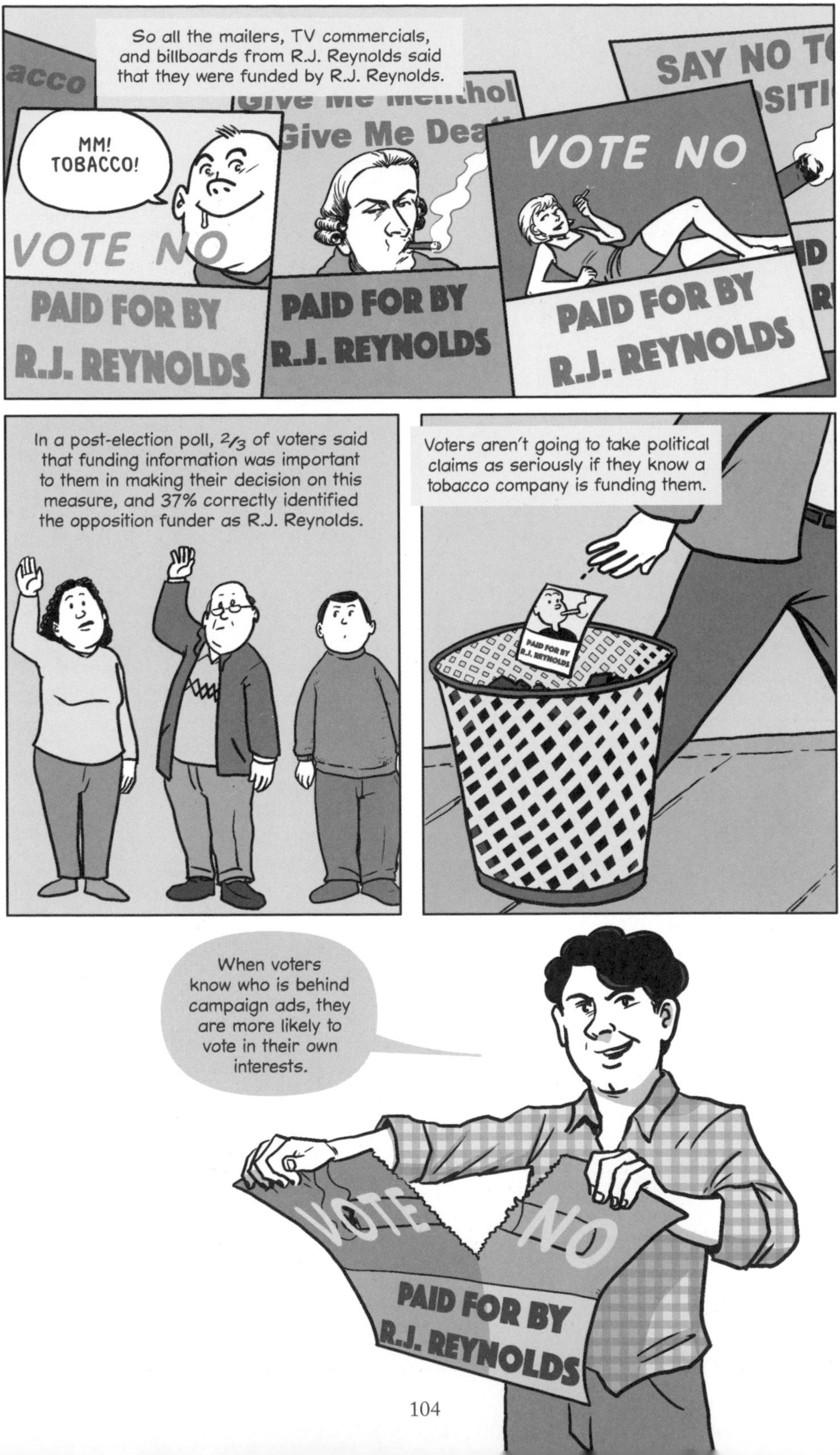
So all the mailers, TV commercials, and billboards from R.J. Reynolds said that they were funded by R.J. Reynolds.
MM! TOBACCO!
VOTE NO
PAID FOR BY R.J. REYNOLDS
Give Me Menthol Give Me Dea
PAID FOR BY R.J. REYNOLDS
SAY NO T
VOTE NO
PAID FOR BY R.J. REYNOLDS
In a post-election poll, 2/3 of voters said that funding information was important to them in making their decision on this measure, and 37% correctly identified the opposition funder as R.J. Reynolds.
Voters aren't going to take political claims as seriously if they know a tobacco company is funding them.
PAID FOR BY R.J. REYNOLDS
When voters know who is behind campaign ads, they are more likely to vote in their own interests.
VOTE NO
PAID FOR BY R.J. REYNOLDS

unlimited money

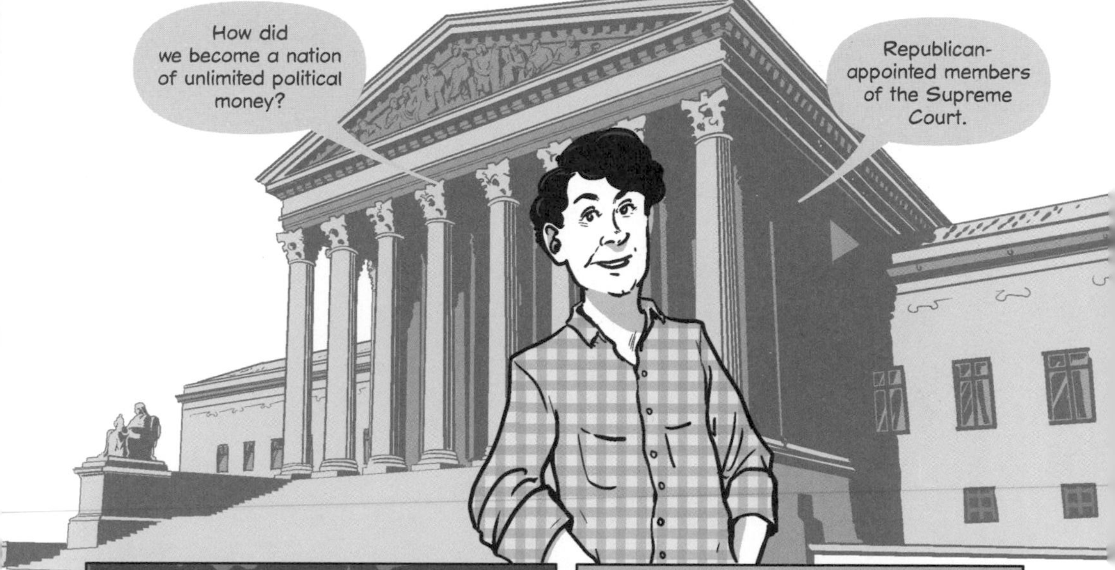
How did we become a nation of unlimited political money?
Republican-appointed members of the Supreme Court.

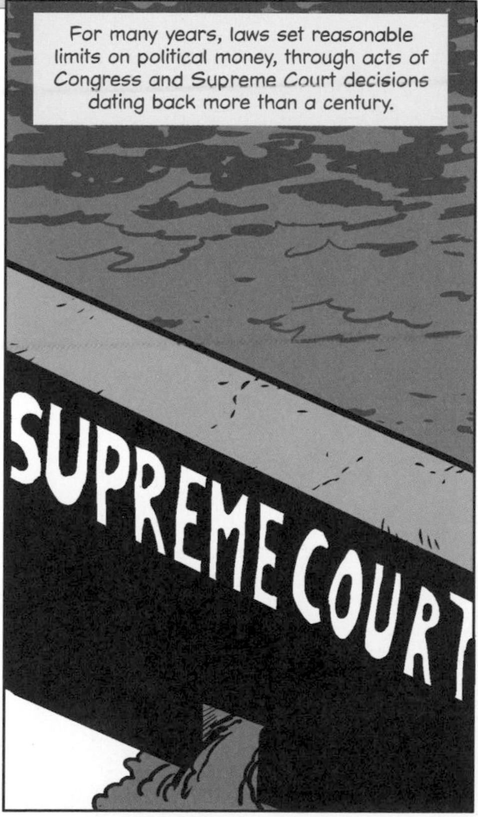
For many years, laws set reasonable limits on political money, through acts of Congress and Supreme Court decisions dating back more than a century.
SUPREME COURT

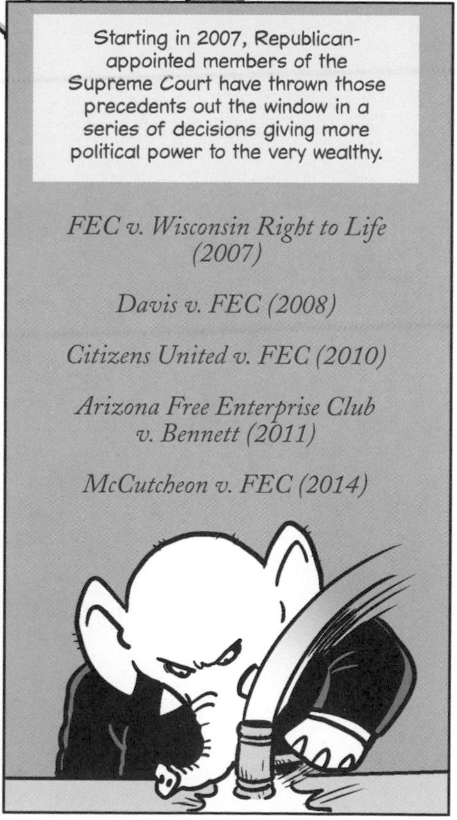
Starting in 2007, Republican-appointed members of the Supreme Court have thrown those precedents out the window in a series of decisions giving more political power to the very wealthy.
FEC v. Wisconsin Right to Life (2007)
Davis v. FEC (2008)
Citizens United v. FEC (2010)
Arizona Free Enterprise Club v. Bennett (2011)
McCutcheon v. FEC (2014)

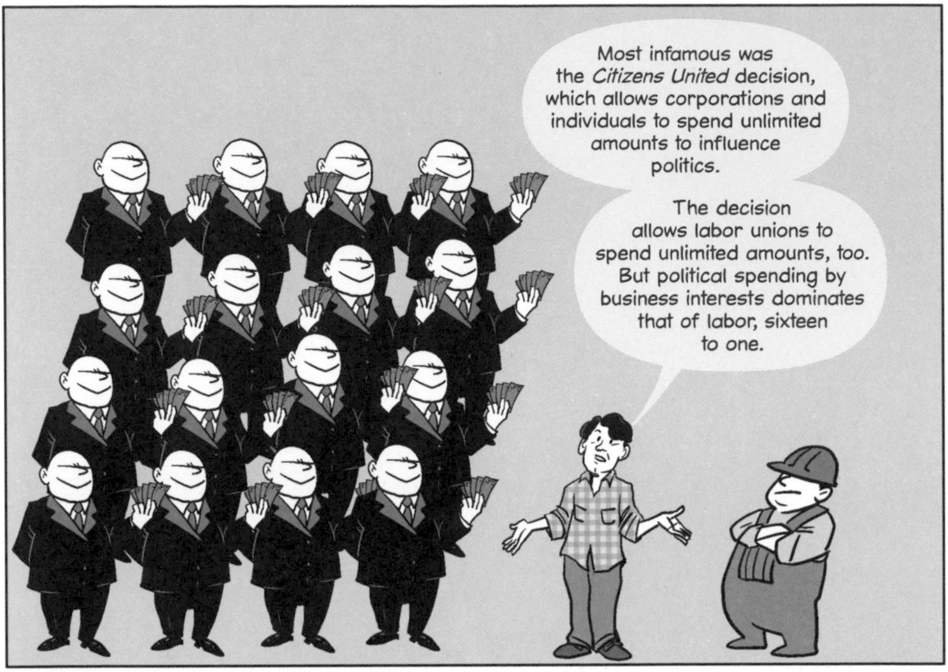
Most infamous was the *Citizens United* decision, which allows corporations and individuals to spend unlimited amounts to influence politics.
The decision allows labor unions to spend unlimited amounts, too. But political spending by business interests dominates that of labor, sixteen to one.

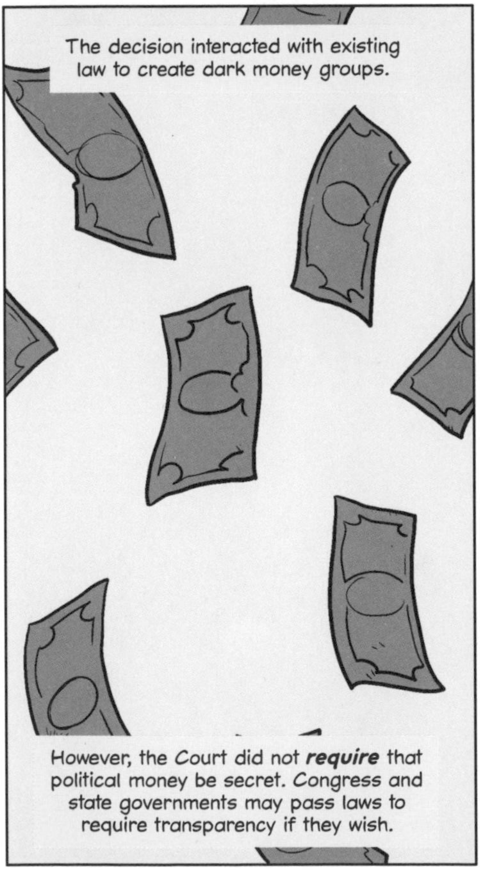
The decision interacted with existing law to create dark money groups.
However, the Court did not ***require*** that political money be secret. Congress and state governments may pass laws to require transparency if they wish.

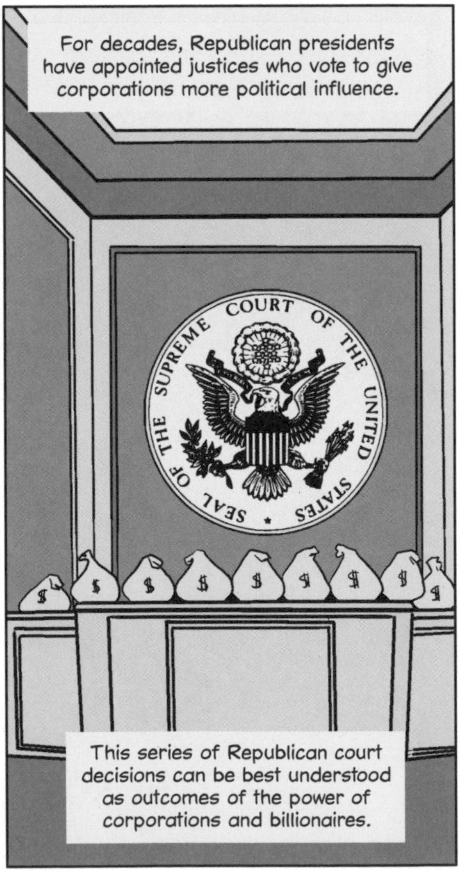
For decades, Republican presidents have appointed justices who vote to give corporations more political influence.
SEAL OF THE SUPREME COURT OF THE UNITED STATES
This series of Republican court decisions can be best understood as outcomes of the power of corporations and billionaires.

rights for the rich

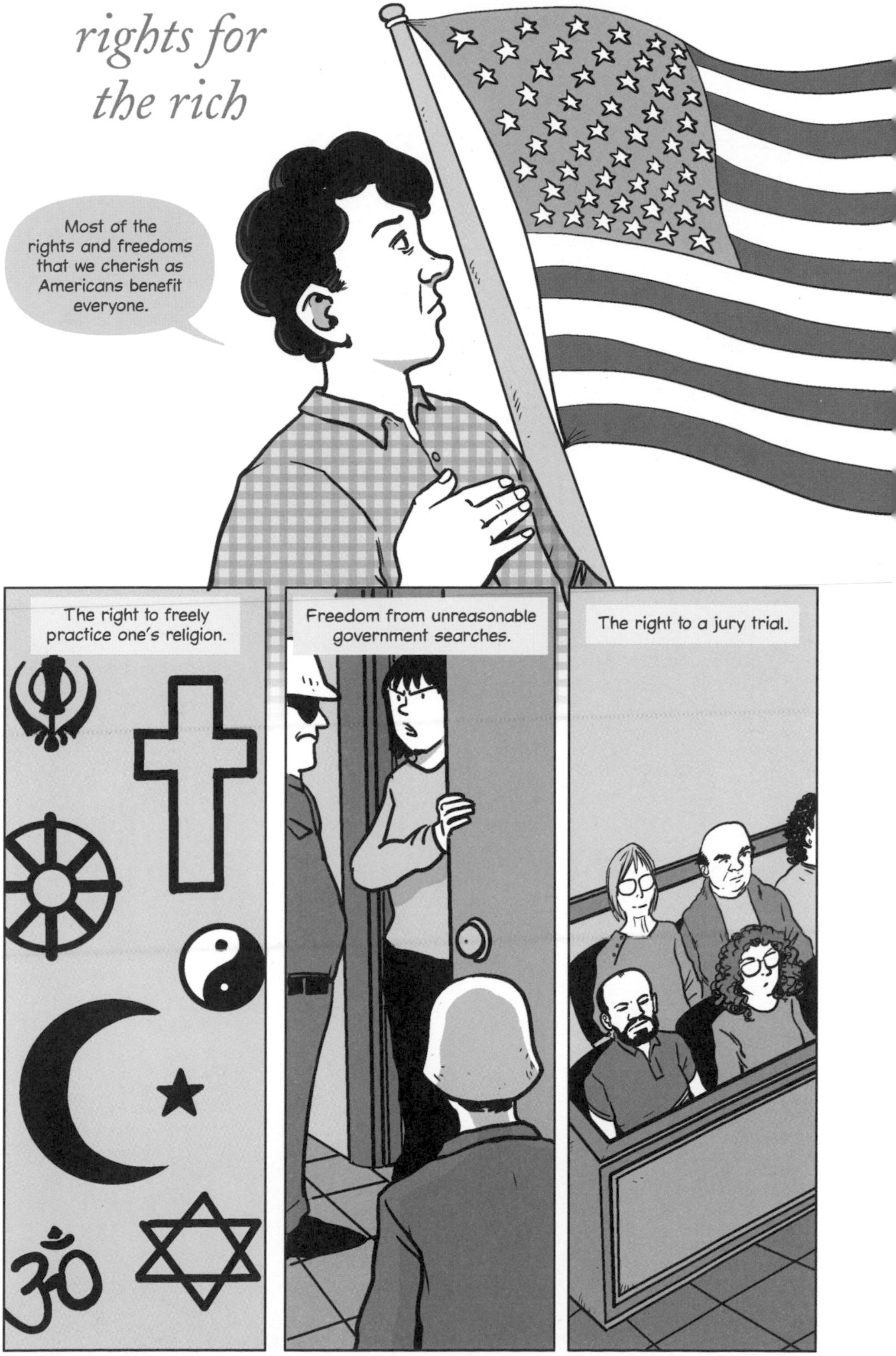
Most of the rights and freedoms that we cherish as Americans benefit everyone.
The right to freely practice one's religion.
Freedom from unreasonable government searches.
The right to a jury trial.

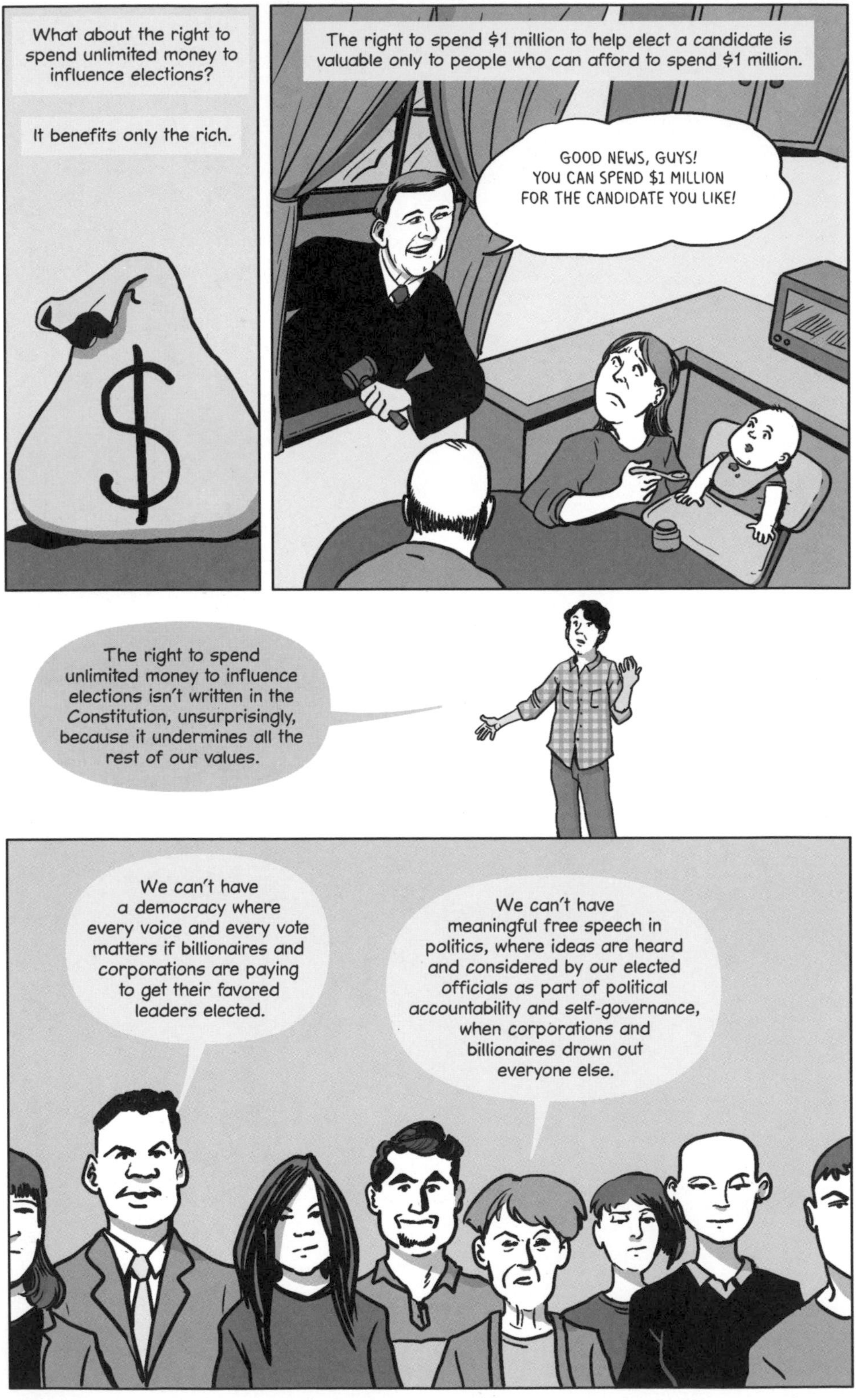
What about the right to spend unlimited money to influence elections?
It benefits only the rich.
The right to spend $1 million to help elect a candidate is valuable only to people who can afford to spend $1 million.
GOOD NEWS, GUYS! YOU CAN SPEND $1 MILLION FOR THE CANDIDATE YOU LIKE!
The right to spend unlimited money to influence elections isn't written in the Constitution, unsurprisingly, because it undermines all the rest of our values.
We can't have a democracy where every voice and every vote matters if billionaires and corporations are paying to get their favored leaders elected.
We can't have meaningful free speech in politics, where ideas are heard and considered by our elected officials as part of political accountability and self-governance, when corporations and billionaires drown out everyone else.

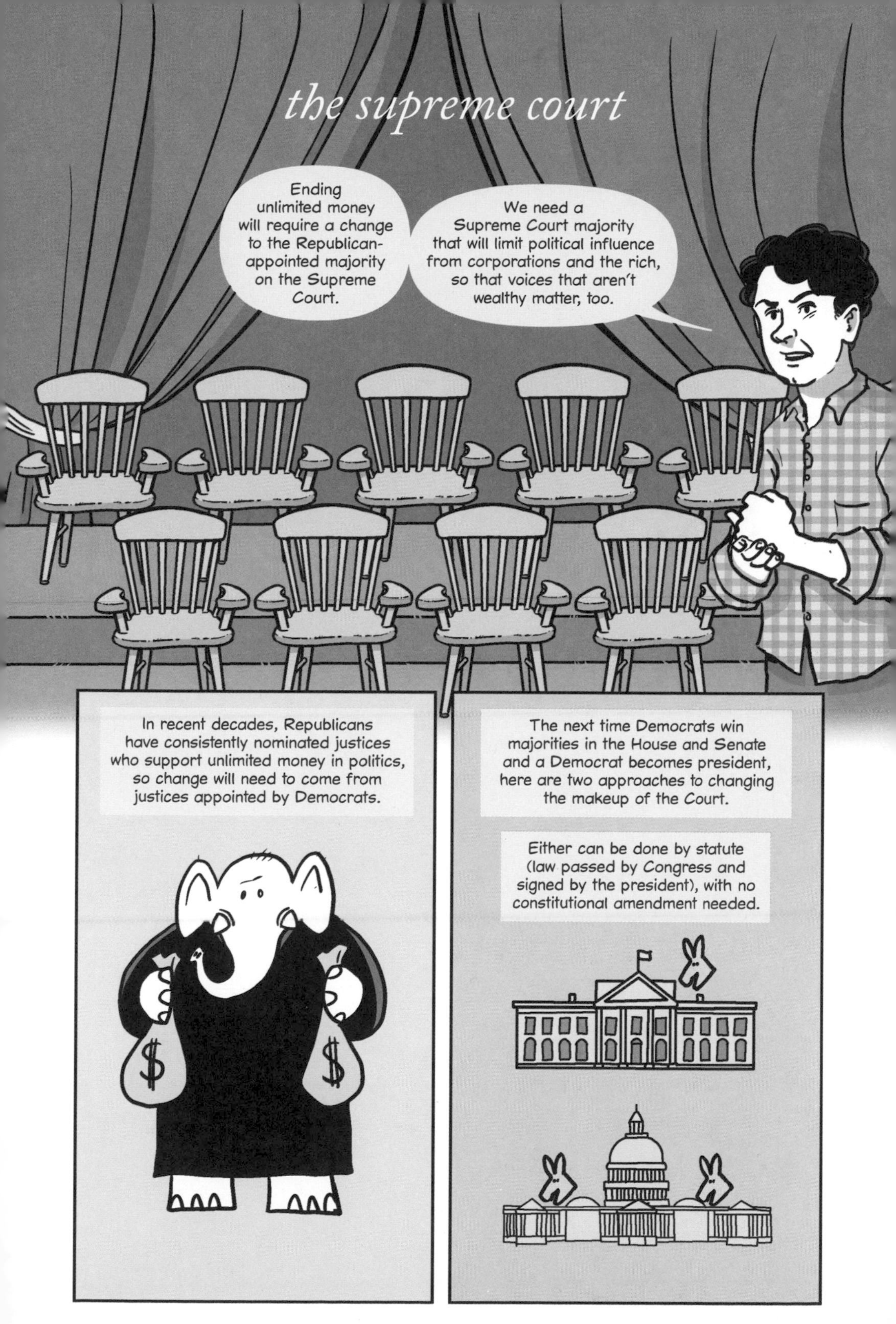
the supreme court
Ending unlimited money will require a change to the Republican-appointed majority on the Supreme Court.
We need a Supreme Court majority that will limit political influence from corporations and the rich, so that voices that aren't wealthy matter, too.
In recent decades, Republicans have consistently nominated justices who support unlimited money in politics, so change will need to come from justices appointed by Democrats.
$
$
The next time Democrats win majorities in the House and Senate and a Democrat becomes president, here are two approaches to changing the makeup of the Court.
Either can be done by statute (law passed by Congress and signed by the president), with no constitutional amendment needed.

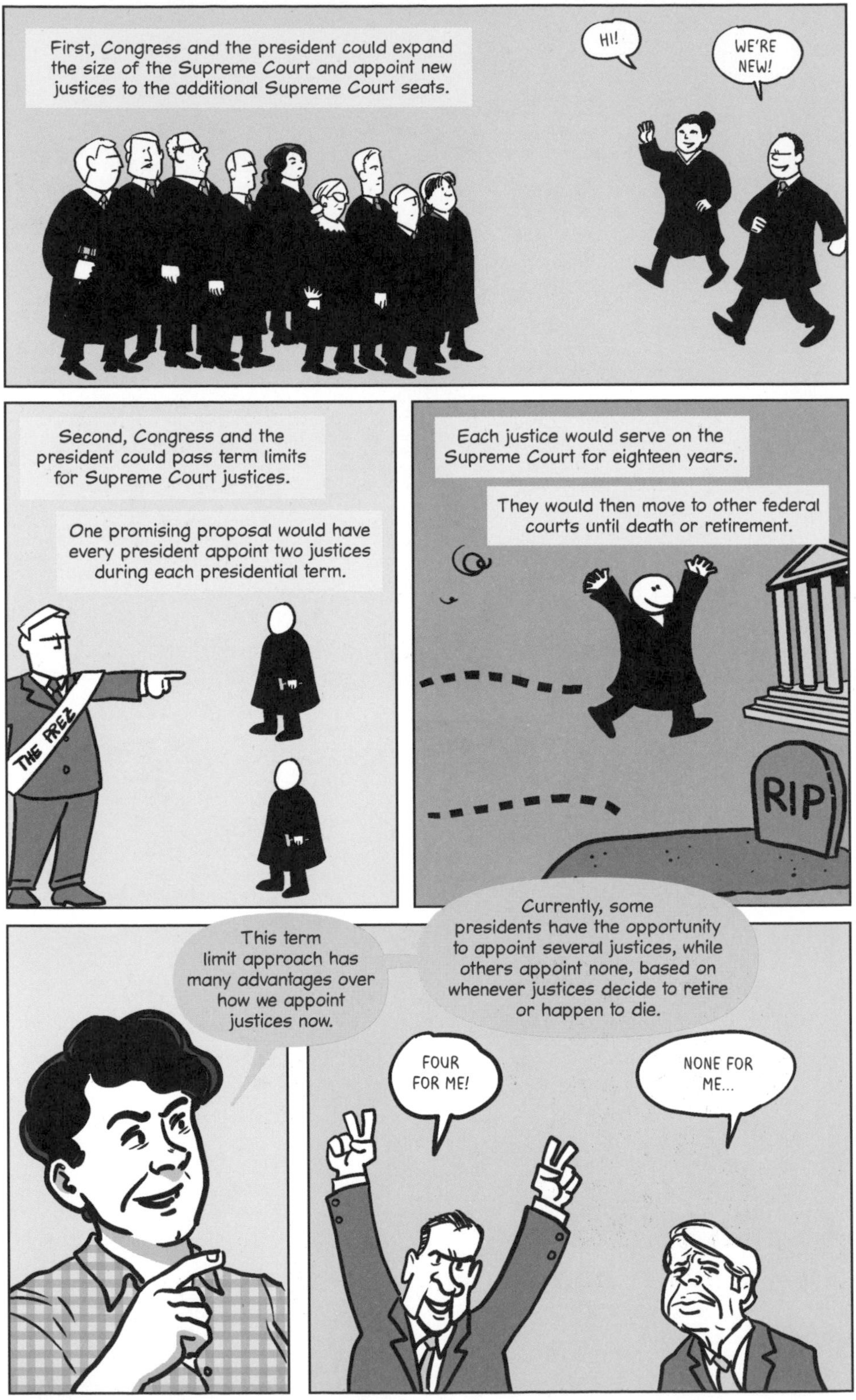
First, Congress and the president could expand the size of the Supreme Court and appoint new justices to the additional Supreme Court seats.
HI!
WE'RE NEW!
Second, Congress and the president could pass term limits for Supreme Court justices.
One promising proposal would have every president appoint two justices during each presidential term.
THE PREZ
Each justice would serve on the Supreme Court for eighteen years.
They would then move to other federal courts until death or retirement.
RIP
This term limit approach has many advantages over how we appoint justices now.
Currently, some presidents have the opportunity to appoint several justices, while others appoint none, based on whenever justices decide to retire or happen to die.
FOUR FOR ME!
NONE FOR ME...

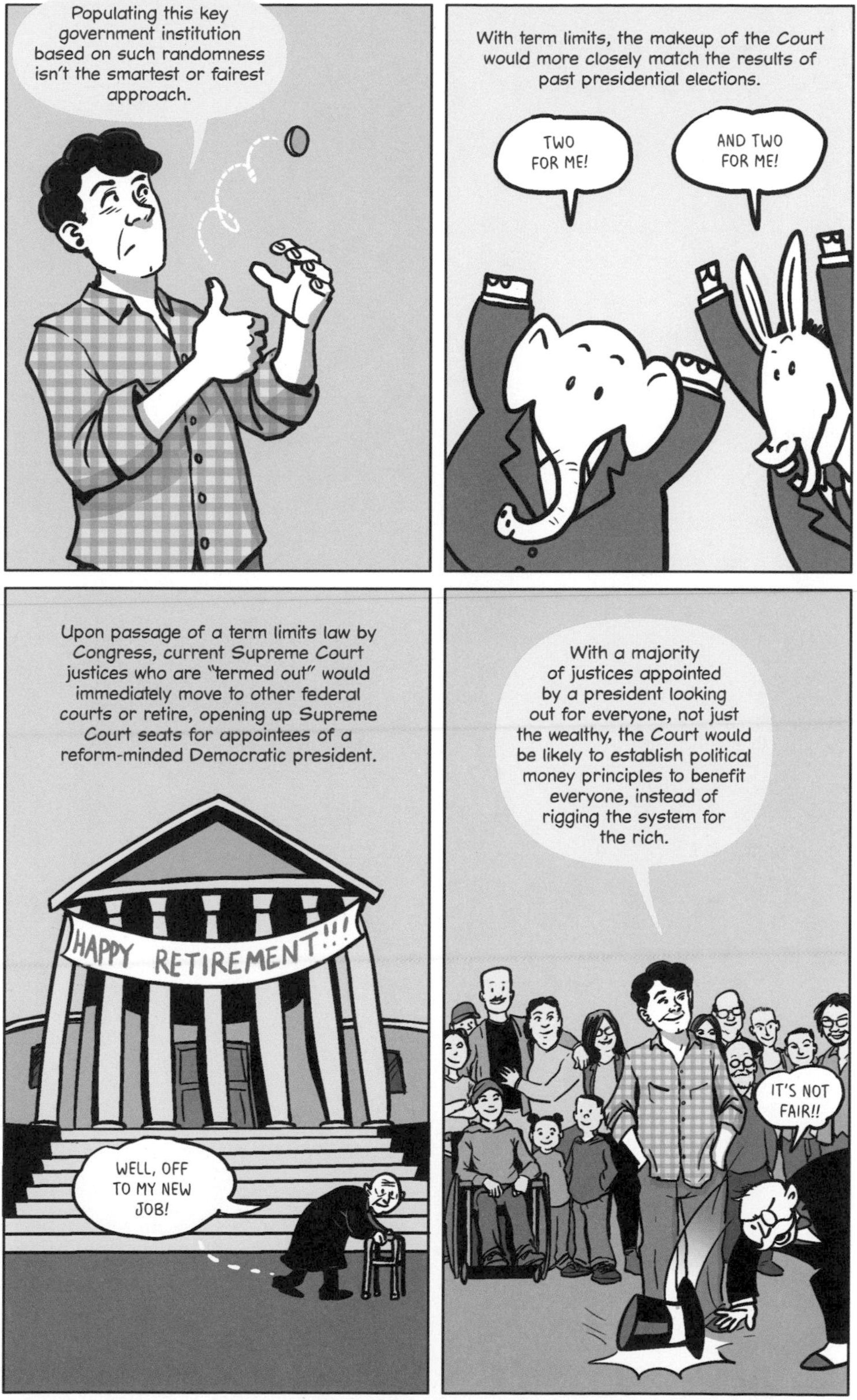
Populating this key government institution based on such randomness isn't the smartest or fairest approach.
With term limits, the makeup of the Court would more closely match the results of past presidential elections.
TWO FOR ME!
AND TWO FOR ME!
Upon passage of a term limits law by Congress, current Supreme Court justices who are "termed out" would immediately move to other federal courts or retire, opening up Supreme Court seats for appointees of a reform-minded Democratic president.
HAPPY RETIREMENT!!!
WELL, OFF TO MY NEW JOB!
With a majority of justices appointed by a president looking out for everyone, not just the wealthy, the Court would be likely to establish political money principles to benefit everyone, instead of rigging the system for the rich.
IT'S NOT FAIR!!

4

the
wealth
hoarders

As we work to unrig the rules so that our country works for everyone, it helps to know who's working to ***rig*** those rules so that our country serves only the very wealthy.
A small group of extremist billionaires has been working for more than a half century to change our country to their liking—in a way that will hollow out our democracy.
They want to turn the United States into a fiefdom where the very wealthy make the laws and control the government.

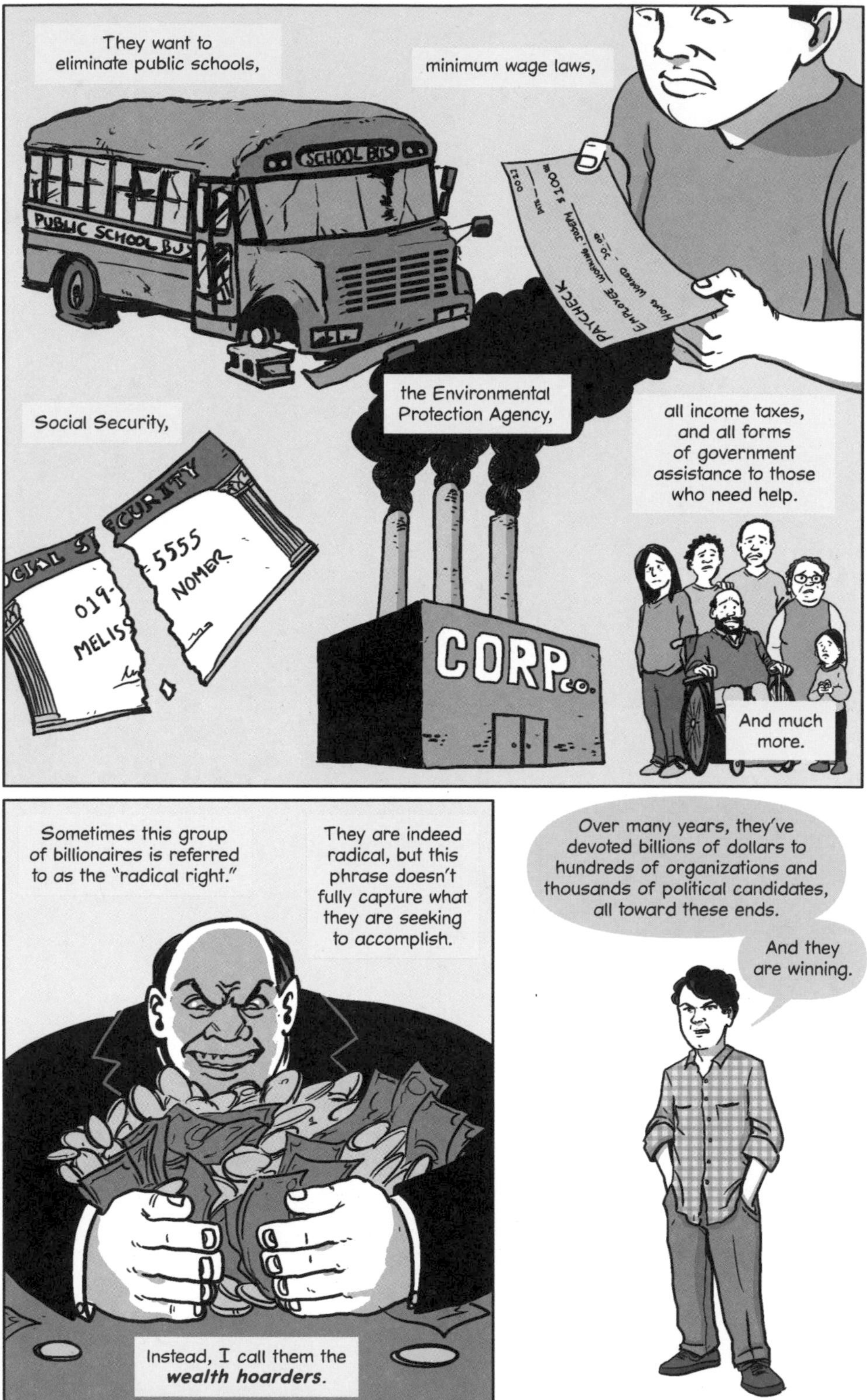
They want to eliminate public schools,
SCHOOL BUS
PUBLIC SCHOOL BUS
minimum wage laws,
PAYCHECK
Social Security,
the Environmental Protection Agency,
CORP co.
all income taxes, and all forms of government assistance to those who need help.
And much more.
Sometimes this group of billionaires is referred to as the "radical right."
They are indeed radical, but this phrase doesn't fully capture what they are seeking to accomplish.
Instead, I call them the ***wealth hoarders***.
Over many years, they've devoted billions of dollars to hundreds of organizations and thousands of political candidates, all toward these ends.
And they are winning.

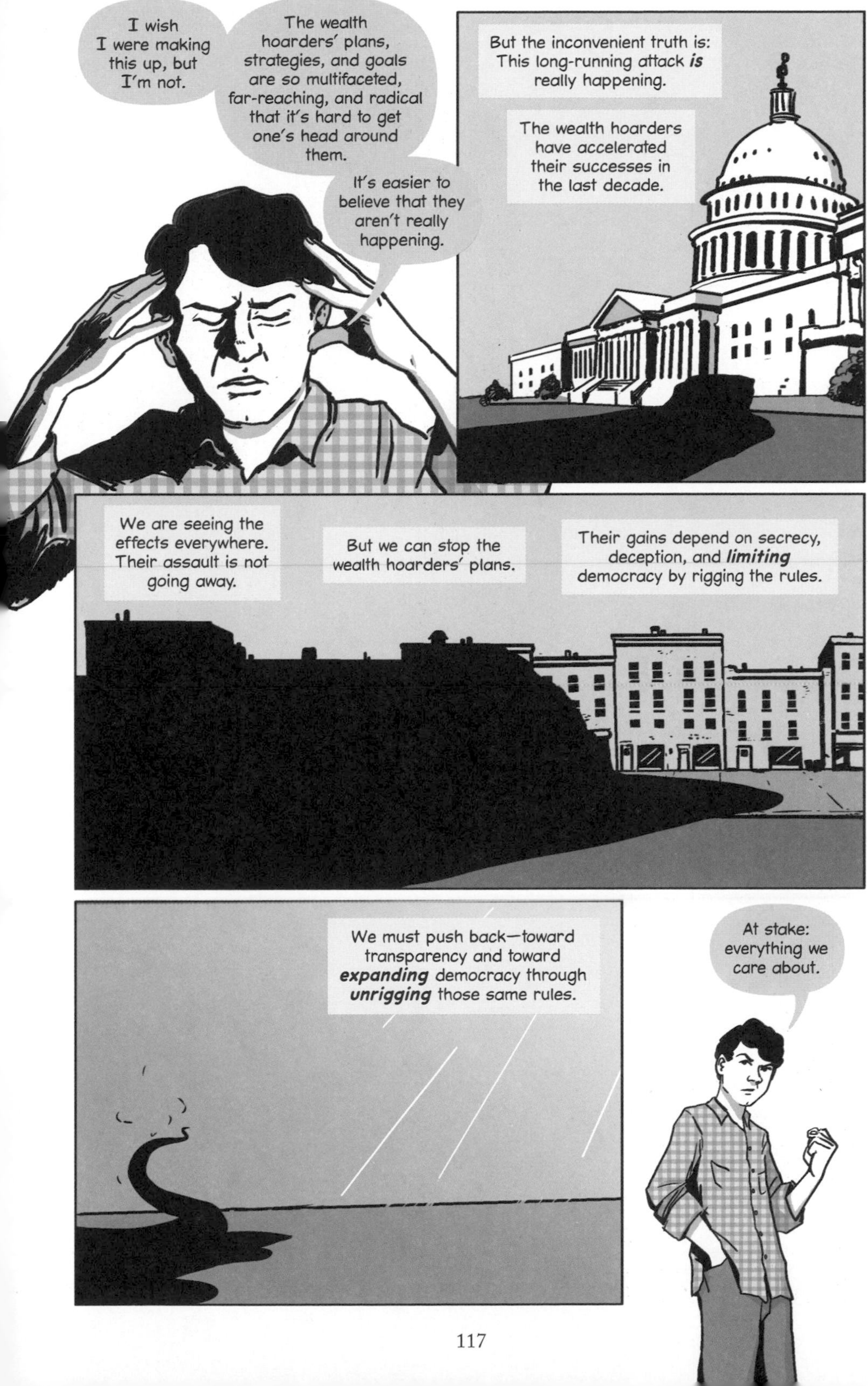
I wish I were making this up, but I'm not.
The wealth hoarders' plans, strategies, and goals are so multifaceted, far-reaching, and radical that it's hard to get one's head around them.
It's easier to believe that they aren't really happening.
But the inconvenient truth is: This long-running attack *is* really happening.
The wealth hoarders have accelerated their successes in the last decade.
We are seeing the effects everywhere. Their assault is not going away.
But we can stop the wealth hoarders' plans.
Their gains depend on secrecy, deception, and ***limiting*** democracy by rigging the rules.
We must push back—toward transparency and toward ***expanding*** democracy through ***unrigging*** those same rules.
At stake: everything we care about.

To stop the wealth hoarder agenda, it helps to better understand the people behind it.

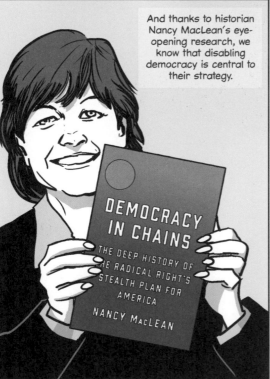

From the groundbreaking work of journalist Jane Mayer, we have a good idea of who these people are and what they seek.

JANE MAYER

DARK MONEY

And thanks to historian Nancy MacLean's eye-opening research, we know that disabling democracy is central to their strategy.

DEMOCRACY IN CHAINS

THE DEEP HISTORY OF THE RADICAL RIGHT'S STEALTH PLAN FOR AMERICA

NANCY MacLEAN

This chapter is based on their work. It's a long chapter, due to its importance.

wealth hoarder leaders

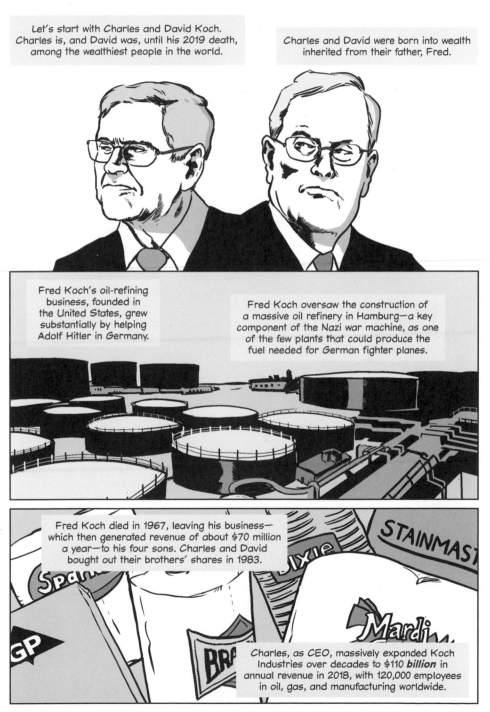

Let's start with Charles and David Koch. Charles is, and David was, until his 2019 death, among the wealthiest people in the world.

Charles and David were born into wealth inherited from their father, Fred.

Fred Koch's oil-refining business, founded in the United States, grew substantially by helping Adolf Hitler in Germany.

Fred Koch oversaw the construction of a massive oil refinery in Hamburg—a key component of the Nazi war machine, as one of the few plants that could produce the fuel needed for German fighter planes.

Fred Koch died in 1967, leaving his business—which then generated revenue of about $70 million a year—to his four sons. Charles and David bought out their brothers' shares in 1983.

Charles, as CEO, massively expanded Koch Industries over decades to $110 **billion** in annual revenue in 2018, with 120,000 employees in oil, gas, and manufacturing worldwide.

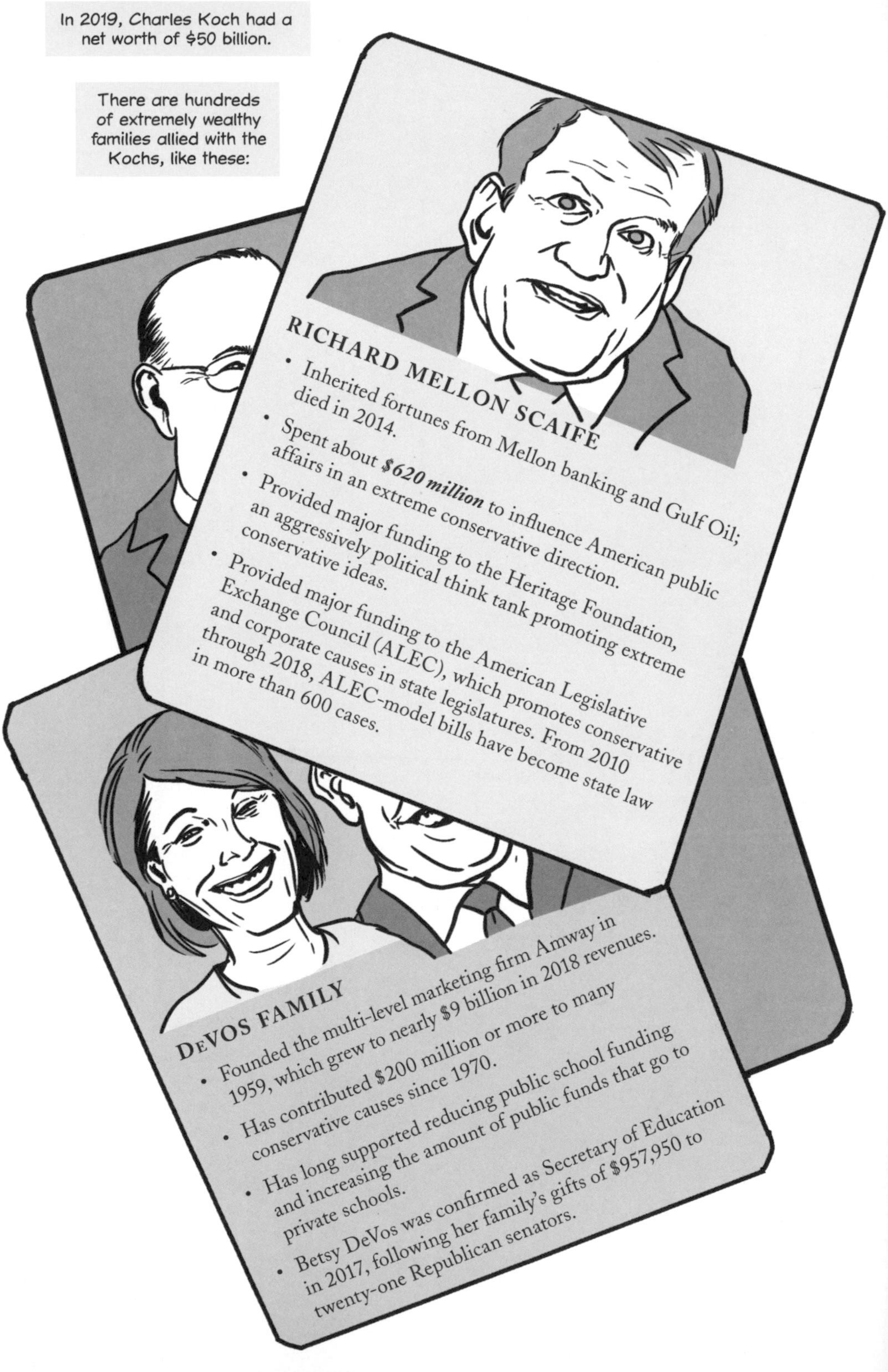
In 2019, Charles Koch had a net worth of $50 billion.
There are hundreds of extremely wealthy families allied with the Kochs, like these:
RICHARD MELLON SCAIFE
• Inherited fortunes from Mellon banking and Gulf Oil; died in 2014.
• Spent about $620 million to influence American public affairs in an extreme conservative direction.
• Provided major funding to the Heritage Foundation, an aggressively political think tank promoting extreme conservative ideas.
• Provided major funding to the American Legislative Exchange Council (ALEC), which promotes conservative and corporate causes in state legislatures. From 2010 through 2018, ALEC-model bills have become state law in more than 600 cases.
DeVOS FAMILY
• Founded the multi-level marketing firm Amway in 1959, which grew to nearly $9 billion in 2018 revenues.
• Has contributed $200 million or more to many conservative causes since 1970.
• Has long supported reducing public school funding and increasing the amount of public funds that go to private schools.
• Betsy DeVos was confirmed as Secretary of Education in 2017, following her family's gifts of $957,950 to twenty-one Republican senators.

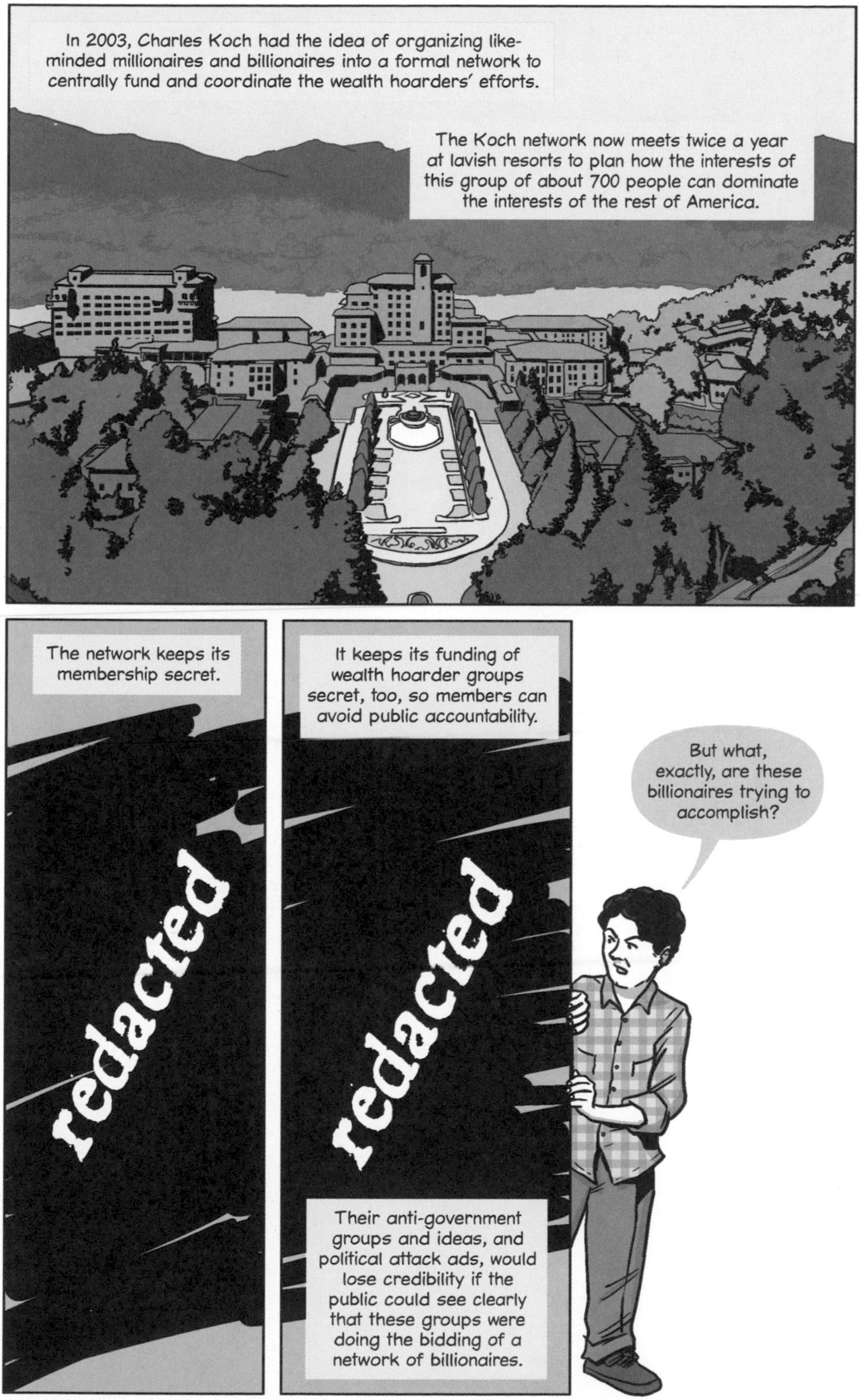
In 2003, Charles Koch had the idea of organizing like-minded millionaires and billionaires into a formal network to centrally fund and coordinate the wealth hoarders' efforts.
The Koch network now meets twice a year at lavish resorts to plan how the interests of this group of about 700 people can dominate the interests of the rest of America.
The network keeps its membership secret.
redacted
It keeps its funding of wealth hoarder groups secret, too, so members can avoid public accountability.
redacted
Their anti-government groups and ideas, and political attack ads, would lose credibility if the public could see clearly that these groups were doing the bidding of a network of billionaires.
But what, exactly, are these billionaires trying to accomplish?

wealth hoarder ideology

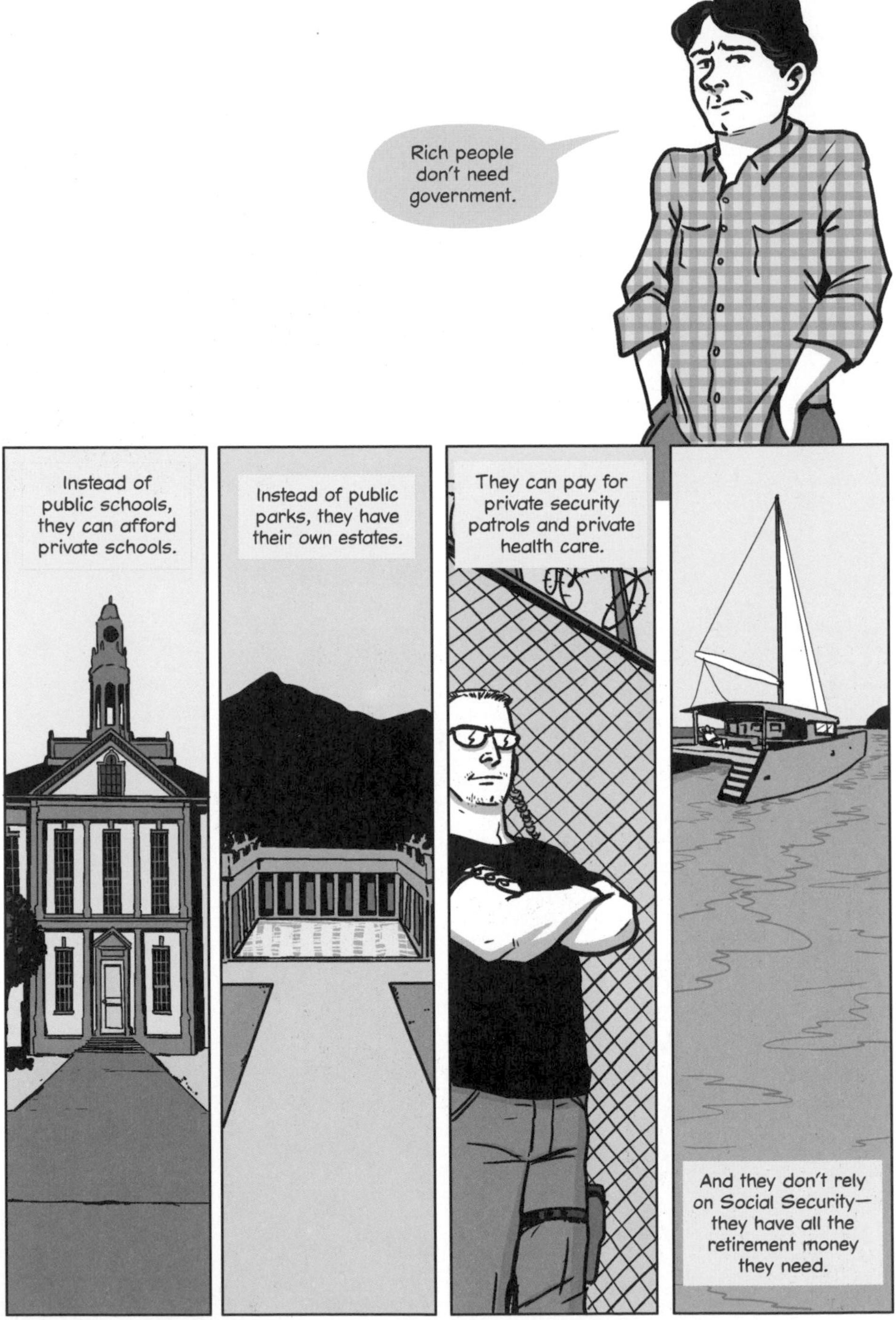
Rich people don't need government.
Instead of public schools, they can afford private schools.
Instead of public parks, they have their own estates.
They can pay for private security patrols and private health care.
And they don't rely on Social Security— they have all the retirement money they need.

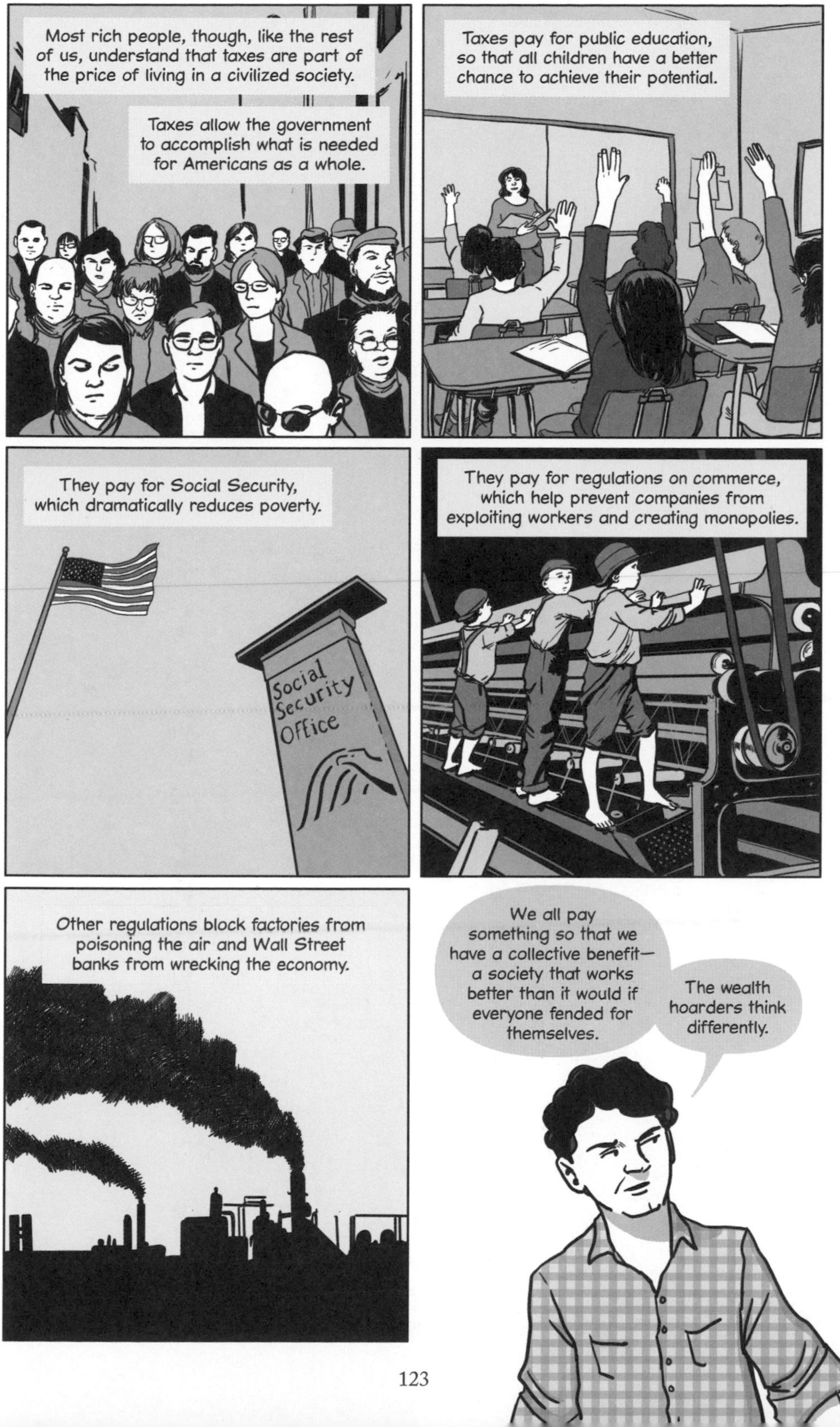
Most rich people, though, like the rest of us, understand that taxes are part of the price of living in a civilized society.
Taxes allow the government to accomplish what is needed for Americans as a whole.
Taxes pay for public education, so that all children have a better chance to achieve their potential.
They pay for Social Security, which dramatically reduces poverty.
Social Security Office
They pay for regulations on commerce, which help prevent companies from exploiting workers and creating monopolies.
Other regulations block factories from poisoning the air and Wall Street banks from wrecking the economy.
We all pay something so that we have a collective benefit— a society that works better than it would if everyone fended for themselves.
The wealth hoarders think differently.

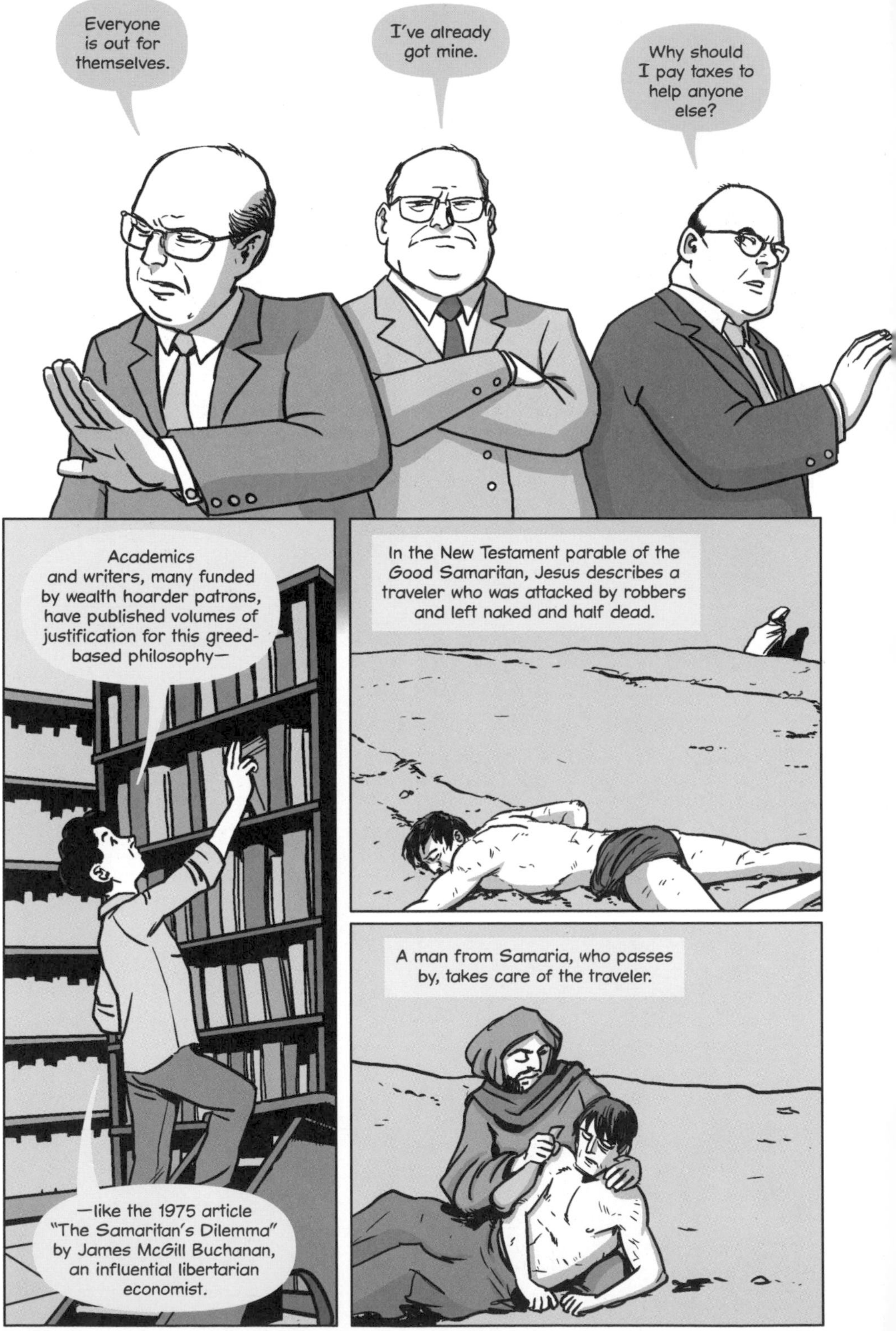
Everyone is out for themselves.
I've already got mine.
Why should I pay taxes to help anyone else?
Academics and writers, many funded by wealth hoarder patrons, have published volumes of justification for this greed-based philosophy—
—like the 1975 article "The Samaritan's Dilemma" by James McGill Buchanan, an influential libertarian economist.
In the New Testament parable of the *Good Samaritan*, Jesus describes a traveler who was attacked by robbers and left naked and half dead.
A man from Samaria, who passes by, takes care of the traveler.

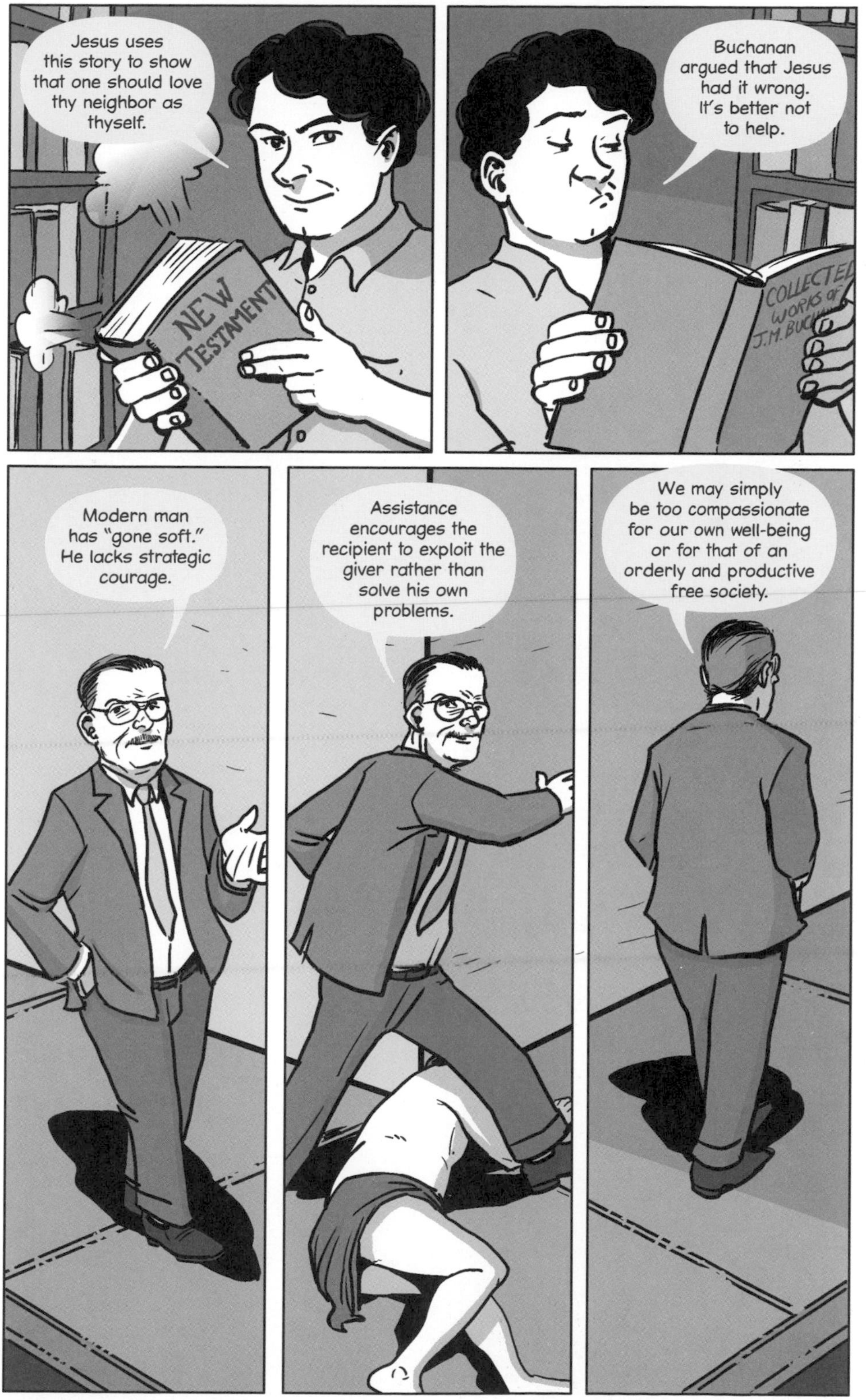
Jesus uses this story to show that one should love thy neighbor as thyself.
NEW TESTAMENT
Buchanan argued that Jesus had it wrong. It's better not to help.
COLLECTED WORKS OF J.M. BUC
Modern man has "gone soft." He lacks strategic courage.
Assistance encourages the recipient to exploit the giver rather than solve his own problems.
We may simply be too compassionate for our own well-being or for that of an orderly and productive free society.

the wealth hoarder agenda

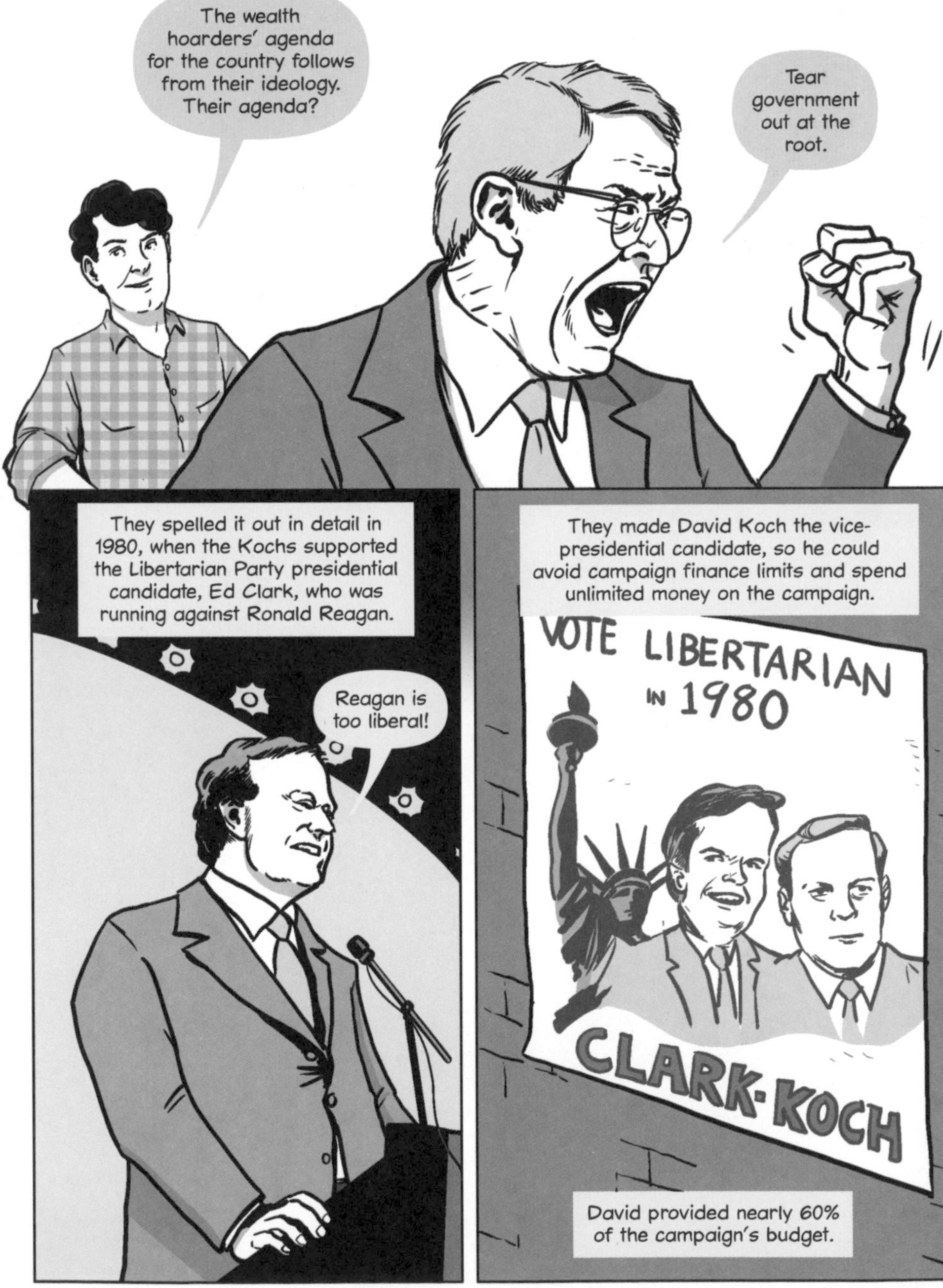

The wealth hoarders' agenda for the country follows from their ideology. Their agenda?
Tear government out at the root.
They spelled it out in detail in 1980, when the Kochs supported the Libertarian Party presidential candidate, Ed Clark, who was running against Ronald Reagan.
Reagan is too liberal!
They made David Koch the vice-presidential candidate, so he could avoid campaign finance limits and spend unlimited money on the campaign.
VOTE LIBERTARIAN IN 1980
CLARK-KOCH
David provided nearly 60% of the campaign's budget.

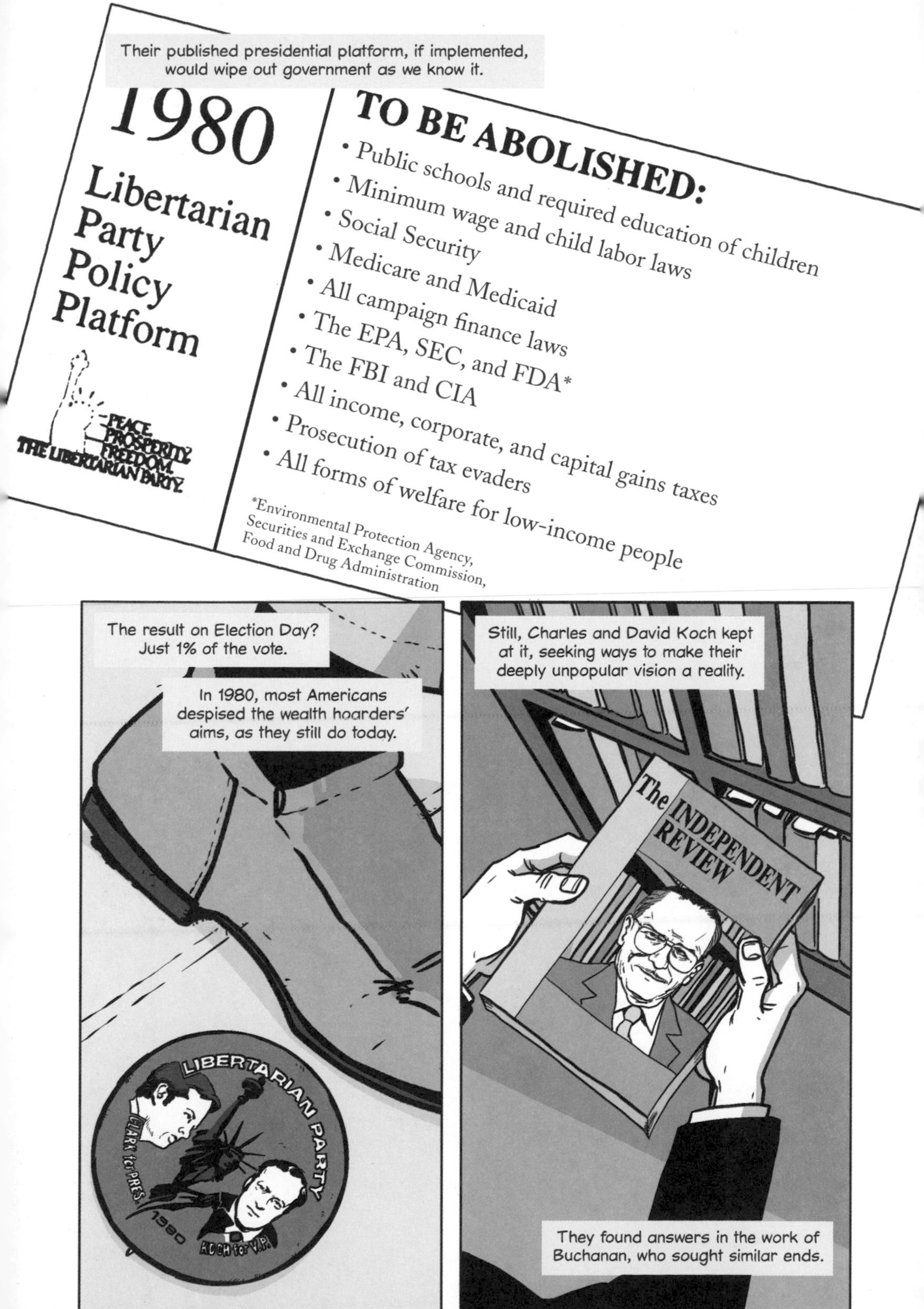
Their published presidential platform, if implemented, would wipe out government as we know it.
1980
Libertarian Party Policy Platform
PEACE. PROSPERITY. FREEDOM. THE LIBERTARIAN PARTY.
TO BE ABOLISHED:
• Public schools and required education of children
• Minimum wage and child labor laws
• Social Security
• Medicare and Medicaid
• All campaign finance laws
• The EPA, SEC, and FDA*
• The FBI and CIA
• All income, corporate, and capital gains taxes
• Prosecution of tax evaders
• All forms of welfare for low-income people
*Environmental Protection Agency, Securities and Exchange Commission, Food and Drug Administration
The result on Election Day? Just 1% of the vote.
In 1980, most Americans despised the wealth hoarders' aims, as they still do today.
LIBERTARIAN PARTY
CLARK for PRES.
1980
KOCH for V.P.
Still, Charles and David Koch kept at it, seeking ways to make their deeply unpopular vision a reality.
The INDEPENDENT REVIEW
They found answers in the work of Buchanan, who sought similar ends.

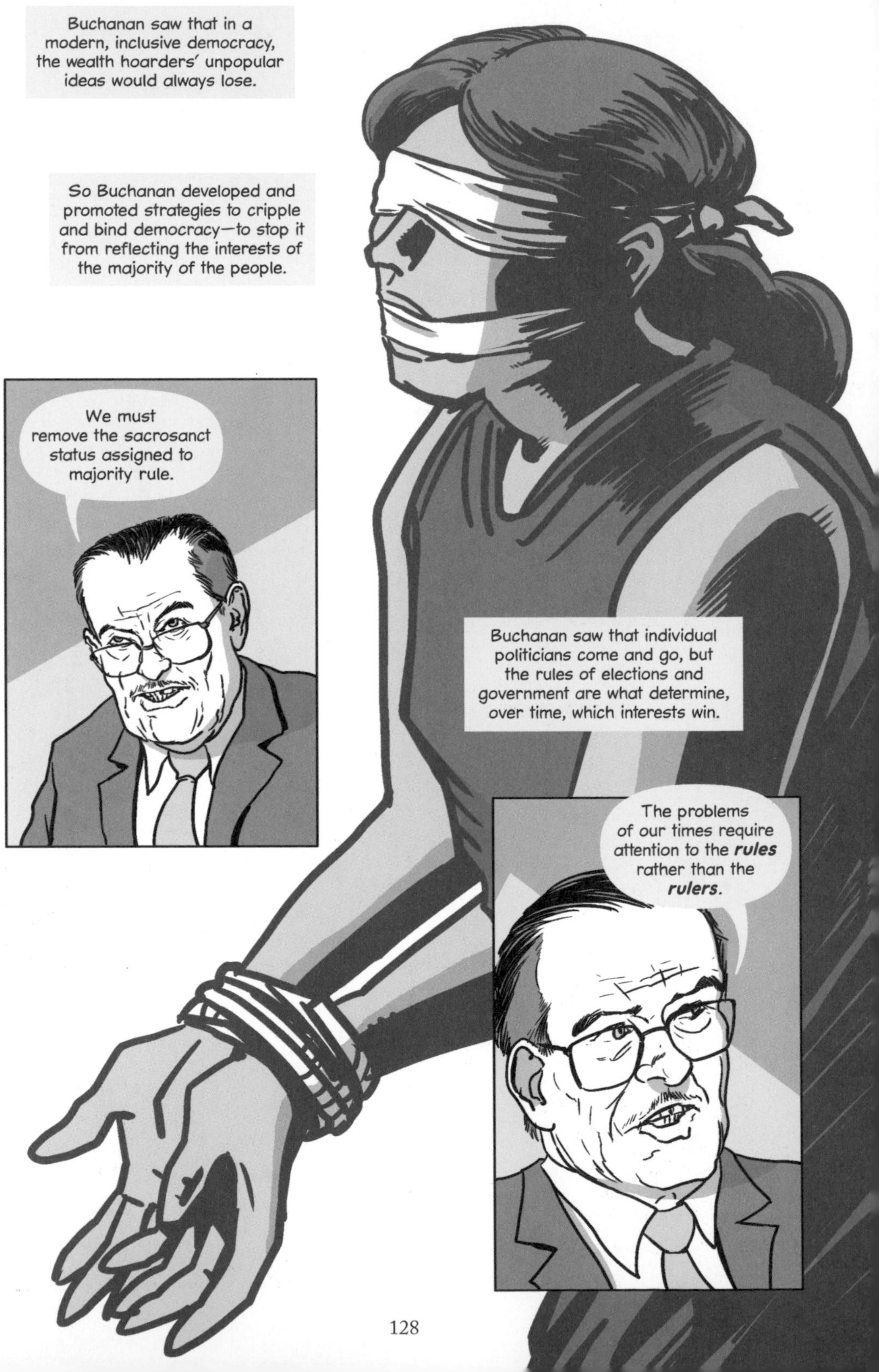
Buchanan saw that in a modern, inclusive democracy, the wealth hoarders' unpopular ideas would always lose.
So Buchanan developed and promoted strategies to cripple and bind democracy—to stop it from reflecting the interests of the majority of the people.
We must remove the sacrosanct status assigned to majority rule.
Buchanan saw that individual politicians come and go, but the rules of elections and government are what determine, over time, which interests win.
The problems of our times require attention to the ***rules*** rather than the ***rulers***.

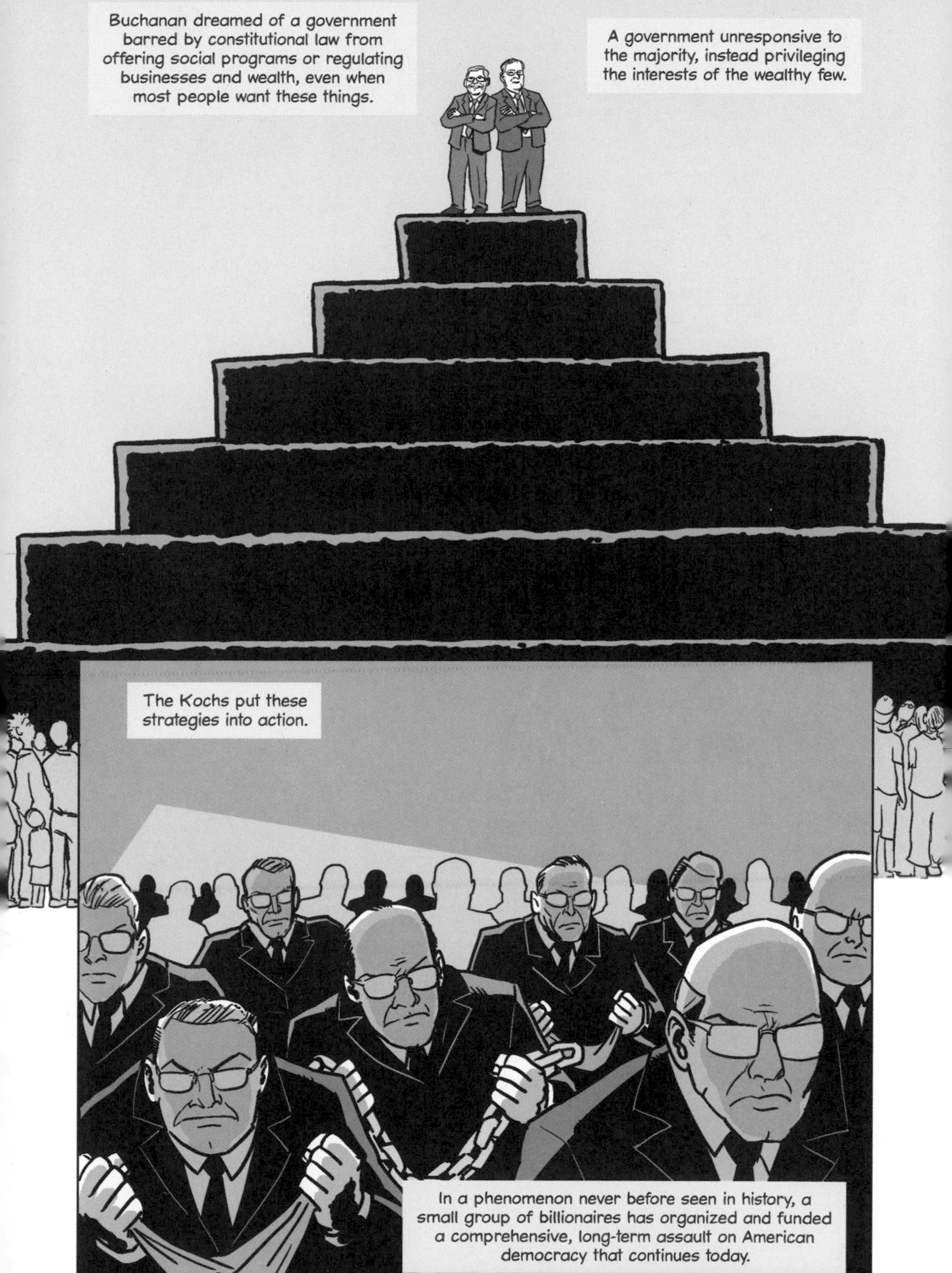
Buchanan dreamed of a government barred by constitutional law from offering social programs or regulating businesses and wealth, even when most people want these things.
A government unresponsive to the majority, instead privileging the interests of the wealthy few.
The Kochs put these strategies into action.
In a phenomenon never before seen in history, a small group of billionaires has organized and funded a comprehensive, long-term assault on American democracy that continues today.

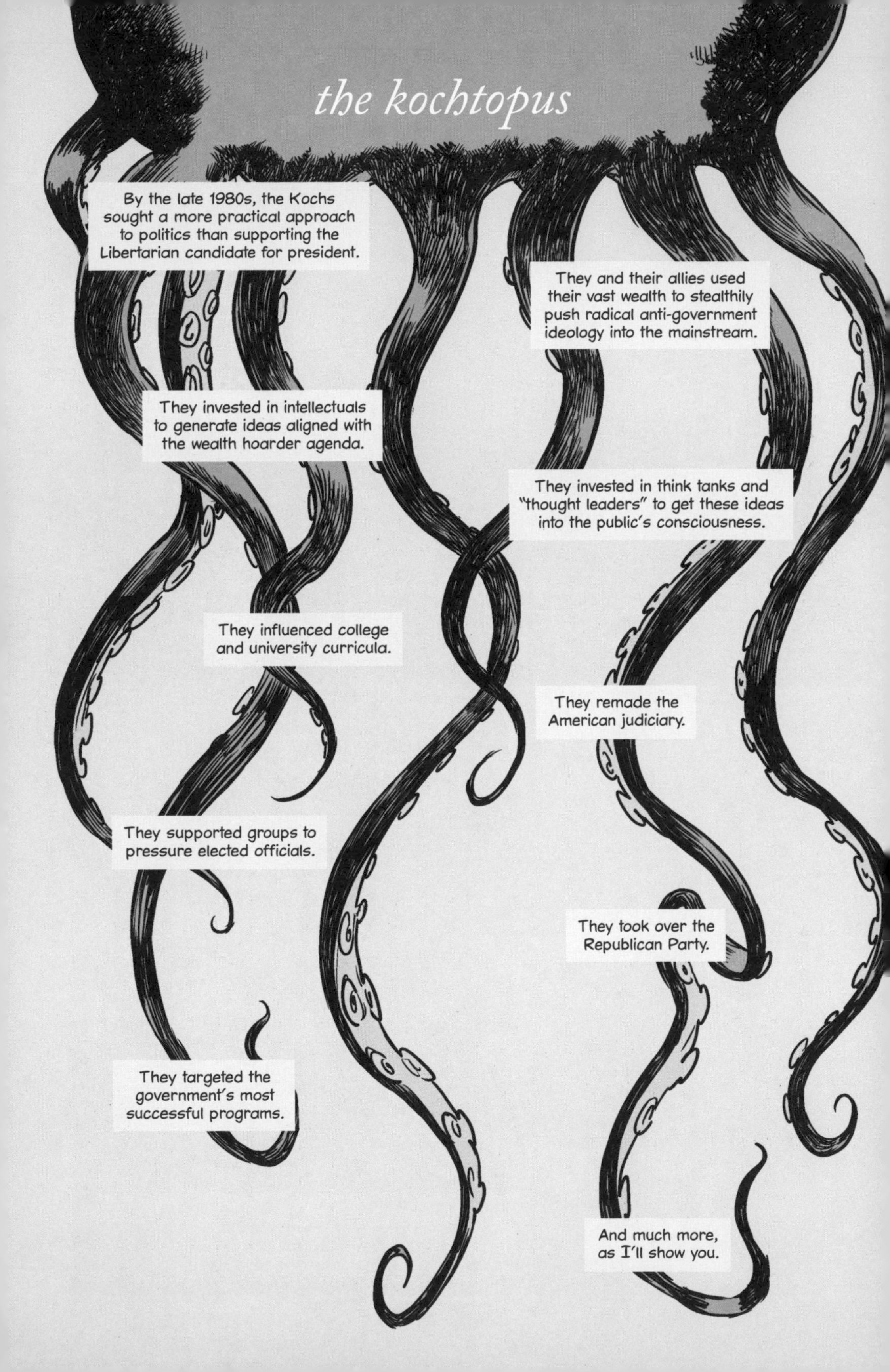
the kochtopus
By the late 1980s, the Kochs sought a more practical approach to politics than supporting the Libertarian candidate for president.
They and their allies used their vast wealth to stealthily push radical anti-government ideology into the mainstream.
They invested in intellectuals to generate ideas aligned with the wealth hoarder agenda.
They invested in think tanks and "thought leaders" to get these ideas into the public's consciousness.
They influenced college and university curricula.
They remade the American judiciary.
They supported groups to pressure elected officials.
They took over the Republican Party.
They targeted the government's most successful programs.
And much more, as I'll show you.

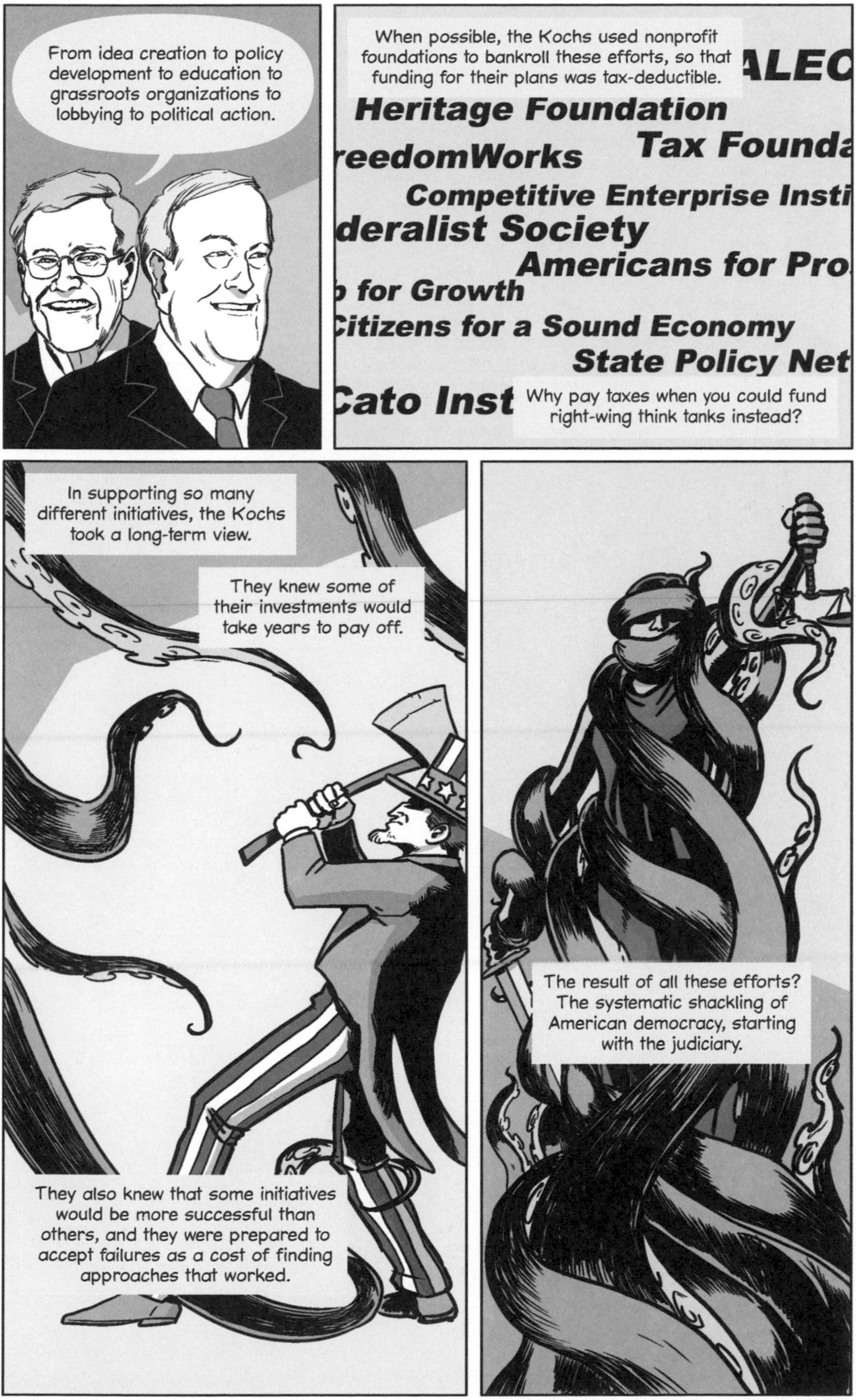
From idea creation to policy development to education to grassroots organizations to lobbying to political action.
When possible, the Kochs used nonprofit foundations to bankroll these efforts, so that funding for their plans was tax-deductible.
ALEC
Heritage Foundation
Tax Founda
reedomWorks
Competitive Enterprise Insti
deralist Society
Americans for Pro
for Growth
itizens for a Sound Economy
State Policy Net
Cato Inst
Why pay taxes when you could fund right-wing think tanks instead?
In supporting so many different initiatives, the Kochs took a long-term view.
They knew some of their investments would take years to pay off.
They also knew that some initiatives would be more successful than others, and they were prepared to accept failures as a cost of finding approaches that worked.
The result of all these efforts? The systematic shackling of American democracy, starting with the judiciary.

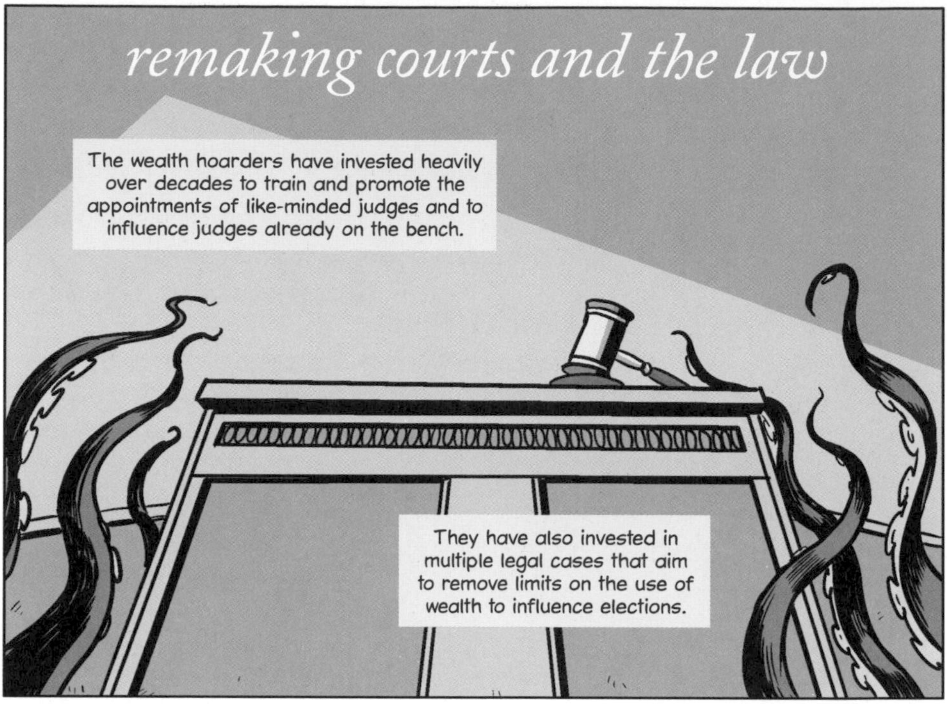
remaking courts and the law
The wealth hoarders have invested heavily over decades to train and promote the appointments of like-minded judges and to influence judges already on the bench.
They have also invested in multiple legal cases that aim to remove limits on the use of wealth to influence elections.

INFLUENCING JUDGES

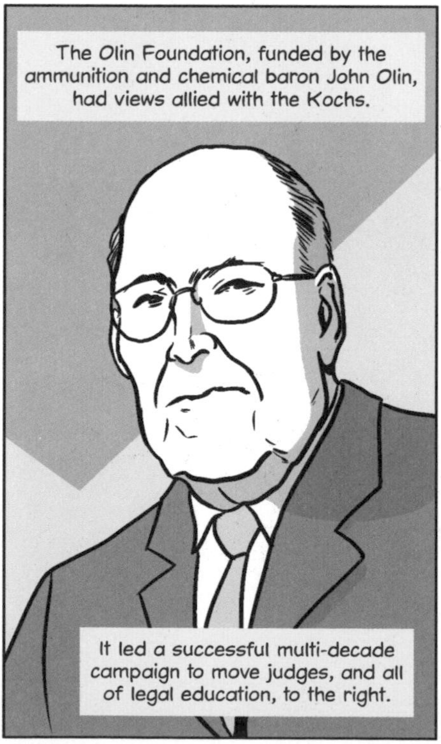
The Olin Foundation, funded by the ammunition and chemical baron John Olin, had views allied with the Kochs.
It led a successful multi-decade campaign to move judges, and all of legal education, to the right.

A type of analysis that applies economic concepts to law was considered a fringe libertarian theory—until the Olin Foundation spent an astonishing $68 million to support it in American law schools from 1985 to 1989.

Law and Economics

Harvard $10 million
Yale $7 million
Chicago $7 million
Columbia $2 million

The foundation even paid students to take law and economics classes.

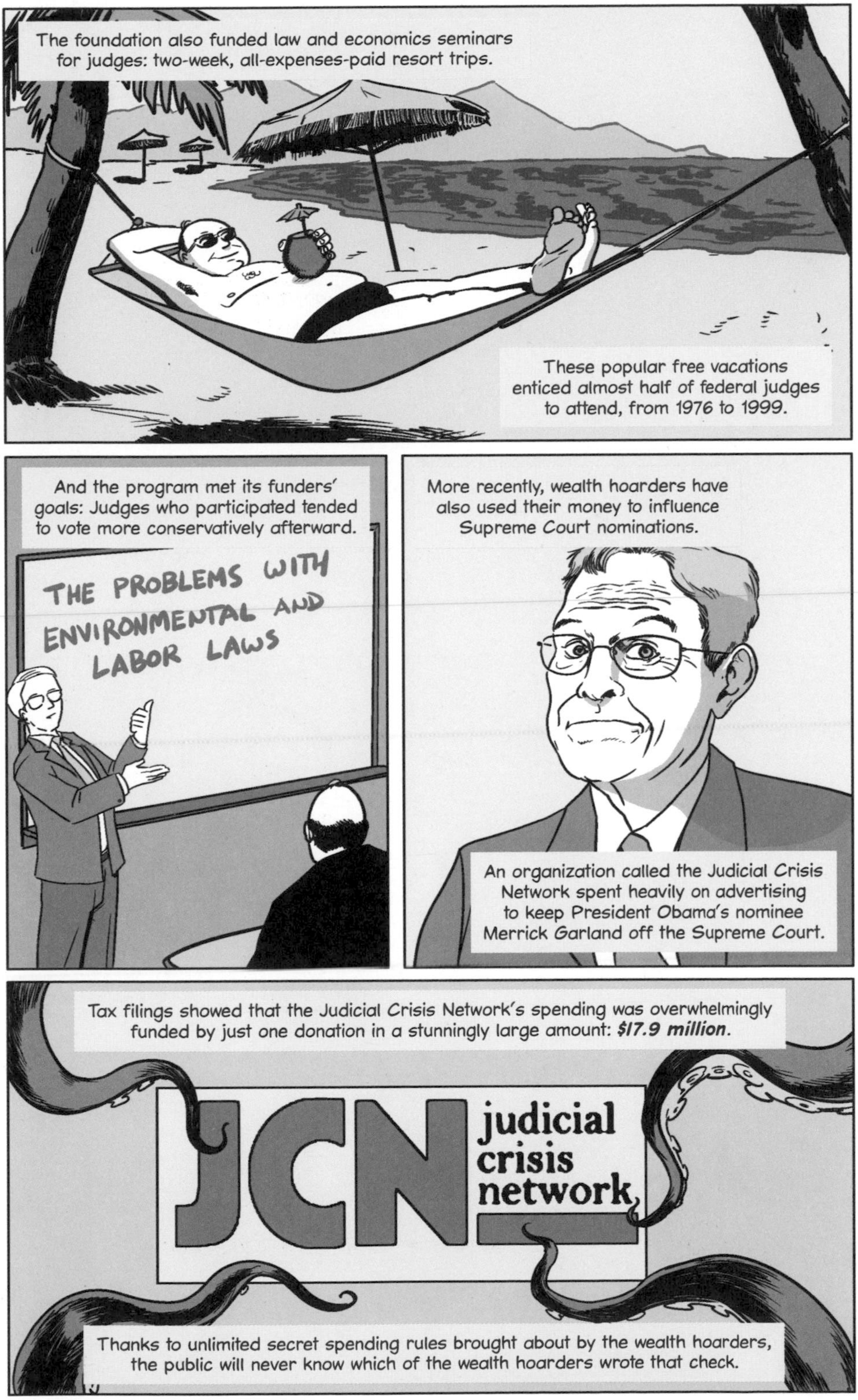

The foundation also funded law and economics seminars for judges: two-week, all-expenses-paid resort trips.
These popular free vacations enticed almost half of federal judges to attend, from 1976 to 1999.
And the program met its funders' goals: Judges who participated tended to vote more conservatively afterward.
THE PROBLEMS WITH ENVIRONMENTAL AND LABOR LAWS
More recently, wealth hoarders have also used their money to influence Supreme Court nominations.
An organization called the Judicial Crisis Network spent heavily on advertising to keep President Obama's nominee Merrick Garland off the Supreme Court.
Tax filings showed that the Judicial Crisis Network's spending was overwhelmingly funded by just one donation in a stunningly large amount: ***$17.9 million***.
JCN judicial crisis network
Thanks to unlimited secret spending rules brought about by the wealth hoarders, the public will never know which of the wealth hoarders wrote that check.

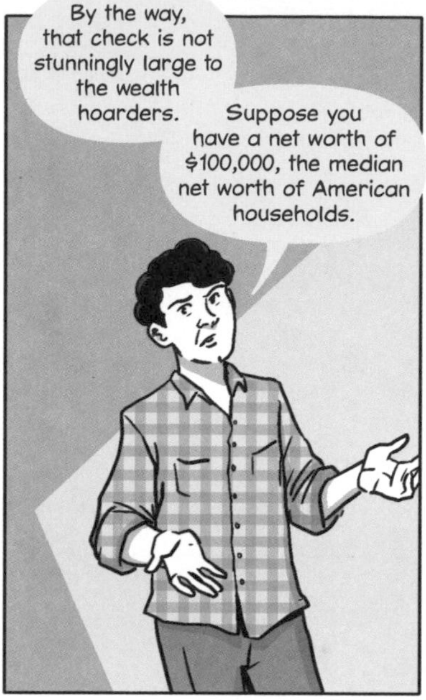
By the way, that check is not stunningly large to the wealth hoarders.
Suppose you have a net worth of $100,000, the median net worth of American households.

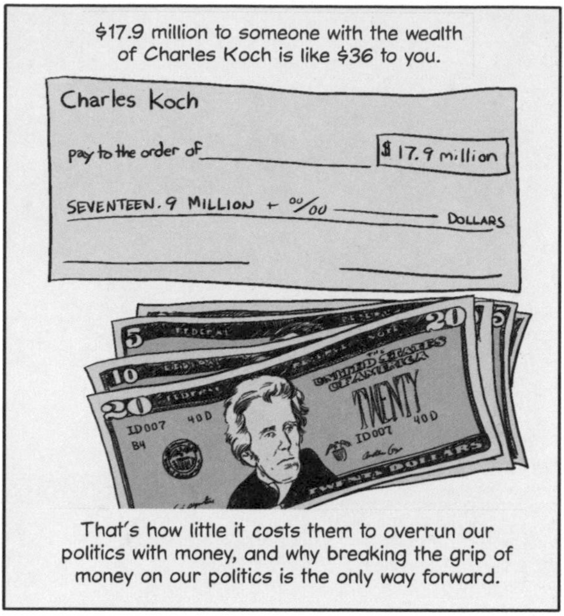
$17.9 million to someone with the wealth of Charles Koch is like $36 to you.
Charles Koch
pay to the order of
$ 17.9 million
SEVENTEEN. 9 MILLION + 00/00
DOLLARS
TWENTY
That's how little it costs them to overrun our politics with money, and why breaking the grip of money on our politics is the only way forward.

UNLIMITED DARK MONEY

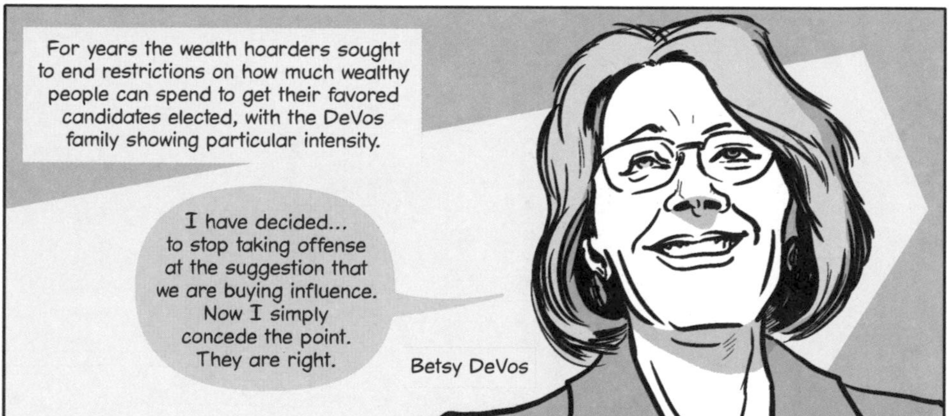
For years the wealth hoarders sought to end restrictions on how much wealthy people can spend to get their favored candidates elected, with the DeVos family showing particular intensity.
I have decided... to stop taking offense at the suggestion that we are buying influence. Now I simply concede the point. They are right.
Betsy DeVos

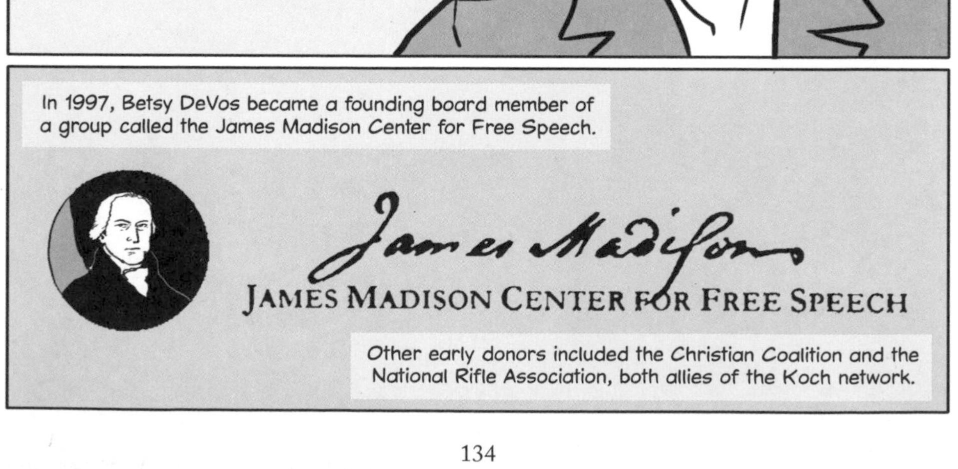
In 1997, Betsy DeVos became a founding board member of a group called the James Madison Center for Free Speech.
James Madison
JAMES MADISON CENTER FOR FREE SPEECH
Other early donors included the Christian Coalition and the National Rifle Association, both allies of the Koch network.

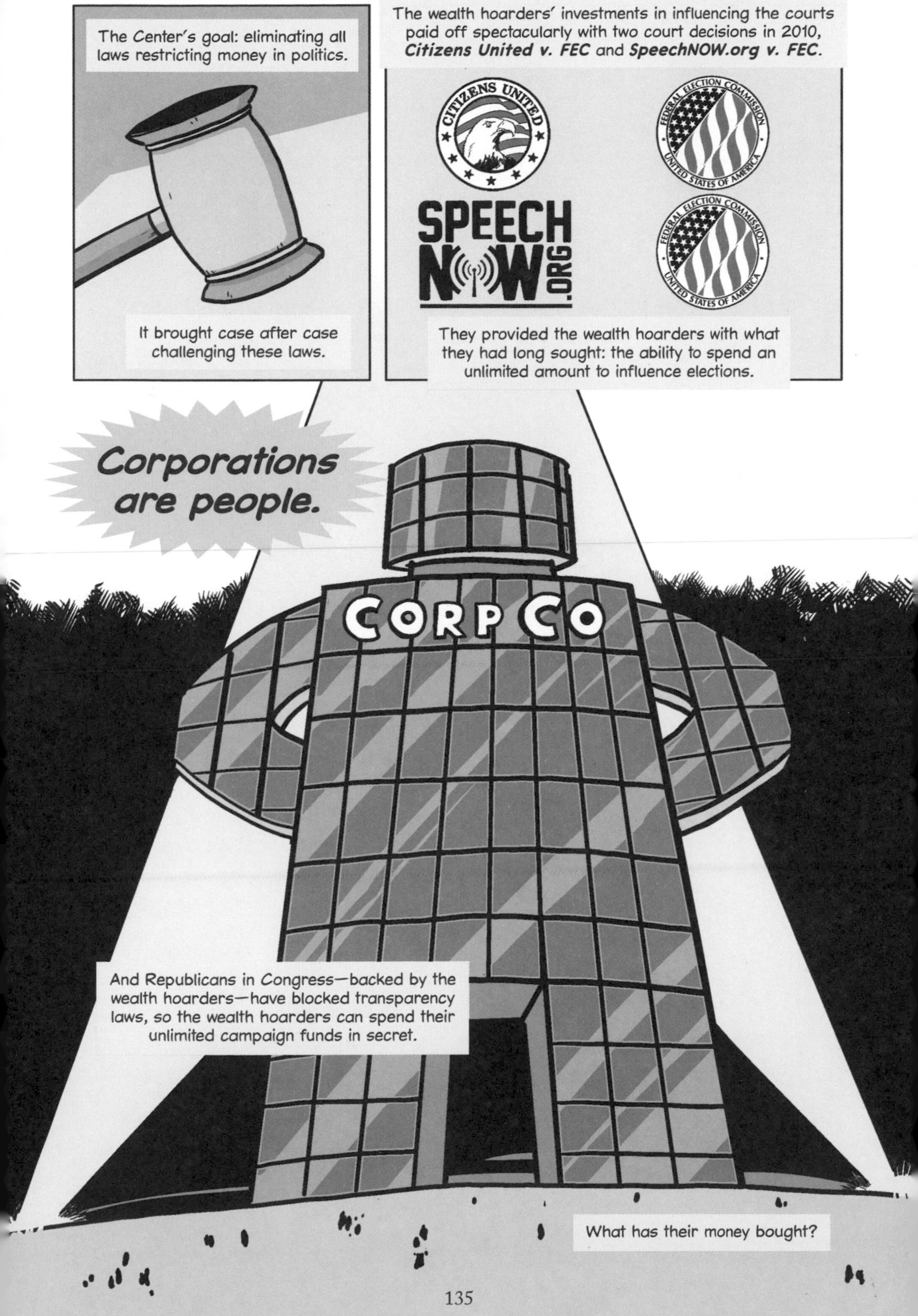
The Center's goal: eliminating all laws restricting money in politics.
It brought case after case challenging these laws.
The wealth hoarders' investments in influencing the courts paid off spectacularly with two court decisions in 2010, ***Citizens United v. FEC*** and ***SpeechNOW.org v. FEC***.
CITIZENS UNITED
FEDERAL ELECTION COMMISSION
UNITED STATES OF AMERICA
SPEECH NOW .ORG
FEDERAL ELECTION COMMISSION
UNITED STATES OF AMERICA
They provided the wealth hoarders with what they had long sought: the ability to spend an unlimited amount to influence elections.
Corporations are people.
CORP CO
And Republicans in Congress—backed by the wealth hoarders—have blocked transparency laws, so the wealth hoarders can spend their unlimited campaign funds in secret.
What has their money bought?

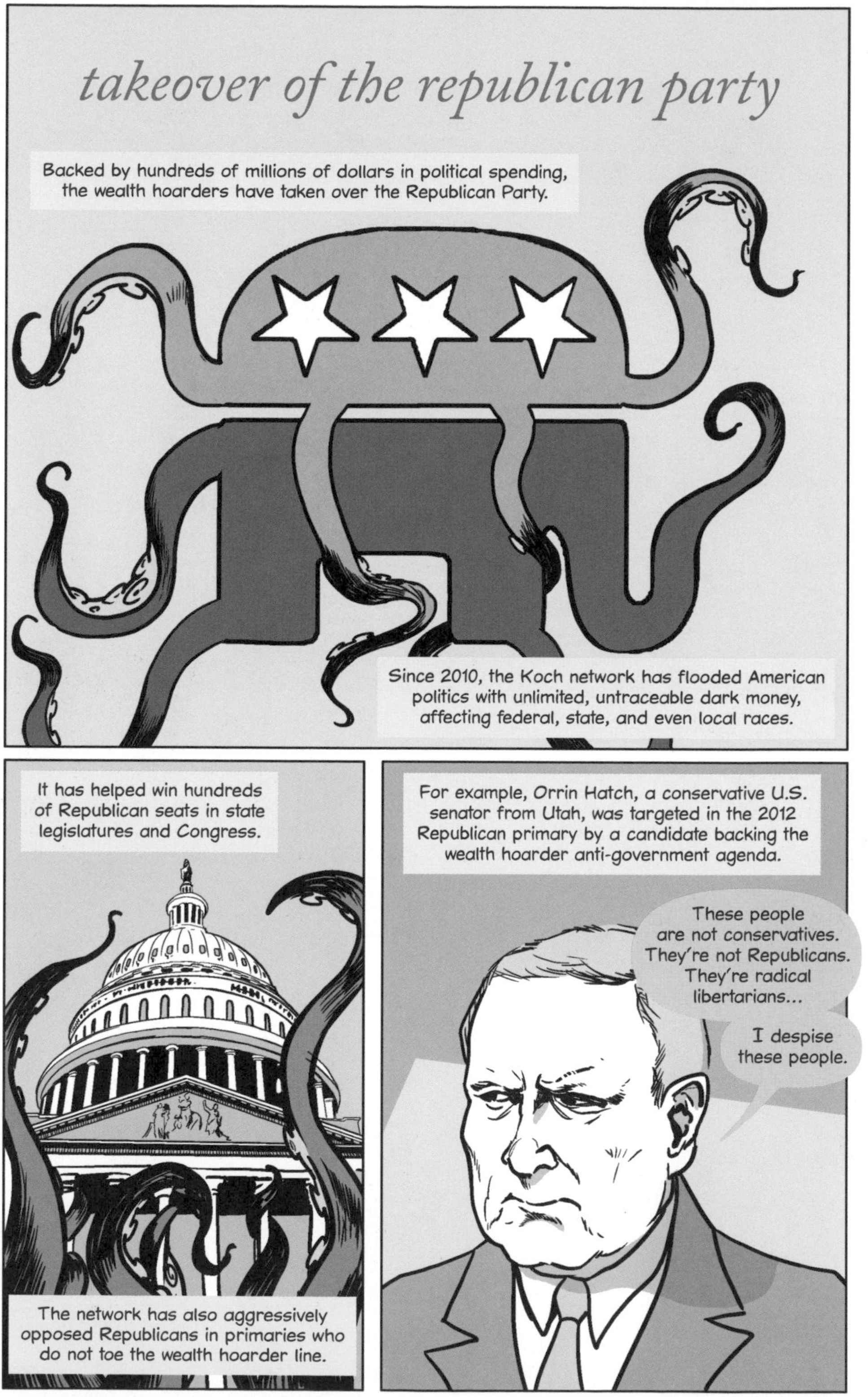
takeover of the republican party
Backed by hundreds of millions of dollars in political spending, the wealth hoarders have taken over the Republican Party.
Since 2010, the Koch network has flooded American politics with unlimited, untraceable dark money, affecting federal, state, and even local races.
It has helped win hundreds of Republican seats in state legislatures and Congress.
The network has also aggressively opposed Republicans in primaries who do not toe the wealth hoarder line.
For example, Orrin Hatch, a conservative U.S. senator from Utah, was targeted in the 2012 Republican primary by a candidate backing the wealth hoarder anti-government agenda.
These people are not conservatives. They're not Republicans. They're radical libertarians...
I despise these people.

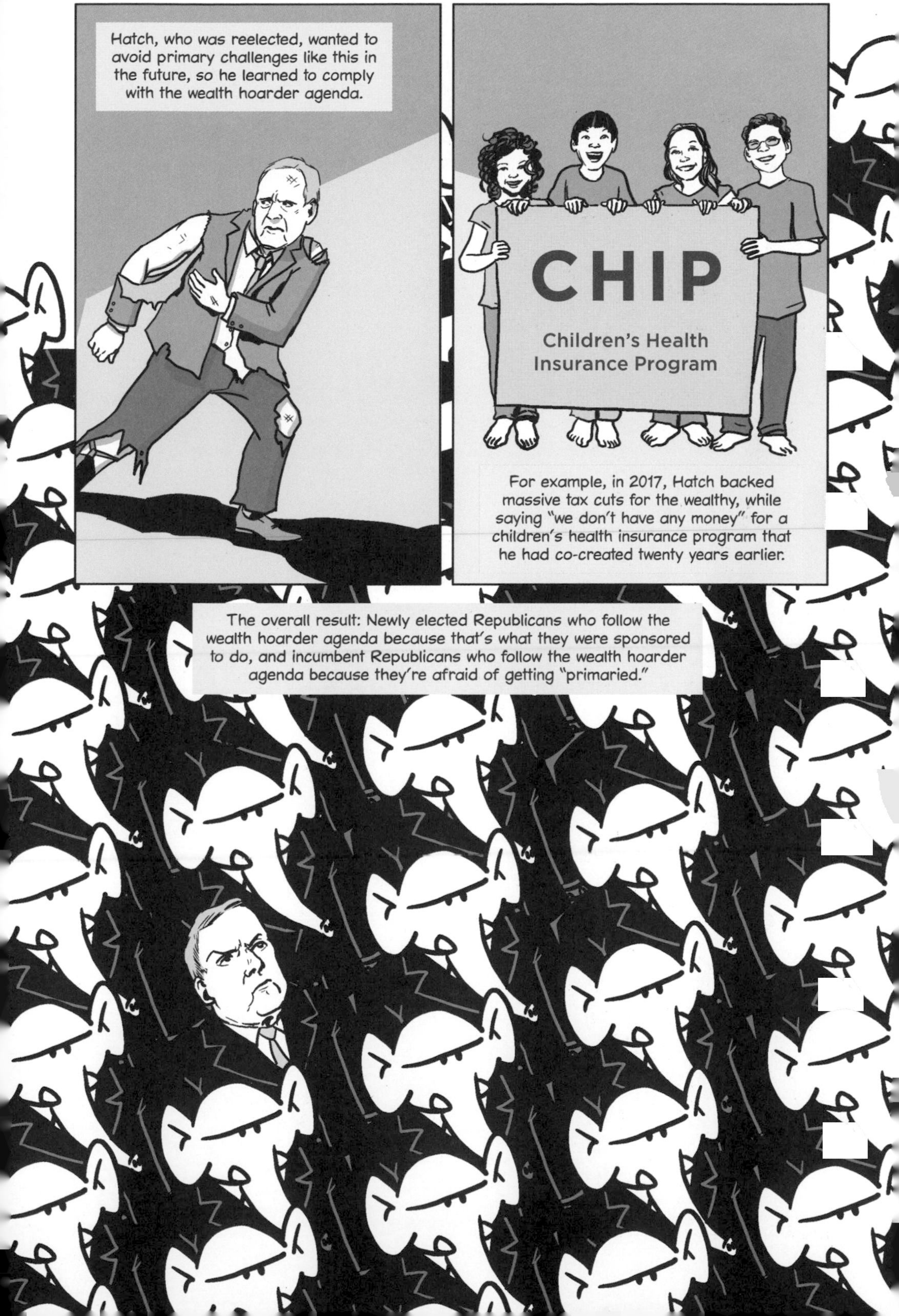
Hatch, who was reelected, wanted to avoid primary challenges like this in the future, so he learned to comply with the wealth hoarder agenda.
CHIP
Children's Health Insurance Program
For example, in 2017, Hatch backed massive tax cuts for the wealthy, while saying "we don't have any money" for a children's health insurance program that he had co-created twenty years earlier.
The overall result: Newly elected Republicans who follow the wealth hoarder agenda because that's what they were sponsored to do, and incumbent Republicans who follow the wealth hoarder agenda because they're afraid of getting "primaried."

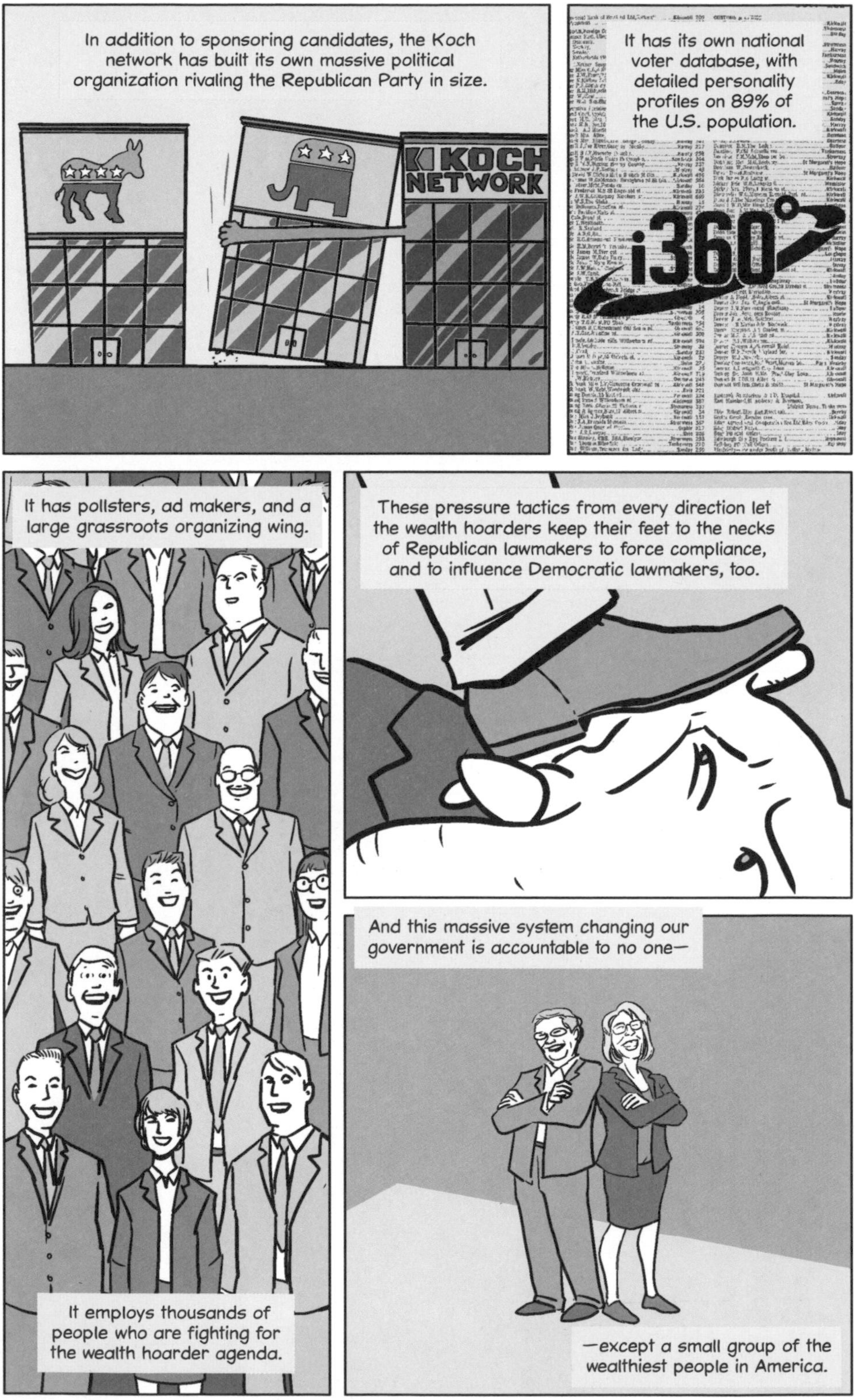

In addition to sponsoring candidates, the Koch network has built its own massive political organization rivaling the Republican Party in size.
KOCH NETWORK
It has its own national voter database, with detailed personality profiles on 89% of the U.S. population.
i360°
It has pollsters, ad makers, and a large grassroots organizing wing.
It employs thousands of people who are fighting for the wealth hoarder agenda.
These pressure tactics from every direction let the wealth hoarders keep their feet to the necks of Republican lawmakers to force compliance, and to influence Democratic lawmakers, too.
And this massive system changing our government is accountable to no one—
—except a small group of the wealthiest people in America.

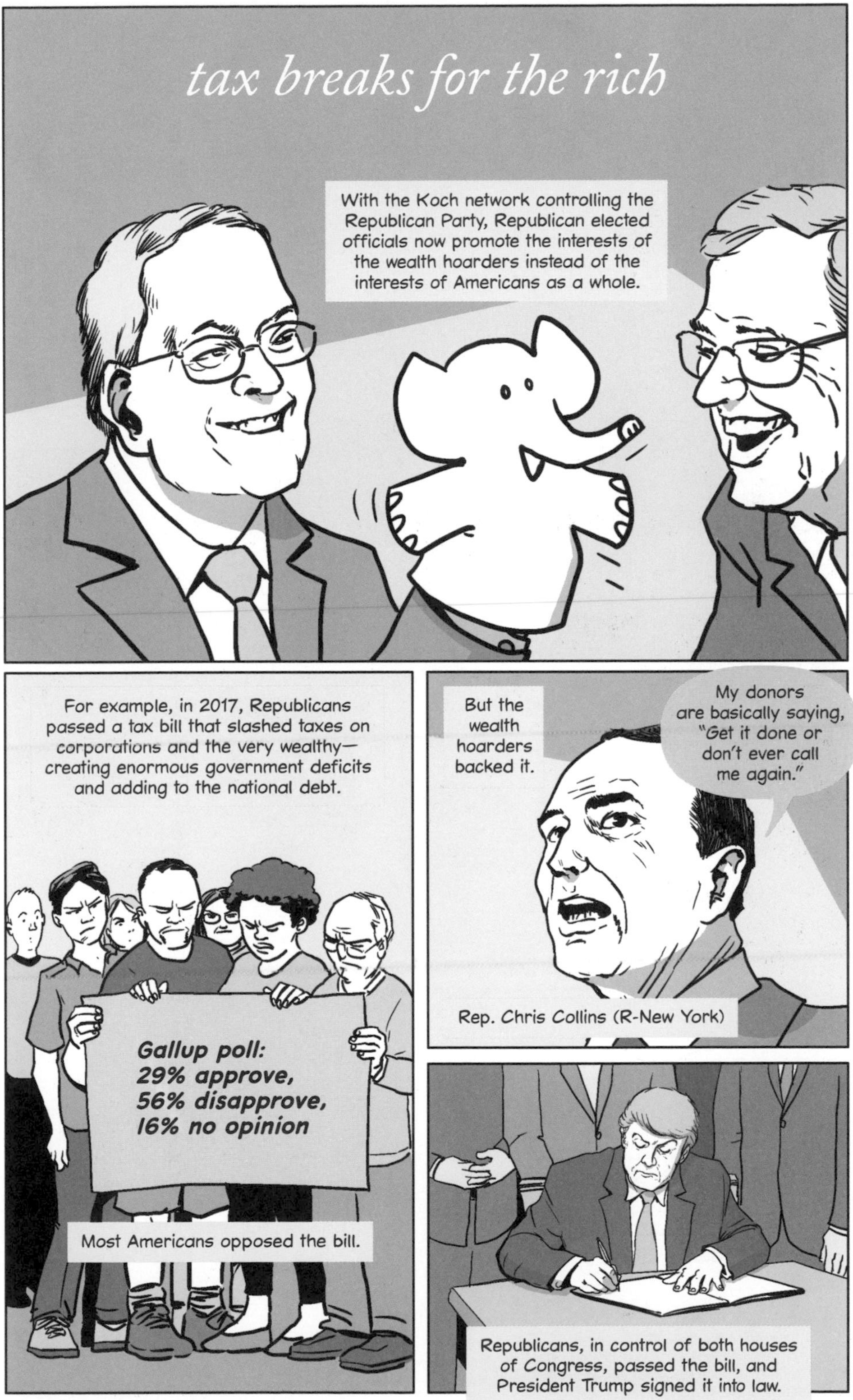
tax breaks for the rich
With the Koch network controlling the Republican Party, Republican elected officials now promote the interests of the wealth hoarders instead of the interests of Americans as a whole.
For example, in 2017, Republicans passed a tax bill that slashed taxes on corporations and the very wealthy—creating enormous government deficits and adding to the national debt.
Gallup poll: 29% approve, 56% disapprove, 16% no opinion
Most Americans opposed the bill.
But the wealth hoarders backed it.
My donors are basically saying, "Get it done or don't ever call me again."
Rep. Chris Collins (R-New York)
Republicans, in control of both houses of Congress, passed the bill, and President Trump signed it into law.

Most people would call it fiscally irresponsible to pass tax cuts while running up debt.

And it's not just cutting taxes.

The wealth hoarders also add to the deficit by supporting enormous government spending on defense without a way to pay for it.

For example, U.S. spending since 9/11 on wars in Iraq, Afghanistan, and elsewhere now exceeds $5.9 trillion.

That's equivalent to **$50,000 for every American household**—almost all of it borrowed money that adds to the national debt.

Why this fiscal irresponsibility? Because huge deficits, driven by tax cuts and military spending, help the wealth hoarders' goals—they constrain what government can do in the future.

Congressiona Budget Offic

breaking government

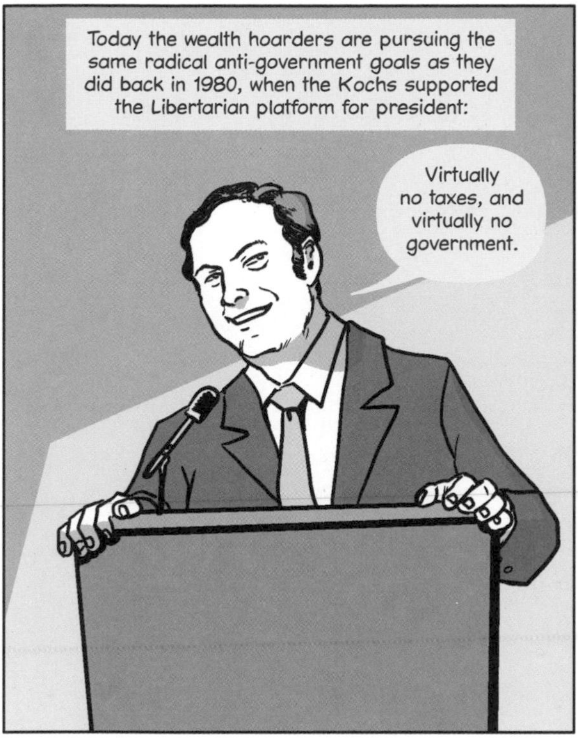
Today the wealth hoarders are pursuing the same radical anti-government goals as they did back in 1980, when the Kochs supported the Libertarian platform for president:
Virtually no taxes, and virtually no government.

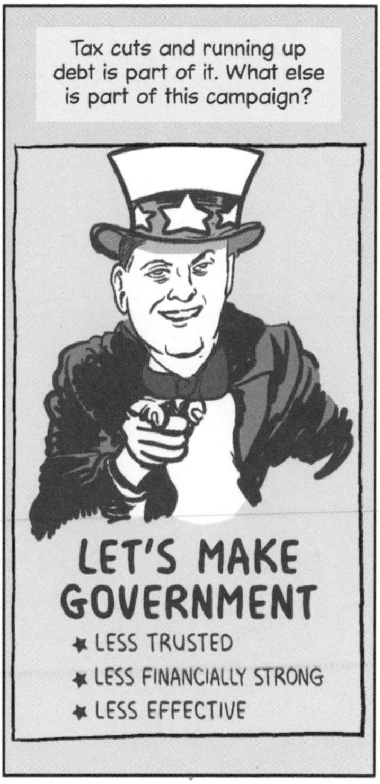
Tax cuts and running up debt is part of it. What else is part of this campaign?
LET'S MAKE GOVERNMENT
★ LESS TRUSTED
★ LESS FINANCIALLY STRONG
★ LESS EFFECTIVE

SABOTAGING GOVERNMENT'S SUCCESSES

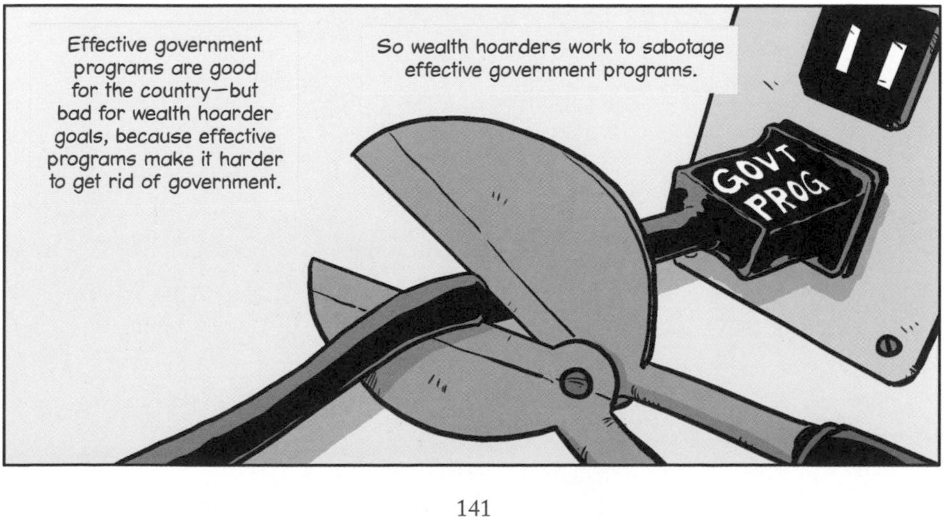
Effective government programs are good for the country—but bad for wealth hoarder goals, because effective programs make it harder to get rid of government.
So wealth hoarders work to sabotage effective government programs.
GOVT PROG

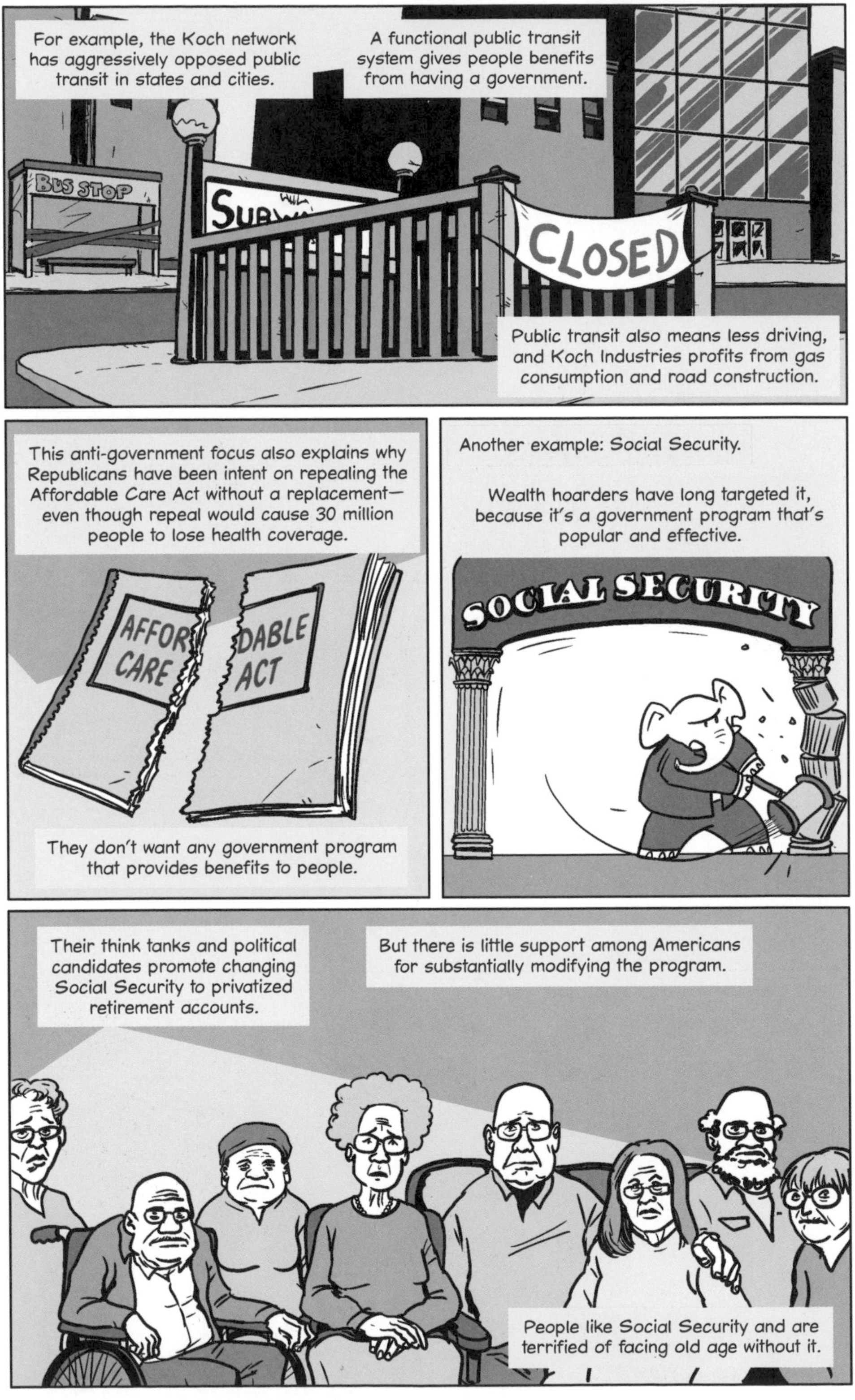
For example, the Koch network has aggressively opposed public transit in states and cities.
A functional public transit system gives people benefits from having a government.
BUS STOP
CLOSED
Public transit also means less driving, and Koch Industries profits from gas consumption and road construction.
This anti-government focus also explains why Republicans have been intent on repealing the Affordable Care Act without a replacement—even though repeal would cause 30 million people to lose health coverage.
AFFOR CARE
DABLE ACT
They don't want any government program that provides benefits to people.
Another example: Social Security.
Wealth hoarders have long targeted it, because it's a government program that's popular and effective.
SOCIAL SECURITY
Their think tanks and political candidates promote changing Social Security to privatized retirement accounts.
But there is little support among Americans for substantially modifying the program.
People like Social Security and are terrified of facing old age without it.

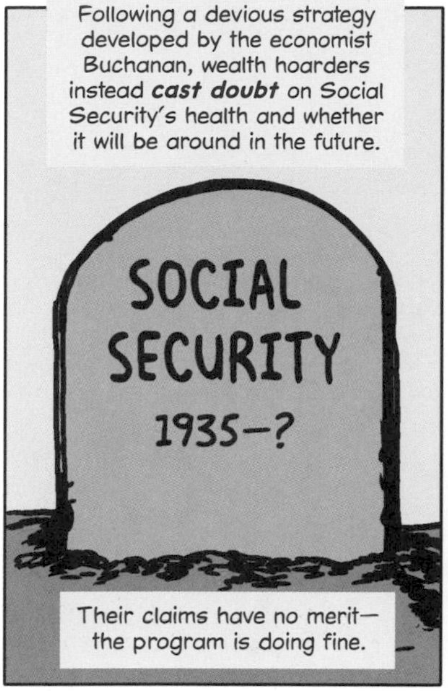
Following a devious strategy developed by the economist Buchanan, wealth hoarders instead ***cast doubt*** on Social Security's health and whether it will be around in the future.
SOCIAL SECURITY 1935–?
Their claims have no merit—the program is doing fine.

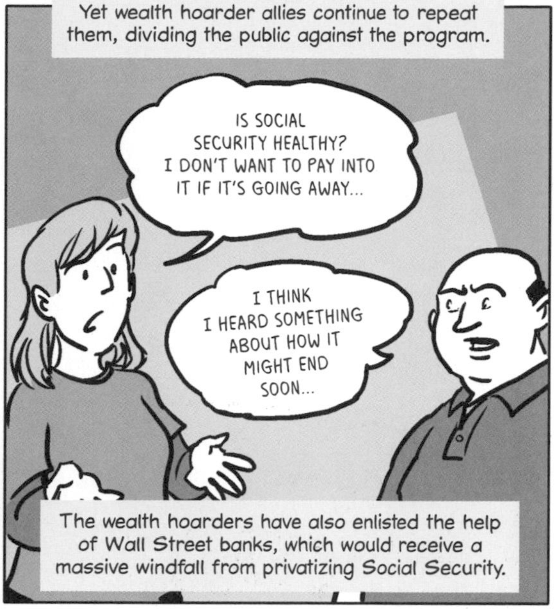
Yet wealth hoarder allies continue to repeat them, dividing the public against the program.
IS SOCIAL SECURITY HEALTHY? I DON'T WANT TO PAY INTO IT IF IT'S GOING AWAY...
I THINK I HEARD SOMETHING ABOUT HOW IT MIGHT END SOON...
The wealth hoarders have also enlisted the help of Wall Street banks, which would receive a massive windfall from privatizing Social Security.

PRIVATIZATION

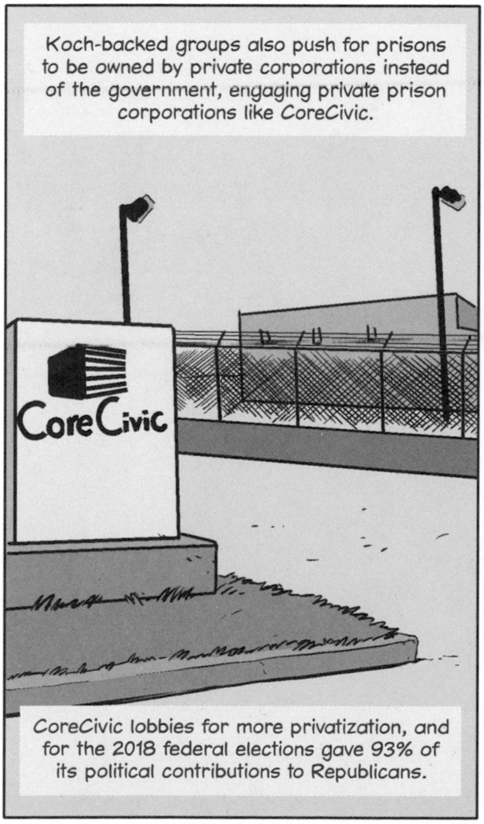
Koch-backed groups also push for prisons to be owned by private corporations instead of the government, engaging private prison corporations like CoreCivic.
CoreCivic
CoreCivic lobbies for more privatization, and for the 2018 federal elections gave 93% of its political contributions to Republicans.

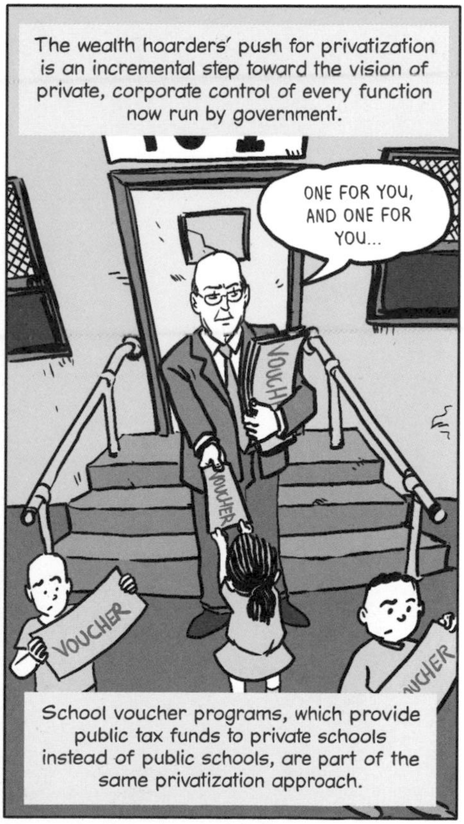
The wealth hoarders' push for privatization is an incremental step toward the vision of private, corporate control of every function now run by government.
ONE FOR YOU, AND ONE FOR YOU...
VOUCHER
VOUCHER
School voucher programs, which provide public tax funds to private schools instead of public schools, are part of the same privatization approach.

FUNDING CLIMATE CHANGE DENIAL

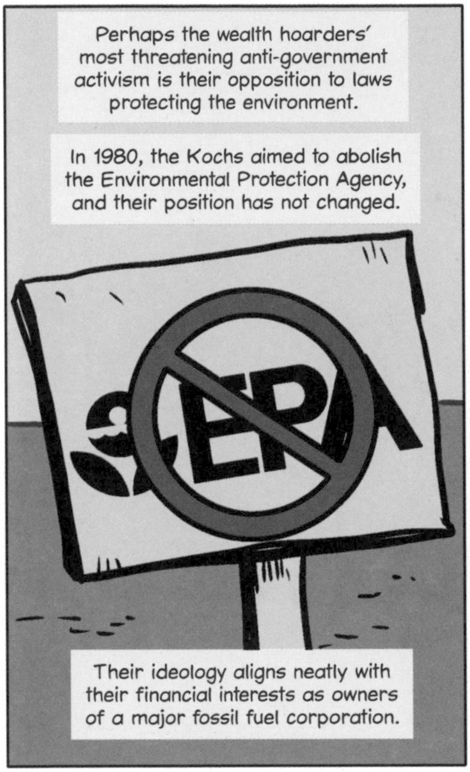
Perhaps the wealth hoarders' most threatening anti-government activism is their opposition to laws protecting the environment.
In 1980, the Kochs aimed to abolish the Environmental Protection Agency, and their position has not changed.
EPA
Their ideology aligns neatly with their financial interests as owners of a major fossil fuel corporation.

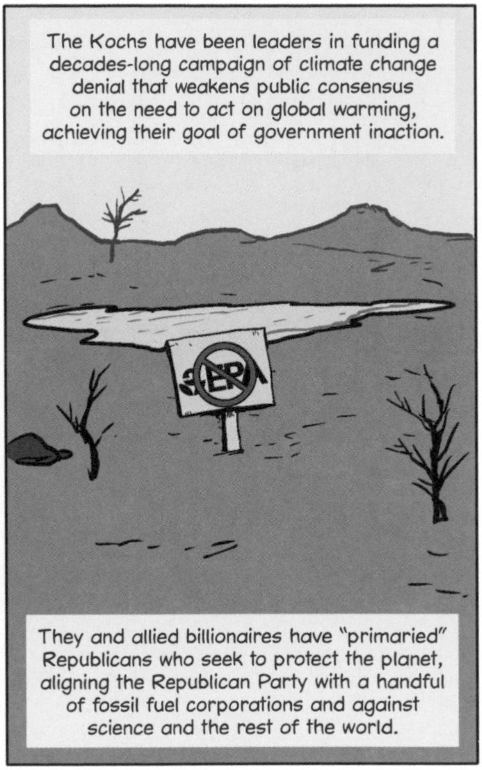
The Kochs have been leaders in funding a decades-long campaign of climate change denial that weakens public consensus on the need to act on global warming, achieving their goal of government inaction.
EPA
They and allied billionaires have "primaried" Republicans who seek to protect the planet, aligning the Republican Party with a handful of fossil fuel corporations and against science and the rest of the world.

BITTER NASTINESS AND PARTISANSHIP

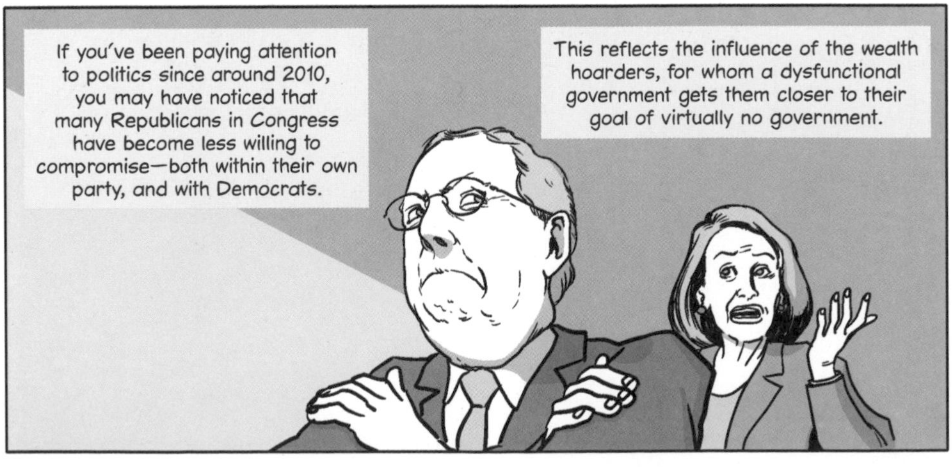
If you've been paying attention to politics since around 2010, you may have noticed that many Republicans in Congress have become less willing to compromise—both within their own party, and with Democrats.
This reflects the influence of the wealth hoarders, for whom a dysfunctional government gets them closer to their goal of virtually no government.

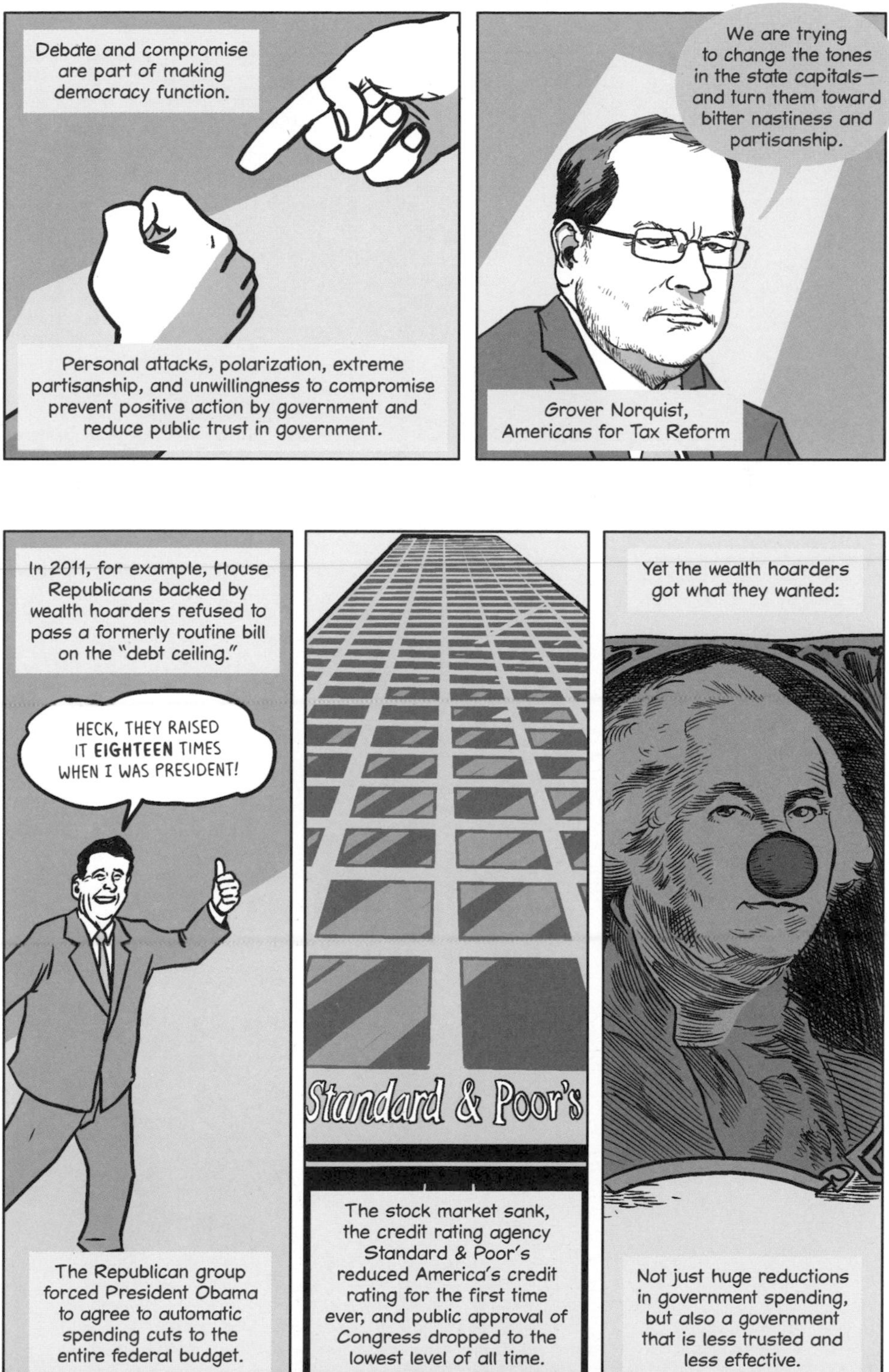
Debate and compromise are part of making democracy function.
Personal attacks, polarization, extreme partisanship, and unwillingness to compromise prevent positive action by government and reduce public trust in government.
We are trying to change the tones in the state capitals—and turn them toward bitter nastiness and partisanship.
Grover Norquist, Americans for Tax Reform
In 2011, for example, House Republicans backed by wealth hoarders refused to pass a formerly routine bill on the "debt ceiling."
HECK, THEY RAISED IT **EIGHTEEN** TIMES WHEN I WAS PRESIDENT!
The Republican group forced President Obama to agree to automatic spending cuts to the entire federal budget.
Standard & Poor's
The stock market sank, the credit rating agency Standard & Poor's reduced America's credit rating for the first time ever, and public approval of Congress dropped to the lowest level of all time.
Yet the wealth hoarders got what they wanted:
Not just huge reductions in government spending, but also a government that is less trusted and less effective.

DECREASING TRUST

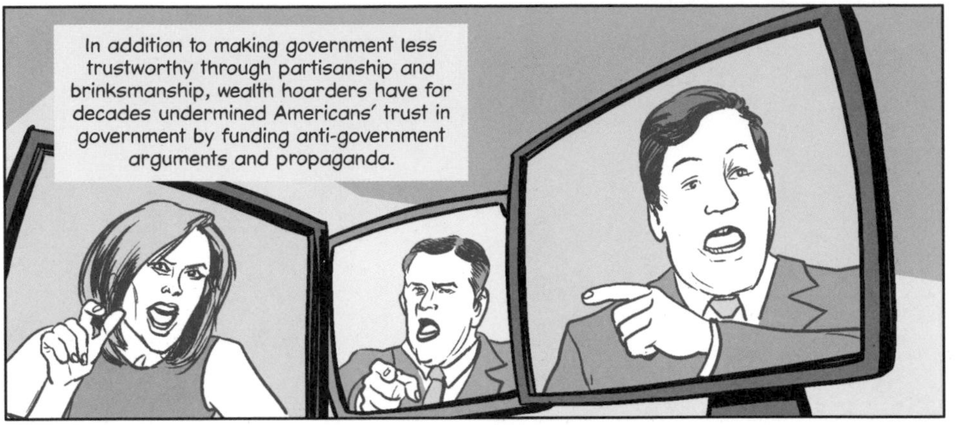
In addition to making government less trustworthy through partisanship and brinksmanship, wealth hoarders have for decades undermined Americans' trust in government by funding anti-government arguments and propaganda.

LAWBREAKERS

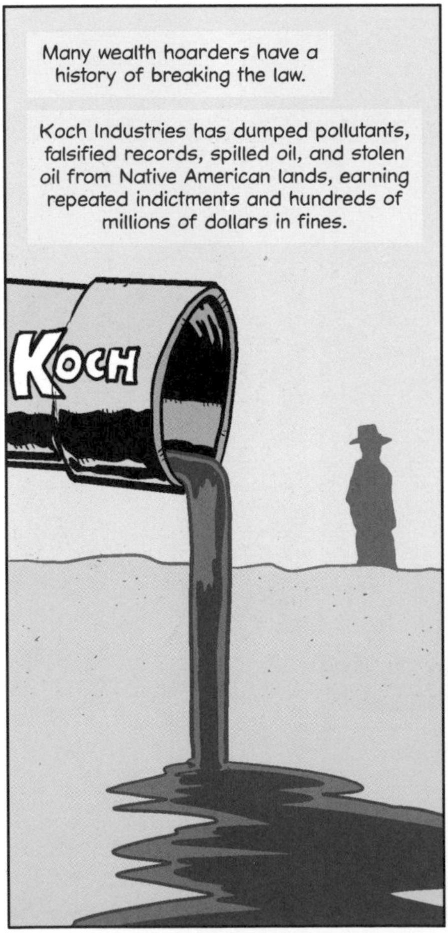
Many wealth hoarders have a history of breaking the law.
Koch Industries has dumped pollutants, falsified records, spilled oil, and stolen oil from Native American lands, earning repeated indictments and hundreds of millions of dollars in fines.
KOCH

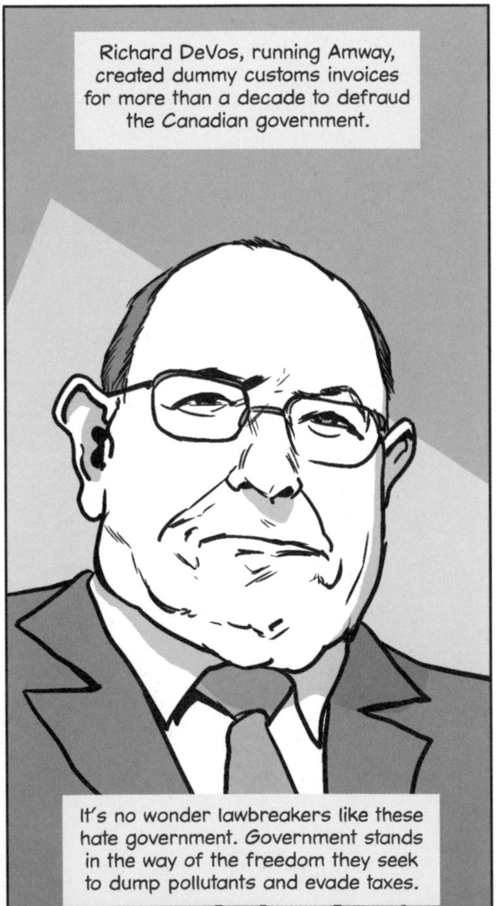
Richard DeVos, running Amway, created dummy customs invoices for more than a decade to defraud the Canadian government.
It's no wonder lawbreakers like these hate government. Government stands in the way of the freedom they seek to dump pollutants and evade taxes.

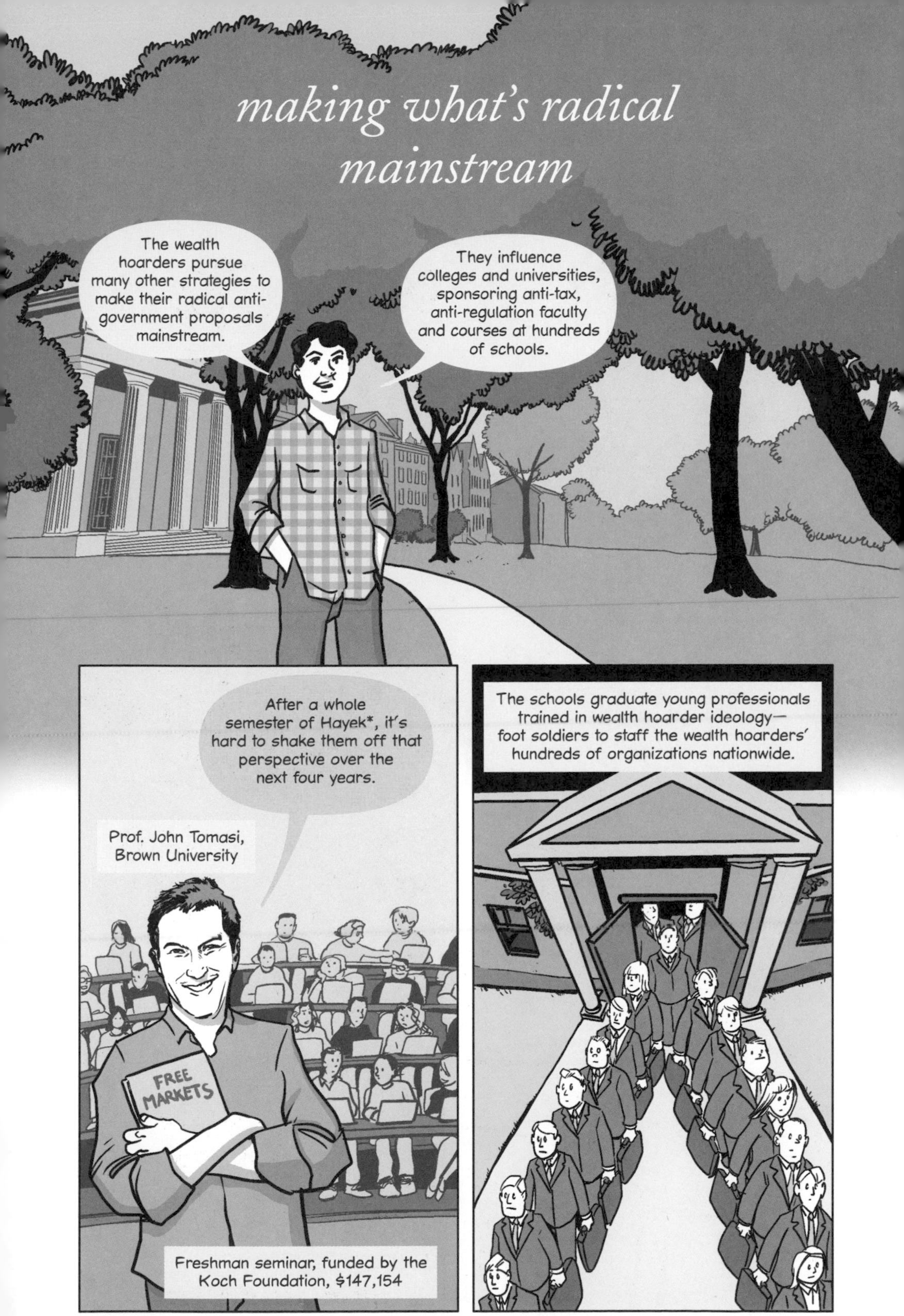
making what's radical mainstream
The wealth hoarders pursue many other strategies to make their radical anti-government proposals mainstream.
They influence colleges and universities, sponsoring anti-tax, anti-regulation faculty and courses at hundreds of schools.
After a whole semester of Hayek*, it's hard to shake them off that perspective over the next four years.
Prof. John Tomasi, Brown University
FREE MARKETS
Freshman seminar, funded by the Koch Foundation, $147,154
The schools graduate young professionals trained in wealth hoarder ideology— foot soldiers to staff the wealth hoarders' hundreds of organizations nationwide.

*Libertarian economist

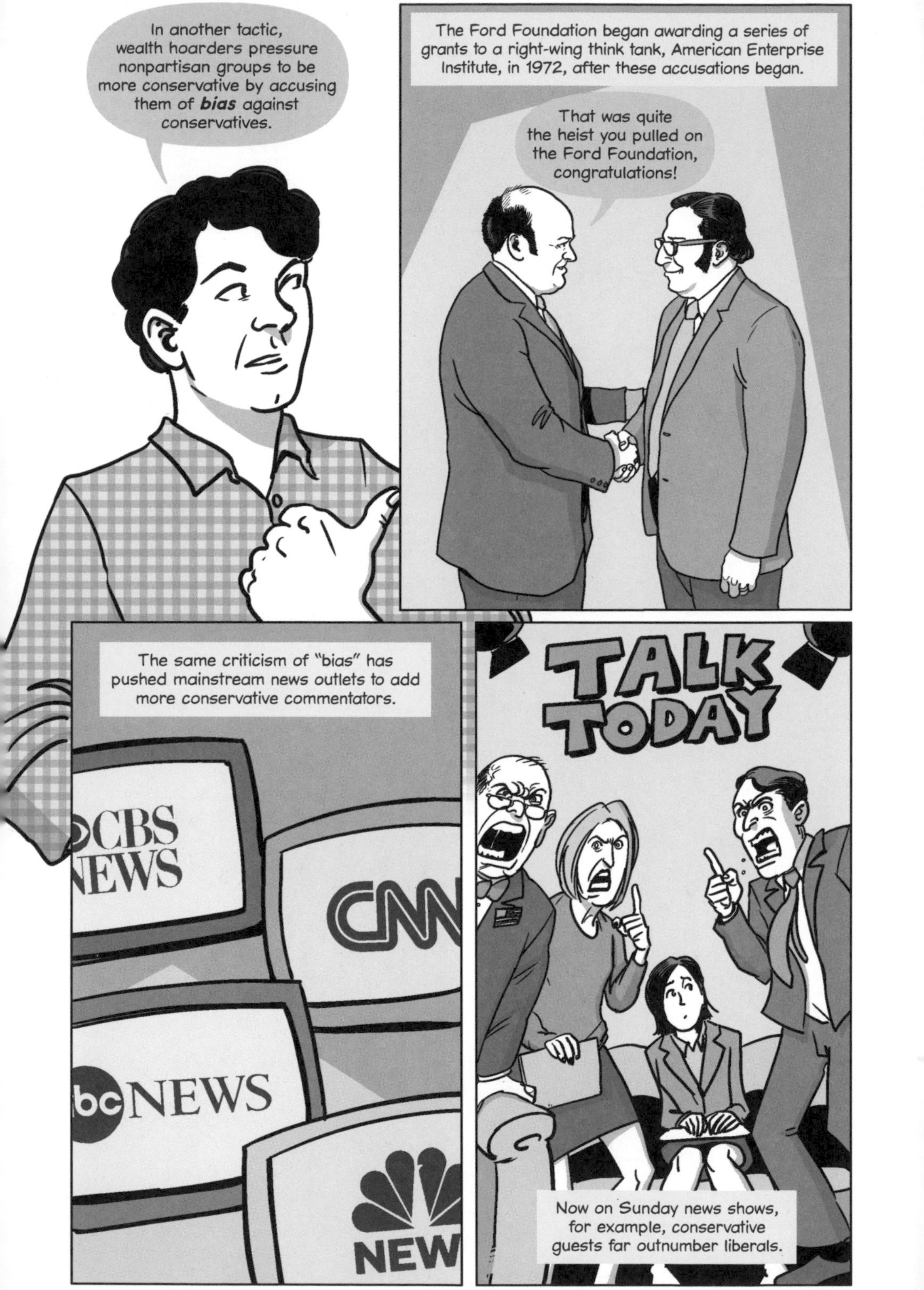
In another tactic, wealth hoarders pressure nonpartisan groups to be more conservative by accusing them of *bias* against conservatives.
The Ford Foundation began awarding a series of grants to a right-wing think tank, American Enterprise Institute, in 1972, after these accusations began.
That was quite the heist you pulled on the Ford Foundation, congratulations!
The same criticism of "bias" has pushed mainstream news outlets to add more conservative commentators.
CBS NEWS
CNN
NEWS
NEW
TALK TODAY
Now on Sunday news shows, for example, conservative guests far outnumber liberals.

disabling democracy

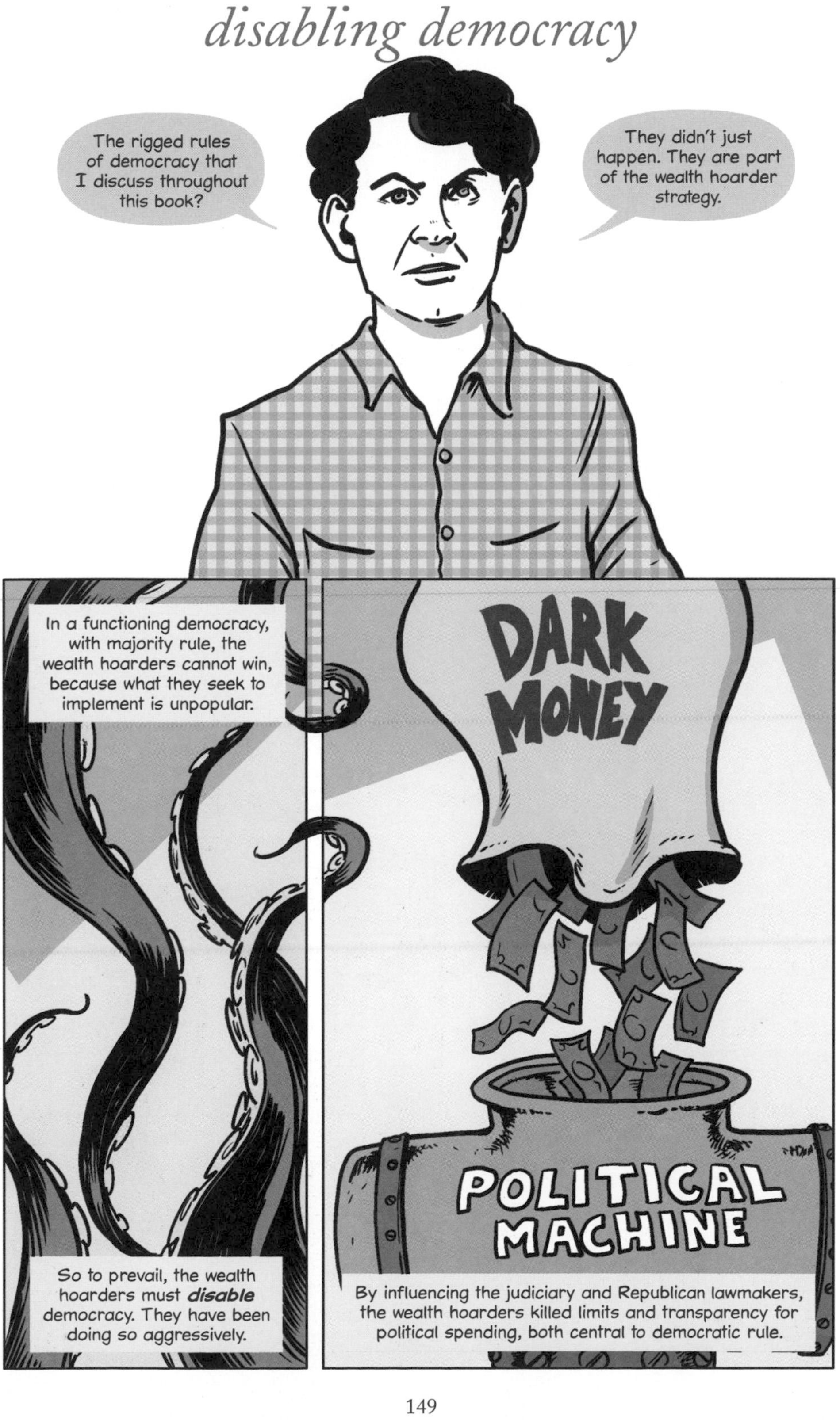

The rigged rules of democracy that I discuss throughout this book?
They didn't just happen. They are part of the wealth hoarder strategy.
In a functioning democracy, with majority rule, the wealth hoarders cannot win, because what they seek to implement is unpopular.
So to prevail, the wealth hoarders must ***disable*** democracy. They have been doing so aggressively.
DARK MONEY
POLITICAL MACHINE
By influencing the judiciary and Republican lawmakers, the wealth hoarders killed limits and transparency for political spending, both central to democratic rule.

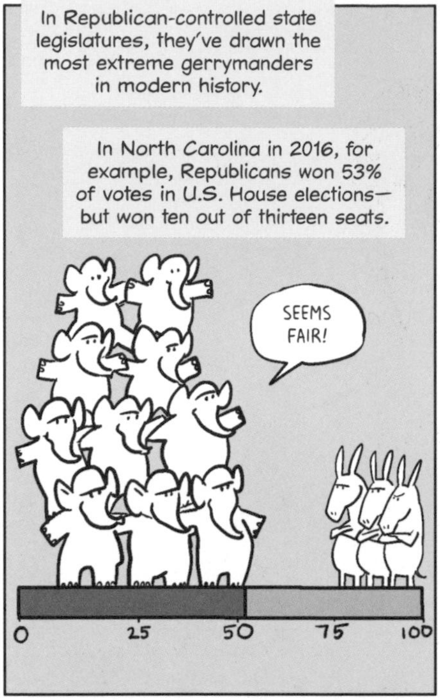
In Republican-controlled state legislatures, they've drawn the most extreme gerrymanders in modern history.
In North Carolina in 2016, for example, Republicans won 53% of votes in U.S. House elections—but won ten out of thirteen seats.
SEEMS FAIR!
0
25
50
75
100

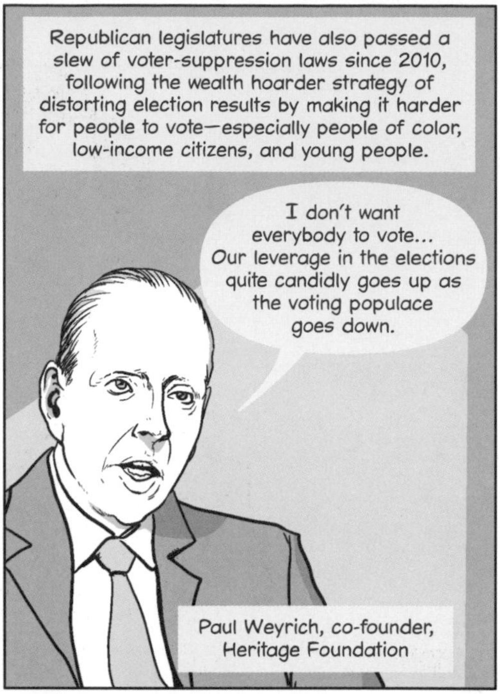
Republican legislatures have also passed a slew of voter-suppression laws since 2010, following the wealth hoarder strategy of distorting election results by making it harder for people to vote—especially people of color, low-income citizens, and young people.
I don't want everybody to vote... Our leverage in the elections quite candidly goes up as the voting populace goes down.
Paul Weyrich, co-founder, Heritage Foundation

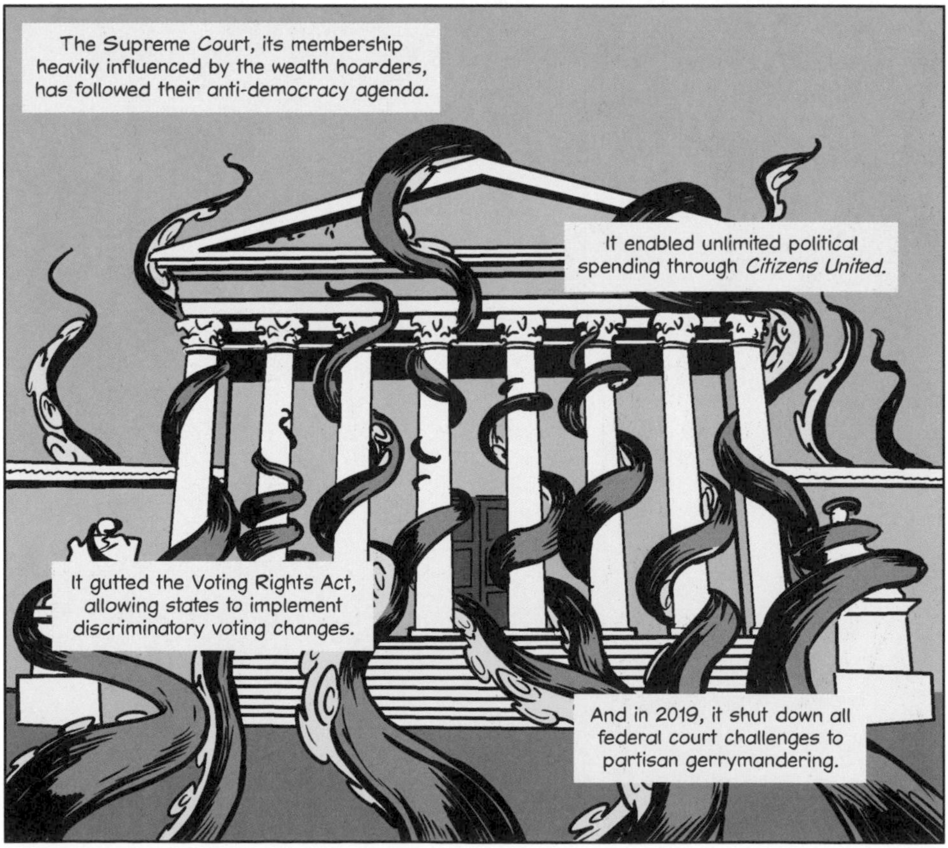
The Supreme Court, its membership heavily influenced by the wealth hoarders, has followed their anti-democracy agenda.
It enabled unlimited political spending through *Citizens United.*
It gutted the Voting Rights Act, allowing states to implement discriminatory voting changes.
And in 2019, it shut down all federal court challenges to partisan gerrymandering.

LOCKING DOWN THE CONSTITUTION

The wealth hoarders' ultimate goal: changing the U.S. Constitution to shackle American democracy so that it benefits the very wealthy and is forever unresponsive to the peoples' will.

Their proposed constitutional changes include:

• Slashing income taxes and eliminating estate taxes.

• Requiring a balanced budget.

Passage of this amendment would force immediate, radical cuts to government spending, with Social Security benefits among the many casualties.

• State legislators, not the people, electing U.S. senators.

The U.S. Constitution allows for a convention to propose changes to it, without going through Congress, if two-thirds of states (that's thirty-four states) agree.

Article. V.

two thirds of both Houses shall deem it necessary, shall propose
several States, shall call a Convention for proposing Amendm
ion, when ratified by the Legislatures of three fourths of the several
proposed by the Congress: Provided that no Amendment which

Lest you think this plan is just a fantasy, twenty-eight states have already passed resolutions for a convention, and the amendments above come from a 2013 book that was a number-one bestseller.

LIBERTY AMENDMENTS

151

the wealth hoarders' endgame

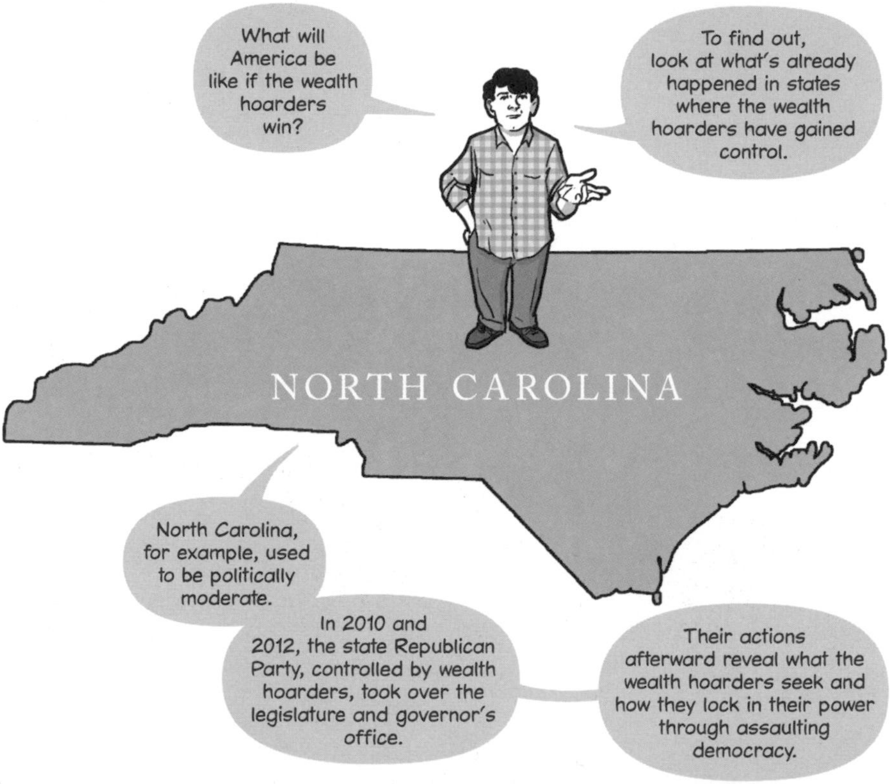

What will America be like if the wealth hoarders win?
To find out, look at what's already happened in states where the wealth hoarders have gained control.
NORTH CAROLINA
North Carolina, for example, used to be politically moderate.
In 2010 and 2012, the state Republican Party, controlled by wealth hoarders, took over the legislature and governor's office.
Their actions afterward reveal what the wealth hoarders seek and how they lock in their power through assaulting democracy.

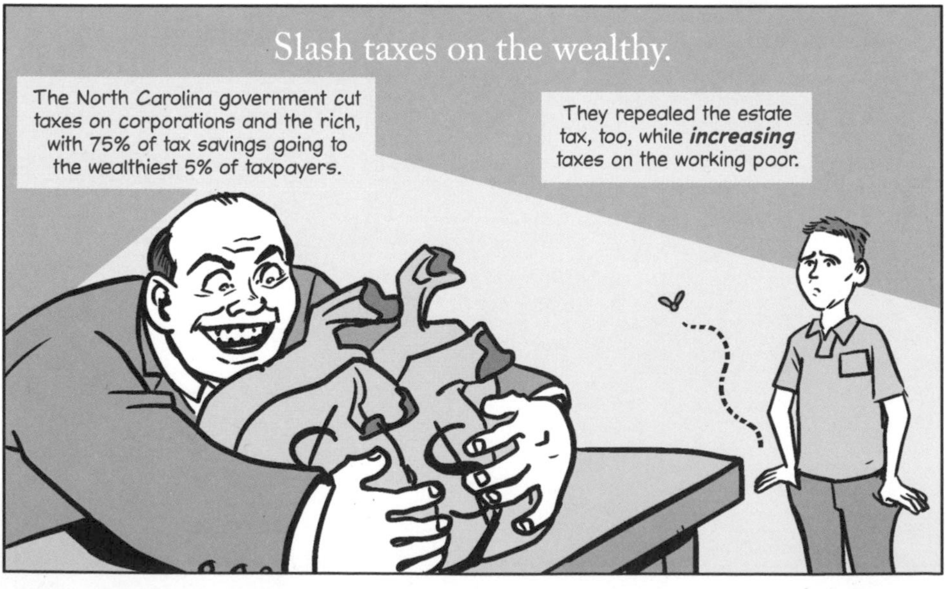

Slash taxes on the wealthy.
The North Carolina government cut taxes on corporations and the rich, with 75% of tax savings going to the wealthiest 5% of taxpayers.
They repealed the estate tax, too, while ***increasing*** taxes on the working poor.

If you're sick and can't pay for medical treatment, tough luck.

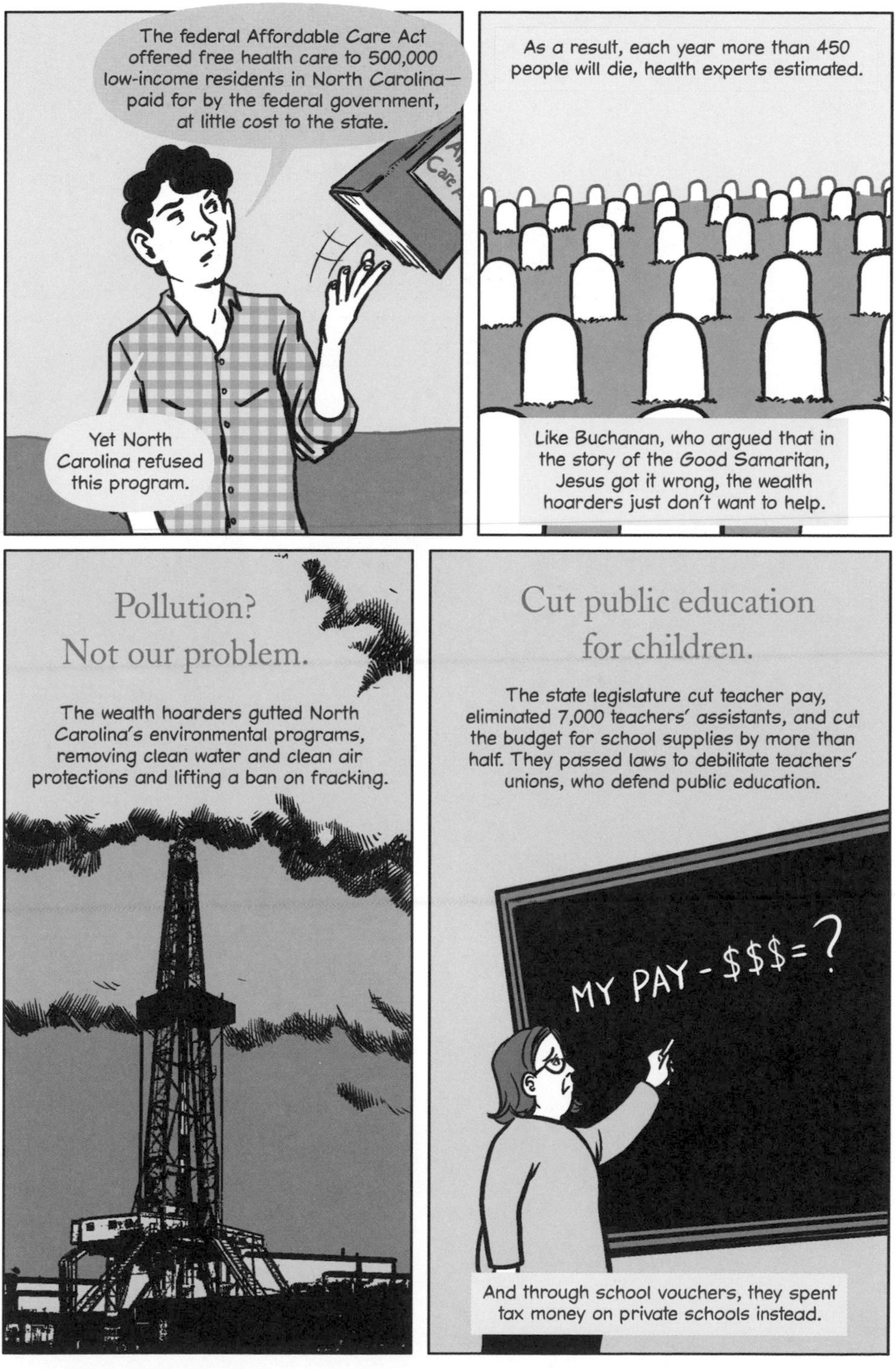

The federal Affordable Care Act offered free health care to 500,000 low-income residents in North Carolina—paid for by the federal government, at little cost to the state.
Yet North Carolina refused this program.
As a result, each year more than 450 people will die, health experts estimated.
Like Buchanan, who argued that in the story of the Good Samaritan, Jesus got it wrong, the wealth hoarders just don't want to help.
Pollution? Not our problem.
The wealth hoarders gutted North Carolina's environmental programs, removing clean water and clean air protections and lifting a ban on fracking.
Cut public education for children.
The state legislature cut teacher pay, eliminated 7,000 teachers' assistants, and cut the budget for school supplies by more than half. They passed laws to debilitate teachers' unions, who defend public education.
MY PAY - $$$ = ?
And through school vouchers, they spent tax money on private schools instead.

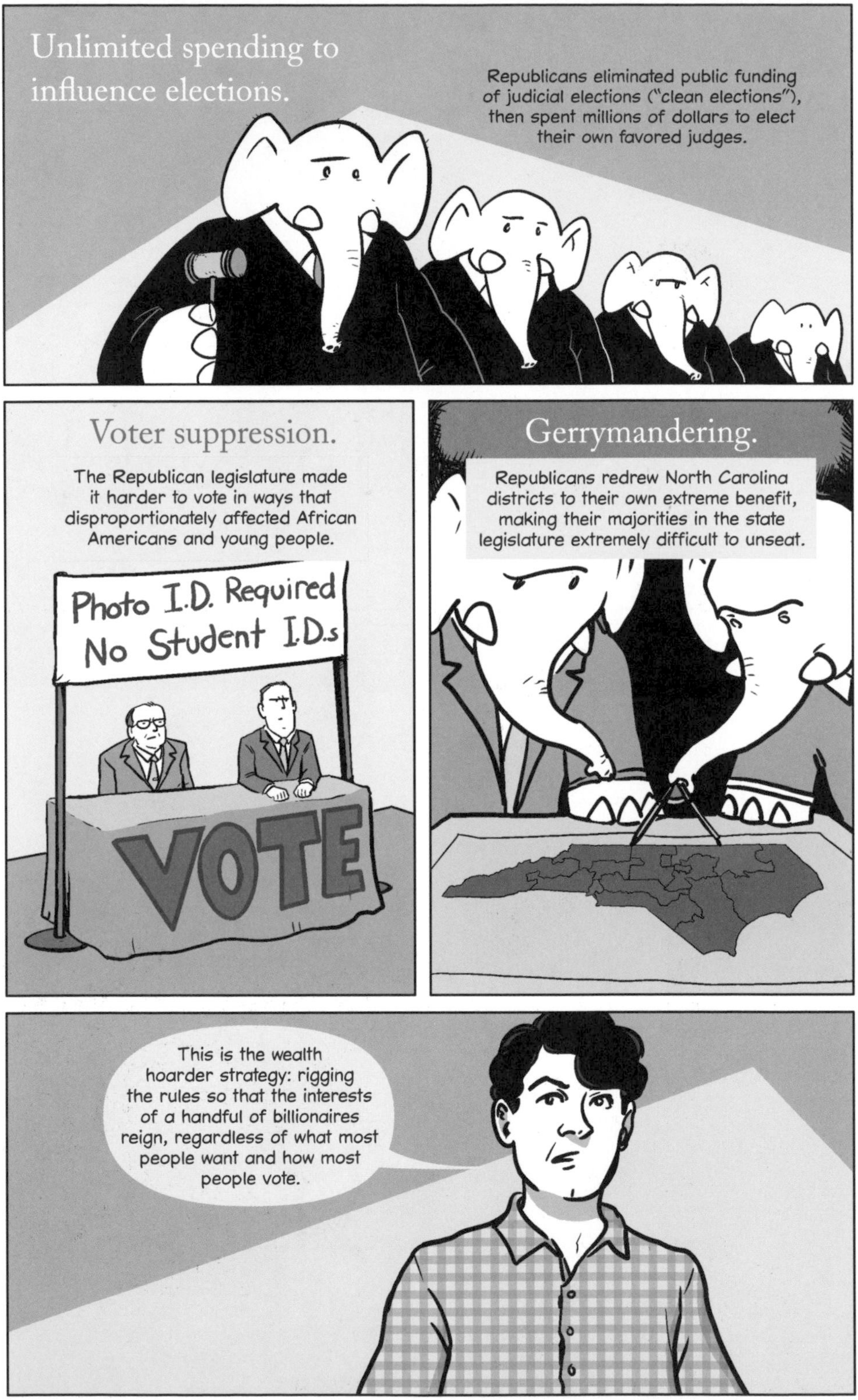

Unlimited spending to influence elections.
Republicans eliminated public funding of judicial elections ("clean elections"), then spent millions of dollars to elect their own favored judges.
Voter suppression.
The Republican legislature made it harder to vote in ways that disproportionately affected African Americans and young people.
Photo I.D. Required
No Student I.D.s
VOTE
Gerrymandering.
Republicans redrew North Carolina districts to their own extreme benefit, making their majorities in the state legislature extremely difficult to unseat.
This is the wealth hoarder strategy: rigging the rules so that the interests of a handful of billionaires reign, regardless of what most people want and how most people vote.

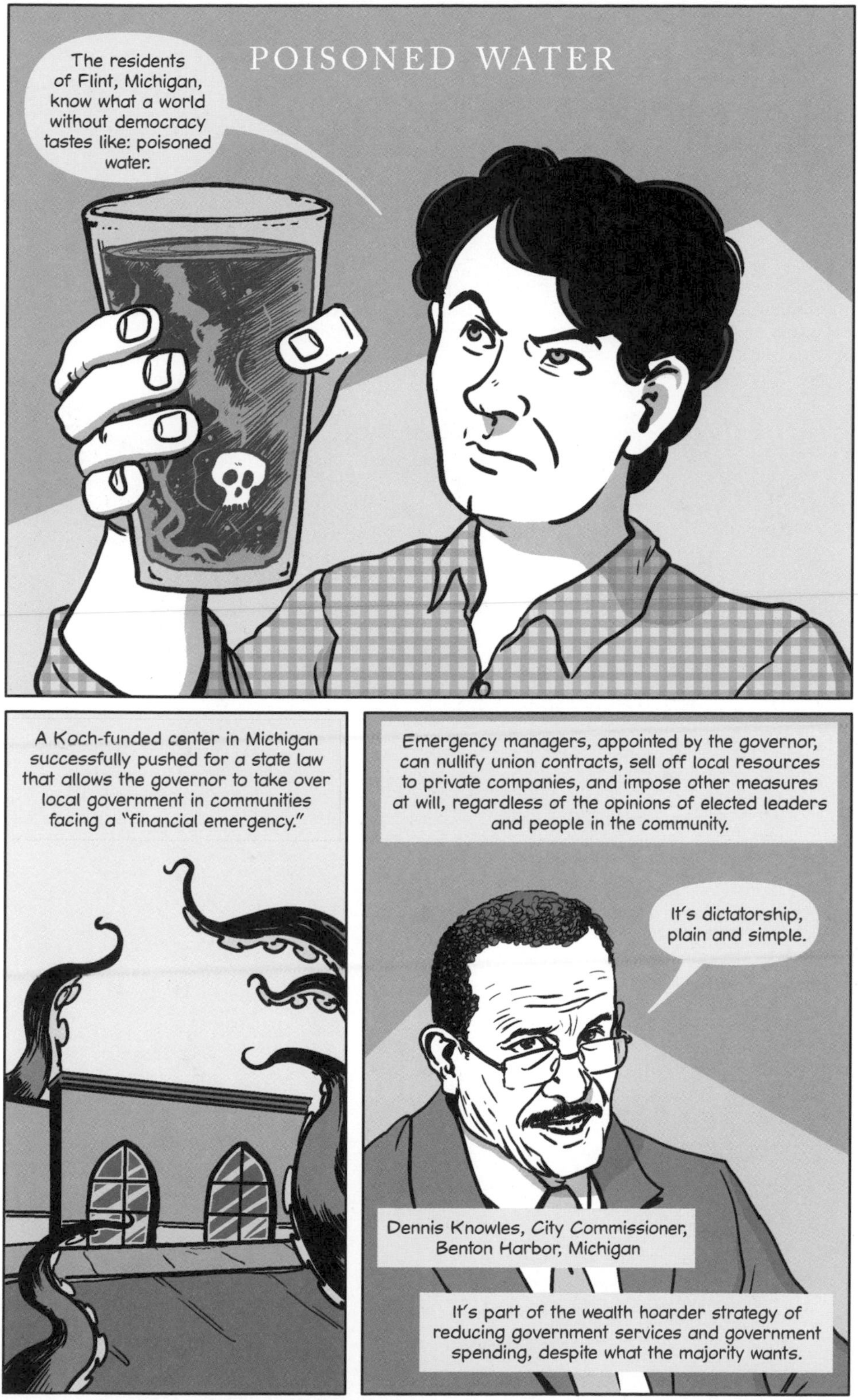
POISONED WATER
The residents of Flint, Michigan, know what a world without democracy tastes like: poisoned water.
A Koch-funded center in Michigan successfully pushed for a state law that allows the governor to take over local government in communities facing a "financial emergency."
Emergency managers, appointed by the governor, can nullify union contracts, sell off local resources to private companies, and impose other measures at will, regardless of the opinions of elected leaders and people in the community.
It's dictatorship, plain and simple.
Dennis Knowles, City Commissioner, Benton Harbor, Michigan
It's part of the wealth hoarder strategy of reducing government services and government spending, despite what the majority wants.

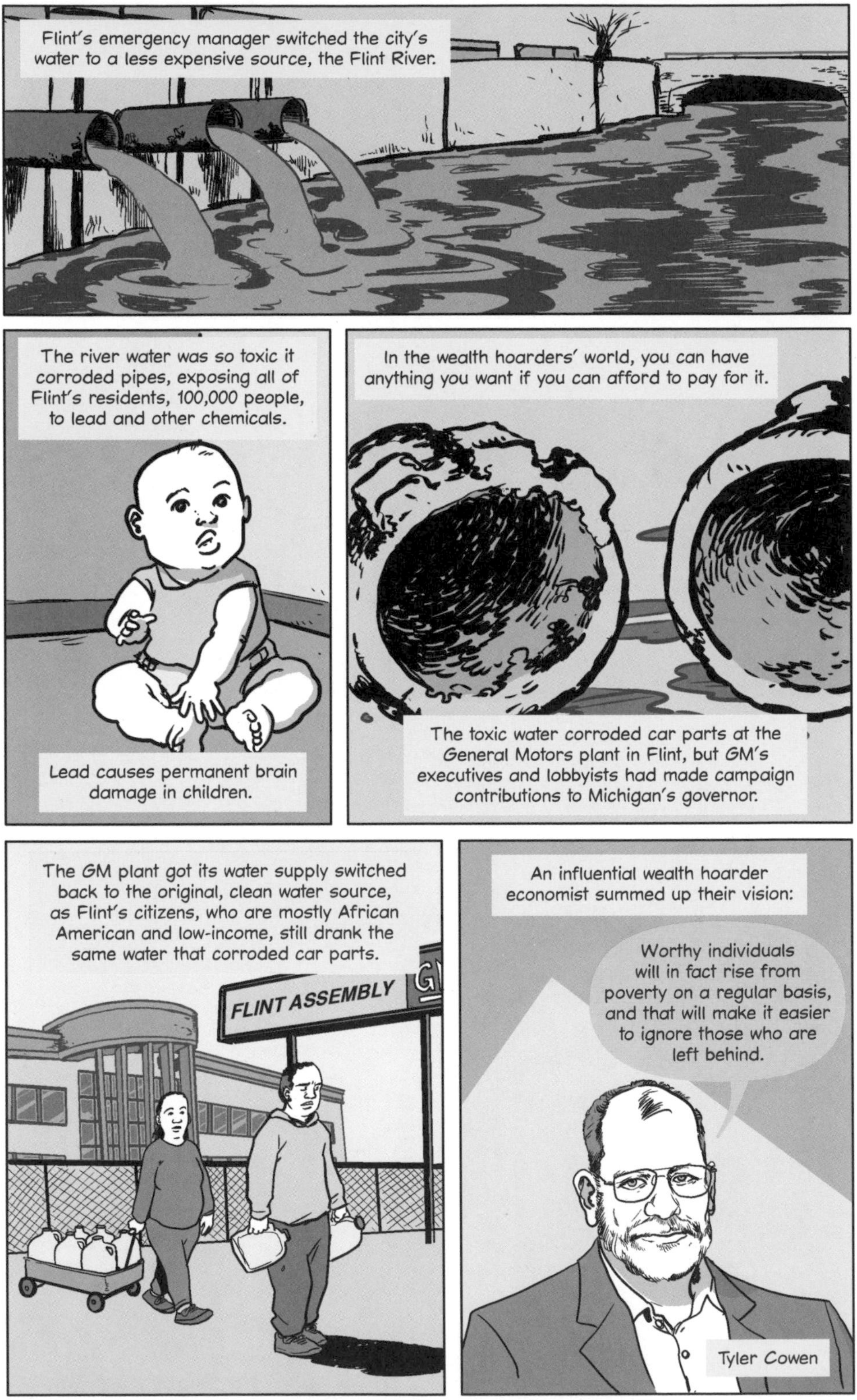
Flint's emergency manager switched the city's water to a less expensive source, the Flint River.
The river water was so toxic it corroded pipes, exposing all of Flint's residents, 100,000 people, to lead and other chemicals.
Lead causes permanent brain damage in children.
In the wealth hoarders' world, you can have anything you want if you can afford to pay for it.
The toxic water corroded car parts at the General Motors plant in Flint, but GM's executives and lobbyists had made campaign contributions to Michigan's governor.
The GM plant got its water supply switched back to the original, clean water source, as Flint's citizens, who are mostly African American and low-income, still drank the same water that corroded car parts.
FLINT ASSEMBLY
An influential wealth hoarder economist summed up their vision:
Worthy individuals will in fact rise from poverty on a regular basis, and that will make it easier to ignore those who are left behind.
Tyler Cowen

secrecy and coercion

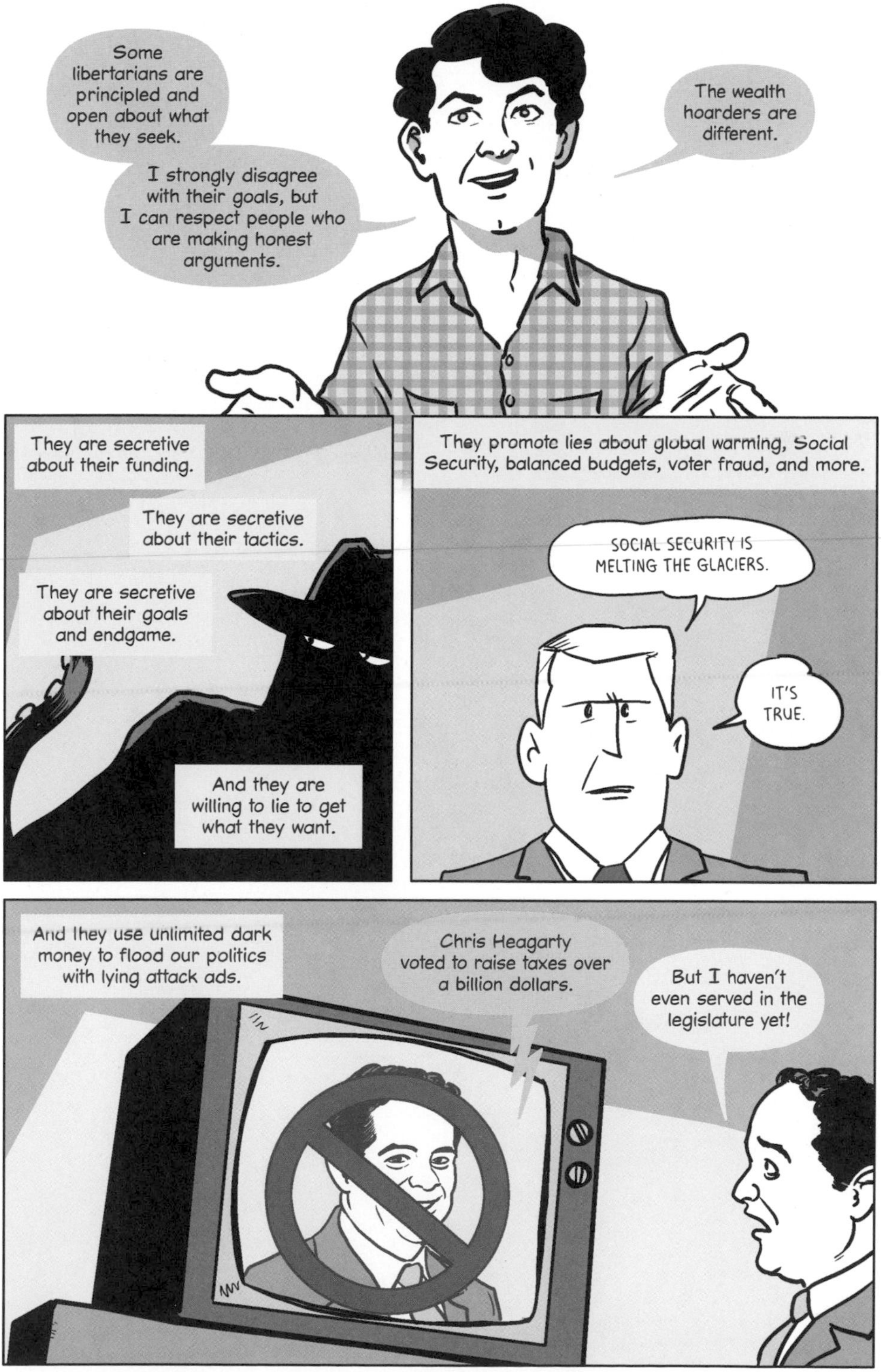
Some libertarians are principled and open about what they seek.
I strongly disagree with their goals, but I can respect people who are making honest arguments.
The wealth hoarders are different.
They are secretive about their funding.
They are secretive about their tactics.
They are secretive about their goals and endgame.
And they are willing to lie to get what they want.
They promote lies about global warming, Social Security, balanced budgets, voter fraud, and more.
SOCIAL SECURITY IS MELTING THE GLACIERS.
IT'S TRUE.
And they use unlimited dark money to flood our politics with lying attack ads.
Chris Heagarty voted to raise taxes over a billion dollars.
But I haven't even served in the legislature yet!

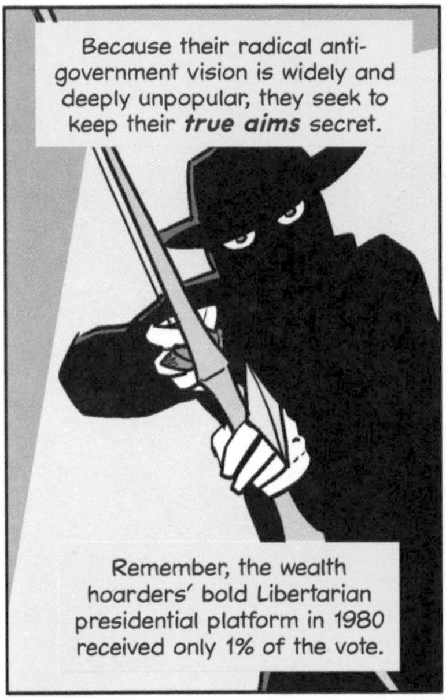
Because their radical anti-government vision is widely and deeply unpopular, they seek to keep their ***true aims*** secret.
Remember, the wealth hoarders' bold Libertarian presidential platform in 1980 received only 1% of the vote.

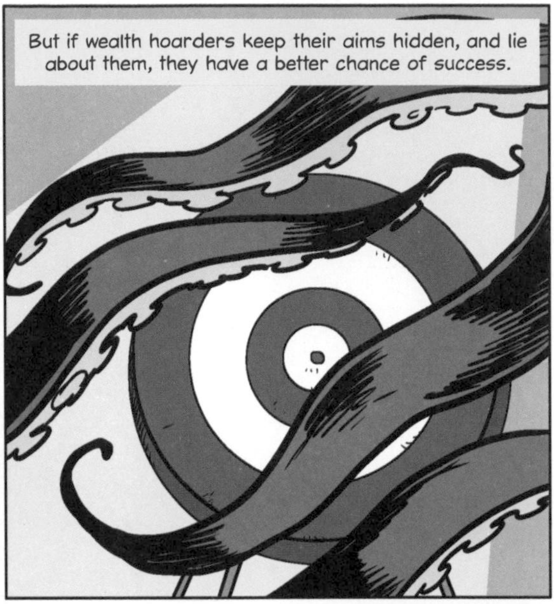
But if wealth hoarders keep their aims hidden, and lie about them, they have a better chance of success.

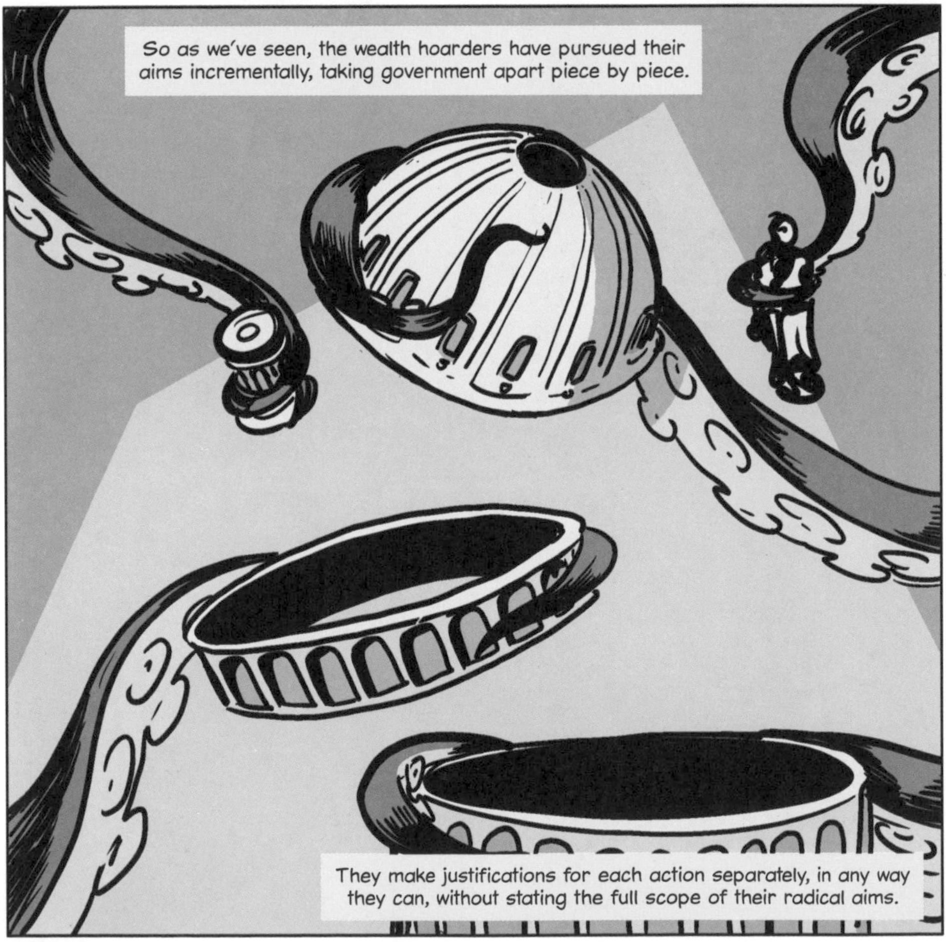
So as we've seen, the wealth hoarders have pursued their aims incrementally, taking government apart piece by piece.
They make justifications for each action separately, in any way they can, without stating the full scope of their radical aims.

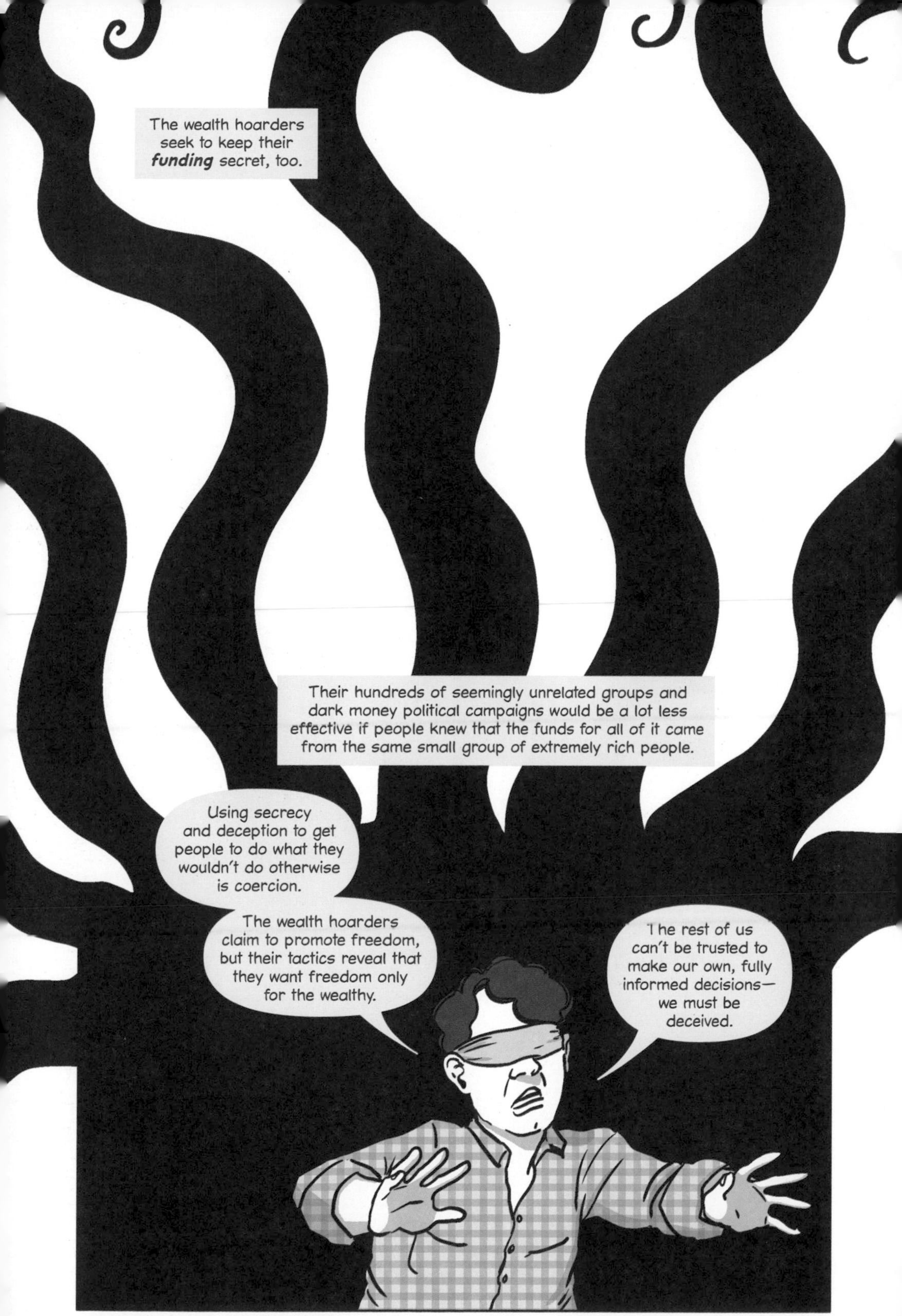
The wealth hoarders seek to keep their *funding* secret, too.
Their hundreds of seemingly unrelated groups and dark money political campaigns would be a lot less effective if people knew that the funds for all of it came from the same small group of extremely rich people.
Using secrecy and deception to get people to do what they wouldn't do otherwise is coercion.
The wealth hoarders claim to promote freedom, but their tactics reveal that they want freedom only for the wealthy.
The rest of us can't be trusted to make our own, fully informed decisions— we must be deceived.

image makeover

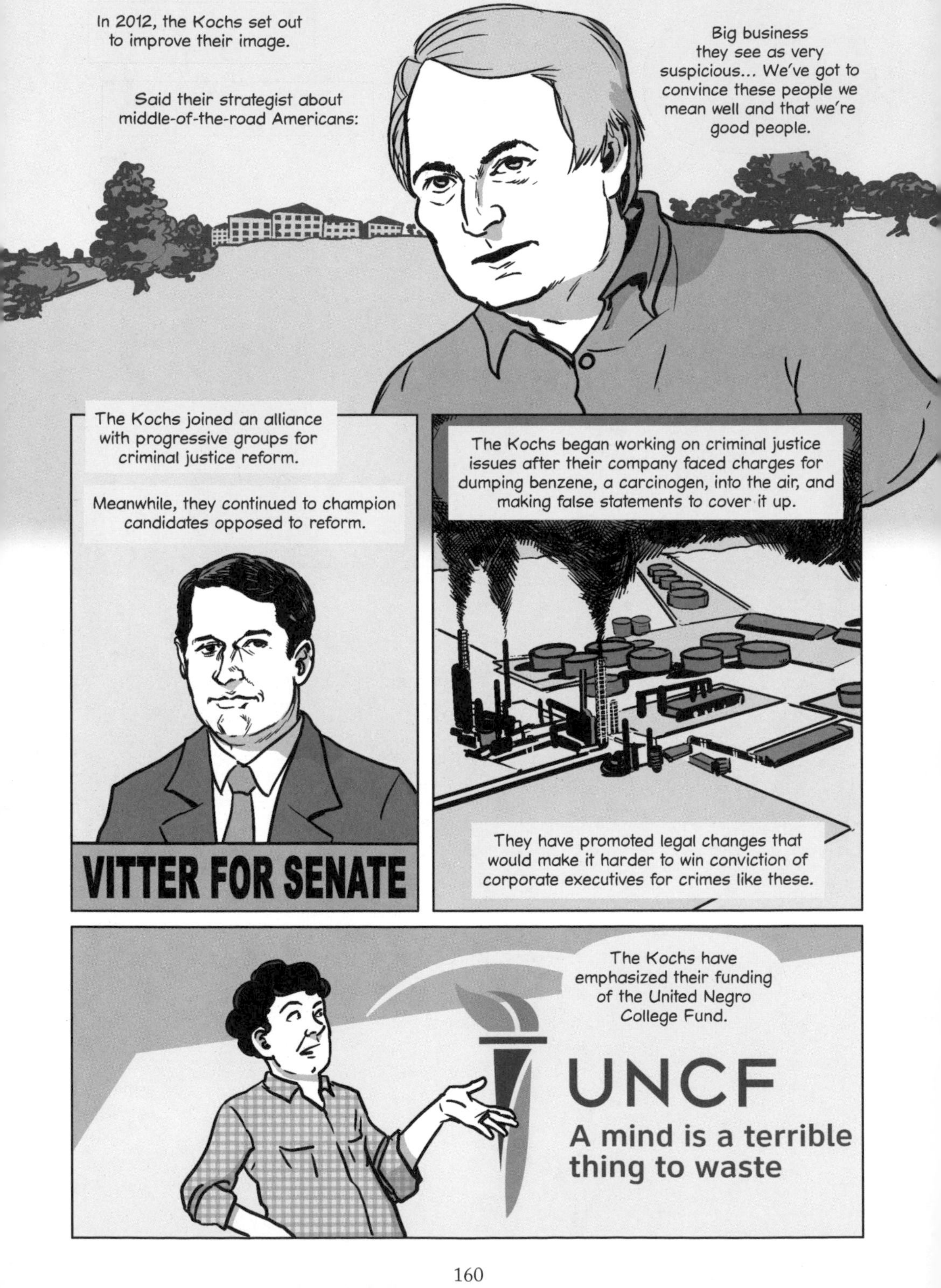
In 2012, the Kochs set out to improve their image.
Said their strategist about middle-of-the-road Americans:
Big business they see as very suspicious... We've got to convince these people we mean well and that we're good people.
The Kochs joined an alliance with progressive groups for criminal justice reform.
Meanwhile, they continued to champion candidates opposed to reform.
VITTER FOR SENATE
The Kochs began working on criminal justice issues after their company faced charges for dumping benzene, a carcinogen, into the air, and making false statements to cover it up.
They have promoted legal changes that would make it harder to win conviction of corporate executives for crimes like these.
The Kochs have emphasized their funding of the United Negro College Fund.
UNCF
A mind is a terrible thing to waste

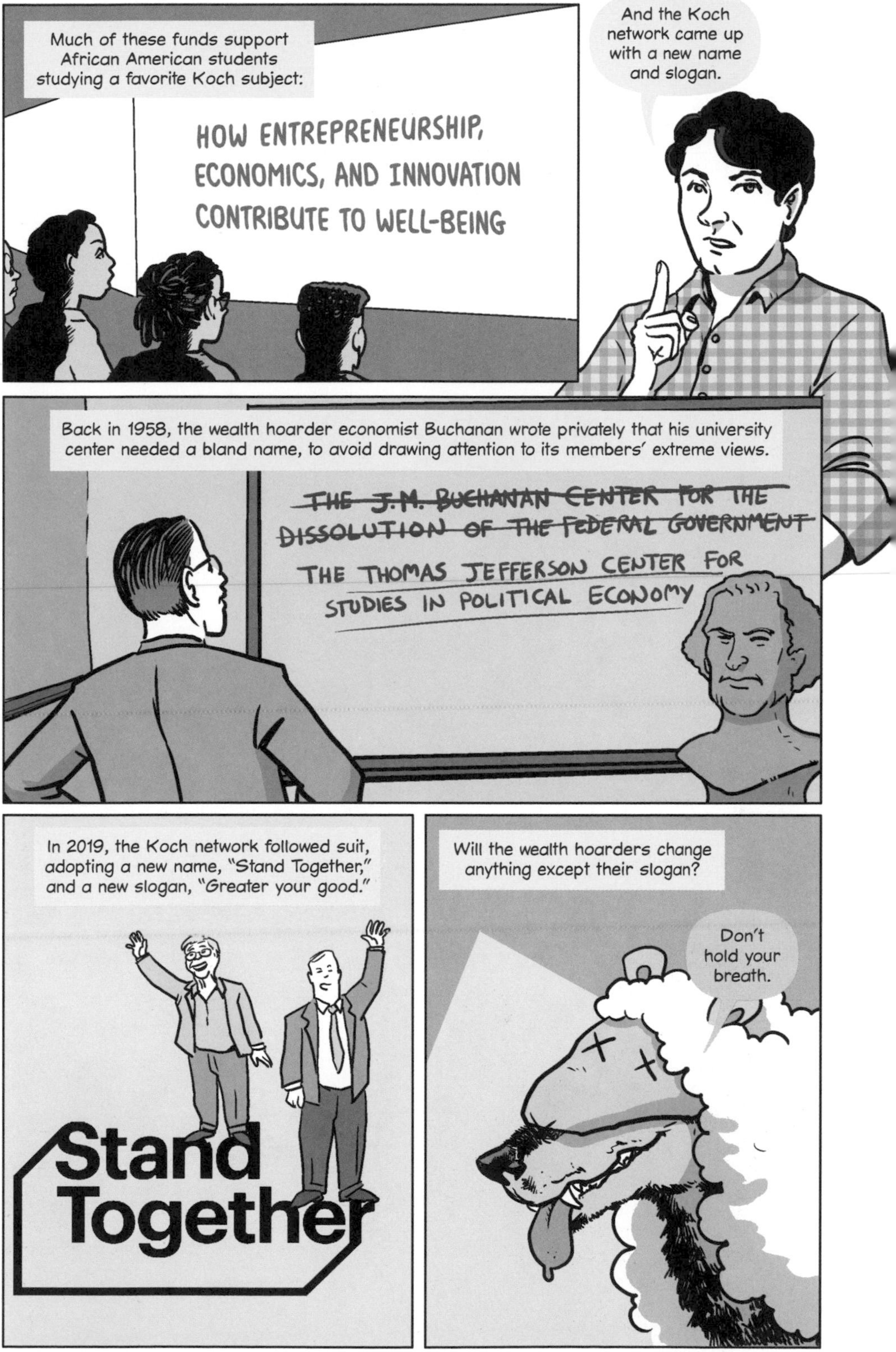
Much of these funds support African American students studying a favorite Koch subject:
HOW ENTREPRENEURSHIP, ECONOMICS, AND INNOVATION CONTRIBUTE TO WELL-BEING
And the Koch network came up with a new name and slogan.
Back in 1958, the wealth hoarder economist Buchanan wrote privately that his university center needed a bland name, to avoid drawing attention to its members' extreme views.
THE J.M. BUCHANAN CENTER FOR THE DISSOLUTION OF THE FEDERAL GOVERNMENT
THE THOMAS JEFFERSON CENTER FOR STUDIES IN POLITICAL ECONOMY
In 2019, the Koch network followed suit, adopting a new name, "Stand Together," and a new slogan, "Greater your good."
Stand Together
Will the wealth hoarders change anything except their slogan?
Don't hold your breath.

how to fight back

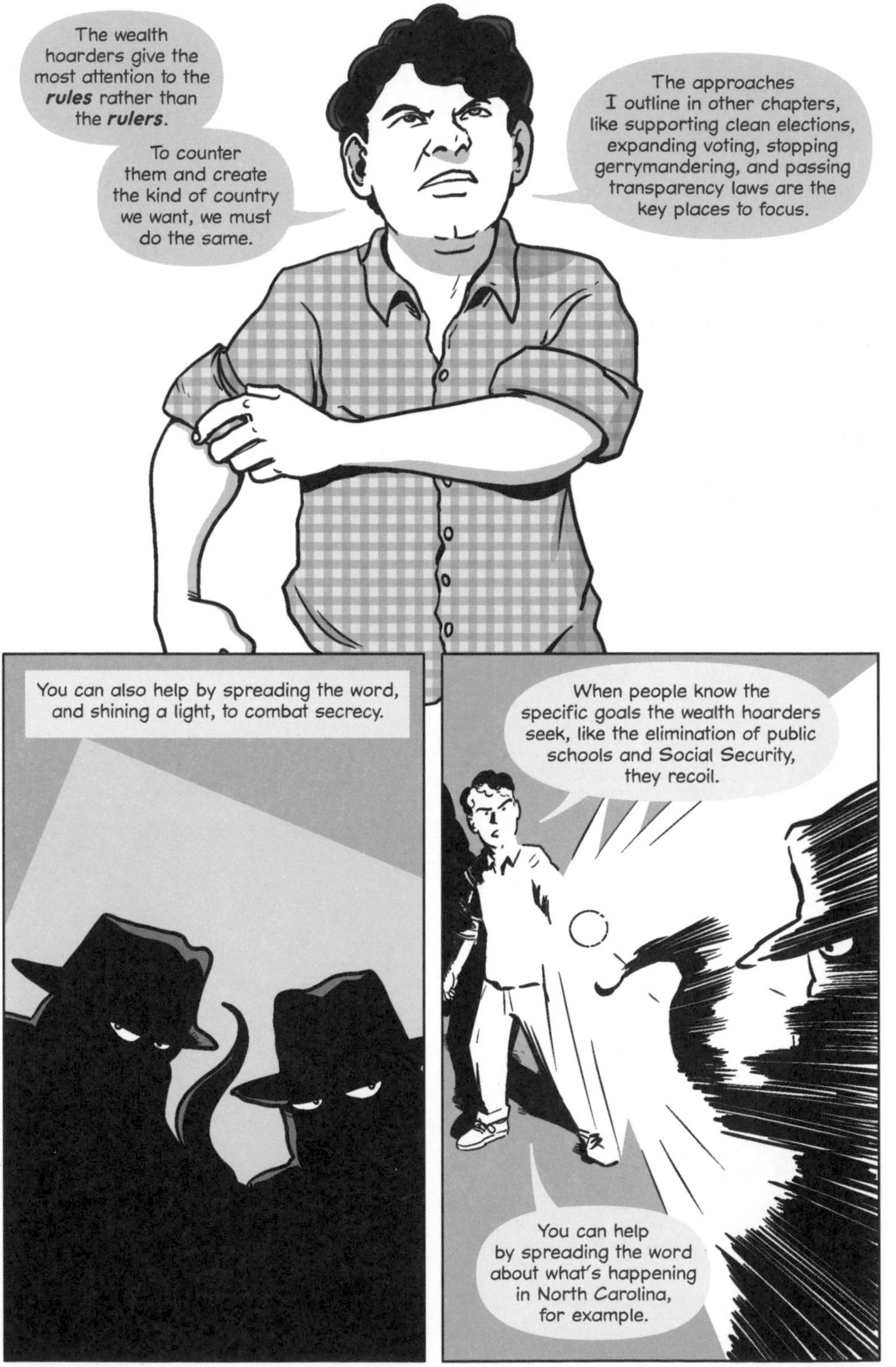

The wealth hoarders give the most attention to the ***rules*** rather than the ***rulers***.
To counter them and create the kind of country we want, we must do the same.
The approaches I outline in other chapters, like supporting clean elections, expanding voting, stopping gerrymandering, and passing transparency laws are the key places to focus.
You can also help by spreading the word, and shining a light, to combat secrecy.
When people know the specific goals the wealth hoarders seek, like the elimination of public schools and Social Security, they recoil.
You can help by spreading the word about what's happening in North Carolina, for example.

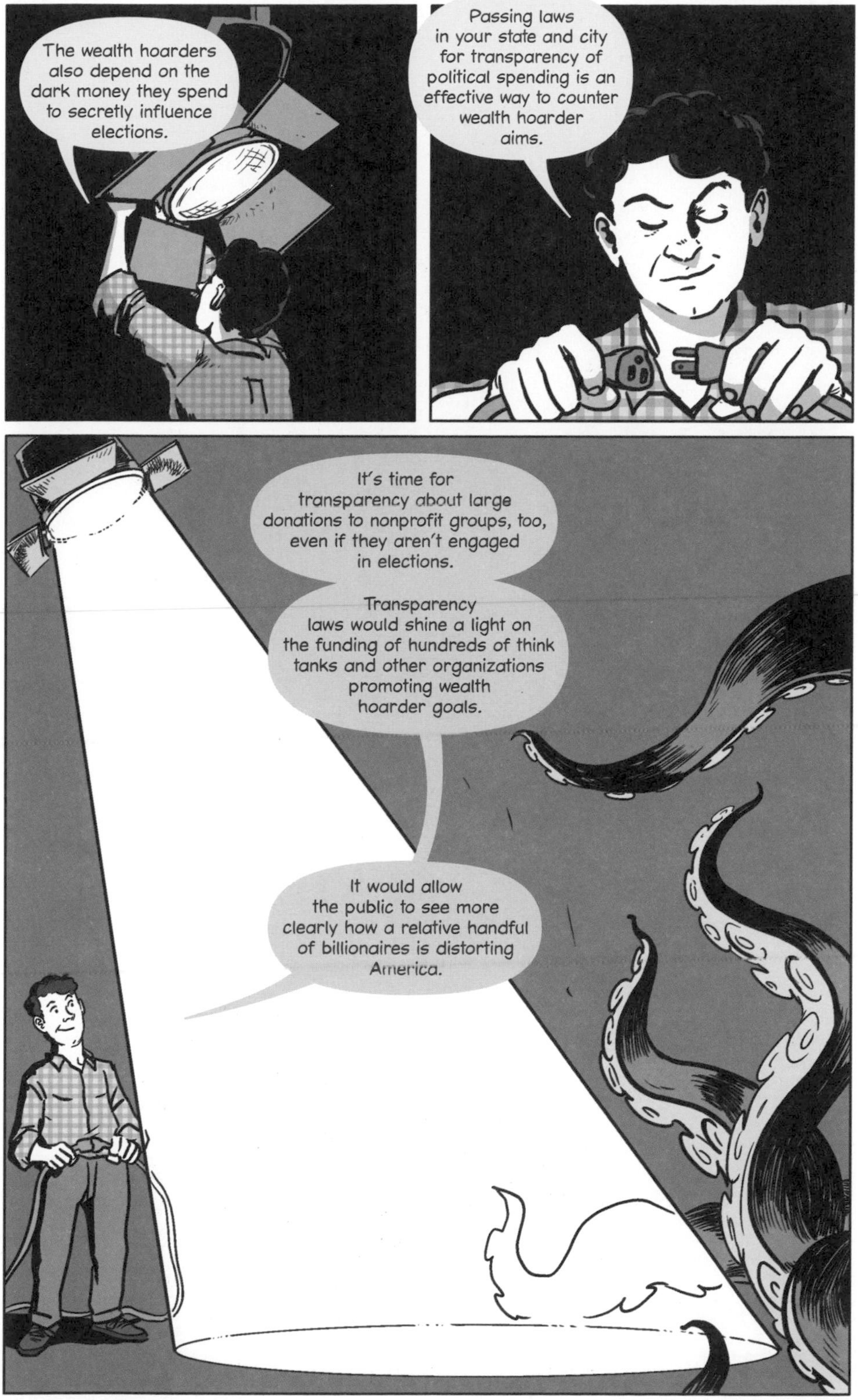
The wealth hoarders also depend on the dark money they spend to secretly influence elections.
Passing laws in your state and city for transparency of political spending is an effective way to counter wealth hoarder aims.
It's time for transparency about large donations to nonprofit groups, too, even if they aren't engaged in elections.
Transparency laws would shine a light on the funding of hundreds of think tanks and other organizations promoting wealth hoarder goals.
It would allow the public to see more clearly how a relative handful of billionaires is distorting America.

FOCUS ON YOUR STATE

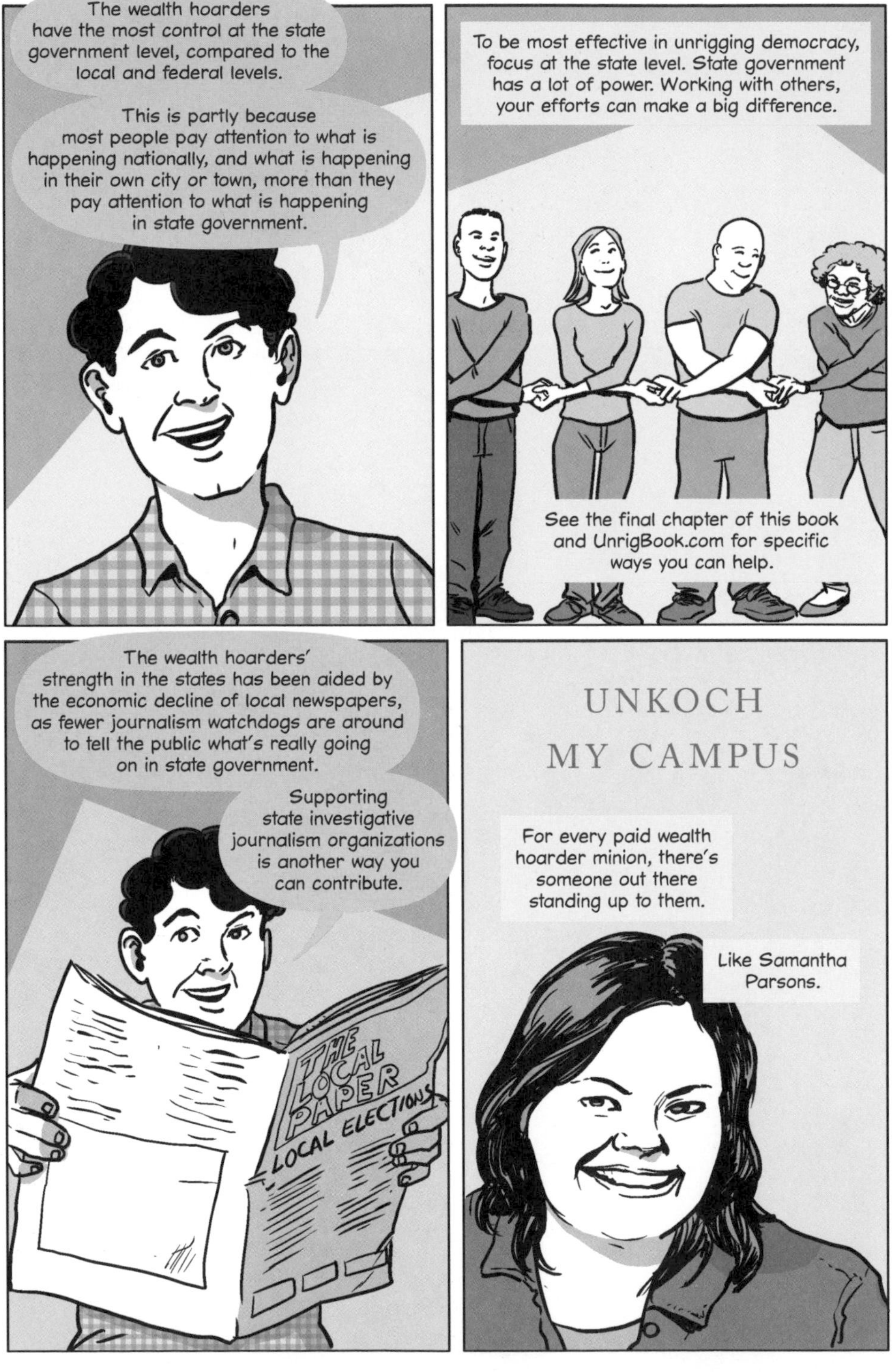

The wealth hoarders have the most control at the state government level, compared to the local and federal levels.
This is partly because most people pay attention to what is happening nationally, and what is happening in their own city or town, more than they pay attention to what is happening in state government.
To be most effective in unrigging democracy, focus at the state level. State government has a lot of power. Working with others, your efforts can make a big difference.
See the final chapter of this book and UnrigBook.com for specific ways you can help.
The wealth hoarders' strength in the states has been aided by the economic decline of local newspapers, as fewer journalism watchdogs are around to tell the public what's really going on in state government.
Supporting state investigative journalism organizations is another way you can contribute.
THE LOCAL PAPER
LOCAL ELECTIONS
UNKOCH MY CAMPUS
For every paid wealth hoarder minion, there's someone out there standing up to them.
Like Samantha Parsons.

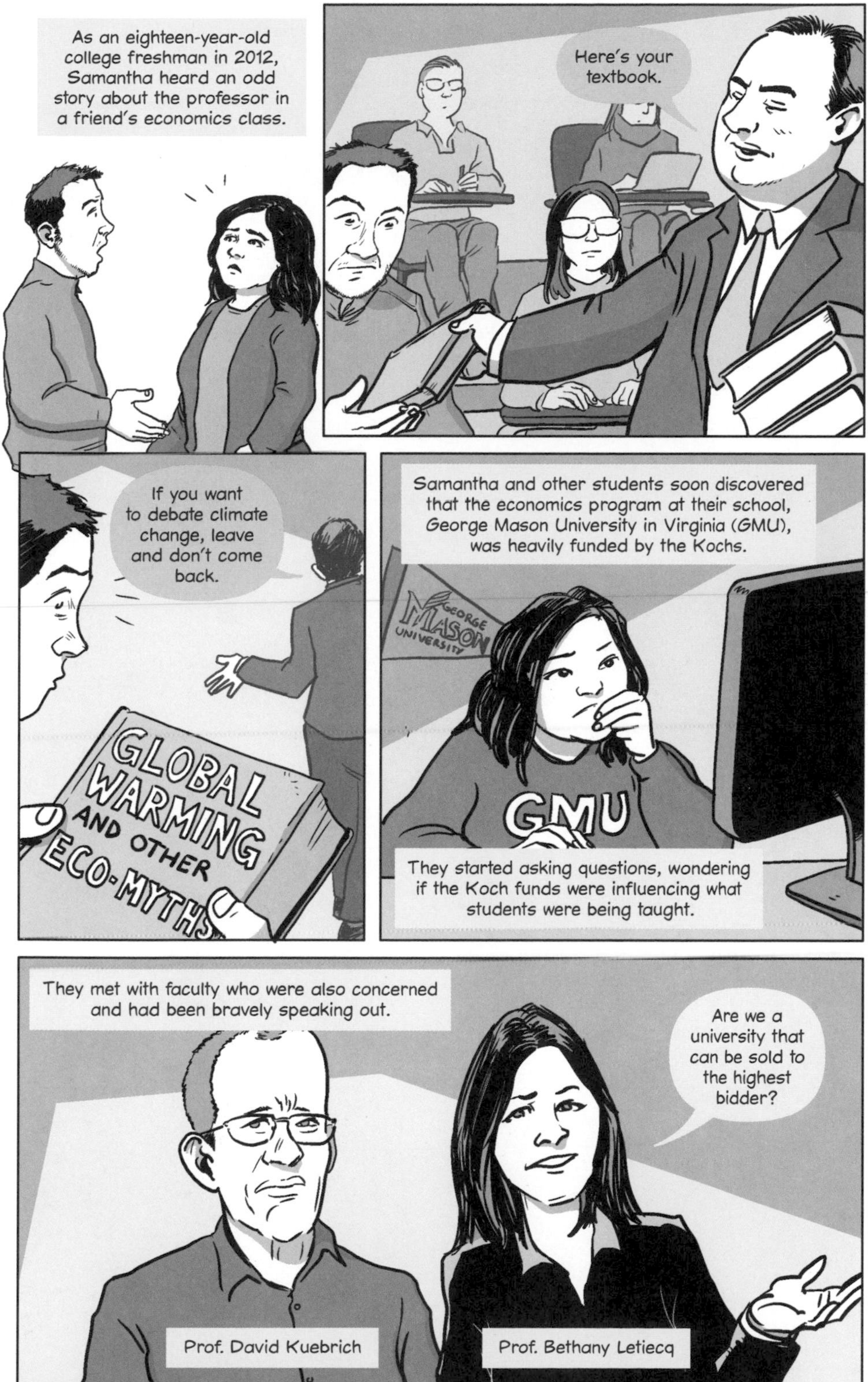

As an eighteen-year-old college freshman in 2012, Samantha heard an odd story about the professor in a friend's economics class.
Here's your textbook.
If you want to debate climate change, leave and don't come back.
GLOBAL WARMING AND OTHER ECO-MYTHS
Samantha and other students soon discovered that the economics program at their school, George Mason University in Virginia (GMU), was heavily funded by the Kochs.
GEORGE MASON UNIVERSITY
GMU
They started asking questions, wondering if the Koch funds were influencing what students were being taught.
They met with faculty who were also concerned and had been bravely speaking out.
Are we a university that can be sold to the highest bidder?
Prof. David Kuebrich
Prof. Bethany Letiecq

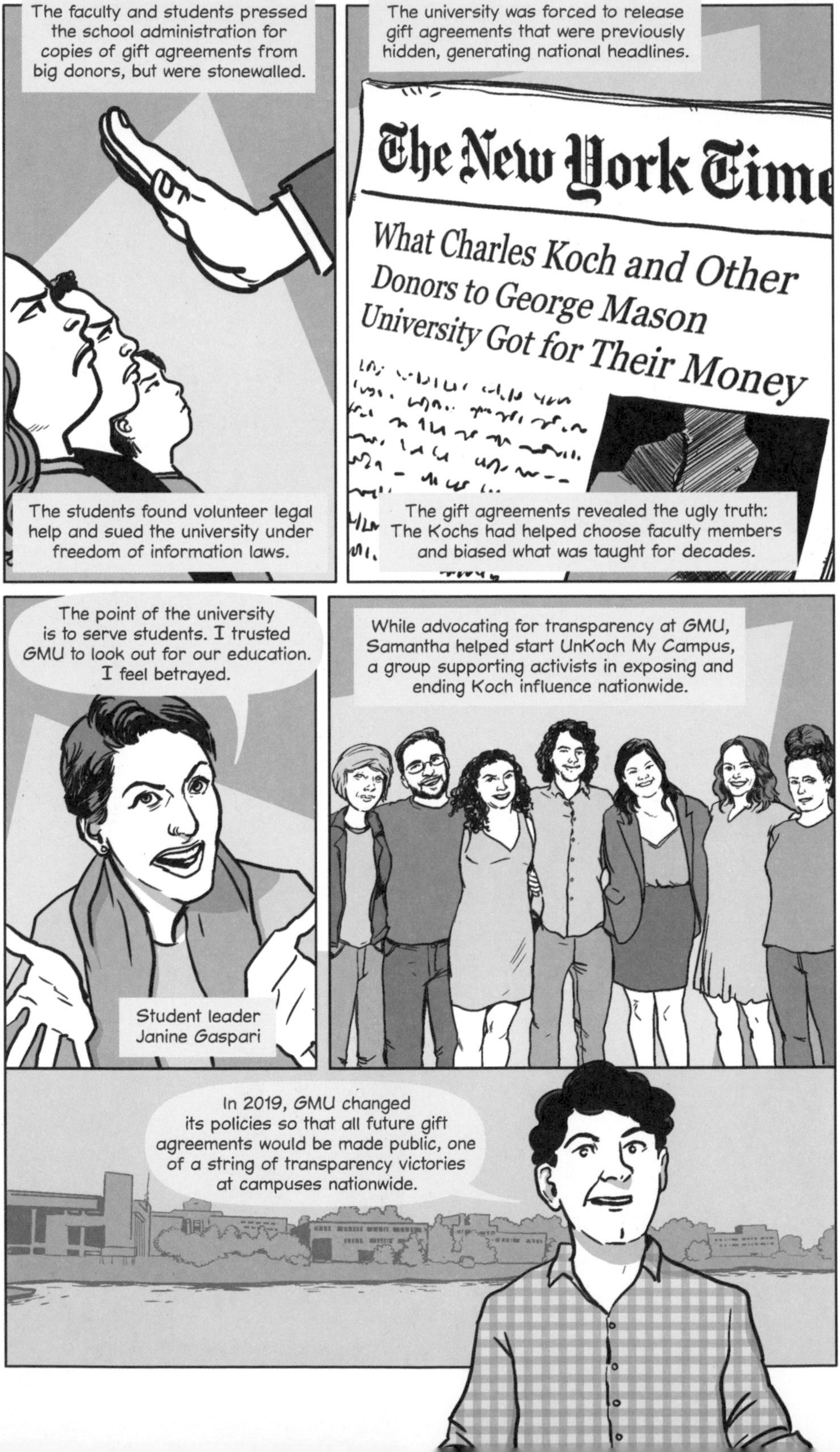
The faculty and students pressed the school administration for copies of gift agreements from big donors, but were stonewalled.
The students found volunteer legal help and sued the university under freedom of information laws.
The university was forced to release gift agreements that were previously hidden, generating national headlines.
The New York Time
What Charles Koch and Other Donors to George Mason University Got for Their Money
The gift agreements revealed the ugly truth: The Kochs had helped choose faculty members and biased what was taught for decades.
The point of the university is to serve students. I trusted GMU to look out for our education. I feel betrayed.
Student leader Janine Gaspari
While advocating for transparency at GMU, Samantha helped start UnKoch My Campus, a group supporting activists in exposing and ending Koch influence nationwide.
In 2019, GMU changed its policies so that all future gift agreements would be made public, one of a string of transparency victories at campuses nationwide.

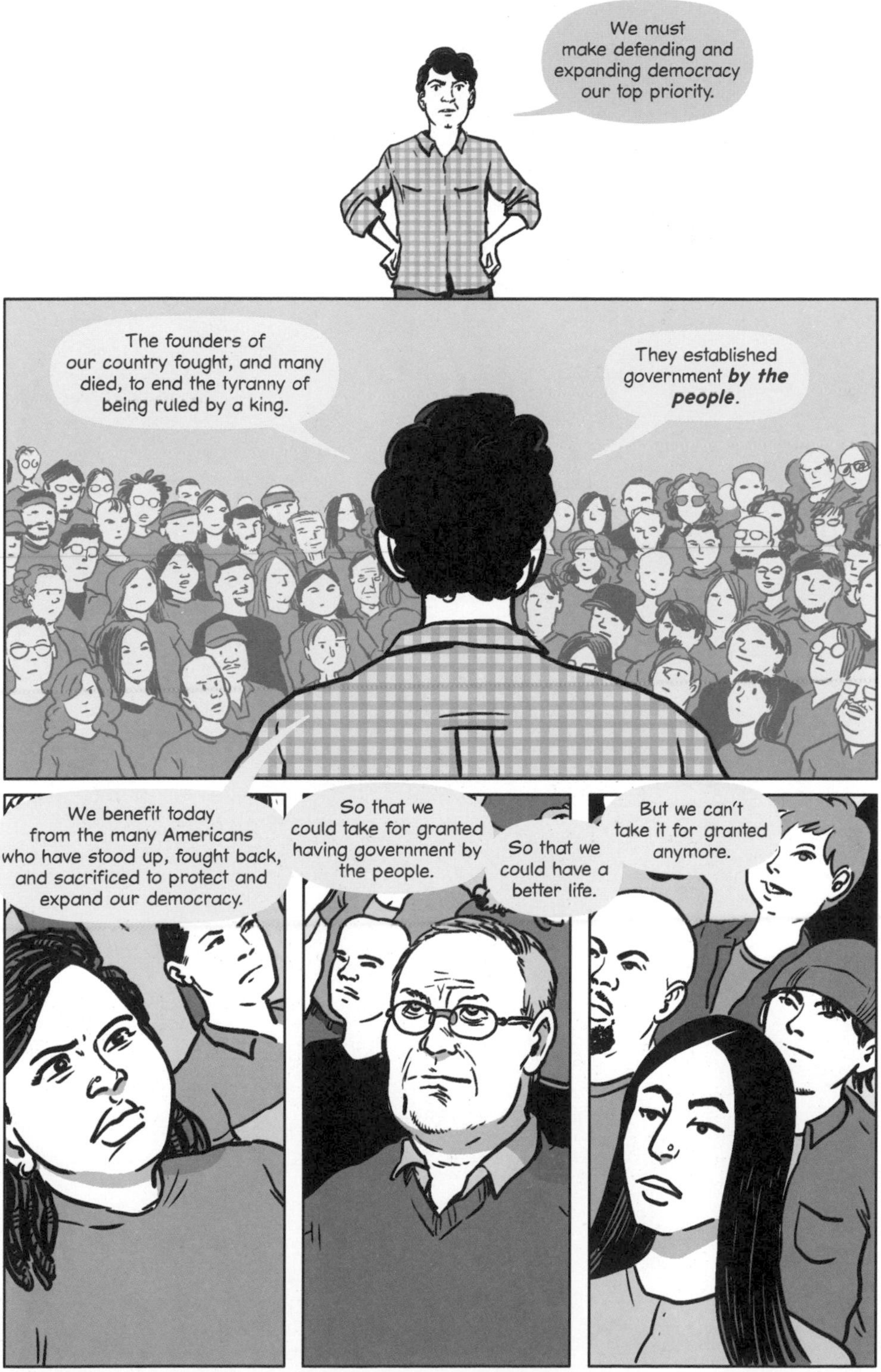
We must make defending and expanding democracy our top priority.
The founders of our country fought, and many died, to end the tyranny of being ruled by a king.
They established government **by the people**.
We benefit today from the many Americans who have stood up, fought back, and sacrificed to protect and expand our democracy.
So that we could take for granted having government by the people.
So that we could have a better life.
But we can't take it for granted anymore.

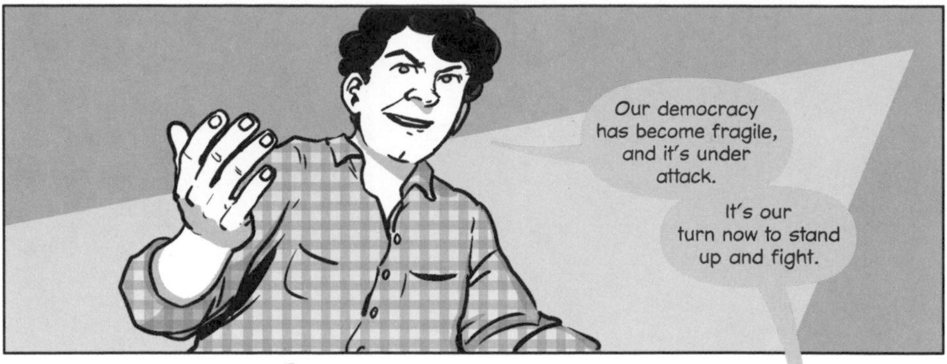
Our democracy has become fragile, and it's under attack.
It's our turn now to stand up and fight.

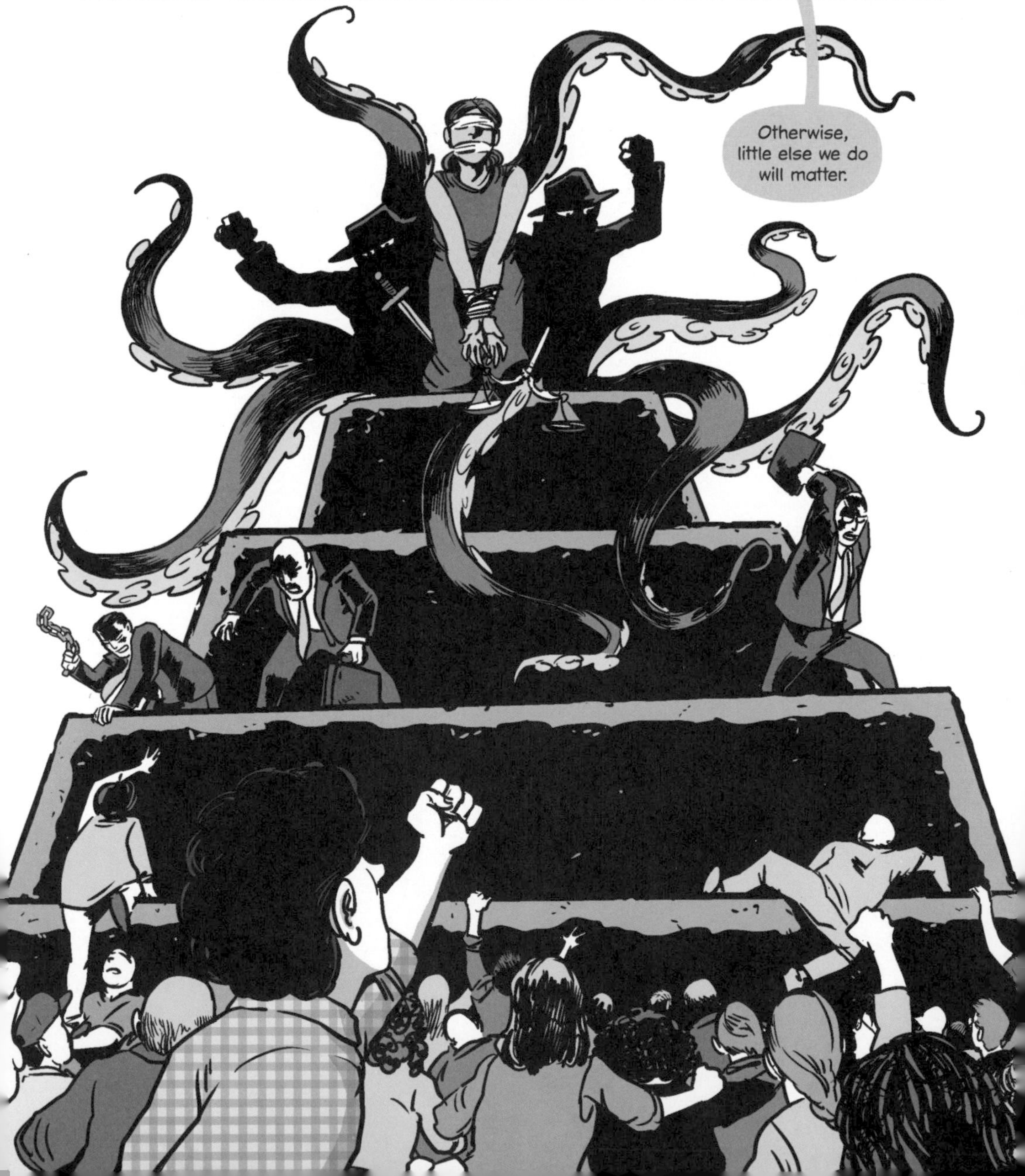
Otherwise, little else we do will matter.

5

who votes

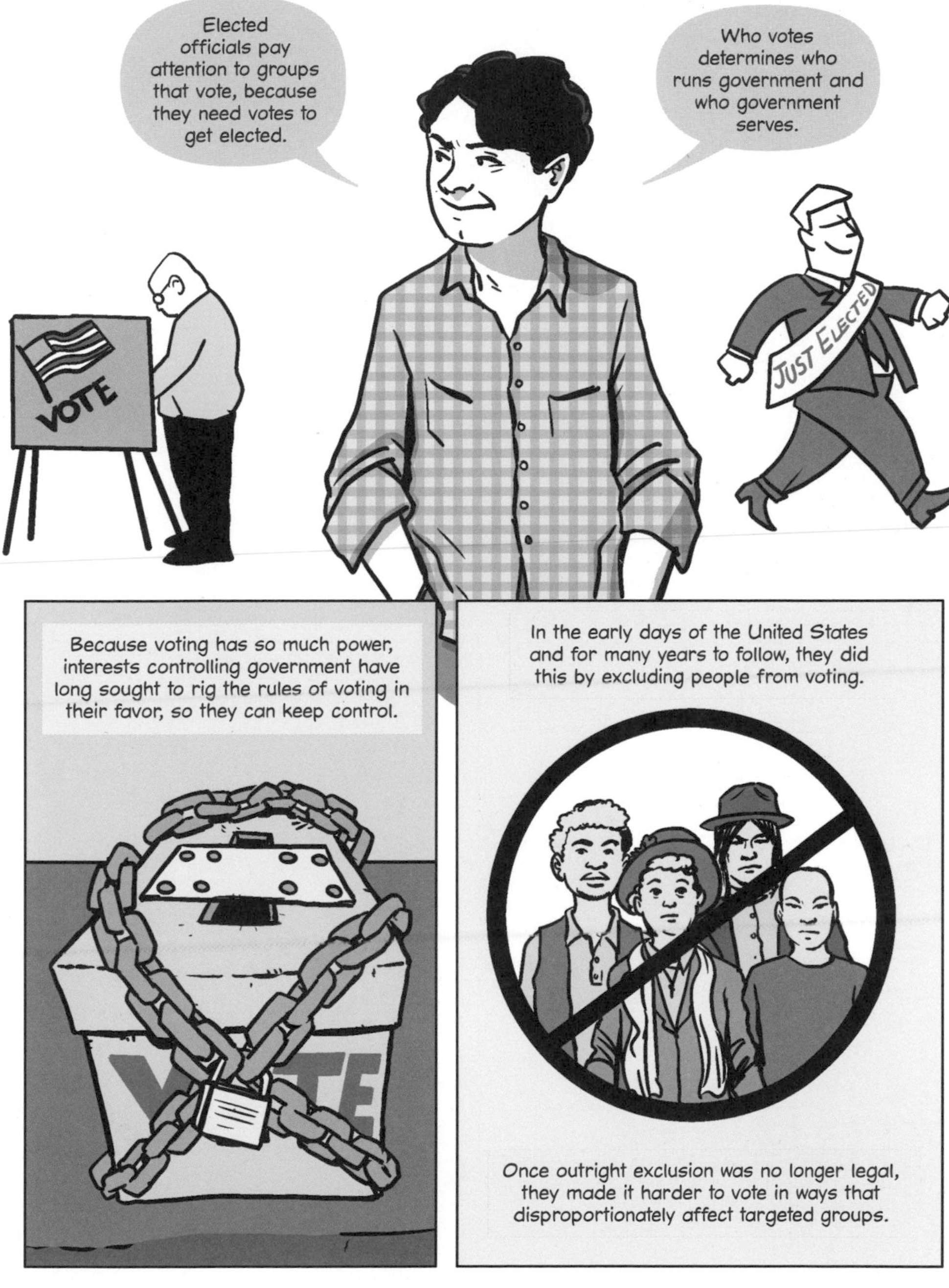
Elected officials pay attention to groups that vote, because they need votes to get elected.
Who votes determines who runs government and who government serves.
VOTE
JUST ELECTED
Because voting has so much power, interests controlling government have long sought to rig the rules of voting in their favor, so they can keep control.
In the early days of the United States and for many years to follow, they did this by excluding people from voting.
Once outright exclusion was no longer legal, they made it harder to vote in ways that disproportionately affect targeted groups.

voter exclusion

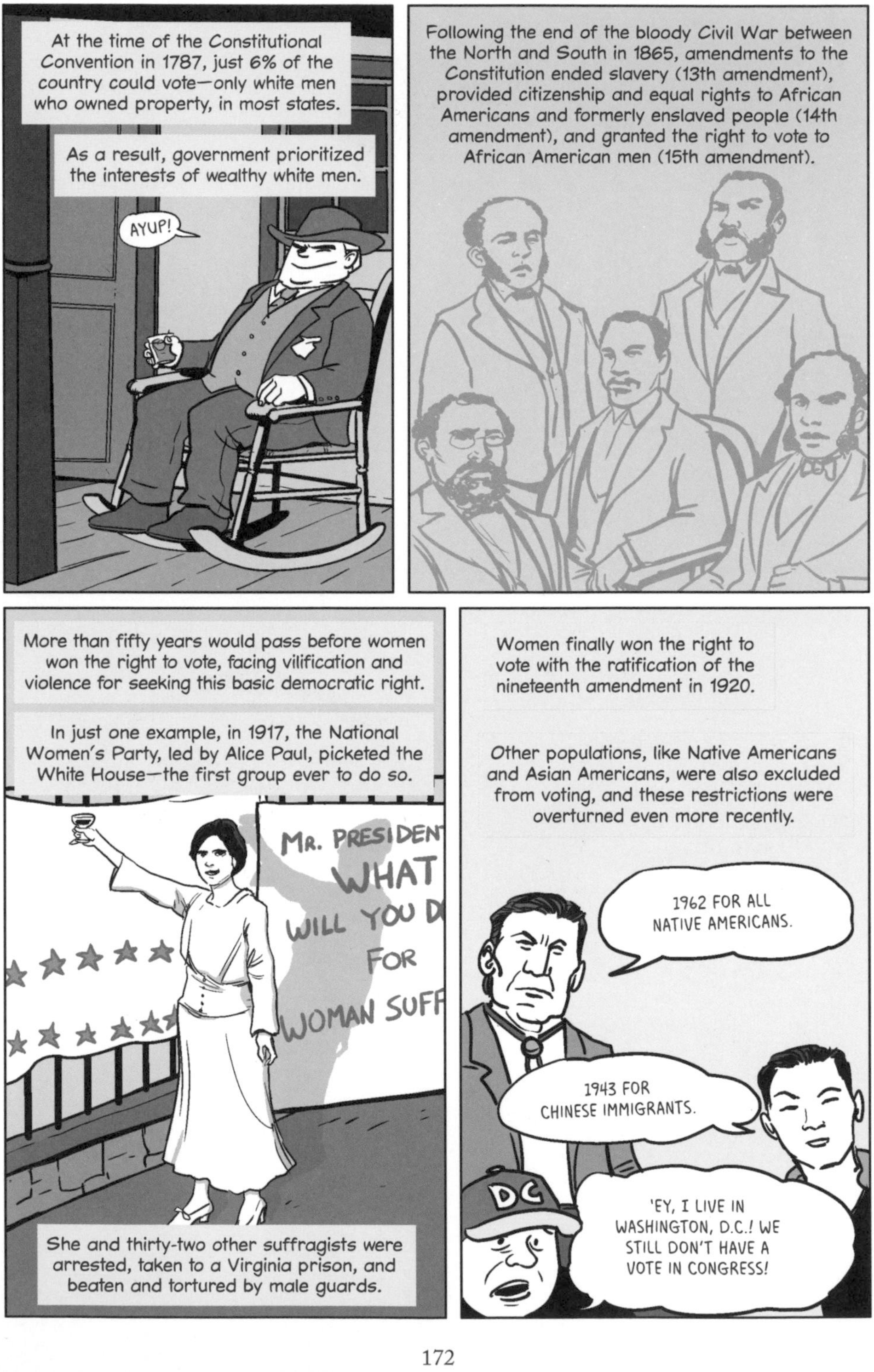
At the time of the Constitutional Convention in 1787, just 6% of the country could vote—only white men who owned property, in most states.
As a result, government prioritized the interests of wealthy white men.
AYUP!
Following the end of the bloody Civil War between the North and South in 1865, amendments to the Constitution ended slavery (13th amendment), provided citizenship and equal rights to African Americans and formerly enslaved people (14th amendment), and granted the right to vote to African American men (15th amendment).
More than fifty years would pass before women won the right to vote, facing vilification and violence for seeking this basic democratic right.
In just one example, in 1917, the National Women's Party, led by Alice Paul, picketed the White House—the first group ever to do so.
MR. PRESIDENT
WHAT
WILL YOU D
FOR
WOMAN SUFF
She and thirty-two other suffragists were arrested, taken to a Virginia prison, and beaten and tortured by male guards.
Women finally won the right to vote with the ratification of the nineteenth amendment in 1920.
Other populations, like Native Americans and Asian Americans, were also excluded from voting, and these restrictions were overturned even more recently.
1962 FOR ALL NATIVE AMERICANS.
1943 FOR CHINESE IMMIGRANTS.
DC
'EY, I LIVE IN WASHINGTON, D.C.! WE STILL DON'T HAVE A VOTE IN CONGRESS!

voter suppression

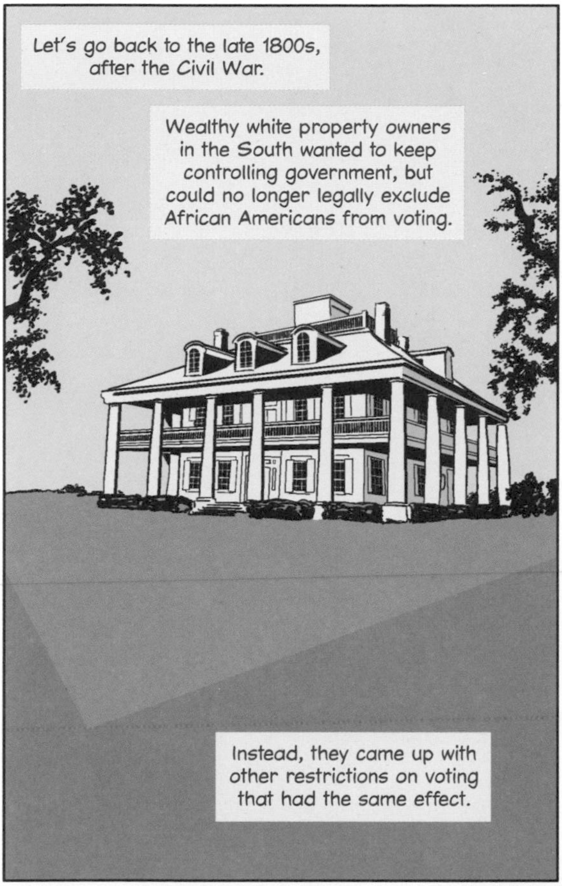

Let's go back to the late 1800s, after the Civil War.
Wealthy white property owners in the South wanted to keep controlling government, but could no longer legally exclude African Americans from voting.
Instead, they came up with other restrictions on voting that had the same effect.

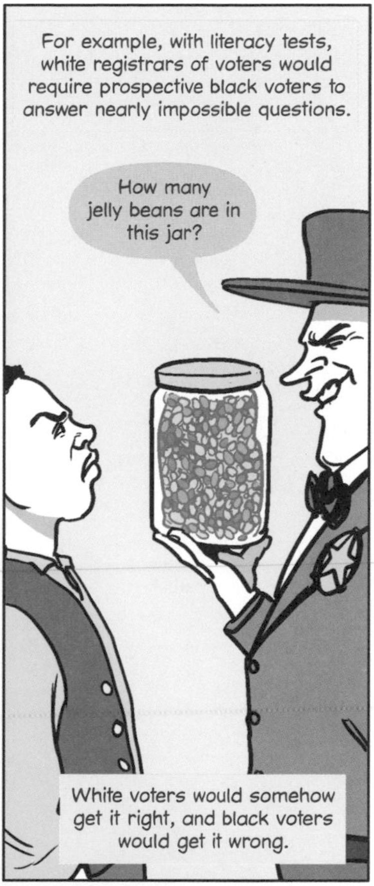

For example, with literacy tests, white registrars of voters would require prospective black voters to answer nearly impossible questions.
How many jelly beans are in this jar?
White voters would somehow get it right, and black voters would get it wrong.

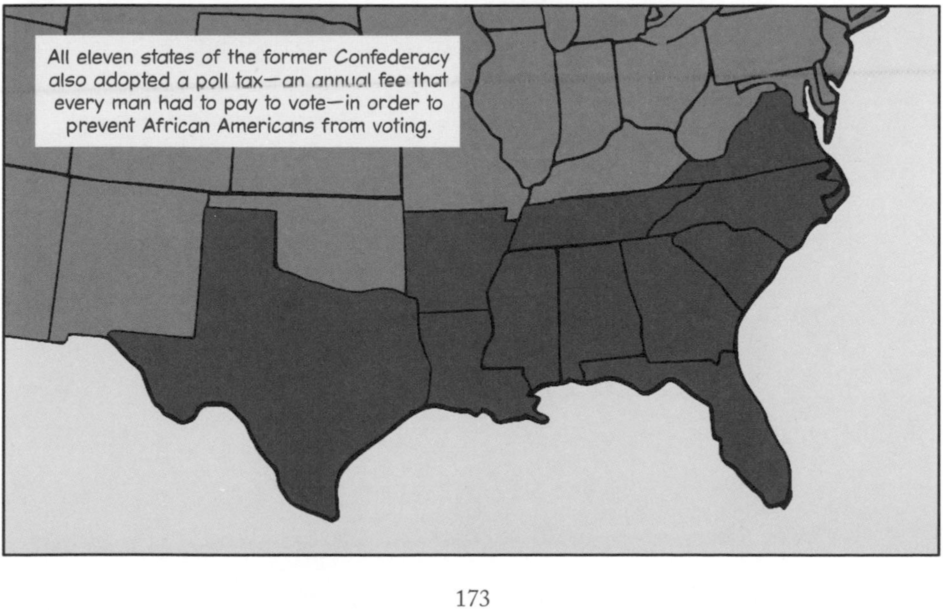

All eleven states of the former Confederacy also adopted a poll tax—an annual fee that every man had to pay to vote—in order to prevent African Americans from voting.

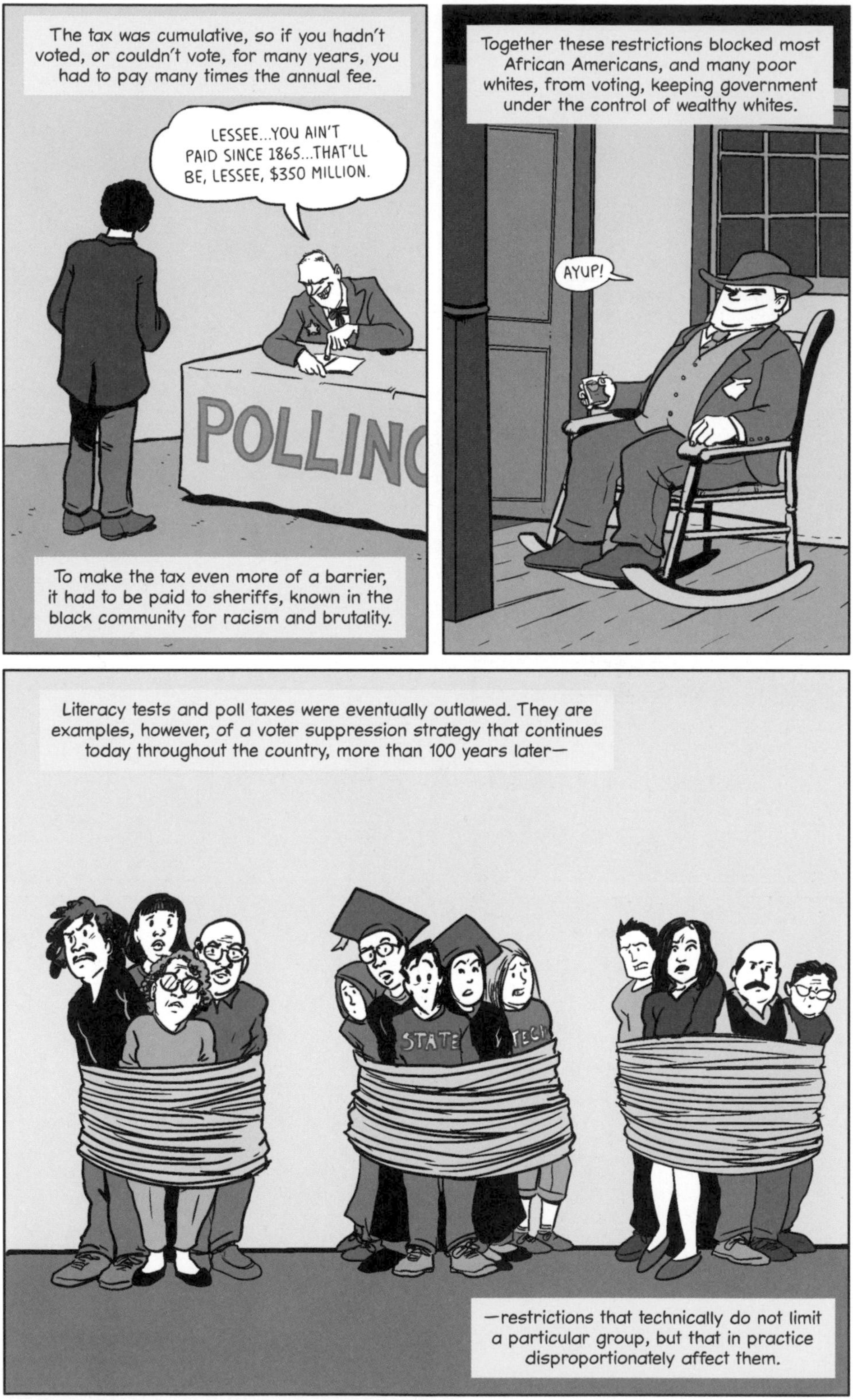
The tax was cumulative, so if you hadn't voted, or couldn't vote, for many years, you had to pay many times the annual fee.
LESSEE...YOU AIN'T PAID SINCE 1865...THAT'LL BE, LESSEE, $350 MILLION.
POLLIN
To make the tax even more of a barrier, it had to be paid to sheriffs, known in the black community for racism and brutality.
Together these restrictions blocked most African Americans, and many poor whites, from voting, keeping government under the control of wealthy whites.
AYUP!
Literacy tests and poll taxes were eventually outlawed. They are examples, however, of a voter suppression strategy that continues today throughout the country, more than 100 years later—
STATE
TECH
—restrictions that technically do not limit a particular group, but that in practice disproportionately affect them.

voter id laws

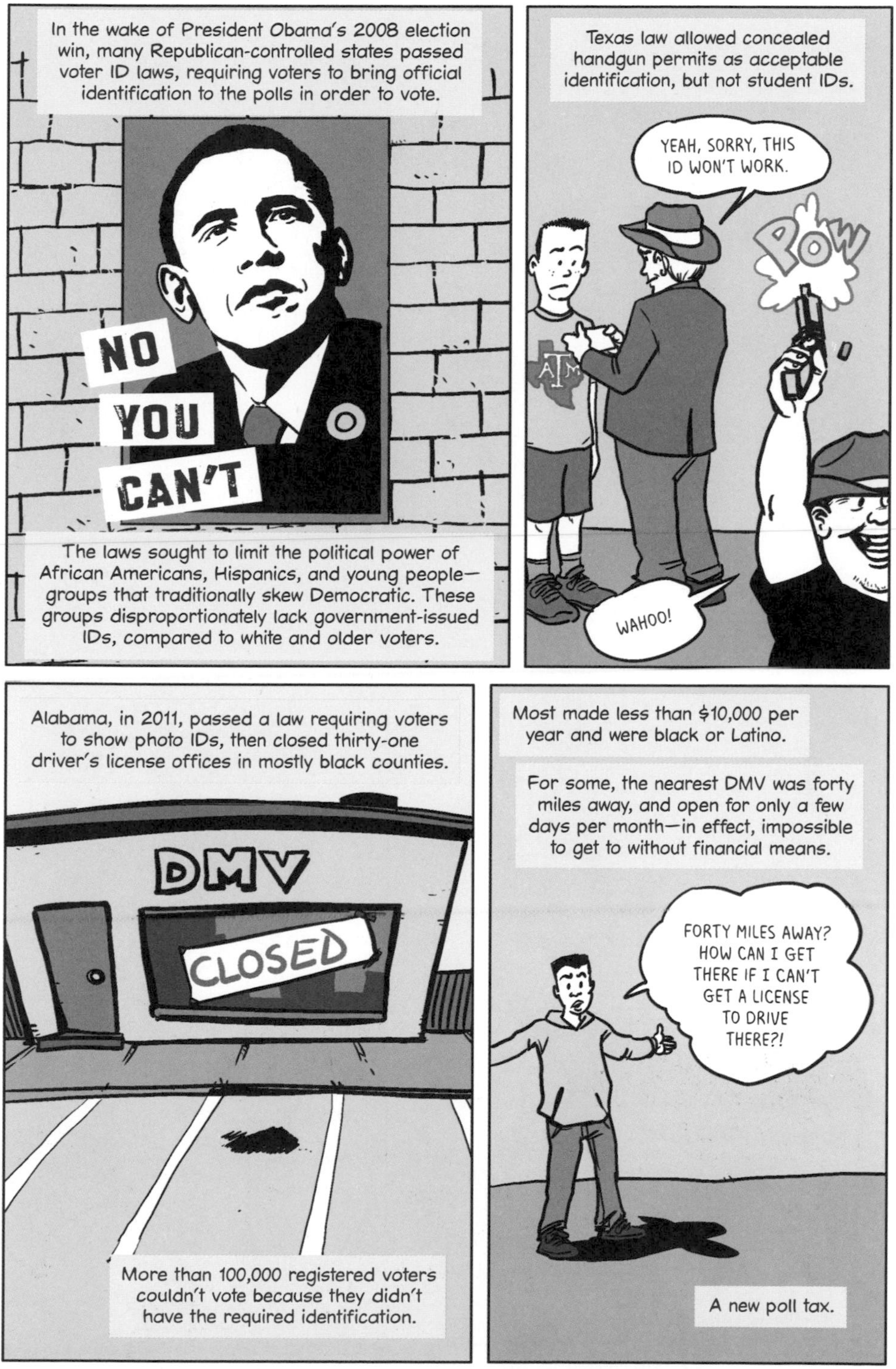
In the wake of President Obama's 2008 election win, many Republican-controlled states passed voter ID laws, requiring voters to bring official identification to the polls in order to vote.
NO YOU CAN'T
The laws sought to limit the political power of African Americans, Hispanics, and young people—groups that traditionally skew Democratic. These groups disproportionately lack government-issued IDs, compared to white and older voters.
Texas law allowed concealed handgun permits as acceptable identification, but not student IDs.
YEAH, SORRY, THIS ID WON'T WORK.
POW
WAHOO!
Alabama, in 2011, passed a law requiring voters to show photo IDs, then closed thirty-one driver's license offices in mostly black counties.
DMV
CLOSED
More than 100,000 registered voters couldn't vote because they didn't have the required identification.
Most made less than $10,000 per year and were black or Latino.
For some, the nearest DMV was forty miles away, and open for only a few days per month—in effect, impossible to get to without financial means.
FORTY MILES AWAY? HOW CAN I GET THERE IF I CAN'T GET A LICENSE TO DRIVE THERE?!
A new poll tax.

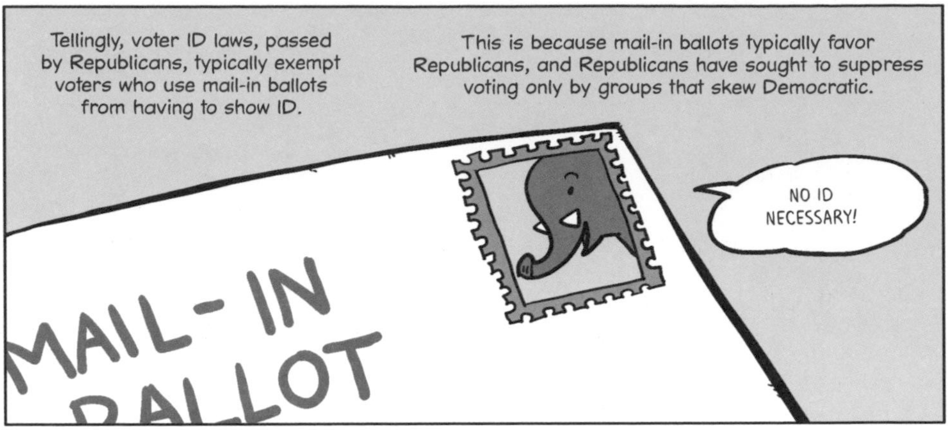
Tellingly, voter ID laws, passed by Republicans, typically exempt voters who use mail-in ballots from having to show ID.
This is because mail-in ballots typically favor Republicans, and Republicans have sought to suppress voting only by groups that skew Democratic.
NO ID NECESSARY!
MAIL-IN BALLOT

limiting early voting

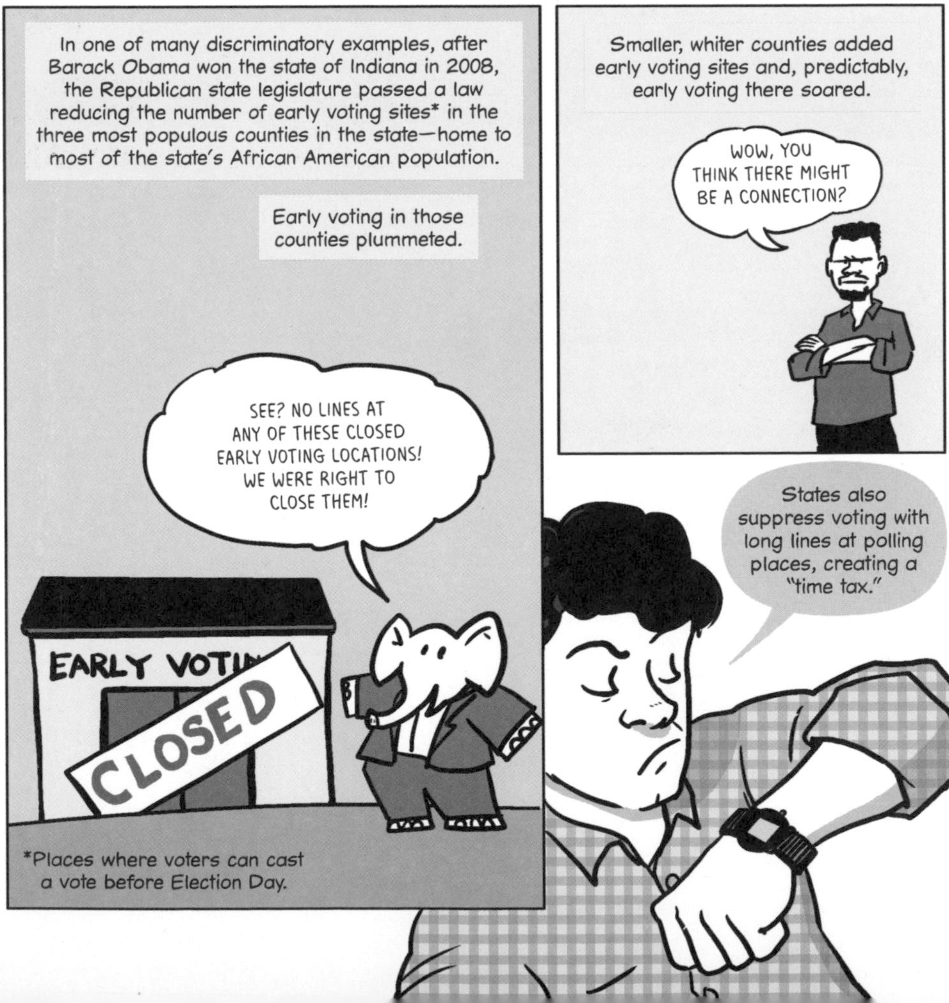
In one of many discriminatory examples, after Barack Obama won the state of Indiana in 2008, the Republican state legislature passed a law reducing the number of early voting sites* in the three most populous counties in the state—home to most of the state's African American population.
Early voting in those counties plummeted.
SEE? NO LINES AT ANY OF THESE CLOSED EARLY VOTING LOCATIONS! WE WERE RIGHT TO CLOSE THEM!
EARLY VOTIN
CLOSED
*Places where voters can cast a vote before Election Day.
Smaller, whiter counties added early voting sites and, predictably, early voting there soared.
WOW, YOU THINK THERE MIGHT BE A CONNECTION?
States also suppress voting with long lines at polling places, creating a "time tax."

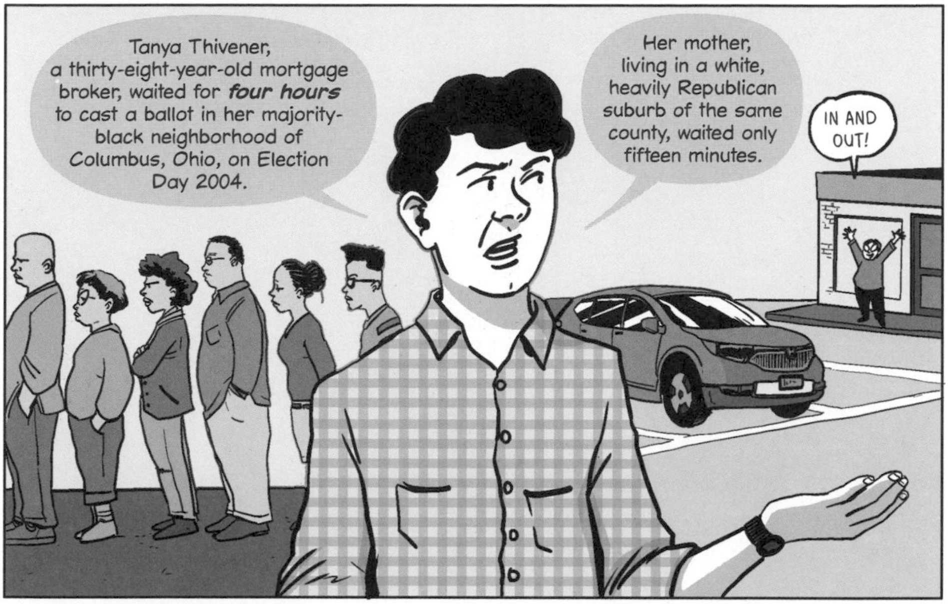
Tanya Thivener, a thirty-eight-year-old mortgage broker, waited for ***four hours*** to cast a ballot in her majority-black neighborhood of Columbus, Ohio, on Election Day 2004.
Her mother, living in a white, heavily Republican suburb of the same county, waited only fifteen minutes.
IN AND OUT!

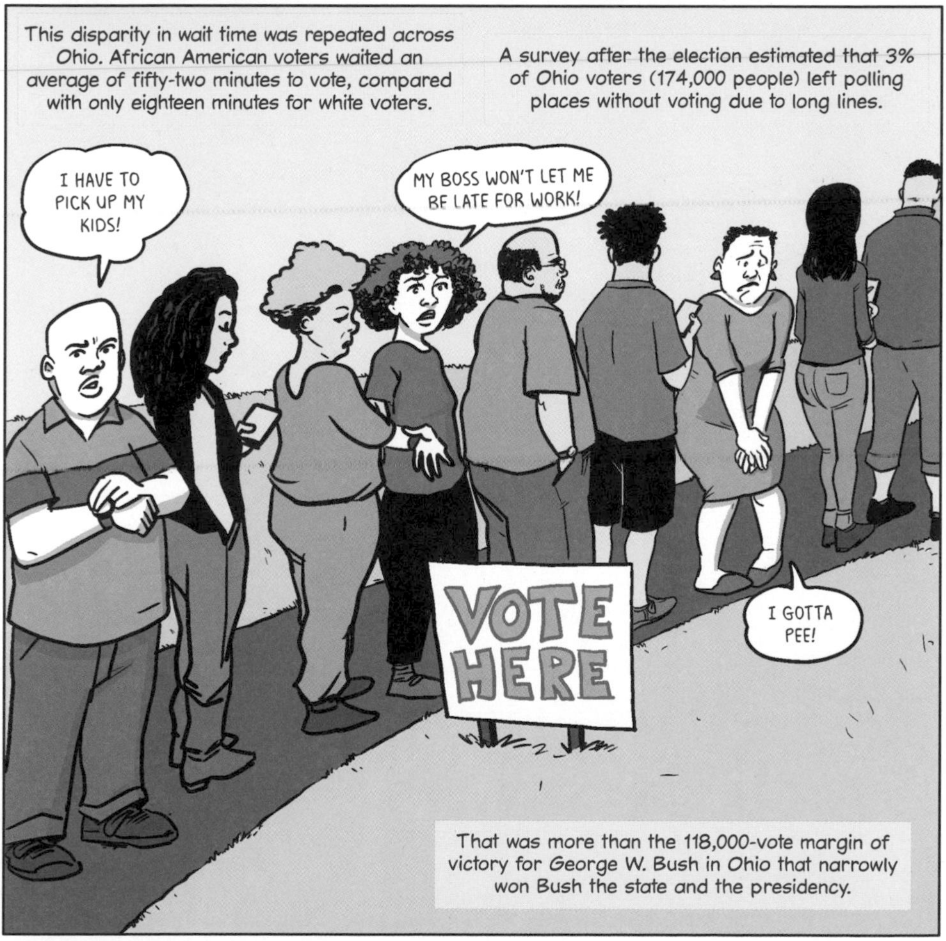
This disparity in wait time was repeated across Ohio. African American voters waited an average of fifty-two minutes to vote, compared with only eighteen minutes for white voters.
A survey after the election estimated that 3% of Ohio voters (174,000 people) left polling places without voting due to long lines.
I HAVE TO PICK UP MY KIDS!
MY BOSS WON'T LET ME BE LATE FOR WORK!
VOTE HERE
I GOTTA PEE!
That was more than the 118,000-vote margin of victory for *George W. Bush* in Ohio that narrowly won Bush the state and the presidency.

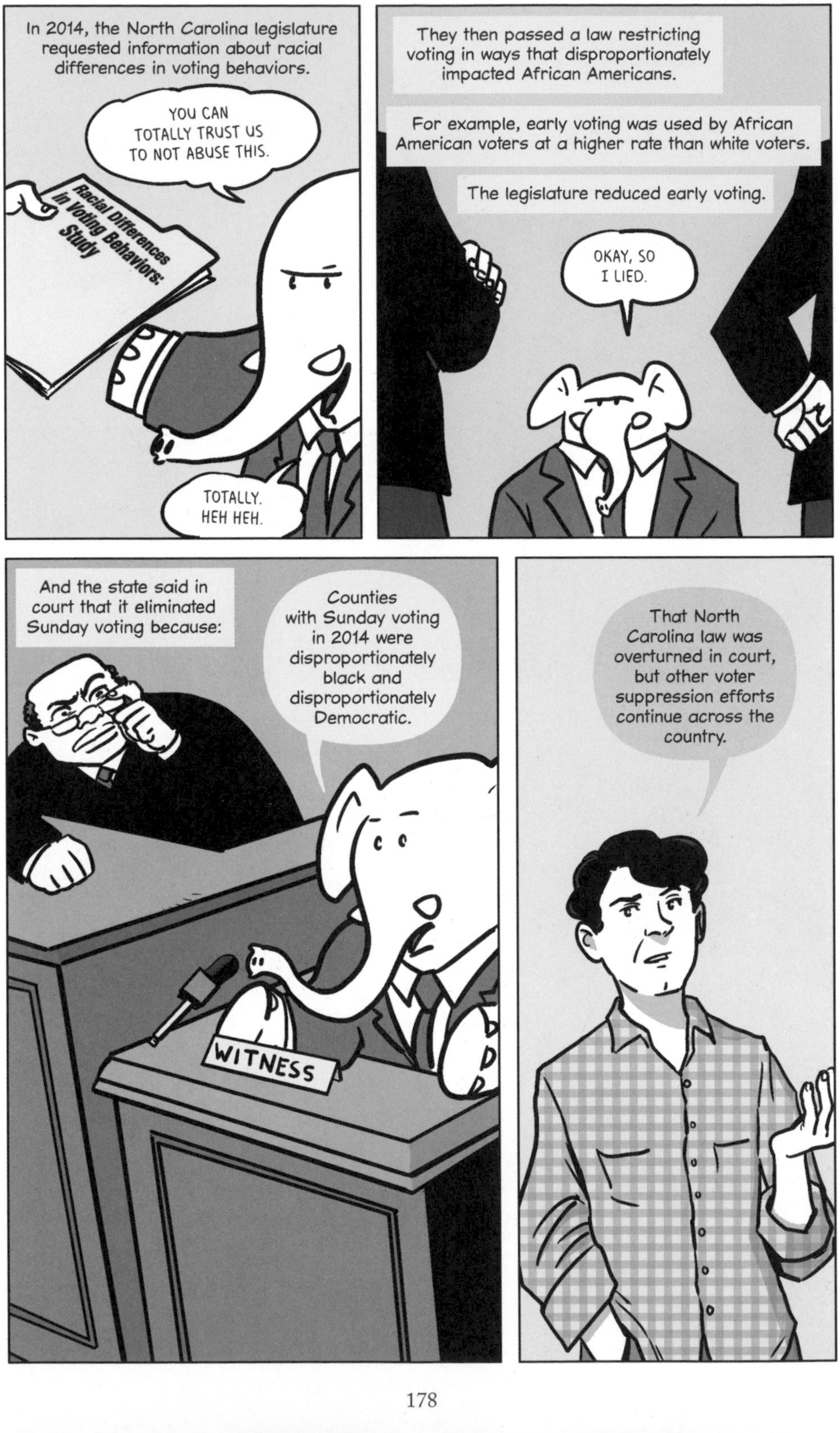
In 2014, the North Carolina legislature requested information about racial differences in voting behaviors.
YOU CAN TOTALLY TRUST US TO NOT ABUSE THIS.
Racial Differences In Voting Behaviors: Study
TOTALLY. HEH HEH.
They then passed a law restricting voting in ways that disproportionately impacted African Americans.
For example, early voting was used by African American voters at a higher rate than white voters.
The legislature reduced early voting.
OKAY, SO I LIED.
And the state said in court that it eliminated Sunday voting because:
Counties with Sunday voting in 2014 were disproportionately black and disproportionately Democratic.
WITNESS
That North Carolina law was overturned in court, but other voter suppression efforts continue across the country.

the voting rights act

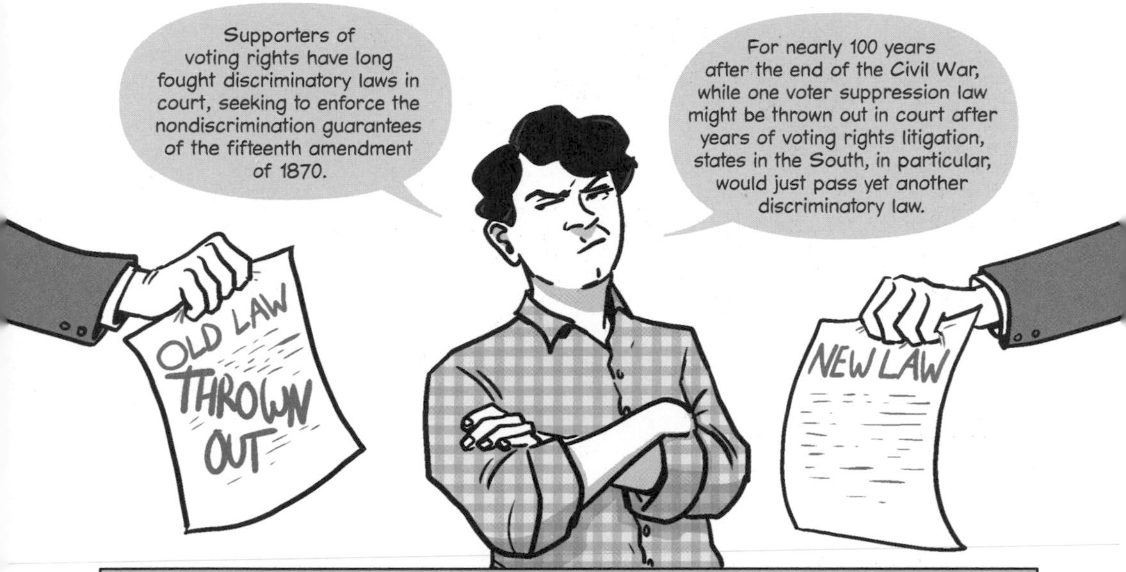
Supporters of voting rights have long fought discriminatory laws in court, seeking to enforce the nondiscrimination guarantees of the fifteenth amendment of 1870.
For nearly 100 years after the end of the Civil War, while one voter suppression law might be thrown out in court after years of voting rights litigation, states in the South, in particular, would just pass yet another discriminatory law.
OLD LAW THROWN OUT
NEW LAW

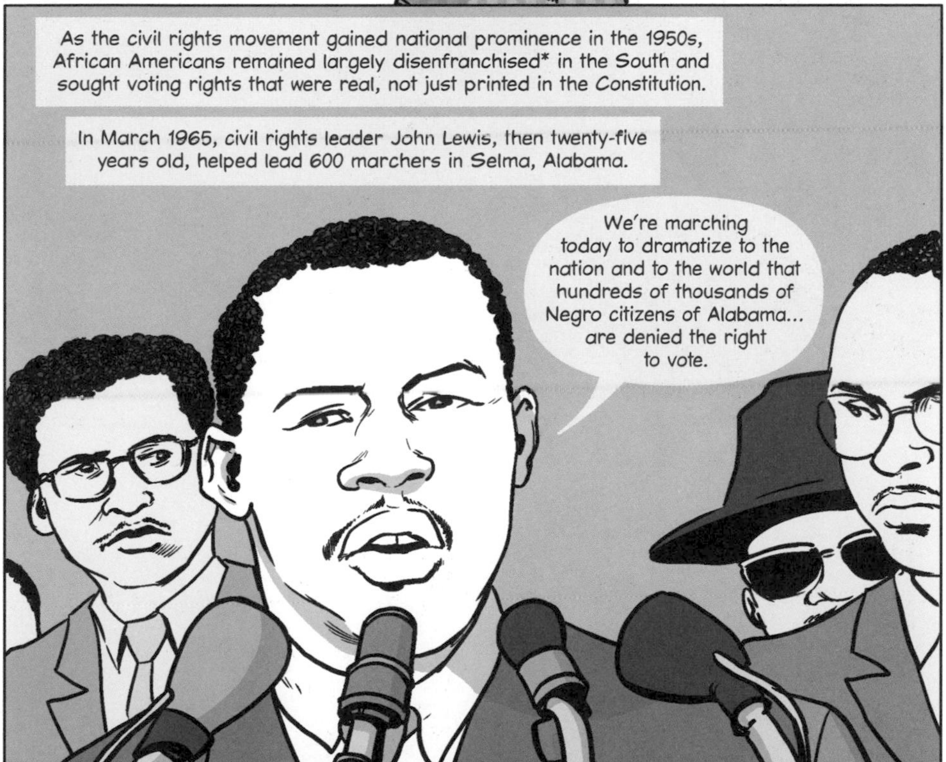
As the civil rights movement gained national prominence in the 1950s, African Americans remained largely disenfranchised* in the South and sought voting rights that were real, not just printed in the Constitution.
In March 1965, civil rights leader John Lewis, then twenty-five years old, helped lead 600 marchers in Selma, Alabama.
We're marching today to dramatize to the nation and to the world that hundreds of thousands of Negro citizens of Alabama... are denied the right to vote.

*Deprived of the right to vote

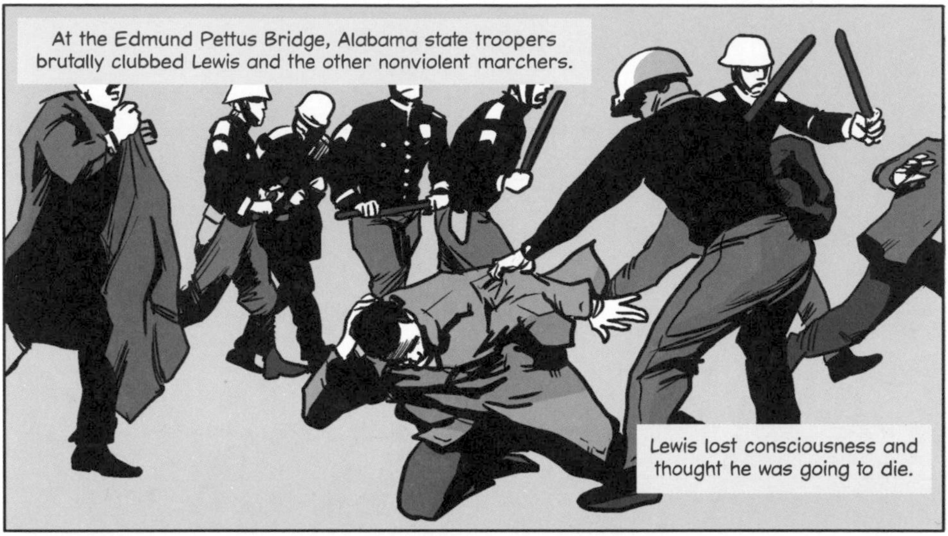
At the Edmund Pettus Bridge, Alabama state troopers brutally clubbed Lewis and the other nonviolent marchers.
Lewis lost consciousness and thought he was going to die.

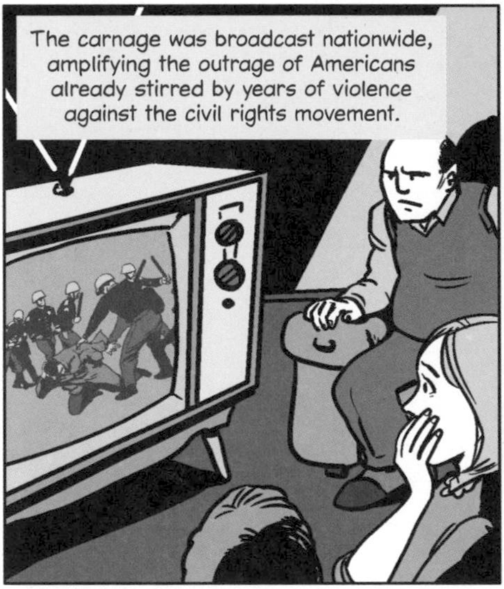
The carnage was broadcast nationwide, amplifying the outrage of Americans already stirred by years of violence against the civil rights movement.

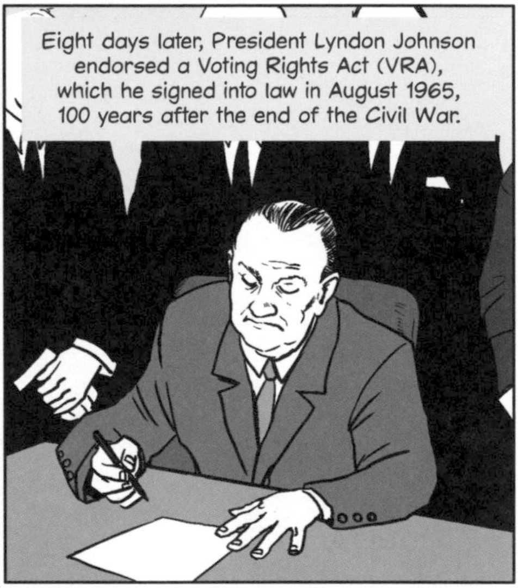
Eight days later, President Lyndon Johnson endorsed a Voting Rights Act (VRA), which he signed into law in August 1965, 100 years after the end of the Civil War.

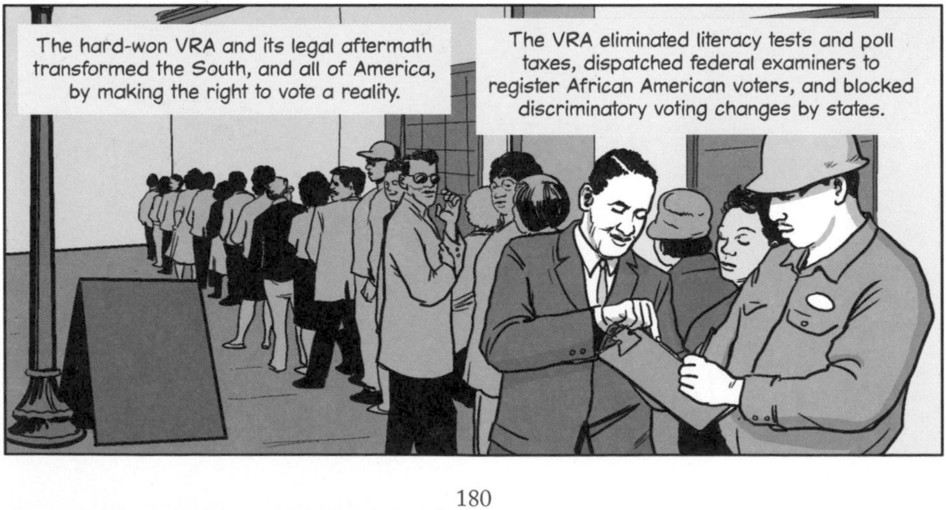
The hard-won VRA and its legal aftermath transformed the South, and all of America, by making the right to vote a reality.
The VRA eliminated literacy tests and poll taxes, dispatched federal examiners to register African American voters, and blocked discriminatory voting changes by states.

In 1966, with enforcement of the new VRA by the U.S. Department of Justice, the number of registered black voters in Selma, Alabama, leaped from 1,516 to 10,186—an almost seven-fold increase.

There were 12,000 registered whites.

REGISTER
Between NOW and AUG 28th
ENROLL
LIBERTY

In the election for county sheriff, a moderate white candidate, Wilson Baker, faced off against segregationist leader and incumbent sheriff Jim Clark—

—who carried a cattle prod to use as a weapon against civil rights activists and wore a pin reading "Never."

With massive voter turnout, black voters backed Baker, voting Clark out of a job and showing the power of the VRA and the right to vote.

VOTE CLARK SHERIFF

The results of the VRA proved similarly dramatic nationwide.

Over the next few decades, the rate of voter registration among African Americans in the South increased from 31% to 73%.

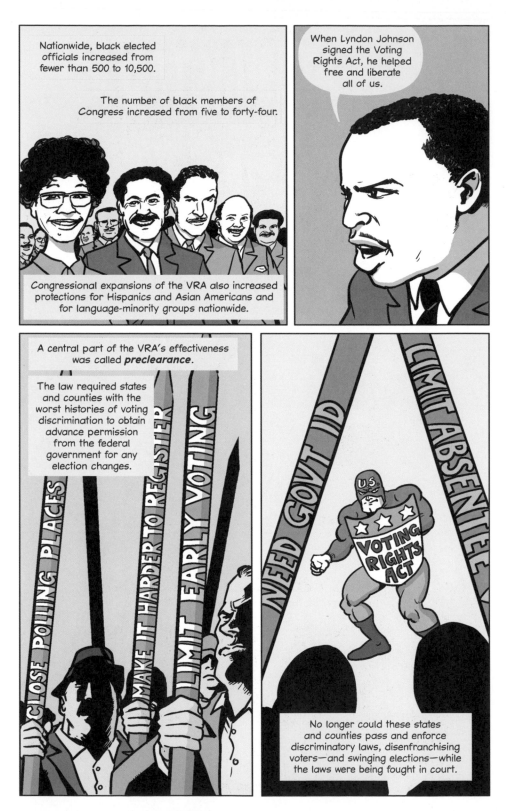

Nationwide, black elected officials increased from fewer than 500 to 10,500.

The number of black members of Congress increased from five to forty-four.

Congressional expansions of the VRA also increased protections for Hispanics and Asian Americans and for language-minority groups nationwide.

When Lyndon Johnson signed the Voting Rights Act, he helped free and liberate all of us.

A central part of the VRA's effectiveness was called **preclearance**.

The law required states and counties with the worst histories of voting discrimination to obtain advance permission from the federal government for any election changes.

CLOSE POLLING PLACES

MAKE IT HARDER TO REGISTER

LIMIT EARLY VOTING

NEED GOV'T ID

LIMIT ABSENTEE

U.S.

VOTING RIGHTS ACT

No longer could these states and counties pass and enforce discriminatory laws, disenfranchising voters—and swinging elections—while the laws were being fought in court.

MAKE IT HARDER

LIMIT VOTER REGIS

NEED GOVT ID

REGIST

U.S.

VOTING RIGHTS

Justice Dept.

ATION

AUTO REGISTRAT

EARLY VOTING

Over decades, the federal government rejected thousands of proposed changes, stopping discriminatory voting changes before states could implement them. Only election changes that were not discriminatory were allowed to go into effect.

For more than forty years, large bipartisan majorities in Congress repeatedly reauthorized (extended) the VRA, with broad consensus on the VRA's effectiveness in countering discrimination and the importance of protecting the foundational right to vote.

Five presidents, all Republicans, signed VRA extensions into law, most recently with a 2006 law that extended the VRA for twenty-five years.

Then, in 2013, five Supreme Court justices gutted the vital preclearance portion of the VRA.

gutting the voting rights act

As the VRA had been proving its effectiveness over nearly fifty years, opponents of the law had been gaining power on the U.S. Supreme Court.

For decades, wealthy libertarian and conservative donors successfully pushed Republican presidents to appoint justices whose views aligned with increased power for corporations and the wealthy.

Attorney John G. Roberts, Jr., had been making arguments against civil rights laws for his entire career.

When Roberts was twenty-five in 1980, he clerked for Supreme Court Justice William Rehnquist, a longtime opponent of civil rights laws.

Rehnquist himself had personally administered literacy tests to Hispanic and black voters in Arizona in the 1960s.

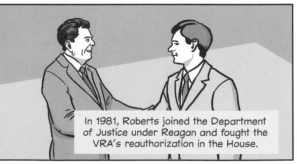

In 1981, Roberts joined the Department of Justice under Reagan and fought the VRA's reauthorization in the House.

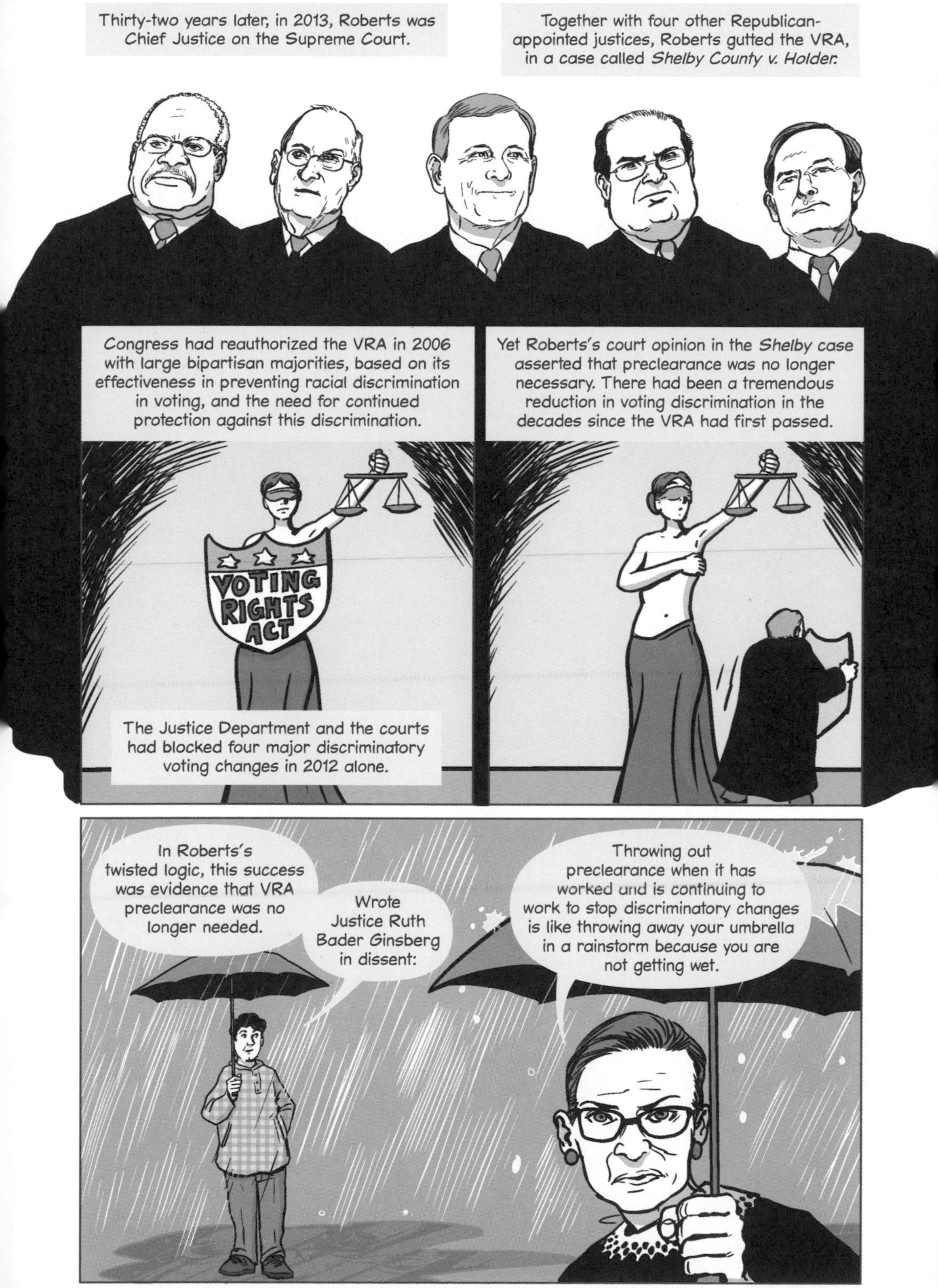
Thirty-two years later, in 2013, Roberts was Chief Justice on the Supreme Court.
Together with four other Republican-appointed justices, Roberts gutted the VRA, in a case called *Shelby County v. Holder.*
Congress had reauthorized the VRA in 2006 with large bipartisan majorities, based on its effectiveness in preventing racial discrimination in voting, and the need for continued protection against this discrimination.
VOTING RIGHTS ACT
The Justice Department and the courts had blocked four major discriminatory voting changes in 2012 alone.
Yet Roberts's court opinion in the *Shelby* case asserted that preclearance was no longer necessary. There had been a tremendous reduction in voting discrimination in the decades since the VRA had first passed.
In Roberts's twisted logic, this success was evidence that VRA preclearance was no longer needed.
Wrote Justice Ruth Bader Ginsberg in dissent:
Throwing out preclearance when it has worked and is continuing to work to stop discriminatory changes is like throwing away your umbrella in a rainstorm because you are not getting wet.

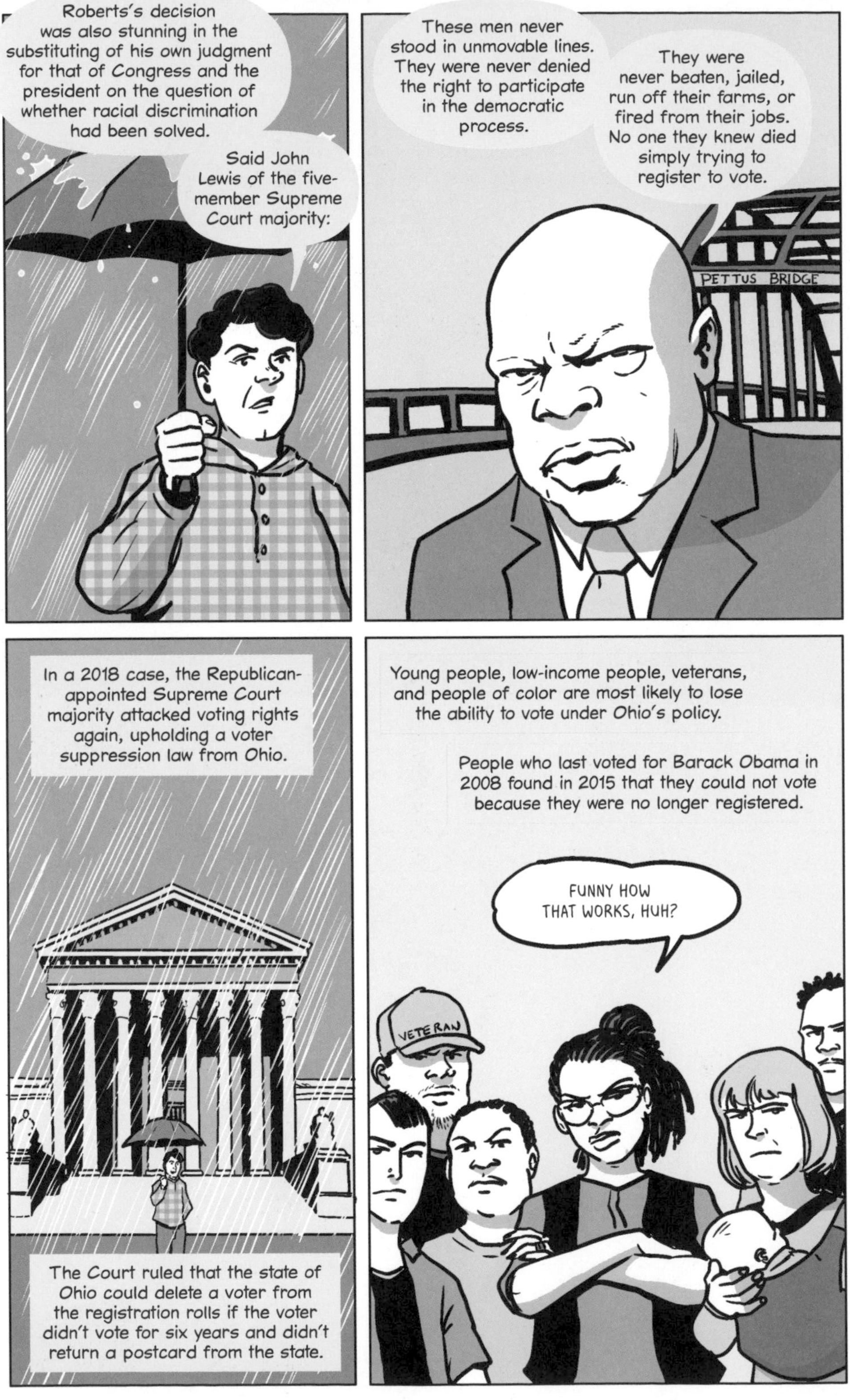
Roberts's decision was also stunning in the substituting of his own judgment for that of Congress and the president on the question of whether racial discrimination had been solved.
Said John Lewis of the five-member Supreme Court majority:
These men never stood in unmovable lines. They were never denied the right to participate in the democratic process.
They were never beaten, jailed, run off their farms, or fired from their jobs. No one they knew died simply trying to register to vote.
PETTUS BRIDGE
In a 2018 case, the Republican-appointed Supreme Court majority attacked voting rights again, upholding a voter suppression law from Ohio.
The Court ruled that the state of Ohio could delete a voter from the registration rolls if the voter didn't vote for six years and didn't return a postcard from the state.
Young people, low-income people, veterans, and people of color are most likely to lose the ability to vote under Ohio's policy.
People who last voted for Barack Obama in 2008 found in 2015 that they could not vote because they were no longer registered.
FUNNY HOW THAT WORKS, HUH?
VETERAN

voting solutions

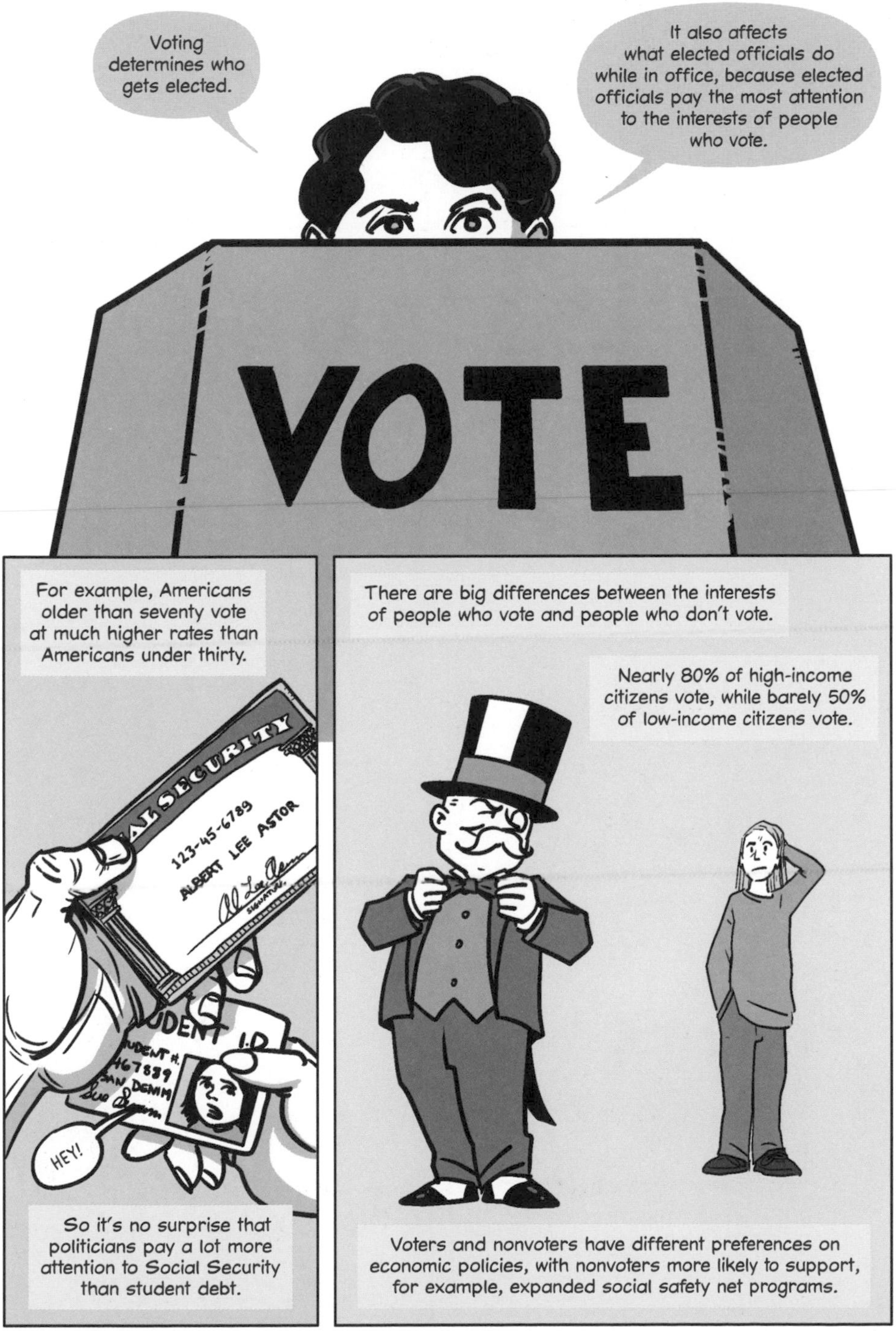

Voting determines who gets elected.
It also affects what elected officials do while in office, because elected officials pay the most attention to the interests of people who vote.
VOTE
For example, Americans older than seventy vote at much higher rates than Americans under thirty.
123-45-6789
ALBERT LEE ASTOR
HEY!
So it's no surprise that politicians pay a lot more attention to Social Security than student debt.
There are big differences between the interests of people who vote and people who don't vote.
Nearly 80% of high-income citizens vote, while barely 50% of low-income citizens vote.
Voters and nonvoters have different preferences on economic policies, with nonvoters more likely to support, for example, expanded social safety net programs.

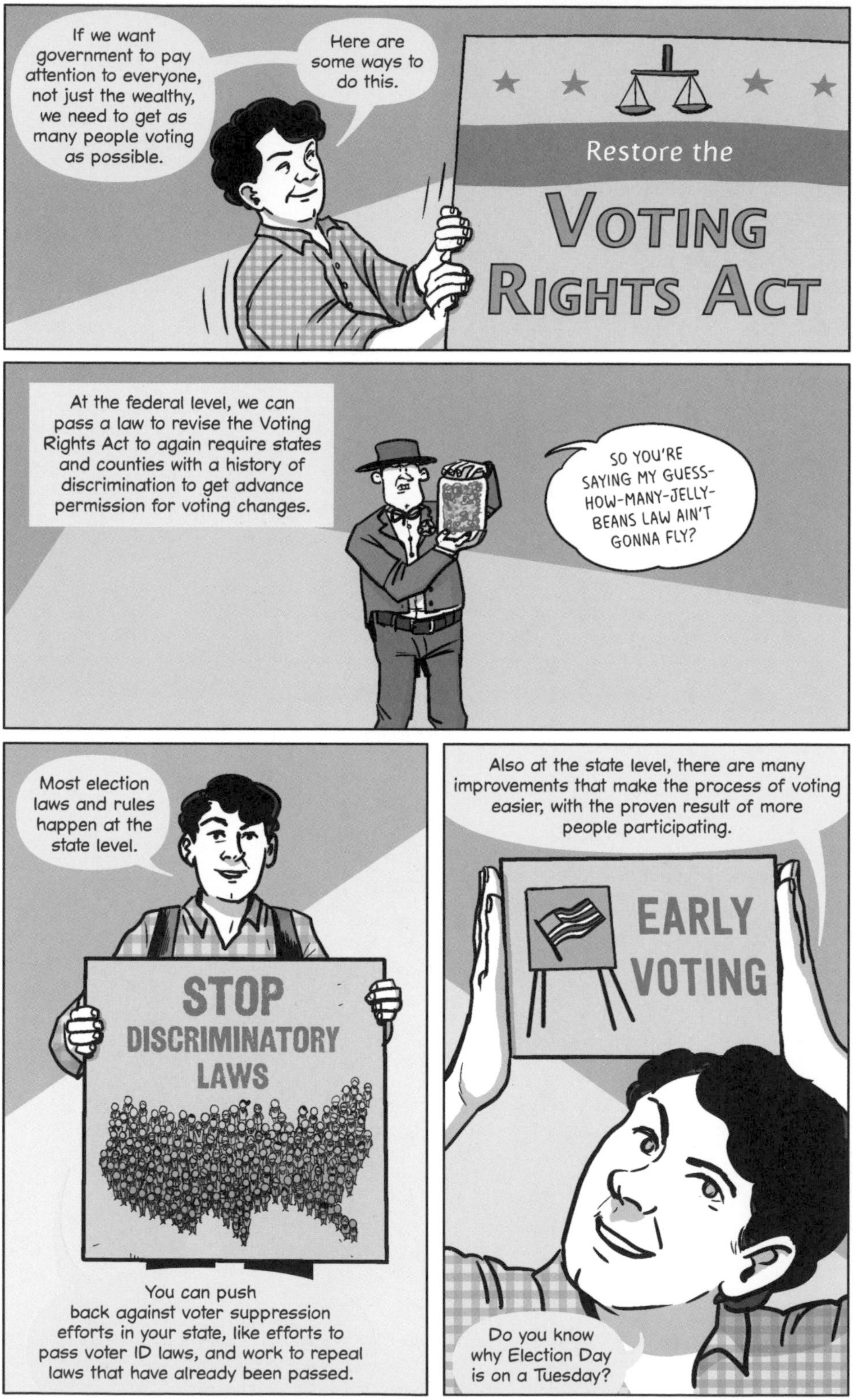

If we want government to pay attention to everyone, not just the wealthy, we need to get as many people voting as possible.
Here are some ways to do this.
Restore the
VOTING RIGHTS ACT
At the federal level, we can pass a law to revise the Voting Rights Act to again require states and counties with a history of discrimination to get advance permission for voting changes.
SO YOU'RE SAYING MY GUESS-HOW-MANY-JELLY-BEANS LAW AIN'T GONNA FLY?
Most election laws and rules happen at the state level.
STOP
DISCRIMINATORY
LAWS
You can push back against voter suppression efforts in your state, like efforts to pass voter ID laws, and work to repeal laws that have already been passed.
Also at the state level, there are many improvements that make the process of voting easier, with the proven result of more people participating.
EARLY
VOTING
Do you know why Election Day is on a Tuesday?

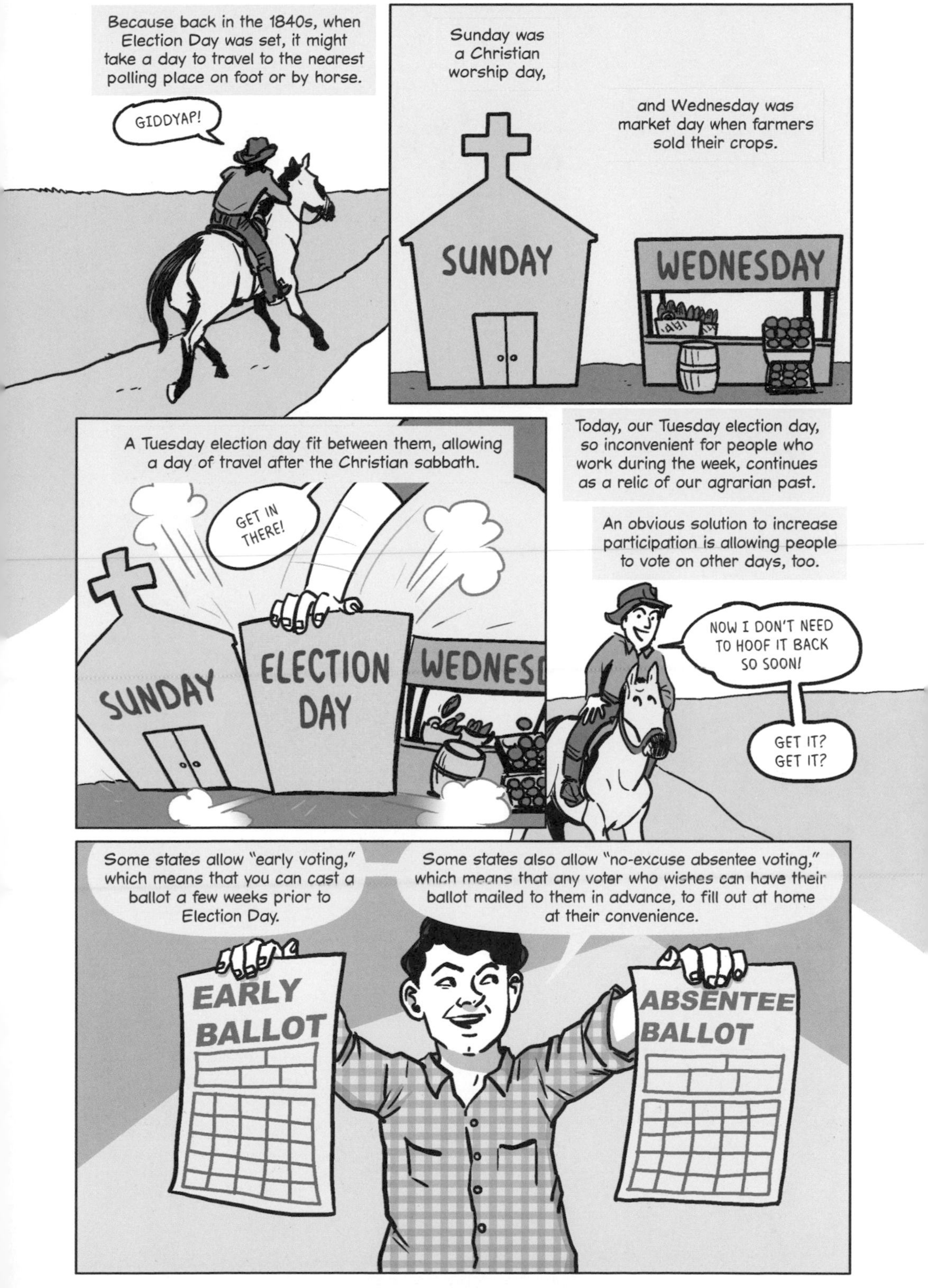
Because back in the 1840s, when Election Day was set, it might take a day to travel to the nearest polling place on foot or by horse.
GIDDYAP!
Sunday was a Christian worship day,
and Wednesday was market day when farmers sold their crops.
SUNDAY
WEDNESDAY
A Tuesday election day fit between them, allowing a day of travel after the Christian sabbath.
GET IN THERE!
SUNDAY
ELECTION DAY
WEDNESD
Today, our Tuesday election day, so inconvenient for people who work during the week, continues as a relic of our agrarian past.
An obvious solution to increase participation is allowing people to vote on other days, too.
NOW I DON'T NEED TO HOOF IT BACK SO SOON!
GET IT? GET IT?
Some states allow "early voting," which means that you can cast a ballot a few weeks prior to Election Day.
Some states also allow "no-excuse absentee voting," which means that any voter who wishes can have their ballot mailed to them in advance, to fill out at home at their convenience.
EARLY BALLOT
ABSENTEE BALLOT

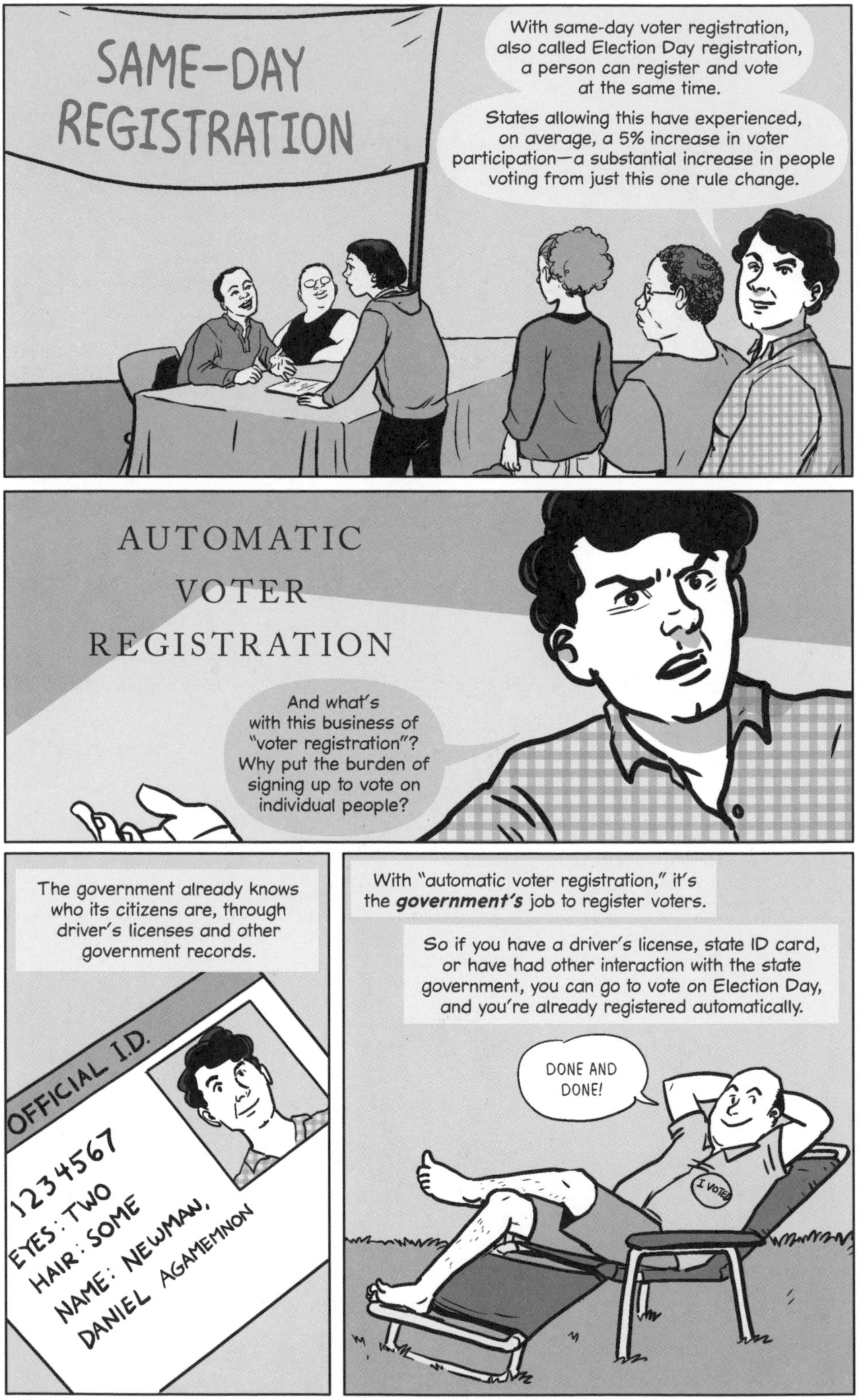

SAME-DAY REGISTRATION
With same-day voter registration, also called Election Day registration, a person can register and vote at the same time.
States allowing this have experienced, on average, a 5% increase in voter participation—a substantial increase in people voting from just this one rule change.
AUTOMATIC VOTER REGISTRATION
And what's with this business of "voter registration"? Why put the burden of signing up to vote on individual people?
The government already knows who its citizens are, through driver's licenses and other government records.
OFFICIAL I.D.
1234567
EYES: TWO
HAIR: SOME
NAME: NEWMAN, DANIEL AGAMEMNON
With "automatic voter registration," it's the ***government's*** job to register voters.
So if you have a driver's license, state ID card, or have had other interaction with the state government, you can go to vote on Election Day, and you're already registered automatically.
DONE AND DONE!
I VOTED

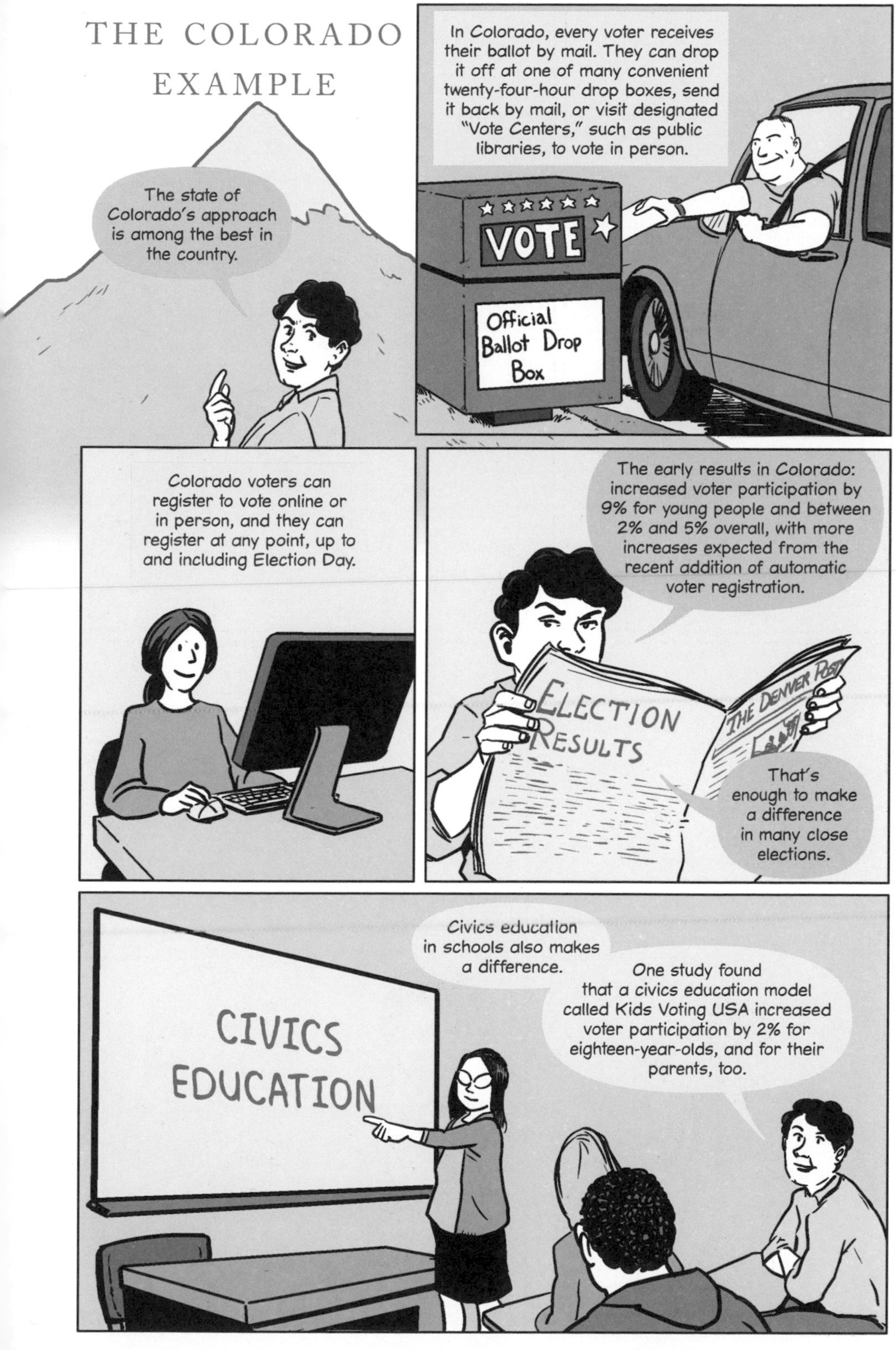
THE COLORADO EXAMPLE
The state of Colorado's approach is among the best in the country.
In Colorado, every voter receives their ballot by mail. They can drop it off at one of many convenient twenty-four-hour drop boxes, send it back by mail, or visit designated "Vote Centers," such as public libraries, to vote in person.
VOTE
Official Ballot Drop Box
Colorado voters can register to vote online or in person, and they can register at any point, up to and including Election Day.
The early results in Colorado: increased voter participation by 9% for young people and between 2% and 5% overall, with more increases expected from the recent addition of automatic voter registration.
ELECTION RESULTS
THE DENVER POST
That's enough to make a difference in many close elections.
Civics education in schools also makes a difference.
CIVICS EDUCATION
One study found that a civics education model called Kids Voting USA increased voter participation by 2% for eighteen-year-olds, and for their parents, too.

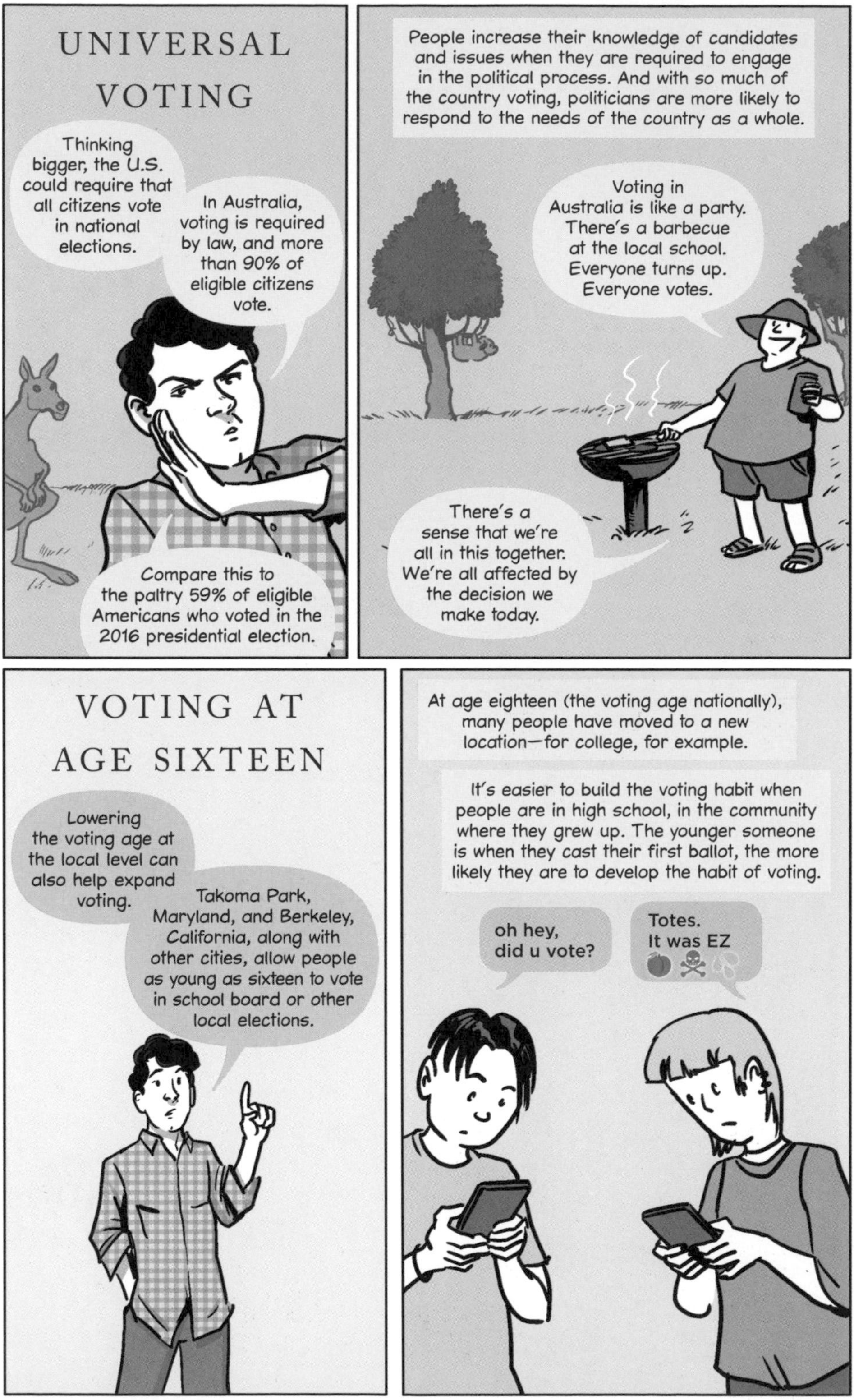
UNIVERSAL VOTING
Thinking bigger, the U.S. could require that all citizens vote in national elections.
In Australia, voting is required by law, and more than 90% of eligible citizens vote.
Compare this to the paltry 59% of eligible Americans who voted in the 2016 presidential election.
People increase their knowledge of candidates and issues when they are required to engage in the political process. And with so much of the country voting, politicians are more likely to respond to the needs of the country as a whole.
Voting in Australia is like a party. There's a barbecue at the local school. Everyone turns up. Everyone votes.
There's a sense that we're all in this together. We're all affected by the decision we make today.
VOTING AT AGE SIXTEEN
Lowering the voting age at the local level can also help expand voting.
Takoma Park, Maryland, and Berkeley, California, along with other cities, allow people as young as sixteen to vote in school board or other local elections.
At age eighteen (the voting age nationally), many people have moved to a new location—for college, for example.
It's easier to build the voting habit when people are in high school, in the community where they grew up. The younger someone is when they cast their first ballot, the more likely they are to develop the habit of voting.
oh hey, did u vote?
Totes. It was EZ

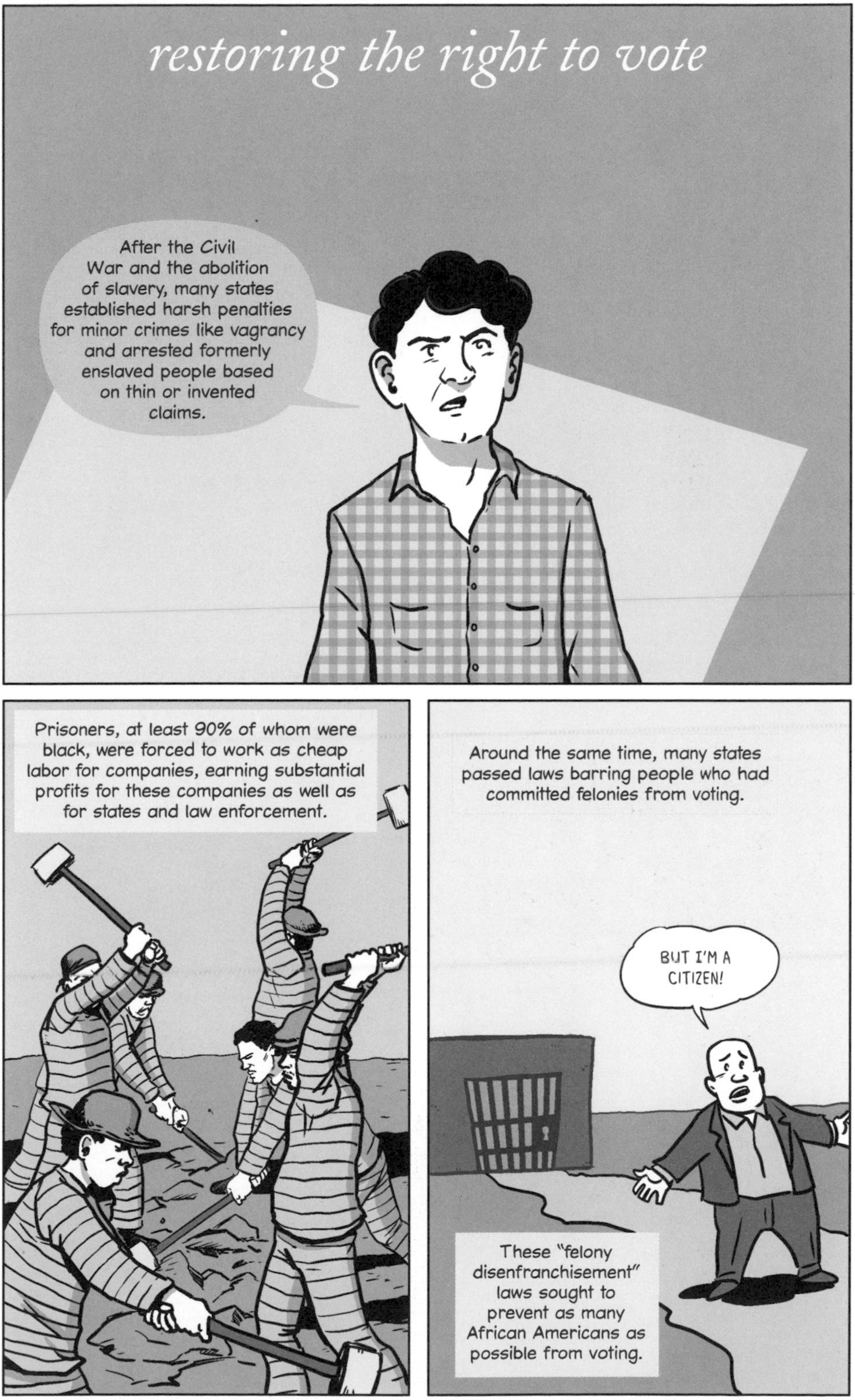
restoring the right to vote
After the Civil War and the abolition of slavery, many states established harsh penalties for minor crimes like vagrancy and arrested formerly enslaved people based on thin or invented claims.
Prisoners, at least 90% of whom were black, were forced to work as cheap labor for companies, earning substantial profits for these companies as well as for states and law enforcement.
Around the same time, many states passed laws barring people who had committed felonies from voting.
BUT I'M A CITIZEN!
These "felony disenfranchisement" laws sought to prevent as many African Americans as possible from voting.

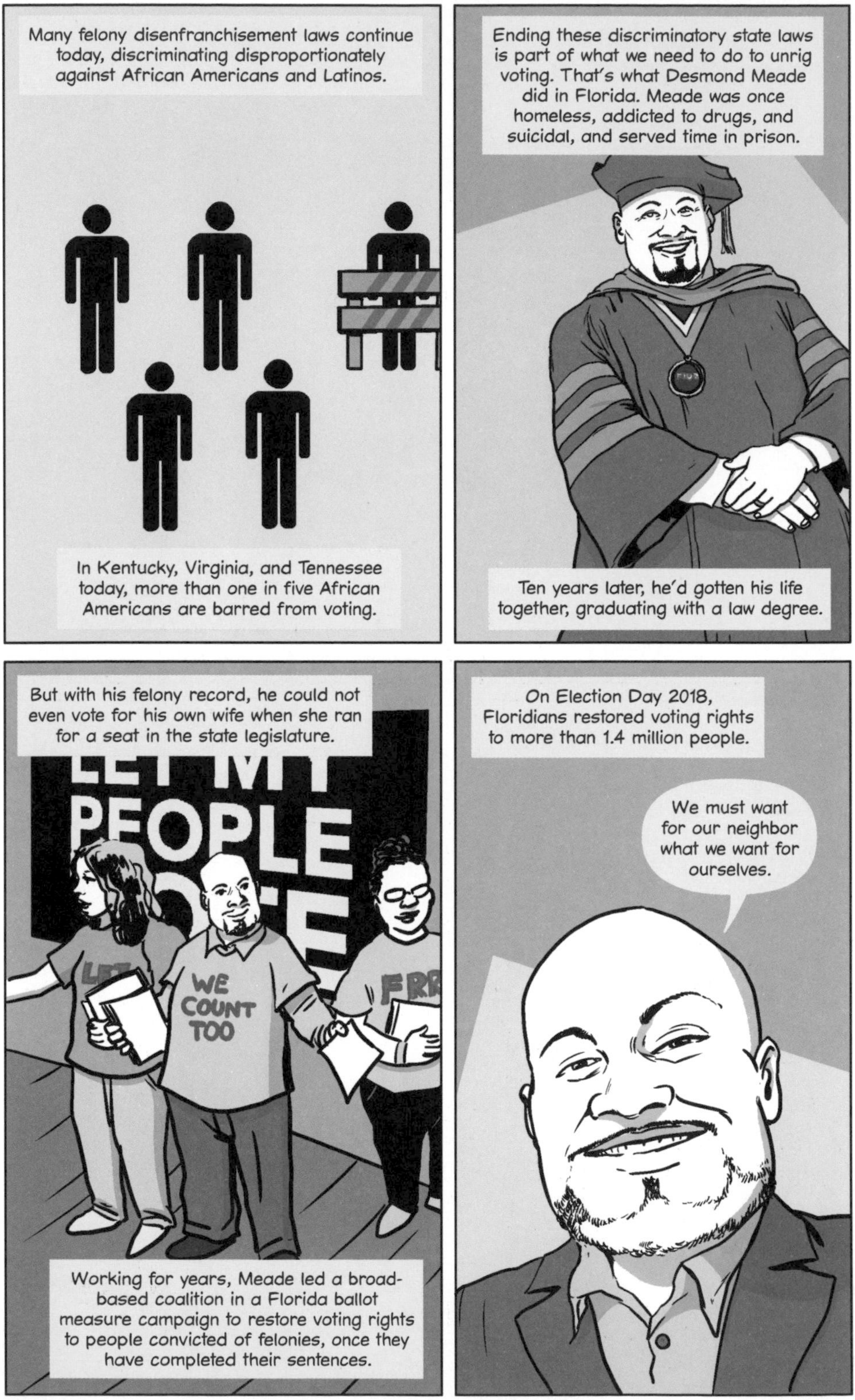
Many felony disenfranchisement laws continue today, discriminating disproportionately against African Americans and Latinos.
In Kentucky, Virginia, and Tennessee today, more than one in five African Americans are barred from voting.
Ending these discriminatory state laws is part of what we need to do to unrig voting. That's what Desmond Meade did in Florida. Meade was once homeless, addicted to drugs, and suicidal, and served time in prison.
Ten years later, he'd gotten his life together, graduating with a law degree.
But with his felony record, he could not even vote for his own wife when she ran for a seat in the state legislature.
PEOPLE
WE COUNT TOO
Working for years, Meade led a broad-based coalition in a Florida ballot measure campaign to restore voting rights to people convicted of felonies, once they have completed their sentences.
On Election Day 2018, Floridians restored voting rights to more than 1.4 million people.
We must want for our neighbor what we want for ourselves.

6

drawing
the
districts

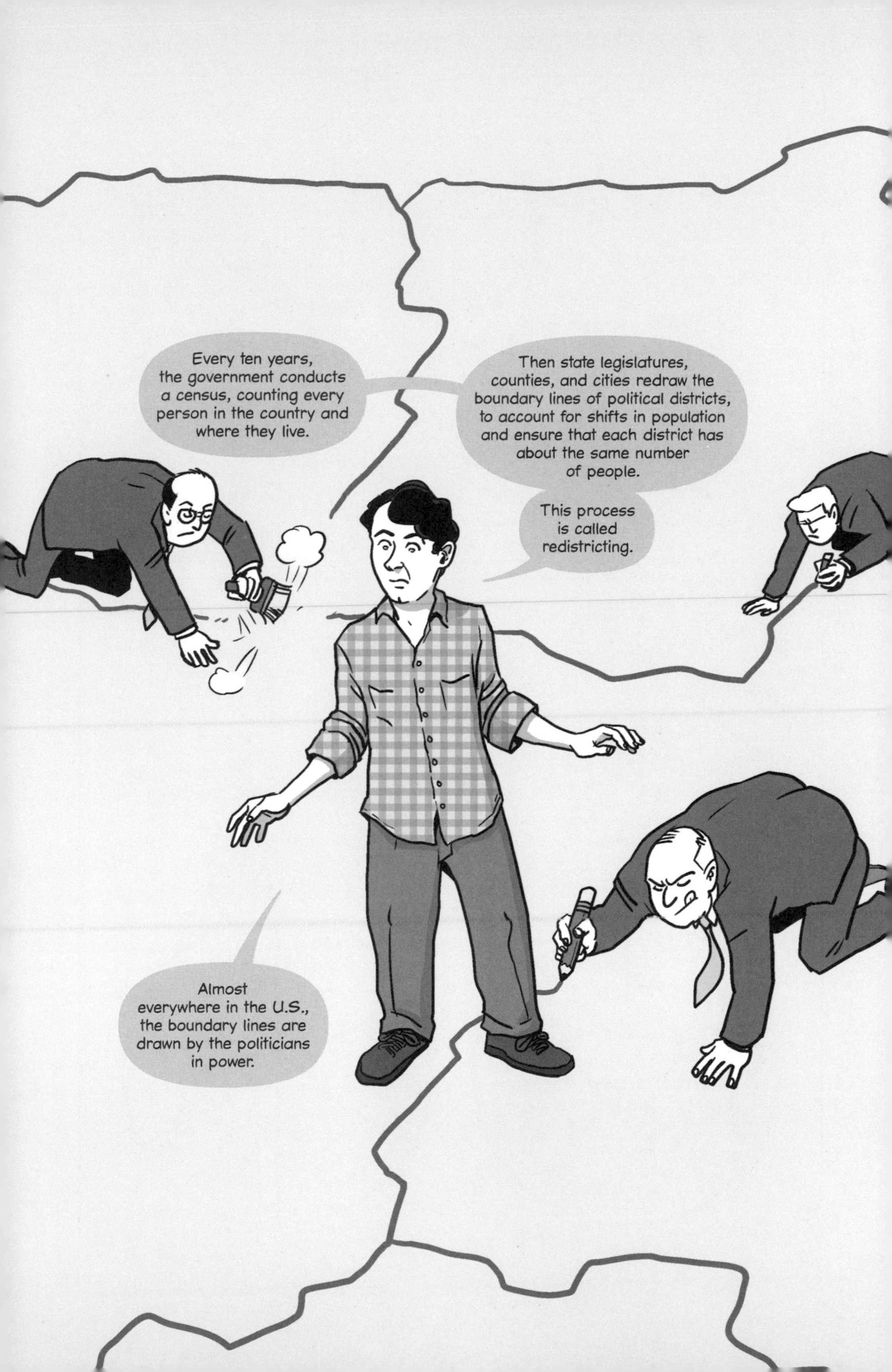
Every ten years, the government conducts a census, counting every person in the country and where they live.
Then state legislatures, counties, and cities redraw the boundary lines of political districts, to account for shifts in population and ensure that each district has about the same number of people.
This process is called redistricting.
Almost everywhere in the U.S., the boundary lines are drawn by the politicians in power.

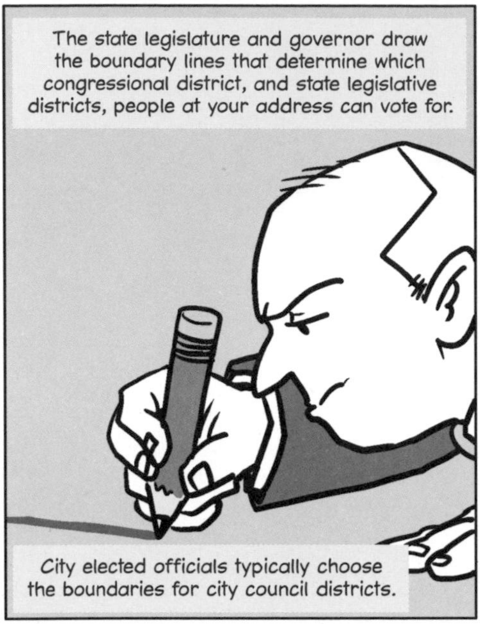
The state legislature and governor draw the boundary lines that determine which congressional district, and state legislative districts, people at your address can vote for.
City elected officials typically choose the boundaries for city council districts.

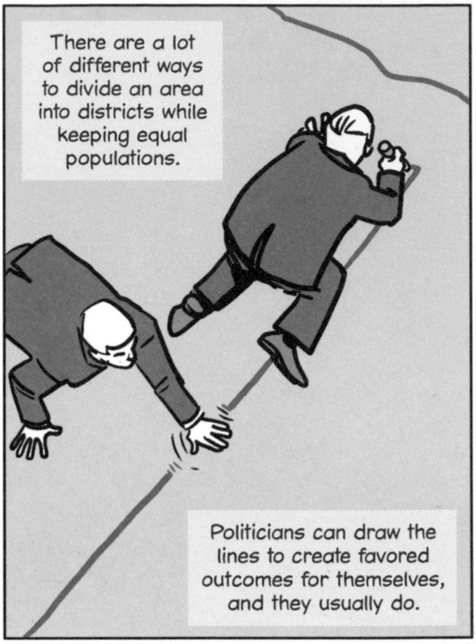
There are a lot of different ways to divide an area into districts while keeping equal populations.
Politicians can draw the lines to create favored outcomes for themselves, and they usually do.

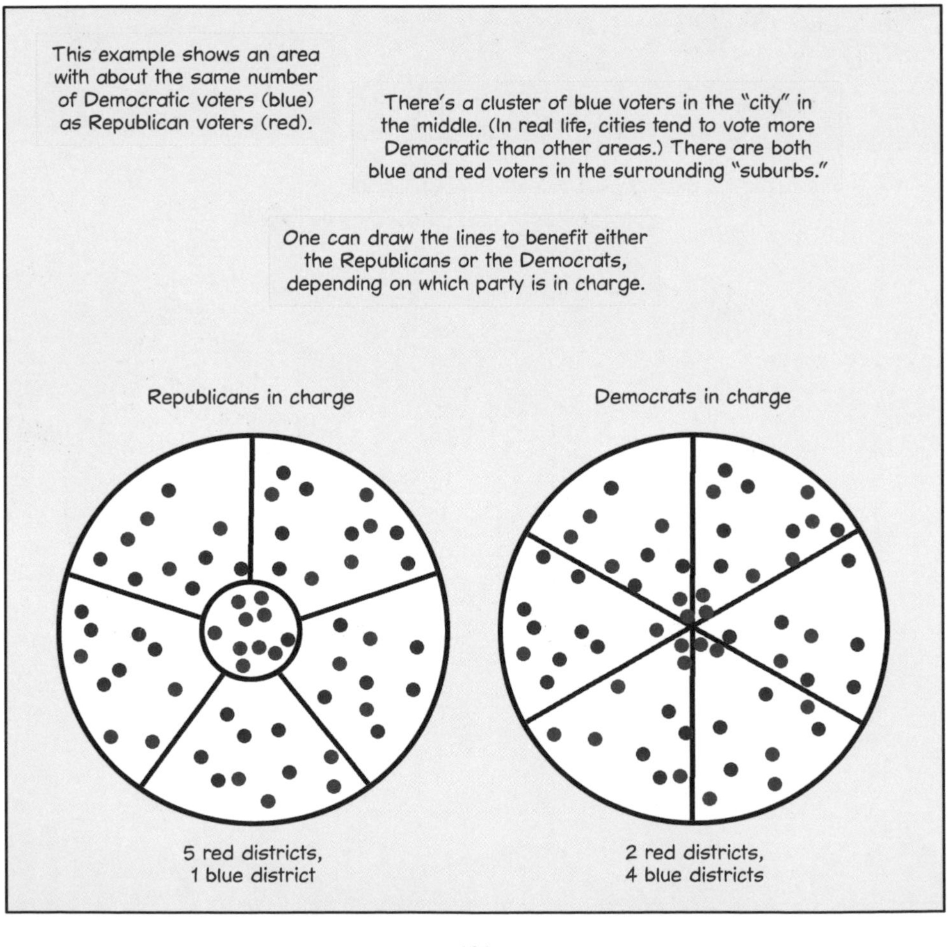
This example shows an area with about the same number of Democratic voters (blue) as Republican voters (red).
There's a cluster of blue voters in the "city" in the middle. (In real life, cities tend to vote more Democratic than other areas.) There are both blue and red voters in the surrounding "suburbs."
One can draw the lines to benefit either the Republicans or the Democrats, depending on which party is in charge.
Republicans in charge
Democrats in charge
5 red districts, 1 blue district
2 red districts, 4 blue districts

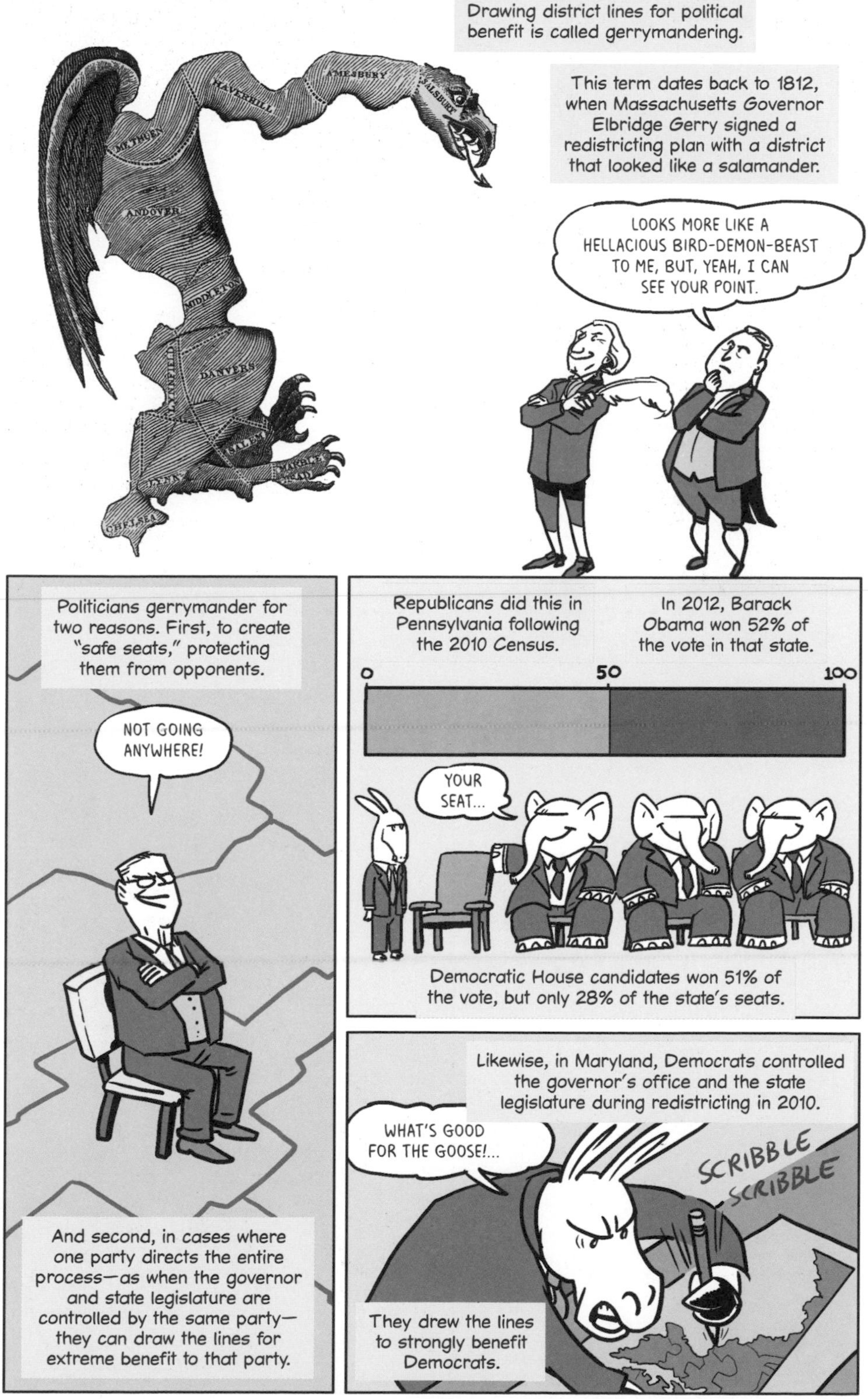
Drawing district lines for political benefit is called gerrymandering.
This term dates back to 1812, when Massachusetts Governor Elbridge Gerry signed a redistricting plan with a district that looked like a salamander.
AMESBURY
HAVERHILL
SALSBURY
METHUEN
ANDOVER
MIDDLETON
LYNNFIELD
DANVERS
SALEM
LYNN
CHELSEA
LOOKS MORE LIKE A HELLACIOUS BIRD-DEMON-BEAST TO ME, BUT, YEAH, I CAN SEE YOUR POINT.
Politicians gerrymander for two reasons. First, to create "safe seats," protecting them from opponents.
NOT GOING ANYWHERE!
And second, in cases where one party directs the entire process—as when the governor and state legislature are controlled by the same party—they can draw the lines for extreme benefit to that party.
Republicans did this in Pennsylvania following the 2010 Census.
In 2012, Barack Obama won 52% of the vote in that state.
0
50
100
YOUR SEAT...
Democratic House candidates won 51% of the vote, but only 28% of the state's seats.
Likewise, in Maryland, Democrats controlled the governor's office and the state legislature during redistricting in 2010.
WHAT'S GOOD FOR THE GOOSE!...
SCRIBBLE
SCRIBBLE
They drew the lines to strongly benefit Democrats.

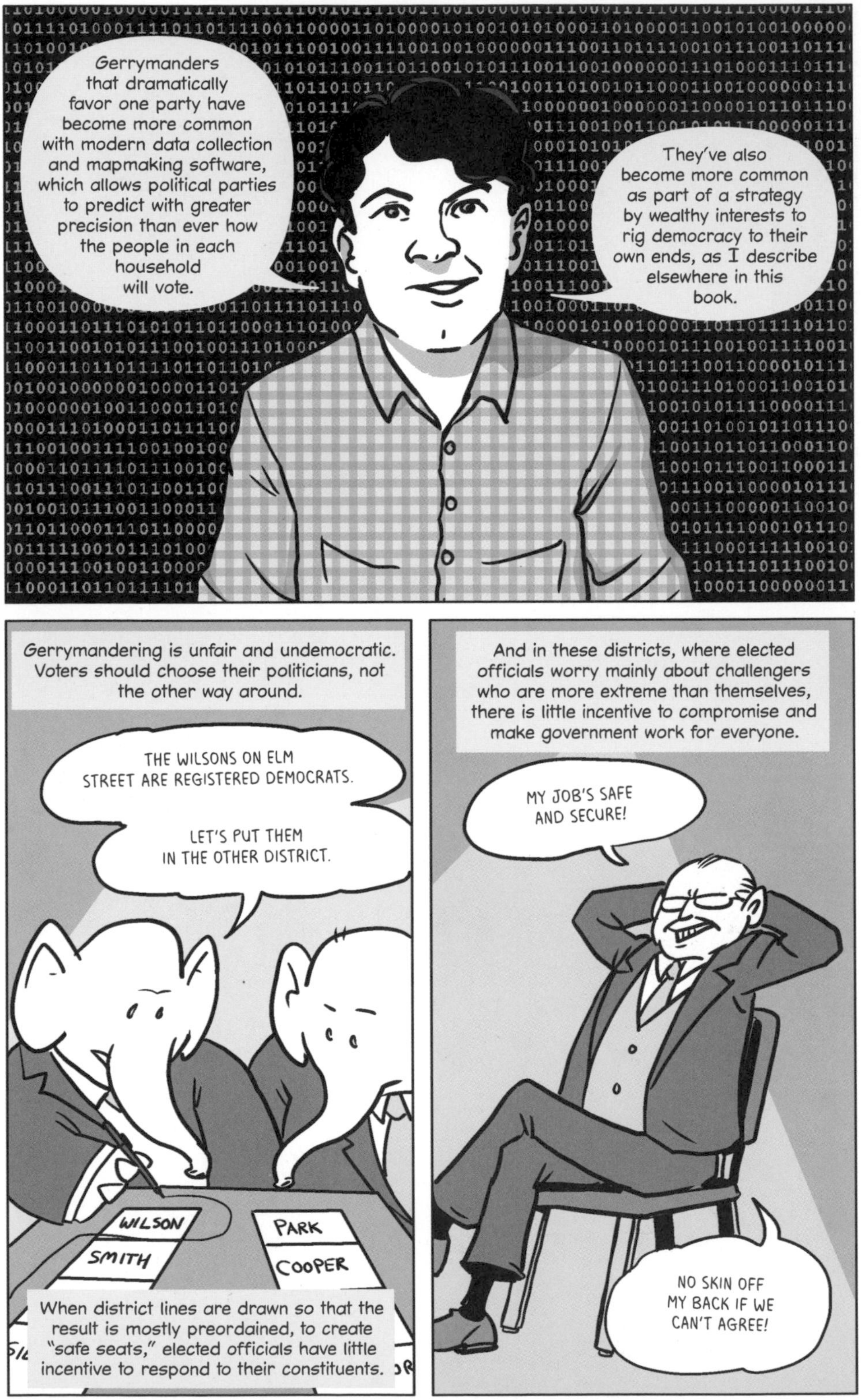

Gerrymanders that dramatically favor one party have become more common with modern data collection and mapmaking software, which allows political parties to predict with greater precision than ever how the people in each household will vote.
They've also become more common as part of a strategy by wealthy interests to rig democracy to their own ends, as I describe elsewhere in this book.
Gerrymandering is unfair and undemocratic. Voters should choose their politicians, not the other way around.
THE WILSONS ON ELM STREET ARE REGISTERED DEMOCRATS.
LET'S PUT THEM IN THE OTHER DISTRICT.
WILSON
SMITH
PARK
COOPER
When district lines are drawn so that the result is mostly preordained, to create "safe seats," elected officials have little incentive to respond to their constituents.
And in these districts, where elected officials worry mainly about challengers who are more extreme than themselves, there is little incentive to compromise and make government work for everyone.
MY JOB'S SAFE AND SECURE!
NO SKIN OFF MY BACK IF WE CAN'T AGREE!

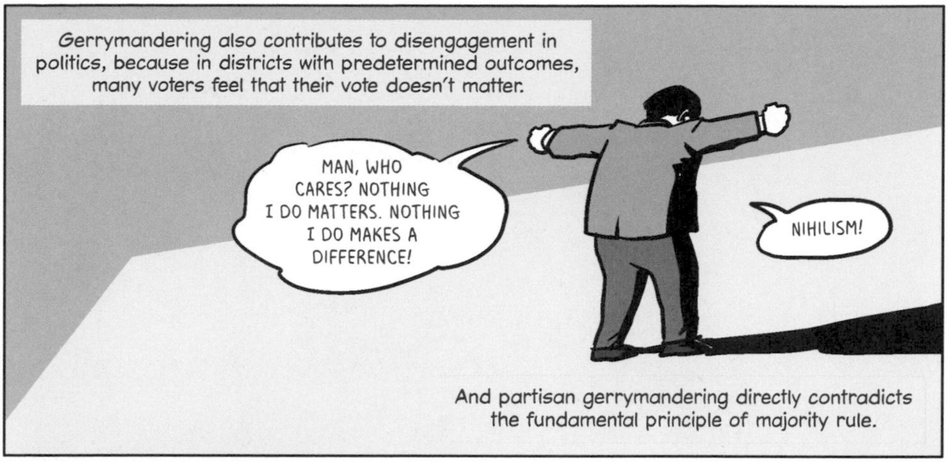
Gerrymandering also contributes to disengagement in politics, because in districts with predetermined outcomes, many voters feel that their vote doesn't matter.
MAN, WHO CARES? NOTHING I DO MATTERS. NOTHING I DO MAKES A DIFFERENCE!
NIHILISM!
And partisan gerrymandering directly contradicts the fundamental principle of majority rule.

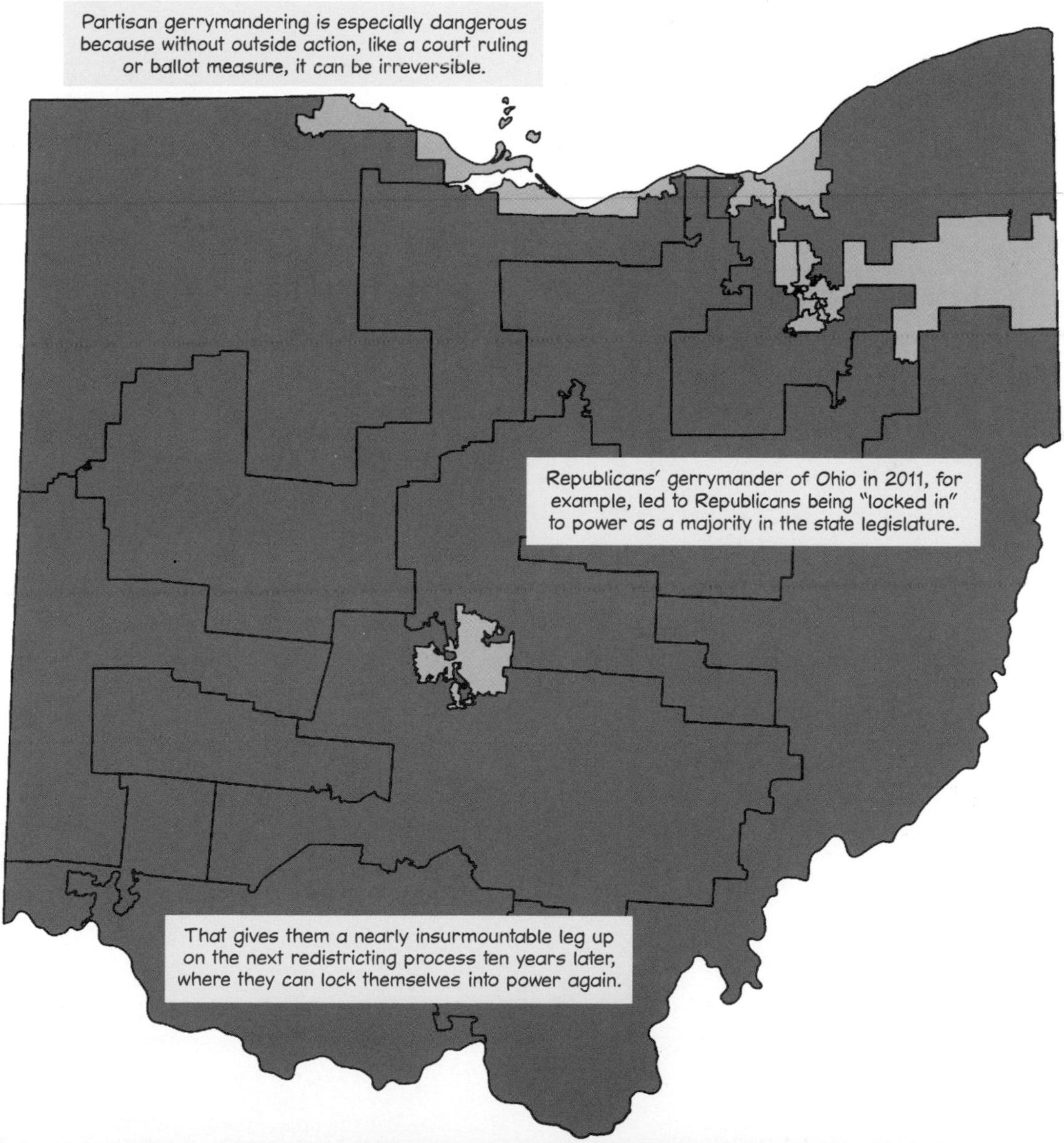
Partisan gerrymandering is especially dangerous because without outside action, like a court ruling or ballot measure, it can be irreversible.
Republicans' gerrymander of *Ohio* in 2011, for example, led to Republicans being "locked in" to power as a majority in the state legislature.
That gives them a nearly insurmountable leg up on the next redistricting process ten years later, where they can lock themselves into power again.

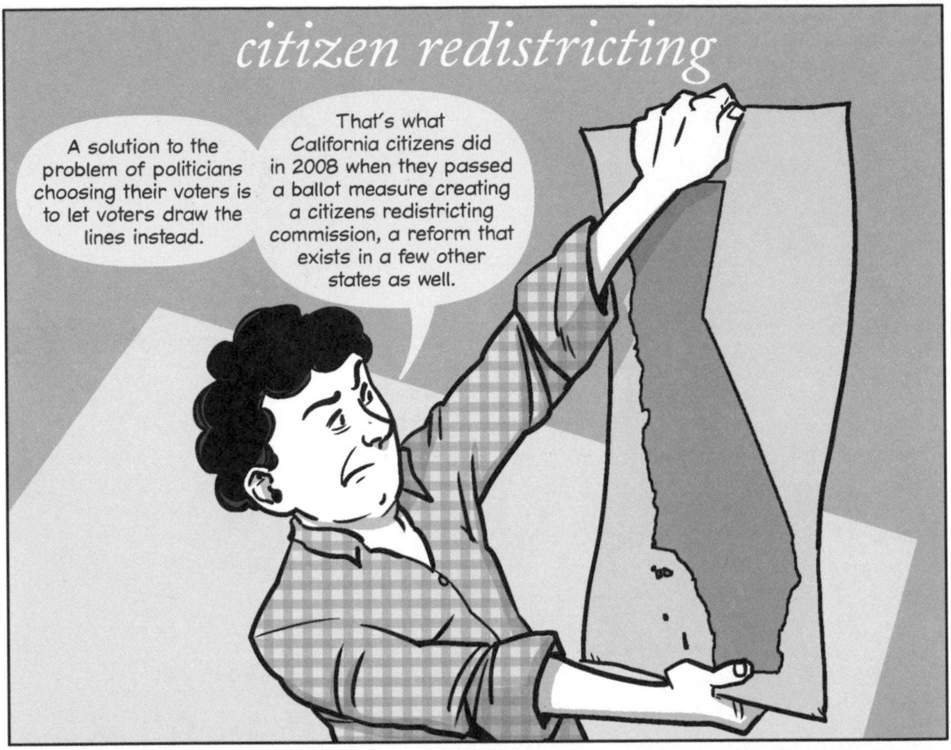
citizen redistricting
A solution to the problem of politicians choosing their voters is to let voters draw the lines instead.
That's what California citizens did in 2008 when they passed a ballot measure creating a citizens redistricting commission, a reform that exists in a few other states as well.

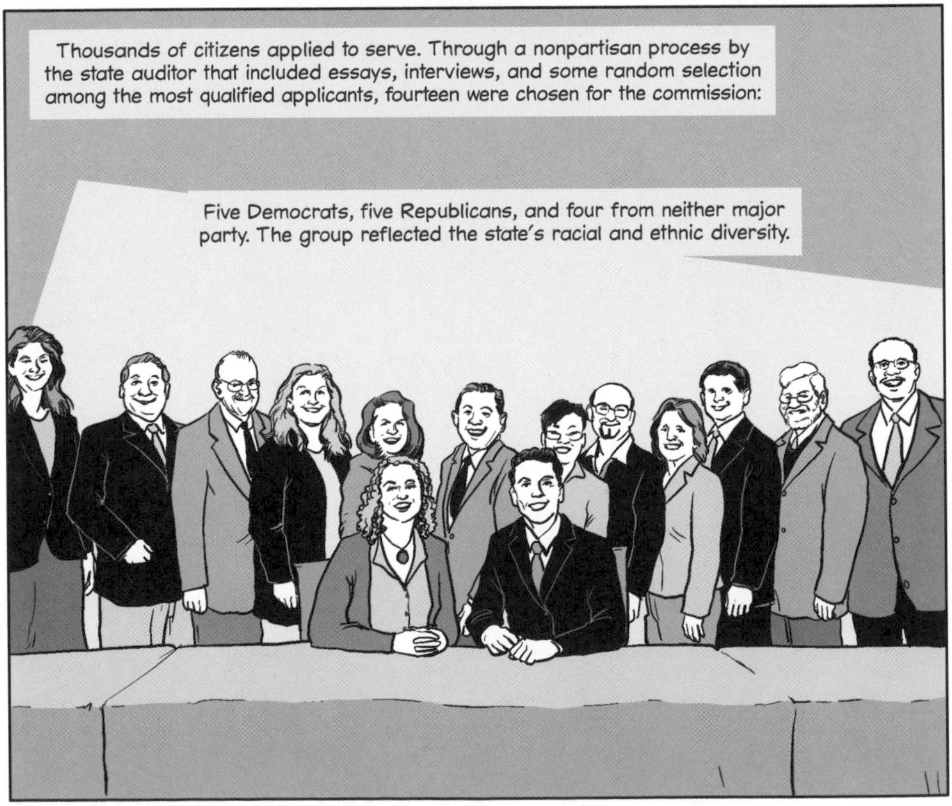
Thousands of citizens applied to serve. Through a nonpartisan process by the state auditor that included essays, interviews, and some random selection among the most qualified applicants, fourteen were chosen for the commission:
Five Democrats, five Republicans, and four from neither major party. The group reflected the state's racial and ethnic diversity.

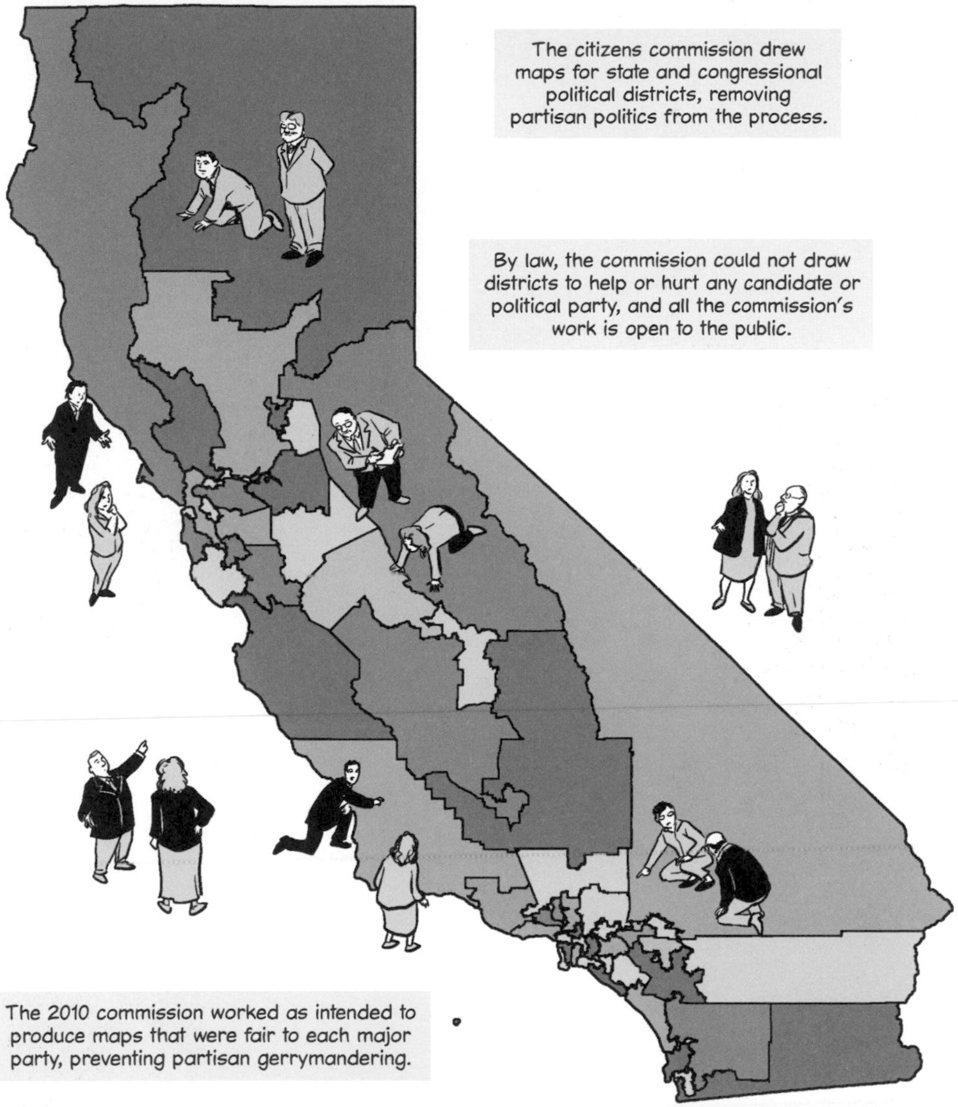
The citizens commission drew maps for state and congressional political districts, removing partisan politics from the process.
By law, the commission could not draw districts to help or hurt any candidate or political party, and all the commission's work is open to the public.
The 2010 commission worked as intended to produce maps that were fair to each major party, preventing partisan gerrymandering.

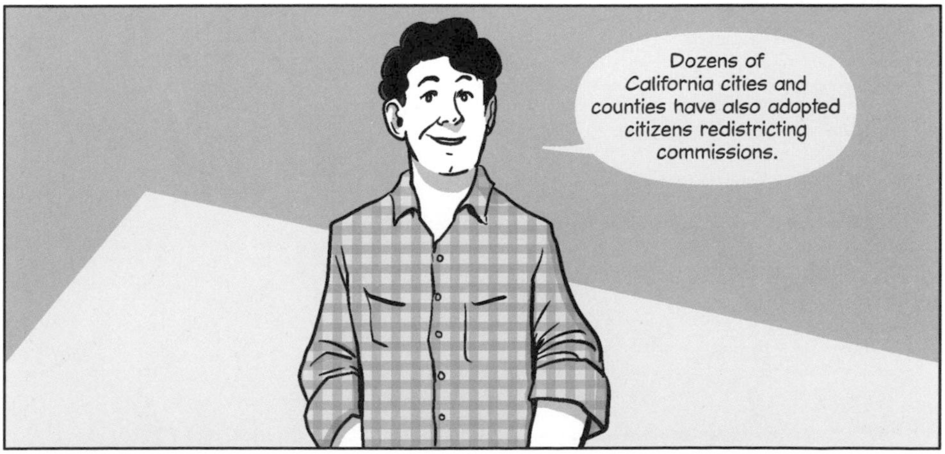
Dozens of California cities and counties have also adopted citizens redistricting commissions.

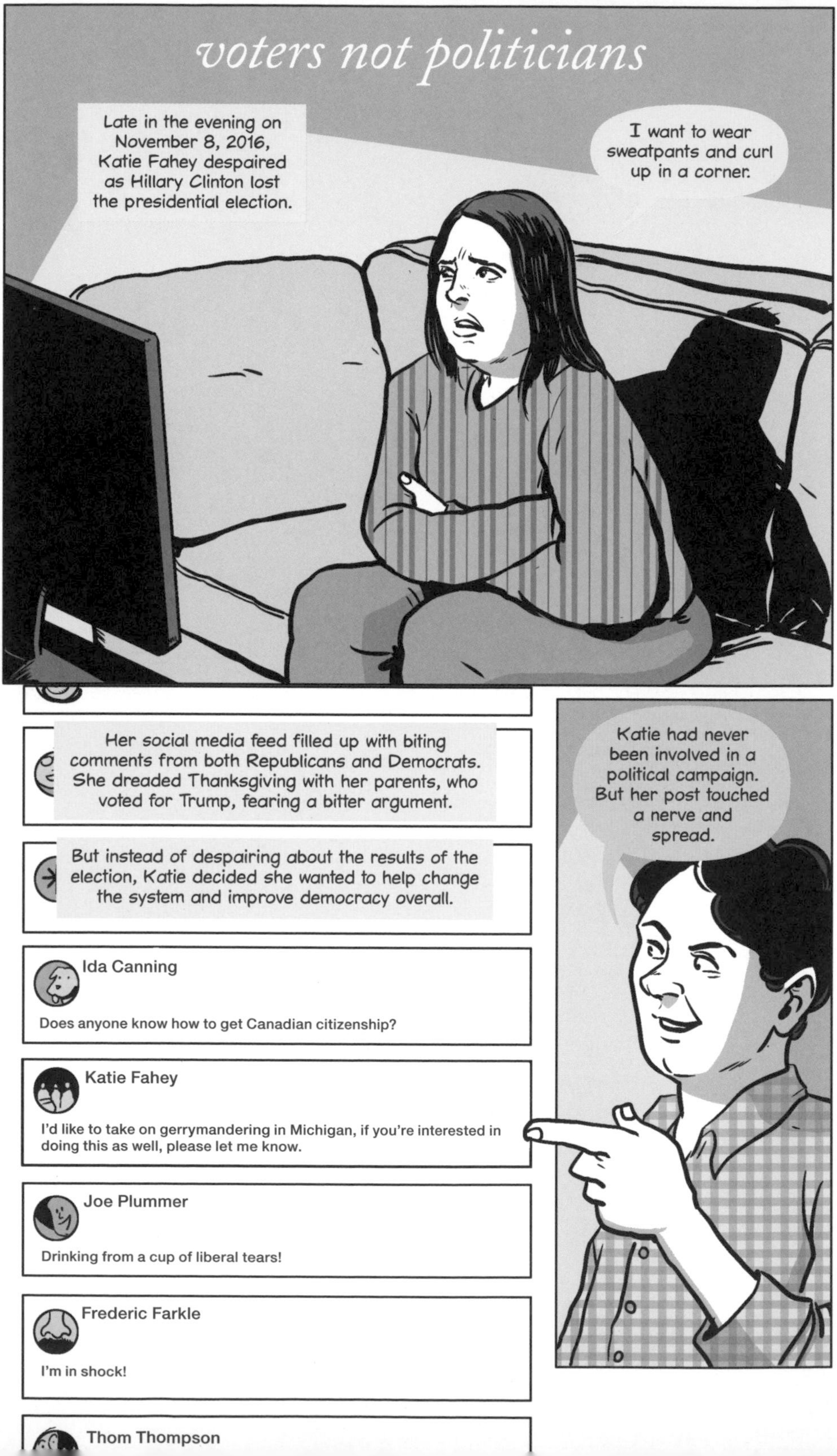
voters not politicians
Late in the evening on November 8, 2016, Katie Fahey despaired as Hillary Clinton lost the presidential election.
I want to wear sweatpants and curl up in a corner.
Her social media feed filled up with biting comments from both Republicans and Democrats. She dreaded Thanksgiving with her parents, who voted for Trump, fearing a bitter argument.
But instead of despairing about the results of the election, Katie decided she wanted to help change the system and improve democracy overall.
Ida Canning
Does anyone know how to get Canadian citizenship?
Katie Fahey
I'd like to take on gerrymandering in Michigan, if you're interested in doing this as well, please let me know.
Katie had never been involved in a political campaign. But her post touched a nerve and spread.
Joe Plummer
Drinking from a cup of liberal tears!
Frederic Farkle
I'm in shock!
Thom Thompson

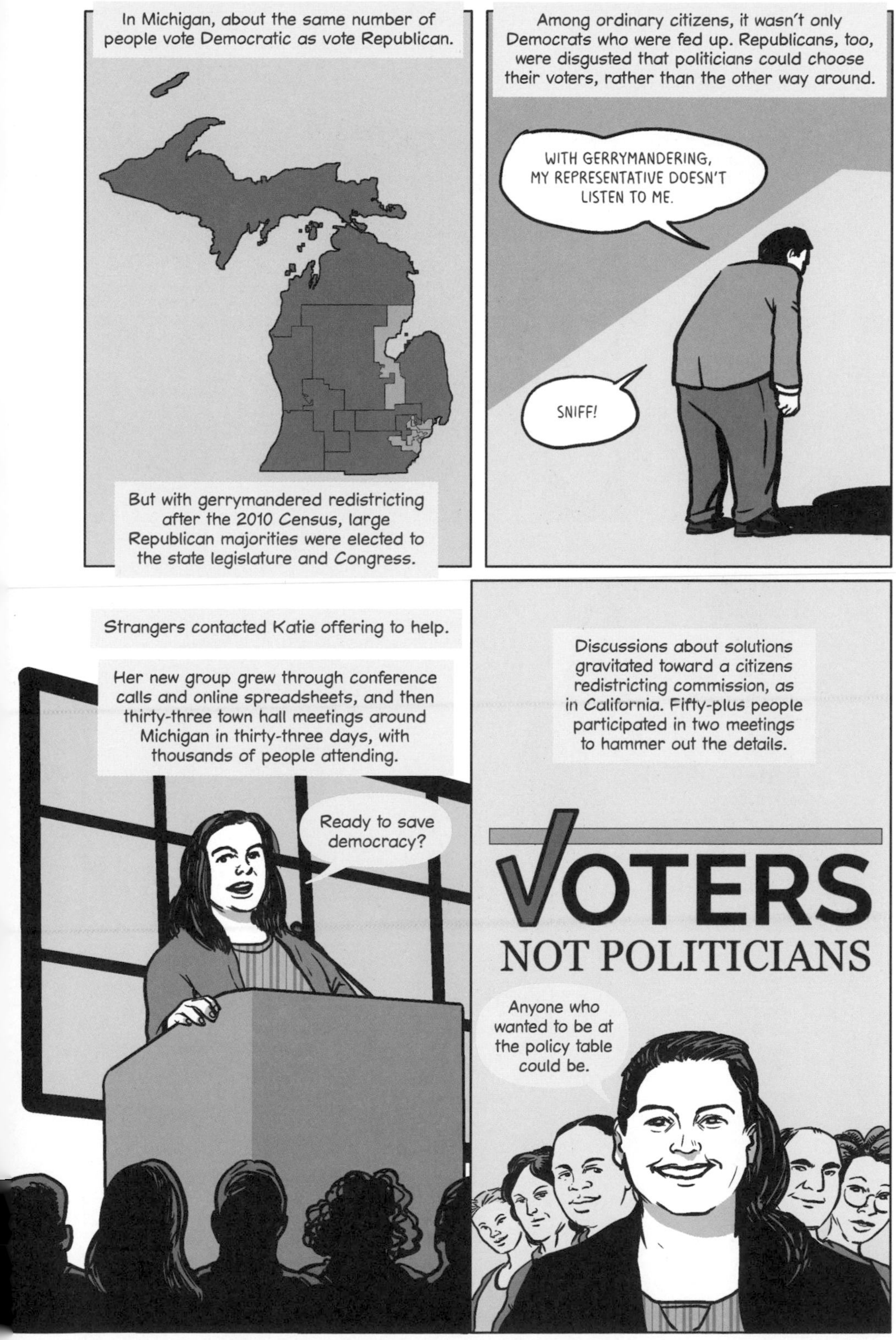
In Michigan, about the same number of people vote Democratic as vote Republican.
But with gerrymandered redistricting after the 2010 Census, large Republican majorities were elected to the state legislature and Congress.
Among ordinary citizens, it wasn't only Democrats who were fed up. Republicans, too, were disgusted that politicians could choose their voters, rather than the other way around.
WITH GERRYMANDERING, MY REPRESENTATIVE DOESN'T LISTEN TO ME.
SNIFF!
Strangers contacted Katie offering to help.
Her new group grew through conference calls and online spreadsheets, and then thirty-three town hall meetings around Michigan in thirty-three days, with thousands of people attending.
Ready to save democracy?
Discussions about solutions gravitated toward a citizens redistricting commission, as in California. Fifty-plus people participated in two meetings to hammer out the details.
VOTERS
NOT POLITICIANS
Anyone who wanted to be at the policy table could be.

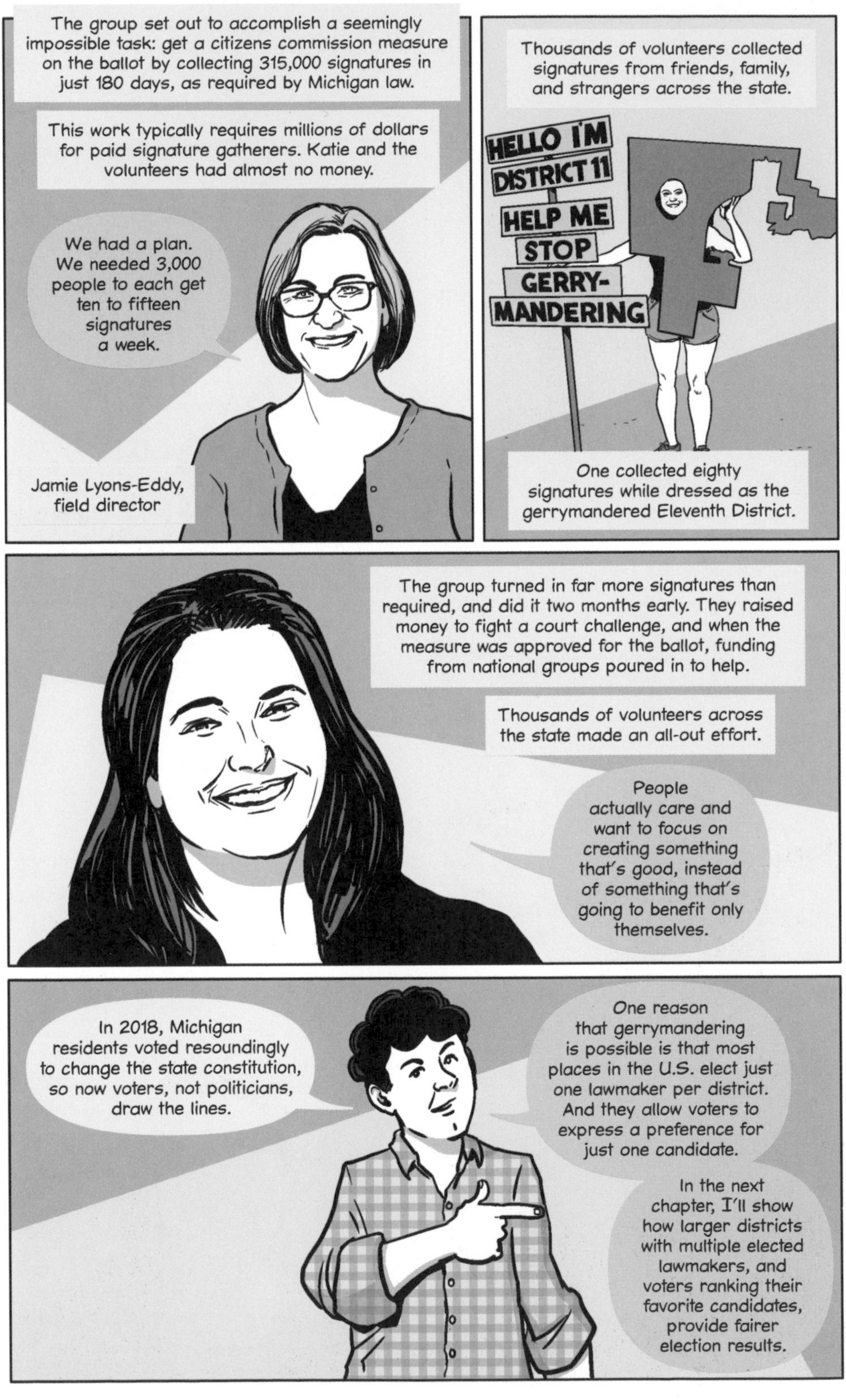
The group set out to accomplish a seemingly impossible task: get a citizens commission measure on the ballot by collecting 315,000 signatures in just 180 days, as required by Michigan law.
This work typically requires millions of dollars for paid signature gatherers. Katie and the volunteers had almost no money.
We had a plan. We needed 3,000 people to each get ten to fifteen signatures a week.
Jamie Lyons-Eddy, field director
Thousands of volunteers collected signatures from friends, family, and strangers across the state.
HELLO I'M
DISTRICT 11
HELP ME
STOP
GERRY-
MANDERING
One collected eighty signatures while dressed as the gerrymandered Eleventh District.
The group turned in far more signatures than required, and did it two months early. They raised money to fight a court challenge, and when the measure was approved for the ballot, funding from national groups poured in to help.
Thousands of volunteers across the state made an all-out effort.
People actually care and want to focus on creating something that's good, instead of something that's going to benefit only themselves.
In 2018, Michigan residents voted resoundingly to change the state constitution, so now voters, not politicians, draw the lines.
One reason that gerrymandering is possible is that most places in the U.S. elect just one lawmaker per district. And they allow voters to express a preference for just one candidate.
In the next chapter, I'll show how larger districts with multiple elected lawmakers, and voters ranking their favorite candidates, provide fairer election results.

7

picking
the

winners

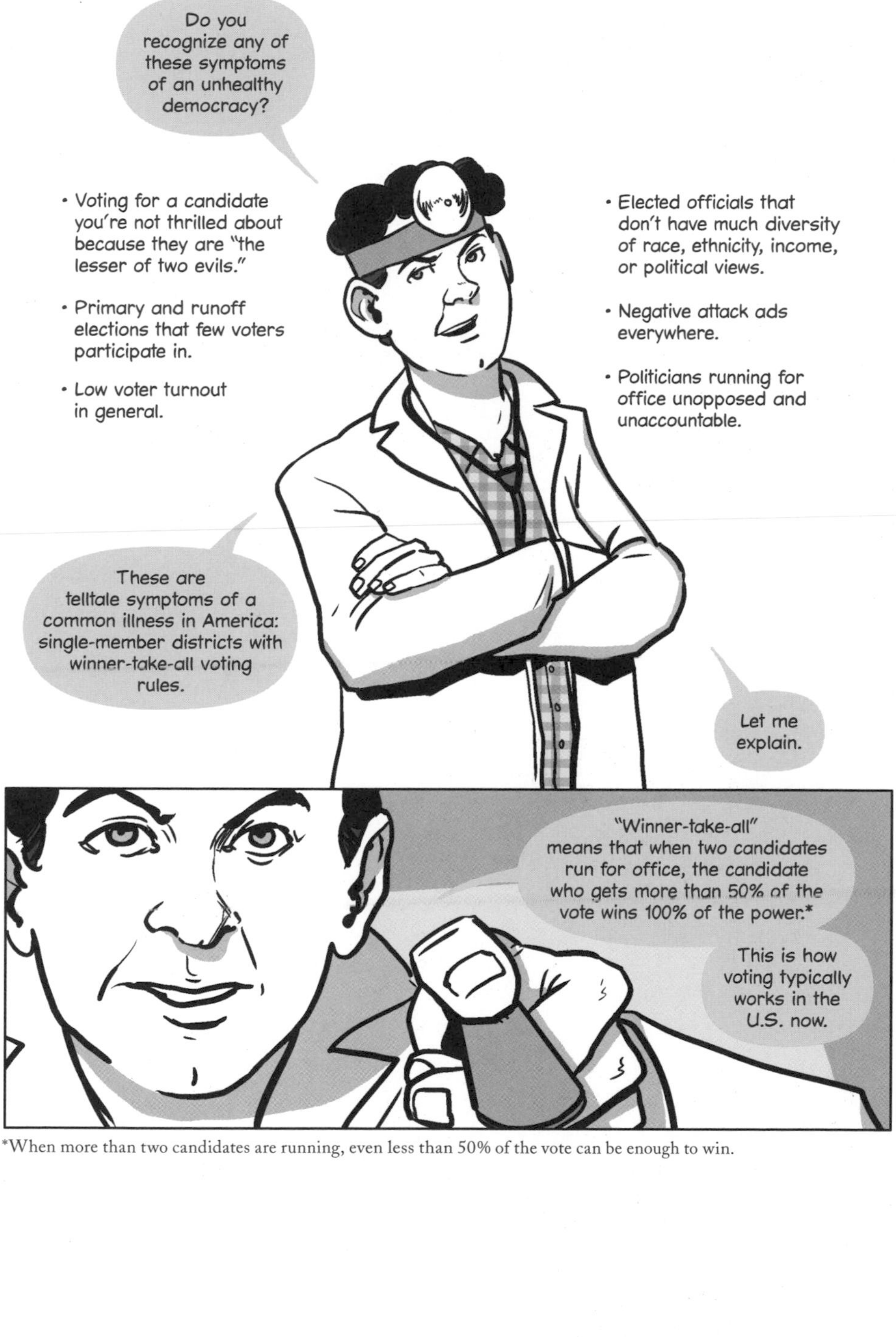
Do you recognize any of these symptoms of an unhealthy democracy?
• Voting for a candidate you're not thrilled about because they are "the lesser of two evils."
• Primary and runoff elections that few voters participate in.
• Low voter turnout in general.
• Elected officials that don't have much diversity of race, ethnicity, income, or political views.
• Negative attack ads everywhere.
• Politicians running for office unopposed and unaccountable.
These are telltale symptoms of a common illness in America: single-member districts with winner-take-all voting rules.
Let me explain.
"Winner-take-all" means that when two candidates run for office, the candidate who gets more than 50% of the vote wins 100% of the power.*
This is how voting typically works in the U.S. now.

*When more than two candidates are running, even less than 50% of the vote can be enough to win.

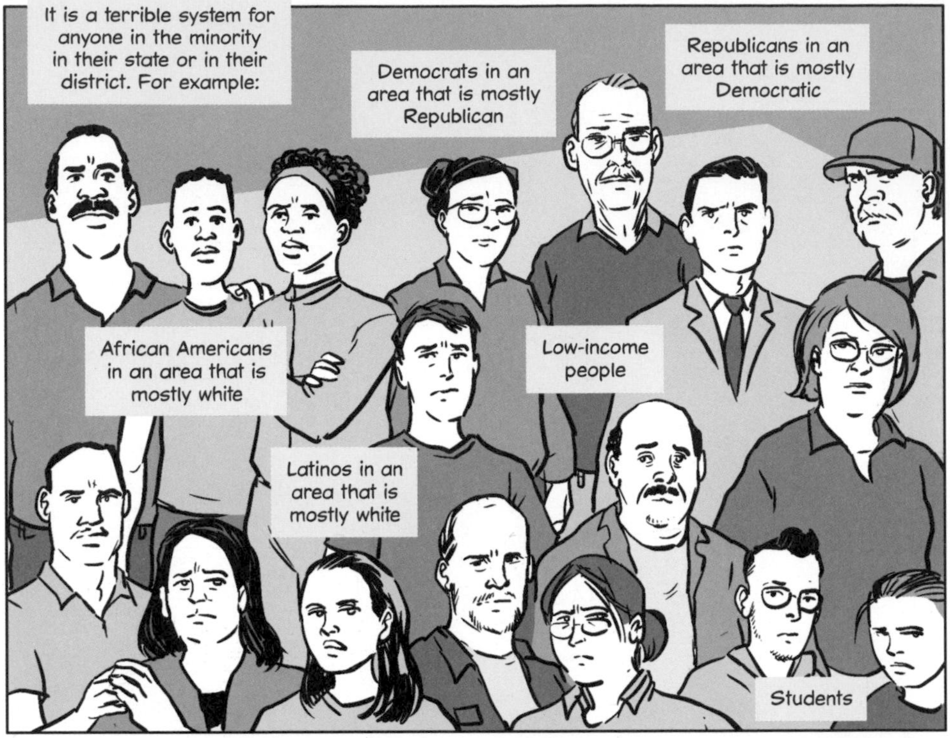
It is a terrible system for anyone in the minority in their state or in their district. For example:
Democrats in an area that is mostly Republican
Republicans in an area that is mostly Democratic
African Americans in an area that is mostly white
Low-income people
Latinos in an area that is mostly white
Students

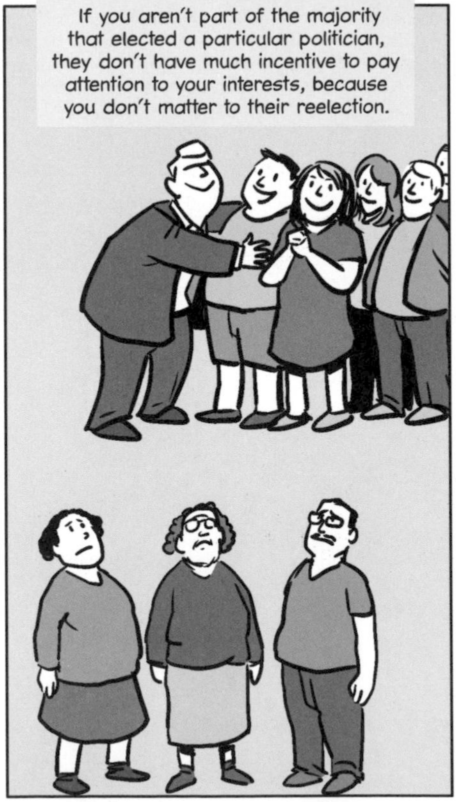
If you aren't part of the majority that elected a particular politician, they don't have much incentive to pay attention to your interests, because you don't matter to their reelection.

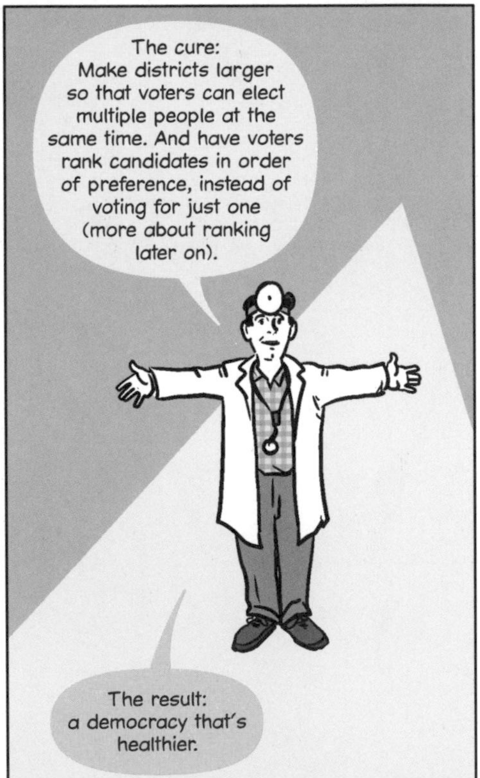
The cure: Make districts larger so that voters can elect multiple people at the same time. And have voters rank candidates in order of preference, instead of voting for just one (more about ranking later on).
The result: a democracy that's healthier.

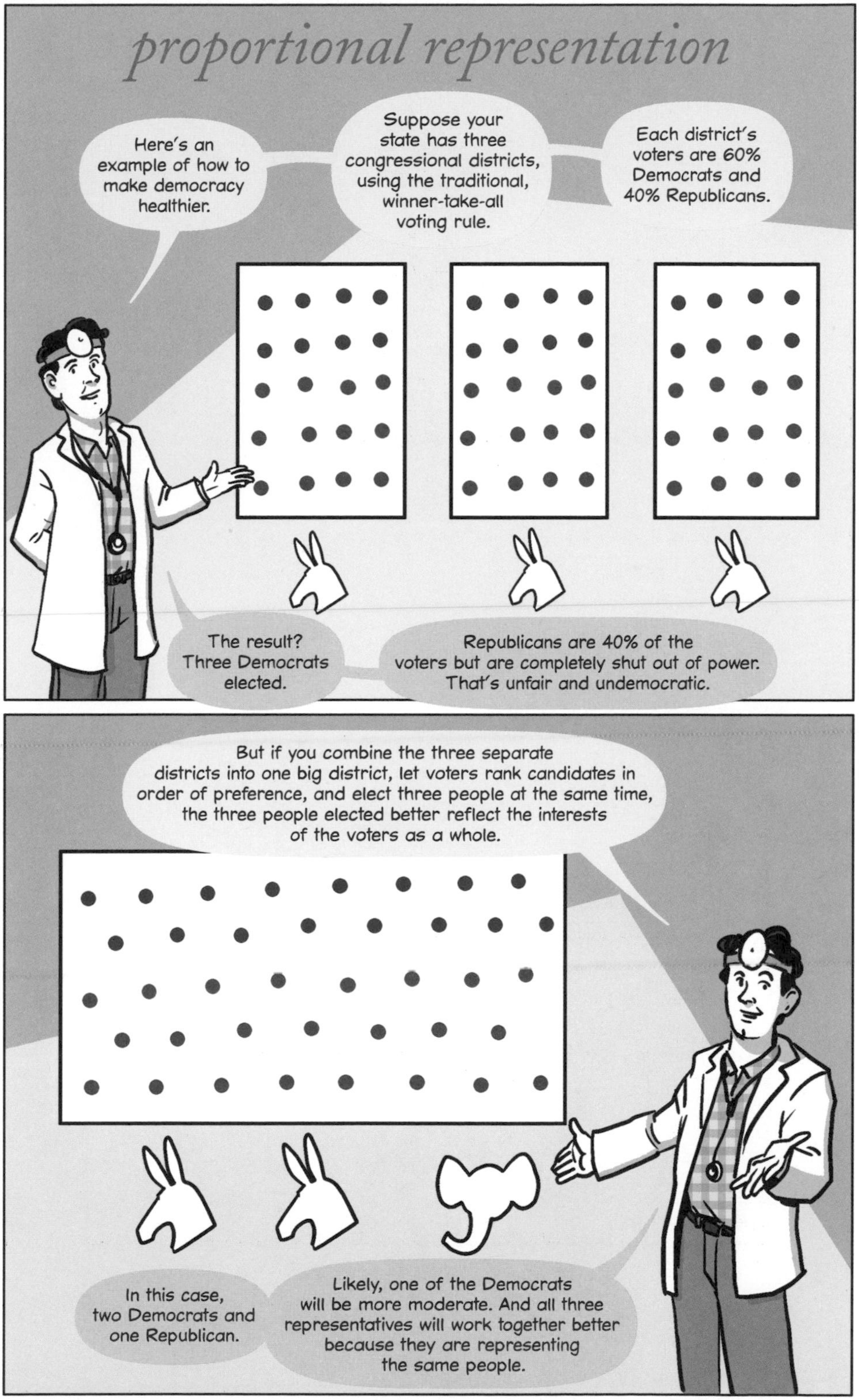

proportional representation
Here's an example of how to make democracy healthier.
Suppose your state has three congressional districts, using the traditional, winner-take-all voting rule.
Each district's voters are 60% Democrats and 40% Republicans.
The result? Three Democrats elected.
Republicans are 40% of the voters but are completely shut out of power. That's unfair and undemocratic.
But if you combine the three separate districts into one big district, let voters rank candidates in order of preference, and elect three people at the same time, the three people elected better reflect the interests of the voters as a whole.
In this case, two Democrats and one Republican.
Likely, one of the Democrats will be more moderate. And all three representatives will work together better because they are representing the same people.

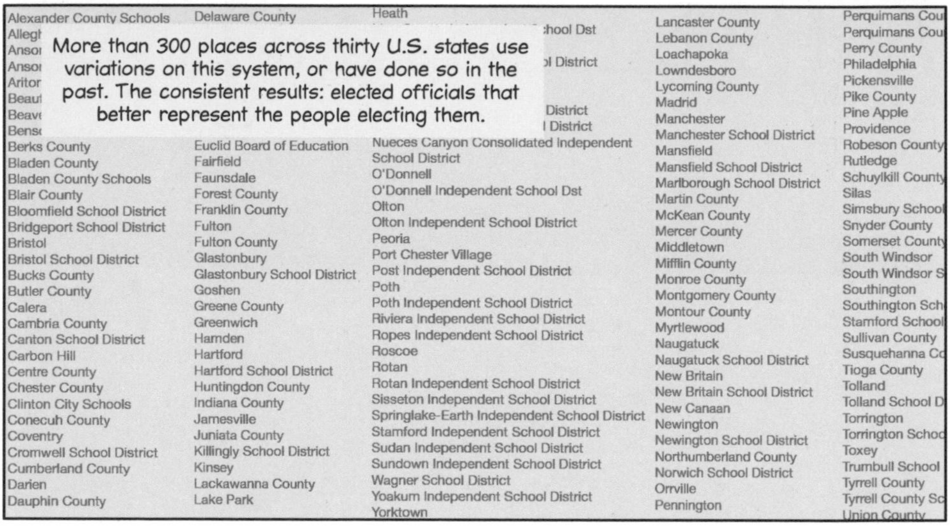

More than 300 places across thirty U.S. states use variations on this system, or have done so in the past. The consistent results: elected officials that better represent the people electing them.

Alexander County Schools	Delaware County	Heath	Lancaster County	Perquimans Cou
Allegh		chool Dst	Lebanon County	Perquimans Cou
Anso			Loachapoka	Perry County
Anso		ol District	Lowndesboro	Philadelphia
Aritor			Lycoming County	Pickensville
Beaut			Madrid	Pike County
Beav		District	Manchester	Pine Apple
Bens		l District	Manchester School District	Providence
Berks County	Euclid Board of Education	Nueces Canyon Consolidated Independent	Mansfield	Robeson County
Bladen County	Fairfield	School District	Mansfield School District	Rutledge
Bladen County Schools	Faunsdale	O'Donnell	Marlborough School District	Schuylkill County
Blair County	Forest County	O'Donnell Independent School Dst	Martin County	Silas
Bloomfield School District	Franklin County	Olton	McKean County	Simsbury School
Bridgeport School District	Fulton	Olton Independent School District	Mercer County	Snyder County
Bristol	Fulton County	Peoria	Middletown	Somerset County
Bristol School District	Glastonbury	Port Chester Village	Mifflin County	South Windsor
Bucks County	Glastonbury School District	Post Independent School District	Monroe County	South Windsor S
Butler County	Goshen	Poth	Montgomery County	Southington
Calera	Greene County	Poth Independent School District	Montour County	Southington Sch
Cambria County	Greenwich	Riviera Independent School District	Myrtlewood	Stamford School
Canton School District	Hamden	Ropes Independent School District	Naugatuck	Sullivan County
Carbon Hill	Hartford	Roscoe	Naugatuck School District	Susquehanna Co
Centre County	Hartford School District	Rotan	New Britain	Tioga County
Chester County	Huntingdon County	Rotan Independent School District	New Britain School District	Tolland
Clinton City Schools	Indiana County	Sisseton Independent School District	New Canaan	Tolland School D
Conecuh County	Jamesville	Springlake-Earth Independent School District	Newington	Torrington
Coventry	Juniata County	Stamford Independent School District	Newington School District	Torrington Schoo
Cromwell School District	Killingly School District	Sudan Independent School District	Northumberland County	Toxey
Cumberland County	Kinsey	Sundown Independent School District	Norwich School District	Trumbull School
Darien	Lackawanna County	Wagner School District	Orrville	Tyrrell County
Dauphin County	Lake Park	Yoakum Independent School District	Pennington	Tyrrell County Sc
		Yorktown		Union County

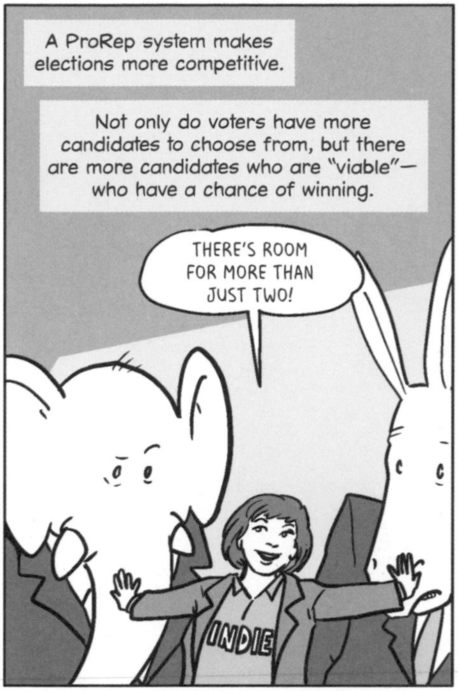
A ProRep system makes elections more competitive.
Not only do voters have more candidates to choose from, but there are more candidates who are "viable"— who have a chance of winning.
THERE'S ROOM FOR MORE THAN JUST TWO!
INDIE

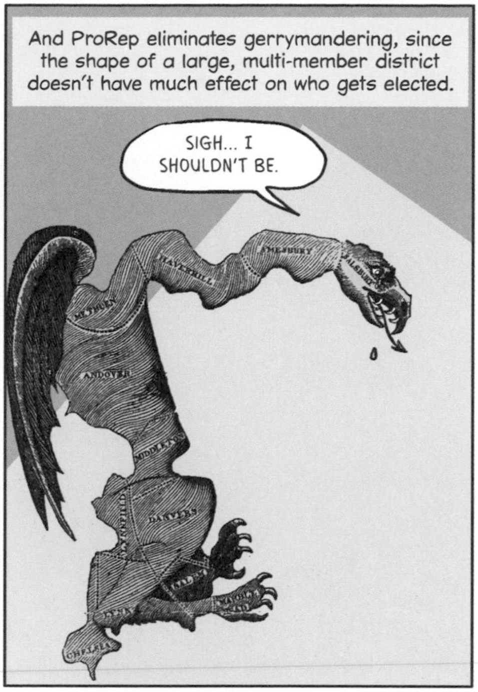
And ProRep eliminates gerrymandering, since the shape of a large, multi-member district doesn't have much effect on who gets elected.
SIGH... I SHOULDN'T BE.

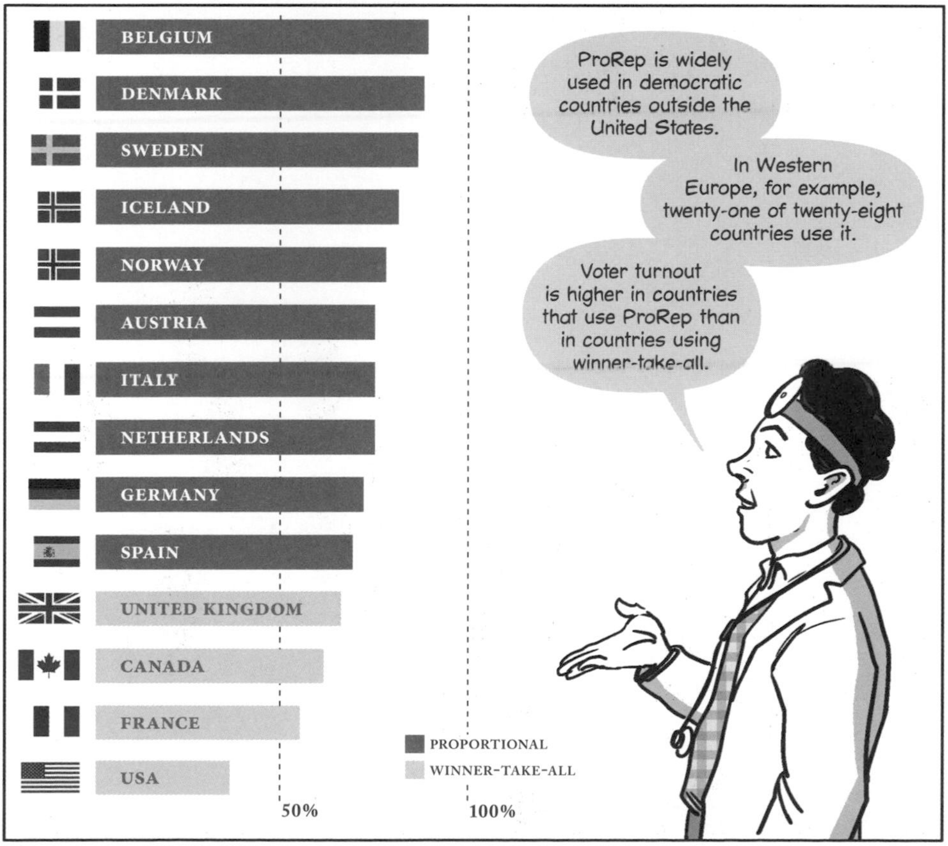
BELGIUM
DENMARK
SWEDEN
ICELAND
NORWAY
AUSTRIA
ITALY
NETHERLANDS
GERMANY
SPAIN
UNITED KINGDOM
CANADA
FRANCE
USA
50%
100%
PROPORTIONAL
WINNER-TAKE-ALL
ProRep is widely used in democratic countries outside the United States.
In Western Europe, for example, twenty-one of twenty-eight countries use it.
Voter turnout is higher in countries that use ProRep than in countries using winner-take-all.

Chart courtesy of Sightline Institute

ranked choice voting

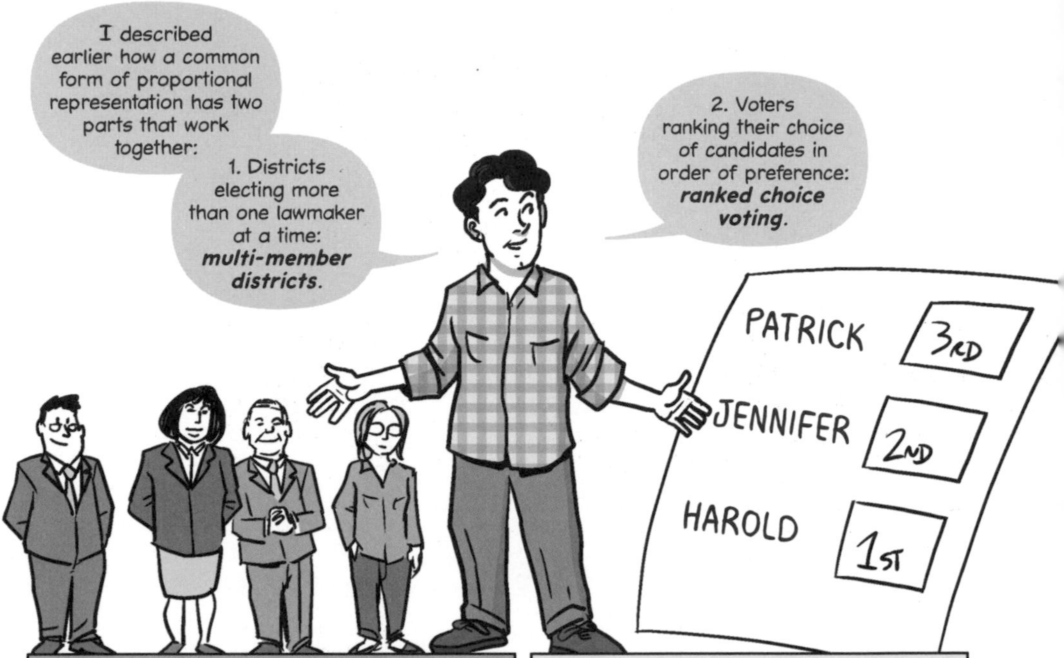
I described earlier how a common form of proportional representation has two parts that work together:
1. Districts electing more than one lawmaker at a time: ***multi-member districts***.
2. Voters ranking their choice of candidates in order of preference: ***ranked choice voting***.
PATRICK 3RD
JENNIFER 2ND
HAROLD 1ST

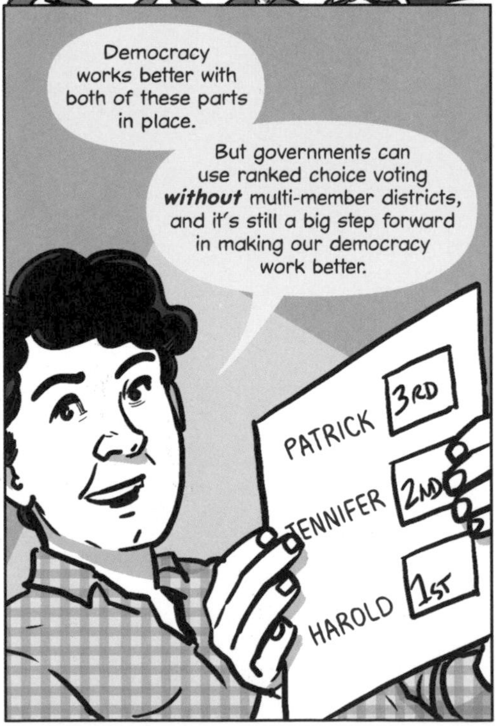
Democracy works better with both of these parts in place.
But governments can use ranked choice voting ***without*** multi-member districts, and it's still a big step forward in making our democracy work better.
PATRICK 3RD
JENNIFER 2ND
HAROLD 1ST

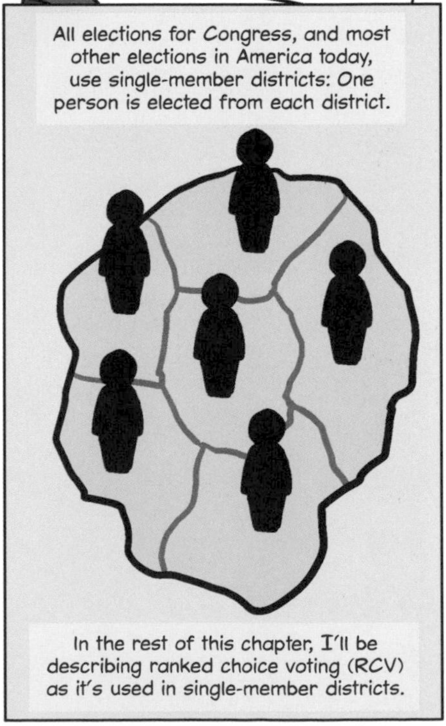
All elections for Congress, and most other elections in America today, use single-member districts: One person is elected from each district.
In the rest of this chapter, I'll be describing ranked choice voting (RCV) as it's used in single-member districts.

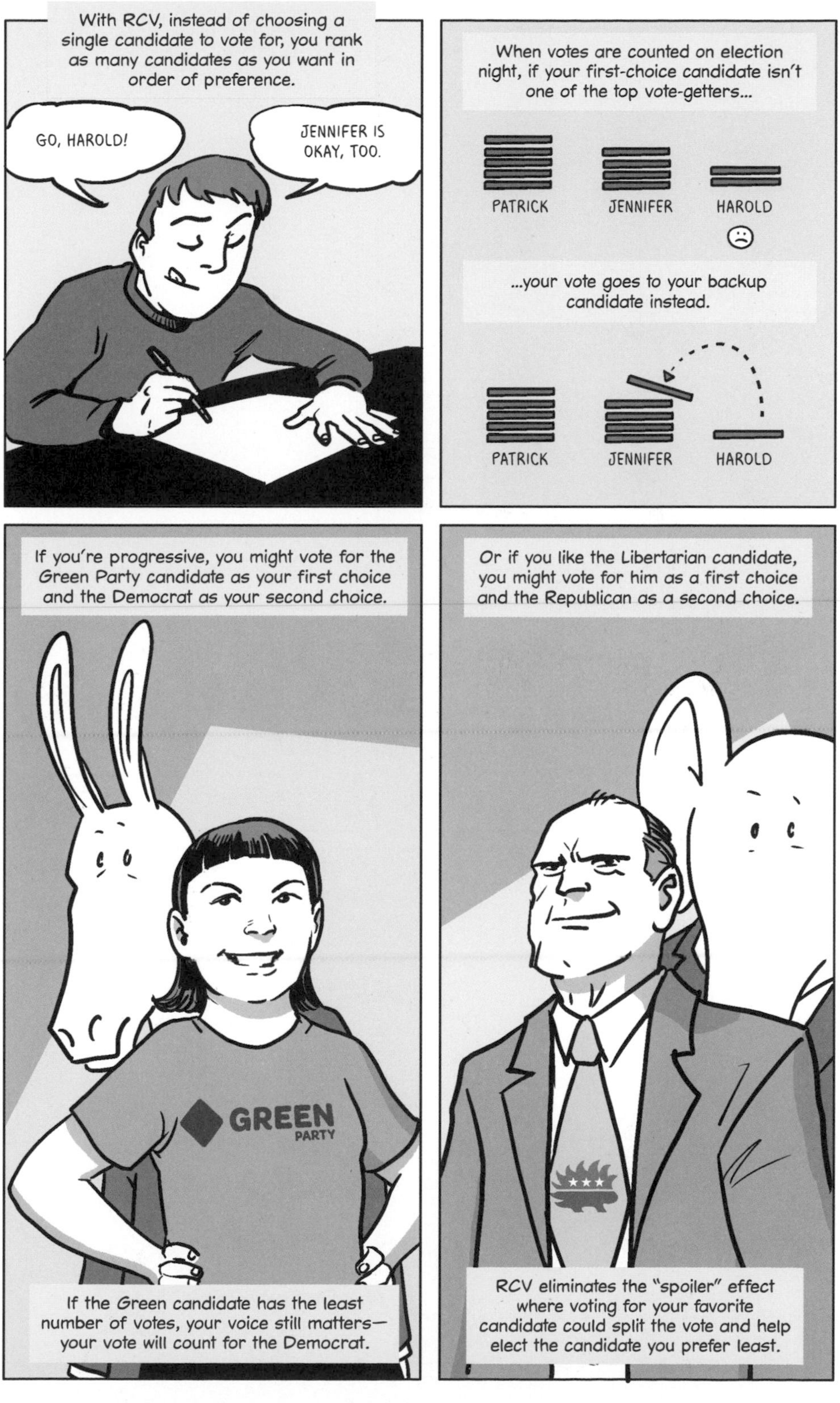

With RCV, instead of choosing a single candidate to vote for, you rank as many candidates as you want in order of preference.
GO, HAROLD!
JENNIFER IS OKAY, TOO.
When votes are counted on election night, if your first-choice candidate isn't one of the top vote-getters...
PATRICK
JENNIFER
HAROLD
...your vote goes to your backup candidate instead.
PATRICK
JENNIFER
HAROLD
If you're progressive, you might vote for the Green Party candidate as your first choice and the Democrat as your second choice.
GREEN PARTY
If the Green candidate has the least number of votes, your voice still matters—your vote will count for the Democrat.
Or if you like the Libertarian candidate, you might vote for him as a first choice and the Republican as a second choice.
RCV eliminates the "spoiler" effect where voting for your favorite candidate could split the vote and help elect the candidate you prefer least.

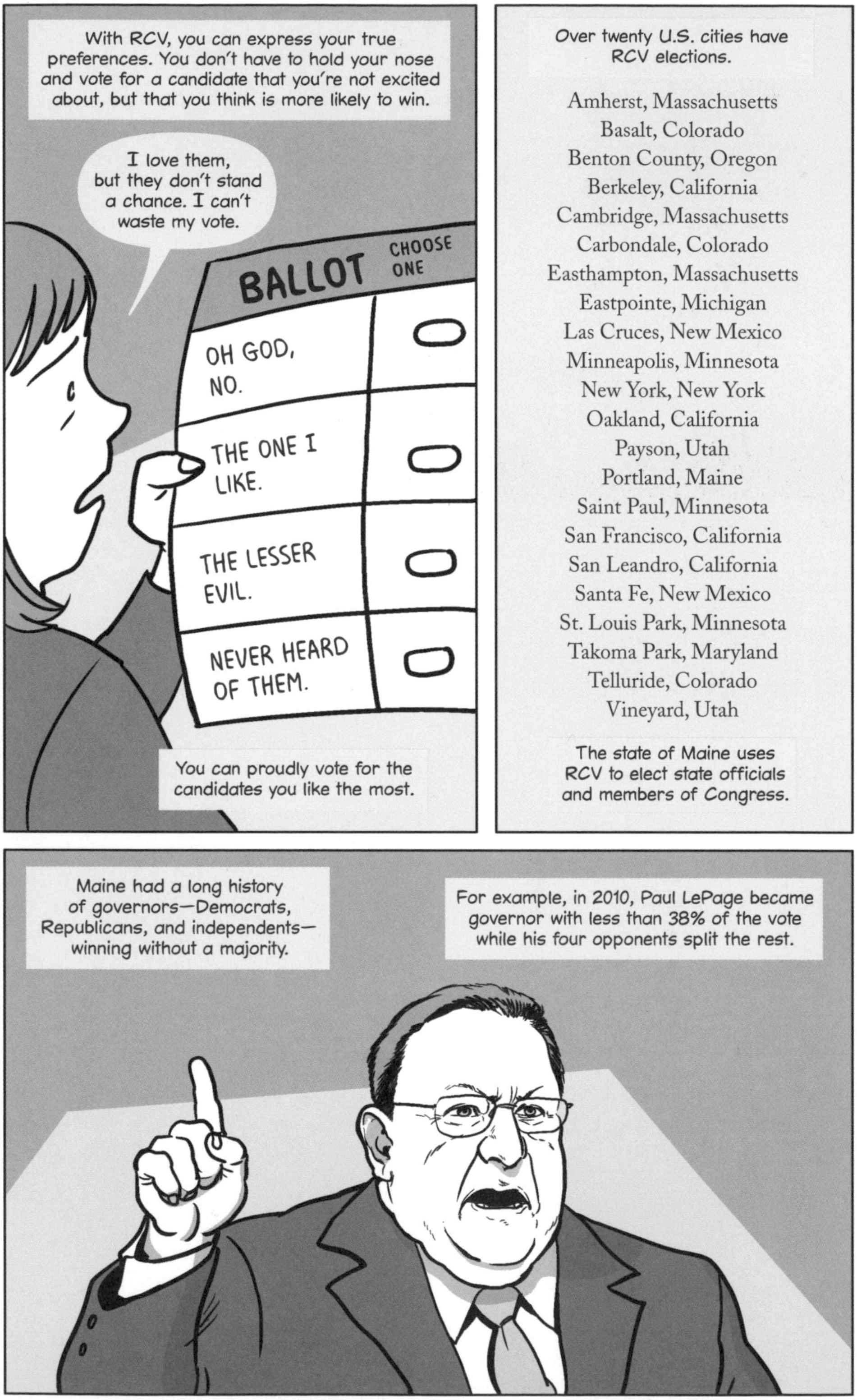
With RCV, you can express your true preferences. You don't have to hold your nose and vote for a candidate that you're not excited about, but that you think is more likely to win.
I love them, but they don't stand a chance. I can't waste my vote.
BALLOT
CHOOSE ONE
OH GOD, NO.
THE ONE I LIKE.
THE LESSER EVIL.
NEVER HEARD OF THEM.
You can proudly vote for the candidates you like the most.
Over twenty U.S. cities have RCV elections.
Amherst, Massachusetts
Basalt, Colorado
Benton County, Oregon
Berkeley, California
Cambridge, Massachusetts
Carbondale, Colorado
Easthampton, Massachusetts
Eastpointe, Michigan
Las Cruces, New Mexico
Minneapolis, Minnesota
New York, New York
Oakland, California
Payson, Utah
Portland, Maine
Saint Paul, Minnesota
San Francisco, California
San Leandro, California
Santa Fe, New Mexico
St. Louis Park, Minnesota
Takoma Park, Maryland
Telluride, Colorado
Vineyard, Utah
The state of Maine uses RCV to elect state officials and members of Congress.
Maine had a long history of governors—Democrats, Republicans, and independents—winning without a majority.
For example, in 2010, Paul LePage became governor with less than 38% of the vote while his four opponents split the rest.

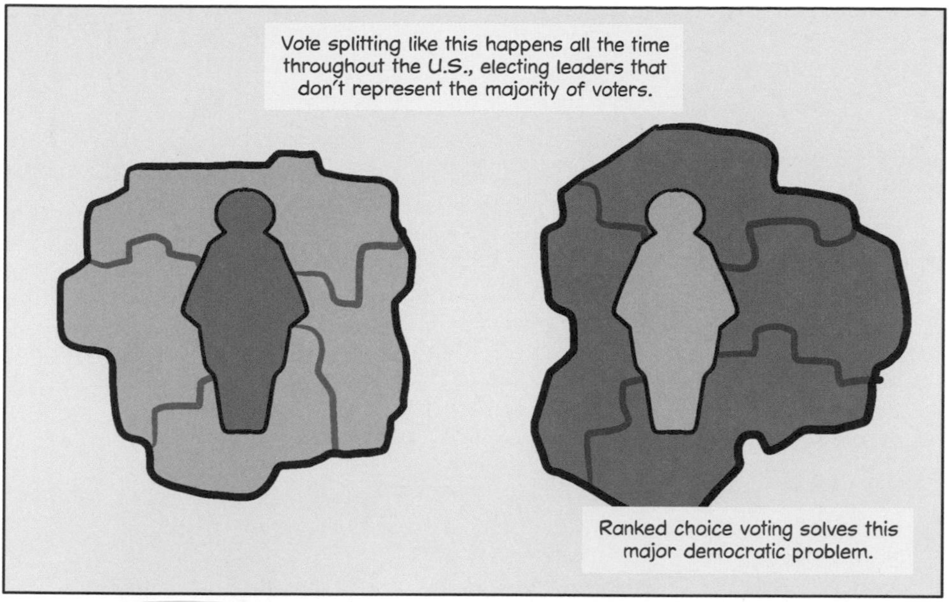
Vote splitting like this happens all the time throughout the U.S., electing leaders that don't represent the majority of voters.
Ranked choice voting solves this major democratic problem.

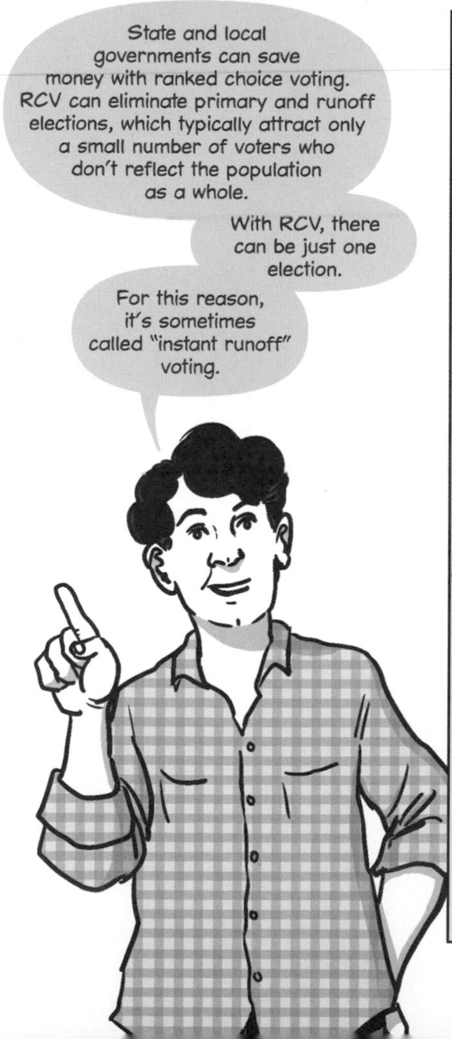
State and local governments can save money with ranked choice voting. RCV can eliminate primary and runoff elections, which typically attract only a small number of voters who don't reflect the population as a whole.
With RCV, there can be just one election.
For this reason, it's sometimes called "instant runoff" voting.

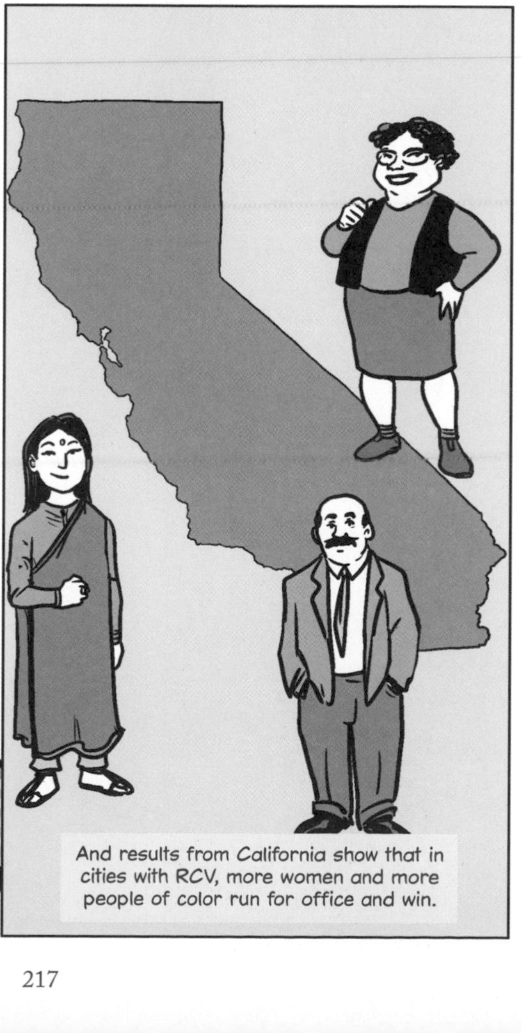
And results from California show that in cities with RCV, more women and more people of color run for office and win.

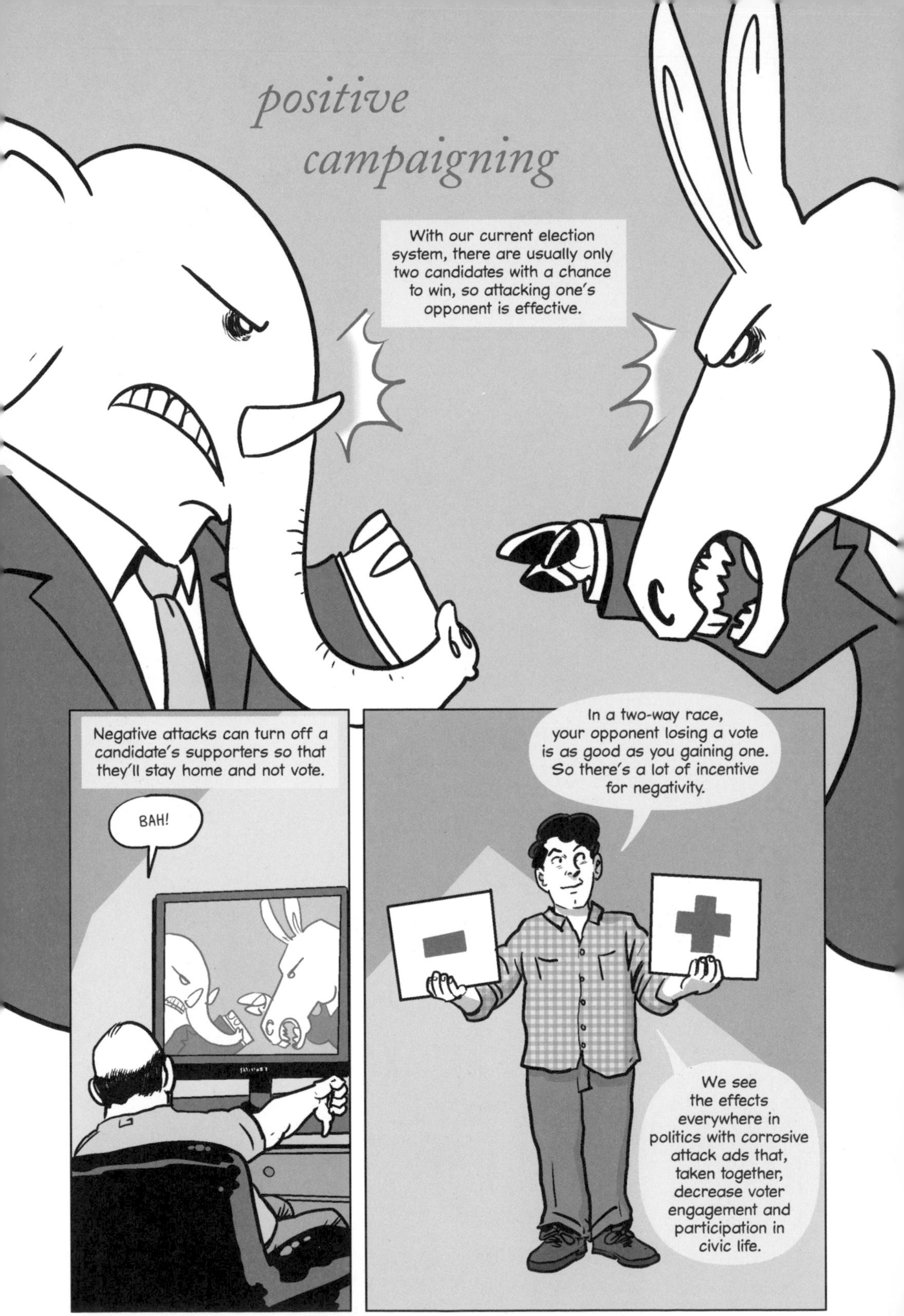
positive campaigning
With our current election system, there are usually only two candidates with a chance to win, so attacking one's opponent is effective.
Negative attacks can turn off a candidate's supporters so that they'll stay home and not vote.
BAH!
In a two-way race, your opponent losing a vote is as good as you gaining one. So there's a lot of incentive for negativity.
We see the effects everywhere in politics with corrosive attack ads that, taken together, decrease voter engagement and participation in civic life.

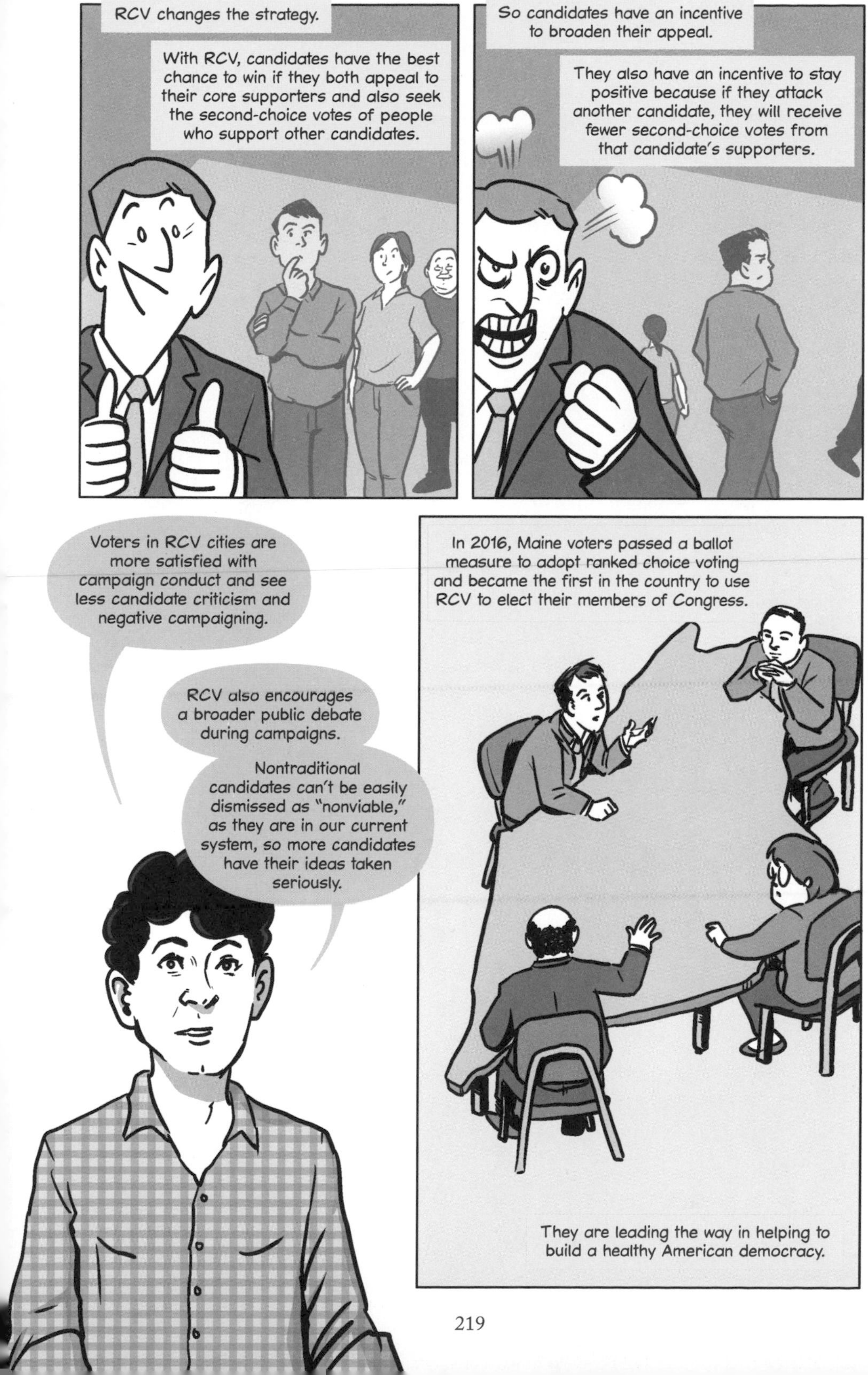
RCV changes the strategy.
With RCV, candidates have the best chance to win if they both appeal to their core supporters and also seek the second-choice votes of people who support other candidates.
So candidates have an incentive to broaden their appeal.
They also have an incentive to stay positive because if they attack another candidate, they will receive fewer second-choice votes from that candidate's supporters.
Voters in RCV cities are more satisfied with campaign conduct and see less candidate criticism and negative campaigning.
RCV also encourages a broader public debate during campaigns.
Nontraditional candidates can't be easily dismissed as "nonviable," as they are in our current system, so more candidates have their ideas taken seriously.
In 2016, Maine voters passed a ballot measure to adopt ranked choice voting and became the first in the country to use RCV to elect their members of Congress.
They are leading the way in helping to build a healthy American democracy.

8
electing
a president

shays' rebellion

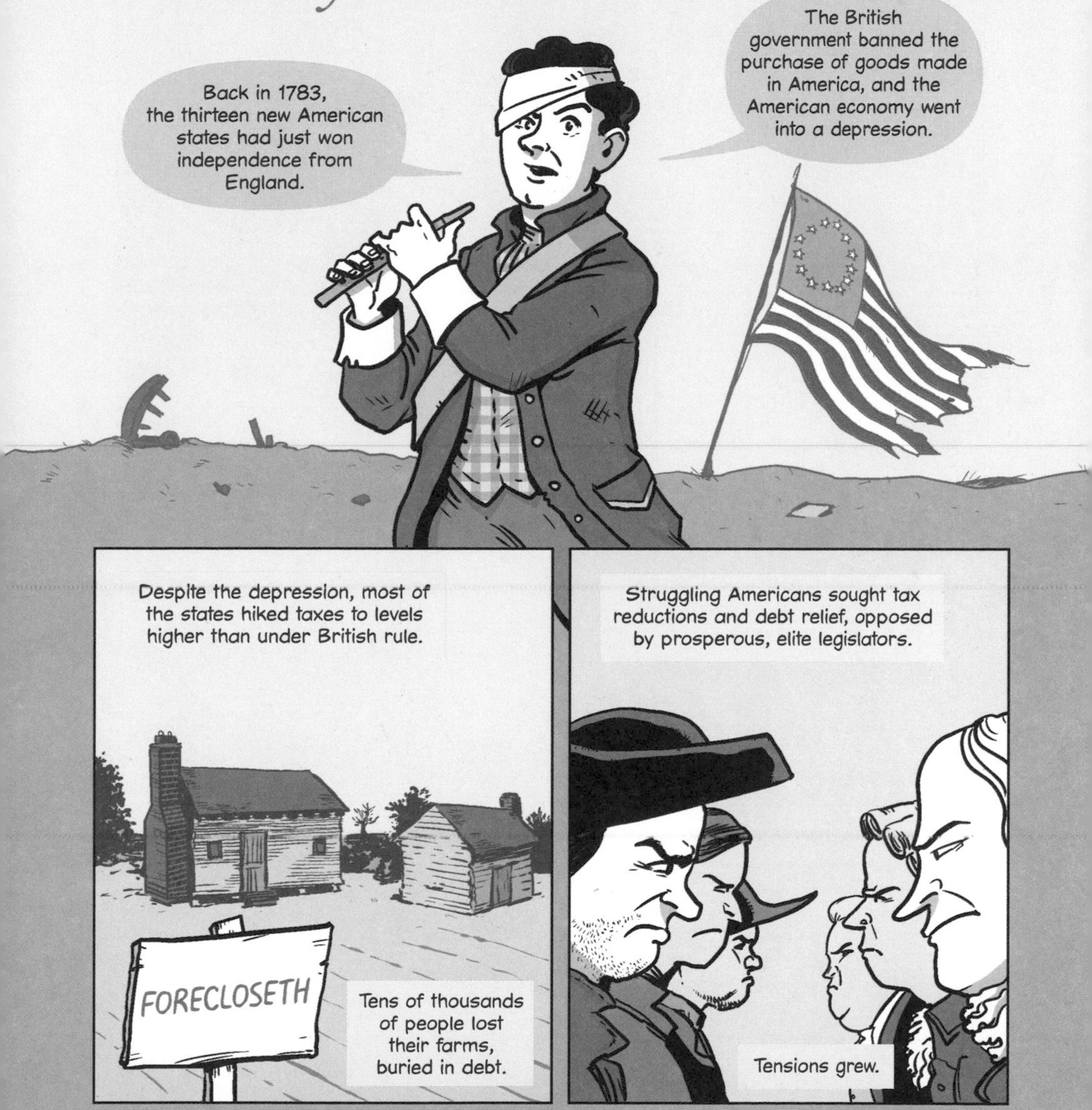
Back in 1783, the thirteen new American states had just won independence from England.
The British government banned the purchase of goods made in America, and the American economy went into a depression.
Despite the depression, most of the states hiked taxes to levels higher than under British rule.
FORECLOSETH
Tens of thousands of people lost their farms, buried in debt.
Struggling Americans sought tax reductions and debt relief, opposed by prosperous, elite legislators.
Tensions grew.

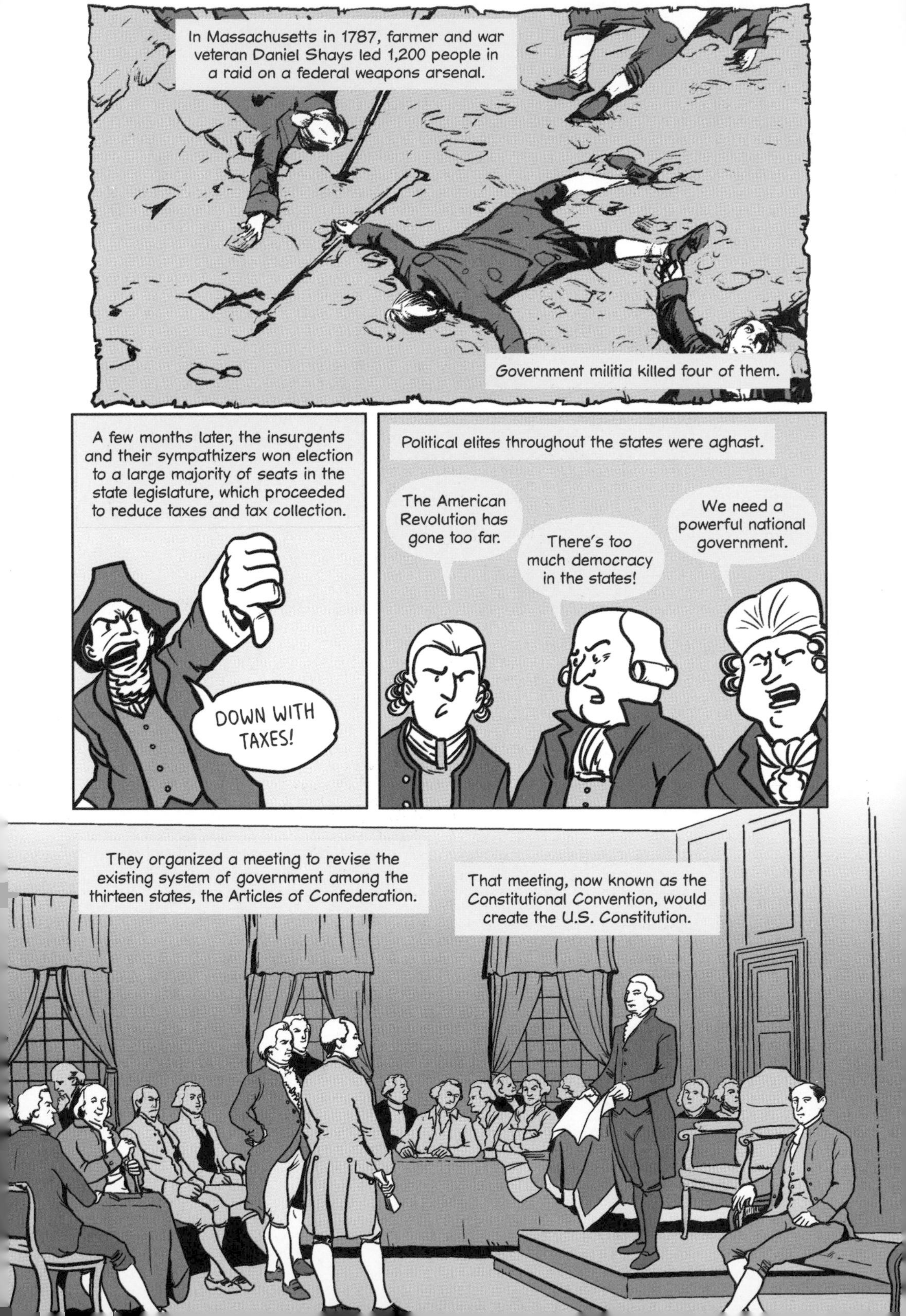
In Massachusetts in 1787, farmer and war veteran Daniel Shays led 1,200 people in a raid on a federal weapons arsenal.
Government militia killed four of them.
A few months later, the insurgents and their sympathizers won election to a large majority of seats in the state legislature, which proceeded to reduce taxes and tax collection.
DOWN WITH TAXES!
Political elites throughout the states were aghast.
The American Revolution has gone too far.
There's too much democracy in the states!
We need a powerful national government.
They organized a meeting to revise the existing system of government among the thirteen states, the Articles of Confederation.
That meeting, now known as the Constitutional Convention, would create the U.S. Constitution.

insulating lawmakers from voters

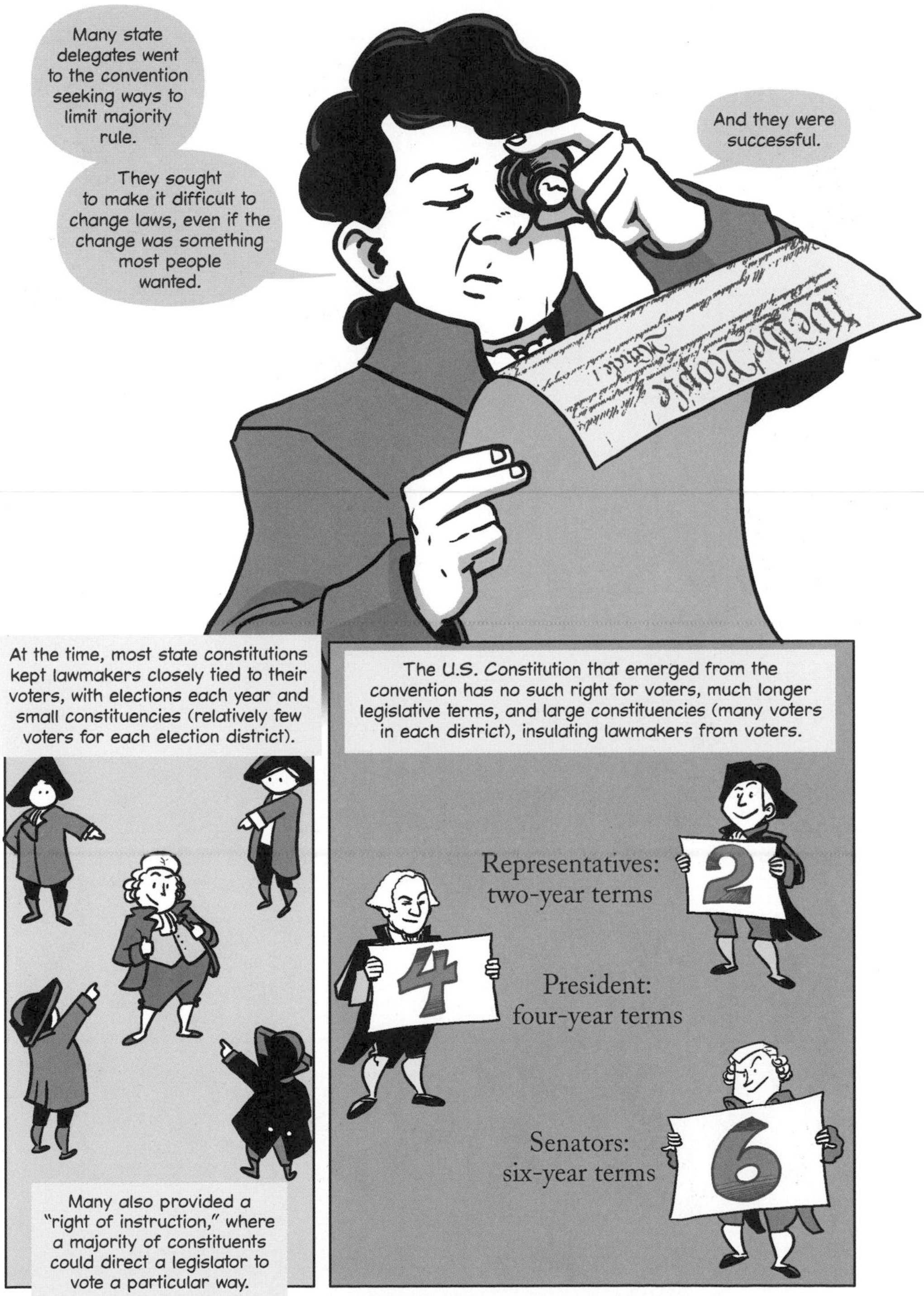
Many state delegates went to the convention seeking ways to limit majority rule.
They sought to make it difficult to change laws, even if the change was something most people wanted.
And they were successful.
At the time, most state constitutions kept lawmakers closely tied to their voters, with elections each year and small constituencies (relatively few voters for each election district).
Many also provided a "right of instruction," where a majority of constituents could direct a legislator to vote a particular way.
The U.S. Constitution that emerged from the convention has no such right for voters, much longer legislative terms, and large constituencies (many voters in each district), insulating lawmakers from voters.
Representatives: two-year terms
2
President: four-year terms
4
Senators: six-year terms
6

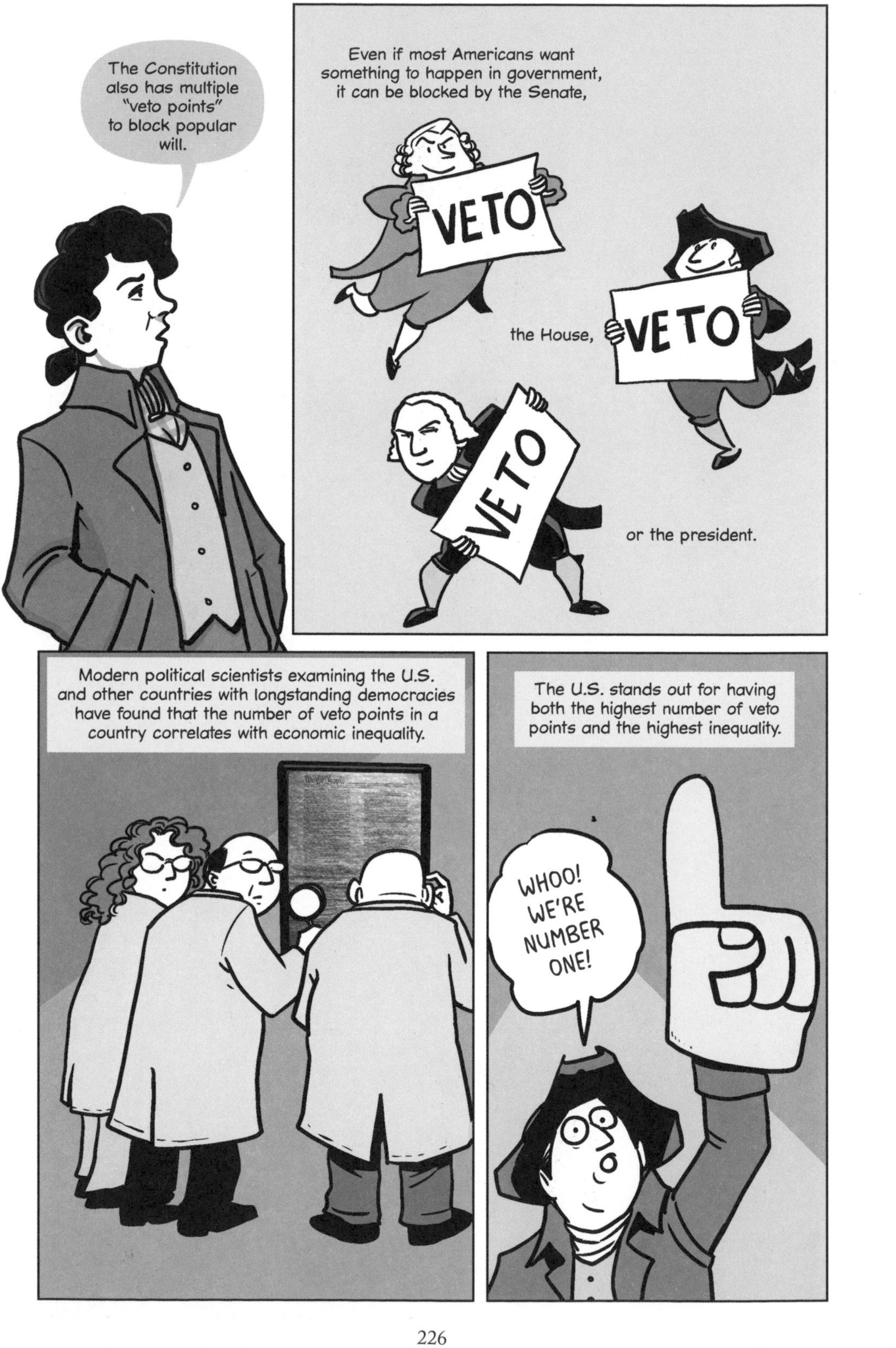
The Constitution also has multiple "veto points" to block popular will.
Even if most Americans want something to happen in government, it can be blocked by the Senate,
VETO
the House,
VETO
VETO
or the president.
Modern political scientists examining the U.S. and other countries with longstanding democracies have found that the number of veto points in a country correlates with economic inequality.
The U.S. stands out for having both the highest number of veto points and the highest inequality.
WHOO! WE'RE NUMBER ONE!

the rules for electing a president

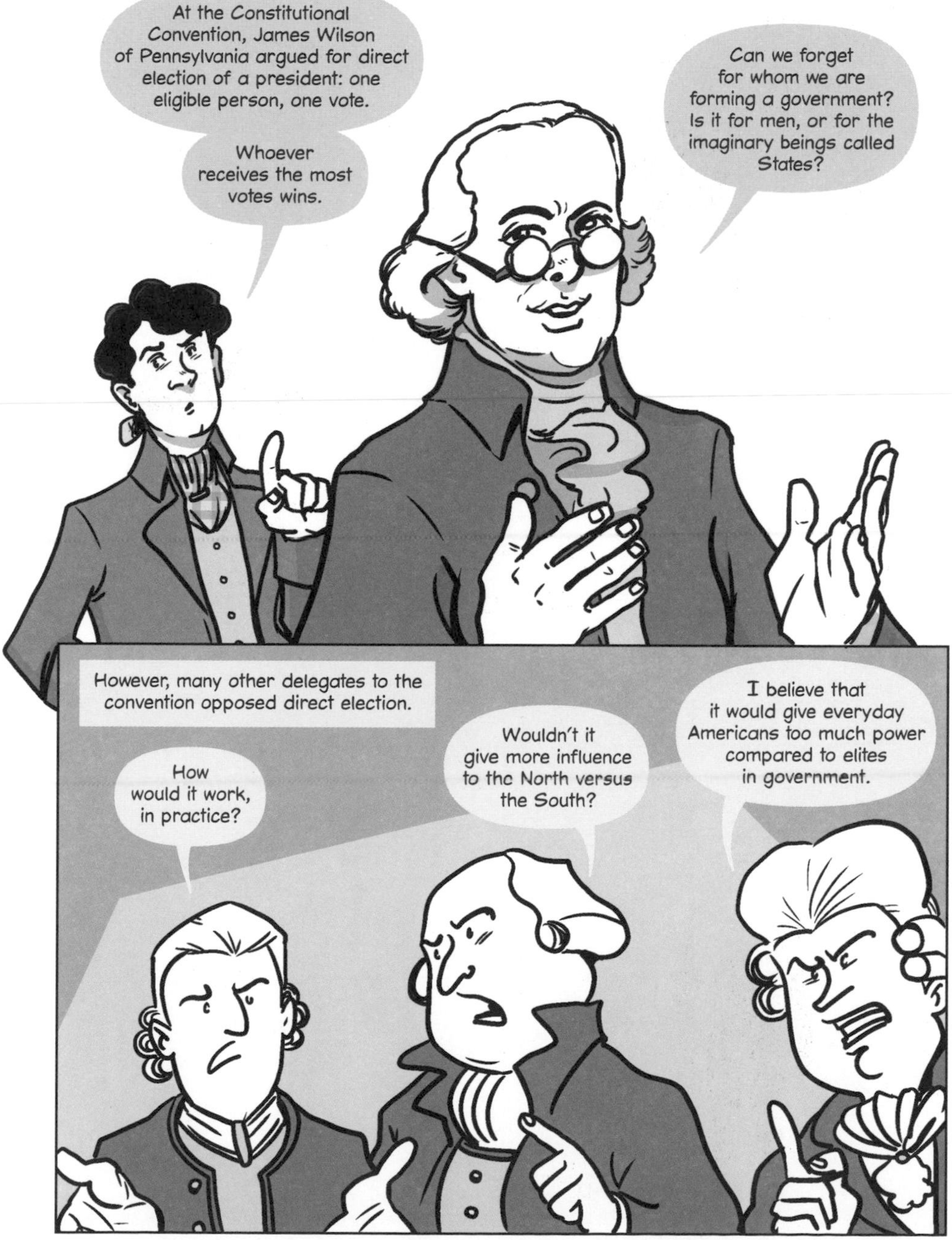
At the Constitutional Convention, James Wilson of Pennsylvania argued for direct election of a president: one eligible person, one vote.
Whoever receives the most votes wins.
Can we forget for whom we are forming a government? Is it for men, or for the imaginary beings called States?
However, many other delegates to the convention opposed direct election.
How would it work, in practice?
Wouldn't it give more influence to the North versus the South?
I believe that it would give everyday Americans too much power compared to elites in government.

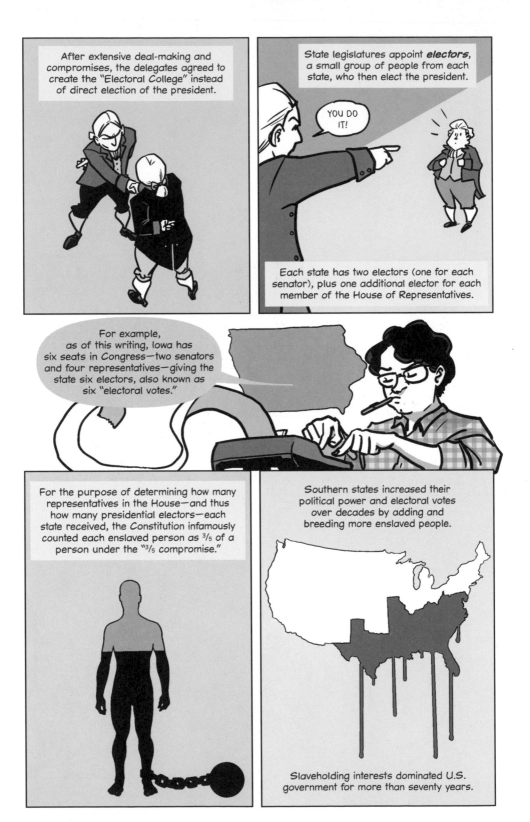

After extensive deal-making and compromises, the delegates agreed to create the "Electoral College" instead of direct election of the president.

State legislatures appoint **electors**, a small group of people from each state, who then elect the president.

YOU DO IT!

Each state has two electors (one for each senator), plus one additional elector for each member of the House of Representatives.

For example, as of this writing, Iowa has six seats in Congress—two senators and four representatives—giving the state six electors, also known as six "electoral votes."

For the purpose of determining how many representatives in the House—and thus how many presidential electors—each state received, the Constitution infamously counted each enslaved person as ³/₅ of a person under the "³/₅ compromise."

Southern states increased their political power and electoral votes over decades by adding and breeding more enslaved people.

Slaveholding interests dominated U.S. government for more than seventy years.

electing a president today

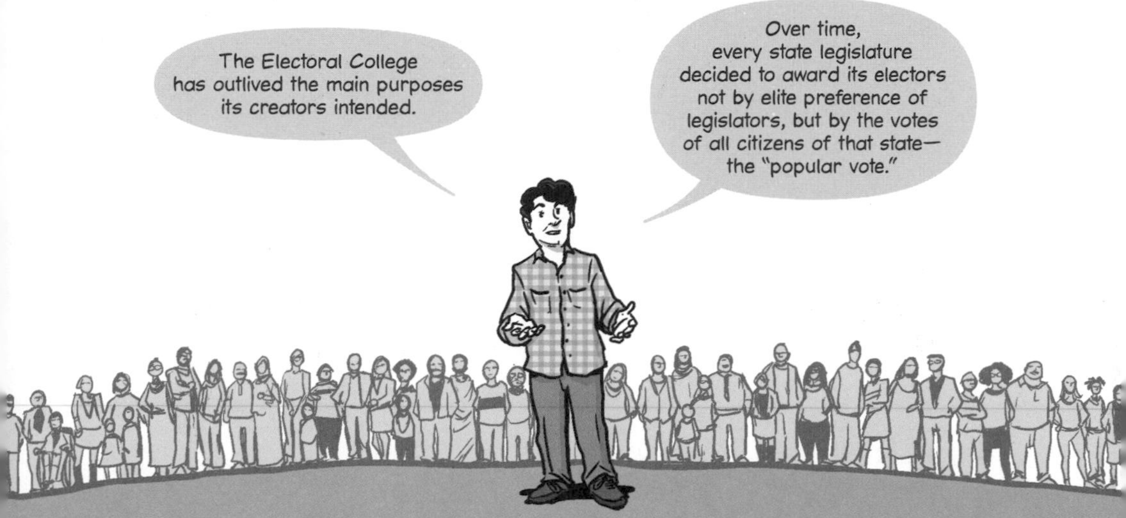
The Electoral College has outlived the main purposes its creators intended.
Over time, every state legislature decided to award its electors not by elite preference of legislators, but by the votes of all citizens of that state—the "popular vote."

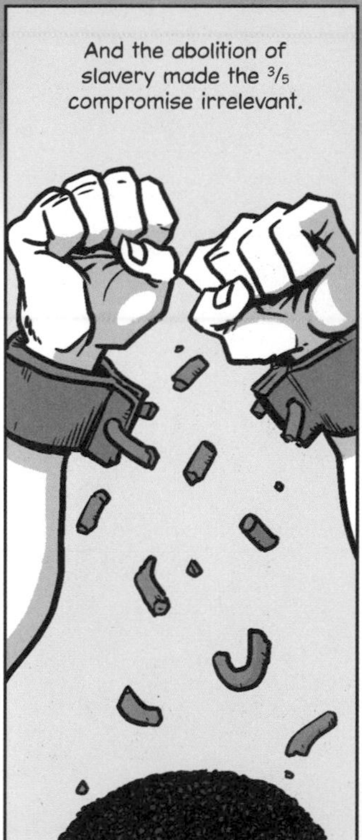
And the abolition of slavery made the 3/5 compromise irrelevant.

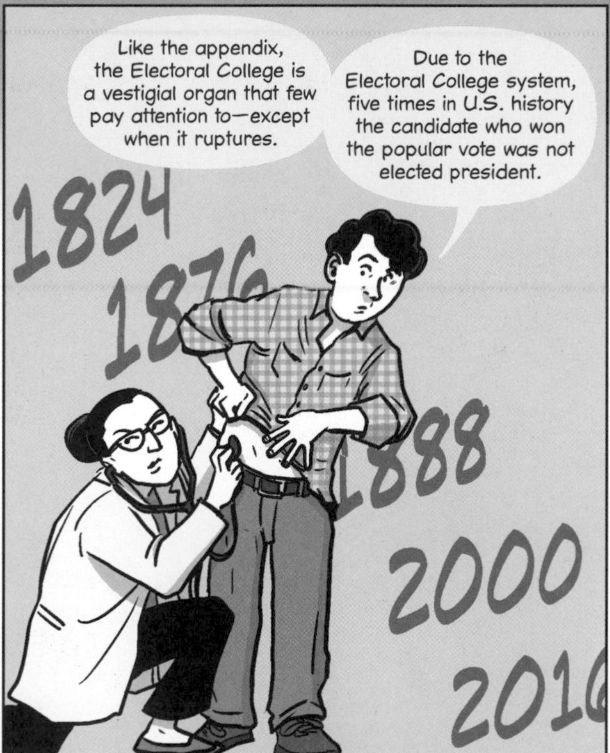
Like the appendix, the Electoral College is a vestigial organ that few pay attention to—except when it ruptures.
Due to the Electoral College system, five times in U.S. history the candidate who won the popular vote was not elected president.
1824
1888
2000

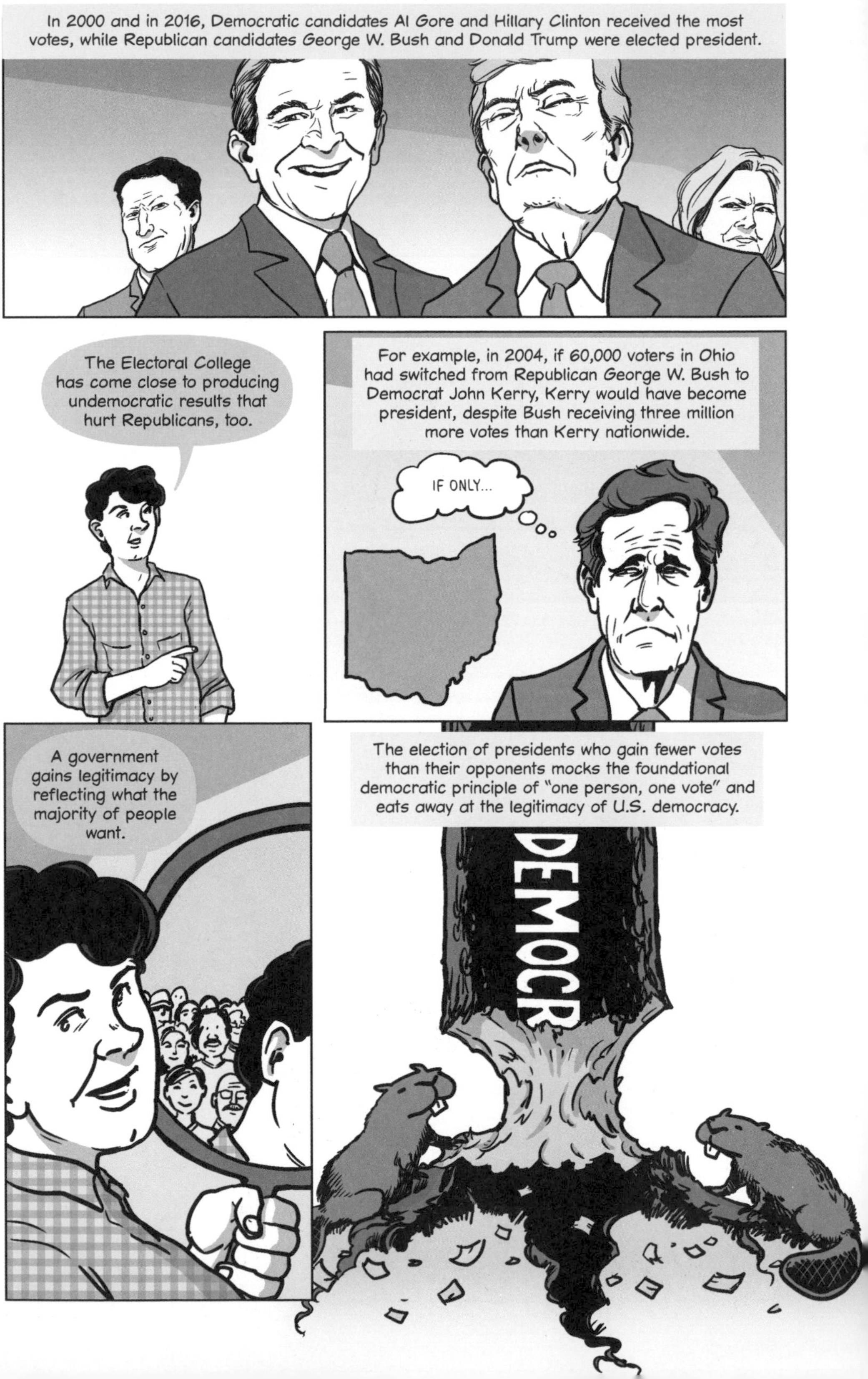
In 2000 and in 2016, Democratic candidates Al Gore and Hillary Clinton received the most votes, while Republican candidates George W. Bush and Donald Trump were elected president.
The Electoral College has come close to producing undemocratic results that hurt Republicans, too.
For example, in 2004, if 60,000 voters in Ohio had switched from Republican George W. Bush to Democrat John Kerry, Kerry would have become president, despite Bush receiving three million more votes than Kerry nationwide.
IF ONLY...
A government gains legitimacy by reflecting what the majority of people want.
The election of presidents who gain fewer votes than their opponents mocks the foundational democratic principle of "one person, one vote" and eats away at the legitimacy of U.S. democracy.
DEMOCR

swing states

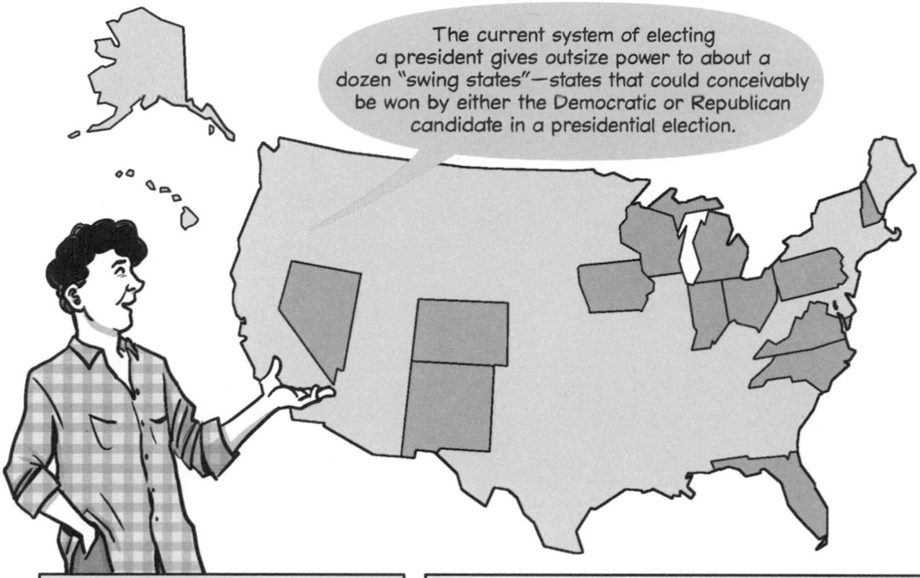
The current system of electing a president gives outsize power to about a dozen "swing states"—states that could conceivably be won by either the Democratic or Republican candidate in a presidential election.

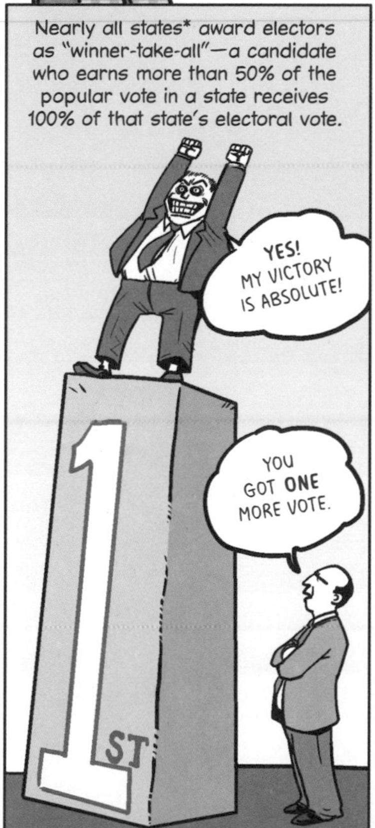
Nearly all states* award electors as "winner-take-all"—a candidate who earns more than 50% of the popular vote in a state receives 100% of that state's electoral vote.
YES! MY VICTORY IS ABSOLUTE!
1 ST
YOU GOT ONE MORE VOTE.
*all except Maine and Nebraska

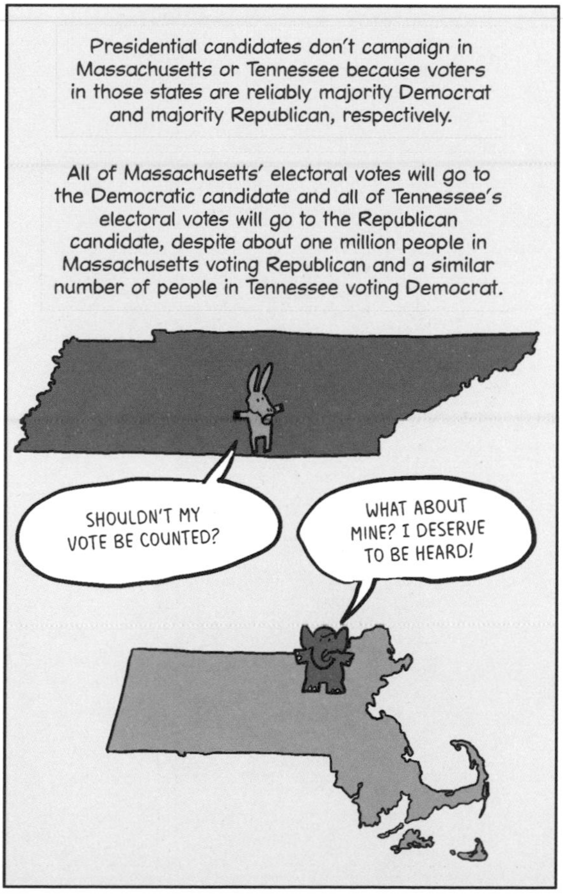
Presidential candidates don't campaign in Massachusetts or Tennessee because voters in those states are reliably majority Democrat and majority Republican, respectively.
All of Massachusetts' electoral votes will go to the Democratic candidate and all of Tennessee's electoral votes will go to the Republican candidate, despite about one million people in Massachusetts voting Republican and a similar number of people in Tennessee voting Democrat.
SHOULDN'T MY VOTE BE COUNTED?
WHAT ABOUT MINE? I DESERVE TO BE HEARD!

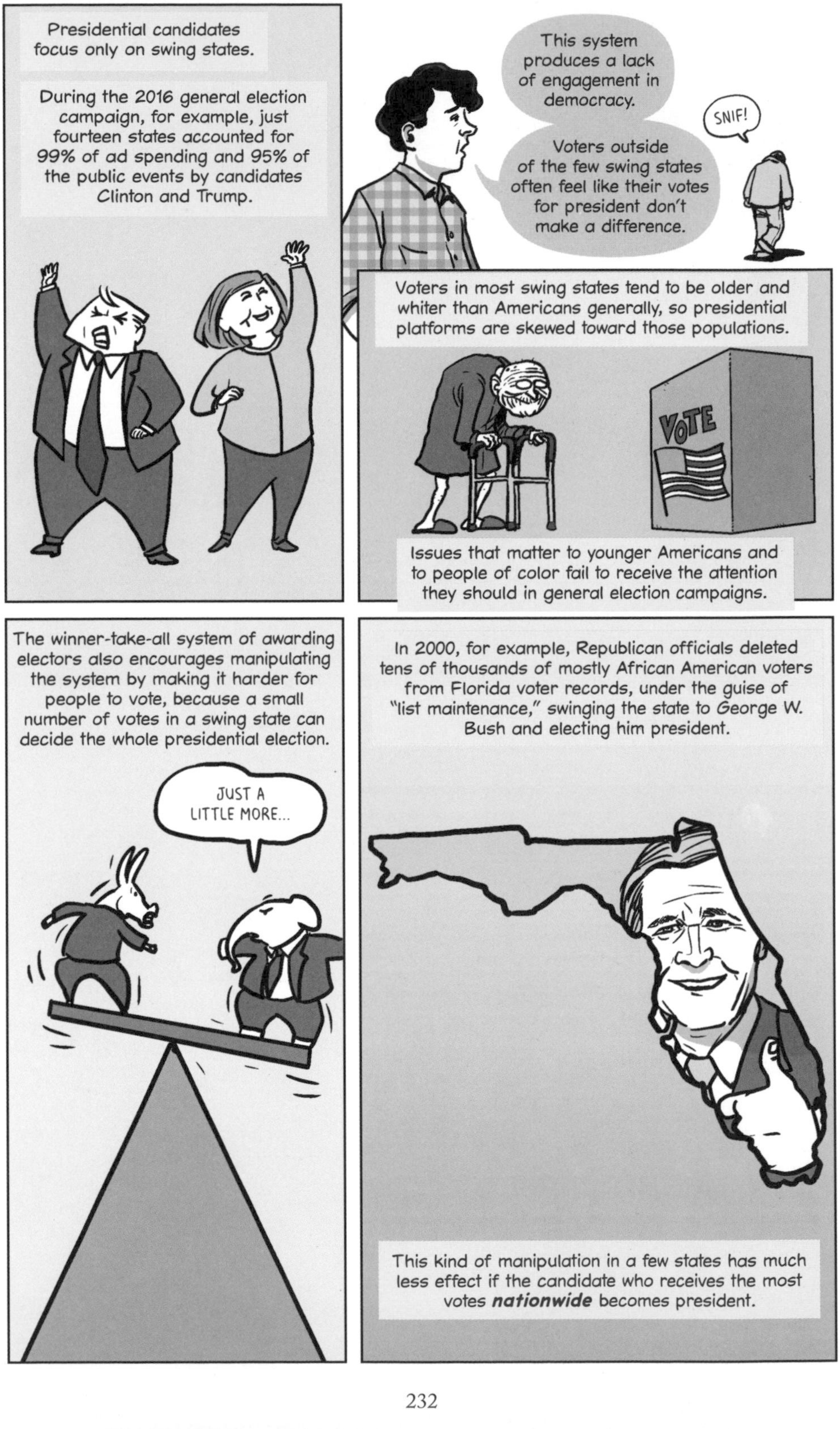
Presidential candidates focus only on swing states.
During the 2016 general election campaign, for example, just fourteen states accounted for 99% of ad spending and 95% of the public events by candidates Clinton and Trump.
This system produces a lack of engagement in democracy.
Voters outside of the few swing states often feel like their votes for president don't make a difference.
SNIF!
Voters in most swing states tend to be older and whiter than Americans generally, so presidential platforms are skewed toward those populations.
VOTE
Issues that matter to younger Americans and to people of color fail to receive the attention they should in general election campaigns.
The winner-take-all system of awarding electors also encourages manipulating the system by making it harder for people to vote, because a small number of votes in a swing state can decide the whole presidential election.
JUST A LITTLE MORE...
In 2000, for example, Republican officials deleted tens of thousands of mostly African American voters from Florida voter records, under the guise of "list maintenance," swinging the state to George W. Bush and electing him president.
This kind of manipulation in a few states has much less effect if the candidate who receives the most votes ***nationwide*** becomes president.

every vote equal

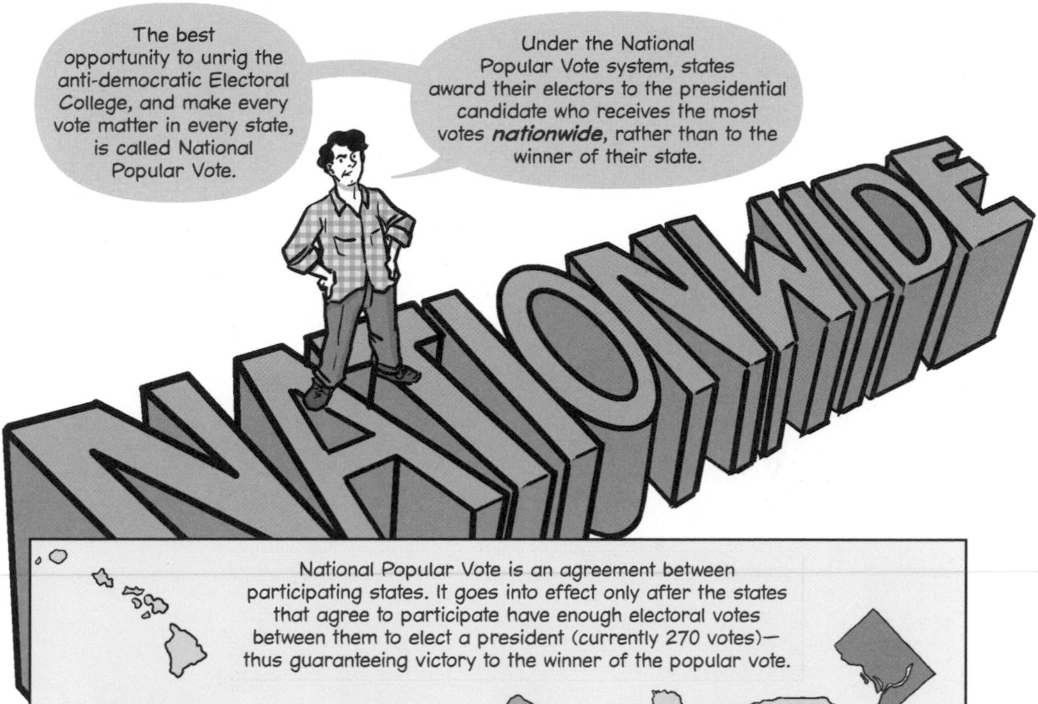

The best opportunity to unrig the anti-democratic Electoral College, and make every vote matter in every state, is called National Popular Vote.
Under the National Popular Vote system, states award their electors to the presidential candidate who receives the most votes ***nationwide***, rather than to the winner of their state.
NATIONWIDE

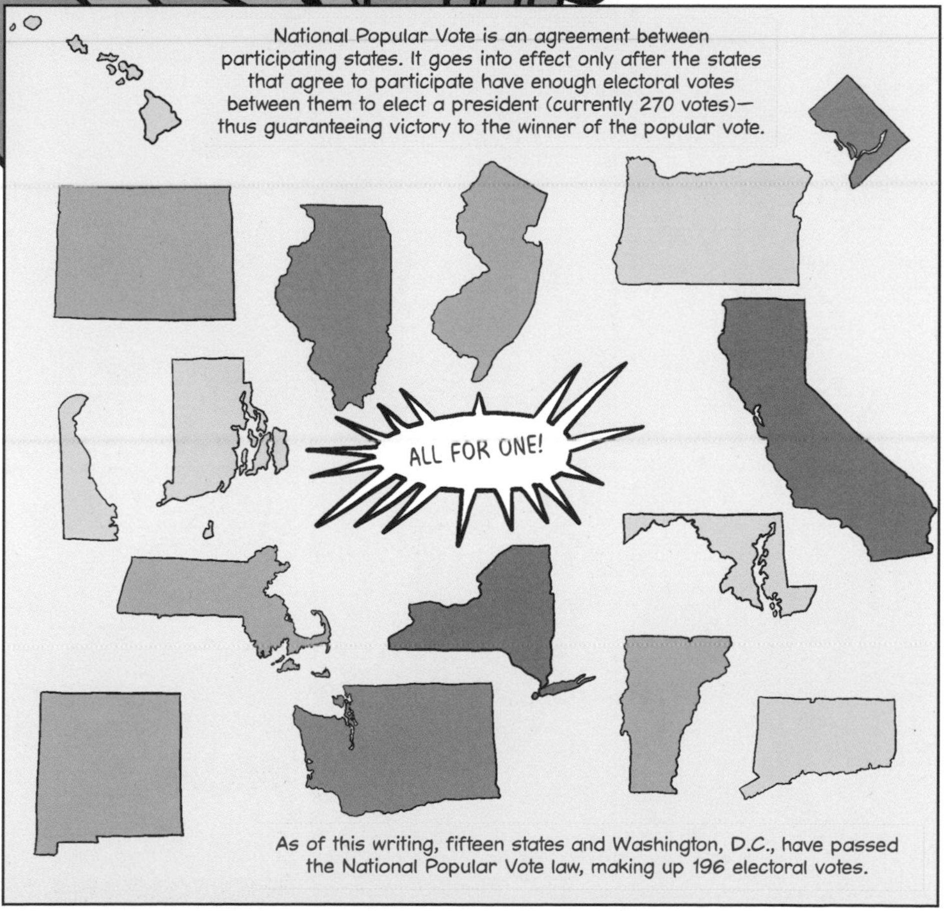

National Popular Vote is an agreement between participating states. It goes into effect only after the states that agree to participate have enough electoral votes between them to elect a president (currently 270 votes)—thus guaranteeing victory to the winner of the popular vote.
ALL FOR ONE!
As of this writing, fifteen states and Washington, D.C., have passed the National Popular Vote law, making up 196 electoral votes.

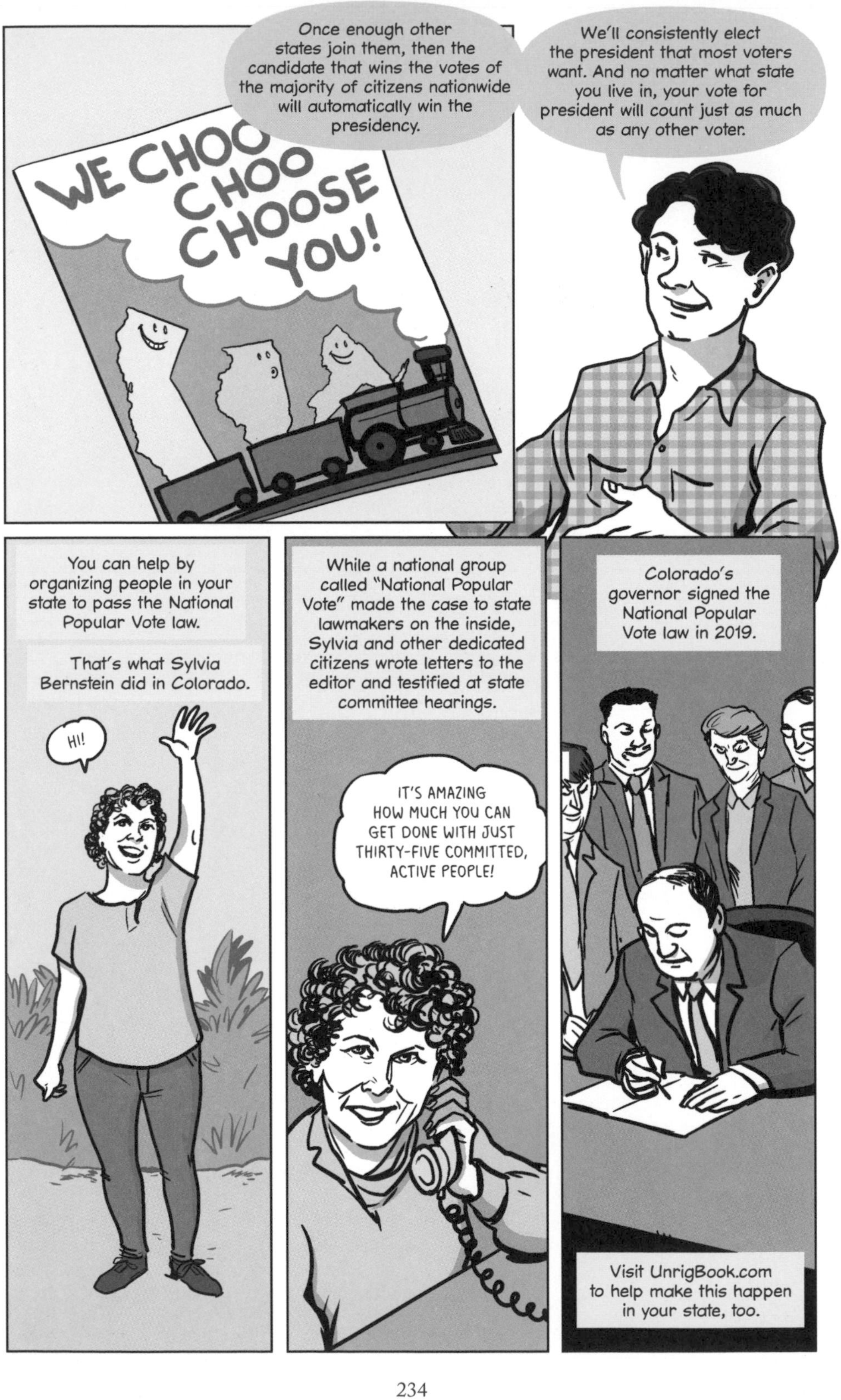
Once enough other states join them, then the candidate that wins the votes of the majority of citizens nationwide will automatically win the presidency.
We'll consistently elect the president that most voters want. And no matter what state you live in, your vote for president will count just as much as any other voter.
WE CHOO CHOO CHOOSE YOU!
You can help by organizing people in your state to pass the National Popular Vote law.
That's what Sylvia Bernstein did in Colorado.
HI!
While a national group called "National Popular Vote" made the case to state lawmakers on the inside, Sylvia and other dedicated citizens wrote letters to the editor and testified at state committee hearings.
IT'S AMAZING HOW MUCH YOU CAN GET DONE WITH JUST THIRTY-FIVE COMMITTED, ACTIVE PEOPLE!
Colorado's governor signed the National Popular Vote law in 2019.
Visit UnrigBook.com to help make this happen in your state, too.

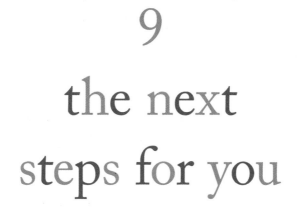

9

the next
steps for you

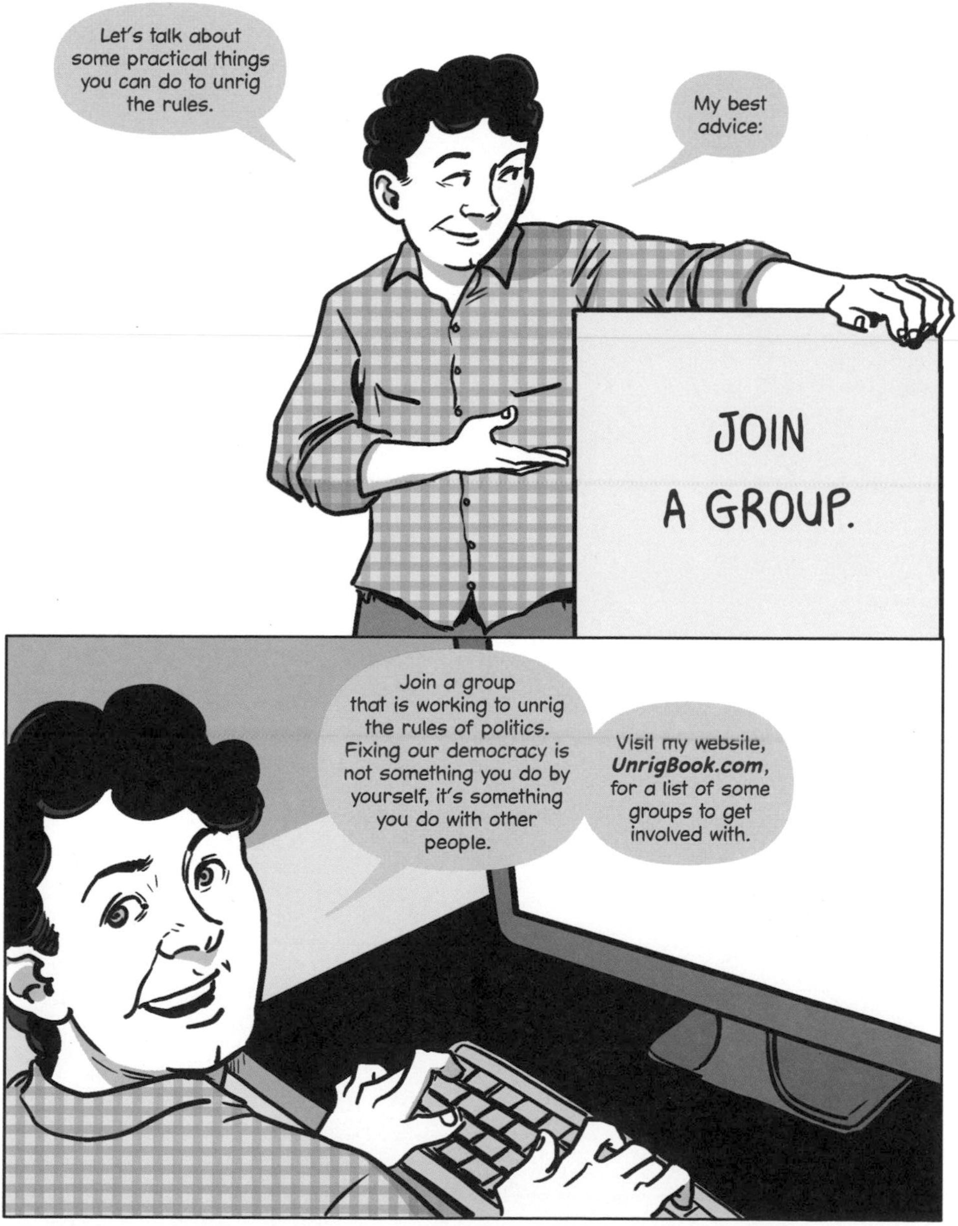
Let's talk about some practical things you can do to unrig the rules.
My best advice:
JOIN A GROUP.
Join a group that is working to unrig the rules of politics. Fixing our democracy is not something you do by yourself, it's something you do with other people.
Visit my website, ***UnrigBook.com***, for a list of some groups to get involved with.

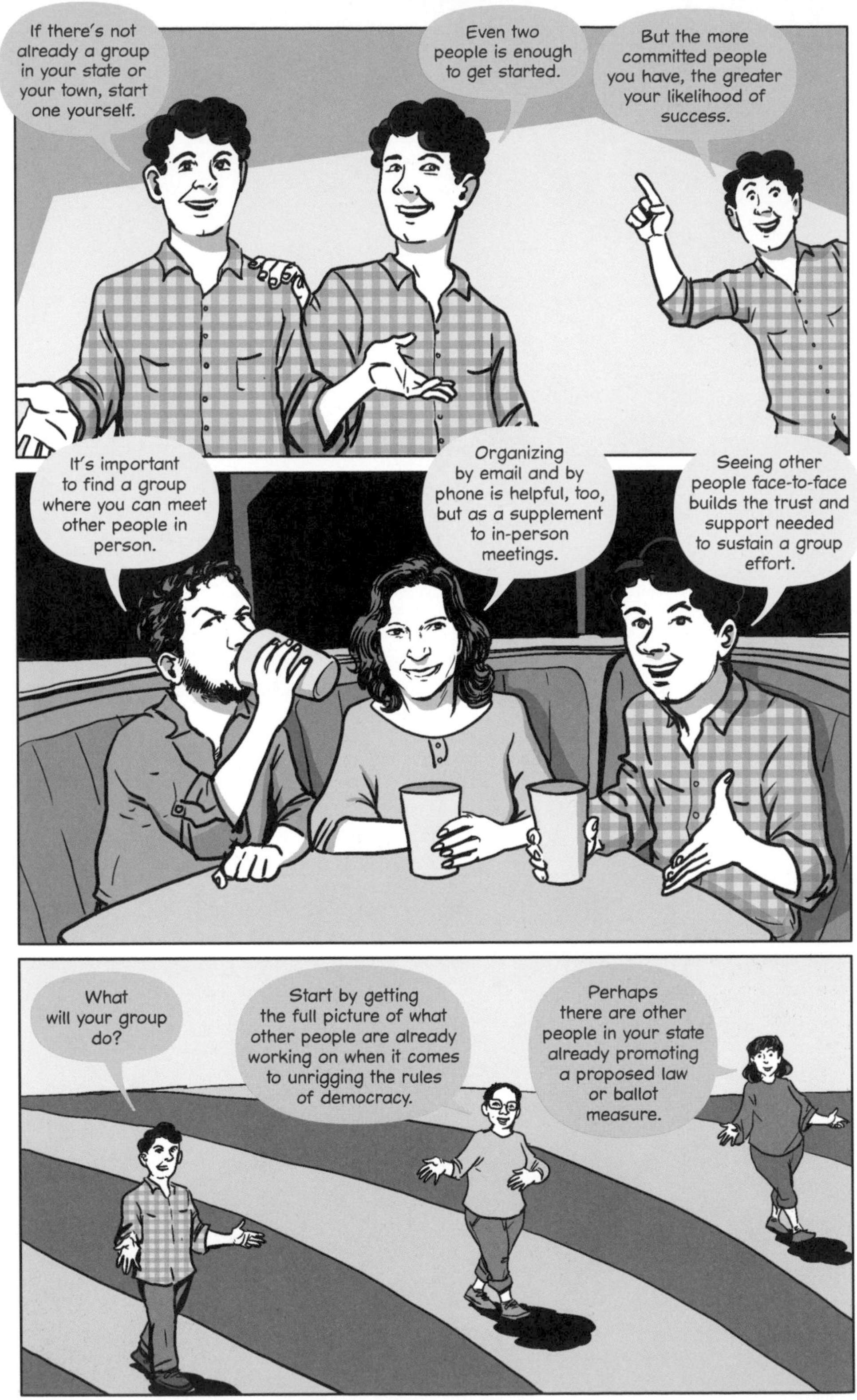
If there's not already a group in your state or your town, start one yourself.
Even two people is enough to get started.
But the more committed people you have, the greater your likelihood of success.
It's important to find a group where you can meet other people in person.
Organizing by email and by phone is helpful, too, but as a supplement to in-person meetings.
Seeing other people face-to-face builds the trust and support needed to sustain a group effort.
What will your group do?
Start by getting the full picture of what other people are already working on when it comes to unrigging the rules of democracy.
Perhaps there are other people in your state already promoting a proposed law or ballot measure.

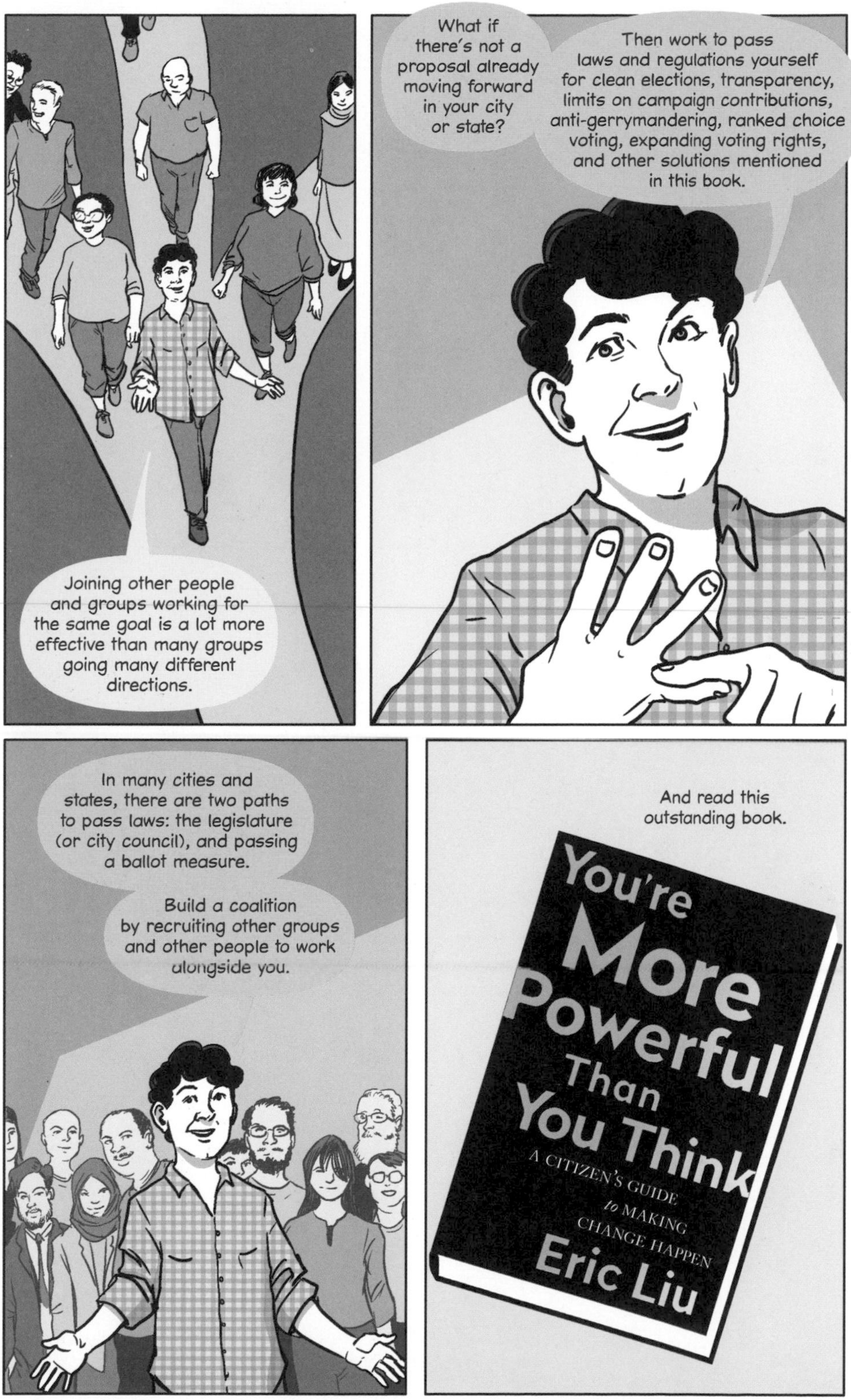
Joining other people and groups working for the same goal is a lot more effective than many groups going many different directions.
What if there's not a proposal already moving forward in your city or state?
Then work to pass laws and regulations yourself for clean elections, transparency, limits on campaign contributions, anti-gerrymandering, ranked choice voting, expanding voting rights, and other solutions mentioned in this book.
In many cities and states, there are two paths to pass laws: the legislature (or city council), and passing a ballot measure.
Build a coalition by recruiting other groups and other people to work alongside you.
And read this outstanding book.
You're More Powerful Than You Think
A CITIZEN'S GUIDE to MAKING CHANGE HAPPEN
Eric Liu

electing candidates

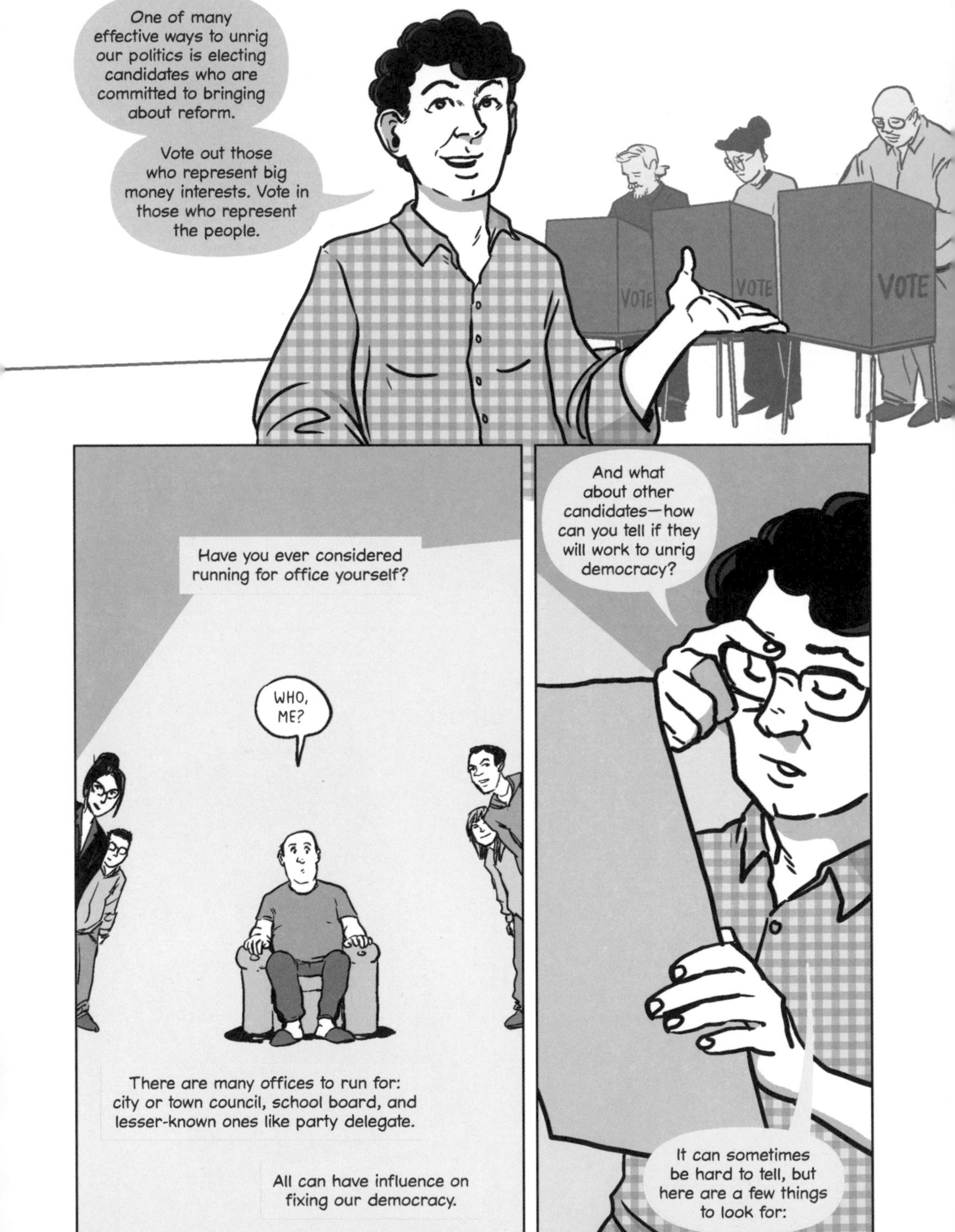
One of many effective ways to unrig our politics is electing candidates who are committed to bringing about reform.
Vote out those who represent big money interests. Vote in those who represent the people.
VOTE
VOTE
VOTE
Have you ever considered running for office yourself?
WHO, ME?
There are many offices to run for: city or town council, school board, and lesser-known ones like party delegate.
All can have influence on fixing our democracy.
And what about other candidates—how can you tell if they will work to unrig democracy?
It can sometimes be hard to tell, but here are a few things to look for:

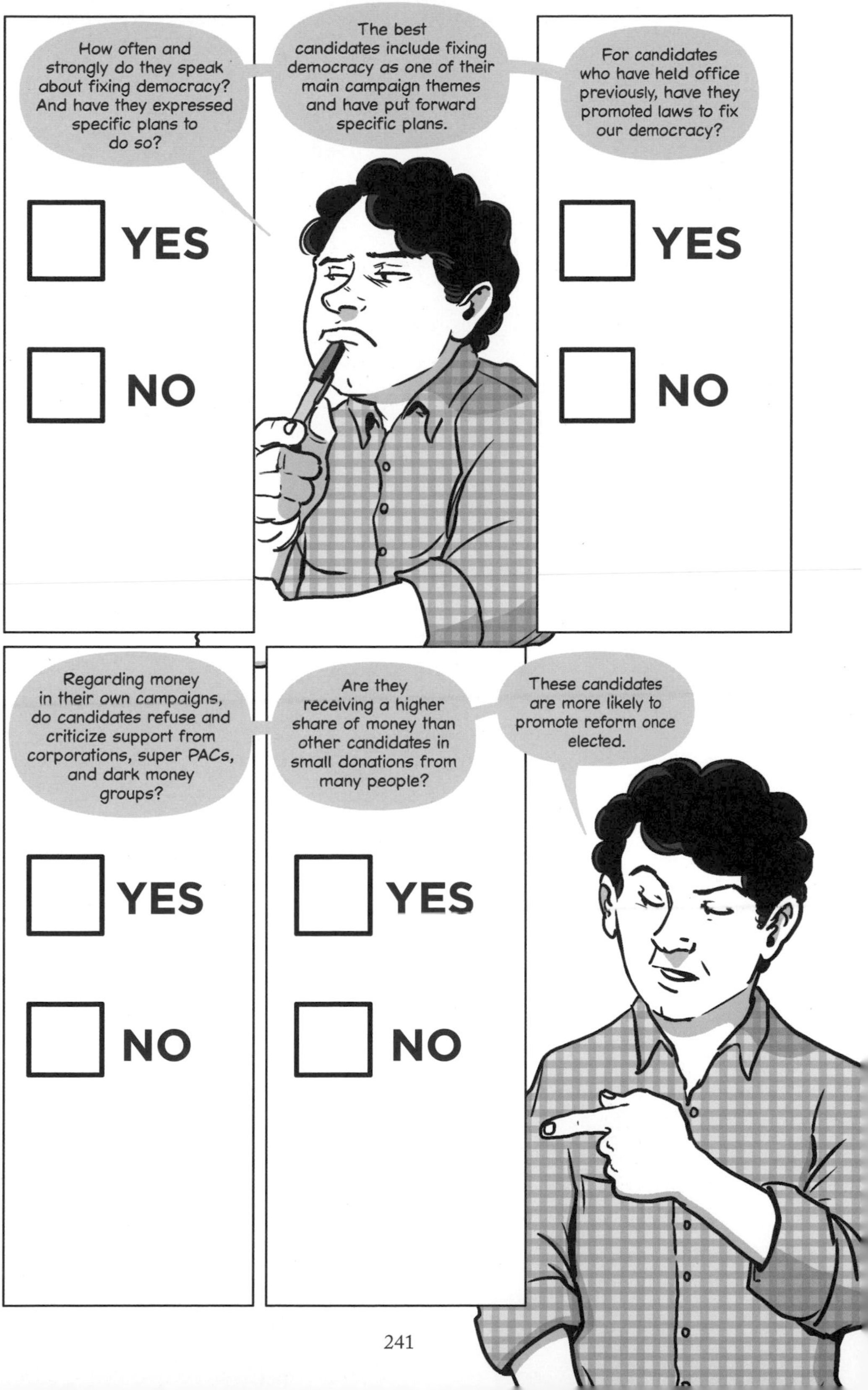
How often and strongly do they speak about fixing democracy? And have they expressed specific plans to do so?
The best candidates include fixing democracy as one of their main campaign themes and have put forward specific plans.
For candidates who have held office previously, have they promoted laws to fix our democracy?
YES
NO
YES
NO
Regarding money in their own campaigns, do candidates refuse and criticize support from corporations, super PACs, and dark money groups?
Are they receiving a higher share of money than other candidates in small donations from many people?
These candidates are more likely to promote reform once elected.
YES
NO
YES
NO

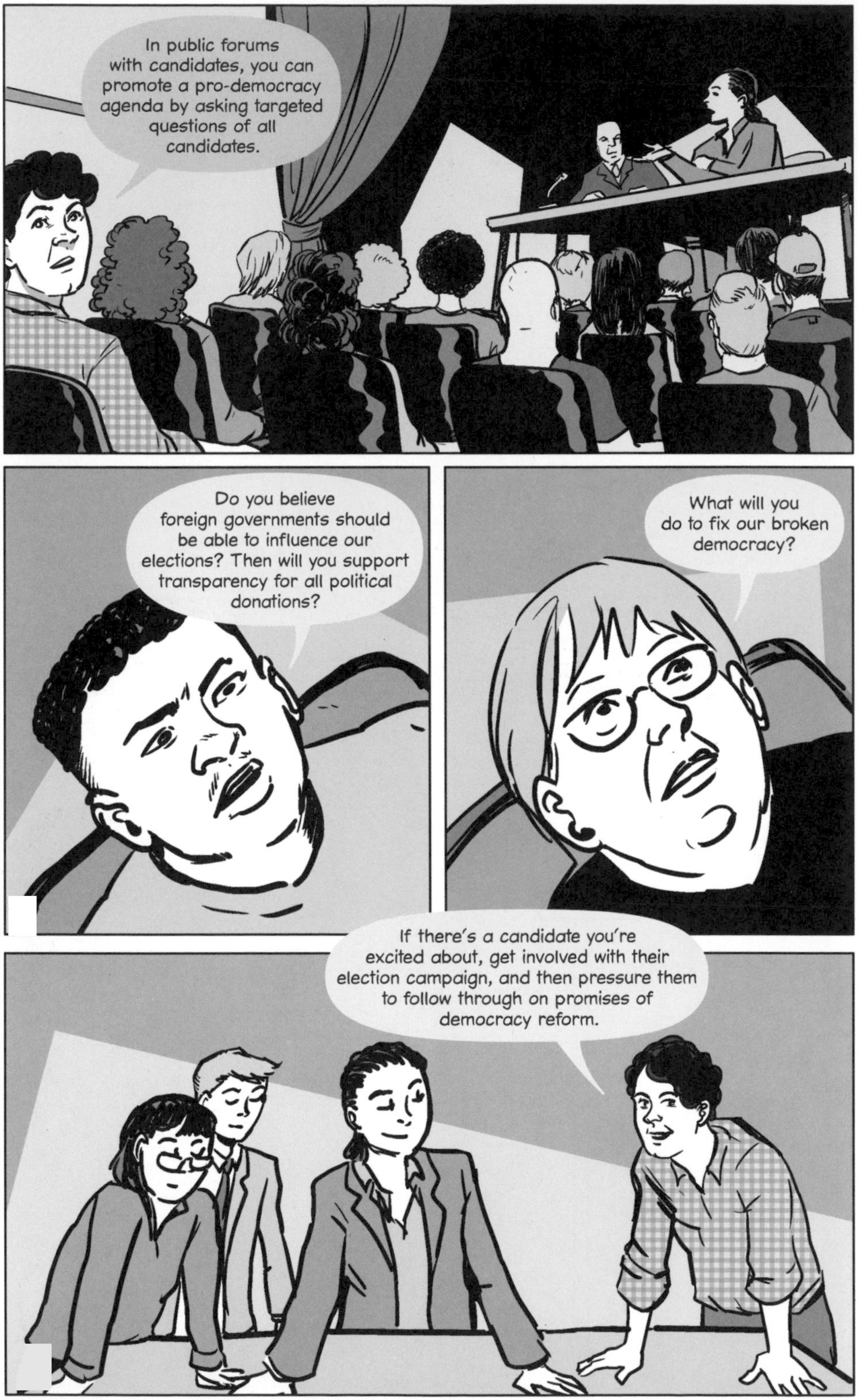
In public forums with candidates, you can promote a pro-democracy agenda by asking targeted questions of all candidates.
Do you believe foreign governments should be able to influence our elections? Then will you support transparency for all political donations?
What will you do to fix our broken democracy?
If there's a candidate you're excited about, get involved with their election campaign, and then pressure them to follow through on promises of democracy reform.

a life of meaning

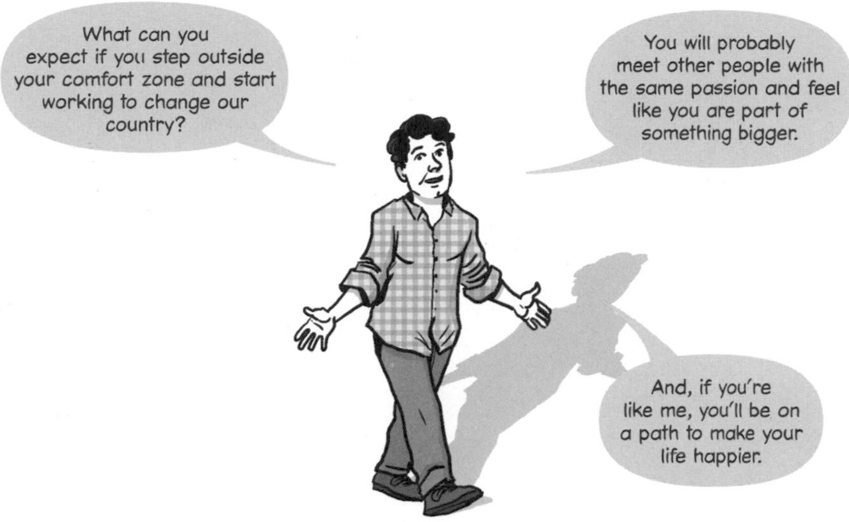
What can you expect if you step outside your comfort zone and start working to change our country?
You will probably meet other people with the same passion and feel like you are part of something bigger.
And, if you're like me, you'll be on a path to make your life happier.

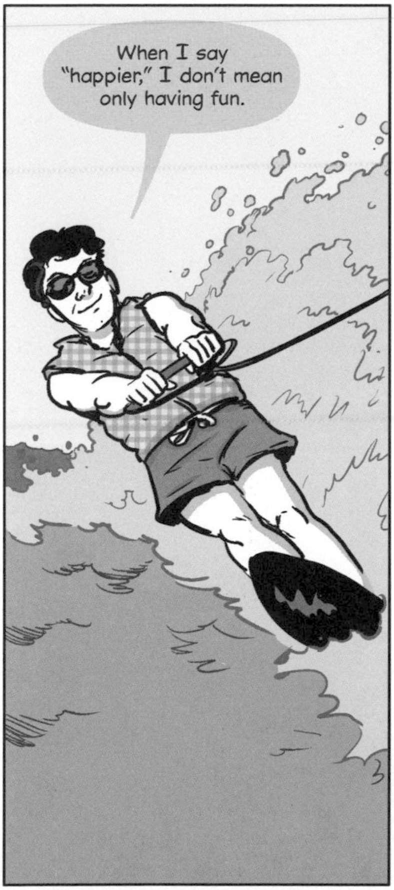
When I say "happier," I don't mean only having fun.

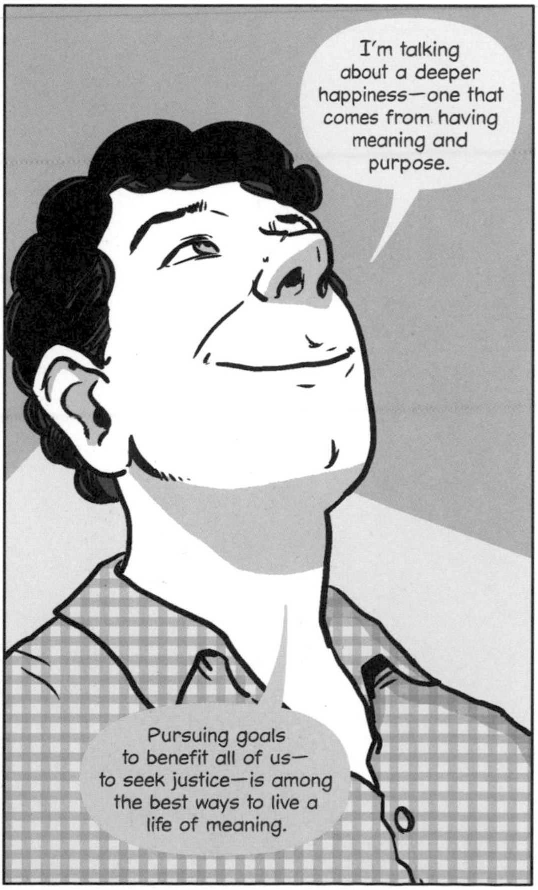
I'm talking about a deeper happiness—one that comes from having meaning and purpose.
Pursuing goals to benefit all of us—to seek justice—is among the best ways to live a life of meaning.

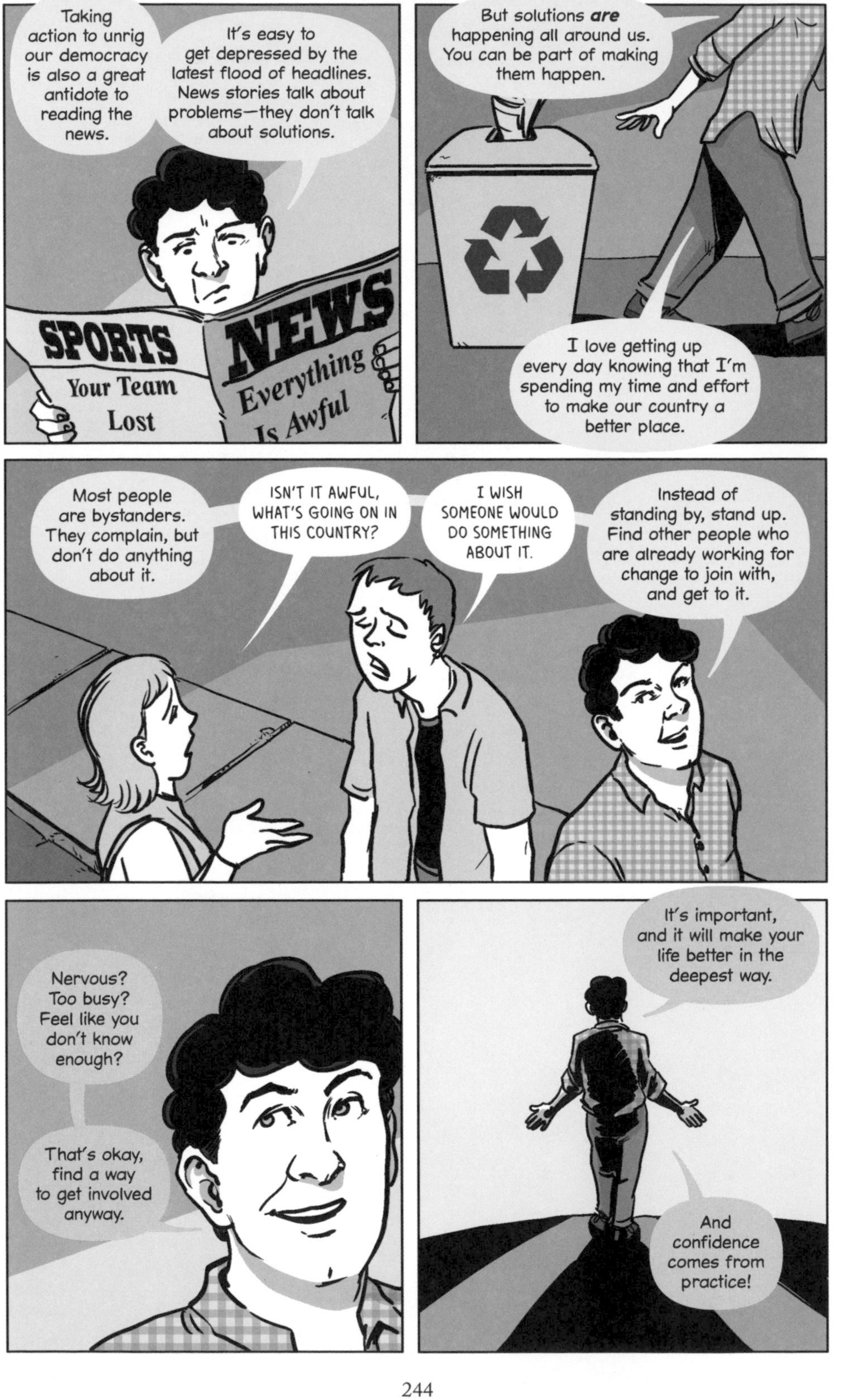

Taking action to unrig our democracy is also a great antidote to reading the news.
It's easy to get depressed by the latest flood of headlines. News stories talk about problems—they don't talk about solutions.
SPORTS
Your Team Lost
NEWS
Everything Is Awful
But solutions **are** happening all around us. You can be part of making them happen.
I love getting up every day knowing that I'm spending my time and effort to make our country a better place.
Most people are bystanders. They complain, but don't do anything about it.
ISN'T IT AWFUL, WHAT'S GOING ON IN THIS COUNTRY?
I WISH SOMEONE WOULD DO SOMETHING ABOUT IT.
Instead of standing by, stand up. Find other people who are already working for change to join with, and get to it.
Nervous? Too busy? Feel like you don't know enough?
That's okay, find a way to get involved anyway.
It's important, and it will make your life better in the deepest way.
And confidence comes from practice!

freedom, justice, and history

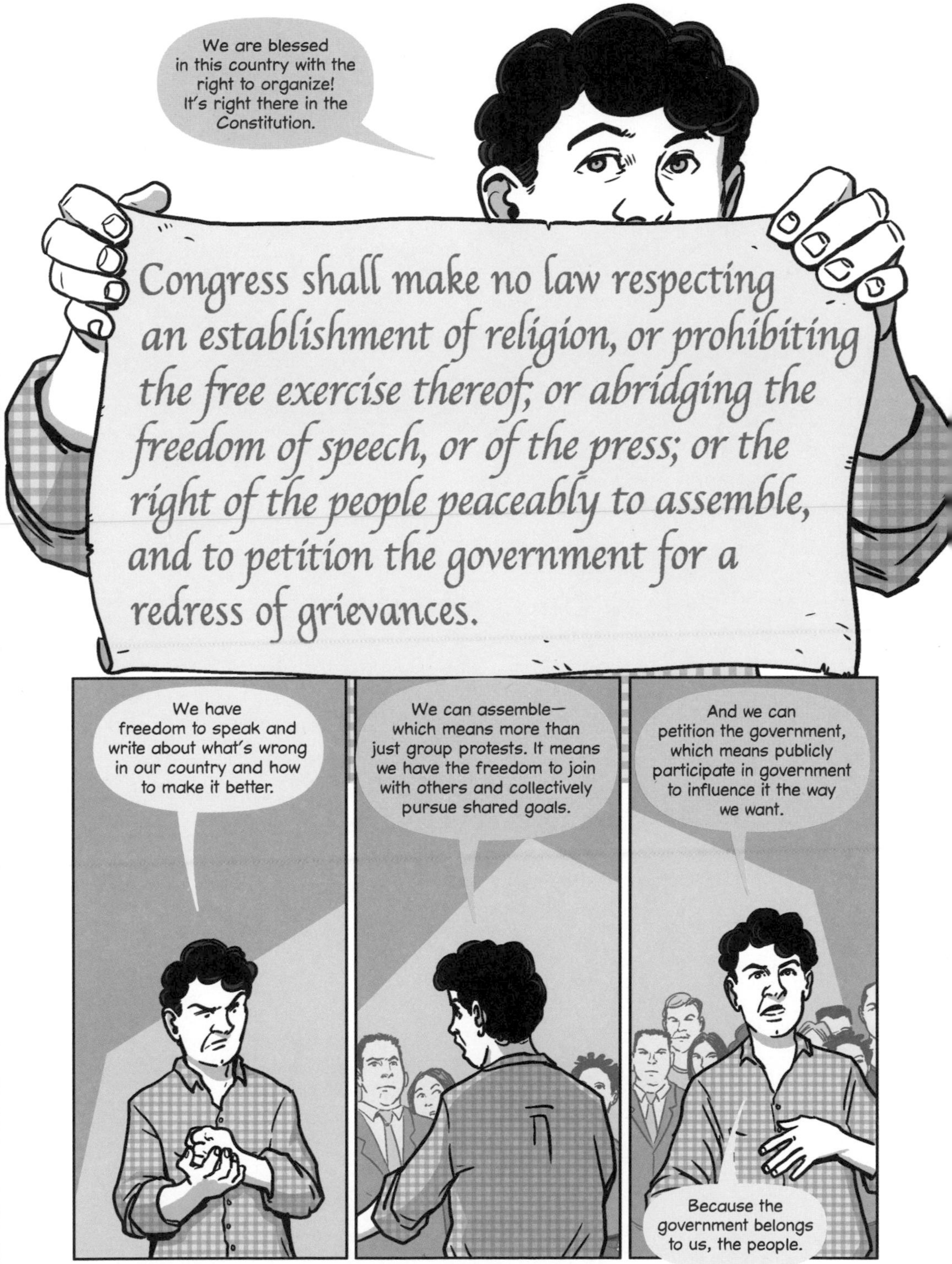
We are blessed in this country with the right to organize! It's right there in the Constitution.
Congress shall make no law respecting an establishment of religion, or prohibiting the free exercise thereof; or abridging the freedom of speech, or of the press; or the right of the people peaceably to assemble, and to petition the government for a redress of grievances.
We have freedom to speak and write about what's wrong in our country and how to make it better.
We can assemble—which means more than just group protests. It means we have the freedom to join with others and collectively pursue shared goals.
And we can petition the government, which means publicly participate in government to influence it the way we want.
Because the government belongs to us, the people.

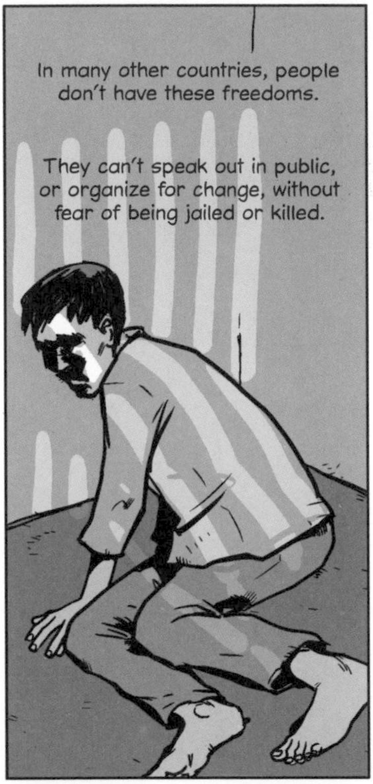
In many other countries, people don't have these freedoms.
They can't speak out in public, or organize for change, without fear of being jailed or killed.

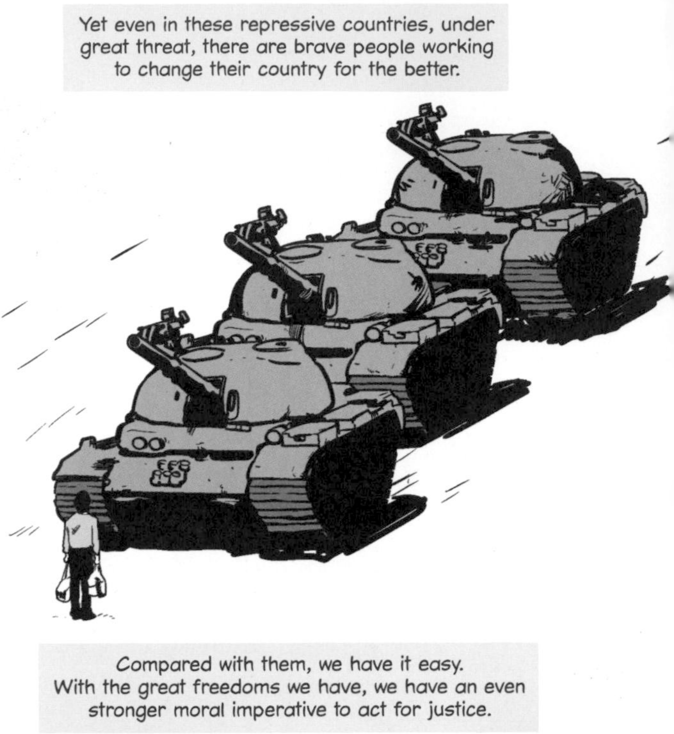
Yet even in these repressive countries, under great threat, there are brave people working to change their country for the better.
Compared with them, we have it easy. With the great freedoms we have, we have an even stronger moral imperative to act for justice.

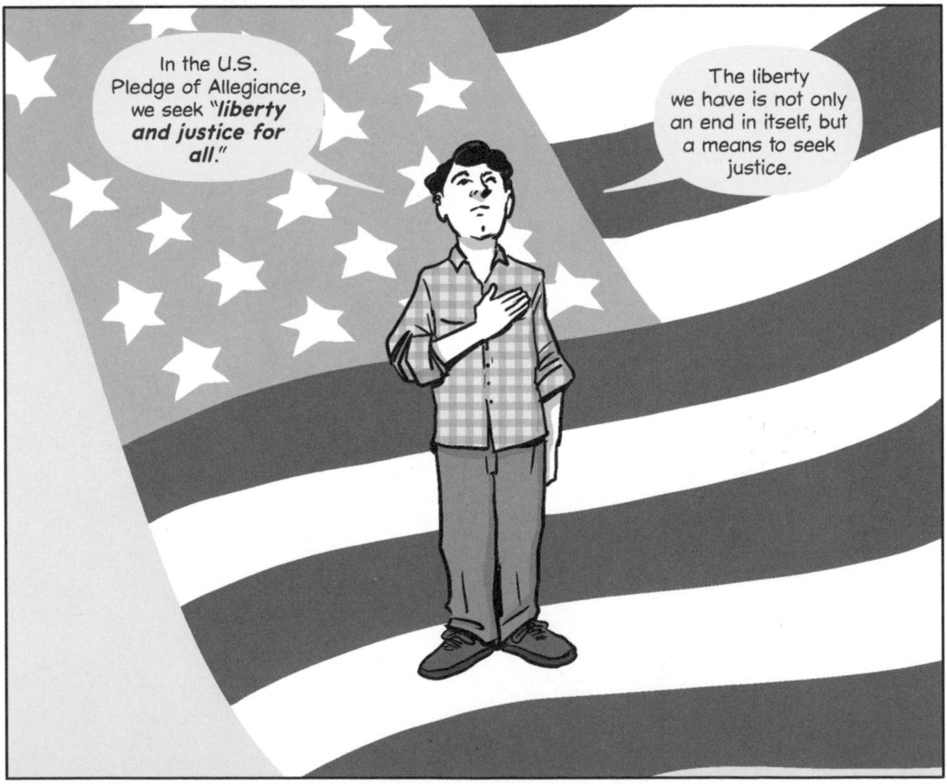
In the U.S. Pledge of Allegiance, we seek "*liberty and justice for all*."
The liberty we have is not only an end in itself, but a means to seek justice.

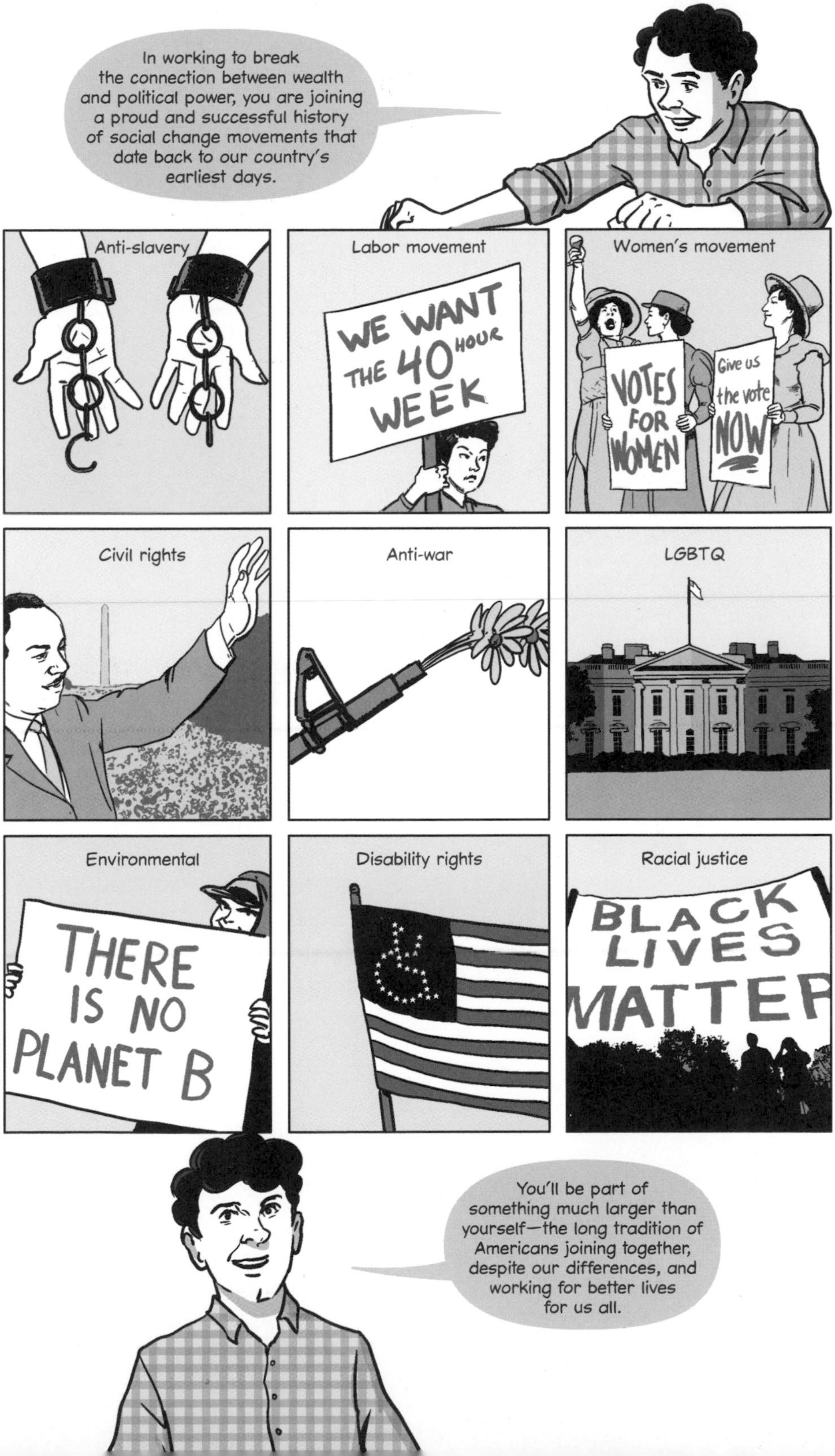
In working to break the connection between wealth and political power, you are joining a proud and successful history of social change movements that date back to our country's earliest days.
Anti-slavery
Labor movement
WE WANT THE 40 HOUR WEEK
Women's movement
VOTES FOR WOMEN
Give us the vote NOW
Civil rights
Anti-war
LGBTQ
Environmental
THERE IS NO PLANET B
Disability rights
Racial justice
BLACK LIVES MATTER
You'll be part of something much larger than yourself—the long tradition of Americans joining together, despite our differences, and working for better lives for us all.

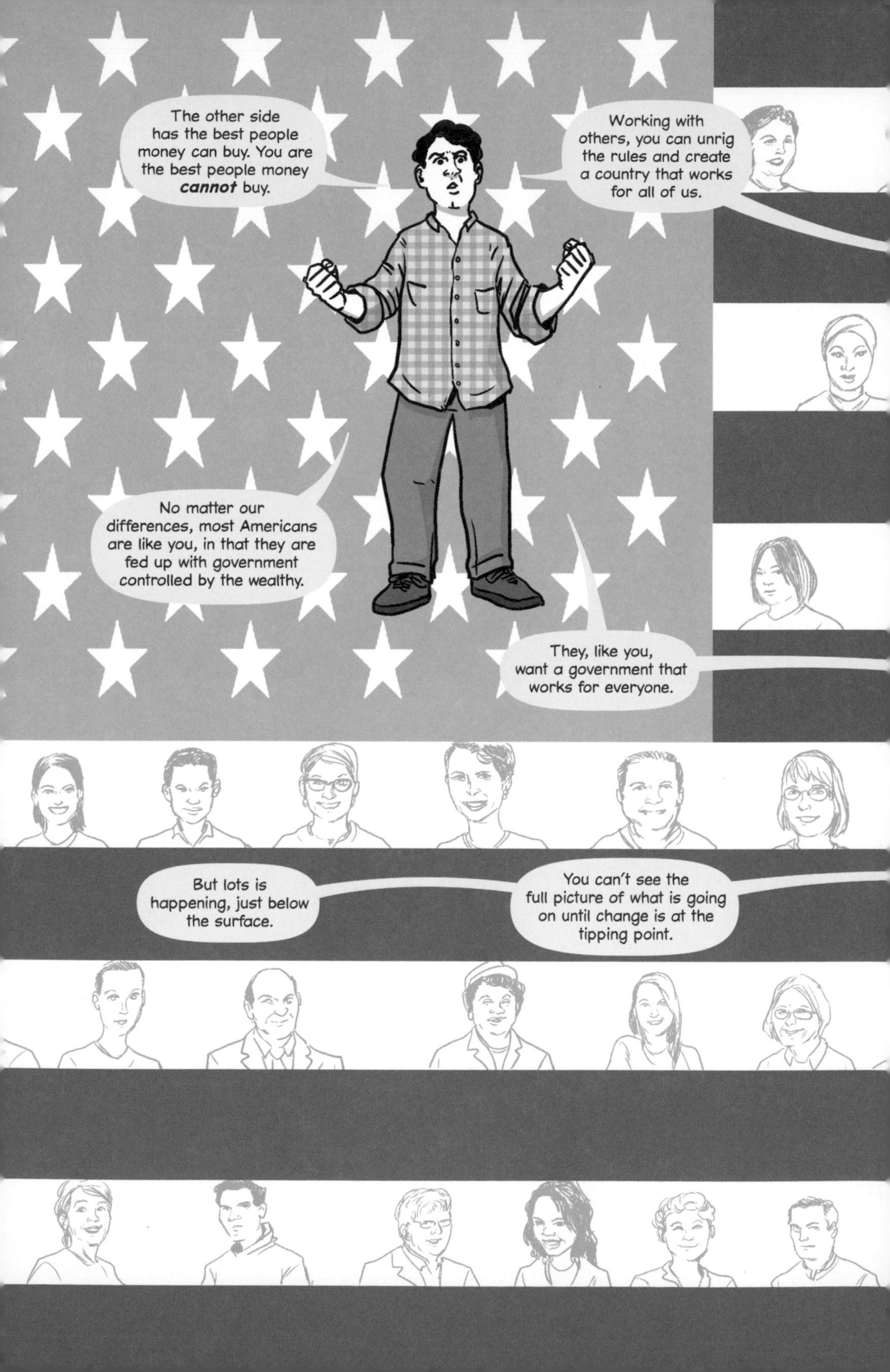
The other side has the best people money can buy. You are the best people money ***cannot*** buy.
Working with others, you can unrig the rules and create a country that works for all of us.
No matter our differences, most Americans are like you, in that they are fed up with government controlled by the wealthy.
They, like you, want a government that works for everyone.
But lots is happening, just below the surface.
You can't see the full picture of what is going on until change is at the tipping point.

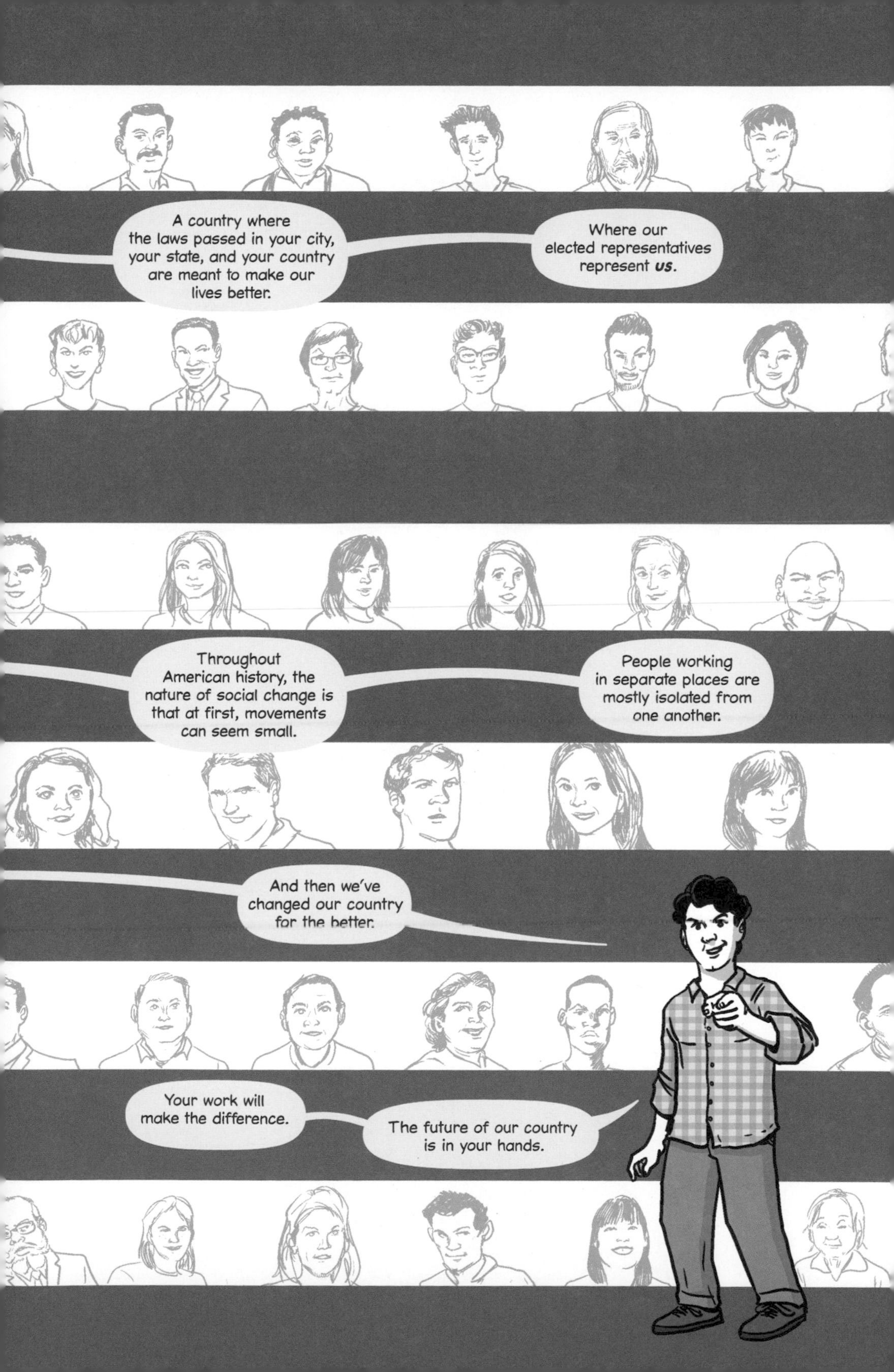
A country where the laws passed in your city, your state, and your country are meant to make our lives better.
Where our elected representatives represent *us*.
Throughout American history, the nature of social change is that at first, movements can seem small.
People working in separate places are mostly isolated from one another.
And then we've changed our country for the better.
Your work will make the difference.
The future of our country is in your hands.

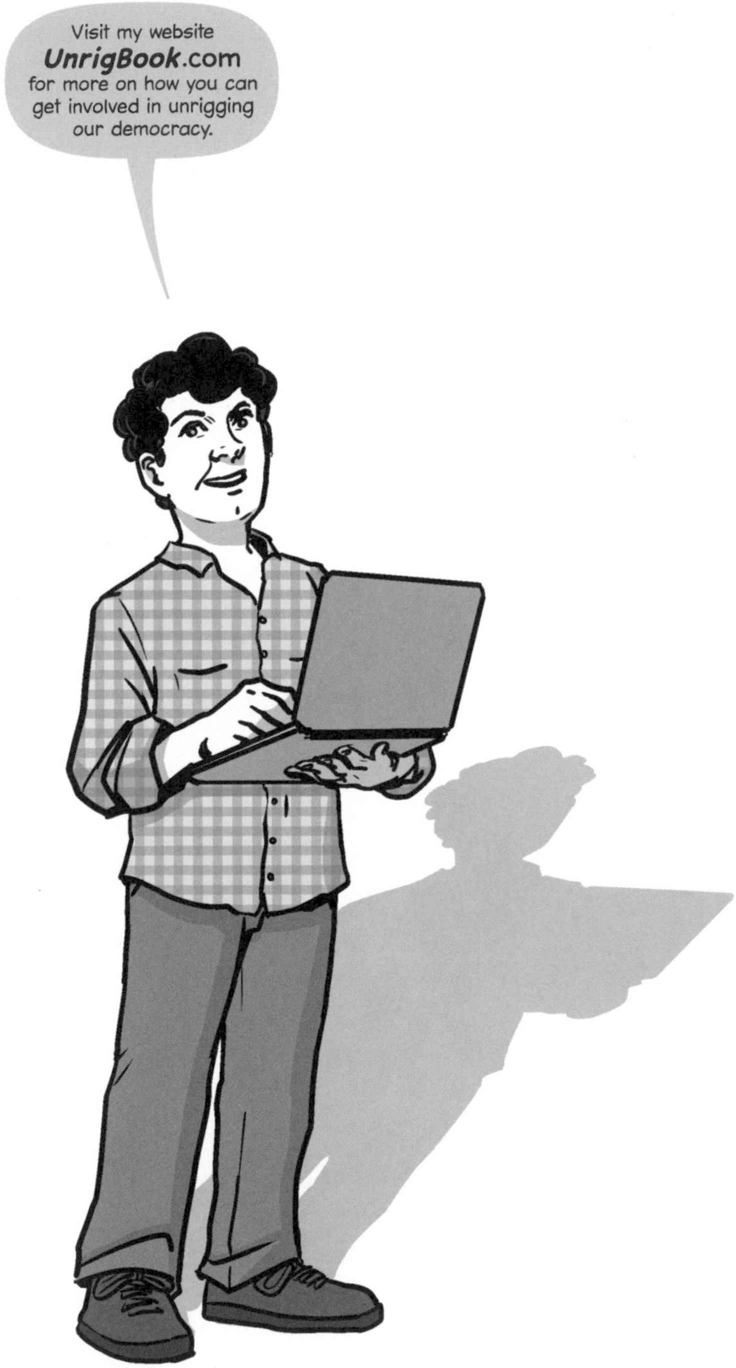
Visit my website UnrigBook.com for more on how you can get involved in unrigging our democracy.

notes

introduction

1 **Fresh/nutritious food bill:** Christian Berthelsen and Lynda Gledhill, "Food Industry's Appetite for Change to Bill Means Schools Can Serve Canned Produce Rather Than Fresh," *San Francisco Chronicle*, September 17, 2005. sfgate.com/health/article/Food-industry-s-appetite-for-change-to-bill-means-2569195.php; Stacy Finz, "Sugary Syrup Fuels Spat over School Food / Original Bill Called for Fresh Produce for Kids," *San Francisco Chronicle*, March 7, 2006. sfgate.com/health/article/Sugary-syrup-fuels-spat-over-school-food-2540046.php.

2 **"gave more than $1 million":** MapLight analysis of data from the National Institute on Money in Politics.

7 **Alcoholic:** Thanks to Lawrence Lessig for this analogy.

1. unrigging the rules

11 **Paul Perry's story:** Interview with Paul Perry, August 14, 2018; "What It's Like to Be Rolodexed: One Candidate's Journey Into the Reality of Political Fundraising," The Intercept, January 31, 2018. theintercept.com/2018/01/31/democratic-party-political-fundraising-dccc/; Paul Perry, "How It Feels to Be Rolodexed," February 11, 2018. medium.com/@pauldavidperry/how-it-feels-to-be-rolodexed-99d9184e34ca. Portions of text © First Look Media. Used with permission.

15 **Teacher and social worker salaries:** 2018 salary figures. "High School Teachers: Occupational Outlook Handbook: U.S. Bureau of Labor Statistics." Accessed August 19, 2019. bls.gov/ooh/education-training-and-library/high-school-teachers.htm; "Social Workers: Occupational Outlook Handbook: U.S. Bureau of Labor Statistics." Accessed August 19, 2019. bls.gov/ooh/community-and-social-service/social-workers.htm.

19 **Teresa Mosqueda's story:** Teresa Mosqueda, "Seattle's Democracy Vouchers Helped Me Get Elected & Here's What I Want You to Know," Bustle, August 14, 2018. bustle.com/p/seattles-democracy-vouchers-helped-me-get-elected-heres-what-i-want-you-to-know-10052772; "Teresa Mosqueda for Seattle City Council Position 8." Accessed January 10, 2019. teamteresa.org/about/.

21 **"Who Funds Seattle's Political Candidates?":** Sightline Institute, July 21, 2015. sightline.org/research_item/who-funds-seattles-political-candidates/.

21 **Map images and demographics of voucher donors:** Win/Win Network and Every Voice Center, "First Look: Seattle's Democracy Voucher Program," November 15, 2017,

3–4. everyvoice.org/wp-content/uploads/2018/08/2017-11-15-Seattle-Post-Election-Report-FINAL.pdf.

24 **Study by the Federal Reserve Board:** Neal Gabler, "The Secret Shame of Middle-Class Americans," *The Atlantic*, May 2016. theatlantic.com/magazine/archive/2016/05/my-secret-shame/476415/; "Federal Reserve Board issues Report on the Economic Well-Being of U.S. Households," Board of Governors of the Federal Reserve System, May 22, 2018. federalreserve.gov/newsevents/pressreleases/other20180522a.htm.

25 **Some of the states and cities with clean elections systems include:**

Arizona: "How Clean Funding Works," Citizens Clean Elections Commission. Accessed May 7, 2019. azcleanelections.gov/en/run-for-office/how-clean-funding-works.

Connecticut: "Model: Connecticut Citizens' Election Program (CEP)," Blueprints for Democracy: A Project of Issue One and the Campaign Legal Center. Accessed May 7, 2019. blueprintsfordemocracy.org/model-public-funding-system.

Maine: "Maine Clean Election Act (MCEA)," Maine Commission on Governmental Ethics & Election Practices. Accessed October 29, 2019. maine.gov/ethics/candidates/maine-clean-election-act.

Minnesota: "Model: Minnesota's Public Subsidy Program," Blueprints for Democracy: A Project of Issue One and the Campaign Legal Center. Accessed May 7, 2019. blueprintsfordemocracy.org/model-public-subsidy-program.

New Mexico: "Campaign Public Financing," Common Cause New Mexico. Accessed May 7, 2019. commoncause.org/new-mexico/our-work/reduce-moneys-influence/campaign-public-financing/.

Tucson, Arizona: "Public Matching Funds: An Introduction," City of Tucson. Accessed May 8, 2019. tucsonaz.gov/files/clerks/pdf/Public_Matching_Funds_Program_Overview.pdf.

Berkeley, California: "Election Information. Public Financing Program," City of Berkeley. Accessed July 24, 2019. cityofberkeley.info/Clerk/Elections/Public_Financing_Program.aspx.

Los Angeles, California: "Campaign Finance Ordinance: Los Angeles Municipal Code 49.7.1. *et seq*.," Los Angeles City Ethics Commission. Accessed October 29, 2019. ethics.lacity.org/wp-content/uploads/laws-campaigns-city-cfo.pdf.

San Francisco, California: "Public Financing Program," San Francisco Ethics Commission, September 22, 2015. sfethics.org/compliance/campaigns/candidates/public-financing-program.

New Haven, Connecticut: "Democracy Fund," City of New Haven. Accessed May 8, 2019. newhavenct.gov/gov/democracy_fund/default.htm.

Montgomery County, Maryland: "Public Campaign Financing - Montgomery County Council," Montgomery County Government. Accessed May 8, 2019. montgomerycountymd.gov/COUNCIL/public_campaign_finance.html.

Albuquerque, New Mexico: "Publicly Financed Candidates - General Information," City of Albuquerque. Accessed May 8, 2019. cabq.gov/vote/candidate-information/publicly-financed-candidates/publicly-financed-candidates-general-information.

Santa Fe, New Mexico: Tripp Stelnicki, "Santa Fe Council OKs Overhaul to Public Campaign Finance," *Santa Fe New Mexican*, December 12, 2018. santafenewmexican.com/news/local_news/santa-fe-council-oks-overhaul-to-public-campaign-finance/article_81762887-46b4-569f-9a53-bce250c1b03c.html.

New York City, New York: "How It Works: New York City's Landmark Campaign Finance Program Provides Public Funds to Candidates for City Office," New York City Campaign Finance Board. Accessed May 8, 2019. nyccfb.info/program/how-it-works/.

Suffolk County, New York: David M. Schwartz, "Suffolk Legislature OKs Public Financing of County Campaigns," *Newsday*, December 19, 2017. newsday.com/long-island/politics/suffolk-public-financing-1.15523881.

Portland, Oregon: "Public Campaign Finance Commission," City of Portland, Oregon. Accessed May 8, 2019. portlandoregon.gov/civic/article/697131.

Seattle, Washington: "Democracy Voucher Program," City of Seattle. Accessed May 7, 2019. seattle.gov/democracyvoucher/about-the-program.

See also: Michael J. Malbin, "Citizen Funding for Elections," The Campaign Finance Institute. Accessed May 19, 2019. cfinst.org/pdf/books-reports/CFI_CitizenFundingforElections.pdf.

28 **Prescription drug discount:** "Ariz. Gov. Napolitano Expands Prescription Drug Discount Card Program to All Residents," *Kaiser Health News*, June 11, 2009. khn.org/morning-breakout/dr00033738/.

31 **Spending on video games:** "U.S. Video Game Sales Reach Record-Breaking $43.4 Billion in 2018," The Entertainment Software Association. Accessed August 19, 2019. theesa.com/press-releases/u-s-video-game-sales-reach-record-breaking-43-4-billion-in-2018/.

31 **Spending on Halloween:** "Halloween Spending to Reach Record $9.1 Billion," National Retail Federation, September 21, 2017. nrf.com/media-center/press-releases/halloween-spending-reach-record-91-billion. Inspired by chart by Bruce Mehlman in Chris Cillizza, "The 2014 Election Cost $3.7 Billion. We Spend Twice That Much on Halloween," *Washington Post*, November 6, 2014. washingtonpost.com/news/the-fix/wp/2014/11/06/the-2014-election-cost-3-7-billion-we-spend-twice-that-much-on-halloween/.

31 **Spending on elections:** Using totals for cycles 2009–16. "Cost of Election," Center for Responsive Politics. Accessed May 8, 2019. opensecrets.org/overview/cost.php.

31 **Hedge fund managers:** From 2009–18, hedge funds and their employees spent $75.1 million on lobbying and $511.7 million on federal campaign contributions, for a sum of $586.8 million invested in political influence. The tax break for carried interest saved them $180 billion over ten years. That's a return on investment of 30,575%. The $18

billion annual carried interest tax break is more than seven times the cost of all spending on federal election campaigns (that's campaigns for U.S. Congress and the president).

Victor Fleischer, "How a Carried Interest Tax Could Raise $180 Billion." *The New York Times*, June 5, 2015. nytimes.com/2015/06/06/business/dealbook/how-a-carried-interest-tax-could-raise-180-billion.html; "Hedge Funds: Long-Term Contribution Trends," Center for Responsive Politics. Accessed May 8, 2019. opensecrets.org/industries/totals.php?cycle=2018&ind=F2700; "Lobbying Spending Database Hedge Funds," Center for Responsive Politics. Accessed May 8, 2019. opensecrets.org/lobby/induscode.php?id=F2700&year=2018.

32 **Cost of Iraq War:** Daniel Trotta, "Iraq War Costs U.S. More than $2 Trillion: Study," *Reuters*, March 14, 2013. reuters.com/article/us-iraq-war-anniversary-idUSBRE92D0PG20130314; Lawrence Lessig, *Republic, Lost* (New York, NY: Twelve, 2011): 269.

33 **Ballot history:** "The History of the Paper Ballot," Fair Vote. Accessed May 8, 2019. archive.fairvote.org/righttovote/pballot.pdf.

38 **New York City's "supermatch" program:** "How It Works."

40 **2013 clean elections campaign contributions:** "Campaigns - Seattle Campaign Finance Disclosure," City of Seattle. Accessed May 21, 2019. web6.seattle.gov/ethics/elections/campaigns.aspx?cycle=2013&type=campaign&IDNum=329&leftmenu=expanded.

41 **Seattle clean elections vote results 2013:** "Election Results General and Special Election," King County Elections. Accessed May 21, 2019. kingcounty.gov/~/media/depts/elections/results/2013/201311.ashx?la=en.

44 **Seattle clean elections vote results 2015:** "Election Results General and Special Election," King County Elections. Accessed May 21, 2019. kingcounty.gov/~/media/depts/elections/results/2015/201511/results.ashx?la=en.

48 **Voter turnout 2016 general election:** "2016 November General Election Turnout Rates," United States Elections Project, September 5, 2018. electproject.org/2016g.

48 **Popular vote 2016 general election:** "Presidential Election Results: Donald J. Trump Wins," *The New York Times*, August 9, 2017. nytimes.com/elections/2016/results/president.

48 **Voter turnout 2016 primary elections:** Drew DeSilver, "Turnout Was High in the 2016 Primary Season, but Just Short of 2008 Record," Pew Research Center, June 10, 2016. pewresearch.org/fact-tank/2016/06/10/turnout-was-high-in-the-2016-primary-season-but-just-short-of-2008-record/.

51 **Infrequent voters who use vouchers:** "Expanding Participation in Municipal Elections: Assessing the Impact of Seattle's Democracy Voucher Program," University of Washington Center for Studies in Demography & Ecology. Accessed May 22, 2019. jenheerwig.com/uploads/1/3/2/1/13210230/mccabe_heerwig_seattle_voucher_4.03.pdf.

57 **Berkeley elections results 2016:** "Election Results - Alameda County Registrar of Voters," Official Election Site of Alameda County. Accessed May 22, 2019. acgov.org/rov/current_election/230/.

2. congress and lobbying

63 **How members of Congress spend their time:** Ezra Klein, "The Most Depressing Graphic for Members of Congress," *Washington Post*, January 14, 2013. washingtonpost.com/news/wonk/wp/2013/01/14/the-most-depressing-graphic-for-members-of-congress/.

65 **Fundraising "call centers":** Norah O'Donnell, "Are Members of Congress Becoming Telemarketers?" *60 Minutes*, CBS News, April 24, 2016. cbsnews.com/news/60-minutes-are-members-of-congress-becoming-telemarketers/.

66 **Steve Israel quote:** Ryan Bort, "John Oliver Breaks Down the Disturbing Truth of Congressional Fundraising," *Newsweek*, April 4, 2016. newsweek.com/john-oliver-last-week-tonight-congressional-fundraising-443675.

67 **Pete DeFazio quote:** *Republic, Lost*, 141.

67 **Rick Nolan quote:** "Are Members of Congress Becoming Telemarketers?"

68 **Elaborate fundraisers:** Kurt Walters, "The 7 Weirdest Political Money Raising Events of 2013," AlterNet, December 27, 2013. alternet.org/2013/12/7-weirdest-political-money-raising-events-2013/.

69 **Eric Fingerhut quote:** *Republic, Lost,* 149.

69 **Rodney Smith quote:** Martin Schram, *Speaking Freely: Former Members of Congress Talk about Money in Politics* (Washington, D.C.: Center for Responsive Politics, 1995): 99.

70 **Tom Harkin quote:** Ed O'Keefe, "Tom Harkin: 'It's Somebody Else's Turn,'" *Washington Post*, January 26, 2013. washingtonpost.com/news/post-politics/wp/2013/01/26/tom-harkin-its-somebody-elses-turn/?utm_term=.13b89e22ef08.

71 **Chris Murphy quote:** Paul Blumenthal, "Chris Murphy: 'Soul-Crushing' Fundraising Is Bad for Congress," HuffPost, May 7, 2013. huffpost.com/entry/chris-murphy-fundraising_n_3232143.

72 **Average expenditure of winning House and Senate candidates:** "Election Trends," Center for Responsive Politics. Accessed July 19, 2019. opensecrets.org/overview/election-trends.php.

72 **U.S. median household income:** Kayla Fontenot, Jessica Semega, and Melissa Kollar, "Income and Poverty in the United States: 2017," U.S. Census Bureau, September 12, 2018. census.gov/library/publications/2018/demo/p60-263.html.

73 **Most Congress members unwilling to support clean elections:** "Cosponsors: H.R.20 - 115th Congress (2017-2018): Government By the People Act of 2017," U.S. Congress, January 24, 2017. congress.gov/bill/115th-congress/house-bill/20/cosponsors.

75 **Committee membership party dues:** Peter Schweizer, *Extortion* (New York: Houghton Mifflin Harcourt, 2013); Jeff Zeleny, "Of Party Dues and Deadbeats on Capitol Hill," *The New York Times*, October 1, 2006. nytimes.com/2006/10/01/us/politics/01dues.html.

75 **Contributions from cosmetic corporations:** MapLight research on contributions to the Senate health committee as of December 7, 2018, from the top 10 beauty companies according to beautypackaging.com/heaps/view/5163/1/.

75 **Lead and other toxins in lipstick and face paint:** "Pretty Scary: Could Halloween Face Paint Cause Lifelong Health Problems?" Campaign for Safe Cosmetics. Accessed May 29, 2019. safecosmetics.org/wp-content/uploads/2015/02/Pretty-Scary.pdf.

76 **Lead and other toxins banned in Canada and Europe:** Ibid.

77 **More than twenty lobbyists per Congress member:** 11,654 lobbyists in 2018. "Lobbying," Center for Responsive Politics. Accessed September 27, 2019. opensecrets. org/lobby/.

77 **Businesses spend thirty-four times as much:** Lee Drutman, *The Business of America is Lobbying*, (New York: Oxford University Press, 2015): 13.

78 **Lobbyists write bills:** Ailsa Chang, "When Lobbyists Literally Write the Bill," NPR, November 11, 2013. npr.org/sections/itsallpolitics/2013/11/11/243973620/when-lobbyists-literally-write-the-bill.

78 **Think tanks:** Eric Lipton and Brooke Williams, "How Think Tanks Amplify Corporate America's Influence," *The New York Times*, August 7, 2016. nytimes.com/2016/08/08/us/politics/think-tanks-research-and-corporate-lobbying.html; John H. Cushman Jr., "Think Tank With Fossil-Fuel Ties Subpoenaed in AG's Climate Inquiry," *InsideClimate News*, April 8, 2016. insideclimatenews.org/news/08042016/think-tank-fossil-fuel-ties-competitive-enterprise-institute-subpoena-attorney-general-climate-change-exxon; Lisa Friedman and Hiroko Tabuchi, "Following the Money That Undermines Climate Science," *The New York Times*, July 10, 2019. nytimes.com/2019/07/10/climate/nyt -climate-newsletter-cei.html.

80 **Revolving door:** Lee Drutman, "About Half of Retiring Senators and a Third of Retiring House Members Register as Lobbyists," *Vox*, January 15, 2016. vox. com/2016/1/15/10775788/revolving-door-lobbying.

81 **Pharmaceutical companies wrote law preventing drug discounts:** Michelle Singer, "Under the Influence." *60 Minutes*, March 29, 2017. cbsnews.com/news/under-the-influence/.

82 **Billy Tauzin's role:** Mike Stuckey, "Tauzin Aided Drug Firms, Then They Hired Him," *NBC News*, March 22, 2006. nbcnews.com/id/11714763/t/tauzin-aided-drug-firms-then-they-hired-him/#.XBlAD1xKhtU.

82 **Tauzin 1,134% salary raise:** Ibid.; "Salaries of Members of Congress: Congressional Votes, 1990-2018," Congressional Research Service, November 26, 2018. everycrsreport. com/files/20181126_97-615_516c618d9fce0f4aecfe680a14f9a56cf3887458.pdf.

83 **Easy-file system, Intuit, H&R Block:** Liz Day, "How the Maker of TurboTax Fought Free, Simple Tax Filing." *ProPublica*, March 26, 2013. propublica.org/article/how-the-maker-of-turbotax-fought-free-simple-tax-filing; Justin Elliott, "Congress Is About to Ban the Government from Offering Free Online Tax Filing. Thank TurboTax," *ProPublica*, April 9, 2019. propublica.org/article/congress-is-about-to-ban-the-government-from-offering-free-online-tax-filing-thank-turbotax; Jessica Huseman, "Filing Taxes Could Be Free and Simple. But H&R Block and Intuit Are Still Lobbying Against It," *ProPublica*, March 20, 2017. propublica.org/article/filing-taxes-could-be-free-simple-hr-block-intuit-lobbying-against-it; Daniel Stevens, "Is Money in Politics to Blame for Complicated Tax Returns?" MapLight, April 12, 2015. maplight.org/story/is-money-in-politics-to-blame-for-complicated-tax-returns/.

87 **Congressional staff stretched thin, underpaid:** "Keeping Congress Competent: Staff Pay, Turnover, And What It Means For Democracy," Sunlight Foundation. Accessed May 30, 2019. sunlightfoundation.com/policy/documents/keeping_congress_competent/.

88 **Office of Technology Assessment:** Kim Zetter, "Of Course Congress Is Clueless About Tech—It Killed Its Tutor," *WIRED*, April 21, 2016. wired.com/2016/04/office-technology-assessment-congress-clueless-tech-killed-tutor/.

88 **Consumer protection agency in Carter era:** Haynes Johnson, "A Carter Issue Turns on Him," *Washington Post*, February 12, 1978. washingtonpost.com/archive/politics/1978/02/12/a-carter-issue-turns-on-him/bc40f9a8-0eec-4899-ae39-26f06eca3286/.

89 **Consumer Nickel Brigade:** David Bollier, "Chapter 3: The Office of Citizen," Ralph Nader, January 6, 2004. nader.org/2004/01/06/chapter-3-the-office-of-citizen/.

3. political money

97 **Ads against John Ward:** *Dark Money*, directed by Kimberly Reed, July 13, 2018. darkmoneyfilm.com/; *Frontline,* "Big Sky, Big Money – Transcript," PBS. Accessed May 30, 2019. pbs.org/wgbh/frontline/film/big-sky-big-money/transcript/.

98 **ARCO and Anaconda Copper Mining company:** Lydia Chavez, "When Arco Left Town," *The New York Times*, July 25, 1982. nytimes.com/1982/07/25/business/when-arco-left-town.html; "Anaconda Closing Open-Pit Copper Mine at Butte," *The New York Times*, April 25, 1982. nytimes.com/1982/04/25/us/anaconda-closing-open-pit-copper-mine-at-butte.html.

98 **Toxic acid from Anaconda Butte mine:** "The Berkeley Pit," Atlas Obscura. Accessed May 30, 2019. atlasobscura.com/places/berkeley-pit.

98 **Dark money in Wisconsin:** Ed Pilkington, "Leaked Documents Reveal Secretive Influence of Corporate Cash on Politics," *The Guardian*, September 14, 2016. theguardian.com/us-news/2016/sep/14/corporate-cash-john-doe-files-scott-walker-wisconsin.

99 Chinese-owned corporation donated to Jeb Bush: Jon Schwarz and Lee Fang, "The Citizens United Playbook: How a Top GOP Lawyer Guided a Chinese-Owned Company Into U.S. Presidential Politics," *The Intercept*, August 3, 2016. theintercept. com/2016/08/03/gop-lawyer-chinese-owned-company-us-presidential-politics/.

100 DISCLOSE Act: Rep. Chris Van Hollen, "H.R.5175 - 111th Congress (2009-2010): DISCLOSE Act," U.S. Congress, April 29, 2010. congress.gov/bill/111th-congress/ house-bill/5175.

101 Federal Election Commission not enforcing law: Dave Levinthal, "FEC Lays Bare Internal Conflicts and Challenges in Letters to Congress," Center for Public Integrity, May 9, 2019. publicintegrity.org/federal-politics/federal-election-commission-congress-fec-conflict/.

101 Republicans in Congress repeatedly protect dark money: Nihal Krishan, "Both Parties Are Addicted to Dark Money. Only One Is Trying to Quit," *Mother Jones*, March 14, 2019. motherjones.com/politics/2019/03/dark-money-democrats-republicans-mitch-mcconnell/.

102 "Badass grandmas": Megan Keller, "North Dakota Activists Dub Themselves 'Badass Grandmas' Taking on Government Corruption," *The Hill*, October 14, 2018. thehill. com/homenews/state-watch/411344-north-dakota-activists-dub-themselves-badass-grandmas-taking-on.

103 San Francisco ban: Madison Park and Roni Selig, "San Francisco Bans Sales of Flavored Tobacco Products," *CNN*, June 6, 2018. cnn.com/2018/06/06/health/san-francisco-flavored-cigarettes-proposition-e/index.html.

103 R.J. Reynolds outspent supporters: "Campaign Finance Dashboards – June 5, 2018 and November 6, 2018 Elections," San Francisco Ethics Commission. Accessed June 1, 2019. sfethics.org/ethics/2018/03/campaign-finance-dashboards-june-5-2018-and-november-6-2018-elections.html.

104 Post-election poll: "San Francisco Measure to Ban Flavored Tobacco Shows Impact of Transparency," Voters' Right To Know, June 8, 2018. votersrighttoknow.org/san-francisco-measure-to-ban-flavored-tobacco-shows-impact-of-transparency/.

106 Business interests outspend labor: "Business-Labor-Ideology Split in PAC & Individual Donations to Candidates, Parties, Super PACs and Outside Spending Groups," Center for Responsive Politics. Accessed June 2, 2019. opensecrets.org/overview/blio. php?cycle=2018.

110 Expanding the Supreme Court: Seth Millstein, "Can Congress Change the Number of Supreme Court Justices? It Hasn't Always Been Nine," Bustle, October 10, 2018. bustle. com/p/can-congress-change-the-number-of-supreme-court-justices-it-hasnt-always-been-nine-12219225.

110 Term limits for justices: "Term Limits," Fix the Court. Accessed June 2, 2019. fixthecourt.com/fix/term-limits/.

4. the wealth hoarders

119 **Fred Koch business history with Hitler:** Jane Mayer, *Dark Money* (New York: Anchor Books, 2017): 34–37.

119 **Revenue at time of Fred Koch's death:** Nancy MacLean, *Democracy in Chains* (New York: Viking, 2017): 129.

119 **Expansion of Koch Industries:** "America's Largest Private Companies." *Forbes.* Accessed June 26, 2019. forbes.com/largest-private-companies/list/; Natalie Jones, "You're Funding the Koch Brothers," *The Guardian*. Accessed June 26, 2019. theguardian.com/us-news/ng-interactive/2018/oct/03/kochs-conservative-patagonia-toilet-paper-interactive.

120 **Charles Koch net worth:** "Billionaires 2019." *Forbes.* Accessed March 5, 2019. forbes.com/billionaires/.

120 **Richard Mellon Scaife inheritance of Mellon banking, Gulf Oil:** *Dark Money*, 6.

120 **Scaife's conservative influence on American public affairs:** Ibid., 73.

120 **Scaife funding to Heritage Foundation:** Ibid., 93.

120 **Scaife funding American Legislative Exchange Council:** Ibid., 109.

120 **ALEC model bills:** Yvonne Wingett Sanchez, and Rob O'Dell, "What Is ALEC? 'The Most Effective Organization' for Conservatives, Says Newt Gingrich," *USA Today*, April 3, 2019. usatoday.com/story/news/investigations/2019/04/03/alec-american-legislative-exchange-council-model-bills-republican-conservative-devos-gingrich/3162357002/.

120 **Amway revenue:** "Amway Reports Sales of $8.8 Billion USD in 2018," Amway Global, February 11, 2019. amwayglobal.com/amway-reports-sales-of-8-8-billion-usd-in-2018/.

120 **DeVos contributions to conservative causes:** *Dark Money*, 286–287.

120 **Betsy DeVos contributions to senators:** Ulrich Boser, Marcella Bombardieri, and C. J. Libassi, "Conflicts of DeVos," Center for American Progress, January 12, 2017. americanprogress.org/issues/education-postsecondary/news/2017/01/12/296231/conflicts-of-devos/.

121 **Koch network:** Jane Mayer, "One Koch Brother Forces the Other Out of the Family Business," *The New Yorker,* June 7, 2018. newyorker.com/news/news-desk/the-meaning-of-a-koch-brothers-retirement.

121 **Meetings at resorts:** Ibid.; Fredreka Schouten, "Koch Tells Donors in Desert: Conservative Political Network Can Increase Tenfold," *USA Today*, January 28, 2018. usatoday.com/story/news/politics/2018/01/28/koch-tells-donors-desert-conservative-political-network-can-increase-tenfold/1072952001/.

123 **Social Security dramatically reduces poverty:** Kathleen Romig, "Social Security Lifts More Americans Above Poverty Than Any Other Program," Center on Budget and Policy Priorities, July 19, 2019. cbpp.org/research/social-security/social-security-lifts-more-americans-above-poverty-than-any-other-program.

124 **"The Samaritan's Dilemma" by James Buchanan:** *Democracy in Chains,* 142–143.

126 **"Tear government out at the root" quote by Koch:** *Dark Money,* 65.

126 **Koch support of Ed Clark:** Ibid., 69; Isaac Chotiner, "American Oligarchs," *Slate,* March 31, 2017. slate.com/news-and-politics/2017/03/the-new-yorkers-jane-mayer-on-the-billionaires-supporting-and-opposing-president-trump.html.

126 **60 percent of campaign budget:** *Dark Money,* 70.

127 **1980 presidential platform:** Ibid., 70.

127 **1 percent of vote:** Ibid.

128 **Buchanan and majority rule:** *Democracy in Chains,* 184.

128 **"The problems of our times require attention to the rules":** Ibid.

131 **"from idea creation. . .to political action":** *Dark Money,* 173.

131 **Groups funded by Koch brothers:** *Democracy in Chains,* xix; Lisa Graves, "ALEC Exposed: The Koch Connection," *The Nation,* July 12, 2011. thenation.com/article/alec-exposed-koch-connection/; Evan Mandery, "Why There's No Liberal Federalist Society," *POLITICO Magazine,* January 23, 2019. politi.co/2FJPQB1.

132 **John Olin ammunition and chemical baron:** *Dark Money,* 115–116.

132 **Legal approach funded by Olin Foundation:** Ibid., 130–131.

132 **Olin Foundation pays students to take Law and Economics:** Ibid., 133.

133 **Law and Economics seminars for judges:** Elliot Ash, Daniel L. Chen, and Suresh Naidu, "Ideas Have Consequences: The Impact of Law and Economics on American Justice," March 20, 2019. elliottash.com/wp-content/uploads/2019/03/ash-chen-naidu-2019-03-20.pdf.

133 **Seminars resulted in judges who voted more conservatively:** Ibid.

133 **Judicial Crisis Network spent heavily to keep Merrick Garland off Court:** Margaret Sessa-Hawkins and Andrew Perez, "Dark Money Group Received Massive Donation in Fight Against Obama's Supreme Court Nominee," MapLight, October 24, 2017. maplight.org/story/dark-money-group-received-massive-donation-in-fight-against-obamas-supreme-court-nominee/.

133 **$17.9 million donation:** Ibid.

134 **Median net worth of American households:** Adrian D. Garcia, "This Is the Median Net Worth By Age—How Do You Compare?" Bankrate, February 7, 2019. bankrate.com/personal-finance/median-net-worth-by-age/.

134 **DeVos, "we are buying influence":** *Dark Money,* 289.

134 **James Madison Center for Free Speech:** Ibid., 288.

136 **Orrin Hatch targeted in primary:** *Democracy in Chains,* xxviii.

136 **Hatch, "These people are not conservatives":** Ibid; Howard Berkes, "GOP-on-GOP Attacks Leave Orrin Hatch Fighting Mad," NPR, April 12, 2012. npr.org/sections/

itsallpolitics/2012/04/12/150506733/tea-party-again-targets-a-utah-gop-senator-and-orrin-hatch-is-fighting-mad.

137 **Hatch backs tax cuts for wealthy while saying no money for children's health:** Dylan Scott, "Orrin Hatch Just Made the Republican Agenda Startlingly Clear," *Vox*, December 5, 2017. vox.com/policy-and-politics/2017/12/5/16733784/senate-tax-bill-orrin-hatch-chip.

138 **Detailed personality profiles on 89 percent of U.S. population:** Calvin Sloan, "Koch Brothers Are Watching You: And New Documents Reveal Just How Much They Know," *Salon*, November 5, 2018. salon.com/2018/11/05/koch-brothers-are-watching-you-and-new-documents-expose-how-much-they-know/.

139 **Koch network organizations and effect:** See, for example, Theda Skocpol and Alexander Hertel-Fernandez, "The Koch Network and Republican Party Extremism," *Perspectives on Politics*, September 2016. doi.org/10.1017/S1537592716001122.

139 **Republicans pass tax bill slashing taxes on corporations and wealthy:** "2017 Tax Law Tilted Toward Wealthy and Corporations," Center on Budget and Policy Priorities, October 25, 2018. cbpp.org/research/federal-tax/2017-tax-law-tilted-toward-wealthy-and-corporations; Chuck Marr, Brendan Duke, and Chye-Ching Huang, "New Tax Law Is Fundamentally Flawed and Will Require Basic Restructuring," Center on Budget and Policy Priorities, August 14, 2018. cbpp.org/research/federal-tax/new-tax-law-is-fundamentally-flawed-and-will-require-basic-restructuring; Frank Sammartino, Philip Stallworth, and David Weiner, "The Effect of the TCJA Individual Income Tax Provisions Across Income Groups and Across the States," Tax Policy Center, March 28, 2018. taxpolicycenter.org/publications/effect-tcja-individual-income-tax-provisions-across-income-groups-and-across-states.

139 **Most Americans opposed the bill:** Lydia Saad, "Independents, Democrats Not on Board With GOP Tax Plan," Gallup.com, December 5, 2017. news.gallup.com/poll/223238/independents-democrats-not-board-gop-tax-plan.aspx.

139 **Chris Collins, "Get it done or don't ever call me again":** Cristina Marcos, "GOP Lawmaker: Donors Are Pushing Me to Get Tax Reform Done," *The Hill*, November 7, 2017. thehill.com/homenews/house/359110-gop-lawmaker-donors-are-pushing-me-to-get-tax-reform-done.

140 **U.S. spending on wars since 9/11:** Neta C. Crawford, "United States Budgetary Costs of the Post-9/11 Wars Through FY2019: $5.9 Trillion Spent and Obligated," Watson Institute, November 14, 2018. watson.brown.edu/costsofwar/files/cow/imce/papers/2018/Crawford_Costs%20of%20War%20Estimates%20Through%20FY2019.pdf.

140 **$50,000 for every American household:** $5.933 trillion war spending since 9/11/2011 (as of November 2018), divided by 118,825,921 U.S. households (2013–17), equals $49,930 per household. "United States Budgetary Costs."; "U.S. Census Bureau QuickFacts: United States," United States Census Bureau. Accessed July 2, 2019. census.gov/quickfacts/fact/table/US/HSD410217.

140 **"Borrowed money that adds to the national debt":** Stephanie Savell, "We Are All Paying the Price for America's Reckless War Spending," *The Nation*, June 28, 2018. thenation.com/article/paying-price-americas-reckless-war-spending/.

142 **Koch network work to defeat public transit:** Hiroko Tabuchi, "How the Koch Brothers Are Killing Public Transit Projects Around the Country," *The New York Times*, June 19, 2018. nytimes.com/2018/06/19/climate/koch-brothers-public-transit.html.

142 **Affordable Care Act repeal would cause 30 million to lose health coverage:** "How Would Repealing the Affordable Care Act Affect Health Care and Jobs in Your State?" *Economic Policy Institute*. Accessed July 2, 2019. epi.org/aca-obamacare-repeal-impact/; Thomas Huelskoetter, "Fact Sheet: Affordable Care Act Repeal," Center for American Progress, December 9, 2016. americanprogress.org/issues/healthcare/reports/2016/12/09/294743/fact-sheet-affordable-care-act-repeal/.

143 **Buchanan contribution to attacks on Social Security:** *Democracy in Chains*, 177–182.

143 **The attacks on Social Security are without merit:** Paul Krugman, "Attacking Social Security," *The New York Times*, August 15, 2010. nytimes.com/2010/08/16/opinion/16krugman.html; "Social Security Works!" *Kirkus Reviews*, January 21, 2015. kirkusreviews.com/book-reviews/nancy-j-altman/social-security-works/.

143 **Privatization of Social Security:** *Democracy in Chains*, 177–182.

143 **Koch-backed groups push for prison privatization:** Ibid., 218–219.

143 **CoreCivic gave 93 percent of political contributions to Republicans 2018:** "CoreCivic Inc: Total Contributions," Center for Responsive Politics. Accessed July 2, 2019. opensecrets.org/orgs/totals.php?id=D000021940&cycle=A.

144 **Koch funding climate change denial:** Jane Mayer, "In the Withdrawal from the Paris Climate Agreement, the Koch Brothers Campaign Becomes Overt," *The New Yorker*, June 5, 2017. newyorker.com/news/news-desk/in-the-withdrawal-from-the-paris-climate-agreement-the-koch-brothers-campaign-becomes-overt.

145 **Grover Norquist, Americans for Tax Reform:** David T. Cook, "Grover Norquist," *Christian Science Monitor*, November 23, 2005. csmonitor.com/2005/1123/p25s02-usmb.html%20.

145 **2011 automatic spending cuts:** *Dark Money*, 364–369.

146 **Koch Industries has dumped pollutants, falsified records:** *Dark Money*, 149–159.

146 **Richard DeVos dummy invoices:** Ibid., 285.

147 **Wealth hoarders influence colleges and universities:** Dave Levinthal, "Koch Brothers' Higher-Ed Investments Advance Political Goals," Center for Public Integrity, October 30, 2015 (updated May 7, 2018). publicintegrity.org/federal-politics/koch-brothers-higher-ed-investments-advance-political-goals/.

147 **"After a whole semester of Hayek":** *Dark Money*, 189.

147 **Koch Foundation spent $147,154 to sponsor freshman course at Brown:** Ibid., 189.

148 **Ford Foundation grant to American Enterprise Institute:** Ibid., 99–100.

148 **Conservative guests outnumber liberals on Sunday news shows:** Emily Crockett, "The Staggering Overrepresentation of White, Conservative Men on Sunday Political Shows," *Vox*, March 15, 2016. vox.com/2016/3/15/11233102/white-conservative-men-sunday-shows; Lis Power and Gabby Miller, "STUDY: Over the Past 3 Months, Guest Panels on Sunday Shows Have Been Overwhelmingly Conservative," Media Matters for America, November 2, 2018. mediamatters.org/blog/2018/11/02/study-over-past-3-months-guest-panels-sunday-shows-have-been-overwhelmingly-conservative/221974.

149 **Strategy of disabling democracy:** Extensively detailed in *Democracy in Chains*.

150 **The most extreme gerrymanders in modern history:** Nicholas O. Stephanopoulos and Eric M. McGhee, "Partisan Gerrymandering and the Efficiency Gap," *The University of Chicago Law Review.* Accessed July 2, 2019. uchicagolawjournalsmshaytiubv.devcloud. acquia-sites.com/sites/lawreview.uchicago.edu/files/04%20Stephanopoulos_McGhee_ART.pdf.

150 **North Carolina gerrymandering 2016:** Mark Olalde, "Redistricting Explained: All Eyes on State Races in 2018," Center for Public Integrity, October 10, 2018 (updated October 26, 2018). publicintegrity.org/state-politics/redistricting-explained-all-eyes-on-state-races-in-2018/.

150 **Paul Weyrich, "I don't want everybody to vote":** Ari Berman, "The GOP War on Voting," *Rolling Stone*, August 30, 2011. rollingstone.com/politics/politics-news/the-gop-war-on-voting-242182/.

151 **Balanced budget would force immediate, radical cuts to government spending:** Richard Kogan, "Constitutional Balanced Budget Amendment Poses Serious Risks," Center on Budget and Policy Priorities, updated March 16, 2018. cbpp.org/research/federal-budget/constitutional-balanced-budget-amendment-poses-serious-risks.

151 **Twenty-eight states have already called for convention:** Jamiles Lartey, "Conservatives Call for Constitutional Intervention Last Seen 230 Years Ago," *The Guardian*, August 11, 2018. theguardian.com/us-news/2018/aug/11/conservatives-call-for-constitutional-convention-alec; Nancy MacLean, "The GOP Tax Bill Could Kill Two Birds with One Stone," The Hill, December 26, 2017. thehill.com/opinion/finance/366488-the-gop-tax-bill-could-kill-two-birds-with-one-stone; States shown on map: Jay Riestenberg, "U.S. Constitution Threatened as Article V Convention Movement Nears Success," Common Cause, March 21, 2018. commoncause.org/resource/u-s-constitution-threatened-as-article-v-convention-movement-nears-success/.

151 **2013 bestselling book:** Mark Levin, *The Liberty Amendments* (New York: Threshold Editions, 2013).

152 **North Carolina taxes:** *Dark Money*, 418.

153 **Affordable Care Act:** Ibid., 418–419.

153 **Gutted environmental programs:** Ibid., 417; Associated Press, "Groups Say NC GOP Has Gutted Pollution Programs," *The Oklahoman*, August 3, 2014. oklahoman.com/article/feed/718449/groups-say-nc-gop-has-gutted-pollution-programs.

153 **Cuts to public education:** *Dark Money*, 419–420; *Democracy in Chains*, 217–218; Jane Mayer, "State for Sale," *The New Yorker*, October 3, 2011. newyorker.com/magazine/2011/10/10/state-for-sale; Lindsay Wagner, "Starving the Schools," NC Policy Watch, December 8, 2015. ncpolicywatch.com/2015/12/08/starving-the-schools/.

154 **Repeal of public funding of judicial elections:** Adam Smith, "North Carolina Legislature Repeals Popular 'Voter Owned Elections' Program," HuffPost, July 26, 2013. huffpost.com/entry/nc-campaign-finance_b_3660472.

154 **Voter suppression:** Ari Berman, "North Carolina Passes the Country's Worst Voter Suppression Law," *The Nation*, July 26, 2013. thenation.com/article/north-carolina-passes-countrys-worst-voter-suppression-law/#sthash.QE1t4Fa3.dpuf.

154 **North Carolina gerrymandering 2012:** *Dark Money*, 410.

155 **Koch-funded center:** *Democracy in Chains*, 214–216.

155 **"It's dictatorship":** Monica Davey, "A State Manager Takes Over and Cuts What a City Can't," *The New York Times*, April 26, 2011. nytimes.com/2011/04/27/us/27michigan.html.

156 **Switched city's water to Flint River:** Rebecca Shabad, "Why Congress Still Isn't Helping Flint," CBS News, May 5, 2016. cbsnews.com/news/why-congress-still-isnt-helping-flint-water-crisis/.

156 **Exposed residents to toxic water:** Ibid.

156 **Contributions by General Motors:** MapLight analysis of campaign finance records from the Michigan Secretary of State and Michigan Campaign Finance Network.

156 **Flint's citizens mostly African American, low-income:** "Flint, MI," Data USA. Accessed July 10, 2019. datausa.io/profile/geo/flint-mi/#economy and datausa.io/profile/geo/flint-mi/#demographics.

156 **"Worthy individuals":** Tyler Cowen, *Average is Over* (New York: Dutton, 2013): 230.

157 **Ad attacking Chris Heagarty:** *Dark Money*, 323–324.

159 **Coercion:** *Democracy in Chains*, 208.

160 **"Big business they see as very suspicious":** Ibid., 438–440.

160 **Koch criminal justice reform:** Ibid., 445–446; "Koch's Criminal Justice Agenda: Protect White-Collar Criminals and Expand the Prison Industrial Complex," UnKoch My Campus. Accessed July 10, 2019. unkochmycampus.org/right-on-crime.

160 **Champion candidates opposed to reform:** *Dark Money*, 445–446. Jane Mayer, "New Koch," *The New Yorker*, January 17, 2016. newyorker.com/magazine/2016/01/25/new-koch.

160 **Koch active in criminal justice reform after environmental crime charges:** *Democracy in Chains*, 445; "Koch Industries Indicted for Environmental Crimes at Refinery," U.S. Department of Justice, September 28, 2000. justice.gov/archive/opa/pr/2000/September/573enrd.htm; "New Koch."

160 **Partnership with United Negro College Fund:** *Democracy in Chains*, 446; "Koch Brothers' $25 Million Gift to UNCF Sparks Controversy," Philanthropy News Digest, June 10, 2014. philanthropynewsdigest.org/news/koch-brothers-25-million-gift-to-uncf-sparks-controversy; "New Koch."

161 **Buchanan university center:** *Democracy in Chains*, 48.

161 **Koch network new name and slogan:** James Hohmann, "The Daily 202: The Koch Network Is Reorganizing Under a New Name and with New Priorities," *Washington Post*, May 20, 2019. washingtonpost.com/news/powerpost/paloma/daily-202/2019/05/20/daily-202-the-koch-network-is-reorganizing-under-a-new-name-and-with-new-priorities/5ce1a94fa7a0a435cff8c0d3/.

162 **"rules rather than the rulers":** *Democracy in Chains*, 184.

165 **GMU economics class:** Rebekah Barber, "Organizing Against Koch Influence on College Campuses," Facing South, March 15, 2019. facingsouth.org/2019/03/organizing-against-koch-influence-college-campuses.

166 **Forced to release gift agreements:** Erica L. Green and Stephanie Saul, "What Charles Koch and Other Donors to George Mason University Got for Their Money," *The New York Times*, May 5, 2018. nytimes.com/2018/05/05/us/koch-donors-george-mason.html.

5. who votes

172 **Six percent of country could vote in 1787:** "How Things Have Changed in Philadelphia since the 1787 Convention," National Constitution Center, May 25, 2016. constitutioncenter.org/blog/how-things-have-changed-since-1787.

172 **National Women's Party:** Terence McArdle, "'Night of Terror': The Suffragists Who Were Beaten and Tortured for Seeking the Vote," *The Washington Post*, November 10, 2017. washingtonpost.com/news/retropolis/wp/2017/11/10/night-of-terror-the-suffragists-who-were-beaten-and-tortured-for-seeking-the-vote/?utm_term=.659202fa071b; "First Picket of White House," NewseumED. Accessed June 5, 2019. newseumed.org/tools/historical-event/first-picket-white-house.

172 **Native Americans, Asian Americans excluded from vote:** "Who Got the Right to Vote When?" *Al Jazeera*. Accessed June 5, 2019. interactive.aljazeera.com/aje/2016/us-elections-2016-who-can-vote/index.html.

173 **Jelly bean test:** Charles E. Cobb, Jr., "The Voting Rights Act, 45 Years Later," The Root, August 6, 2010. theroot.com/the-voting-rights-act-45-years-later-1790880503; Associated Press, "Exhibit Traces History of Voting Rights Act," MSNBC, August 5, 2005. nbcnews.com/id/8839169/ns/us_news-life/t/exhibit-traces-history-voting-rights-act/; Ari Berman, *Give Us the Ballot* (New York: Picador, 2015): 33.

173 **All eleven Confederate states adopt poll tax:** Kelly Phillips Erb, "For Election Day, A History of the Poll Tax in America," *Forbes*, November 5, 2018. forbes.com/sites/kellyphillipserb/2018/11/05/just-before-the-elections-a-history-of-the-poll-tax-in-america/.

174 **Voting laws restricted African Americans, poor whites:** Carol Anderson, *One Person, No Vote* (New York: Bloomsbury Publishing, 2018): 7–9.

175 **Many Republican-controlled states passed voter ID laws:** *Give Us the Ballot*, 260.

175 **Groups that traditionally skew democratic:** "A Deep Dive Into Party Affiliation," Pew Research Center, April 7, 2015. people-press.org/2015/04/07/a-deep-dive-into-party-affiliation/.

175 **Texas law:** Ibid., 257.

175 **Alabama law:** *One Person, No Vote*, 66–68.

176 **Voter ID laws exempt mail-in ballots:** *Give Us the Ballot*, 297; Mark Joseph Stern, "Vote Fraud Exists. Republican Restrictions Won't Stop It," *Slate*, September 1, 2016. slate.com/news-and-politics/2016/09/voter-fraud-exists-through-absentee-ballots-but-republicans-wont-stop-it.html.

176 **Mail-in ballots typically favor Republicans:** Liam Stack, "Millions Have Voted Early in the Midterms. Here's What That Means—and What it Doesn't," *The New York Times*, October 23, 2018. nytimes.com/2018/10/23/us/politics/early-voting-midterms.html.

176 **Indiana law:** *One Person, No Vote*, 151–152.

176 **"Time tax":** Stateline, "Voting Lines Are Shorter—But Mostly for Whites," HuffPost, February, 15, 2018. huffpost.com/entry/voting-lines-are-shorter-but-mostly-for-whites_b_5a85a1bbe4b00e7aba2d2978.

177 **Tanya Thivener:** Michael Powell and Peter Slevin, "Several Factors Contributed to 'Lost' Voters in Ohio." *Washington Post*, December 15, 2004. washingtonpost.com/archive/politics/2004/12/15/several-factors-contributed-to-lost-voters-in-ohio/73aefa72-c8e5-4657-9e85-5ec8b2451202/.

177 **Fifty-two minute average wait time:** *Give Us the Ballot*, 221.

177 **Ohio survey on leaving polling places:** Ibid.

178 **Voter suppression in North Carolina:** Christopher Ingraham, "The 'Smoking Gun' Proving North Carolina Republicans Tried to Disenfranchise Black Voters," *Washington Post*, July 29, 2016. washingtonpost.com/news/wonk/wp/2016/07/29/the-smoking-gun-proving-north-carolina-republicans-tried-to-disenfranchise-black-voters/.

179 **John Lewis in Selma, Alabama:** *Give Us the Ballot*, 5.

180 **Voting Rights Act:** Ibid., 5–6.

181 **VRA effects on registered black voters in Selma:** Ibid., 49.

181 **Selma county sheriff election:** Ibid., 49–53.

181 **Jim Clark :** Ibid., 16–17.

181 **Results of VRA dramatic nationwide:** Ibid., 6.

182 **Lewis quote about Lyndon Johnson:** Ibid.

182 **Preclearance provision in Voting Rights Act:** "The Voting Rights Act," Brennan Center for Justice. Accessed June 5, 2019. brennancenter.org/issues/the-voting-rights-act.

183 **Federal government rejected thousands of discriminatory voting law changes:** Andrew Cohen, "After 50 Years, the Voting Rights Act's Biggest Threat: The Supreme Court," *The Atlantic*, February 22, 2013. theatlantic.com/national/archive/2013/02/after-50-years-the-voting-rights-acts-biggest-threat-the-supreme-court/273257/.

183 **Voting Rights Act extended for twenty-five years:** Jeffrey Toobin, "Voter, Beware," *The New Yorker*, February 22, 2009. newyorker.com/magazine/2009/03/02/voter-beware.

183 **Supreme Court guts preclearance provision of VRA:** Adam Liptak "Supreme Court Invalidates Key Part of Voting Rights Act," *The New York Times*, June 25, 2013. nytimes.com/2013/06/26/us/supreme-court-ruling.html.

184 **John Roberts clerk for William Rehnquist:** *Give Us the Ballot*, 146.

184 **Rehnquist literacy tests:** Ibid., 147.

184 **Roberts's opposition to VRA reauthorization:** Ibid., 149.

185 **Justice Department, courts block four discriminatory voting changes:** Ibid., 277.

185 **Ruth Bader Ginsburg quote:** Ibid., 281.

186 **John Lewis quote:** Ibid., 283.

186 **Ohio voter suppression law upheld:** Richard Wolf, "Supreme Court Says States Can Remove Voters Who Skip Elections, Ignore Warnings," *USA Today*, June 11, 2018. usatoday.com/story/news/politics/2018/06/11/supreme-court-states-purge-voters-who-dont-vote/587316002/.

187 **Politicians pay more attention to voters than nonvoters:** Jan Leighley and Jonathan Nagler, *Who Votes Now?* (Princeton: Princeton University Press, 2014): 2.

187 **Older Americans vote at higher rates:** Asma Khalid, Don Gonyea, and Leila Fadel, "On The Sidelines of Democracy: Exploring Why So Many Americans Don't Vote," NPR, September 10, 2018. npr.org/2018/09/10/645223716/on-the-sidelines-of-democracy-exploring-why-so-many-americans-dont-vote.

187 **High-income and low-income citizen voting rates:** *Who Votes Now?*, 1.

187 **Nonvoters and voters have different preferences:** "On the Sidelines of Democracy."

189 **Election Day history:** John Cunningham, "Why Are U.S. Elections Held on Tuesdays?" *Encyclopedia Britannica*. Accessed June 11, 2019. britannica.com/story/why-are-us-elections-held-on-tuesdays; "Why Tuesday?" whytuesday.org/.

189 **"No excuse absentee voting":** "Absentee and Early Voting," National Conference of State Legislatures, July 30, 2019. ncsl.org/research/elections-and-campaigns/absentee-and-early-voting.aspx.

190 **Same-day voter registration:** "Same Day Voter Registration," National Conference of State Legislatures, June 28, 2019. ncsl.org/research/elections-and-campaigns/same-day-registration.aspx.

190 **Automatic voter registration:** "Automatic Voter Registration," Brennan Center for Justice, July 10, 2019. brennancenter.org/analysis/automatic-voter-registration.

191 **Colorado approach to voter registration:** Allegra Chapman and Amber McReynolds, "The Colorado Voting Experience: A Model That Encourages Full Participation," Common Cause, July 9, 2019. commoncause.org/resource/the-colorado-voting-experience-a-model-that-encourages-full-participation/.

191 **Increased voter participation in Colorado:** Danielle Root and Liz Kennedy, "Increasing Voter Participation in America," Center for American Progress, June 11, 2018. americanprogress.org/issues/democracy/reports/2018/07/11/453319/increasing-voter-participation-america/.

191 **Civics education model Kids Voting USA:** Ibid.

192 **Voting rate in Australia:** Tacey Rychter, "How Compulsory Voting Works: Australians Explain." *The New York Times*, October 22, 2018. nytimes.com/2018/10/22/world/australia/compulsory-voting.html.

192 **Fifty-nine percent of eligible Americans voted in 2016:** "2016 November General Election Turnout Rates," United States Elections Project, September 5, 2018. electproject.org/2016g.

192 **Required voting results in more knowledgeable voters:** "How Compulsory Voting Works."

192 **"Voting in Australia is like a party":** Ibid.

192 **Takoma Park, Maryland, voting at age sixteen:** "Register to Vote," City of Takoma Park. Accessed June 11, 2019. takomaparkmd.gov/register-to-vote/.

192 **Berkeley, California, voting at age sixteen:** "Berkeley, CA," Vote16 USA. Accessed June 11, 2019. vote16usa.org/project/berkeley-ca/.

192 **Early voting develops voting as habit:** "Lower the Voting Age for Local Elections," FairVote. Accessed June 11, 2019. fairvote.org/lower_the_voting_age.

193 **Former slaves penalized, arrested for minor crimes, invented claims:** Emily Bazelon, "Will Florida's Ex-Felons Finally Regain the Right to Vote?" *The New York Times*, September 26, 2018. nytimes.com/2018/09/26/magazine/ex-felons-voting-rights-florida.html.

193 **Prisoners forced to work as cheap labor:** Erin Kelley, "Racism & Felony Disenfranchisement: An Intertwined History," Brennan Center for Justice. Accessed June 11, 2019. brennancenter.org/sites/default/files/publications/Disenfranchisement_History.pdf.

193 **Felony disenfranchisement laws to prevent African Americans from voting:** Ibid.

194 **More than one in five African Americans barred from voting:** Christopher Uggen, Ryan Larson, and Sarah Shannon, "6 Million Lost Voters: State-Level Estimates of Felony Disenfranchisement, 2016," The Sentencing Project, October 6, 2016. sentencingproject.org/publications/6-million-lost-voters-state-level-estimates-felony-disenfranchisement-2016/.

194 **Desmond Meade story:** Stacey Abrams, "Desmond Meade," *Time*, April 16, 2019. time. com/collection-post/5567673/desmond-meade/; Nick Ducassi, "Life Takes a New Track after Prison, Law School," *FIU Magazine*, December 22, 2014. news.fiu.edu/2014/12/ life-takes-a-new-track-after-prison-law-school/83069.

194 **Voting rights restored to more than 1.4 million people:** "We Made History!" Florida Rights Restoration Coalition. Accessed April 29, 2019. floridarrc.com/.

194 **Meade quote:** Flegan Morez, Twitter post, March 30, 2019, 7:38 p.m., twitter.com/ FleganMorez/status/1112182344486715392.

6. drawing the districts

198 **Redistricting process:** Justin Levitt, "Who Draws the Lines," All About Redistricting. Accessed June 16, 2019. redistricting.lls.edu/who.php.

198 **Redistricting diagram:** Michael Li and Annie Lo, "What Is Extreme Gerrymandering?" Brennan Center for Justice. Accessed March 22, 2019. brennancenter. org/blog/what-is-extreme-gerrymandering.

199 **Reasons to gerrymander:** "Why Do Politicians Gerrymander?" *The Economist*, October 27, 2013. economist.com/the-economist-explains/2013/10/27/why-do-politicians-gerrymander.

199 **Pennsylvania gerrymandering:** Alex Wagner, "When Republicans Draw District Boundaries, They Can't Lose. Literally." *The New York Times*, June 21, 2016. nytimes. com/2016/06/26/books/review/rated-by-david-daley.html.

199 **Maryland gerrymandering:** Christopher Ingraham, "How Maryland Democrats Pulled Off Their Aggressive Gerrymander," *The Washington Post*, March 28, 2018. washingtonpost.com/news/wonk/wp/2018/03/28/how-maryland-democrats-pulled-off-their-aggressive-gerrymander/.

200 **Gerrymandering more common:** Richard Pildes, "Why Gerrymandering Is Going to Get Even Worse," *The Washington Post*, April 26, 2018. washingtonpost.com/news/ monkey-cage/wp/2018/04/26/yes-gerrymandering-is-getting-worse-and-will-get-worse-still-this-explains-why/.

200 **Modern data collection and mapmaking software:** Vann R. Newkirk, II, "How Redistricting Became a Technological Arms Race," *The Atlantic*, October 28, 2017. theatlantic.com/politics/archive/2017/10/gerrymandering-technology-redmap-2020/543888/.

202 **Members of redistricting commission:** "FAQ," California Citizens Redistricting Commission. Accessed June 21, 2019. wedrawthelines.ca.gov/faq/.

202 **Thousands of applicants:** "Background on Commission," California Citizens Redistricting Commission. Accessed June 21, 2019. wedrawthelines.ca.gov/commission/.

203 **Commission produced fair maps:** Eric McGhee, "Assessing California's Redistricting Commission: Effects on Partisan Fairness and Competitiveness," Public Policy Institute of California. Accessed June 21, 2019. ppic.org/wp-content/uploads/r-0317emr.pdf.

203 **California jurisdictions adopted redistricting commissions:** "Frequently Asked Questions," California Local Redistricting Project. Accessed June 21, 2019. localredistricting.org/faq.

204 **"Voters Not Politicians" story:** Riley Beggin, "One Woman's Facebook Post Leads to Michigan Vote Against Gerrymandering," *Bridge*, November 7, 2018. bridgemi.com/ public-sector/one-womans-facebook-post-leads-michigan-vote-against-gerrymandering; Tina Rosenberg, "Putting the Voters in Charge of Fair Voting," *The New York Times*, January 23, 2018. nytimes.com/2018/01/23/opinion/michigan-gerrymandering-fair-voting.html; Erick Trickey, "A Grassroots Call to Ban Gerrymandering," *The Atlantic*, September 23, 2018. theatlantic.com/politics/archive/2018/09/a-grassroots-movement-in-michigan-has-gerrymandering-in-the-crosshairs/570949/; B. David Zarley, "Inside the Movement to End Partisan Gerrymandering in Michigan," A Beautiful Perspective, July 19, 2018. abeautifulperspective.com/2018/07/gerrymandering-michigan-citizens-draw-districts/; "Michigan's Anti-Gerrymandering Proposal Is Approved. Now What?" *Detroit Free Press*, November 7, 2018. freep.com/story/news/politics/ elections/2018/11/07/proposal-2-anti-gerrymandering-michigan/1847402002/.

7. picking the winners

211 **Proportional representation system:** "How Proportional Representation Elections Work," FairVote. Accessed June 23, 2019. fairvote.org/how_proportional_ representation_elections_work.

212 **More than 300 places:** Margaret Morales, "Over 300 Places in the United States Have Used Fair Voting Methods," Sightline Institute, November 8, 2017. sightline. org/2017/11/08/over-300-places-in-the-united-states-have-used-fair-voting-methods/.

213 **ProRep is widely used:** FairVote.org, "Proportional Representation Voting Systems," FairVote. Accessed June 23, 2019. fairvote.org/proportional_representation_voting_ systems.

213 **Twenty-one of twenty-eight countries:** Ibid.

213 **Chart:** "Questions about Proportional Representation You Were Afraid to Ask," Sightline Institute, October 18, 2018. sightline.org/2018/10/18/questions-about-proportional-representation-you-were-afraid-to-ask/.

213 **Higher voter turnout in proportional representation democracies:** Ibid.

215 **Ranked choice voting eliminates spoiler effect:** "Correcting the Spoiler Effect," FairVote. Accessed June 23, 2019. archive3.fairvote.org/reforms/instant-runoff-voting/ irv-and-the-status-quo/spoiler-effect.

216 **Ranked choice voting cities:** "Ranked Choice Voting / Instant Runoff," FairVote. Accessed June 23, 2019. fairvote.org/rcv.

217 **More women and people of color run for office and win:** Sarah John, et al. "The Impact of Ranked Choice Voting on Representation." Accessed June 23, 2019. fairvote.app.box. com/v/RCV-Representation-BayArea.

219 **Voters in ranked choice voting cities are more satisfied:** "Data on Ranked Choice Voting," FairVote. Accessed June 23, 2019. fairvote.org/data_on_rcv.

219 **Nontraditional candidates dismissed, which suppresses debate:** Rob Richie, "Should We Choose Ranked Choice Voting?" *Cato Unbound*, December 5, 2016. cato-unbound. org/print-issue/2164.

219 **Maine first state to use ranked choice voting:** "The Committee for Ranked Choice Voting," The Committee for Ranked Choice Voting 2020. Accessed June 23, 2019. rcvmaine.com/.

8. electing a president

223 **Tens of thousands of people lost their farms:** Michael J. Klarman, *The Framers' Coup: The Making of the United States Constitution* (New York: Oxford University Press, 2016): 76.

223 **Shays' Rebellion:** "Shays' Rebellion," History.com. November 12, 2009/updated September 9, 2019. history.com/topics/early-us/shays-rebellion.

224 **Insurgents and sympathizers win seats in state legislature, reduce taxes:** *The Framers' Coup*, 97–98.

225 **State delegates to convention sought to limit majority rule:** Ibid., 606–609.

225 **Characteristics of most state constitutions at the time:** Ibid., 245.

225 **Longer legislative terms, large constituencies:** Ibid., 244–245.

226 **Veto points:** Alfred Stepan and Juan J. Linz. "Comparative Perspectives on Inequality and the Quality of Democracy in the United States," *Perspectives on Politics* 9, no. 4 (December 2011). doi.org/10.1017/S1537592711003756.

227 **James Wilson:** Holly Munson, "Say What?: 'Imaginary Beings Called States.'" National Constitution Center, October 7, 2011. constitutioncenter.org/blog/say-what-imaginary-beings-called-states.

227 **Many delegates opposed direct election:** Christopher F. Petrella, "Slavery, Democracy, and the Racialized Roots of the Electoral College," African American Intellectual History Society, November 14, 2016. aaihs.org/slavery-democracy-and-the-racialized-roots-of-the-electoral-college/.

228 **Electoral College:** Andrew Prokop, "Why the Electoral College is the Absolute Worst, Explained," *Vox*, December 19, 2016. vox.com/policy-and-politics/2016/11/7/12315574/electoral-college-explained-presidential-elections-2016; "How the Electoral College

Works," University of Missouri–Kansas City. Accessed June 25, 2019. law2.umkc.edu/faculty/projects/ftrials/conlaw/electoralworks.htm.

228 **Iowa seats in Congress:** "Iowa Senators, Representatives, and Congressional District Maps - GovTrack.Us." Accessed June 25, 2019. govtrack.us/congress/members/IA.

228 **3/5 compromise:** "The 'Three-Fifths' Compromise," African American Registry. Accessed June 25, 2019. aaregistry.org/story/the-three-fifths-compromise/; "Slavery, Democracy, and the Racialized Roots of the Electoral College."

229 **Five times presidential candidate won popular vote not election:** "Electoral College Fast Facts," US House of Representatives: History, Art & Archives." Accessed June 25, 2019. history.house.gov/Institution/Electoral-College/Electoral-College/.

230 **Al Gore, Hillary Clinton win popular vote, lose Electoral College:** "Electoral College Box Scores 2000-2016," National Archives and Records Administration – U.S. Electoral College. Accessed June 24, 2019. archives.gov/federal-register/electoral-college/scores2.html.

230 **Ohio John Kerry, George W. Bush example:** "President / Vice President: November 2, 2004," Ohio Secretary of State. Accessed June 24, 2019. sos.state.oh.us/elections/election-results-and-data/2004-elections-results/president--vice-president-november-2-2004/.

230 **Bush won popular vote by three million:** "Electoral College Box Scores 2000-2016."

231 **About a dozen swing states:** "A Recent Voting History of the 15 Battleground States," National Constitution Center, November 6, 2016. constitutioncenter.org/blog/voting-history-of-the-15-battleground-states.

231 **Disproportionate power in swing states:** Lawrence Lessig, "Electoral College Confusions," The Hill, October 31, 2018. thehill.com/blogs/congress-blog/politics/413998-electoral-college-confusions.

231 **Republican vote in Massachusetts:** "Massachusetts Election Results 2016," *The New York Times*, August 1, 2017. nytimes.com/elections/2016/results/massachusetts; Ken Belson, "Massachusetts - Election 2012," *The New York Times*. Accessed June 25, 2019. nytimes.com/elections/2012/results/states/massachusetts.html.

231 **Democratic vote in Tennessee:** "Tennessee Election Results 2016," *The New York Times*. August 1, 2017. nytimes.com/elections/2016/results/tennessee; Patricia Cohen, "Tennessee - Election 2012," *The New York Times*. Accessed June 25, 2019. nytimes.com/elections/2012/results/states/tennessee.html.

232 **Clinton, Trump campaigns dedicate most of ad spending and visits to fourteen states:** George Pillsbury and Julian Johannesen, "America Goes to the Polls 2016," Nonprofit VOTE. Accessed June 25, 2019. nonprofitvote.org/documents/2017/03/america-goes-polls-2016.pdf/.

232 **Voters in swing states tend to be older, whiter:** "Equal Votes: Our Fight to Fix the Electoral College," Equal Citizens. Accessed June 25, 2019. equalcitizens.us/equal-votes/.

232 **Issues of younger Americans and people of color fail to receive attention:** Ibid.

232 **Republican officials delete African American voters from Florida records 2000:**
"Voting Irregularities in Florida During the 2000 Presidential Election," U.S.
Commission on Civil Rights. Accessed June 25, 2019. usccr.gov/pubs/vote2000/report/
exesum.htm.

233 **National Popular Vote Interstate Compact:** "Electoral College Confusions"; "Why the
Electoral College Is the Absolute Worst, Explained."

234 **Sylvia Bernstein story:** Sylvia Bernstein, "Sylvia Bernstein: Colorado Should
Join National Popular Vote Movement," *Boulder Daily Camera*, January 24, 2019.
dailycamera.com/2019/01/24/sylvia-bernstein-colorado-should-join-national-popular-
vote-movement/; Conrad Swanson, "Bill to Change How We Elect Presidents
Advances Through Colorado House Committee," Colorado Politics, February 13, 2019.
coloradopolitics.com/news/bill-to-change-how-we-elect-presidents-advances-through-
colorado/article_4deb9242-2ef6-11e9-a81f-db5088bcfed0.html.

9. the next steps for you

241 **How to find who has contributed money to a candidate:**

Federal candidates (candidates for Congress and president): MapLight.org,
OpenSecrets.org, and FEC.gov.

State candidates: the Secretary of State or other government office in your state that
collects campaign contribution reports, and FollowTheMoney.org.

Local candidates (such as city and county offices): the office of city or county clerk, or
other government office that collects campaign contribution reports in your area.

index

justices and unlimited political money, 105–109; term limits for justices, 110–111; VRA gutting by, 183–186; wealth hoarder influence on, 133, 150
Swing states, 231–232

Tauzin, Billy, 82
Taxes: closing tax loopholes, 31; constitutional changes proposed by wealth hoarders, 151; easy-file system for, 82–84, 86; election costs paid from, 29; elimination of income taxes, 116; estate taxes, 151, 152; income taxes, 151, 152; paying taxes for the collective benefit of everyone, 123–125; salaries of politicians paid from, 29, 62; Shays' rebellion for tax reduction, 223–224; tax breaks for the rich, 139–140
Tax preparation industry, 82–84, 86
Tennessee, 194, 231
Texas, 175
Tobacco industry, 103–104
Tomasi, John, 147
Trump, Donald, 48, 139, 230, 232
Tweeten, Kathy, 102

United Negro College Fund (UNCF), 160–161
United States: credit rating reduction, 145; defense spending in, 140; national debt in, 140; rights and freedoms in, 107–108, 245–249
Universal voting, 192
UnKoch My Campus, 164–166
unrigbook.com, 8, 234, 237, 250
Utah, 216

Virginia, 165–166, 194
Vote Clean Seattle, 34–44
Voter ID laws, 175–176
Voter registration: automatic registration, 190; rules that make it harder to vote, 4, 150; same-day registration, 190; Voting Rights Act, 150, 179–186
Voting and voters: age for voting, 192; communities of color, 46–47, 49; early voting, 176–178, 188–189; exclusions on who could vote, 171–172; high-propensity voters, 45–48; limitations on majority rule, 225–228; lower-income communities, 46–47, 49, 187; outreach by campaigns to people who don't usually vote, 46–48; preclearance and election changes, 182–186;

presidential election rules, 227–234; ranked choice voting, 210, 214–219; restoring voting rights, 193–194; rules to control who votes, 171–186; unrigging the rules to limit voting, 187–194; voter suppression, 150, 154, 173–174, 188; young people, 46–47, 49
Voting Rights Act, 150, 179–186

Ward, John, 97–98
Wealth hoarders: anti-government agenda and goals of, 115–117, 126–151, 157–159; anti-government ideology of, 122–125; constitutional changes proposed by, 151; defense spending support from, 140; disabling democracy as goal and strategy of, 115–118, 128–138, 149–151; endgame of, 152–159; fighting back against agenda of, 118, 162–168; image makeover of, 160–161; influence to mainstream radical ideas, 130, 147–151; law-breaking by, 146, 160; leaders of, 119–121; partisanship and brinksmanship tactics of, 144–146; sabotage of effective programs by, 141–144; secretive and coercive actions of, 157–159, 162–163
Wealthy people and interests: clean elections to end influence on government by, 23–28; dependence on money from by candidates, 15–18, 23–27; political power of wealthier communities, 49–52; rules that allow political power and influence of, 2–5, 29–30, 93–99; unlimited political money spending by and influence of, 94–99, 105–109, 133–135, 149, 150; unrigging the rules to limit democracy by, 117, 162–168, 245–249
Weyrich, Paul, 150
Wisconsin, 98–99

You're More Powerful Than You Think (Liu), 239

acknowledgments

Thank you to all the courageous activists working to improve our democracy. Your challenges and triumphs inspire others. Thank you in particular to Sylvia Bernstein, Ellen Chaffee, Katie Fahey, Estevan Muñoz-Howard, Samantha Parsons, and Paul Perry for sharing your stories with me. My deepest appreciation to George O'Connor, whose extraordinary art brings this book to life. Thank you to all who lent their time and expertise to reviewing and improving sections: Steven Addis, John Brautigam, Jay Costa, Laura Curlin, Lee Drutman, Kristin Eberhard, Caroline Fredrickson, Gerry Hebert, Nicolas Heidorn, Pedro Hernandez, Chris Hughes, Michael Klarman, Carlton Larson, Lawrence Lessig, Nancy MacLean, Dan Maffei, Greg Moore, Michael Newman, Rochelle Newman, Janet Nudelman, Nick Nyhart, North Carolina Justice Center, Ann Ravel, Steve Silberstein, Melanie Sloan, Abdi Soltani, Hamsini Sridharan, Jonathan Stein, Sam Wang, and Michelle Whittaker. All opinions and any errors are my own. Thank you to Bo Bogatin for legal work, Kristin Barendsen for editing, Ayça Güralp for research, Simone Parisi for reference checking, Frank Bass for fact-checking, Alyssa Bernardino for fact-checking and extensive work on the endnotes, and Sean Dugar for his thoughtful comments on all the text and art. My appreciation to editor Mark Siegel for championing this project throughout, and to Robyn Chapman and the whole team at First Second Books. My ace editors, DeAnna Dalton and Alec Saslow, were with me at every step, from the earliest concept paper to the final proofread. Thank you to the rest of the MapLight team, too: Doug Edwards, Jim Heerwagen, Shel Kaphan, Irene Litherland, Như Tiên Lư, John O'Farrell, Chad Outler, Andrew Perez, Bergen Smith, Leon Smith, and Chelsea Whitman. All author proceeds from this book go to MapLight, a nonprofit working to unrig U.S. democracy. Thank you also to Daphne Anshel, Kate Gustin, Jonathan Gustin, Lee Notowich, and to the sustaining, unfailing support of my wife, Belinda Lyons-Newman. This book is for my young daughters. May we build a stronger democracy for them and for all of us.

—*Daniel G. Newman*

Thanks to Daniel Newman for writing this important book, and more thanks to Mark Siegel for thinking of me to draw it. Special thanks to Robyn, Kirk, Andrew, Molly, Sunny, and the rest of the crew at First Second for all the work they did to bring this behemoth of a project to finish. Extra-special thanks to "To Be Perfectly" Frank Reynoso for supplying the colors that tie this book together. And supremely grateful thanks to my friends and family (especially Nicole) who endured my endless griping and cries of "nihilism" as I worked through some of the darkest and scariest parts of the manuscript.

—*George O'Connor*

Daniel G. Newman is a national expert on government accountability and money in politics. He is president and co-founder of MapLight, a nonpartisan nonprofit that promotes transparency and political reform, earning a Knight-Batten Award for Innovations in Journalism, a James Madison Freedom of Information Award, a Library Journal Best Reference award, and a Webby Award nomination for Best Politics Website. Newman has appeared in hundreds of media outlets, including CNN, CBS, MSNBC, FOX Business, and NPR. He led a ballot measure campaign establishing public funding of elections in Berkeley, California, and was named one of Fast Company's 100 Most Creative People in Business. Newman received an MA in political psychology from U.C. Berkeley and a BA from Brown, and was a Fellow at the Safra Center for Ethics at Harvard. He lives in the San Francisco Bay Area.

George O'Connor is a *New York Times*–bestselling author and illustrator of the Olympians series as well as the graphic novels *Journey into Mohawk Country* and *Ball Peen Hammer*. His next major project is *Asgardians*, a four-volume exploration of Norse mythology in comics form, coming soon from First Second. In addition to his graphic novel career, O'Connor has published several children's picture books. He lives in Brooklyn with his three cats—two evil, one slightly less so. You can learn more about his works at georgeoconnorbooks.com.